D0988390

The Mini
OXFORD
School
German
DICTIONARY

Editorial Manager: Valerie Grundy
Editors: Neil and Roswitha Morris

OXFORD UNIVERSITY PRESS

Oxford University Press, Great Clarendon Street, Oxford OX2 6

Oxford New York
Athens Auckland Bangkok Bogotá Buenos Aires
Calcutta Cape Town Chennai Dar es Salaam
Delhi Florence Hong Kong Istanbul Karachi
Kuala Lumpur Madras Madrid Melbourne
Mexico City Mumbai Nairobi Paris São Paolo
Singapore Taipei Tokyo Toronto

and associated companies in
Berlin Ibadan

Oxford is a trade mark of Oxford University Press

© **Oxford University Press 1998**

First published 1998
5 7 9 10 8 6

A CIP catalogue record for this book is available from the British Lib

ISBN 0-19-910452-2

Typeset by
Selwood Systems, Midsomer Norton

Printed and bound in Great Britain by
Omnia Books Ltd, Glasgow

INTRODUCTION

Learning a new language is an exciting experience. It can also sometimes seem confusing and difficult. Feeling secure and at ease in using a bilingual dictionary is essential to the building of confidence in understanding and using a foreign language.

This dictionary has been specially written for students who are preparing for exams. We have paid particular attention to making the dictionary as user-friendly as possible. With the help of colour headwords, easy-to-follow signposts and simple example phrases, the right translation can quickly be found. The things students need to know about words in German are clearly shown. These include main parts of irregular verbs, noun plurals, and the case taken by prepositions.

We have adopted a simplified version of traditional bilingual entry layout. This means that the dictionary is ideal for learning basic dictionary skills, which can subsequently be built upon as the student moves towards larger, more complex dictionaries. We have done our best to make this dictionary a practical, easy-to-use tool for learning and understanding German.

Throughout the writing of this dictionary we have worked in close consultation with students, teachers, and examining boards. We gratefully acknowledge the examining boards AQA (NEAB and SEG), OCR (MEG), and EDEXCEL (ULEAC), who have read and commented on the dictionary text.

HOW A BILINGUAL DICTIONARY WORKS

A bilingual dictionary is a dictionary that has two languages in it. When you look up a word in one of the languages, the dictionary gives the translation for that word in the other language. The two languages in this dictionary are English and German. This dictionary is divided into two halves separated by red-edged pages in the middle. In the first half you look up German words to find out what they mean in English and in the second half you look up English words and find out how to say them in German.

The words you look up are in red and in the first half of the dictionary you will find **German** words in alphabetical order from a to z and in the second half **English** words from a to z. In a dictionary, these are called **headwords** because each one of them comes at the **head** of an **entry**. In the **entry** you can find **translations** but also other sorts of information which you can use to make sure you get the correct translation. The different sorts of information are typed in different ways to help you see clearly which is which. Here is a guide to the different things you will find in an entry:

headword	a word you look up in the dictionary
translation	translations are the only things that are in 'ordinary' type in an entry. They are always typed like this, and something that is typed in a different way can never be a translation
part of speech	tells you whether the word you are looking up is a verb, an adjective, or another part of speech. One headword can have more than one part of speech. **Book** can be a noun *(she was reading a book)* or a verb *(remember to book a table)*
(signpost)	helpful information to guide you to the right translation, to show you how to use the translation, or to give you essential information about either the headword or the translation
example	a phrase using the word you have looked up. If these appear in the entry you are looking at, you should read through them carefully to see if one of them is close to what you want to understand or say
der/die/das	gender: after a German noun to tell you whether it is masculine *(der)*, feminine *(die)*, or neuter *(das)*
(PL *die........***)**	plural: shows the plural form of a German noun
●	indicates a phrasal verb such as *to carry on*
★	indicates an idiomatic expression such as *to look on the bright side*
✧	indicates an irregular German verb
SEP	indicates that a German verb is separable such as *ablenken* (PERF *lenkt ab*)
Δ	indicates a new spelling of a German word (see page xii)

vi

You can think of a dictionary entry as being made out of different sorts of building bricks. In the entries below you can see how they fit together to help you to find what you need. The more you use your dictionary the more confident you will feel about finding your way around it.

GERMAN–ENGLISH

headword in red for easy look-up → **abergläubisch** *adjective* superstitious. ← part of speech

abfahren ◇ *verb* (PRES **fährt ab**, IMPERF **fuhr ab**, PERF **ist abgefahren**) to leave; **Peter fährt morgen ganz früh ab** Peter is leaving very early tomorrow morning; **wann fährt der Zug nach Berlin ab?** when does the Berlin train leave? ← main forms of irregular verb

gender → **Abfahrt** *die* (PL die **Abfahrten**) 1 departure; 2 run (*on a ski slope*); 3 exit (*on a motorway*).

Abfall *der* (PL die **Abfälle**) rubbish. ← noun plurals in bold for easy look-up

Abfalleimer *der* (PL die **Abfalleimer**) rubbish bin.

typical examples to show German context → **abfliegen** ◇ *verb* (IMPERF **flog ab**, PERF **ist abgeflogen**) 1 to take off; **die Maschine ist mit zehn Minuten Verspätung abgeflogen** the plane took off ten minutes late; 2 to leave (*by plane*); **ich fliege um elf Uhr ab** my plane leaves at 11 o'clock.

Abflug *der* (PL die **Abflüge**) departure.

ENGLISH–GERMAN

case governed by German preposition

based *adjective* **1 to be based on** basieren auf (+DAT); **the film is based on a true story** der Film basiert auf einer wahren Geschichte; **2 to be based in** wohnen in (+DAT); **he's based in Bristol** er wohnt in Bristol.

essential structures for expression in German

new spelling

basement *noun* Kellergeschoss△ *das* (PL *die* Kellergeschosse).

plural form

irregular verb

bear *noun* Bär *der* (PL *die* Bären). *verb* **1** ertragen ◇; **I can't bear the idea** ich kann den Gedanken nicht ertragen; **2 to bear something in mind** an etwas +(ACC) denken; **I'll bear it in mind** ich denke daran.

case of 'etwas' shown in translation of example

perfect formed with 'sein'

blush *verb* erröten (PERF *sein*).

bolt *noun* (*on a door*) Riegel *der* (PL *die* Riegel). *verb* **1** (*lock*) verriegeln; **2** (*gobble down*) runterschlingen ◇ SEP (*informal*).

gender

separable verb

informal word or expression

◇ IRREGULAR VERB: See the verb tables in the centre of the dictionary

A STEP-BY-STEP GUIDE TO FINDING THE TRANSLATION YOU NEED

Finding a word in the dictionary

You will be using this dictionary to do one of the following things:

1 look up a German word or phrase to find out what it means
2 look up an English word or phrase to find out how to say it in German.

1 Finding out what a German word means

First of all, look for it in the first half of the dictionary where you can find the German word and expressions with their English translations You will see that the top of every page is marked with this red box

No matter what you are using the dictionary to find out, you will alwa start by looking up a headword. Here are the German headwords **Ampel, Amsel, Amt, amtlich,** and **amüsant** with their entries.

> **Ampel** *die* (PL *die* **Ampeln**) traffic lights.
>
> **Amsel** *die* (PL *die* **Amseln**) blackbird.
>
> **Amt** *das* (PL *die* **Ämter**) 1 office; 2 exchange (*telephone*).
>
> **amtlich** *adjective* official.
>
> **amüsant** *adjective* amusing.

Suppose you want to find out what the German word **Bürste** means. You will look through the first half of your dictionary until you come to the bit which has all the German words beginning with **b.** You now need to find the page or pages containing German words beginning with **bu,** then **bur,** then **burs,** then **burs** The dictionary helps you to do this by showing you the alphabetic range of words that you can find on the two pages you can see when you have the dictionary open.

For instance, if you look at pages 52-53, you will see **Brühwürfel** and **campen** at the top of the pages. If you look down the first column on page 53, you will find **Bürste** between **Büroklammer** and **bürsten**. You will know that all German nouns start with a capital letter. Notice that this makes no difference to the alphabetical order, nor do accented letters like **ü**.

> **Büro** das (PL die Büros) office.
>
> **Büroklammer** die (PL die
> Büroklammern) paper clip.
>
> **Bürste** die (PL die Bürsten) brush.
>
> **bürsten** verb (PERF hat gebürstet)
> to brush.

When you look at the entry for **Bürste** you will find the translation you are looking for: **Bürste** means **brush**.

> **Bürste** die (PL die Bürsten) brush.

You can also see what the gender of **Bürste** is. Nouns in German are either masculine, feminine, or neuter. These are shown in the dictionary as *der*, *die*, or *das*. You can see that **Bürste** says *die*. **Bürste** is a feminine noun.

It often happens that a German word has more than one translation in English. If you look at the entry for **Tor** on page 235 you will see that it is divided into sections numbered **1** and **2**.

> **Tor** das (PL die Tore) **1** gate; **2** goal.

The first translation is **gate** and the second is **goal**. You will need to look at both translations and see which fits best in the German sentence you are trying to understand, so:

> **Uli hat das Tor geöffnet** *means* Uli opened the gate
>
> BUT
>
> **Uli steht im Tor** *means* Uli's in goal

In English, the plural of most nouns is formed by adding **-s** (**book/books**). In German there are quite a lot of ways of forming the plural and these are not always easy to recognize. To help you with this, we show the plural form after every noun headword.

For instance, if you are trying to find out what the German word **Häuser** means, you can see immediately that it is the plural of **Haus** and so it means **houses**.

> **Haus** *das* (PL *die* **Häuser**) **1** house;
> **2 nach Hause** home; **zu Hause** at
> home.

German like English has certain words that you would use when chatting with friends but not in more formal situations. German words like this are marked (*informal*) like **flitzen** here:

> **flitzen** *verb* (*informal*) (PERF **ist**
> **geflitzt**) **1** to dash; **2** to whizz.

2 Finding an English word and how to say it in German

You can see that it is quite easy once you know how the dictionary works to look up a German word and find out what it means. Students usually find it harder to use the dictionary to find out how to say something in German. This dictionary is written specially to help you do this and to make it easy to find the right way of saying things in German.

| ENGLISH–GERMAN |

Suppose you want to know how to say **garden** in German. Look up the word in the second part of the dictionary where the top of every page is marked with this box framed in red.

If you follow the same way of going through the alphabetical order of the headwords as you did when you were looking up a German word, you will find **garden** on page 417.

Now you can see that the German word for **garden** is **Garten**. But if you want to make a sentence using a noun like **Garten** you need to know its gender. The dictionary shows you that it is *der* **Garten** so **in the garden** will be **im Garten**.

It is not always as easy as this to know which German word you need. Sometimes there will be more than one German word for the English word you are looking up. When the dictionary entry gives you more than just one translation, it is very important to take the time to read through the whole entry. If you look up **plug** the entry looks like this:

> **plug** *noun* **1** (*electrical*) Stecker *der*
> (PL *die* Stecker); **2** (*in a bath or sink*)
> Stöpsel *der* (PL *die* Stöpsel); **to pull
> out the plug** den Stöpsel
> herausziehen.

You can see that **1** tells you that the German word for an electrical plug is **Stecker** and **2** tells you that the word for a plug in a bath or a sink is **Stöpsel**.

Remember that information which is either in brackets or italics or both is there to help you, but it *will never be* the translation itself. Wherever there is more than one translation, depending on what meaning of the English word you are looking for, the dictionary will always help you to choose the right one.

Often it is not enough to find the translation of one word. In the case of more common words the dictionary also gives you a selection of phrases you will often want to use. In the entry for **hair** below you can find out how to use the translation **Haare** in different expressions:

> **hair** *noun* **1** Haare (*plural*); **to comb
> your hair** sich ←(DAT) die Haare
> kämmen; **to wash your hair** sich
> ←(DAT) die Haare waschen; **to have
> your hair cut** sich ←(DAT) die Haare
> schneiden lassen; **she's had her hair
> cut** sie hat sich die Haare schneiden
> lassen; **2 a hair** ein Haar.

THE GERMAN SPELLING REFORM

The German spelling reform was adopted by German-speaking countries in July 1996. It was agreed that both old and new spellings would be acceptable until 2005, by which time the new spellings should be included in all written texts.

The main changes to the spelling of German words include:
- After a short vowel, **ss** is used instead of **ß**. For example: **daß** becomes **dass**, **Schloß** becomes **Schloss**.
- Capital letters are now used more often, especially for adjectives used as nouns. For example: **recht haben** becomes **Recht haben**, **es tut mir leid** becomes **es tut mir Leid**.
- Words which were previously one word are now often spelt as two words. For example: **stehenlassen** becomes **stehen lassen**, **wieviel** becomes **wie viel**.

In the headword list of this dictionary you will find all the new spellings. They are marked Δ and there is a note at the foot of each page explaining that this symbol signals a new spelling. However, since you may come across old spellings if you are reading pre-reform German material, we have also given as headwords all the most frequent old spellings which could cause problems in looking up. These are cross-referred to the new spellings.

The same symbol Δ is used on the English-German side of the dictionary to signal new spellings in translations of English headwords.

A a

Aal der (PL die Aale) eel.

ab preposition ←(+DAT) from; **ab Montag** from Monday; **Kinder ab sechs Jahren** children from the age of six.
adverb **1** off; **der Henkel ist ab** the handle has come off; **ab ins Bett!** (informal) off (you go) to bed!; **2 ab und zu** now and again.

abbiegen ◇ verb (IMPERF **bog ab**, PERF **ist abgebogen**) **1** to turn off; **nach rechts abbiegen** to turn off to the right; **2 biegen Sie an der Ampel (nach) links ab** turn left at the lights.

Abbildung die (PL die Abbildungen) illustration.

abbrechen ◇ verb (PRES **bricht ab**, IMPERF **brach ab**, PERF **hat abgebrochen**) **1** to break off (a branch, negotiations); **Ruth brach ein paar Zweige ab** Ruth broke off a few branches; **2** to pull down (a building); **3** to cut short; **leider mussten wir unsere Ferien vorzeitig abbrechen** unfortunately we had to cut short our holidays; **er hat sein Studium aus finanziellen Gründen abgebrochen** he left university for financial reasons; **4** (PERF **ist abgebrochen**) **der Ast ist abgebrochen** the branch has broken off.

Abend der (PL die Abende) evening;

am Abend in the evening; **heute Abend** △ this evening, tonight; **gestern Abend** △ yesterday evening, last night; **wann esst ihr zu Abend?** when do you have dinner?

Abendessen das (PL die Abendessen) dinner (in the evening); **was gibt es zum Abendessen?** what are we having for dinner?

Abendbrot das evening meal.

Abendkurs der (PL die Abendkurse) evening course.

abends adverb in the evening.

Abenteuer das (PL die Abenteuer) adventure.

aber conjunction but; **es ist zwar nützlich, aber zu teuer** it's useful, but too expensive.
adverb really; **das ist aber sehr nett von dir** that's really nice of you; **du bist aber groß!** aren't you tall!; **aber ja!** but of course!; **jetzt ist aber Schluss!** that's it now!

abergläubisch adjective superstitious.

abfahren ◇ verb (PRES **fährt ab**, IMPERF **fuhr ab**, PERF **ist abgefahren**) to leave; **Peter fährt morgen ganz früh ab** Peter is leaving very early tomorrow morning; **wann fährt der Zug nach Berlin ab?** when does the Berlin train leave?

Abfahrt die (PL die Abfahrten) **1** departure; **2** run (on a ski slope); **3** exit (on a motorway).

Abfall der (PL die Abfälle) rubbish.

△ NEW SPELLING: See page xii

Abfalleimer der (PL die Abfalleimer) rubbish bin.

abfliegen ◇ verb (IMPERF flog ab, PERF ist abgeflogen) **1** to take off; **die Maschine ist mit zehn Minuten Verspätung abgeflogen** the plane took off ten minutes late; **2** to leave (by plane); **ich fliege um elf Uhr ab** my plane leaves at 11 o'clock.

Abflug der (PL die Abflüge) departure.

abfragen verb (PERF hat abgefragt) **1** to test; **sie fragt ihn Vokabeln ab** she's testing him on his vocabulary; **2** to call up (on a computer); **Adressen am Computer abfragen** to call up addresses on the computer.

Abgase (plural noun) exhaust fumes.

abgeben ◇ verb (PRES gibt ab, IMPERF gab ab, PERF hat abgegeben) **1** to hand in (homework, an application, lost property); **2** to pass (in football); **den Ball abgeben** to pass the ball; **3** sich mit etwas abgeben to spend time on something; **mit solchen Typen würde ich mich nicht abgeben** I wouldn't associate with blokes like that; **4** jemandem etwas abgeben to give someone something; **gib mir ein Stück von deiner Schokolade ab** give me a piece of your chocolate; **5** er wird einen guten Lehrer abgeben he'll make a good teacher.

abgelegen adjective remote.

abgemacht adjective agreed.

Abgeordnete der/die (PL die Abgeordneten) member of parliament.

Abhang der (PL die Abhänge) slope.

abhängen[1] ◇ verb (IMPERF hing ab, PERF hat abgehangen) **von jemandem abhängen** to depend on somebody; **von etwas abhängen** to depend on something; **es hängt vom Wetter ab, ob wir am Wochenende nach Wales fahren** whether or not we are going to Wales at the weekend depends on the weather.

abhängen[2] verb (PERF hat abgehängt) **1** to unhitch (a trailer); **2** to uncouple (a train carriage); **3** (informal) to shake off; **die Einbrecher hängten die Polizei schnell ab** the burglars soon shook off the police.

abheben ◇ verb (IMPERF hob ab, PERF hat abgehoben) **1** to lift off; **2** to withdraw (money); **3** to answer the phone; **ich habe schon zweimal angerufen, aber niemand hat abgehoben** I've rung twice before, but nobody answered.

abholen verb (PERF hat abgeholt) **1** to collect; **2** to pick up; **ich hole dich am Bahnhof ab** I'll pick you up at the station.

Abitur das (PL die Abiture) A levels (German students usually take Abitur at 19, sitting exams in four subjects, which they have to pass to go on to university); **sein Abitur machen** to do your A levels.

Abiturient der (PL die Abiturienten) A-level student.

◇ IRREGULAR VERB: See the verb table in the centre of the dictionary

Abiturientin die (PL die Abiturientinnen) A-level student.

Abkommen das (PL die Abkommen) agreement.

abkürzen verb (PERF hat abgekürzt) 1 to abbreviate; **wie kürzt man das Wort ab?** how do you abbreviate that word?; 2 **den Weg abkürzen** to take a short cut.

Abkürzung die (PL die Abkürzungen) 1 abbreviation; **die Abkürzung für Europäische Union ist EU** the abbreviation for European Union is EU; 2 short cut.

abladen ◇ verb (PRES lädt ab, IMPERF lud ab, PERF hat abgeladen) to unload.

ablaufen ◇ verb (PRES läuft ab, IMPERF lief ab, PERF ist abgelaufen) 1 to expire (passport, contract); 2 to drain off; **das Badewasser ablaufen lassen** to let the bathwater out; 3 to go off; **wie ist die Besprechung abgelaufen?** how did the meeting go?

ablegen verb (PERF hat abgelegt) 1 to take off; 2 **abgelegte Kleidung** cast-offs.

ablehnen verb (PERF hat abgelehnt) 1 to turn down (a position, money, an invitation); 2 to reject (an applicant, a suggestion).

ablenken verb (PERF hat abgelenkt) 1 to distract; **jemanden von seiner Arbeit ablenken** to distract somebody from their work; 2 **jemanden von seinen Sorgen ablenken** to take somebody's mind off their worries; 3 to divert

(attention, suspicion); **vom Thema ablenken** to change the subject.

abliefern verb (PERF hat abgeliefert) 1 to deliver; 2 to hand in (an essay, a form, lost property); 3 to drop off; **die Kinder abliefern** to drop the children off.

abmachen verb (PERF hat abgemacht) 1 to take off; **kannst du den Deckel abmachen?** can you take off the lid?; 2 to agree; **wir müssen noch einen Termin für unser nächstes Treffen abmachen** we still have to agree on a date for our next meeting; **abgemacht!** agreed!; 3 to sort out; **das müsst ihr untereinander abmachen** you'll have to sort that out amongst yourselves.

Abmachung die (PL die Abmachungen) agreement.

abnehmen ◇ verb (PRES nimmt ab, IMPERF nahm ab, PERF hat abgenommen) 1 to take off (remove); 2 **kann ich dir etwas abnehmen?** (carry) can I take something (for you)?; (help) can I do anything for you?; 3 **jemandem etwas abnehmen** to take something off somebody; **sie nehmen einem schnell zwanzig Mark ab** they'll soon take 20 marks off you; 4 to buy; 5 to decrease (in number); 6 to lose weight; **er hat schon vier Kilo abgenommen** he's already lost four kilos; 7 to answer the phone; 8 **das nehme ich dir nicht ab** (informal) I don't buy that.

Abonnement das (PL die Abonnements) subscription.

△ NEW SPELLING: See page xii

abonnieren verb (PERF hat abonniert) to subscribe to.

abraten ◇ verb (PRES rät ab, IMPERF riet ab, PERF hat abgeraten) jemandem von etwas abraten to advise somebody against something.

abräumen verb (PERF hat abgeräumt) to clear away.

abreagieren verb (PERF hat abreagiert) 1 seine Wut an jemandem abreagieren to take your anger out on somebody; 2 sich abreagieren to calm down.

Abreise die departure.

abreisen verb (PERF ist abgereist) to leave.

abreißen ◇ verb (IMPERF riss ab △, PERF hat abgerissen) 1 to tear down (a poster, notice); 2 PERF ist abgerissen) to come off (a button, for example).

Absage die (PL die Absagen) refusal.

absagen verb (PERF hat abgesagt) 1 to cancel; 2 eine Einladung absagen to turn down an invitation.

Absatz der (PL die Absätze) 1 heel (of a shoe); 2 paragraph.

abschaffen verb (PERF hat abgeschafft) 1 to abolish (a regulation, capital punishment); 2 to get rid of; wir haben unseren Hund abgeschafft we got rid of our dog.

abscheulich adjective horrible.

abschicken verb (PERF hat abgeschickt) to send off.

Abschied der (PL die Abschiede) 1 parting; 2 farewell; 3 Abschied nehmen to say goodbye.

Abschleppdienst der breakdown service.

abschleppen verb (PERF hat abgeschleppt) 1 to tow away; 2 sich mit den Koffern abschleppen (informal) to struggle along with the suitcases; 3 jemanden abschleppen (informal) to pick somebody up.

abschließen ◇ verb (IMPERF schloss ab △, PERF hat abgeschlossen) to lock.

Abschlussprüfung △ die (PL die Abschlussprüfungen) final exam.

abschneiden ◇ verb (IMPERF schnitt ab, PERF hat abgeschnitten) 1 to cut off; ich schneide dir eine Scheibe Brot ab I'll cut you a slice of bread; 2 gut/schlecht abschneiden to do well/badly.

abschrecken verb (PERF hat abgeschreckt) to deter.

abschreiben ◇ verb (IMPERF schrieb ab, PERF hat abgeschrieben) to copy.

abseits adverb 1 far away; etwas abseits a little way away; 2 offside (in soccer).

Absender der (PL die Absender) sender.

absetzen verb (PERF hat abgesetzt) 1 to take off (your hat, glasses); 2 to put down (a bag, suitcase); 3 to drop off; ich setze euch am Bahnhof ab I'll drop you off at the station; 4 die

◇ IRREGULAR VERB: See the verb table in the centre of the dictionary

Pille **absetzen** to stop taking the pill.

Absicht die (PL die **Absichten**) intention.

absichtlich adverb intentionally.

absolut adjective absolute. adverb absolutely; **das ist absolut unmöglich** that's absolutely impossible.

abspülen verb (PERF hat abgespült) 1 to rinse, to rinse off; 2 to do the washing up.

Abstand der (PL die **Abstände**) 1 distance; **in zwanzig Meter Abstand** at a distance of 20 metres; **Abstand halten** to keep your distance; 2 interval.

abstauben verb (PERF hat abgestaubt) to dust.

abstellen verb (PERF hat abgestellt) 1 to turn off (the radio, a tap); 2 to put down (a suitcase, the shopping); 3 to park (the car).

Abstimmung die (PL die **Abstimmungen**) vote.

abstreiten ◇ verb (IMPERF stritt ab, PERF hat abgestritten) to deny.

abstürzen verb (PERF ist abgestürzt) 1 to fall; 2 to crash (a plane).

Abteil das (PL die **Abteile**) compartment.

Abteilung die (PL die **Abteilungen**) department.

Abtreibung die (PL die **Abtreibungen**) abortion.

abtrocknen verb (PERF hat abgetrocknet) 1 to dry up; 2 **sich abtrocknen** to dry yourself.

abwägen verb (IMPERF wog ab, PERF hat abgewogen) to weigh up.

abwärts adverb down.

Abwasch der washing-up.

abwaschen ◇ verb (PRES wäscht ab, IMPERF wusch ab, PERF hat abgewaschen) 1 to wash up (the dishes); 2 to wash off (dirt, marks).

Abwasser das (PL die **Abwässer**) sewage.

Abwechslung die (PL die **Abwechslungen**) change; **zur Abwechslung** for a change.

abwerten verb (PERF hat abgewertet) to devalue.

abwertend adjective pejorative.

abwesend adjective absent.

Abwesenheit die absence.

abwischen verb (PERF hat abgewischt) to wipe.

abzählen verb (PERF hat abgezählt) to count.

Abzeichen das (PL die **Abzeichen**) badge.

abziehen ◇ verb (IMPERF zog ab, PERF hat abgezogen) 1 to take off (a sheet, backing); **die Betten abziehen** to strip the beds; 2 to take out (a key); 3 to deduct, to take away; 4 to withdraw (troops); 5 (PERF ist abgezogen) to escape (steam or smoke, for example); 6 (PERF ist abgezogen) sie sind

△ NEW SPELLING: See page xii

gleich nach dem Essen **abgezogen** (*informal*) they pushed off straight after the meal.

abzielen *verb* (PERF hat abgezielt) etwas zielt auf etwas ab something is aimed at something.

ach *exclamation* oh!

Achsel *die* (PL die Achseln) shoulder.

acht *number* eight; um acht (Uhr) at eight (o'clock); um halb acht at half past seven.

Acht[1] *die* (PL die Achten) eight; eine Acht schreiben to write an eight.

Acht[2] *die* 1 Acht geben △ to pay attention; er sollte in der Schule besser Acht geben he should pay more attention at school; 2 auf etwas/jemanden Acht geben to look after something/somebody; 3 gib Acht! watch out!; 4 sich in Acht nehmen △ to be careful; 5 etwas außer Acht lassen △ to disregard something.

Achtel *das* (PL die Achtel) eighth.

achten *verb* (PERF hat geachtet) 1 to respect (*a person, an opinion*); 2 auf etwas achten to pay attention to something; 3 auf jemanden achten to look after somebody; 4 nicht darauf! don't take any notice of it!

achter, achte, achtes *adjective* eighth; jede achte Kiste every eighth crate; mein achter Geburtstag my eighth birthday; sie ging als Achte durchs Ziel she finished eighth.

Achterbahn *die* (PL die Achterbahnen) roller coaster.

achtgeben SEE Acht[2].

achthundert *number* eight hundred.

achtmal *adverb* eight times.

Achtung *die* 1 respect; Achtung vor jemandem haben to have respect for somebody; 2 Achtung! look out!; Achtung, fertig, los! on your marks, get set, go!; 'Achtung Stufe' 'mind the step'.

achtzehn *number* eighteen.

achtzig *number* eighty.

Acker *der* (PL die Äcker) field.

addieren *verb* (PERF hat addiert) to add.

Ader *die* (PL die Adern) vein.

Adjektiv *das* (PL die Adjektive) adjective.

Adler *der* (PL die Adler) eagle.

adoptieren *verb* (PERF hat adoptiert) to adopt.

Adoption *die* (PL die Adoptionen) adoption.

Adoptiveltern *plural noun* adoptive parents.

Adoptivkind *das* (PL die Adoptivkinder) adopted child.

Adresse *die* (PL die Adressen) address.

adressieren *verb* (PERF hat adressiert) to address; an wen soll ich den Brief adressieren? who shall I address the letter to?

✧ IRREGULAR VERB: *See the verb table in the centre of the dictionary.*

Advent der Advent.

Adventskalender der (PL die Adventskalender) Advent calendar.

Adventskranz der (PL die Adventskränze) Advent wreath.

Adverb das (PL die Adverbien) adverb.

aerobic das aerobics.

Affe der (PL die Affen) 1 monkey; 2 ape.

Afrika das Africa; **aus Afrika** from Africa; **nach Afrika** to Africa.

Afrikaner der (PL die Afrikaner) African.

Afrikanerin die (PL die Afrikanerinnen) African.

afrikanisch adjective African.

Agentur die (PL die Agenturen) agency.

aggressiv adjective aggressive.

ähneln verb (PERF hat geähnelt) 1 to resemble; **er ähnelt seinem Vater sehr** he's very like his father; 2 **sich ähneln** to be alike.

ahnen verb (PERF hat geahnt) 1 to know; **das konnte ich wirklich nicht ahnen** I had no way of knowing that; **wer soll denn ahnen, dass …?** who would know that …?; 2 to suspect; **so etwas habe ich doch schon geahnt** I did suspect something like that.

ähnlich adjective 1 similar; 2 **jemandem ähnlich sein** to be like somebody; **jemandem ähnlich sehen** to look like somebody;

3 **ähnlich wie** like; 4 **das sieht dir ähnlich!** (informal) that's just like you!

Ähnlichkeit die (PL die Ähnlichkeiten) similarity.

Ahnung die 1 idea; **hast du eine Ahnung, wie er heißt?** have you got any idea what he's called?; 2 **keine Ahnung!** no idea!; **er hat von Mode absolut keine Ahnung** he doesn't know a thing about fashion; 3 premonition.

ahnungslos adjective unsuspecting.

Ahorn der (PL die Ahorne) maple.

Aids das Aids.

Akademiker der (PL die Akademiker) university graduate.

Akademikerin die (PL die Akademikerinnen) university graduate.

akademisch adjective academic.

Akkusativ der (PL die Akkusative) accusative.

Akne die acne.

Akte die (PL die Akten) file.

Aktentasche die (PL die Aktentaschen) briefcase.

Aktion die (PL die Aktionen) 1 action; **in Aktion treten** to go into action; 2 campaign.

aktiv adjective active.

Aktiv das active.

aktuell adjective 1 topical; **ein aktuelles Thema** a topical issue;

△ NEW SPELLING: *See page xii*

2 nicht mehr aktuell no longer relevant; **3** current; eine aktuelle Sendung a current-affairs programme.

Akzent der (PL die Akzente)
1 accent; mit starkem Akzent sprechen to speak with a strong accent; **2** accent (on a letter); **3** stress; den Akzent auf etwas legen to stress something.

albern adjective silly.
adverb in a silly way.

Album das (PL die Alben) album.

Algebra die algebra.

Alkohol der alcohol.

alkoholfrei adjective non-alcoholic.

Alkoholiker der (PL die Alkoholiker) alcoholic.

Alkoholikerin die (PL die Alkoholikerinnen) alcoholic.

alkoholisch adjective alcoholic.

All das space; einen Satelliten ins All schicken to send a satellite into space.

alle SEE aller.

Allee die (PL die Alleen) avenue.

allein adjective, adverb **1** alone; sie waren allein im Zimmer they were alone in the room; jemanden allein lassen to leave somebody alone; **2** on your own; sie hat das ganz allein gezeichnet she drew it all on her own; **3** von allein by yourself, by itself (automatically); eine allein stehendΔ single; **5** eine allein

erziehende MutterΔ a single mother; der/die allein Erziehende single parent; **6** nicht allein not only; **7** allein der Gedanke the mere thought.

alleinerziehend, alleinstehend SEE allein.

aller, alle, alles pronoun **1** all; all meine Freunde all my friends; alles Geld all the money; alle miteinander all together; alle Jungen in der Schule all the boys in the school; alle Bewohner der Stadt sind dagegen all the people of the town are against it; alles Gute! all the best!; Getränke aller Art all kinds of drinks; **3** alle (plural) all; alle waren da they were all there; wir alle we all, all of us; wir haben alle gesehen we saw all of them; **4** ohne allen Grund without any reason; **5** alle beide both of them; **6** every; alle Tage every day, alle fünf Minuten every five minutes; **7** alles everything, everybody (people).
adjective alle sein (informal) to be all gone.

allerbester, allerbeste, allerbestes adjective **1** very best; **2** am allerbesten best of all.

allerdings adverb **1** though; das Essen ist gut, allerdings ziemlich teuer the food's good, though rather expensive; **2** certainly (yes); 'tut das weh?' – 'allerdings!' 'does it hurt?' – 'it certainly does!'.

Allergie die (PL die Allergien) allergy.

allergisch adjective allergic.

◇ IRREGULAR VERB: See the verb table in the centre of the dictionary

llerheiligen *das* All Saints' Day.

llerlei *adjective* all sorts of; **allerlei Ausreden** all sorts of excuses.

llerletzter, allerletzte, allerletztes *adjective* very last.

lles SEE aller.

llgemein *adjective* **1** general; **im Allgemeinen** △ in general. *adverb* **1** generally; **2 es ist allgemein bekannt, dass** … it is common knowledge that …

llmählich *adjective* gradual. *adverb* gradually; **wir sollten allmählich gehen** it's time we got going.

lltäglich *adjective* everyday (*event, sight*).

lltag *der* **1** daily routine; **2** weekday.

lltags *adverb* on weekdays.

lpen *plural noun* **die Alpen** the Alps.

lphabet *das* (PL die **Alphabete**) alphabet.

lphabetisch *adjective* alphabetical.

lptraum *der* (PL die **Alpträume**) nightmare.

ls *conjunction* **1** when; **als meine Freundin hier war** when my friend was here; **erst als** only when; **2** than (*as a comparison*); **er ist jünger als sie** he's younger than her; **3 lieber … als** … rather … than …; **ich ginge lieber ins Kino als zum Essen** I'd rather go to the cinema than for a

meal; **4** as; **als Frau kann ich das verstehen** as a woman, I can sympathize; **gerade als ich gehen wollte** just as I was about to leave; **5 als ob** as if; **als ob ich das nicht wüsste!** as if I didn't know that!

also *adverb, conjunction* **1** so; **ich konnte ihn telefonisch nicht erreichen, also habe ich ihm ein Fax geschickt** I couldn't get through to him on the phone, so I sent him a fax; **2** then; **also kommst du mit?** you're coming too, then?; **also gut** all right then; **3** well; **also, wie gesagt** well, as I said before; **4 na also!** there you are!

alt *adjective* **1** old; **wie alt bist du?** how old are you?; **alt werden** to grow old; **2 alles beim Alten lassen** to leave everything as it was.

Altar *der* (PL die **Altäre**) altar.

Alter *das* (PL die **Alter**) **1** age; **in deinem Alter** at your age; **im Alter von zwanzig** at the age of twenty; **2** old age; **im Alter** in old age.

älter *adjective* **1** older; **mein Rad ist älter als deins** my bike is older than yours; **2** elder; **mein älterer Bruder** my elder brother; **3** elderly.

altern *verb* (PERF **ist gealtert**) to age.

Alternative *die* (PL die **Alternativen**) alternative.

Altersgrenze *die* (PL die **Altersgrenzen**) age limit.

Altersheim *das* (PL die **Altersheime**) old people's home.

△ NEW SPELLING: *See page xii*

ältester, älteste, ältestes *adjective* 1 oldest; 2 eldest; **der älteste Sohn** the eldest son.

Altglas *das* used glass.

Altglascontainer *der* (PL die Altglascontainer) bottle bank.

altmodisch *adjective* old-fashioned.

Altpapier *das* waste paper.

Altstadt *die* (PL die Altstädte) old town.

Alufolie *die* tin foil.

Aluminium *das* aluminium.

am = an dem; 1 **am Freitag** on Friday; 2 **am besten** the best; 3 **am teuersten** (the) most expensive; 4 **am höchsten** the highest; 5 **am Abend** in the evening.

Ameise *die* (PL die Ameisen) ant.

Amerika *das* America.

Amerikaner *der* (PL die Amerikaner) American.

Amerikanerin *die* (PL die Amerikanerinnen) American.

amerikanisch *adjective* American.

Ampel *die* (PL die Ampeln) traffic lights.

Amsel *die* (PL die Amseln) blackbird.

Amt *das* (PL die Ämter) 1 office; 2 exchange (*telephone*).

amtlich *adjective* official.

amüsant *adjective* amusing.

amüsieren *verb* (PERF **hat amüsiert**) 1 to amuse; 2 **sich amüsieren** to enjoy oneself;

amüsier dich gut! enjoy yourself!; 3 **sich über etwas amüsieren** to find something funny.

an *preposition* ←(+DAT *or* +ACC) (*the dative is used when talking about position; the accusative shows movement or a change of place*) 1 **an der Spitze** at the top; **sich an den Tisch setzen** to sit down at the table; **er arbeitet an der Schule** he works at the school; 2 on (*attached to, when talking about time*); **das Bild hängt an der Wand** the picture is on the wall; **an dem Tag** on that day; **ich habe am fünften März Geburtstag** my birthday is on the fifth of March; 3 to; **einen Brief an jemanden schicken** to send a letter to somebody; 4 **an einer Krankheit sterben** to die of a disease; 5 **an jemanden denken** to think of somebody; 6 **sich an etwas erinnern** to remember something; 7 **an** (*und für*) **sich** actually; **an sich ist das kein Problem** actually, it's no problem; 8 **es liegt an dir, jetzt etwas zu unternehmen** it's up to you to do something now.
adverb 1 on; **das Licht ist an** the light's on; 2 **ohne etwas an** with nothing on; 3 **an die dreißig Mark** about thirty marks; 4 **von heute an** from today.

Ananas *die* (PL die Ananas) pineapple.

anbieten ✧ *verb* (IMPERF **bot an**, PERF **hat angeboten**) to offer; **Anna bot mir an, mich nach Hause zu bringen** Anna offered to take me home.

✧ IRREGULAR VERB: *See the verb table in the centre of the dictionary*

nblick der (PL die Anblicke) sight.

nbrennen ◇ verb (IMPERF brannte
an, PERF ist angebrannt) to burn; das
Essen ist angebrannt the food's
burnt.

ndenken das (PL die Andenken)
1 souvenir; 2 zum Andenken an
unsere Ferien to remind us of our
holiday.

nderer, andere, anderes
adjective 1 other; ich nehme das
andere T-Shirt I'll have the other T-
shirt; 2 different; 3 ein anderer/
eine andere/ein anderes another;
ein anderes Mal another time.
pronoun 1 der/die/das andere the
other one; nicht dieses Buch,
sondern das andere not that book,
but the other one; die anderen the
others; die anderen kommen
später the others are coming later;
2 andere other ones (things, toys,
etc.); 3 ein anderer/eine
andere/ein anderes a different one
(a thing); someone else (a person);
4 kein anderer no one else; 5 unter
anderem among other things;
6 etwas anderes something else;
7 alles andere everything else.

ndererseits adverb on the other
hand.

ndermal adverb ein andermal
another time.

ndern verb (PERF hat geändert)
1 to change; 2 to alter (a garment);
3 sich ändern to change; sie hat
sich sehr geändert she's changed a
lot.

nders adverb 1 differently;

2 anders aussehen to look
different; 3 niemand anders
nobody else; jemand anders
somebody else; 4 anders als
different from; du bist ganz anders
als ich you're quite different from
me; 5 irgendwo anders
somewhere else.

anderthalb number one and a half.

Anerkennung die 1 appreciation;
2 recognition (of a king, state).

Anfall der (PL die Anfälle) fit.

Anfang der (PL die Anfänge)
1 beginning, start; am Anfang at
the beginning; von Anfang an from
the start; 2 zu Anfang at first.

anfangen ◇ verb (PRES fängt an,
IMPERF fing an, PERF hat
angefangen) 1 to begin, to start; die
Schule fängt um acht an school
starts at eight; mit etwas anfangen
to start (on) something; 2 bei einer
Firma anfangen to start working for
a firm; 3 was soll ich damit
anfangen? what am I supposed to
do with that?; 4 damit kann ich
nichts anfangen it's no good to
me (it's no use); it doesn't mean
anything to me (I don't understand
it).

Anfänger der (PL die Anfänger)
beginner.

Anfängerin die (PL die
Anfängerinnen) beginner.

anfassen verb (PERF hat
angefasstΔ) 1 to touch; 2 to tackle
(a problem, a task); 3 to treat (a
person); 4 mit anfassen to lend a

△ NEW SPELLING: See page xii

hand; **5 sich anfassen** to feel; **es fasst sich weich an** it feels soft; **6 jemanden anfassen** to take somebody's hand; **sie hat ihre Mutter angefasst** she took her mother's hand; **fasst euch an!** hold hands!

anfragen verb (PERF **hat angefragt**) to enquire, to ask.

anfreunden verb (PERF **hat sich angefreundet**) **1 sich anfreunden** to make friends; **sie freundet sich mit allen möglichen Leuten an** she makes friends with all sorts of people; **2 sich anfreunden** to become friends; **wir haben uns angefreundet** we've become friends.

Anführungszeichen plural noun inverted commas.

Angabe die (PL die **Angaben**) **1** piece of information; **2** serve (in tennis); **das ist nur Angabe** he is/she is/they are only showing off.

angeben ◇ verb (PRES **gibt an**, IMPERF **gab an**, PERF **hat angegeben**) **1** to give (your name, a reason); **2** to show off; **3** to indicate (on a map); **4** to serve (in tennis).

Angeber der (PL die **Angeber**) show-off.

Angeberin die (PL die **Angeberinnen**) show-off.

Angebot das (PL die **Angebote**) offer.

angehen ◇ verb (IMPERF **ging an**, PERF **ist angegangen**) **1** to come on (a radio, heating, a light); **2** to

concern; **das geht auch dich etwas an** it concerns you too; **das geht dich nichts an** it's none of your business; **3** (PERF **hat angegangen**) to tackle (problems, difficulty, work).

Angehörige der/die (PL die **Angehörigen**) relative.

Angel die (PL die **Angeln**) fishing rod.

Angelegenheit die (PL die **Angelegenheiten**) **1** matter; **2** business; **das ist meine Angelegenheit** that's my business.

angeln verb (PERF **hat geangelt**) **1** fish; **angeln gehen** to go fishing; **2** to catch (a fish).

Angelrute die (PL die **Angelruten**) fishing rod.

angenehm adjective pleasant. exclamation pleased to meet you! (when introduced to somebody).

Angestellte der/die (PL die **Angestellten**) employee.

angewiesen adjective dependent **auf etwas angewiesen sein** to be dependent on something; **auf jemanden angewiesen sein** to be dependent on somebody.

angewöhnen verb (PERF **hat angewöhnt**) **1 jemandem etwas angewöhnen** to get somebody used to something; **2 sich etwas angewöhnen** to get into the habit of doing something; **ich habe es mir angewöhnt, früh aufzustehen** I've got into the habit of getting up early.

Angewohnheit die (PL die **Angewohnheiten**) habit.

◇ IRREGULAR VERB: See the verb table in the centre of the dictionary

angreifen ◇ verb (IMPERF **griff an**, PERF **hat angegriffen**) 1 to attack; 2 to affect (your health, voice).

Angriff der (PL die **Angriffe**) attack.

Angst die (PL die **Ängste**) 1 fear; 2 **Angst haben** to be afraid; **vor jemandem Angst haben** to be afraid of somebody; **mir ist Angst** I'm afraid; 3 **jemandem Angst machen** to frighten somebody; 4 **Angst vor einer Prüfung haben** to be worried about an exam; **Angst um jemanden haben** to be worried about somebody.

ängstlich adjective 1 nervous; 2 frightened; 3 anxious.

anhaben ◇ verb (informal) (PRES **hat an**, IMPERF **hatte an**, PERF **hat angehabt**) to have on; **sie hat heute das neue Kleid an** she's got her new dress on today.

anhalten ◇ verb (PRES **hält an**, IMPERF **hielt an**, PERF **hat angehalten**) 1 to stop; 2 **den Atem anhalten** to hold your breath; 3 to last; **das schöne Wetter wird nicht lange anhalten** the nice weather won't last long; 4 **jemanden zur Arbeit anhalten** to urge somebody to work.

Anhalter der (PL die **Anhalter**) hitchhiker; **per Anhalter fahren** to hitchhike.

Anhalterin die (PL die **Anhalterinnen**) hitchhiker.

Anhang der (PL die **Anhänge**) appendix.

Anhänger der (PL die **Anhänger**) 1 supporter; 2 trailer; 3 label (on a suitcase); 4 pendant; 5 loop (for hanging up).

Anhängerin die (PL die **Anhängerinnen**) supporter.

anhören verb (PERF **hat angehört**) 1 to listen to (music, a CD); **sich etwas anhören** to listen to something; **ich kann ihn mir nicht länger anhören** I can't listen to him any longer; 2 **sich anhören** to sound; **sich gut anhören** to sound good; 3 **jemandem etwas anhören** to hear something in somebody's voice; **man hörte ihr die Verzweiflung an** you could hear the despair in her voice.

anklagen verb (PERF **hat angeklagt**) to accuse.

Ankleidekabine die (PL die **Ankleidekabinen**) changing cubicle.

ankommen ◇ verb (IMPERF **kam an**, PERF **ist angekommen**) 1 to arrive; **gut ankommen** to arrive safely; 2 **(bei jemandem) gut ankommen** (informal) to go down well (with somebody); 3 **ankommen auf** to depend on; **es kommt ganz darauf an** it all depends; 4 **es drauf ankommen lassen** (informal) to take a chance; 5 **auf ein paar Minuten kommt es nicht an** a few minutes don't matter.

ankündigen verb (PERF **hat angekündigt**) to announce.

Ankunft die (PL die **Ankünfte**) arrival.

Ankunftstafel die (PL die **Ankunftstafeln**) arrivals board.

△ NEW SPELLING: See page xii

Ankunftszeit die (PL die Ankunftszeiten) time of arrival.

Anlage die (PL die Anlagen) 1 gardens; 2 investment; **das Haus ist eine gute Anlage** the house is a good investment; 3 plant (industrial, for recycling, for example); 4 enclosure; **als Anlage** enclosed; 5 system (music, loudspeakers, etc.); 6 installation (military).

Anlass △ der (PL die Anlässe) 1 cause; **der Anlass ihres Streits** the cause of their row; **Anlass zu etwas geben** to give cause for something; 2 occasion; **ein festlicher Anlass** a festive occasion; **aus Anlass ihres Geburtstags** on the occasion of her birthday.

Anleitung die (PL die Anleitungen) instructions.

anmachen verb (PERF hat angemacht) 1 to turn on (the light, radio, TV); 2 to light (a fire); 3 to dress (salad); 4 (informal) to chat up (a person).

Anmeldeformular das (PL die Anmeldeformulare) registration form.

anmelden verb (PERF hat angemeldet) 1 to register (a car, change of address); 2 **jemanden anmelden** to enrol somebody; 3 **jemanden anmelden** to make an appointment for somebody; **sind Sie angemeldet?** do you have an appointment? 4 **ein Gespräch anmelden** to book a call (on the

phone); 5 **sich anmelden** to say that you're coming; 6 **sich anmelden** to register your new address (in Germany a change of address has to be registered at the 'Einwohnermeldeamt'); **sich polizeilich anmelden** to register with the police; 7 **sich anmelden** to make an appointment; **sich beim Arzt anmelden** to make an appointment with the doctor; 8 **sich anmelden** to enrol; **sich zu einem Abendkurs anmelden** to enrol for an evening course.

Anmeldung die (PL die Anmeldungen) 1 registration; 2 appointment.

annehmen ◇ verb (PRES nimmt an, IMPERF nahm an, PERF hat angenommen) 1 to accept (an invitation, help, a verdict); 2 to take (a call, name); 3 to adopt (a child, habit); 4 to assume; **angenommen, dass ...** assuming that ...; 5 to suppose.

annehmbar adjective acceptable.

Annonce die (PL die Annoncen) (small) ad.

anordnen verb (PERF hat angeordnet) 1 to arrange; 2 to order.

anpassen verb (PERF hat sich angepasst △) **sich anpassen** to adapt.

anpassungsfähig adjective adaptable.

anprobieren verb (PERF hat anprobiert) to try on.

◇ IRREGULAR VERB: See the verb table in the centre of the dictionary

Anruf der (PL die Anrufe) (phone) call.

Anrufbeantworter der (PL die Anrufbeantworter) answering machine.

anrufen ◇ verb (IMPERF **rief an**, PERF **hat angerufen**) 1 to ring, to phone; **ich rufe schnell mal meine Mutter an** I'll just quickly ring my mother; 2 to call to (a passer-by).

ans = an das; **ans Telefon gehen** to answer the phone.

Ansage die (PL die Ansagen) announcement.

Ansager der (PL die Ansager) announcer.

Ansagerin die (PL die Ansagerinnen) announcer.

anschalten verb (PERF **hat angeschaltet**) to switch on.

anschauen verb (PERF **hat angeschaut**) 1 to look at; 2 **sich etwas anschauen** to look at something, to watch something (on TV); **sie schauten sich den neuen Film an** they saw the new film.

anscheinend adverb apparently.

Anschlag der (PL die Anschläge) 1 notice; 2 attack; **ein Anschlag auf den Präsidenten** an attack on the president.

Anschlagbrett das (PL die Anschlagbretter) notice board.

anschlagen ◇ verb (PRES **schlägt an**, IMPERF **schlug an**, PERF **hat angeschlagen**) 1 to put up (a notice, an announcement); 2 to chip.

anschließen ◇ verb (IMPERF **schloss an** △, PERF **hat angeschlossen**) 1 to connect; 2 **sich an etwas anschließen** to follow something; **an den Vortrag schließt sich eine Diskussion an** the talk will be followed by a discussion; 3 **sich jemandem anschließen** to join somebody; **sich einer Gruppe anschließen** to join a group.

anschließend adverb 1 afterwards; 2 **anschließend an das Essen** after the meal.

Anschluss △ der (PL die Anschlüsse) 1 connection; 2 **Anschluss finden** to make friends; 3 **den Anschluss verlieren** to lose contact; 4 **im Anschluss an** after.

anschnallen verb (PERF **hat sich angeschnallt**) **sich anschnallen** to fasten your seat belt.

Anschrift die (PL die Anschriften) address.

Anschuldigung die (PL die Anschuldigungen) accusation.

ansehen ◇ verb (PRES **sieht an**, IMPERF **sah an**, PERF **hat angesehen**) 1 to look at; **sie sah mich nicht an** she didn't look at me; 2 **sich etwas ansehen** to look at something; (on TV) to watch something; **sich einen Film ansehen** to see a film; 3 **sich eine Stadt ansehen** to look round a town; 4 to regard; **ich sehe ihn als meinen Freund an** I regard him as a friend.

△ NEW SPELLING: See page xii

Ansehen das 1 respect; 2 reputation.

Ansicht die (PL die Ansichten) view; **meiner Ansicht nach** in my view.

Ansichtskarte die (PL die Ansichtskarten) picture postcard.

ansprechen ◇ verb (PRES **spricht an**, IMPERF **sprach an**, PERF **hat angesprochen**) 1 to speak to; 2 to appeal to; **die Musik spricht mich an** the music appeals to me; 3 to mention; **er hat den Skandal, in den sie verwickelt war, angesprochen** he mentioned the scandal she was involved in; 4 **auf etwas ansprechen** to respond to something (a treatment, for example).

Anspruch der (PL die Ansprüche) 1 demand; **keine Ansprüche stellen** to make no demands; 2 claim; 3 **Anspruch auf etwas haben** to be entitled to something; 4 **viel Zeit in Anspruch nehmen** to take up a lot of time; 5 **etwas in Anspruch nehmen** to take advantage of something (an offer, for example).

anständig adjective 1 decent; 2 respectable.

anstarren verb (PERF **hat angestarrt**) to stare at.

anstatt preposition ←(+GEN) instead of.
conjunction **anstatt zu arbeiten** instead of working.

ansteckend adjective infectious.

anstelle preposition ←(+GEN) instead of.

anstellen verb (PERF **hat angestellt**) 1 to employ; 2 to turn on (the TV, radio); 3 to do; **was stellt ihr heute Abend noch an?** what are you doing tonight?; **wie kann ich es nur anstellen, dass …?** what can I do to …?; 4 **sich anstellen** to queue; 5 **sich anstellen** to make a fuss; **stell dich nicht so an!** don't make such a fuss!

anstreichen ◇ verb (IMPERF **strich an**, PERF **hat angestrichen**) to paint.

anstrengen verb (PERF **hat angestrengt**) 1 to tire; **ihr Besuch hat mich sehr angestrengt** their visit tired me out; 2 **sich anstrengen** to make an effort.

anstrengend adjective tiring.

Anstrengung die (PL die Anstrengungen) effort.

Antarktis die **die Antarktis** the Antarctic.

Anteil der (PL die Anteile) 1 share; **mein Anteil an dem Gewinn** my share of the profit; 2 **Anteil nehmen** to sympathize; 3 **Anteil nehmen an** to take an interest in.

Antenne die (PL die Antennen) aerial.

Antibiotikum das (PL die Antibiotika) antibiotic.

antik adjective antique.

Antiquitäten plural noun antiques.

Antrag der (PL die Anträge)

◇ IRREGULAR VERB: See the verb table in the centre of the dictionary

application; **einen Antrag stellen** to make an application.

Antragsformular das (PL die Antragsformulare) application form.

Antwort die (PL die Antworten) answer, reply; **jemandem eine Antwort geben** to give somebody an answer.

antworten verb (PERF hat geantwortet) to answer, to reply; **auf etwas antworten** to answer something; **jemandem antworten** to reply to somebody.

Anwalt der (PL die Anwälte) lawyer.

Anwältin die (PL die Anwältinnen) lawyer.

Anweisung die (PL die Anweisungen) instruction.

anwenden verb (PERF hat angewendet) 1 to use (a method, process, medicine); 2 to apply (a rule, law).

anwesend adjective present.

Anzahl die number.

anzahlen verb (PERF hat angezahlt) to pay a deposit; **hundert Mark anzahlen** to pay a hundred marks deposit; **ein Auto anzahlen** to pay a deposit on a car.

Anzahlung die (PL die Anzahlungen) deposit.

Anzeichen das (PL die Anzeichen) sign.

Anzeige die (PL die Anzeigen) 1 advertisement; 2 report (to the police); **(eine) Anzeige gegen jemanden erstatten** to report somebody to the police.

anzeigen verb (PERF hat angezeigt) 1 to report; **jemanden anzeigen** to report somebody to the police; 2 to show (the time, a date).

anziehen ◇ verb (IMPERF zog an, PERF hat angezogen) 1 to attract; 2 to put on (clothes, the brakes); 3 to dress (a child or doll); **gut angezogen** well dressed; 4 **sich anziehen** to get dressed; 5 **was soll ich anziehen?** what shall I wear?

Anzug der (PL die Anzüge) suit.

anzünden verb (PERF hat angezündet) to light.

Apfel der (PL die Äpfel) apple.

Apfelsaft der (PL die Apfelsäfte) apple juice.

Apfelsine die (PL die Apfelsinen) orange.

Apotheke die (PL die Apotheken) chemist's, pharmacy.

Apotheker der (PL die Apotheker) chemist, pharmacist.

Apothekerin die (PL die Apothekerinnen) chemist, pharmacist.

Apparat der (PL die Apparate) 1 set (TV, radio); 2 camera; 3 phone; **am Apparat!** speaking!; 4 gadget.

Appartement das (PL die Appartements) flat.

Appetit der appetite; **guten Appetit!** enjoy your meal!

△ NEW SPELLING: See page xii

Aprikose die (PL die Aprikosen) apricot.

April der April; **am ersten April** on the first of April; **April, April!** April fool!; **jemanden in den April schicken** to play an April fool trick on somebody.

Äquator der equator.

Araber der (PL die Araber) Arab.

Araberin die (PL die Araberinnen) Arab.

arabisch adjective 1 Arab; 2 Arabian; 3 Arabic (number); **die arabische Sprache** Arabic.

Arbeit die (PL die Arbeiten) 1 work; **viel Arbeit haben** to have a lot of work; **von der Arbeit kommen** to come from work; 2 job; 3 test (at school); 4 **sich viel Arbeit machen** to go to a lot of trouble.

arbeiten verb (PERF **hat gearbeitet**) to work.

Arbeiter der (PL die Arbeiter) worker.

Arbeiterin die (PL die Arbeiterinnen) worker.

Arbeitgeber der (PL die Arbeitgeber) employer.

Arbeitnehmer der (PL die Arbeitnehmer) employee.

Arbeitsamt das (PL die Arbeitsämter) job centre.

arbeitslos adjective unemployed.

Arbeitslose der/die (PL die Arbeitslosen) unemployed person; **die Arbeitslosen** the unemployed.

Arbeitslosigkeit die unemployment.

Arbeitspraktikum das (PL die Arbeitspraktika) work experience.

Arbeitsplatz der (PL die Arbeitsplätze) 1 job; 2 desk.

Architekt der (PL die Architekten) architect.

Architektin die (PL die Architektinnen) architect.

Architektur die architecture.

Ärger der 1 annoyance; 2 trouble; **Ärger mit dem Auto haben** to have trouble with the car.

ärgerlich adjective 1 annoying; 2 annoyed; **er war darüber sehr ärgerlich** he was very annoyed about it.

ärgern verb (PERF **hat geärgert**) 1 to annoy; 2 **sich ärgern** to be annoyed, to get annoyed; **ich habe mich darüber geärgert** I was annoyed about it; **sich über jemanden ärgern** to get annoyed with somebody.

artig adjective well-behaved.

Arktis die die Arktis the Arctic; **in der Arktis** in the Arctic.

arm adjective poor.

Arm der (PL die Arme) arm; **jemanden auf den Arm nehmen** (informal) to pull somebody's leg.

Armband das (PL die Armbänder) bracelet.

Armbanduhr die (PL die Armbanduhren) wrist-watch.

◇ IRREGULAR VERB: See the verb table in the centre of the dictionary

Armee die (PL die Armeen) army.

Ärmel der (PL die Ärmel) sleeve.

Ärmelkanal der (English) Channel.

Armut die poverty.

arrangieren verb (PERF hat arrangiert) 1 to arrange; 2 sich arrangieren to come to an arrangement.

Art die (PL die Arten) 1 way; auf diese Art in this way; auf seine Art in his own way; 2 kind; diese Art (von) Buch this kind of book; Bücher aller Art all kinds of books; 3 species; 4 nature; es ist nicht seine Art, das zu tun it's not (in) his nature to do that.

Artikel der (PL die Artikel) article.

Arznei die medicine.

Arzneimittel das (PL die Arzneimittel) drug.

Arzt der (PL die Ärzte) doctor.

Ärztin die (PL die Ärztinnen) doctor.

ärztlich adjective medical.
adverb sich ärztlich behandeln lassen to have medical treatment.

As SEE Ass.

Asche die (PL die Aschen) ash.

Aschenbecher der (PL die Aschenbecher) ashtray.

Aschermittwoch der Ash Wednesday.

Asiat der (PL die Asiaten) Asian.

Asiatin die (PL die Asiatinnen) Asian.

asiatisch adjective Asian.

Asien das Asia; nach Asien to Asia.

aß SEE essen.

Ass △ das (PL die Asse) ace.

Assistent der (PL die Assistenten) assistant.

Assistentin die (PL die Assistentinnen) assistant.

Ast der (PL die Äste) branch.

Asthma das asthma.

Astrologie die astrology.

Astronaut der (PL die Astronauten) astronaut.

Astronomie die astronomy.

Asyl das (PL die Asyle) 1 asylum; um politisches Asyl bitten to apply for political asylum; 2 hostel (for the homeless).

Asylant der (PL die Asylanten) asylum-seeker.

Atelier das (PL die Ateliers) (artist's) studio.

Atem der breath; außer Atem sein to be out of breath.

atemlos adjective breathless.

Athlet der (PL die Athleten) athlete.

Athletin die (PL die Athletinnen) athlete.

Atlantik der der Atlantik the Atlantic (Ocean); im Atlantik in the Atlantic.

Atlas der (PL die Atlanten) atlas.

atmen verb (PERF hat geatmet) to breathe.

△ NEW SPELLING: See page xii

Atmosphäre die (PL die Atmosphären) atmosphere.

Atom das (PL die Atome). atom.

atomar adjective atomic.

Atomwaffen plural noun nuclear weapons.

atomwaffenfrei adjective nuclear-free.

attraktiv adjective attractive.

ätzend adjective **1** corrosive; **2** caustic (wit, remark).

au exclamation **1** ouch!; **2** oh! (when surprised or enthusiastic); **au ja!** oh yes!

auch adverb **1** also, too; **Sophie war auch dabei** Sophie was also there, Sophie was there too; **ich auch** me too; **nicht nur … sondern auch …** not only … but also …; **2** 'ich gehe jetzt' – 'ich auch' 'I'm going now' – 'so am I'; **'er schläft' – 'sie auch'** 'he's asleep' – 'so is she'; **3** 'ich bin nicht müde' – 'ich auch nicht' 'I'm not tired'–'neither am I'; **das weiß ich auch nicht** I don't know either; **4** auch wenn even if; **5** wann auch whenever; **was auch** whatever; **wo auch** wherever; **wer auch** whoever; **6** wie dem auch sei however that may be; **7** lügst du auch nicht? you're not lying, are you?

auf preposition ←(+DAT or +ACC) (the dative is used when talking about position; the accusative shows movement or a change of place) **1** on; **das Buch liegt auf dem Tisch** the book's on the table; **er hat das** Buch auf den Tisch gelegt he put the book on the table; **2** ich war auf der Party** I was at the party; **ich gehe auf eine Party** I'm going to a party; **ich war auf der Post** I was at the post office; **er ist auf die Post gegangen** he went to the post office; **3** auf der Straße** in the street; **4** auf diese Art** in this way; **auf Deutsch** in German; **5** for (indicating time or distance); **er ist auf ein paar Tage verreist** he's gone away for a few days; **6** auf seinen Rat hin** on his advice; **7** auf Wiedersehen!** goodbye!
adverb **1** open; **die Tür ist auf** the door is open; **Mund auf!** open your mouth!; **2** up (out of bed); **auf sein** to be up; **er ist schon auf** he's already up; **3** auf einmal** suddenly; **4** auf einmal** at once (at the same time); **5** auf und ab** up and down; **6** sich auf und davon machen** to make off.

aufbekommen ◇ verb (IMPERF bekam auf, PERF hat aufbekommen) **1** to get open; **2** Hausaufgaben aufbekommen** to be given homework.

aufbewahren verb (PERF hat aufbewahrt) to keep.

aufblasen ◇ verb (PRES bläst auf, IMPERF blies auf, PERF hat aufgeblasen) to blow up.

aufbleiben ◇ verb (IMPERF blieb auf, PERF ist aufgeblieben) **1** to stay open; **wie lange bleiben die Geschäfte auf?** how long do the shops stay open?; **2** to stay up (not go to bed).

◇ IRREGULAR VERB: See the verb table in the centre of the dictionary

aufbringen ◇ *verb* (IMPERF **brachte auf**, PERF **hat aufgebracht**) **1** to raise (*money*); **2** to find (*patience, strength*); **3** to open; **ich kann die Tür nicht aufbringen** I can't open the door; **4 jemanden aufbringen** to make somebody angry; **5 Verständnis für etwas aufbringen** to be able to understand something.

aufeinander *adverb* **1** one on top of the other; **die Bretter aufeinander legen** to put the planks one on top of the other; **2 aufeinander liegen** △ to lie on top of each other; **3 aufeinander folgen** to follow one another; **4 aufeinander warten** to wait for each other; **5 aufeinander schießen** to shoot at each other; **6 aufeinander fahren** to collide with each other.

Aufenthalt *der* (PL **die Aufenthalte**) **1** stay; **2** stop (*pause in a journey*); **zehn Minuten Aufenthalt haben** to stop for ten minutes.

Auffahrt *die* (PL **die Auffahrten**) **1** drive; **2** slip road.

auffallend *adjective* striking.

auffangen ◇ *verb* (PRES **fängt auf**, IMPERF **fing auf**, PERF **hat aufgefangen**) to catch.

aufführen *verb* (PERF **hat aufgeführt**) **1** to perform (*a play*); **2** to list (*words, items*); **3 sich aufführen** to behave.

Aufführung *die* (PL **die Aufführungen**) performance.

Aufgabe *die* (PL **die Aufgaben**)

1 task; **2** exercise (*at school*); **3** question (*in a test or an exam*); **4 Aufgaben** homework.

aufgeben ◇ *verb* (PRES **gibt auf**, IMPERF **gab auf**, PERF **hat aufgegeben**) **1** to give up; **ich gebe auf!** I give up!; **2** to post; **3** to check in (*luggage*); **4** to place (*an advertisement, order*); **5 Hausaufgaben aufgeben** to set homework.

aufgehen ◇ *verb* (IMPERF **ging auf**, PERF **ist aufgegangen**) **1** to open (*of a door or flower, for example*); **2** to come undone (*of a knot or zip, for example*); **3** to rise (*of the sun, moon*); **4** to realize; **es ist mir aufgegangen, dass ...** I've realized that ...; **5** to work out (*in maths*); **zehn durch drei geht nicht auf** three into ten won't go.

aufgeregt *adjective* excited.

aufgeschlossen *adjective* open-minded.

aufgrund *preposition* ←(+GEN) **1** because of; **2** on the strength of.

aufhaben ◇ *verb* (PRES **hat auf**, IMPERF **hatte auf**, PERF **hat aufgehabt**) **1** to have on (*a hat*); **2 den Mund aufhaben** to have your mouth open; **3 etwas aufhaben** to have homework to do; **viel aufhaben** to have a lot of homework; **4** to be open; **der Laden hat abends auf** the shop is open in the evening.

aufhalten ◇ *verb* (PRES **hält auf**, IMPERF **hielt auf**, PERF **hat aufgehalten**) **1** to hold open (*a*

△ NEW SPELLING: *See page xii*

door); **2** to hold up, to keep (*somebody from doing something*); **3 die Hand aufhalten** to hold out your hand; **4 die Augen aufhalten** to keep your eyes open; **5** to check (*inflation, an advance, unemployment*); **6 sich aufhalten** to stay; **7 sich mit etwas aufhalten** to spend your time on something.

aufhängen verb (PERF **hat aufgehängt**) **1** to hang up (*washing*); **2 sich aufhängen** to hang yourself.

aufheben ✧ verb (IMPERF **hob auf**, PERF **hat aufgehoben**) **1** to pick up (*from the ground*); **2** to keep; **3** to abolish (*a law*); **4 gut aufgehoben sein** to be well looked after.

aufheitern verb (PERF **hat aufgeheitert**) **1** to cheer up; **2 sich aufheitern** to brighten up (*of the weather*).

aufhören verb (PERF **hat aufgehört**) **1** to stop; **aufhören zu arbeiten** to stop working.

aufklären verb (PERF **hat aufgeklärt**) **1** to solve (*a crime*); **2** to explain (*an event, incident*); **3 ein Kind aufklären** to tell a child the facts of life; **4 sich aufklären** to be solved (*a misunderstanding or mystery*); **5 sich aufklären** to clear up; **das Wetter klärt sich auf** the weather is clearing up.

Aufkleber der (PL die **Aufkleber**) sticker.

auflegen verb (PERF **hat aufgelegt**) **1** to put on; **2** to hang up (*when phoning*); **3** to publish; **ein Buch neu auflegen** to reprint a book.

auflösen verb (PERF **hat aufgelöst**) **1** to dissolve; **2** to close (*an account*); **3 sich auflösen** to dissolve; **4 sich auflösen** to break up (*of a crowd, demonstration*); **5 der Nebel hat sich aufgelöst** the fog has lifted; **6 in Tränen aufgelöst sein** to be in floods of tears.

aufmachen verb (PERF **hat aufgemacht**) **1** to open; **2 jemandem aufmachen** to open the door to somebody; **3** to undo (*a zip, knot*); **4 sich aufmachen** to set out.

aufmerksam adjective **1** attentive; **2 auf etwas aufmerksam werden** to notice something; **3 jemanden auf etwas aufmerksam machen** to draw somebody's attention to something.

aufmuntern verb (PERF **hat aufgemuntert**) to cheer up.

Aufnahme die (PL die **Aufnahmen**) **1** photograph; **2** recording; **3** admission (*to hospital, to a club*); **4** welcome.

Aufnahmeprüfung die (PL die **Aufnahmeprüfungen**) entrance exam.

aufnehmen ✧ verb (PRES **nimmt auf**, IMPERF **nahm auf**, PERF **hat aufgenommen**) **1** to receive (*guests*); **2** to take up (*an idea, activity, a theme*); **3** to admit (*to hospital, to a club*); **4** to photograph; **5** to film; **6** to record (*a song*); **7 es mit jemandem aufnehmen können**

✧ **IRREGULAR VERB: See the verb table in the centre of the dictionary**

to be a match for somebody; **8 to take** (*food, news*); **etwas gelassen aufnehmen** to take something calmly.

aufpassen verb (PERF **hat aufgepasst** ∆) **1** to pay attention; **2** to watch out; **3 auf jemanden aufpassen** to look after somebody; **4 auf etwas aufpassen** to keep an eye on something; **pass auf meine Tasche auf** keep an eye on my bag.

aufräumen verb (PERF **hat aufgeräumt**) to tidy up.

aufrecht adjective upright.

aufregen verb (PERF **hat aufgeregt**) **1** to excite; **2** to annoy; **3 sich aufregen** to get worked up.

aufregend adjective exciting.

aufs = auf das.

Aufsatz der (PL die **Aufsätze**) essay.

aufschieben ◊ verb (IMPERF **schob auf**, PERF **hat aufgeschoben**) **1** to put off (*an arrangement*); **2** to slide open.

aufschließen ◊ verb (IMPERF **schloss auf** ∆, PERF **hat aufgeschlossen**) to unlock.

Aufschnitt der sliced cold meat and cheese.

aufschreiben ◊ verb (IMPERF **schrieb auf**, PERF **hat aufgeschrieben**) to write down.

aufsehen ◊ verb (PRES **sieht auf**, IMPERF **sah auf**, PERF **hat aufgesehen**) to look up.

aufsetzen verb (PERF **hat aufgesetzt**) **1** to put on; **2** to draft; **3 sich aufsetzen** to sit up.

Aufsicht die **1** supervision; **2** supervisor.

Aufstand der (PL die **Aufstände**) rebellion.

aufstehen ◊ verb (IMPERF **stand auf**, PERF **ist aufgestanden**) **1** to get up; **2** (PERF **hat aufgestanden**) to be open.

aufstellen verb (PERF **hat aufgestellt**) **1** to put up; **2** to set up (*skittles, chess pieces*); **3 eine Mannschaft aufstellen** to pick a team; **4 eine Liste aufstellen** to draw up a list; **5 sich aufstellen** to line up.

auftauen verb (PERF **ist aufgetaut**) **1** to thaw; **2** to defrost; **die Erdbeeren sind aufgetaut** the strawberries have defrosted; **3** (PERF **hat aufgetaut**) to defrost; **ich habe die Erbeeren aufgetaut** I've defrosted the strawberries.

aufteilen verb (PERF **hat aufgeteilt**) to divide up.

Auftrag der (PL die **Aufträge**) **1** job; **2** order (*in business*); **etwas in Auftrag geben** to order something; **3** instructions; **einen Auftrag ausführen** to carry out an instruction; **4 im Auftrag von** on behalf of.

auftreten ◊ verb (PRES **tritt auf**, IMPERF **trat auf**, PERF **ist aufgetreten**) **1** to appear (*on stage*); **2** to arise (*a problem, difficulty*); **3** to behave; **4** to tread.

∆ NEW SPELLING: See page xii

aufwachen *verb* (PERF **ist aufgewacht**) to wake up.

aufwachsen ◇ *verb* (PRES **wächst auf**, IMPERF **wuchs auf**, PERF **ist aufgewachsen**) to grow up.

aufwecken *verb* (PERF **hat aufgeweckt**) to wake up.

aufziehen ◇ *verb* (IMPERF **zog auf**, PERF **hat aufgezogen**) 1 to wind up (*a clock or toy*); 2 to draw (*curtains*); 3 **jemanden aufziehen** (*informal*) to tease somebody; 4 to bring up (*a child*).

Aufzug *der* (PL **die Aufzüge**) lift; **ich fahre mit dem Aufzug runter** I'm going down in the lift.

Auge *das* (PL **die Augen**) 1 eye; 2 **unter vier Augen** in private.

Augenblick *der* (PL **die Augenblicke**) moment; **im Augenblick** at the moment.

Augenbraue *die* (PL **die Augenbrauen**) eyebrow.

August *der* August.

aus *preposition* ←(+DAT) 1 out of; **er hat es aus dem Fenster geworfen** he threw it out of the window; 2 from; **aus Spanien** from Spain; **aus Erfahrung** from experience; 3 made of; **aus Holz** made of wood; 4 **aus Spaß** for fun; 5 **aus der Mode** out of fashion; 6 **aus Versehen** by mistake; 7 **aus welchem Grund?** for what reason?; 8 **aus ihr ist eine gute Rechtsanwältin geworden** she made a good lawyer; **aus ihm ist nichts geworden** he never made

anything of his life. *adverb* 1 off (*of a TV, radio*); **das Licht ist aus** the light is off; **Licht aus!** lights out!; 2 finished; **wenn das Spiel aus ist** when the game has finished; 3 **von mir aus** as far as I'm concerned; 4 **von sich aus** of your own accord.

ausbeuten *verb* (PERF **hat ausgebeutet**) to exploit.

ausbilden *verb* (PERF **hat ausgebildet**) to train.

Ausbildung *die* 1 training; 2 education.

Ausdruck[1] *der* (PL **die Ausdrücke**) expression; **etwas zum Ausdruck bringen** to express something.

Ausdruck[2] *der* (PL **die Ausdrucke**) print-out.

ausdrucken *verb* (PERF **hat ausgedruckt**) to print out.

ausdrücken *verb* (PERF **hat ausgedrückt**) 1 to squeeze (*oranges, lemons*); 2 to express; 3 **sich ausdrücken** to express oneself.

auseinander *adverb* 1 apart; **etwas auseinander nehmen** △ to take something apart; **auseinander halten** △ to tell apart; 2 **auseinander gehen** △ to part; 3 **auseinander schreiben** to write as separate words; 4 **sich mit einem Problem auseinander setzen** △ to come to grips with a problem; 5 **sich mit jemandem auseinander setzen** △ to have it out with somebody.

◇ IRREGULAR VERB: *See the verb table in the centre of the dictionary*

Ausfahrt die (PL die Ausfahrten)
1 exit; 2 'Ausfahrt freihalten' 'keep clear'.

ausfallen ◇ verb (PRES fällt aus, IMPERF fiel aus, PERF ist ausgefallen)
1 to be cancelled; etwas ausfallen lassen to cancel something; 2 to fall out (hair); 3 to fail (an engine, brakes, a signal); 4 to break down (a machine, a car, heating); 5 to turn out; gut ausfallen to turn out well.

Ausflug der (PL die Ausflüge) outing, trip; einen Ausflug machen to go on an outing.

Ausfuhr die export.

ausführen verb (PERF hat ausgeführt) 1 to carry out (a plan); 2 to export (goods); 3 to take out; er hat seine Freundin zum Essen ausgeführt he took his girlfriend out for a meal; 4 den Hund ausführen to take the dog for a walk.

ausführlich adjective detailed. adverb in detail.

ausfüllen verb (PERF hat ausgefüllt) 1 to fill in; 2 ihr Beruf als Lehrerin füllt sie ganz aus teaching gives her great satisfaction.

Ausgabe die (PL die Ausgaben) 1 edition; 2 issue; 3 Ausgaben expenditure.

Ausgang der (PL die Ausgänge) 1 exit; 'kein Ausgang' 'no exit'; 2 end, ending; 3 result (of a game, discussion).

ausgeben ◇ verb (PRES gibt aus, IMPERF gab aus, PERF hat ausgegeben) 1 to spend; 2 to hand out; 3 Fahrkarten ausgeben to issue tickets; 4 to serve (food); 5 sich ausgeben als to pretend to be; 6 einen ausgeben (informal) to treat everybody (to a round of drinks for example).

ausgebucht adjective fully booked.

ausgehen ◇ verb (PRES geht aus, IMPERF ging aus, PERF ist ausgegangen) 1 to go out; 2 to run out (of supplies); 3 to end; schlecht ausgehen to end badly; 4 davon ausgehen, dass ... to assume that ...

ausgerechnet adverb 1 ausgerechnet heute today of all days; 2 ausgerechnet sie she of all people.

ausgeschlossen adjective out of the question.

ausgezeichnet adjective excellent.

aushalten ◇ verb (PRES hält aus, IMPERF hielt aus, PERF hat ausgehalten) 1 to stand; 2 es ist nicht zum Aushalten it's unbearable.

Aushilfe die (PL die Aushilfen) temporary assistant, temp.

auskennen ◇ verb (IMPERF kannte sich aus, PERF hat sich ausgekannt) 1 sich auskennen to know your way around; 2 sich gut mit etwas auskennen to know a lot about something.

auskommen ◇ verb (IMPERF kam aus, PERF ist ausgekommen) 1 to manage; mit fünfzig Mark

△ NEW SPELLING: See page xii

auskommen to manage on fifty marks; **2 mit jemandem gut auskommen** to get on well with somebody.

Auskunft die (PL die **Auskünfte**) **1** information; **2** information desk; **3** enquiries (when phoning).

auslachen verb (PERF hat **ausgelacht**) to laugh at.

ausladen ◇ verb (PRES **lädt aus**, IMPERF **lud aus**, PERF hat **ausgeladen**) **1** to unload; **2 jemanden ausladen** (informal) to put somebody off.

Ausland das im Ausland abroad; ins Ausland reisen to travel abroad.

Ausländer der (PL die **Ausländer**) foreigner.

Ausländerin die (PL die **Ausländerinnen**) foreigner.

ausländisch adjective foreign.

Auslandsgespräch das (PL die **Auslandsgespräche**) international call.

ausleeren verb (PERF hat **ausgeleert**) to empty.

ausleihen ◇ verb (IMPERF **lieh aus**, PERF hat **ausgeliehen**) **1** to lend; **2 etwas ausleihen** to borrow something.

ausmachen verb (PERF hat **ausgemacht**) **1** to turn off; **2** to put out; **3** to arrange; **wir haben ausgemacht, dass wir uns heute Abend treffen** we've arranged to meet up this evening; **4 das macht mir nichts aus** I don't mind; **macht es Ihnen etwas aus, wenn ...?**

would you mind if ...?; **5 viel ausmachen** to make a great difference.

Ausnahme die (PL die **Ausnahmen**) exception.

ausnutzen verb (PERF hat **ausgenutzt**) **1** to use; **2** to take advantage of.

auspacken verb (PERF hat **ausgepackt**) to unpack.

Auspuff der (PL die **Auspuffe**) exhaust.

ausrechnen verb (PERF hat **ausgerechnet**) to work out.

Ausrede die (PL die **Ausreden**) excuse.

ausreichend adjective **1** sufficient; **2** fair, pass (as a mark at school).

Ausreise die (PL die **Ausreisen**) departure (from a country).

ausrichten verb (PERF hat **ausgerichtet**) **jemandem etwas ausrichten** to tell somebody something.

Ausrufezeichen das (PL die **Ausrufezeichen**) exclamation mark.

ausruhen verb (PERF hat sich **ausgeruht**) sich ausruhen to have a rest.

Ausrüstung die equipment.

ausschalten verb (PERF hat **ausgeschaltet**) **1** to switch off; **2** to eliminate.

ausschneiden ◇ verb (IMPERF **schnitt aus**, PERF hat **ausgeschnitten**) to cut out.

◇ IRREGULAR VERB: *See the verb table in the centre of the dictionary*

Ausschuss ∆ *der* (PL *die* **Ausschüsse**) committee.

aussehen ◇ *verb* (PRES **sieht aus**, IMPERF **sah aus**, PERF **hat ausgesehen**) to look.

Aussehen *das* appearance.

außen *adverb* 1 (on the) outside; **von außen** from the outside; 2 **nach außen** outwards.

Außenminister *der* (PL *die* **Außenminister**) Foreign Secretary, Foreign Minister.

außer *preposition* ←(+DAT) 1 apart from, except (for); **alle außer ihm** everyone except (for) him; 2 out of; **außer Sicht** out of sight; **außer Betrieb** out of order; 3 **außer Haus** out; 4 **außer sich sein** to be beside yourself.
conjunction 1 except; **außer sonntags** except Sundays; 2 **außer wenn** unless.

außerdem *adverb* 1 as well; 2 besides.

äußerer, äußere, äußeres *adjective* 1 external (*injury, circumstances*); 2 outer (*layer, circle*); 3 outward (*appearance, effect*).

außergewöhnlich *adjective* unusual.

außerhalb *preposition* ←(+GEN) outside.
adverb **außerhalb wohnen** to live out of town.

äußerlich *adjective* 1 external; 2 outward (*appearance*).

außerordentlich *adjective* extraordinary.

äußerst *adverb* extremely.

Äußerung *die* (PL *die* **Äußerungen**) remark.

Aussicht *die* (PL *die* **Aussichten**) 1 prospect; **etwas in Aussicht haben** to have the prospect of something; **keine Aussichten auf Erfolg haben** to have no chance of success; 2 view; **ein Zimmer mit Aussicht aufs Meer** a room with a view of the sea.

Aussprache *die* (PL *die* **Aussprachen**) 1 pronunciation; 2 talk.

aussprechen ◇ *verb* (PRES **spricht aus**, IMPERF **sprach aus**, PERF **hat ausgesprochen**) 1 to pronounce; 2 to express; 3 **lassen Sie ihn aussprechen** let him finish (*speaking*); 4 **sich aussprechen** to talk; **sich mit jemandem aussprechen** to have a talk with somebody; 5 **sich gegen etwas aussprechen** to come out against something; **sich für etwas aussprechen** to come out in favour of something; 6 **sich lobend über jemanden aussprechen** to speak highly of somebody.

aussteigen ◇ *verb* (IMPERF **stieg aus**, PERF **ist ausgestiegen**) 1 to get out; 2 to get off.

ausstellen *verb* (PERF **hat ausgestellt**) 1 to display (*in a shop*); 2 to exhibit; 3 to make out (*a certificate, bill*); 4 to issue (*a passport*); 5 to switch off.

∆ NEW SPELLING: *See page xii*

Ausstellung die (PL die Ausstellungen) exhibition.

ausstreichen ◇ verb (IMPERF strich aus, PERF hat ausgestrichen) to cross out.

aussuchen verb (PERF hat ausgesucht) 1 to choose; 2 sich etwas aussuchen to choose something.

Austausch der of exchange.

austauschen verb (PERF hat ausgetauscht) 1 to exchange; 2 to replace; 3 to substitute (a player).

Auster die (PL die Austern) oyster.

austragen ◇ verb (PRES trägt aus, IMPERF trug aus, PERF hat ausgetragen) to deliver (post); to hold (a race).

Australien das Australia; aus Australien from Australia.

Australier der (PL die Australier) Australian.

Australierin die (PL die Australierinnen) Australian.

australisch adjective Australian.

austreten ◇ verb (PRES tritt aus, IMPERF trat aus, PERF hat ausgetreten) 1 to stamp out (a cigarette or fire); 2 to wear out (shoes); 3 (PERF ist ausgetreten) aus einem Klub austreten to leave a club; ich trete aus I'm leaving; 4 (informal) (PERF ist ausgetreten) to go to the loo.

austrinken ◇ verb (IMPERF trank aus, PERF hat ausgetrunken) to drink up.

Ausverkauf der (PL die Ausverkäufe) sale.

ausverkauft adjective 1 sold out; 2 ein ausverkauftes Haus a full house (at the cinema or theatre).

Auswahl die (PL die Auswahlen) choice, selection; wenig Auswahl haben to have a limited selection.

auswärts adverb 1 away (in sport); auswärts spielen to play away; 2 auswärts essen to eat out; 3 sie arbeitet auswärts she doesn't work locally.

Auswärtsspiel das (PL die Auswärtsspiele) away game.

Ausweg der (PL die Auswege) way out.

Ausweis der (PL die Ausweise) 1 identity card; 2 card (for students or members); 3 pass.

auswendig adverb by heart.

auswirken verb (PERF hat sich ausgewirkt) sich auf etwas auswirken to have an effect on something.

ausziehen ◇ verb (IMPERF zog aus, PERF hat ausgezogen) 1 to take off (clothes); 2 to undress; 3 sich ausziehen to get undressed; 4 (PERF ist ausgezogen) to move out (move house).

Auto das (PL die Autos) car; Auto fahren to drive.

Autobahn die (PL die Autobahnen) motorway.

Autofahrer der (PL die Autofahrer) motorist.

◇ IRREGULAR VERB: *See the verb table in the centre of the dictionary*

Autogramm das (PL die Autogramme) autograph.

Automat der (PL die Automaten) machine.

automatisch adjective automatic.

Autor der (PL die Autoren) author.

Autorin die (PL die Autorinnen) authoress.

Autorität die authority.

Autostopp der per Autostopp fahren to hitchhike.

Autotelefon das (PL die Autotelefone) car phone.

Autounfall der (PL die Autounfälle) car accident.

Autoverleih der (PL die Autoverleihe) car hire (firm).

Axt die (PL die Äxte) axe.

B b

Baby das (PL die Babys) baby.

Bach der (PL die Bäche) stream.

Backe die (PL die Backen) cheek.

backen ◇ verb (PRES bäckt, IMPERF backte, PERF hat gebacken) to bake.

Bäcker der (PL die Bäcker) 1 baker; 2 beim Bäcker at the baker's.

Bäckerei die (PL die Bäckereien) baker's.

Backofen der (PL die Backöfen) oven.

Backpflaume die (PL die Backpflaumen) prune.

Bad das (PL die Bäder) 1 bath; 2 bathroom; 3 pool (for swimming).

Badeanzug der (PL die Badeanzüge) swimsuit.

Badehose die (PL die Badehosen) swimming trunks.

Bademütze die (PL die Bademützen) bathing cap.

baden verb (PERF hat gebadet) 1 to have a bath; 2 to bathe (in the sea); 3 to bath (wash somebody).

Badetuch das (PL die Badetücher) bath towel.

Badewanne die (PL die Badewannen) bath (tub).

Badezimmer das (PL die Badezimmer) bathroom.

Bahn die (PL die Bahnen) 1 railway; 2 train; mit der Bahn fahren to go by train; 3 tram; 4 track (in sport); 5 lane (on a track); 6 path; auf die schiefe Bahn geraten to go off the rails.

Bahnhof der (PL die Bahnhöfe) (railway) station.

Bahnsteig der (PL die Bahnsteige) platform.

Bahnübergang der (PL die Bahnübergänge) level crossing.

bald adverb 1 soon; bis bald! see you soon!; 2 wird's bald! (informal) get a move on!; 3 almost; ich hätte bald vergessen, ihn

△ NEW SPELLING: See page xii

anzurufen I almost forgot to ring him.

Balken der (PL die Balken) beam.

Balkon der (PL die Balkons) balcony.

Ball der (PL die Bälle) 1 ball; **Ball spielen** to play ball; 2 ball; **auf dem Ball** at the ball.

Ballett das (PL die Ballette) ballet.

Balletttänzer △ der (PL die Balletttänzer) ballet dancer.

Balletttänzerin △ die (PL die Balletttänzerinnen) ballet dancer.

Ballon der (PL die Ballons) balloon.

Banane die (PL die Bananen) banana.

band SEE **binden**.

Band[1] das (PL die Bänder) 1 ribbon; 2 tape (for recording); **etwas auf Band aufnehmen** to tape something; 3 production line; **am Band arbeiten** to work on the production line; 4 **am laufenden Band** (informal) nonstop.

Band[2] der (PL die Bände) volume.

Band[3] die (PL die Bands) band.

Bank[1] die (PL die Bänke) bench.

Bank[2] die (PL die Banken) bank; **ich muss erst zur Bank gehen** I have to go to the bank first.

Bankkonto das (PL die Bankkonten) bank account.

Banknote die (PL die Banknoten) banknote.

bankrott adjective bankrupt;

bankrott gehen/machen to go bankrupt.

bar adjective (in) cash.

Bar die (PL die Bars) bar.

Bär der (PL die Bären) bear.

Bardame die (PL die Bardamen) barmaid.

barfuß adjective barefoot.

Bargeld das cash.

Barkeeper der (PL die Barkeeper) barman.

Barren der (PL die Barren) 1 bar; 2 parallel bars.

Bart der (PL die Bärte) beard.

bärtig adjective bearded.

Basel das Basle.

Basis die (PL die Basen) basis.

Bass △ der (PL die Bässe) bass.

basta exclamation and that's that!

basteln verb (PERF hat gebastelt) 1 to make (things); 2 **sie bastelt gern** she likes making things.

bat SEE **bitten**.

Batterie die (PL die Batterien) battery.

Bau der (PL die Bauten) 1 construction; **im Bau sein** to be under construction; 2 building; 3 building site; **auf dem Bau arbeiten** to work on a building site.

Bauarbeiter der (PL die Bauarbeiter) builder.

Bauch der (PL die Bäuche) stomach, belly.

◊ IRREGULAR VERB: *See the verb table in the centre of the dictionary*

Bauchschmerzen *plural noun* stomachache.

bauen *verb* (PERF hat gebaut) 1 to build; 2 einen Unfall bauen (*informal*) to have an accident.

Bauer *der* (PL die Bauern) 1 farmer; 2 pawn (*in chess*).

Bäuerin *die* (PL die Bäuerinnen) 1 farmer; 2 farmer's wife.

Bauernhof *der* (PL die Bauernhöfe) farm.

Baum *der* (PL die Bäume) tree.

Baumwolle *die* cotton.

Bausparkasse *die* (PL die Bausparkassen) building society.

Baustelle *die* (PL die Baustellen) building site.

Bayer *der* (PL die Bayern) Bavarian.

Bayerin *die* (PL die Bayerinnen) Bavarian.

Bayern *das* Bavaria; aus Bayern from Bavaria.

bayrisch *adjective* Bavarian.

beabsichtigen *verb* (PERF hat beabsichtigt) to intend.

beachten *verb* (PERF hat beachtet) 1 to take notice of; beachte ihn einfach nicht just don't take any notice of him; 2 to observe; 3 to follow (*a rule, advice*); 4 to obey; die Verkehrsregeln beachten to obey traffic regulations.

Beamte *der* (PL die Beamten) 1 civil servant (*in Germany all public employees, such as teachers and policemen, are 'Beamte'*); 2 official.

Beamtin *die* (PL die Beamtinnen) 1 civil servant; 2 official.

beanspruchen *verb* (PERF hat beansprucht) 1 to claim (*benefit*); 2 to take up (*time, space*); jemanden beanspruchen to take up somebody's time; 3 to demand (*energy, attention*); die Arbeit beansprucht sie sehr her work is very demanding; 4 to take advantage of (*hospitality, services, help*); ich möchte Ihre Geduld nicht zu sehr beanspruchen I don't want to try your patience.

Beanstandung *die* (PL die Beanstandungen) complaint.

beantragen *verb* (PERF hat beantragt) to apply for.

beantworten *verb* (PERF hat beantwortet) to answer.

bearbeiten *verb* (PERF hat bearbeitet) 1 to deal with; einen Antrag bearbeiten to deal with an application; 2 to adapt (*a play*); 3 to treat (*wood, for example*); er hat die Oberfläche mit Wachs bearbeitet he's treated the surface with wax; 4 jemanden bearbeiten, dass er etwas macht (*informal*) to work on somebody so that he does something (*persuade*).

beaufsichtigen *verb* (PERF hat beaufsichtigt) to supervise.

Becher *der* (PL die Becher) 1 beaker, mug; 2 pot, carton (*of yoghurt, cream*).

△ NEW SPELLING: *See page xii*

Becken das (PL die Becken)
1 basin; 2 pool (for swimming);
3 pelvis.

bedanken verb (PERF hat sich
bedankt) sich bedanken to say
thank you; vergiss nicht, dich zu
bedanken don't forget to say thank
you; ich habe mich bei ihm bedankt
I thanked him.

Bedarf der 1 need; 2 bei Bedarf if
required; 3 demand; je nach
Bedarf according to demand.

bedauerlicherweise adverb
unfortunately.

bedauern verb (PERF hat bedauert)
1 to regret; ich bedaure kein Wort I
don't regret a single word; 2 ich
bedaure sehr, dass du nicht
kommen kannst I'm very sorry that
you can't come; bedaure! sorry!;
3 jemanden bedauern to feel sorry
for somebody.

bedecken verb (PERF hat bedeckt)
to cover.

bedeckt adjective 1 covered;
2 overcast (weather); gestern war
es den ganzen Tag bedeckt it was
overcast all day yesterday.

bedenken ✧ verb (IMPERF
bedachte, PERF hat bedacht) to
consider.

Bedenken plural noun 1 doubts;
Bedenken haben to have doubts;
2 ohne Bedenken without
hesitation.

bedenklich adjective 1 worrying;
die Situation ist sehr bedenklich
the situation is very worrying;
2 dubious; er hat bedenkliche
Mittel angewendet, um sein Ziel zu
erreichen he's used dubious
methods to achieve his aims;
3 serious.

bedeuten verb (PERF hat bedeutet)
to mean.

bedeutend adjective 1 important;
2 considerable.

Bedeutung die (PL die
Bedeutungen) 1 meaning;
2 importance.

bedienen verb (PERF hat bedient)
1 to serve; hier wird man sehr
schnell bedient you get served very
quickly here; 2 to operate; 3 sich
bedienen to help oneself.

Bedienung die (PL die
Bedienungen) 1 service;
Bedienung inbegriffen service
included; 2 waiter, waitress; 3 shop
assistant; 4 operation (of a
machine).

Bedingung die (PL die
Bedingungen) condition; nur unter
der Bedingung, dass du
mitkommst only on condition that
you're coming with us.

bedrohen verb (PERF hat bedroht)
to threaten.

Bedrohung die (PL die
Bedrohungen) threat.

beeilen verb (PERF hat sich beeilt)
sich beeilen to hurry (up); beeilt
euch! hurry up!

beeindrucken verb (PERF hat
beeindruckt) to impress.

beeinflussen verb (PERF hat
beeinflusst) to influence.

✧ IRREGULAR VERB: See the verb table in the centre of the dictionary

beenden verb (PERF hat beendet) to end.

Beerdigung die (PL die Beerdigungen) funeral.

Beere die (PL die Beeren) berry.

Beet das (PL die Beete) 1 bed (of flowers); 2 patch (of vegetables).

befahl SEE befehlen.

Befehl der (PL die Befehle) 1 order; 2 command; **den Befehl über etwas haben** to be in command of something.

befehlen ✧ verb (PRES befiehlt, IMPERF befahl, PERF hat befohlen) 1 **jemandem etwas befehlen** to order somebody to do something; 2 to give orders.

befestigen verb (PERF hat befestigt) 1 to fix; **etwas an der Wand befestigen** to fix something to the wall; 2 to fasten.

befinden ✧ verb (IMPERF befand sich, PERF hat sich befunden) **sich befinden** to be; **sie befindet sich zur Zeit in Deutschland** she's in Germany at the moment.

befolgen verb (PERF hat befolgt) to follow.

befördern verb (PERF hat befördert) 1 to carry (people by bus or train); 2 to transport (goods by train or lorry); 3 to promote; **er ist zum Kommissar befördert worden** he's been promoted to superintendent.

befragen verb (PERF hat befragt) to question.

befreien verb (PERF hat befreit) 1 to free; 2 to exempt; **jemanden vom Wehrdienst befreien** to exempt somebody from military service; 3 **sich befreien** to free oneself.

Befreiung die liberation.

befreunden verb (PERF hat sich befreundet) **sich befreunden** to make friends.

befreundet adjective **mit jemandem befreundet sein** to be friends with somebody; **wir sind schon lange gut befreundet** we've been close friends for a long time.

befriedigen verb (PERF hat befriedigt) to satisfy.

befriedigend adjective satisfactory.

Befugnis die (PL die Befugnisse) authority.

begabt adjective gifted, talented.

Begabung die gift, talent.

begann SEE beginnen.

begegnen verb (PERF ist begegnet) 1 **jemandem begegnen** to meet somebody; **etwas begegnen** to meet something; 2 **sich begegnen** to meet (each other).

Begegnung die (PL die Begegnungen) meeting.

begehen ✧ verb (IMPERF beging, PERF hat begangen) to commit.

begeistern verb (PERF hat begeistert) 1 **jemanden für etwas begeistern** to fill somebody with enthusiasm for something; 2 **sich begeistern** to get enthusiastic.

△ NEW SPELLING: See page xii

begeistert *adjective* enthusiastic.

Begeisterung *die* enthusiasm.

Beginn *der* beginning; **zu Beginn** at the beginning.

beginnen ◇ *verb* (IMPERF **begann**, PERF **hat begonnen**) to begin, to start.

begleiten *verb* (PERF **hat begleitet**) to accompany; **er hat mich nach Hause begleitet** he took me home.

beglückwünschen *verb* (PERF **hat beglückwünscht**) to congratulate.

begonnen SEE **beginnen**.

begraben ◇ *verb* (PRES **begräbt**, IMPERF **begrub**, PERF **hat begraben**) to bury.

begreifen ◇ *verb* (IMPERF **begriff**, PERF **hat begriffen**) to understand.

Begriff *der* (PL *die* **Begriffe**) 1 concept; **davon kann ich mir keinen Begriff machen** I can't imagine that; **ein Begriff aus der Malerei** a painting term; 3 **im Begriff sein, etwas zu tun** to be about to do something; 4 **für meine Begriffe** to my mind; 5 **schwer von Begriff** (*informal*) slow on the uptake.

Begründung *die* (PL *die* **Begründungen**) reason.

begrüßen *verb* (PERF **hat begrüßt**) 1 to greet; 2 to welcome.

Begrüßung *die* welcome.

begünstigen *verb* (PERF **hat begünstigt**) to favour.

behaglich *adjective* cosy.

behalten ◇ *verb* (PRES **behält**, IMPERF **behielt**, PERF **hat behalten**) 1 to keep; **du kannst die CD behalten** you can keep the CD; 2 to remember (*a name*).

Behälter *der* (PL *die* **Behälter**) container.

behandeln *verb* (PERF **hat behandelt**) 1 to treat; **er ist sehr schlecht behandelt worden** he's been treated very badly; **einen Patienten behandeln** to treat a patient; 2 to deal with (*a subject, question*).

Behandlung *die* (PL *die* **Behandlungen**) treatment.

behaupten *verb* (PERF **hat behauptet**) 1 to claim; 2 **sich behaupten** to assert oneself.

Behauptung *die* (PL *die* **Behauptungen**) claim.

beherrschen *verb* (PERF **hat beherrscht**) 1 to rule over (*a country, people*); 2 to control; 3 to know; 4 **sich beherrschen** to control oneself.

behilflich *adjective* **jemandem behilflich sein** to help somebody.

behindert *adjective* disabled, handicapped.

Behinderte *der/die* (PL *die* **Behinderten**) disabled person, handicapped person.

Behinderung *die* 1 obstruction; 2 handicap, disability.

Behörde *die* (PL *die* **Behörden**) authority, authorities.

◇ IRREGULAR VERB: *See the verb table in the centre of the dictionary*

behüten verb (PERF hat behütet) to protect.

bei preposition ←(+DAT) 1 near; **die Diskothek beim Bahnhof** the disco near the station; 2 at (indicating a place or time); **bei mir** at my place; **beim Arzt** at the doctor's; **bei Beginn** at the beginning; 3 **bei seinen Eltern wohnen** to live with your parents; 4 **bei uns in der Firma** in our firm; **bei guter Gesundheit** in good health; 5 **bei einem Verlag arbeiten** to work for a publisher; 6 **bei Regen** if it rains; **bei Nebel** in fog; **bei Tag** by day; 7 **etwas bei sich haben** to have something on you; 8 **bei Morris** c/o Morris; 9 **sich bei jemandem entschuldigen** to apologize to somebody; 10 **bei der hohen Miete** with the high rent; 11 **beim Fahren** while driving; **beim Lesen sein** to be reading; **beim Frühstück** at breakfast; 12 **bei der Ankunft** on arrival.

beibringen ◆ verb (PRES bringt bei, IMPERF brachte bei, PERF hat beigebracht) **jemandem etwas beibringen** to teach somebody something.

Beichte die (PL die Beichten) confession.

beichten verb (PERF hat gebeichtet) to confess.

beide adjective, pronoun 1 both; **ihr beide** both of you; **er hat seine beiden Eltern verloren** he has lost both his parents; 2 **die ersten beiden** the first two; **eins von beiden** one of the two; 3 **keiner von**

beiden neither (of them); 4 **beides** both; **er kann beides – Klavier und Gitarre spielen** he can do both – play the piano and the guitar; 5 **dreißig beide** thirty all (in tennis).

beieinander adverb together.

Beifahrer der (PL die Beifahrer) passenger.

Beifahrerin die (PL die Beifahrerinnen) passenger.

Beifall der applause.

Beil das (PL die Beile) axe.

Beilage die (PL die Beilagen) 1 supplement (to a paper); 2 side-dish; **als Beilage Reis und Spinat** served with rice and spinach.

beiläufig adjective casual.

beilegen verb (PERF hat beigelegt) to enclose.

beiliegen ◆ verb (PRES liegt bei, IMPERF lag bei, PERF hat beigelegen) to be enclosed; **ein Scheck liegt bei** please find enclosed a cheque.

beiliegend adjective enclosed.

Beileid das condolences; **jemandem sein Beileid aussprechen** to offer your condolences to somebody.

beim = bei dem.

Bein das (PL die Beine) leg.

beinahe adverb almost.

Beinbruch der (PL die Beinbrüche) broken leg; **das ist doch kein Beinbruch** (informal) it's not the end of the world.

△ NEW SPELLING: See page xii

beisammen *adverb* together.

beiseite *adverb* 1 aside; **etwas beiseite schieben** to push something aside; 2 **etwas beiseite legen** to put something by; 3 **das Geld beiseite schaffen** to hide the money away.

Beispiel *das* (PL *die* **Beispiele**) example; **zum Beispiel** for example; **mit gutem Beispiel vorangehen** to set a good example.

beispielsweise *adverb* for example.

beißen ◇ *verb* (IMPERF **biss** △, PERF **hat gebissen**) 1 to bite; 2 to sting (*of smoke, for example*); 3 **sich beißen** to clash; **die Farben beißen sich** the colours clash.

Beitrag *der* (PL *die* **Beiträge**) 1 contribution; 2 subscription; 3 premium (*insurance fee*); 4 article (*in a newspaper*).

beitragen ◇ *verb* (PRES **trägt bei**, IMPERF **trug bei**, PERF **hat beigetragen**) **zu etwas beitragen** to contribute to something.

beitreten ◇ *verb* (PRES **tritt bei**, IMPERF **trat bei**, PERF **ist beigetreten**) to join; **ich trete dem Fußballverein bei** I'm joining the football club.

bekam SEE **bekommen**.

bekämpfen *verb* (PERF **hat bekämpft**) 1 to fight; 2 **sich bekämpfen** to fight.

bekannt *adjective* 1 well known; 2 familiar; **das kommt mir bekannt vor** that seems familiar; 3 **mit jemandem bekannt sein** to know

somebody; 4 **für etwas bekannt sein** to be (well) known for something; 5 **jemanden bekannt machen** to introduce somebody; 6 **das ist mir bekannt** I know that; 7 **etwas bekannt geben/machen** to announce something; 8 **bekannt werden** to become known.

Bekannte *der/die* (PL *die* **Bekannten**) 1 acquaintance; 2 friend.

bekanntlich *adverb* **Rauchen ist bekanntlich schädlich** as you know, smoking is bad for you.

beklagen *verb* (PERF **hat sich beklagt**) **sich beklagen** to complain.

Bekleidung *die* clothes, clothing.

bekommen ◇ *verb* (IMPERF **bekam**, PERF **hat bekommen**) 1 to get; **Angst bekommen** to get frightened; 2 to catch (*a cold, the train*); 3 **ein Kind bekommen** to have a baby; 4 **was bekommen Sie?** (*in a shop*) can I help you?; (*in a restaurant*) what would you like?; 5 **was bekommen Sie dafür?** how much is it?; 6 (PERF **ist bekommen**) **fettes Essen bekommt mir nicht** fatty food doesn't agree with me; 7 (PERF **ist bekommen**) **die Ferien sind mir gut bekommen** the holiday did me good.

Belag *der* (PL *die* **Beläge**) 1 covering; 2 coating; 3 topping (*on bread*); 4 lining (*of brakes*).

belasten *verb* (PERF **hat belastet**) 1 to burden; 2 to put weight on (*foot*); 3 to pollute (*the* *atmosphere*); **4** to debit (*an account*); **5** to incriminate.

belästigen *verb* (PERF hat belästigt) **1** to bother; **2** to harass.

Belastung *die* **1** strain; **2** load; **3** burden; **4** pollution.

belegen *verb* (PERF hat belegt) **1** to cover; **2** eine Scheibe Brot mit Käse belegen to put some cheese on a slice of bread; **3** to enrol for (*a course*); **4** to reserve (*a seat*); **5** den ersten Platz belegen to come first; **6** to prove (*facts*).

belegt *adjective* **1** occupied; **2** der Platz ist belegt this seat is taken; **3** ein belegtes Brot an open sandwich; **4** die Nummer ist belegt (*when phoning*) the number's engaged.

beleidigen *verb* (PERF hat beleidigt) to insult.

Beleidigung *die* (PL die Beleidigungen) insult.

Beleuchtung *die* lighting.

Belgien *das* Belgium.

Belgier *der* (PL die Belgier) Belgian.

Belgierin *die* (PL die Belgierinnen) Belgian.

belgisch *adjective* Belgian.

Belichtung *die* exposure.

beliebig *adjective* any; eine beliebige Zahl any number you like.
adverb beliebig lange as long as you like; beliebig viele as many as you like.

beliebt *adjective* popular.

Beliebtheit *die* popularity.

bellen *verb* (PERF hat gebellt) to bark.

belohnen *verb* (PERF hat belohnt) to reward.

Belohnung *die* (PL die Belohnungen) reward.

belügen *verb* (IMPERF belog, PERF hat belogen) to lie to.

bemerkbar *adjective* sich bemerkbar machen to attract attention, to become noticeable.

bemerken *verb* (PERF hat bemerkt) **1** to notice; **2** to remark; **3** nebenbei bemerkt by the way.

Bemerkung *die* (PL die Bemerkungen) remark.

bemitleiden *verb* (PERF hat bemitleidet) to pity.

bemühen *verb* (PERF hat sich bemüht) **1** sich bemühen to try; sich sehr bemühen to try hard; er bemüht sich um eine Stelle he's trying to get a job; **2** sich um jemanden bemühen to try to help somebody; **3** bitte, bemühen Sie sich nicht please don't trouble yourself.

Bemühung *die* (PL die Bemühungen) effort.

benachrichtigen *verb* (PERF hat benachrichtigt) **1** to inform; **2** to notify (*officially*).

benachteiligt *adjective* disadvantaged.

△ NEW SPELLING: *See page xii*

benehmen ◇ verb (PRES **benimmt sich**, IMPERF **benahm sich**, PERF **hat sich benommen**) **sich benehmen** to behave; **benimm dich!** behave yourself!

Benehmen das behaviour.

beneiden verb (PERF **hat beneidet**) to envy; **jemanden um etwas beneiden** to envy somebody something.

benoten verb (PERF **hat benotet**) to mark.

benutzen verb (PERF **hat benutzt**) to use.

Benutzer der (PL die **Benutzer**) user.

Benutzung die use.

Benzin das petrol.

beobachten verb (PERF **hat beobachtet**) to observe, to watch.

bequem adjective **1** comfortable; **2 machen Sie es sich bequem** make yourself at home; **3** lazy; **4** easy; **eine bequeme Lösung finden** to find an easy way out.

beraten ◇ verb (PRES **berät**, IMPERF **beriet**, PERF **hat beraten**) **1** to advise; **2 jemanden gut/schlecht beraten** to give somebody good/bad advice; **3 sich beraten lassen** to get advice; **4 gut beraten sein** to be well advised; **5 über etwas (a plan, matter)**; **6 sich über etwas beraten** to discuss something.

Berater der (PL die **Berater**) adviser.

Beratung die (PL die **Beratungen**) **1** advice; **2** discussion; **3** consultation (with a doctor).

berauben verb (PERF **hat beraubt**) to rob.

berechnen verb (PERF **hat berechnet**) **1** to charge; **jemandem zehn Mark für etwas berechnen** to charge somebody ten marks for something; **2 jemandem zuviel berechnen** to overcharge somebody; **3** to calculate.

Bereich der (PL die **Bereiche**) **1** area; **2** field (in a profession).

bereit adjective ready.

bereiten verb (PERF **hat bereitet**) **1** to make (coffee, tea); **2** to cause (trouble, difficulty); **leider hat es uns Schwierigkeiten bereitet** unfortunately it caused us some trouble; **3** to give (a surprise, pleasure).

bereits adverb already.

bereuen verb (PERF **hat bereut**) to regret.

Berg der (PL die **Berge**) **1** mountain; **2** hill.

bergab adverb downhill.

Bergarbeiter der (PL die **Bergarbeiter**) miner.

bergauf adverb uphill.

bergen ◇ verb (PRES **birgt**, IMPERF **barg**, PERF **hat geborgen**) to rescue.

Bergsteigen das mountaineering.

Bergsteiger der (PL die **Bergsteiger**) mountaineer, climber.

Bergsteigerin die (PL die **Bergsteigerinnen**) mountaineer, climber.

◇ IRREGULAR VERB: See the verb table in the centre of the dictionary

Bergwacht *die* mountain rescue.

Bergwerk *das* (PL *die* **Bergwerke**) mine.

Bericht *der* (PL *die* **Berichte**) report.

berichten *verb* (PERF **hat berichtet**)
1 to report; **die Zeitungen haben nichts davon berichtet** the newspapers didn't report anything about it; 2 **jemandem über etwas berichten** to tell somebody about something; **er hat mir über seine Ferien in Amerika berichtet** he told me about his holiday in America.

berücksichtigen *verb* (PERF **hat berücksichtigt**) to take into account.

Beruf *der* (PL *die* **Berufe**)
1 occupation; 2 profession; **ich bin Lehrerin von Beruf** I'm a teacher by profession; 3 trade; 4 **was sind Sie von Beruf?** what do you do for a living?

beruflich *adjective* 1 professional; 2 vocational (*training*).
adverb 1 **beruflich erfolgreich sein** to be successful in your career; 2 **viel beruflich unterwegs sein** to be away a lot on business.

Berufsberatung *die* careers advice.

Berufsschule *die* (PL *die* **Berufsschulen**) technical college.

berufstätig *adjective* working.

Berufsverkehr *der* rush-hour traffic.

beruhigen *verb* (PERF **hat beruhigt**)
1 to calm down; 2 to reassure; 3 **sich beruhigen** to calm down.

Beruhigungsmittel *das* (PL *die* **Beruhigungsmittel**) sedative, tranquillizer.

berühmt *adjective* famous.

berühren *verb* (PERF **hat berührt**)
1 to touch; 2 to touch on (*a topic, an issue*); 3 to affect; **ihre Geschichte berührte ihn seltsam** he was strangely affected by her story; 4 **sich berühren** to touch.

besaß SEE **besitzen**.

beschädigen *verb* (PERF **hat beschädigt**) to damage.

beschaffen[1] *verb* (PERF **hat beschafft**) to get; **kannst du mir nicht einen Job beschaffen?** can't you get me a job?

beschaffen[2] *adjective* so **beschaffen sein, dass …** to be such that …

beschäftigen *verb* (PERF **hat beschäftigt**) 1 to occupy (*keep busy*); 2 to employ (*people*); 3 **sich beschäftigen** to occupy yourself; 4 **ich beschäftige mich mit den Kindern** I'm busy with the children; 5 **sich mit einem Fall beschäftigen** to deal with a case; **sein Aufsatz beschäftigt sich mit der Umweltverschmutzung** his essay deals with environmental pollution.

beschäftigt *adjective* 1 busy; 2 employed.

Beschäftigung *die* (PL *die* **Beschäftigungen**) 1 occupation; 2 activity.

Bescheid *der* (PL *die* **Bescheide**)
1 information; 2 jemandem

△ NEW SPELLING: See page xii

Bescheid sagen to let somebody know; **3 über etwas Bescheid wissen** to know about something.

bescheiden *adjective* modest.

Bescheinigung *die* (PL die Bescheinigungen) **1** certificate; **eine Bescheinigung des Arztes** a doctor's certificate; **2** (written) confirmation.

beschimpfen *verb* (PERF hat beschimpft) to abuse.

beschlagnahmen *verb* (PERF hat beschlagnahmt) to confiscate.

beschleunigen *verb* (PERF hat beschleunigt) **1** to speed up; **2** to accelerate; **der Lastwagen hinter uns hat plötzlich beschleunigt** the lorry behind us suddenly accelerated.

beschließen ◇ *verb* (IMPERF beschloss △, PERF hat beschlossen) to decide.

Beschluss △ *der* (PL die Beschlüsse) decision.

beschreiben ◇ *verb* (IMPERF beschrieb, PERF hat beschrieben) to describe.

Beschreibung *die* (PL die Beschreibungen) description.

beschuldigen *verb* (PERF hat beschuldigt) to accuse.

beschützen *verb* (PERF hat beschützt) to protect.

Beschwerde *die* (PL die Beschwerden) complaint.

beschweren *verb* (PERF hat sich beschwert) **sich beschweren** to complain; **ich habe mich bei den Nachbarn über ihn beschwert** I've complained to the neighbours about him.

beschwipst *adjective* tipsy.

beseitigen *verb* (PERF hat beseitigt) to remove.

Besen *der* (PL die Besen) broom.

besetzen *verb* (PERF hat besetzt) **1** to occupy; **2** to fill (*a post, role*); **3** to trim, to edge (*with lace or fur*).

besetzt *adjective* **1** occupied; **2 besetzt sein** to be engaged (*a phone, toilet*); **3** taken (*a table, seat*); **der Platz ist besetzt** this seat is taken; **4** full (*of a train, bus*); **der Zug ist voll besetzt** the train is full up.

Besetztzeichen *das* (PL die Besetztzeichen) engaged tone.

besichtigen *verb* (PERF hat besichtigt) **1** to look round (*a town, museum*); **2** to see (*sights, a house*).

Besichtigung *die* (PL die Besichtigungen) visit.

besinnungslos *adjective* unconscious.

Besitz *der* **1** property; **2 im Besitz einer Sache sein** to be in possession of something.

besitzen ◇ *verb* (IMPERF besaß, PERF hat besessen) **1** to own; **sie besitzen ein Haus in Italien** they own a house in Italy; **2** to have (*talent, a quality*).

Besitzer *der* (PL die Besitzer) owner.

◇ IRREGULAR VERB: See the verb table in the centre of the dictionary

Besitzerin die (PL die Besitzerinnen) owner.

besonderer, besondere, besonderes adjective 1 special; unter besonderen Umständen in special circumstances; 2 particular; ohne besondere Begeisterung without any particular enthusiasm; 3 keine besonderen Kennzeichen no distinguishing features.

Besonderheit die (PL die Besonderheiten) 1 special feature; 2 peculiarity.

besonders adverb particularly.

besorgen verb (PERF hat besorgt) to get; ich kann dir Karten besorgen I can get you tickets.

besorgt adjective worried.

besprechen ◇ verb (PRES bespricht, IMPERF besprach, PERF hat besprochen) 1 to discuss; ich muss es erst mit meinen Eltern besprechen I'll have to discuss it with my parents first; 2 to review (a book, film).

Besprechung die (PL die Besprechungen) 1 meeting (at work); 2 discussion; 3 review (of a film, play).

besser adjective, adverb better; alles besser wissen to know better.

Besserung die 1 improvement; 2 gute Besserung! get well soon!

beständig adjective 1 constant; 2 settled (weather).

Bestandteil der (PL die Bestandteile) component.

bestätigen verb (PERF hat bestätigt) 1 to confirm; 2 to acknowledge (receipt); 3 sich bestätigen to be confirmed, to prove to be true.

beste SEE bester.

Bestechung die (PL die Bestechungen) bribery.

Besteck das (PL die Bestecke) cutlery.

bestehen ◇ verb (IMPERF bestand, PERF hat bestanden) 1 to exist; 2 es besteht die Gefahr, dass ... there is a danger that ...; noch besteht die Hoffnung, dass ... there is still hope that ...; 3 to pass; eine Prüfung bestehen to pass an exam; 4 auf etwas bestehen to insist on something; 5 aus etwas bestehen to consist of something; 6 aus etwas bestehen to be made of something.

bestellen verb (PERF hat bestellt) 1 to order (goods); 2 to reserve (tickets); 3 to tell; jemandem etwas bestellen to tell somebody something; 4 bestell ihm schöne Grüße give him my regards; 5 kann ich etwas bestellen? can I take a message?; 6 to send for; jemanden zu sich bestellen to send for somebody.

Bestellung die (PL die Bestellungen) 1 order (for goods); 2 reservation (for tickets).

bestens adverb very well; das hat ja bestens geklappt that worked out very well.

△ NEW SPELLING: See page xii

bester, beste, bestes *adjective*
1 best; **sein bestes Buch** his best book; 2 **ich halte es für das Beste** △, **wenn …** I think it would be best if …; **sein Bestes tun** to do your best; 3 **einen Witz zum Besten geben** △ to tell a joke; 4 **jemanden zum Besten halten** △ to pull somebody's leg.
adverb **am besten** best; **du bleibst am besten zu Hause** you'd best stay at home; **es ist am besten, wenn wir gleich anfangen** it's best if we get started straight away.

bestimmen *verb* (PERF **hat bestimmt**) 1 to fix (*a time, price*); 2 **etwas allein bestimmen** to decide (on) something on your own; **er bestimmt immer, was wir machen** he always decides what we're going to do; 3 to be in charge; 4 **für jemanden bestimmt sein** to be meant for somebody; 5 **für etwas bestimmt sein** to be intended for something (*a donation for a good cause, for example*).

bestimmt *adjective* 1 certain; **zu einer bestimmten Zeit** at a certain time; 2 particular; **suchen Sie etwas Bestimmtes?** are you looking for anything in particular?; 3 definite.
adverb 1 certainly, definitely; **ich komme ganz bestimmt** I'm definitely coming; 2 **er hat es bestimmt vergessen** he's bound to have forgotten; 3 **du weißt es doch bestimmt noch** surely you must remember it.

Bestimmung *die* (PL *die* **Bestimmungen**) regulation.

bestrafen *verb* (PERF **hat bestraft**) to punish.

bestreiten ◇ *verb* (IMPERF **bestritt**, PERF **hat bestritten**) 1 to deny; 2 to dispute; **das möchte ich nicht bestreiten** I'm not disputing it; 3 to pay for.

bestürzt *adjective* upset.

Besuch *der* (PL *die* **Besuche**) 1 visit; 2 attendance (*at school*); 3 **Besuch haben** to have visitors/a visitor; 4 **bei Freunden zu Besuch sein** to be staying with friends; **zu Besuch kommen** to be visiting.

besuchen *verb* (PERF **hat besucht**) 1 to visit; 2 to go to (*an exhibition, the theatre*); **die Schule besuchen** to go to school; 3 to attend (*a lecture*).

Besucher *der* (PL *die* **Besucher**) visitor.

Besucherin *die* (PL *die* **Besucherinnen**) visitor.

betätigen *verb* (PERF **hat betätigt**) 1 to operate; 2 **die Bremse betätigen** to apply the brakes; 3 **sich politisch betätigen** to be involved in politics; 4 **sich künstlerisch betätigen** to do art; 5 **sich als Reporter betätigen** to work as a reporter.

Betäubungsmittel *das* (PL *die* **Betäubungsmittel**) anaesthetic.

Bete *die* **Rote Bete** △ beetroot.

beteiligen *verb* (PERF **hat beteiligt**) 1 to give a share to; **jemanden mit**

◇ **IRREGULAR VERB: See the verb table in the centre of the dictionary**

zehn Prozent an einem Geschäft beteiligen to give somebody a ten percent share of a business; **2 sich an etwas beteiligen** to take part in something; **3 kann ich mich an eurem Spiel beteiligen?** can I join in your game?

beten *verb* (PERF **hat gebetet**) to pray.

Beton *der* concrete.

betonen *verb* (PERF **hat betont**) to stress.

Betonung *die* (PL *die* **Betonungen**) stress.

Betrag *der* (PL *die* **Beträge**) amount.

betragen ◇ *verb* (PRES **beträgt**, IMPERF **betrug**, PERF **hat betragen**) **1** to amount to, to come to; **2 sich betragen** to behave; **haben sich die Kinder gut betragen?** did the children behave well?

Betragen *das* behaviour.

betreffen ◇ *verb* (PRES **betrifft**, IMPERF **betraf**, PERF **hat betroffen**) to concern; **was mich betrifft** as far as I'm concerned.

betreten ◇ *verb* (PRES **betritt**, IMPERF **betrat**, PERF **hat betreten**) **1** to enter; **2 'Betreten verboten'** 'keep out', 'keep off' (*the grass, for example*).

Betrieb *der* (PL *die* **Betriebe**) **1** business, firm; **2** activity; **es war viel Betrieb** it was very busy; **3 in Betrieb sein** to be working (*of a machine*); **4 außer Betrieb sein** to be out of order; **5 eine Maschine in**

Betrieb setzen to start up a machine.

Betriebsferien *plural noun* firm's holiday; **'Betriebsferien'** 'closed for the holidays'.

betrinken ◇ *verb* (IMPERF **betrank sich**, PERF **hat sich betrunken**) **sich betrinken** to get drunk.

betrog SEE **betrügen**.

Betrug *der* **1** deception; **2** fraud.

betrügen ◇ *verb* (IMPERF **betrog**, PERF **hat betrogen**) **1** to cheat; **jemanden um tausend Mark betrügen** to cheat somebody out of a thousand marks; **2** to be unfaithful to, to cheat on; **sie hat ihren Mann betrogen** she's been unfaithful to her husband.

betrunken *adjective* drunk.

Bett *das* (PL *die* **Betten**) bed; **ins Bett gehen** to go to bed.

Bettbezug *der* (PL *die* **Bettbezüge**) duvet cover.

betteln *verb* (PERF **hat gebettelt**) to beg.

Bettlaken *das* (PL *die* **Bettlaken**) sheet.

Bettler *der* (PL *die* **Bettler**) beggar.

Bettlerin *die* (PL *die* **Bettlerinnen**) beggar.

Bettwäsche *die* bed linen.

Bettzeug *das* bedding.

beugen *verb* (PERF **hat gebeugt**) **1** to bend; **2** to decline, to conjugate (*in grammar*); **3 sich nach vorn beugen** to bend forwards; **sich über**

△ NEW SPELLING: *See page xii*

etwas beugen to bend over something; **4 sich aus dem Fenster beugen** to lean out of the window; **5 sich beugen** to submit.

Beule die (PL die **Beulen**) **1** bump; **2** lump; **3** dent.

beurteilen verb (PERF **hat beurteilt**) to judge.

Beutel der (PL die **Beutel**) bag.

Bevölkerung die (PL die **Bevölkerungen**) population.

bevor conjunction **1** before; **2 bevor nicht** until; **bevor er nicht unterschrieben hat** until he has signed.

bevorzugen verb (PERF **hat bevorzugt**) to prefer.

bewachen verb (PERF **hat bewacht**) to guard.

bewaffnen verb (PERF **hat bewaffnet**) to arm.

bewaffnet adjective armed.

bewährt adjective **1** reliable; **2** proven (method, design); **3 ein bewährtes Rezept** a well-tried recipe.

bewegen[1] verb (PERF **hat bewegt**) **1** to move; **2 sich bewegen** to take exercise; **3 sich bewegen** to move.

bewegen[2] ◇ verb (IMPERF **bewog**, PERF **hat bewogen**) **jemanden dazu bewegen, etwas zu tun** to persuade somebody to do something.

bewegt adjective eventful.

Bewegung die (PL die **Bewegungen**) **1** movement;

2 exercise; **3 eine Maschine in Bewegung setzen** to start (up) a machine; **4 sich in Bewegung setzen** to start to move.

Beweis der (PL die **Beweise**) **1** proof; **2 belastende Beweise** incriminating evidence; **3** token, sign.

beweisen ◇ verb (IMPERF **bewies**, PERF **hat bewiesen**) **1** to prove; **2** to show.

bewerben ◇ verb (PRES **bewirbt sich**, IMPERF **bewarb sich**, PERF **hat sich beworben**) **sich bewerben** to apply; **sich um eine Stelle bewerben** to apply for a job.

Bewerber der (PL die **Bewerber**) applicant.

Bewerberin die (PL die **Bewerberinnen**) applicant.

Bewerbung die (PL die **Bewerbungen**) application.

bewohnen verb (PERF **hat bewohnt**) to live in.

Bewohner der (PL die **Bewohner**) **1** resident; **2** inhabitant (of a region).

Bewohnerin die (PL die **Bewohnerinnen**) **1** resident; **2** inhabitant (of a region).

bewölkt adjective cloudy.

Bewölkung die clouds.

bewundern verb (PERF **hat bewundert**) to admire.

Bewunderung die admiration.

bewusst △ adjective **1** conscious;

◇ IRREGULAR VERB: *See the verb table in the centre of the dictionary*

2 deliberate; 3 **sich etwas bewusst sein** to be aware of something; **ich war mir der Folgen bewusst** I was aware of the consequences.

bewusstlos Δ *adjective* unconscious.

Bewusstsein Δ *das* 1 consciousness; 2 **bei vollem Bewusstsein sein** to be fully conscious; 3 **mir kam zu(m) Bewusstsein, dass ...** I realized that ...

bezahlen *verb* (PERF **hat bezahlt**) 1 to pay; 2 to pay for (*goods, food*); **er hat das Essen bezahlt** he paid for the meal.

Bezahlung *die* payment.

bezeichnend *adjective* typical.

beziehen ◇ *verb* (IMPERF **bezog**, PERF **hat bezogen**) 1 to cover; 2 **das Bett frisch beziehen** to put clean sheets on the bed; 3 to move into; **wann kannst du die neue Wohnung beziehen?** when will you be able to move into the new flat?; 4 to get (*goods, a pension*); 5 to take (*a newspaper*); 6 **sich auf etwas/jemanden beziehen** to refer to something/somebody; 7 **es bezieht sich** it's clouding over.

Beziehung *die* (PL die **Beziehungen**) 1 connection; 2 relationship; 3 **Beziehungen** contacts; **Anna hat gute Beziehungen** Anna has good contacts; 4 **diplomatische Beziehungen** diplomatic relations; 5 **in dieser Beziehung** in this respect; 6 **eine Beziehung zu etwas**

haben to be able to relate to something (*to art, pop music, for example*).

beziehungsweise *conjunction* 1 or rather; 2 respectively.

Bezirk *der* (PL die **Bezirke**) district.

Bezug *der* (PL die **Bezüge**) 1 cover (*of a cushion, duvet, etc.*); 2 connection; **keinen Bezug zu etwas haben** to be unable to relate to something; 3 **auf etwas Bezug nehmen** to refer to something; 4 **in Bezug auf** regarding; 5 **mit Bezug auf Ihr Angebot** with reference to your offer.

bezweifeln *verb* (PERF **hat bezweifelt**) to doubt.

BH *der* (PL die **BHs**) bra.

Bibel *die* (PL die **Bibeln**) bible; **die Bibel** the Bible.

Bibliothek *die* (PL die **Bibliotheken**) library.

biegen ◇ *verb* (IMPERF **bog**, PERF **hat gebogen**) 1 to bend; 2 **sich biegen** to bend; 3 (PERF **ist gebogen**) to turn; **um die Ecke biegen** to turn the corner.

Biene *die* (PL die **Bienen**) bee.

Bier *das* (PL die **Biere**) beer.

Bierdeckel *der* (PL die **Bierdeckel**) beer mat.

bieten ◇ *verb* (IMPERF **bot**, PERF **hat geboten**) 1 to offer; 2 to bid (*at an auction*); 3 **es bietet sich die Möglichkeit** there is a possibility; 4 to present (*a sight*); 5 **das lasse**

ich mir nicht bieten! I won't put up with it!

Bikini der (PL die Bikinis) bikini.

Bild das (PL die Bilder) 1 picture; **jemanden ins Bild setzen** to put somebody in the picture; 2 scene.

bilden verb (PERF hat gebildet) 1 to form; 2 sich bilden to form; 3 sich bilden to educate yourself.

Bildschirm der (PL die Bildschirme) screen.

bildschön adjective (very) beautiful.

Bildung die 1 formation; 2 education.

billig adjective cheap.

Billion die (PL die Billionen) billion (a million million).

bin SEE sein.

Binde die (PL die Binden) 1 bandage; 2 sanitary towel.

binden ♦ verb (IMPERF band, PERF hat gebunden) 1 to tie; 2 to bind (a book); 3 to make up (a bouquet); 4 to thicken (a sauce); 5 sich binden to commit oneself.

Bindestrich der (PL die Bindestriche) hyphen.

Bindfaden der (PL die Bindfäden) (piece of) string.

Bindung die (PL die Bindungen) 1 tie; 2 relationship; 3 binding (on a ski).

Biokost die health food.

Biologie die biology.

biologisch adjective biological.

Birke die (PL die Birken) birch tree.

Birne die (PL die Birnen) 1 pear; 2 bulb.

bis preposition ←(+ACC) 1 as far as; **dieser Zug fährt nur bis Passau** this train only goes as far as Passau; 2 up to; **Kinder bis zehn zahlen die Hälfte** children up to ten pay half; **bis jetzt** up to now; **bis zu** up to; 3 until, till (with time); 4 by; **bis dahin** by then; 5 bis auf except for; **alle sind durchgefallen bis auf die zwei Mädchen** everyone failed except for the two girls; 6 bis bald! see you soon!; 7 von München bis Salzburg from Munich to Salzburg; **von Montag bis Freitag** from Monday to Friday; **zwei bis drei Mark** two to three marks. conjunction until, till; **sie bleibt, bis es dunkel wird** she's staying until it gets dark.

Bischof der (PL die Bischöfe) bishop.

bisher adverb so far.

bisherig adjective previous.

biss △ SEE beißen.

Biss △ der (PL die Bisse) bite.

bisschen △ pronoun 1 ein bisschen a bit; **ein bisschen Brot** a bit of bread; 2 kein bisschen not a bit.

bissig adjective 1 vicious; 'Vorsicht bissiger Hund!' beware of the dog!'; 2 cutting (remark, tone).

bist SEE sein.

bitte adverb 1 please; 'möchten Sie

♦ IRREGULAR VERB: See the verb table in the centre of the dictionary

Kuchen?' – 'ja bitte' 'would you like some cake?' – 'yes please'; 2 you're welcome (*in reply to thanks*); 3 come in (*after a knock on the door*); 4 (*in a shop*) bitte? yes, please?; 5 wie bitte? sorry?

Bitte *die* (PL *die* Bitten) request.

bitten ◇ *verb* (IMPERF bat, PERF hat gebeten) to ask; jemanden um etwas bitten to ask somebody for something.

bitter *adjective* bitter.

blamieren *verb* (PERF hat blamiert) 1 to disgrace; 2 jemanden blamieren to embarrass somebody; 3 sich blamieren to make a fool of yourself.

Blase *die* (PL *die* Blasen) 1 bubble; 2 blister; 3 bladder.

blasen ◇ *verb* (PRES bläst, IMPERF blies, PERF hat geblasen) to blow.

Blasinstrument *das* (PL *die* Blasinstrumente) wind instrument.

Blaskapelle *die* (PL *die* Blaskapellen) brass band.

blass △ *adjective* pale.

Blatt *das* (PL *die* Blätter) 1 leaf; 2 sheet; ein Blatt Papier a sheet of paper; 3 page; 4 newspaper.

blau *adjective* 1 blue; ein blau gestreiftes Kleid a dress with blue stripes; 2 ein blaues Auge haben to have a black eye; 3 ein blauer Fleck a bruise; 4 blau sein (*informal*) to be tight; 5 eine Fahrt ins Blaue a mystery tour.

Blech *das* (PL *die* Bleche) 1 sheet

metal; 2 tin; 3 baking tray; 4 brass (*in music*).

Blei *das* lead.

bleiben ◇ *verb* (IMPERF blieb, PERF ist geblieben) 1 to stay, to remain; 2 to be left; 3 bleiben Sie am Apparat hold the line; 4 bei etwas bleiben to stick to something; 5 ruhig bleiben to keep calm; 6 wo bleibt er so lange? where has he got to?; 7 etwas bleiben lassen to not do something; wenn du nicht mitkommen willst, dann lass es eben bleiben if you don't want to come, then don't.

bleich *adjective* pale.

Bleichmittel *das* (PL *die* Bleichmittel) bleach.

bleifrei *adjective* unleaded.

Bleistift *der* (PL *die* Bleistifte) pencil.

Bleistiftspitzer *der* (PL *die* Bleistiftspitzer) pencil sharpener.

blenden *verb* (PERF hat geblendet) 1 to dazzle; 2 to blind.

blendend *adjective* 1 marvellous; 2 es geht mir blendend I feel great; wir haben uns blendend amüsiert we had a great time.

Blick *der* (PL *die* Blicke) 1 look; 2 glance; 3 auf den ersten Blick at first sight; 4 view; ein Zimmer mit Blick aufs Meer a room with a sea view.

blicken *verb* (PERF hat geblickt) 1 to look; 2 sich blicken lassen to show your face.

blieb SEE bleiben.

△ NEW SPELLING: See page xii

blies SEE **blasen**.

blind adjective blind.

Blinddarm der (PL die **Blinddärme**) appendix.

Blinddarmentzündung die (PL die **Blinddarmentzündungen**) appendicitis.

Blinde der/die (PL die **Blinden**) blind person, blind man/woman.

blinzeln verb (PERF hat geblinzelt) to blink.

blinken verb (PERF hat geblinkt) 1 to flash; 2 to indicate (of a car).

Blinker der (PL die **Blinker**) indicator.

Blitz der (PL die **Blitze**) 1 (flash of) lightning; 2 flash.

blitzen verb (PERF hat geblitzt) 1 to flash; 2 to sparkle; 3 es hat geblitzt there was a flash of lightning.

Block der (PL die **Blöcke**) 1 pad (for writing on); 2 (PL die **Blocks**) block (of flats).

Blockflöte die (PL die **Blockflöten**) recorder.

blöd adjective stupid.

Blödsinn der nonsense.

blond adjective blonde, fair-haired.

bloß adverb 1 only; es kostet bloß fünf Mark it's only five marks; 2 warum hat er das bloß gemacht? why on earth did he do it?; 3 was mache ich bloß? whatever shall I do?; 4 fass das bloß nicht an! don't touch it!
adjective 1 bare (feet); mit bloßem Auge with the naked eye; 2 mere

(words, suspicion); der bloße Gedanke daran the mere thought of it.

Blume die (PL die **Blumen**) flower.

Blumenkohl der cauliflower.

Bluse die (PL die **Blusen**) blouse.

Blut das blood.

Blutdruck der blood pressure.

Blüte die (PL die **Blüten**) blossom.

bluten verb (PERF hat geblutet) to bleed.

Blutprobe die (PL die **Blutproben**) blood test.

Bock der (PL die **Böcke**) 1 buck; 2 billy-goat; 3 ram; 4 Bock auf etwas haben (informal) to fancy something; 5 einen Bock schießen (informal) to make a blunder.

Bockwurst die (PL die **Bockwürste**) frankfurter.

Boden der (PL die **Böden**) 1 ground; 2 floor; 3 bottom (of a container); 4 loft, attic.

Bodensee der Lake Constance.

bog SEE **biegen**.

Bogen der (PL die **Bögen**) 1 curve; 2 arch; 3 turn (in skiing).

Bohne die (PL die **Bohnen**) bean.

bohren verb (PERF hat gebohrt) to drill.

Bohrer der (PL die **Bohrer**) drill.

Bohrinsel die (PL die **Bohrinseln**) oil rig.

◇ IRREGULAR VERB: See the verb table in the centre of the dictionary

Bohrmaschine die (PL die Bohrmaschinen) electric drill.

Bombe die (PL die Bomben) bomb.

Bonbon der (PL die Bonbons) sweet.

Boot das (PL die Boote) boat.

Bord[1] das (PL die Borde) shelf.

Bord[2] der an Bord on board; über Bord overboard.

Bordkarte die (PL die Bordkarten) boarding card.

borgen (PERF hat geborgt) 1 to borrow; 2 sich etwas borgen to borrow something; ich habe es mir von ihr geborgt I borrowed it from her; 3 jemandem etwas borgen to lend somebody something; Evi hat mir ihr Buch geborgt Evi lent me her book.

Börse die (PL die Börsen) stock exchange.

Borste die (PL die Borsten) bristle.

böse adjective 1 bad; 2 wicked; 3 naughty (child); 4 angry; böse werden to get angry; ich bin ihm böse I'm angry with him; 5 auf jemanden böse sein to be cross with somebody.

boshaft adjective malicious.

bot SEE bieten.

Bote der (PL die Boten) messenger.

Botin die (PL die Botinnen) messenger.

Botschaft die (PL die Botschaften) 1 message; 2 embassy.

Botschafter der (PL die Botschafter) ambassador.

Botschafterin die (PL die Botschafterinnen) ambassador.

Bowle die (PL die Bowlen) punch (for drinking).

boxen verb (PERF hat geboxt) 1 to box; 2 to punch.

Boxer der (PL die Boxer) boxer.

brach SEE brechen.

brachte SEE bringen.

Branche die (PL die Branchen) (line of) business.

Branchenverzeichnis das (PL die Branchenverzeichnisse) classified directory.

Brand der (PL die Brände) fire.

Brandung die surf.

brannte SEE brennen.

braten ◇ verb (PRES brät, IMPERF briet, PERF hat gebraten) 1 to fry; 2 to roast.

Braten der (PL die Braten) 1 roast; 2 joint.

Brathähnchen das (PL die Brathähnchen) roast chicken.

Bratkartoffeln plural noun fried potatoes.

Bratpfanne die (PL die Bratpfannen) frying pan.

Bratwurst die (PL die Bratwürste) fried sausage.

Brauch der (PL die Bräuche) custom.

△ NEW SPELLING: See page xii

brauchbar *adjective* 1 usable; 2 useful.

brauchen *verb* (PERF hat gebraucht) 1 need; ich brauche eine neue Birne für meine Lampe I need a new bulb for my light; du brauchst nur auf den Knopf zu drücken all you need to do is press the button; du brauchst nicht zu gehen you needn't go; 2 sie braucht es nur zu sagen she only has to say; 3 to take (*time*); wie lange brauchst du mit dem Auto? how long does it take you by car?; 4 ich könnte es gut brauchen I could do with it.

brauen *verb* (PERF hat gebraut) to brew.

Brauerei die (PL die Brauereien) brewery.

braun *adjective* 1 brown; 2 braun werden to get a tan; braun (gebrannt) sein to be tanned.

Bräune die tan.

Brause die (PL die Brausen) fizzy drink.

Braut die (PL die Bräute) bride.

Bräutigam der (PL die Bräutigame) bridegroom.

Brautjungfer die (PL die Brautjungfern) bridesmaid.

Brautpaar das (PL die Brautpaare) bride and groom.

brav *adjective* good.

BRD die (*Bundesrepublik Deutschland*) FRG (*Federal Republic of Germany*).

brechen ◇ *verb* (PRES bricht, IMPERF brach, PERF hat gebrochen) 1 to break (*an agreement, a record*); 2 sich den Arm brechen to break your arm; 3 to vomit; 4 (PERF ist gebrochen) to break; der Ast ist gebrochen the branch broke.

breit *adjective* 1 wide; 2 broad; 3 die breite Masse the general public.

Breite die (PL die Breiten) width.

Bremse die (PL die Bremsen) 1 brake; 2 horsefly.

bremsen *verb* (PERF hat gebremst) 1 to brake; 2 to slow down (*development, production*); 3 jemanden bremsen (*informal*) to stop somebody; er ist nicht mehr zu bremsen there's no stopping him.

Bremslicht das (PL die Bremslichter) brake light.

Bremspedal das (PL die Bremspedale) brake pedal.

brennen ◇ *verb* (IMPERF brannte, PERF hat gebrannt) 1 to burn; 2 to be on (*of a light*); das Licht brennen lassen to leave the light on; 3 to sting (*of a wound or sore*); 4 das Haus brennt the house is on fire; es brennt! fire!; 5 darauf brennen, etwas zu tun to be dying to do something.

Brennnessel △ die (PL die Brennnesseln) stinging nettle.

Brennpunkt der (PL die Brennpunkte) focus.

Brett das (PL die Bretter) 1 board; 2 plank; 3 shelf.

◇ IRREGULAR VERB: *See the verb table in the centre of the dictionary*

Brezel die (PL die Brezeln) pretzel.

bricht SEE **brechen**.

Brief der (PL die Briefe) letter.

Brieffreund der (PL die Brieffreunde) pen friend.

Brieffreundin die (PL die Brieffreundinnen) pen friend.

Briefkasten der (PL die Briefkästen) 1 letterbox; 2 postbox.

Briefmarke die (PL die Briefmarken) stamp.

Brieftasche die (PL die Brieftaschen) wallet.

Briefträger der (PL die Briefträger) postman.

Briefträgerin die (PL die Briefträgerinnen) postwoman.

Briefumschlag der (PL die Briefumschläge) envelope.

Briefwechsel der correspondence.

briet SEE **braten**.

Brillant der (PL die Brillanten) diamond.

Brille die (PL die Brillen) glasses, spectacles.

bringen ◇ verb (IMPERF **brachte**, PERF **hat gebracht**) 1 to bring; 2 to take; Peter bringt dich nach Hause Peter will take you home; 3 **die Kinder ins Bett bringen** to put the children to bed; 4 **einen Film im Fernsehen bringen** to show a film on television; 5 to publish (an article); 6 to yield (interest, a profit);

7 **jemanden dazu bringen, etwas zu tun** to get somebody to do something; 8 **mit sich bringen** to entail; 9 **etwas hinter sich bringen** to get something over and done with; 10 **es weit bringen** to go far; 11 **jemanden auf eine Idee bringen** to give somebody an idea; 12 **es zu nichts bringen** to get nowhere; 13 **das bringt's nicht!** (informal) that's no use!

Brise die (PL die Brisen) breeze.

Brite der (PL die Briten) Briton; **die Briten** the British.

Britin die (PL die Britinnen) Briton.

britisch adjective British.

Brokkoli der broccoli.

Brombeere die (PL die Brombeeren) blackberry.

Brosche die (PL die Broschen) brooch.

Broschüre die (PL die Broschüren) brochure.

Brot das (PL die Brote) 1 bread; **ein Brot** a loaf of bread; 2 **ein Brot** a slice of bread.

Brötchen das (PL die Brötchen) roll.

Bruch der (PL die Brüche) 1 break; 2 fracture; 3 hernia; 4 fraction.

Bruchteil der (PL die Bruchteile) fraction.

Brücke die (PL die Brücken) bridge.

Bruder der (PL die Brüder) brother.

Brühe die (PL die Brühen) 1 broth; 2 stock (for cooking).

△ NEW SPELLING: See page xii

Brühwürfel der (PL die Brühwürfel) stock cube.

brüllen verb (PERF hat gebrüllt) to roar.

brummen verb (PERF hat gebrummt) 1 to buzz; 2 to growl (of a bear); 3 to hum (of an engine).

Brunnen der (PL die Brunnen) 1 well; 2 fountain.

Brust die (PL die Brüste) 1 chest; 2 breast.

Brustschwimmen das breaststroke.

brutto adverb gross.

BSE das (bovine spongiforme Enzephalopathie) BSE.

Bub der (PL die Buben) boy.

Buch das (PL die Bücher) book.

Buche die (PL die Buchen) beech.

buchen verb (PERF hat gebucht) to book.

Bücherei die (PL die Büchereien) library.

Bücherregal das (PL die Bücherregale) bookcase.

Buchhalter der (PL die Buchhalter) accountant, bookkeeper.

Buchhalterin die (PL die Buchhalterinnen) accountant, bookkeeper.

Buchhandlung die (PL die Buchhandlungen) bookshop.

Büchse die (PL die Büchsen) tin, can.

Büchsenöffner der (PL die Büchsenöffner) tin opener.

Buchstabe der (PL die Buchstaben) letter (of the alphabet); ein großer Buchstabe a capital letter; ein kleiner Buchstabe a small letter.

buchstabieren verb (PERF hat buchstabiert) to spell.

Bucht die (PL die Buchten) bay.

bücken (PERF hat sich gebückt) sich bücken to bend down.

Buddhismus der Buddhism.

Bude die (PL die Buden) 1 hut; 2 stall; 3 meine Bude (informal) my room, my pad.

Büfett das (PL die Büfetts) buffet.

Bügel der (PL die Bügel) hanger.

Bügeleisen das (PL die Bügeleisen) iron.

bügeln verb (PERF hat gebügelt) to iron.

Bühne die (PL die Bühnen) stage.

Bulle der (PL die Bullen) 1 bull; 2 (informal) cop.

Bummel der (PL die Bummel) stroll (around town).

bummeln verb (PERF ist gebummelt) 1 to stroll; wir sind durch die Stadt gebummelt we strolled around town; 2 (PERF hat gebummelt) to dawdle.

Bund[1] der (PL die Bünde) 1 association; 2 waistband.

Bund[2] das (PL die Bunde) bunch.

◇ IRREGULAR VERB: See the verb table in the centre of the dictionary

Bundesbürger der (PL die Bundesbürger) German citizen.

Bundeskanzler der (PL die Bundeskanzler) Federal Chancellor.

Bundesland das (PL die Bundesländer) (federal) state.

Bundesliga die (PL die Bundesligen) (German) national league.

Bundesrat der Upper House (of the German Parliament).

Bundesrepublik die Federal Republic.

Bundesstraße die (PL die Bundesstraßen) A road, major road.

Bundestag der Lower House (of the German Parliament).

Bundeswehr die (German) Army.

bunt adjective colourful.

Buntstift der (PL die Buntstifte) coloured pencil.

Burg die (PL die Burgen) castle.

Bürger der (PL die Bürger) citizen.

Bürgerin die (PL die Bürgerinnen) citizen.

Bürgermeister der (PL die Bürgermeister) mayor.

Bürgersteig der (PL die Bürgersteige) pavement.

Büro das (PL die Büros) office.

Büroklammer die (PL die Büroklammern) paper clip.

Bürste die (PL die Bürsten) brush.

bürsten verb (PERF hat gebürstet) to brush.

Bus der (PL die Busse) bus; ich fahre mit dem Bus I'm going by bus.

Busbahnhof der (PL die Busbahnhöfe) bus station.

Busch der (PL die Büsche) bush.

Busen der (PL die Busen) bosom.

Busfahrer der (PL die Busfahrer) bus driver.

Busfahrerin die (PL die Busfahrerinnen) bus driver.

Busfahrkarte die (PL die Busfahrkarten) bus ticket.

Bushaltestelle die (PL die Bushaltestellen) bus stop.

Bußgeld das (PL die Bußgelder) fine.

Buslinie die (PL die Buslinien) bus route.

Büstenhalter der (PL die Büstenhalter) bra.

Butter die butter.

Butterbrot das (PL die Butterbrote) sandwich, bread and butter.

bzw. = beziehungsweise.

C c

Café das (PL die Cafés) café.

Cafeteria die (PL die Cafeterias) cafeteria.

campen verb (PERF hat gecampt) to camp.

△ NEW SPELLING: See page xii

Camping das camping.

Campingkocher der (PL die Campingkocher) camping stove.

Campingplatz der (PL die Campingplätze) campsite.

CD die (PL die CDs) CD.

CD-Spieler der (PL die CD-Spieler) CD player.

Cello das (PL die Cellos) cello.

Champignon der (PL die Champignons) mushroom.

Chance die (PL die Chancen) chance.

Chaos das chaos.

chaotisch adjective chaotic.

Charakter der (PL die Charaktere) character.

charmant adjective charming.

Charterflug der (PL die Charterflüge) charter flight.

Chauvinist der (PL die Chauvinisten) chauvinist.

Chef der (PL die Chefs) 1 head (of a firm); 2 boss.

Chefin die (PL die Chefinnen) 1 head (of a firm); 2 boss.

Chemie die chemistry.

Chemiker der (PL die Chemiker) chemist.

Chemikerin die (PL die Chemikerinnen) chemist.

chemisch adjective 1 chemical; 2 chemische Reinigung dry-cleaning; dry-cleaner's.

China das China.

Chinese der (PL die Chinesen) Chinese; die Chinesen the Chinese.

Chinesin die (PL die Chinesinnen) Chinese.

chinesisch adjective Chinese.

Chipkarte die (PL die Chipkarten) smart card.

Chips plural noun crisps.

Chirurg der (PL die Chirurgen) surgeon.

Chirurgin die (PL die Chirurginnen) surgeon.

Chlor das chlorine.

Chor der (PL die Chöre) choir.

Christ der (PL die Christen) Christian.

Christin die (PL die Christinnen) Christian.

christlich adjective Christian.

Christus der Christ.

circa adverb approximately.

Clown der (PL die Clowns) clown.

Cola™ die (PL die Colas) Coke™.

Comic der (PL die Comics) cartoon.

Comic-Heft das (PL die Comic-Hefte) comic.

Computer der (PL die Computer) computer.

Computerspiel das (PL die Computerspiele) computer game.

Container der (PL die Container) 1 container; 2 skip.

◇ IRREGULAR VERB: See the verb table in the centre of the dictionary

Cordsamt *der* corduroy.

Couch *die* (PL die **Couchs**) sofa.

Couchtisch *der* (PL die **Couchtische**) coffee table.

Cousin *der* (PL die **Cousins**) cousin.

Cousine *die* (PL die **Cousinen**) cousin.

Creme *die* (PL die **Cremes**) 1 cream; 2 cream dessert.

Curry *das* 1 curry; 2 curry powder.

Currywurst *die* (PL die **Currywürste**) curried sausage.

Cursor *der* (PL die **Cursors**) cursor.

D d

da *adverb* 1 there; **da draußen** out there; **da drüben** over there; **da sein** to be there; **man muss pünktlich da sein** you have to be there on time; 2 **ist noch Brot da?** is there any bread left?; 3 here; **sind alle da?** is everyone here?; **da sind deine Handschuhe** here are your gloves; 4 **ist Sabine da?** is Sabine about?; 5 **von da an** from then on; 6 **ich bin wieder da** I'm back; 7 so (*therefore*); **der Bus war weg, da bin ich gelaufen** the bus had gone, so I walked; 8 **da kann man nichts machen** there's nothing you can do about it; 9 **da, wo die Straße nach Stuttgart abzweigt** at the turning for Stuttgart.
conjunction as, since; **da es gerade regnet** as it's raining.

dabei *adverb* 1 (*included or next to*) with it/him/her/them; **sie hatten die Kinder dabei** they had the children with them; 2 **dicht dabei** close by; 3 (*referring to something already mentioned*) about it; **das Wichtigste dabei** the most important thing about it; 4 at the same time; **er malte ein Bild und sang dabei** he painted a picture and sang at the same time; 5 during this; 6 **jemandem dabei helfen, etwas zu tun** to help somebody do something; 7 **was hast du dir denn dabei gedacht?** what were you thinking of?; 8 **dabei sein**△ to be there; **er ist dabei gewesen** he was there; 9 **was ist denn dabei?** so what?; 10 **dabei sein, etwas zu tun** to be just doing something; **ich war gerade dabei zu gehen** I was just about to leave; 11 **dabei bleiben** to stick with it (*an opinion, for example*); 12 and yet, even though.

dabeibleiben ◇ *verb* (IMPERF **blieb dabei**, PERF **ist dabeigeblieben**) 1 to stay on (*at an organisation*); 2 **er hat mit dem Training begonnen, ist aber nicht dabeigeblieben** he started training, but didn't keep it up.

dabeisein SEE **dabei**.

Dach *das* (PL die **Dächer**) roof.

Dachboden *der* (PL die **Dachböden**) loft, attic.

dachte SEE **denken**.

Dackel *der* (PL die **Dackel**) dachshund.

dadurch *adverb* 1 through it/them; **das Wasser muss dadurch**

△ NEW SPELLING: See page xii

gelaufen sein the water must have run through it; **2** as a result; **3** in this way; **ich nehme die U-Bahn, dadurch bin ich eine halbe Stunde eher da** I'll take the tube, that way I'll be there half an hour earlier. *conjunction* **dadurch, dass** because.

dafür *adverb* **1** for it/them; **dafür kriegt man nicht viel** you won't get much for it/them; **2** instead; **wenn er schon nicht auf die Party gehen will, kann er dich dafür zum Essen einladen** if he doesn't want to go to the party he can take you for a meal instead; **3** but then (*on the other hand*); **4 dafür, dass** considering (that); **5 ich kann nichts dafür** it's not my fault.

dagegen *adverb* **1** against it/them; **ich bin dagegen** I'm against it; **2** for it/them (*when swapping*); **3** into it; **das Auto ist dagegen gefahren** the car drove into it; **4** by comparison; **5 hast du was dagegen?** do you mind?; **6** however.

daheim *adverb* at home.

daher *adverb* **1** from there; **2** that's why.

dahin *adverb* **1** there; **2 bis dahin** (*in the past*) until then; (*in the future*) by then; **3 jemanden dahin bringen, dass er etwas tut** to get somebody to do something.

dahinten *adverb* over there.

dahinter *adverb* **1** behind it/them; **2 dahinter kommen Δ** to get to the bottom of it; **ich bin endlich dahinter**

gekommen I finally got to the bottom of it.

dalassen ◇ *verb* (PRES **lässt da** Δ, IMPERF **ließ da**, PERF **hat dagelassen**) to leave there.

damals *adverb* at that time; then; **wir wohnten damals in Berlin** we were then living in Berlin.

Dame *die* (PL *die* **Damen**) **1** lady; **2** queen (*in chess or cards*); **3** draughts.

Damenbinde *die* (PL *die* **Damenbinden**) sanitary towel.

damit *adverb* **1** with it/them; **ich wi damit spielen** I want to play with it **hör auf damit!** stop it!; **2** by it; **wa meinst du damit?** what do you mean by that?; **3 damit hat es noch Zeit** there's no hurry (about that); **4** therefore, because of that; **sie hat den zweiten Satz verloren und damit das Spiel** she lost the secon set and because of it the match. *conjunction* so that; **ich habe es aufgeschrieben, damit du es nicht vergisst** I wrote it down so that you won't forget.

Damm *der* (PL *die* **Dämme**) **1** dam; **2** embankment.

dämmern *verb* (PERF **hat gedämmert**) es **dämmert** it is getting light; it is getting dark.

Dämmerung *die* **1** dawn; **2** dusk.

Dampf *der* (PL *die* **Dämpfe**) steam.

dampfen *verb* (PERF **hat gedampft**) to steam.

dämpfen *verb* (PERF **hat gedämpft**)

◇ IRREGULAR VERB: *See the verb table in the centre of the dictionary*

1 to steam (*in cooking*); **2** to muffle (*a sound*); **3** to dampen (*somebody's enthusiasm*).

Dampfer *der* (PL *die* **Dampfer**) steamer.

danach *adverb* **1** after it/them; **2** afterwards; **kurz danach** shortly afterwards; **3** danach suchen to look for it/them; **4** danach riechen to smell of it; **5** accordingly; **6** es sieht danach aus it looks like it.

Däne *der* (PL *die* **Dänen**) Dane.

daneben *adverb* **1** next to it/them; **2** by comparison.

Dänemark *das* Denmark.

Dänin *die* (PL *die* **Däninnen**) Dane.

dänisch *adjective* Danish.

dank *preposition* ←(+GEN *or* +DAT) thanks to.

Dank *der* **1** thanks; **mit Dank zurück** thanks for the loan; **2** vielen Dank thank you very much.

dankbar *adjective* **1** grateful; **2** rewarding.

danke *exclamation* thank you, thanks; **danke schön** thank you very much; **(nein) danke** no thank you, no thanks.

danken *verb* (PERF hat gedankt) **1** to thank; **2** nichts zu danken don't mention it.

dann *adverb* then.

daran *adverb* **1** on it/them; **2** daran denken to think of it/them; **3** dicht daran close to it/them; **4** nahe daran sein, etwas zu tun to be on the point of doing something; **5** about it/them; **daran ist nichts zu machen** there is nothing you can do about it; **6** es liegt daran, dass ... it is because ...; **7** er ist daran gestorben he died of it.

darauf *adverb* **1** on it/them; **2** darauf warten to wait for it; **3** darauf antworten to reply to it; **4** after that; **kurz darauf** shortly after that; **5** am Tag darauf the day after; **6** am darauf folgenden Tag △ the following day; **7** es kommt darauf an, ob ... it depends whether ...

daraufhin *adverb* as a result.

daraus *adverb* **1** out of it/them, from it/them; **2** was ist daraus geworden? what has become of it/them?; **3** mach dir nichts daraus don't worry about it.

darf, darfst SEE **dürfen**.

darin *adverb* **1** in it/them; **2** in that respect; **der Unterschied liegt darin, dass** ... the difference is that ...

Darm *der* (PL *die* **Därme**) intestine(s).

darstellen *verb* (PERF hat dargestellt) **1** to represent; **2** to portray; **dieses Gemälde stellt Szenen aus dem Bürgerkrieg dar** this painting portrays scenes from the civil war; **3** to describe; **er stellt es so dar, als sei es meine Schuld** the way he describes it, it's all my fault; **4** to play (*in the theatre*).

Darsteller *der* (PL *die* **Darsteller**) actor.

Darstellerin die (PL die Darstellerinnen) actress.

darüber adverb 1 over it/them; 2 about it; darüber sprechen to talk about it; 3 more; dreißig Mark oder darüber thirty marks or more.

darum adverb 1 round it/them; 2 darum bitten to ask for it; 3 that's why; darum komme ich nicht that's why I'm not coming; 4 ich sorge mich darum I worry about it; 5 es geht darum, zu gewinnen the main thing is to win; 6 darum geht es nicht that's not the point; 7 because of that; darum, weil because.

darunter adverb 1 under it/them; 2 im Stock darunter on the floor below; 3 among them; mehrere Schüler, darunter zwei Zehnjährige a number of pupils, among them two ten year olds; 4 less; dreißig Mark oder darunter thirty marks or less; 5 was verstehen Sie darunter? what do you understand by that?

das article (neuter) 1 the; das Haus the house; 2 that; das Mädchen war es it was that girl; das da that one. pronoun 1 which, that; das Kleid, das ich im Schaufenster gesehen habe the dress which I saw in the window; 2 das mit der Spitze the one with the lace; 3 who; das Mädchen, das gegenüber wohnt the girl who lives opposite; 4 that; das wusste ich nicht I didn't know that; das geht that's all right.

dasein SEE da.

Dasein das existence.

dass Δ conjunction 1 that; ich freue mich, dass ... I'm very pleased that ...; 2 ich verstehe nicht, dass Karin ihn mag I don't understand why Karin likes him.

dasselbe pronoun the same, the same one.

Daten plural noun data.

Datenbank die (PL die Datenbanken) database.

Datenverarbeitung die data processing.

datieren verb (PERF hat datiert) to date.

Dativ der (PL die Dative) dative.

Datum das (PL die Daten) date.

Dauer die 1 duration; 2 length; 3 für die Dauer von fünf Jahren for (a period of) five years; 4 von Dauer sein to last; 5 auf die Dauer in the long run; auf Dauer permanently.

Dauerkarte die (PL die Dauerkarten) season ticket.

dauern verb (PERF hat gedauert) 1 to last; 2 lange dauern to take a long time; es hat vier Wochen gedauert, bis der Brief hier ankam it took four weeks for the letter to arrive.

dauernd adjective constant. adverb constantly.

Dauerwelle die (PL die Dauerwellen) perm.

Daumen der (PL die Daumen) thumb.

◆ IRREGULAR VERB: *See the verb table in the centre of the dictionary*

Daunendecke die (PL die Daunendecken) duvet.

davon adverb 1 from it/them; 2 about it; **ich weiß nichts davon** I don't know anything about it; 3 of it/them; **die Hälfte davon** half of it/them; 4 **das kommt davon** (informal) it serves you right; 5 **was habe ich davon?** what's the point?; 6 **abgesehen davon** apart from that.

davor adverb 1 in front of it/them; 2 beforehand; 3 **Angst davor haben** to be frightened of it/them; 4 **kurz davor sein, etwas zu tun** to be on the point of doing something.

dazu adverb 1 to it/them; 2 in addition; **noch dazu** in addition (to it); 3 with it; **was isst du dazu?** what are you having with it?; 4 **ich habe keine Lust dazu** I don't feel like it; 5 **jemanden dazu bringen, etwas zu tun** to get somebody to do something; 6 **ich bin nicht dazu gekommen** I didn't get round to it; 7 **er ist nicht dazu bereit** he's not prepared to do it.

dazugeben ◇ verb (PRES **gibt dazu**, IMPERF **gab dazu**, PERF **hat dazugegeben**) to add.

dazugehören verb (PERF **hat dazugehört**) 1 to belong to it/them; 2 to go with it/them (of accessories); **alles, was dazugehört** everything that goes with it.

dazukommen ◇ verb (IMPERF **kam dazu**, PERF **ist dazugekommen**) 1 to arrive; 2 to be added; 3 **kommt noch etwas dazu?** would you like anything else?

dazwischen adverb 1 in between; 2 between them; **der Unterschied dazwischen** the difference between them.

dazwischenkommen ◇ verb (PRES **kommt dazwischen**, IMPERF **kam dazwischen**, PERF **ist dazwischengekommen**) to crop up.

DB die (Deutsche Bundesbahn) German railways.

DDR die (Deutsche Demokratische Republik) GDR, East Germany; **in der ehemaligen DDR** in the former East Germany.

Debatte die (PL die **Debatten**) debate.

Decke die (PL die **Decken**) 1 blanket, cover; 2 (table)cloth; **ich habe eine neue Decke aufgelegt** I've put on a new tablecloth; 3 ceiling.

Deckel der (PL die **Deckel**) 1 lid; 2 top.

decken verb (PERF **hat gedeckt**) 1 to cover; 2 **ein Tuch über etwas decken** to spread a cloth over something; 3 **den Tisch decken** to lay the table; 4 **jemanden decken** to cover up for somebody; 5 **einen Spieler decken** to mark a player (in sport).

definieren verb (PERF **hat definiert**) to define.

dehnbar adjective elastic.

dehnen verb (PERF **hat gedehnt**) to stretch.

dein adjective your.

△ NEW SPELLING: See page xii

deiner, deine, deins *pronoun*
yours; **meine Uhr ist kaputt, kann
ich deine haben?** my watch is
broken, can I take yours?

deinetwegen *adverb* 1 because of
you; 2 for your sake.

deins SEE **deiner**.

deklinieren *verb* (PERF **hat
dekliniert**) to decline.

Delle *die* (PL *die* **Dellen**) dent.

Delphin *der* (PL *die* **Delphine**)
dolphin.

dem *article* (*dative*) 1 (to) the; **2 es
liegt auf dem Tisch** it's on the table.
pronoun 1 him; **gib es dem** give
it to him; 2 to it, to that one; 3 to
whom; **der Mann, dem ich das Geld
gegeben habe** the man I gave the
money to; 4 which; **das Messer, mit
dem ich Zwiebeln schneide** the
knife that I cut onions with.

demnächst *adverb* shortly.

Demokratie *die* (PL *die*
Demokratien) democracy.

demokratisch *adjective*
democratic.

Demonstrant *der* (PL *die*
Demonstranten) demonstrator.

Demonstrantin *die* (PL *die*
Demonstrantinnen) demonstrator.

Demonstration *die* (PL *die*
Demonstrationen) demonstration.

demonstrieren *verb* (PERF **hat
demonstriert**) to demonstrate.

den *article* (*accusative*) 1 the; **2 ich
habe mir den Arm gebrochen** I've
broken my arm.

pronoun 1 him; **kennst du den?** do
you know him?; 2 it, that one; **den
kannst du gerne haben** you're
welcome to it; **ich nehme den** I'll
take that one; 3 who(m); 4 which;
**der Mantel, den ich mir gekauft
habe** the coat I bought.

denen *pronoun* (*dative plural*)
1 (to) them; 2 that, (to) whom; **die
Menschen, denen sie geholfen hat**
the people she helped.

denkbar *adjective* conceivable.

denken ♦ *verb* (IMPERF **dachte**, PERF
hat gedacht) 1 to think; **ich denke
oft an dich** I often think of you;
2 das kann ich mir denken I can
imagine.

Denkmal *das* (PL *die* **Denkmäler**)
monument.

denn *conjunction* 1 because, for;
2 mehr denn je more than ever.
adverb 1 **wo denn?** where?; **2 was
ist denn los?** so what's the matter?;
3 warum denn nicht? why ever
not?; 4 **es sei denn** unless.

dennoch *conjunction* nevertheless.

deprimiert *adjective* depressed.

der *article* 1 (*masculine*) the; **der
Mann** the man; 2 (*feminine and
plural genitive*) of the; **die Katze der
Frau** the woman's cat; **der Ball der
Kinder** the children's ball; 3 (*dative*)
(to) the; **ich gab es der Frau** I gave
it to the woman.
pronoun 1 who; **der Mann, der hier
wohnt** the man who lives here;
2 which; **der Regenschirm, der mir**

♦ **IRREGULAR VERB: See the verb table in the centre of the dictionary**

gehört the umbrella which is mine; 3 **der da** that one; 4 him, he.

deren *pronoun* 1 their; **die Kinder und deren Hund** the children and their dog; 2 whose; 3 of which.

derselbe *pronoun* the same, the same one.

des *article* 1 of the; **das Klingeln des Telefons** the ringing of the phone; 2 **der Ball des Jungen** the boy's ball.

deshalb *adverb* 1 therefore; 2 that's why.

desinfizieren *verb.* (PERF **hat desinfiziert**) to disinfect.

dessen *pronoun* 1 his; 2 its; 3 whose; **der Junge, dessen Mutter weint** the boy whose mother is crying; 4 of which.

desto *adverb* the; **je mehr, desto besser** the more the better.

deswegen *conjunction* 1 therefore; 2 that's why.

Detektiv *der* (PL die **Detektive**) detective.

deutlich *adjective* clear. *adverb* **ich konnte ihn deutlich sehen** I could clearly see him.

deutsch *adjective* German.

Deutsch *das* German; **auf Deutsch** in German; **fließend Deutsch sprechen** to speak fluent German.

Deutsche *der/die* (PL die **Deutschen**) German; **er ist Deutscher** he's German.

Deutschland *das* Germany; **nach Deutschland** to Germany.

Devisen *plural noun* foreign currency.

Dezember *der* December; **am ersten Dezember** on the first of December; **im Dezember** in December.

Dezimalzahl *die* (PL die **Dezimalzahlen**) decimal (number).

d.h. (*das heißt*) i.e.

Dia *das* (PL die **Dias**) slide.

diagonal *adjective* diagonal.

Diagramm *das* (PL die **Diagramme**) diagram.

Dialekt *der* (PL die **Dialekte**) dialect.

Dialog *der* (PL die **Dialoge**) dialogue.

Diamant *der* (PL die **Diamanten**) diamond.

Diät *die* (PL die **Diäten**) diet; **jemanden auf Diät setzen** (*informal*) to put somebody on a diet.

dich *pronoun* 1 you; 2 yourself.

dicht *adjective* 1 thick (*fog*); 2 dense; 3 watertight; 4 airtight; 5 **er ist nicht ganz dicht** (*informal*) he's off his head. *adverb* 1 densely; 2 tightly; 3 close; **geh nicht so dicht an den Käfig** don't go so close to the cage; **dicht bei** close to.

Dichter *der* (PL die **Dichter**) poet.

Dichterin *die* (PL die **Dichterinnen**) poet.

Dichtung *die* (PL die **Dichtungen**) 1 poetry; 2 seal, washer.

△ NEW SPELLING: *See page xii*

dick *adjective* 1 thick; 2 swollen (*ankle, tonsils*); 3 fat (*person*).

Dickkopf *der* (PL die Dickköpfe) 1 stubborn person; 2 einen Dickkopf haben to be stubborn.

die *article* (*feminine and plural*) the; die Frau the woman; die Bücher the books.
pronoun (*feminine and plural*) 1 who; die Frau, die hier wohnt the woman who lives here; die Frau, die ich kenne the woman I know; die Kinder, die ich gefragt habe the children I asked; 2 which; die Tasche, die ich gekauft habe the bag I bought; 3 she, her; 4 them; ich meine die I mean them; 5 die da that one; (*plural*) those.

Dieb *der* (PL die Diebe) thief.

Diebin *die* (PL die Diebinnen) thief.

Diebstahl *der* (PL die Diebstähle) theft.

Diele *die* (PL die Dielen) 1 hall; 2 floorboard.

dienen *verb* (PERF hat gedient) to serve.

Dienst *der* (PL die Dienste) service; Dienst haben to work, to be on duty (*of a soldier or doctor*).

Dienstag *der* (PL die Dienstage) Tuesday; am Dienstag on Tuesday.

dienstags *adverb* on Tuesdays.

dienstfrei *adjective* 1 ein dienstfreier Tag a day off; 2 dienstfrei haben to have time off, to be off duty.

dienstlich *adverb* on business.

Dienstreise *die* (PL die Dienstreisen) business trip.

diese SEE dieser.

Diesel *der* diesel.

dieselbe *pronoun* the same, the same one.

dieser, diese, dieses *adjective* 1 this; 2 these; diese Äpfel these apples.
pronoun 1 this one; mir gefällt dieses am besten I like this one best; 2 these ones.

diesmal *adverb* this time.

Digitaluhr *die* (PL die Digitaluhren) 1 digital watch; 2 digital clock.

Diktat *das* (PL die Diktate) dictation.

Ding *das* (PL die Dinge) thing; vor allen Dingen above all; das war ein Ding (*informal*) that was quite something.

Dings *der/die/das* thingummy.

Dinosaurier *der* (PL die Dinosaurier) dinosaur.

Diplom *das* (PL die Diplome) diploma.

dir *pronoun* 1 you, to you; sie hat es dir gegeben she gave it to you; ich verspreche dir, dass ... I promise you that ...; 2 Freunde von dir friends of yours; 3 yourself.

direkt *adjective* direct.

Direktor *der* (PL die Direktoren) 1 director; 2 headmaster, principal; 3 manager (*of a bank, theatre*).

Direktorin *die* (PL die Direktorinnen) 1 director;

✧ IRREGULAR VERB: *See the verb table in the centre of the dictionary*

2 headmistress, principal;
3 manager (*of a bank, theatre*).

Direktübertragung *die* (PL *die*
Direktübertragungen) live
transmission.

Dirigent *der* (PL *die* Dirigenten)
conductor.

dirigieren *verb* (PERF **hat dirigiert**)
to conduct.

Diskette *die* (PL *die* Disketten)
floppy disk.

Diskothek *die* (PL *die* Diskotheken)
disco, discotheque.

Diskriminierung *die*
discrimination; **die Diskriminierung
von Frauen** discrimination against
women.

Diskussion *die* (PL *die*
Diskussionen) discussion; **zur
Diskussion stehen** to be under
discussion.

diskutieren *verb* (PERF **hat
diskutiert**) to discuss.

Disziplin *die* (PL *die* Disziplinen)
discipline.

DJH *die* (*Deutsche Jugendherberge*)
German youth hostel (association).

DM *die* (*Deutsche Mark*) DM,
Deutschmark.

D-Mark *die* (PL *die* D-Mark)
Deutschmark, German mark.

doch *adverb* **1** yes (*when you are
contradicting somebody*); '**hast du
keinen Hunger?**' – '**doch!**' 'aren't
you hungry?' – 'yes, I am!'; **2** after
all; **sie hat ihn doch eingeladen** she

invited him after all; **sie ist doch
nicht gekommen** she hasn't come
after all; **3 er hat doch meinen Brief
bekommen?** he did get my letter,
didn't he?; **sie kommt doch?** she's
coming, isn't she?; **4** anyway; **du
hörst ja doch nicht auf mich** you
won't listen to me anyway; **5 pass
doch auf!** do be careful!
conjunction but.

Doktor *der* (PL *die* Doktoren) doctor;
den Doktor machen to do a
doctorate.

Dokument *das* (PL *die* Dokumente)
document.

Dokumentarfilm *der* (PL *die*
Dokumentarfilme) documentary.

Dokumentarsendung *die* (PL *die*
Dokumentarsendungen)
documentary (programme).

dolmetschen *verb* (PERF **hat
gedolmetscht**) to interpret.

Dolmetscher *der* (PL *die*
Dolmetscher) interpreter.

Dolmetscherin *die* (PL *die*
Dolmetscherinnen) interpreter.

Dom *der* (PL *die* Dome) cathedral.

Donau *die* Danube.

Donner *der* thunder.

donnern *verb* (PERF **hat gedonnert**)
to thunder.

Donnerstag *der* (PL *die*
Donnerstage) Thursday; **am
Donnerstag** on Thursday.

donnerstags *adverb* on Thursdays.

doof *adjective* (*informal*) stupid.

△ NEW SPELLING: *See page xii*

Doppel das (PL die Doppel)
1 duplicate; 2 doubles (in sport).

Doppelbett das (PL die Doppelbetten) double bed.

Doppelfenster das (PL die Doppelfenster) double-glazed window; **wir haben Doppelfenster** we've got double glazing.

Doppelhaus das (PL die Doppelhäuser) semi-detached house.

doppelt adjective 1 double; 2 in doppelter Ausführung in duplicate; 3 die doppelte Menge twice the amount.
adverb 1 doubly; 2 twice; doppelt so viel twice as much; sich doppelt anstrengen to try twice as hard.

Doppelzimmer das (PL die Doppelzimmer) double room.

Dorf das (PL die Dörfer) village.

Dorn der (PL die Dornen) thorn.

dort adverb there; dort drüben over there.

dorther adverb from there.

dorthin adverb there; geht ihr jetzt dorthin? are you going there now?

Dose die (PL die Dosen) tin, can.

Dosenöffner der (PL die Dosenöffner) tin opener.

Dosis die (PL die Dosen) dose.

Dotter der (PL die Dotter) yolk.

Dozent der (PL die Dozenten) lecturer.

Dozentin die (PL die Dozentinnen) lecturer.

Drache der (PL die Drachen) dragon.

Drachen der (PL die Drachen) kite.

Drachenfliegen das hang-gliding.

Draht der (PL die Drähte) 1 wire; 2 er ist auf Draht (informal) he's on the ball.

Drama das (PL die Dramen) drama.

Dramatik die drama.

dran adverb SEE daran; 1 ich bin dran it's my turn; wer ist dran? whose turn is it?; 2 gut dran sein to be well off; 3 arm dran sein to be in a bad way; 4 spät dran sein to be late.

drängen verb (PERF hat gedrängt) 1 to push; 2 to press, to urge (somebody); 3 sich drängen to crowd; die Leute drängten sich vor der Kasse people crowded around the box-office.

drankommen ◇ verb (IMPERF kam dran, PERF ist drangekommen) to have your turn; wer kommt dran? whose turn is it?

drauf adverb SEE darauf; 1 drauf und dran sein, etwas zu tun to be on the point of doing something; 2 gut drauf sein (informal) to be in a good mood.

draußen adverb outside.

Dreck der dirt.

dreckig adjective dirty, filthy.

Drehbuch das (PL die Drehbücher) 1 screenplay; 2 script.

drehen verb (PERF hat gedreht) 1 to turn; an etwas drehen to turn

◇ IRREGULAR VERB: See the verb table in the centre of the dictionary

something; **2** to shoot (*a film*);
3 sich drehen to turn; **4 sich im
Kreis drehen** to rotate; **5 es dreht
sich um ihr Taschengeld** it's about
her pocket money.

drei *number* three.

Drei *die* (PL *die* **Dreien**) three.

Dreieck *das* (PL *die* **Dreiecke**)
triangle.

dreieckig *adjective* triangular.

dreifach *adjective* triple.

dreihundert *number* three
hundred.

dreimal *adverb* three times.

dreißig *number* thirty.

dreiviertel *number* three-quarters.

Dreiviertelstunde *die* (PL *die*
Dreiviertelstunden) three-quarters
of an hour.

dreizehn *number* thirteen.

drin *adverb* SEE **darin; drin sein** to
be inside.

dringend *adjective* urgent.

drinnen *adverb* **1** inside; **2** indoors.

dritt *adverb* **sie sind zu dritt** there
are three of them.

dritte SEE **dritter.**

Drittel *das* (PL *die* **Drittel**) third.

drittens *adverb* thirdly.

dritter, dritte, drittes *adjective*
third; **zum dritten Mal** for the third
time; **ein Dritter** a third person;
jeder Dritte, der mitwollte every

third person who wanted to come;
die Dritte Welt the Third World.

Droge *die* (PL *die* **Drogen**) drug.

drogenabhängig *adjective*
addicted to drugs.

Drogenabhängige *der/die* (PL *die*
Drogenabhängigen) drug addict.

Drogenabhängigkeit *die* drug
addiction.

drogensüchtig *adjective* addicted
to drugs.

Drogensüchtige *der/die* (PL *die*
Drogensüchtigen) drug addict.

Drogerie *die* (PL *die* **Drogerien**)
chemist's.

Drogist *der* (PL *die* **Drogisten**)
chemist.

Drogistin *die* (PL *die* **Drogistinnen**)
chemist.

drohen *verb* (PERF **hat gedroht**) to
threaten; **jemandem drohen** to
threaten somebody.

Drohung *die* (PL *die* **Drohungen**)
threat.

drüben *adverb* over there.

Druck *der* **1** pressure; **jemanden
unter Druck setzen** to put pressure
on somebody; **2** printing; **3** (PL *die*
Drucke) print.

drucken *verb* (PERF **hat gedruckt**) to
print.

drücken *verb* (PERF **hat gedrückt**)
1 to press; **2 an der Tür drücken** to
push the door; **'bitte drücken'**
'push'; **3** to hug; **4** to pinch (*of
shoes*); **5 die Preise drücken** to

△ NEW SPELLING: *See page xii*

force down prices; **6 sich vor etwas drücken** (*informal*) to get out of something; **du hast dich mal wieder vor dem Aufräumen gedrückt** you've got out of tidying up again.

Drucker der (PL die **Drucker**) printer.

Druckknopf der (PL die **Druckknöpfe**) press stud.

Drucksache die (PL die **Drucksachen**) printed matter.

Druckschrift die (PL die **Druckschriften**) 1 block letters; 2 type; 3 pamphlet.

Drüse die (PL die **Drüsen**) gland.

Dschungel der (PL die **Dschungel**) jungle.

du pronoun 1 you; **2 du sagen** to say 'du' (to each other); **per du sein** to be on familiar terms ('*du' is used when talking to family members, close friends, or people of your own age; otherwise 'Sie' is used*).

Dudelsack der (PL die **Dudelsäcke**) bagpipes.

Duft der (PL die **Düfte**) fragrance, scent.

duften verb (PERF **hat geduftet**) to smell; **nach Lavendel duften** to smell of lavender.

dumm adjective 1 stupid; **2 das wird mir jetzt zu dumm** (*informal*) I've had enough of it; **3 so etwas Dummes!** how annoying!; **4 der Dumme sein** to draw the short straw.

dummerweise adverb stupidly.

Dummheit die (PL die

Dummheiten) 1 stupidity; 2 stupid thing; **mach keine Dummheiten** don't do anything stupid.

Dummkopf der (PL die **Dummköpfe**) fool.

Dünger der (PL die **Dünger**) fertilizer.

dunkel adjective 1 dark; **ein dunkler Anzug** a dark suit; **2 im Dunkeln** in the dark; **3** vague (*idea*); **4** shady (*business*); **5** deep (*voice*).

Dunkelheit die darkness, dark.

dünn adjective 1 thin; 2 weak (*coffee, tea*).

Dunst der (PL die **Dünste**) haze.

Duo das (PL die **Duos**) duet.

durch preposition ←(+ACC) 1 through; **er ist durch das Fernsehen bekannt geworden** he's become famous through television; 2 by; **durch Boten** by courier; **3 acht durch zwei ist vier** eight divided by two is four; **4** due to. adverb 1 through; **die ganze Nacht durch** all through the night; **2 den Winter durch** throughout the winter; **3 durch und durch** completely; **4 es war acht Uhr durch** (*informal*) it was gone eight o'clock.

durcharbeiten verb (PERF **hat durchgearbeitet**) 1 to work through; **die Nacht durcharbeiten** to work through the night; **2 sich durch etwas durcharbeiten** to work your way through something.

durchaus adverb absolutely.

durchblicken verb (PERF **hat**

durchgeblickt) 1 (*informal*) to understand; 2 **durchblicken lassen, dass ...** to hint that ...

durchbrechen ◇ *verb* (PRES **bricht durch,** IMPERF **brach durch,** PERF **hat durchgebrochen**) 1 to snap, to break in two; 2 (PERF **ist durchgebrochen**) **das Brett ist durchgebrochen** the board has snapped.

durcheinander *adverb* 1 in a mess; **mein Zimmer ist durcheinander** my room is (in) a mess; 2 **die Akten durcheinander bringen** △ to muddle up the files; **Karl hat ihre Namen durcheinander gebracht** Karl got their names mixed up; 3 confused; **bring mich nicht durcheinander** don't confuse me; 4 **sie haben alle durcheinander geredet** they all talked at once.

Durcheinander *das* 1 muddle; 2 mess; **in der Wohnung herrschte ein fürchterliches Durcheinander** the flat was a terrible mess; 3 confusion; **im allgemeinen Durcheinander** in the general confusion.

durcheinanderbringen SEE **durcheinander**.

durchfahren ◇ *verb* (PRES **fährt durch,** IMPERF **fuhr durch,** PERF **ist durchgefahren**) 1 to drive through; 2 to go through; 3 **der Zug fährt (in Stuttgart) durch** the train doesn't stop (in Stuttgart).

Durchfall *der* diarrhoea.

durchfallen ◇ *verb* (PRES **fällt durch,** IMPERF **fiel durch,** PERF **ist**

durchgefallen) 1 to fall through; 2 to fail (*an exam*).

durchführen *verb* (PERF **hat durchgeführt**) to carry out.

Durchgang *der* (PL **die Durchgänge**) 1 passage; 2 '**Durchgang verboten**' 'no entry'; 3 round (*in sport*).

Durchgangsverkehr *der* through traffic.

durchgehen ◇ *verb* (IMPERF **ging durch,** PERF **ist durchgegangen**) 1 to go through; 2 (*informal*) to escape; 3 **jemandem etwas durchgehen lassen** to let somebody get away with something.

durchkommen ◇ *verb* (IMPERF **kam durch,** PERF **ist durchgekommen**) 1 to come through; 2 to get through (*on the phone, in an exam*); 3 to pull through (*after an illness*).

durchlassen ◇ *verb* (PRES **lässt durch** △ IMPERF **ließ durch,** PERF **hat durchgelassen**) 1 to let through; 2 to let in.

durchmachen *verb* (PERF **hat durchgemacht**) 1 to go through; 2 to work through (*your lunch break, for example*); 3 **wir haben die Nacht durchgemacht** we made a night of it.

Durchmesser *der* (PL **die Durchmesser**) diameter.

durchnehmen ◇ *verb* (PRES **nimmt durch,** IMPERF **nahm durch,** PERF **hat durchgenommen**) to do (*a topic at school*).

△ NEW SPELLING: *See page xii*

durchs = durch das.

Durchsage die (PL die Durchsagen) announcement.

Durchschnitt der (PL die Durchschnitte) average; **im Durchschnitt** on average.

durchschnittlich adjective average.
adverb on average.

durchsetzen verb (PERF hat durchgesetzt) 1 to carry through; 2 sich durchsetzen to assert yourself; 3 sich durchsetzen to catch on (of a fashion, an idea).

durchsichtig adjective transparent.

durchstreichen ✧ verb (IMPERF strich durch, PERF hat durchgestrichen) to cross out.

Durchzug der draught.

dürfen ✧ verb (PRES darf, IMPERF durfte, PERF hat gedurft or hat dürfen) 1 to be allowed; sie darf das nicht she's not allowed to do that; er hat nicht gedurft he wasn't allowed to; 2 Klaus hat sie im Krankenhaus besuchen dürfen Klaus was allowed to visit her in hospital; 3 darf ich? may I?; 4 das dürfen Sie nicht vergessen you mustn't forget that; du darfst es nicht alles so ernst nehmen you mustn't take it all so seriously; 5 du darfst froh sein, dass sonst nichts passiert ist you should be glad that nothing else happened; das darf einfach nicht passieren that just shouldn't happen; das dürfte nicht schwierig sein that shouldn't be

difficult; 6 das darf nicht wahr sein! I don't believe it!; 7 was darf es sein? can I help you?; 8 das dürfte der Grund sein that's probably the reason.

durfte, durften, durftest, durftet SEE dürfen.

Dürre die (PL die Dürren) drought.

Durst der thirst; Durst haben to be thirsty.

durstig adjective thirsty.

Dusche die (PL die Duschen) shower.

duschen verb (PERF hat geduscht) 1 to have a shower; 2 sich duschen to have a shower.

Düsenflugzeug das (PL die Düsenflugzeuge) jet (plane).

düster adjective 1 gloomy (future, thoughts); 2 dark.

Dutzend das (PL die Dutzende) dozen.

duzen verb (PERF hat geduzt) to call somebody 'du'; wollen wir uns duzen? shall we say 'du' to each other? ('du' is used when talking to family members, close friends, or people of your own age).

dynamisch adjective dynamic.

D-Zug der (PL die D-Züge) fast train, express.

✧ IRREGULAR VERB: See the verb table in the centre of the dictionary

E e

Ebbe die (PL die Ebben) low tide.

eben adjective 1 flat; 2 level. adverb 1 just; Gabi war eben hier Gabi was just here; eben noch just now; 2 eben! exactly!

Ebene die (PL die Ebenen) 1 plain; 2 level; 3 plane (in geometry).

ebenso adverb just as; Ulla hat den Film ebenso oft gesehen wie du Ulla's seen the film just as often as you; ich habe ebenso viel Arbeit wie du I've got just as much work as you.

Echo das (PL die Echos) echo.

echt adjective real, genuine; die Kette ist aus echtem Gold the necklace is real gold. adverb (informal) really; das ist echt gut that's really good.

Eckball der (PL die Eckbälle) corner (kick).

Ecke die (PL die Ecken) corner; um die Ecke round the corner.

eckig adjective square.

Edelstein der (PL die Edelsteine) precious stone.

EDV die (elektronische Datenverarbeitung) electronic data processing, EDP.

Efeu der (PL die Efeus) ivy.

EG die (Europäische Gemeinschaft) EC.

egal adjective 1 das ist mir egal it's all the same to me; 2 egal, wie groß no matter how big; egal, ob es will oder nicht (it doesn't matter) whether he wants to or not.

egoistisch adjective selfish.

ehe conjunction before; ehe ich nicht weiß, was er will, mache ich nichts I won't do anything before I know what he wants.

Ehe die (PL die Ehen) marriage.

Ehefrau die (PL die Ehefrauen) wife.

ehemalig adjective former.

Ehemann der (PL die Ehemänner) husband.

Ehepaar das (PL die Ehepaare) married couple.

eher adverb 1 earlier, sooner; je eher, desto besser the sooner the better; 2 rather; eher gehe ich zu Fuß, als Geld für ein Taxi auszugeben I'd rather walk than pay for a taxi; 3 more; das ist schon eher möglich that's more likely.

Ehre die (PL die Ehren) honour.

Ehrgeiz der ambition.

ehrgeizig adjective ambitious.

ehrlich adjective honest.

Ehrlichkeit die honesty.

Ei das (PL die Eier) egg.

Eiche die (PL die Eichen) oak.

△NEW SPELLING: See page xii

Eichhörnchen *das* (PL *die* Eichhörnchen) squirrel.

Eid *der* (PL *die* Eide) oath.

Eidechse *die* (PL *die* Eidechsen) lizard.

Eierbecher *der* (PL *die* Eierbecher) egg-cup.

Eierschale *die* (PL *die* Eierschalen) eggshell.

Eifer *der* eagerness.

Eifersucht *die* jealousy.

eifersüchtig *adjective* jealous; **auf jemanden eifersüchtig sein** to be jealous of somebody.

eifrig *adjective* eager.

Eigelb *das* (PL *die* Eigelb(e)) egg yolk.

eigen *adjective* own; **sie ist erst siebzehn und hat schon ihr eigenes Auto** she's only seventeen and she's already got her own car.

Eigenart *die* (PL *die* Eigenarten) peculiarity.

eigenartig *adjective* peculiar.

Eigenschaft *die* (PL *die* Eigenschaften) **1** quality; **2** characteristic.

eigensinnig *adjective* obstinate.

eigentlich *adjective* actual. *adverb* actually; **eigentlich habe ich keine Lust, heute ins Kino zu gehen** actually I don't fancy going to the cinema today.

Eigentum *das* property.

Eigentümer *der* (PL *die* Eigentümer) owner.

eignen *verb* (PERF **hat sich geeignet**) **sich eignen** to be suitable.

Eile *die* hurry.

eilen *verb* **1** (PERF **ist geeilt**) to hurry; **2** (PERF **hat geeilt**) to be urgent; **das eilt nicht** it's not urgent.

eilig *adjective* **1** urgent; **2** hurried; **3** es eilig haben to be in a hurry.

Eilzug *der* (PL *die* Eilzüge) fast stopping train.

Eimer *der* (PL *die* Eimer) bucket.

ein, eine, ein *article* a, an; **ein Haus** a house; **eine Allergie** an allergy; **ein bisschen mehr** a bit more; **was für ein Kleid hast du gekauft?** what sort of dress did you buy?
adjective **1** one; **sie haben nur ein Kind** they've got just one child; **eines Abends** one evening; **2 einer Meinung sein** to be of the same opinion; **3 ein für allemal** once and for all.

einander *pronoun* each other, one another.

Einbahnstraße *die* (PL *die* Einbahnstraßen) one-way street.

Einband *der* (PL *die* Einbände) cover.

einbauen *verb* (PERF **hat eingebaut**) **1** to fit; **2** to install.

Einbauküche *die* (PL *die* Einbauküchen) fitted kitchen.

einbiegen ◇ *verb* (IMPERF **bog ein**, PERF **ist eingebogen**) to turn; **der Radfahrer bog langsam in die Seitenstraße ein** the cyclist turned slowly down the side street.

◇ IRREGULAR VERB: *See the verb table in the centre of the dictionary*

einbilden verb (PERF hat sich eingebildet) 1 sich einbilden to imagine; das bildest du dir nur ein you're only imagining it; 2 Till bildet sich viel ein Till is very conceited.

Einbildung die imagination; das ist alles nur Einbildung it's all in the mind.

einbrechen ⬦ verb (PRES bricht ein, IMPERF brach ein, PERF ist eingebrochen) to break in; in unserem Haus sind Diebe eingebrochen thieves broke into our house; bei unseren Nachbarn ist eingebrochen worden our neighbours have been burgled.

Einbrecher der (PL die Einbrecher) burglar.

Einbruch der (PL die Einbrüche) 1 burglary; 2 vor Einbruch der Dunkelheit before it gets dark; 3 bei Einbruch der Nacht at nightfall.

eindeutig adjective 1 clear; 2 definite (proof).

Eindruck der (PL die Eindrücke) impression.

eindrucksvoll adjective impressive.

eine SEE ein, einer.

eineinhalb number one and a half.

einer, eine, ein(e)s pronoun 1 one; einer von uns one of us; wie soll das einer wissen? how is one supposed to know?; 2 somebody; 3 kaum einer hardly anyone; 4 you; das macht einen müde it makes you tired.

einerseits adverb on the one hand;

einerseits sagt sie, dass sie kein Geld hat, andererseits kauft sie sich dauernd neue Sachen on the one hand she claims to have no money, on the other hand she's constantly buying new things.

eines SEE einer.

einfach adjective 1 simple; 2 easy; 3 single (ticket, knot). adverb simply.

Einfachheit die simplicity.

Einfahrt die (PL die Einfahrten) 1 entrance; 2 arrival (of a train); 3 slip road (on a motorway).

Einfall der (PL die Einfälle) idea.

einfallen ⬦ verb (PRES fällt ein, IMPERF fiel ein, PERF ist eingefallen) 1 jemandem einfallen to occur to somebody; 2 ihr Name fällt mir nicht ein I can't think of her name; 3 was fällt dir eigentlich ein? what do you think you're doing?; 4 sich etwas einfallen lassen to think of something.

Einfamilienhaus das (PL die Einfamilienhäuser) detached family house.

Einfluss Δ der (PL die Einflüsse) influence.

einfrieren ⬦ verb (IMPERF fror ein, PERF ist eingefroren) 1 to freeze; 2 (PERF hat eingefroren) to freeze (food in the freezer).

Einfuhr die (PL die Einfuhren) import.

einführen verb (PERF hat

Δ NEW SPELLING: See page xii

eingeführt 1 to import; 2 to introduce.

Einführung die (PL die Einführungen) introduction.

Eingabe die input (of data).

eingeben ◇ verb (PRES gibt ein, IMPERF gab ein, PERF hat eingegeben) 1 to hand in; 2 to input, to key in.

eingebildet adjective 1 conceited; 2 imaginary (illness).

Eingeborene der/die (PL die Eingeborenen) native.

eingehen ◇ verb (IMPERF ging ein, PERF ist eingegangen) 1 to shrink (of clothes); 2 to die (of plants); 3 to arrive (of goods); 4 auf etwas eingehen to go into something; sie ging näher darauf ein she went into it in more detail; 5 auf etwas nicht eingehen to ignore something; 6 auf etwas eingehen to agree to something; Oliver ist auf unseren Plan eingegangen Oliver agreed to our plan; 7 ein Risiko eingehen to take a risk.

eingeschrieben adjective registered; ein eingeschriebener Brief a registered letter.

eingestellt adjective 1 auf etwas eingestellt sein to be prepared for something; 2 fortschrittlich eingestellt sein to be progressively minded.

eingewöhnen verb (PERF hat sich eingewöhnt) sich eingewöhnen to settle in.

eingießen ◇ verb (IMPERF goss ein △, PERF hat eingegossen) to pour.

Eingriff der (PL die Eingriffe) 1 intervention; 2 operation (surgical).

einheimisch adjective 1 native; 2 local.

Einheit die (PL die Einheiten) 1 unity; 2 unit (of drink, soldiers).

Einheitspreis der (PL die Einheitspreise) 1 standard price; 2 flat fare.

einholen verb (PERF hat eingeholt) 1 to catch up with; 2 to make up (time, a delay); 3 to buy; einholen gehen to go shopping.

einhundert number one hundred.

einige SEE einiger.

einigen verb (PERF hat sich geeinigt) sich einigen to come to an agreement; sich auf etwas einigen to agree on something.

einiger, einige, einiges adjective, pronoun 1 some; vor einiger Zeit some time ago; 2 several; 3 nur einige waren noch da there were only a few left; 4 einiges quite a lot; wir haben einiges gesehen we saw quite a lot (of things); 5 einiges some things; einiges hat uns nicht gefallen there were some things we didn't like.

einigermaßen adverb 1 fairly; 2 fairly well; 3 'wie geht es dir?' – 'einigermaßen' 'how are you?' – 'so-so'.

einiges SEE einiger.

◇ IRREGULAR VERB: See the verb table in the centre of the dictionary

Einigung *die* agreement.

Einkauf *der* (PL *die* Einkäufe) 1 purchase; 2 shopping; **Einkäufe machen** to do some shopping.

einkaufen *verb* (PERF hat eingekauft) 1 to buy; **ich habe vergessen Milch einzukaufen** I forgot to buy milk; 2 to shop; **wir kaufen meist im Supermarkt ein** we usually shop at the supermarket; **einkaufen gehen** to go shopping.

Einkaufsbummel *der* (PL *die* Einkaufsbummel) shopping spree.

Einkaufswagen *der* (PL *die* Einkaufswagen) shopping trolley.

Einkaufszentrum *das* (PL *die* Einkaufszentren) shopping centre.

Einkommen *das* (PL *die* Einkommen) income.

einladen ◇ *verb* (PRES lädt ein, IMPERF lud ein, PERF hat eingeladen) 1 to invite; **jemanden zum Abendessen einladen** to invite somebody for dinner; 2 **jemanden ins Kino einladen** to take somebody to the cinema; 3 to treat; **ich lade euch ein** I'll treat you; 4 to load (*goods*).

Einladung *die* (PL *die* Einladungen) invitation.

einleben *verb* (PERF hat sich eingelebt) **sich einleben** to settle down.

Einleitung *die* (PL *die* Einleitungen) introduction.

einlösen *verb* (PERF hat eingelöst) to cash.

einmal *adverb* 1 once (*in the past*); **es war einmal …** once upon a time …; 2 one day (*in the future*); 3 **auf einmal** suddenly; 4 **auf einmal** at the same time; **sie kamen alle auf einmal** they all came at the same time; 5 **nicht einmal** not even; (*an organisation*) 6 noch einmal again; 7 **es geht nun einmal nicht** it's just not possible.

einmalig *adjective* 1 unique; 2 fantastic; 3 single, one-off (*payment*).

einmischen *verb* (PERF hat sich eingemischt) **sich einmischen** to interfere.

einordnen *verb* (PERF hat eingeordnet) 1 to put in order; 2 **sich einordnen** (*with other people*); 3 **sich einordnen** to get in lane (*when driving*).

einpacken *verb* (PERF hat eingepackt) 1 to pack; 2 to wrap.

einreichen *verb* (PERF hat eingereicht) to hand in.

Einreise *die* (PL *die* Einreisen) entry.

einreisen *verb* (PERF ist eingereist) to enter a country; **er reiste nach Italien ein** he entered Italy.

einrichten *verb* (PERF hat eingerichtet) 1 to furnish; 2 to set up (*an organisation*); 3 to arrange; **kannst du es so einrichten, dass du vormittags da bist?** can you arrange to be here in the morning?; 4 **sich einrichten** to furnish your home; 5 **sich einrichten** to economize; 6 **sich auf etwas**

△ NEW SPELLING: *See page xii*

einrichten to prepare for something.

Einrichtung die (PL die Einrichtungen) 1 furnishing; 2 furnishings; 3 setting up; 4 institution; **staatliche Einrichtungen** state institutions.

eins number one; **eins zu eins** one all; **es ist eins** it's one o'clock. pronoun SEE **einer**. adjective **mir ist alles eins** it's all the same to me.

Eins die (PL die Einsen) one.

einsam adjective lonely.

einsammeln verb (PERF hat eingesammelt) to collect.

Einsatz der 1 use; 2 stake (when betting).

einschalten verb (PERF hat eingeschaltet) 1 to switch on (a radio, TV); 2 **sich einschalten** to intervene.

einschlafen ✧ verb (PRES schläft ein, IMPERF schlief ein, PERF ist eingeschlafen) to go to sleep.

einschließen ✧ verb (IMPERF schloss ein △, PERF hat eingeschlossen) 1 to lock in; 2 to include; 3 **sich einschließen** to lock yourself in.

einschließlich preposition ←(+GEN) including; **einschließlich der Unkosten** including expenses. adverb inclusive.

einschränken verb (PERF hat eingeschränkt) 1 to restrict; 2 to cut back; 3 **sich einschränken** to economize.

einschreiben ✧ verb (IMPERF schrieb sich ein, PERF hat sich eingeschrieben) 1 **sich einschreiben** to enrol (at university); 2 **sich einschreiben** to put your name down.

Einschreiben das (PL die Einschreiben) registered letter, registered parcel; **per Einschreiben** registered.

einsehen ✧ verb (PRES sieht ein, IMPERF sah ein, PERF hat eingesehen) 1 to realize; 2 to see; **das sehe ich nicht ein** I don't see why.

einseitig adjective one-sided.

einsenden ✧ verb (IMPERF sendete ein/sandte ein, PERF hat eingesendet/hat eingesandt) to send in.

einsetzen verb (PERF hat eingesetzt) 1 to put in (a missing part), to insert; 2 to use; **während der Weltmeisterschaft wurden Sonderzüge eingesetzt** special train were put on during the World Cup; 3 to stake (money); 4 to start (of rain, snow); 5 **sich für jemanden einsetzen** to support somebody.

Einsicht die 1 insight; 2 sense; 3 **zu der Einsicht kommen, dass …** to come to realize that …

einsperren verb (PERF hat eingesperrt) to lock up.

Einspruch der (PL die Einsprüche) objection.

✧ IRREGULAR VERB: See the verb table in the centre of the dictionary

einst *adverb* 1 once; 2 one day (*in the future*).

einstecken *verb* (PERF hat eingesteckt) 1 to put in (*a coin*); 2 einen Brief einstecken to post a letter; 3 to plug in; 4 etwas einstecken to put something in your pocket or bag, to take something; 5 (*informal*) to take (*insults*).

einsteigen ◇ *verb* (IMPERF stieg ein, PERF ist eingestiegen) 1 to get in; 2 to get on (*a bus or train*).

einstellen *verb* (PERF hat eingestellt) 1 to employ (*in a job*); 2 to adjust (*a machine*); 3 to focus (*a camera*); 4 to tune into (*a radio station*); 5 to stop; 6 sich auf etwas einstellen to prepare yourself for something; 7 sich schnell auf eine neue Situation einstellen to adjust quickly to a new situation.

Einstellung *die* (PL die Einstellungen) 1 employment; 2 adjustment; 3 stopping; 4 take (*of a film*); 5 attitude; seine politische Einstellung his political views.

Einstieg *der* (PL die Einstiege) entrance.

einstürzen *verb* (PERF ist eingestürzt) to collapse.

einstweilen *adverb* 1 for the time being; 2 meanwhile.

eintausend *number* one thousand.

einteilen *verb* (PERF hat eingeteilt) 1 to divide up; 2 sich seine Zeit gut einteilen to organize your time well.

Eintopf *der* (PL die Eintöpfe) stew.

Eintrag *der* (PL die Einträge) entry.

eintragen ◇ *verb* (PRES trägt ein, IMPERF trug ein, PERF hat eingetragen) 1 to enter, to write; 2 sich eintragen to put your name down.

einträglich *adjective* profitable.

eintreffen ◇ *verb* (PRES trifft ein, IMPERF traf ein, PERF ist eingetroffen) 1 to arrive; 2 to come true.

eintreten ◇ *verb* (PRES tritt ein, IMPERF trat ein, PERF ist eingetreten) 1 to enter; 2 in einen Klub eintreten to join a club; für jemanden eintreten to stand up for somebody.

Eintritt *der* 1 entrance; 2 admission; 'Eintritt frei' 'admission free'.

Eintrittskarte *die* (PL die Eintrittskarten) (admission) ticket.

Eintrittspreis *der* (PL die Eintrittspreise) admission charge.

einverstanden *adjective* 1 einverstanden sein to agree; einverstanden! okay!; 2 mit jemandem einverstanden sein to approve of somebody.

Einwand *der* (PL die Einwände) objection.

Einwanderer *der* (PL die Einwanderer) immigrant.

Einwanderin *die* (PL die Einwanderinnen) immigrant.

einwandern *verb* (PERF ist eingewandert) to immigrate.

△ NEW SPELLING: *See page xii*

einweichen verb (PERF hat eingeweicht) to soak (*washing*).

einwerfen ◇ verb (PRES wirft ein, IMPERF warf ein, PERF hat eingeworfen) 1 to post; 2 to put in (*a coin, money*); 3 to throw in; 4 to smash.

Einwohner der (PL die Einwohner) inhabitant.

Einzahl die singular.

einzahlen verb (PERF hat eingezahlt) to pay in.

Einzel das (PL die Einzel) singles (*in sport*).

Einzelheit die (PL die Einzelheiten) detail.

Einzelkarte die (PL die Einzelkarten) single ticket.

Einzelkind das (PL die Einzelkinder) only child.

einzeln adjective 1 single; 2 individual; 3 odd (*sock, for example*).
adverb 1 individually; 2 separately, one at a time; **bitte einzeln eintreten** please enter one at a time.

Einzelne △ der/die/das (PL die Einzelnen) 1 der/die Einzelne the individual; 2 Einzelne some; 3 ein Einzelner/eine Einzelne/ein Einzelnes a single one; jeder/jede/jedes Einzelne every single one; 4 im Einzelnen in detail; ins Einzelne gehen to go into detail.

Einzelzimmer das (PL die Einzelzimmer) single room.

einziehen ◇ verb (IMPERF zog ein,

PERF hat eingezogen) 1 to collect (*payment*); 2 to draw in (*its feelers, claws*); 3 den Kopf einziehen to duck; 4 (PERF ist eingezogen) to move in; wann zieht ihr in die neue Wohnung ein? when are you moving into your new flat?; 5 (PERF ist eingezogen) to soak in.

einzig adjective only; ein einziges Mal only once.

Einzige △ der/die/das (PL die Einzigen) 1 der/die/das Einzige the only one; 2 ein Einziger/eine Einzige/ein Einziges a single one; kein Einziger/keine Einzige/kein Einziges not a single one; 3 das Einzige, was mich stört the only thing that bothers me.

Eis das 1 ice; 2 ice cream.

Eisbahn die (PL die Eisbahnen) skating rink.

Eisbär der (PL die Eisbären) polar bear.

Eisbecher der (PL die Eisbecher) ice-cream sundae.

Eisdiele die (PL die Eisdielen) ice-cream parlour.

Eisen das iron.

Eisenbahn die (PL die Eisenbahnen) railway.

eisern adjective iron.

Eishockey das ice hockey.

eisig adjective icy.

eiskalt adjective 1 ice-cold (*drink*); 2 freezing cold.

Eislaufen das ice-skating.

◇ IRREGULAR VERB: *See the verb table in the centre of the dictionary*

Eiswürfel der (PL die **Eiswürfel**) ice cube.

Eiszapfen der (PL die **Eiszapfen**) icicle.

eitel adjective vain.

Eitelkeit die vanity.

Eiter der pus.

Eiweiß das 1 egg-white; 2 protein.

Ekel der disgust.

ekelhaft adjective disgusting.

ekeln verb (PERF **hat sich geekelt**) **sich vor etwas ekeln** to find something disgusting.

eklig adjective disgusting.

Ekzem das (PL die **Ekzeme**) eczema.

Elefant der (PL die **Elefanten**) elephant.

elegant adjective elegant.

Elektriker der (PL die **Elektriker**) electrician.

elektrisch adjective electrical.

Elektrizität die electricity.

Elektroherd der (PL die **Elektroherde**) electric cooker.

Elektronik die electronics.

elektronisch adjective electronic.

Elektrorasierer der (PL die **Elektrorasierer**) electric razor.

elend adjective 1 miserable; 2 terrible.

Elend das misery.

elf number eleven.

Elfe die (PL die **Elfen**) fairy.

Elfmeter der (PL die **Elfmeter**) penalty (in soccer).

Ellbogen der (PL die **Ellbogen**) elbow.

Eltern plural noun parents.

Email das (PL die **Emails**) enamel.

E-Mail die (PL die **E-Mails**) E-mail.

empfahl SEE **empfehlen**.

Empfang der (PL die **Empfänge**) 1 reception; 2 receipt (of goods or a letter).

empfangen ✧ verb (PRES **empfängt**, IMPERF **empfing**, PERF **hat empfangen**) to receive.

Empfängnisverhütung die contraception.

Empfangsdame die (PL die **Empfangsdamen**) receptionist.

empfehlen ✧ verb (PRES **empfiehlt**, IMPERF **empfahl**, PERF **hat empfohlen**) to recommend.

empfindlich adjective 1 sensitive; 2 delicate; 3 touchy.

empfing SEE **empfangen**.

empfohlen SEE **empfehlen**.

empört adjective indignant.

Ende das (PL die **Enden**) 1 end; **Ende April** at the end of April; **am Ende der Straße** at the end of the road; **2 am Ende** in the end; **3** ending (of a film, novel); **4 zu Ende sein** to be finished, to be over; **5 Ende gut, alles gut** all's well that ends well.

△ NEW SPELLING: *See page xii*

enden verb (PERF **hat geendet**) to
end.

endgültig adjective **1** final (consent,
decision); **2** definite.

Endivie die (PL die **Endivien**) endive.

endlich adverb finally, at last; **na
endlich!** at last!

endlos adjective endless.

Endspiel das (PL die **Endspiele**)
final.

Endstation die (PL die
Endstationen) terminus.

Endung die (PL die **Endungen**)
ending.

Energie die energy.

energisch adjective energetic.

eng adjective **1** narrow; **2** tight;
3 close; **eng befreundet sein** to be
close friends.

Engel der (PL die **Engel**) angel.

England das England; **aus England**
from England.

Engländer der (PL die **Engländer**)
Englishman.

Engländerin die (PL die
Engländerinnen) Englishwoman.

englisch adjective English; **auf
Englisch** in English.

Enkel der (PL die **Enkel**) grandson.

Enkelin die (PL die **Enkelinnen**)
granddaughter.

Enkelkind das (PL die **Enkelkinder**)
grandchild.

entdecken verb (PERF **hat
entdeckt**) to discover.

Entdeckung die (PL die
Entdeckungen) discovery.

Ente die (PL die **Enten**) duck.

entfernen verb (PERF **hat entfernt**)
to remove.

entfernt adjective **1** distant; **2 zehn
Kilometer entfernt** ten kilometres
away.
adverb **entfernt verwandt sein** to
be distantly related.

Entfernung die (PL die
Entfernungen) distance.

entführen verb (PERF **hat entführt**)
1 to kidnap; **2** to hijack.

entgegen preposition ←(+DAT)
contrary to.

entgegengesetzt adjective
1 opposite; **2** opposing (views).

entgegenkommen ◇ verb (IMPERF
kam entgegen, PERF **ist
entgegengekommen**) **1** to come
towards; **2 jemandem
entgegenkommen** to come to meet
somebody; **3 jemandem auf
halbem Wege entgegenkommen**
to meet somebody halfway;
**4 jemandem freundlich
entgegenkommen** to be
accommodating towards somebody.

entgegenkommend adjective
1 obliging; **2 der entgegen-
kommende Verkehr** the oncoming
traffic.

Entgelt das payment.

Enthaarungsmittel das (PL die

Enthaarungsmittel) hair remover, depilatory.

enthalten ◇ verb (PRES enthält, IMPERF enthielt, PERF hat enthalten) **1** to contain; **2** sich einer Sache enthalten to abstain from something; sich der Stimme enthalten to abstain; (PERF ist enthalten) in etwas enthalten sein to be included in something; im Preis enthalten included in the price.

entkommen ◇ verb (IMPERF entkam, PERF ist entkommen) to escape.

entlang preposition ←(+ACC or +DAT) along; die Straße entlang along the road; am Fluss entlang along the river.

entlanggehen ◇ verb (IMPERF ging entlang, PERF ist entlanggegangen) to walk along.

entlanglaufen ◇ verb (PRES läuft entlang, IMPERF lief entlang, PERF ist entlanggelaufen) to run along.

entlassen ◇ verb (PRES entlässt Δ, IMPERF entließ, PERF hat entlassen) **1** to dismiss (from a job); **2** to discharge (from hospital); **3** to release (from prison).

Entlassung die (PL die Entlassungen) **1** dismissal; **2** discharge; **3** release.

entmutigen verb (PERF hat entmutigt) to discourage.

entschädigen verb (PERF hat entschädigt) to compensate.

Entschädigung die compensation.

entscheiden ◇ verb (IMPERF entschied, PERF hat entschieden) **1** to decide (on); **2** sich entscheiden to decide.

Entscheidung die (PL die Entscheidungen) decision.

entschließen ◇ verb (IMPERF entschloss sich Δ, PERF hat sich entschlossen) **1** sich entschließen to decide; **2** sich anders entschließen to change your mind; Karl hat sich anders entschlossen Karl has changed his mind.

entschlossen adjective determined.

Entschluss Δ der (PL die Entschlüsse) decision.

entschuldigen verb (PERF hat entschuldigt) **1** to excuse; entschuldigen Sie bitte excuse me; **2** sich entschuldigen to apologize; ich habe mich bei Michi entschuldigt I apologized to Michi.

Entschuldigung die (PL die Entschuldigungen) **1** apology; **2** jemanden um Entschuldigung bitten to apologize to somebody; **3** Entschuldigung! sorry!; **4** Entschuldigung (with a question or request) excuse me; Entschuldigung, können Sie mir sagen, wie ich zum Bahnhof komme? excuse me, could you tell me the way to the station?; **5** excuse.

Entsetzen das horror.

Δ NEW SPELLING: See page xii

entsetzlich adjective 1 horrible; 2 terrible.

entsetzt adjective horrified.

entspannen verb (PERF hat sich entspannt) 1 sich entspannen to relax; 2 sich entspannen to ease (of a situation).

entsprechen ◇ verb (PRES entspricht, IMPERF entsprach, PERF hat entsprochen) 1 den Anforderungen entsprechen to meet the requirements; 2 einer Sache entsprechen to correspond to something; 3 to agree with (the truth, a description); 4 to comply with (certain standards).

entsprechend adjective 1 corresponding; 2 appropriate. preposition ←(+DAT) in accordance with.

entstehen ◇ verb (IMPERF entstand, PERF ist entstanden) 1 to develop; 2 to result (of damage).

enttäuschen verb (PERF hat enttäuscht) to disappoint.

Enttäuschung die (PL die Enttäuschungen) disappointment.

entweder conjunction either; entweder heute oder morgen either today or tomorrow.

entwerten verb (PERF hat entwertet) 1 to devalue; 2 to punch (a ticket in a machine found on trains, trams, buses, and on the platform; you have to punch your ticket before each journey).

Entwerter der (PL die Entwerter) ticket-punching machine (these machines are found on trains, trams, buses, and on the platform; you have to punch your ticket before each journey).

entwickeln verb (PERF hat entwickelt) 1 to develop; 2 to display (ability, a characteristic); 3 sich entwickeln to develop.

Entwicklung die (PL die Entwicklungen) 1 development; 2 developing.

Entwicklungsland das (PL die Entwicklungsländer) developing country.

Entwurf der (PL die Entwürfe) 1 design; 2 draft.

entzückend adjective delightful.

entzünden verb (PERF hat entzündet) 1 to light (a fire, match); 2 sich entzünden to become inflamed; 3 sich entzünden to ignite.

Entzündung die (PL die Entzündungen) inflammation.

Enzian der (PL die Enziane) gentian.

Epidemie die (PL die Epidemien) epidemic.

er pronoun 1 he; 2 it; 'wo ist mein Mantel?' – 'er liegt auf dem Stuhl' 'where's my coat?' – 'it's on the chair'; 3 him (stressed); er war es it was him.

erben verb (PERF hat geerbt) to inherit.

erblich adjective hereditary.

Erbschaft die (PL die Erbschaften) inheritance.

◇ IRREGULAR VERB: See the verb table in the centre of the dictionary

Erbse *die* (PL *die* Erbsen) pea.

Erdbeben *das* (PL *die* Erdbeben) earthquake.

Erdbeere *die* (PL *die* Erdbeeren) strawberry.

Erde *die* 1 earth, soil; 2 ground; **auf der Erde** on the ground; 3 Earth; 4 earth (*for electricity*).

Erdgeschoss △ *das* (PL *die* Erdgeschosse) ground floor; **im Erdgeschoss** on the ground floor.

Erdkunde *die* geography.

Erdnuss △ *die* (PL *die* Erdnüsse) peanut.

ereignen *verb* (PERF hat sich ereignet) **sich ereignen** to happen.

Ereignis *das* (PL *die* Ereignisse) event.

erfahren ◇ *verb* (PRES erfährt, IMPERF erfuhr, PERF hat erfahren) 1 to hear, to learn; 2 to experience. *adjective* experienced.

Erfahrung *die* (PL *die* Erfahrungen) experience.

erfinden ◇ *verb* (IMPERF erfand, PERF hat erfunden) to invent.

Erfindung *die* (PL *die* Erfindungen) invention.

Erfolg *der* (PL *die* Erfolge) 1 success; **Erfolg haben** to be successful; 2 **Erfolg versprechend** △ promising; 3 **viel Erfolg!** good luck!

erfolglos *adjective* unsuccessful.

erfolgreich *adjective* successful.

erfolgversprechend SEE Erfolg.

erforderlich *adjective* necessary.

erforschen *verb* (PERF hat erforscht) 1 to explore; 2 to investigate.

erfreulicherweise *adverb* happily.

erfreut *adjective* pleased.

Erfrischung *die* (PL *die* Erfrischungen) refreshment.

erfüllen *verb* (PERF hat erfüllt) to fulfil; **sich erfüllen** to come true.

Ergebnis *das* (PL *die* Ergebnisse) result.

ergreifen ◇ *verb* (IMPERF ergriff, PERF hat ergriffen) 1 to seize, to grab; 2 to take (*measures, an opportunity*); 3 to take up (*a job, career*); 4 to move; **die Nachricht von ihrem Tod hat uns tief ergriffen** the news of her death moved us deeply; 5 **die Flucht ergreifen** to flee.

ergreifend *adjective* moving.

erhalten ◇ *verb* (PRES erhält, IMPERF erhielt, PERF hat erhalten) 1 to receive; 2 to preserve.

erhältlich *adjective* obtainable.

erheben ◇ *verb* (IMPERF erhob, PERF hat erhoben) 1 to raise; 2 to charge (*a fee*); 3 **Protest erheben** to protest; 4 **sich erheben** to rise up (*in a rebellion*).

erheblich *adjective* considerable.

erheitern *verb* (PERF hat erheitert) to amuse.

△ NEW SPELLING: *See page xii*

erhitzen verb (PERF **hat erhitzt**) to heat.

erhöhen verb (PERF **hat erhöht**) **1** to increase; **2 sich erhöhen** to rise.

Erhöhung die (PL die **Erhöhungen**) increase.

erholen verb (PERF **hat sich erholt**) **1 sich erholen** to have a rest; **ich habe mich in den Ferien gut erholt** I had a good rest on holiday; **2 sich von einer Krankheit erholen** to recover from an illness.

erholsam adjective restful.

Erholung die rest; **Iris ist zur Erholung in die Berge gefahren** Iris went to the mountains for a rest.

erinnern verb (PERF **hat erinnert**) **1** to remind; **2 sich erinnern** to remember.

Erinnerung die (PL die **Erinnerungen**) **1** memory; **2** souvenir.

erkälten verb (PERF **hat sich erkältet**) **1 sich erkälten** to catch a cold; **2 erkältet sein** to have a cold; **Ben ist erkältet** Ben has a cold.

Erkältung die (PL die **Erkältungen**) cold.

erkennen ◇ verb (IMPERF **erkannte**, PERF **hat erkannt**) **1** to recognize; **2** to realize.

erklären verb (PERF **hat erklärt**) **1** to explain; **2** to declare; **3 sich zu etwas bereit erklären** to agree to something.

Erklärung die (PL die **Erklärungen**)

1 explanation; **2** declaration; **3 eine öffentliche Erklärung** a public statement.

erkundigen verb (PERF **hat sich erkundigt**) **1** to enquire; **2** to ask about; **Susi hat sich nach dir erkundigt** Susi was asking about you.

Erkundigung die (PL die **Erkundigungen**) enquiry.

erlauben verb (PERF **hat erlaubt**) **1** to allow; **jemandem etwas erlauben** to allow somebody to do something; **2 sich etwas erlauben** to allow yourself something; **3 sich alles erlauben** to do as you please; **4 erlauben Sie mal!** (informal) do you mind!

Erlaubnis die permission.

erleben verb (PERF **hat erlebt**) **1** to experience; **2** to have (a disappointment, an experience); **eine Überraschung erleben** to have a surprise; **3 er hat die Geburt seines Enkels nicht mehr erlebt** he didn't live to see the birth of his grandson.

Erlebnis das (PL die **Erlebnisse**) experience.

erledigen verb (PERF **hat erledigt**) to deal with, to do.

erledigt adjective **1** settled; **2** (informal) worn out.

Erleichterung die relief.

erleiden ◇ verb (IMPERF **erlitt**, PERF **hat erlitten**) to suffer.

Erlös der (PL die **Erlöse**) proceeds.

◇ IRREGULAR VERB: *See the verb table in the centre of the dictionary*

ermäßigen verb (PERF hat ermäßigt) to reduce.

Ermäßigung die (PL die Ermäßigungen) reduction.

ermorden verb (PERF hat ermordet) to murder.

ermutigen verb (PERF hat ermutigt) to encourage.

ernähren verb (PERF hat ernährt) 1 to feed; 2 sich von Nudeln ernähren to live on pasta; 3 to support (a family).

Ernährung die 1 diet; eine gesunde Ernährung a healthy diet; 2 nutrition.

erneuern verb (PERF hat erneuert) to renew.

erneut adjective renewed. adverb once again.

ernst adjective serious.

Ernst der 1 seriousness; 2 im Ernst seriously; 3 ist das dein Ernst? are you serious?

ernsthaft adjective serious.

ernstlich adjective serious.

Ernte die (PL die Ernten) harvest.

ernten verb (PERF hat geerntet) to harvest.

erobern verb (PERF hat erobert) to conquer.

Eroberung die (PL die Eroberungen) conquest.

eröffnen (PERF hat eröffnet) to open.

Eröffnung die (PL die Eröffnungen) opening.

erraten ◇ verb (PRES errät, IMPERF erriet, PERF hat erraten) to guess.

Erreger der (PL die Erreger) germ.

Erregung die excitement.

erreichen verb (PERF hat erreicht) 1 to reach; 2 den Zug erreichen to catch the train; 3 to achieve (a goal, aim); 4 Irene ist telefonisch zu erreichen Irene can be contacted by phone.

erröten verb (PERF ist errötet) to blush.

Ersatz der replacement, substitute.

Ersatzreifen der (PL die Ersatzreifen) spare tyre.

Ersatzteil das (PL die Ersatzteile) spare part.

erscheinen ◇ verb (IMPERF erschien, PERF ist erschienen) to appear.

erschöpft adjective exhausted.

erschrecken verb 1 (PERF hat erschreckt) to scare; 2 ◇ (PRES erschrickt, IMPERF erschrak, PERF ist erschrocken) to get a fright.

erschreckend adjective alarming.

erschrocken adjective 1 frightened; 2 startled.

ersetzen verb (PERF hat ersetzt) to replace; jemandem einen Schaden ersetzen to compensate somebody for damages.

Ersparnisse plural noun savings.

erst adverb 1 first; erst einmal first of all; 2 only; eben erst only just; 3 not until; erst nächste Woche not

△ NEW SPELLING: See page xii

until next week; **Oma war erst
zufrieden, als die ganze Familie da
war** granny was not happy until all
the family were there.

erstaunen verb (PERF **hat erstaunt**)
to astonish.

erstaunlich adjective astonishing.

erstaunt adjective amazed; **über
etwas erstaunt sein** to be amazed
about something.

Erste △ der/die/das (PL die **Ersten**)
1 der/die **Erste** the first (one); **das
Erste** the first (thing); 2 **Dirk kam
als Erster** Dirk arrived first;
Marianne ging als Erste Marianne
left first; 3 **als Erster/Erste etwas
tun** to be the first to do something;
4 **als Erstes** first of all; 5 **fürs Erste**
for the time being.

erstens adverb firstly.

erster, erste, erstes adjective
first; **mein erstes Rad war rot** my
first bike was red; **der erste April** the
first of April; **erste Hilfe** △ first aid.

erstklassig adjective first-class.

erstmals adverb for the first time.

erteilen verb (PERF **hat erteilt**) to
give (advice, information).

ertragen ◇ verb (PRES **erträgt**,
IMPERF **ertrug**, PERF **hat ertragen**) to
bear.

ertrinken ◇ verb (IMPERF **ertrank**,
PERF **ist ertrunken**) to drown.

erwachsen adjective grown-up.

Erwachsene der/die (PL die
Erwachsenen) adult, grown-up.

Erwachsenenbildung die adult
education.

erwähnen verb (PERF **hat erwähnt**)
to mention.

erwarten verb (PERF **hat erwartet**)
to expect.

Erwartung die (PL die
Erwartungen) expectation.

erzählen verb (PERF **hat erzählt**) to
tell.

Erzählung die (PL die **Erzählungen**)
story.

Erzeugnis das (PL die **Erzeugnisse**)
product.

erziehen ◇ verb (IMPERF **erzog**, PERF
hat erzogen) 1 to bring up; 2 to
educate.

Erziehung die 1 upbringing;
2 education.

es pronoun 1 it; **es regnet** it is
raining; 2 **es gibt** there is, there
are; 3 'wo ist das Baby?' – 'es
schläft' 'where's the baby?' –
'he's/she's asleep'.

Esel der (PL die **Esel**) donkey.

essbar △ adjective edible.

essen ◇ verb (PRES **isst** △, IMPERF **aß**,
PERF **hat gegessen**) to eat.

Essen das 1 meal; 2 food.

Essig der vinegar.

Essiggurke die (PL die
Essiggurken) gherkin.

Esskastanie △ die (PL die
Esskastanien) sweet chestnut.

◇ IRREGULAR VERB: *See the verb table in the centre of the dictionary*

Fach

Esszimmer △ das (PL die Esszimmer) dining room.

Etage die (PL die Etagen) floor; in der zweiten Etage on the second floor.

Etagenbett das (PL die Etagenbetten) bunk beds.

ethnisch adjective ethnic.

Etikett das (PL die Etikette) label.

Etui das (PL die Etuis) case.

etwa adverb 1 about; er ist etwa so groß wie du he's about as tall as you; 2 for example; 3 nicht etwa, dass … not that …; 4 hat Klaus etwa Angst gehabt? Klaus wasn't scared, was he?

etwas pronoun, adverb 1 something; 2 anything; sonst noch etwas? anything else?; 3 some; etwas von dem Geld some of the money; noch etwas Kaffee? (some) more coffee?; 4 a little; nur etwas Zucker only a little sugar; etwas lauter singen to sing a little louder.

EU die (Europäische Union) EU.

euch pronoun 1 you; ich habe euch eingeladen I've invited you; 2 to you; Eva hat es euch geschenkt Eva gave it to you; 3 (reflexive) yourselves.

euer adjective your.

Eule die (PL die Eulen) owl.

eurer, eure, eures pronoun yours.

Euro der (PL die Euros) (European currency) Euro.

Europa das Europe.

Europäer der (PL die Europäer) European.

Europäerin die (PL die Europäerinnen) European.

europäisch adjective European.

evangelisch adjective Protestant.

eventuell adjective possible. adverb possibly.

ewig adjective eternal. adverb forever.

Ewigkeit die eternity.

Examen das (PL die Examen) examination, exam.

Exemplar das (PL die Exemplare) 1 copy; 2 specimen.

existieren verb (PERF hat existiert) to exist.

explodieren verb (PERF ist explodiert) to explode.

Explosion die (PL die Explosionen) explosion.

extra adverb 1 separately; 2 extra; 3 specially; 4 (informal) on purpose.

extrem adjective extreme.

F f

fabelhaft adjective fabulous, fantastic.

Fabrik die (PL die Fabriken) factory.

Fach das (PL die Fächer) 1 compartment; 2 drawer; 3 subject (at school).

△ NEW SPELLING: See page xii

Facharzt der (PL die **Fachärzte**) specialist.

Fachärztin die (PL die **Fachärztinnen**) specialist.

Fachfrau die (PL die **Fachfrauen**) expert.

Fachmann der (PL die **Fachleute**) expert.

Faden der (PL die **Fäden**) thread.

fähig adjective 1 capable; 2 able.

Fähigkeit die (PL die **Fähigkeiten**) ability.

Fahne die (PL die **Fahnen**) flag.

Fahrausweis der (PL die **Fahrausweise**) ticket.

Fahrbahn die (PL die **Fahrbahnen**) 1 carriageway; 2 road.

Fähre die (PL die **Fähren**) ferry.

fahren ◇ verb (PRES **fährt**, IMPERF **fuhr**, PERF **ist gefahren**) 1 to go; **mit dem Zug nach Wien fahren** to go to Vienna by train; **ich bin mit dem Auto gefahren** I went by car; 2 to drive; **Hanna ist sehr schnell gefahren** Hanna drove very fast; 3 to ride (of a cyclist); 4 to run (of a train, bus); **der Zug fährt nicht an Sonn- und Feiertagen** the train doesn't run on Sundays and public holidays; 5 to leave; **wann fahrt ihr?** when are you leaving? 6 **was ist in sie gefahren?** (informal) what's got into her? 7 (PERF **hat gefahren**) to drive; **er hat Doris nach Hause gefahren** he drove Doris home; **ich**

habe das Auto in die Garage gefahren I drove the car into the garage.

Fahrer der (PL die **Fahrer**) driver.

Fahrerflucht die hit-and-run driving; **Fahrerflucht begehen** to be involved in a hit-and-run.

Fahrerin die (PL die **Fahrerinnen**) driver.

Fahrgast der (PL die **Fahrgäste**) passenger.

Fahrkarte die (PL die **Fahrkarten**) ticket.

Fahrkartenausgabe die ticket office.

Fahrkartenautomat der (PL die **Fahrkartenautomaten**) ticket machine.

Fahrkartenschalter der (PL die **Fahrkartenschalter**) ticket office.

fahrlässig adjective negligent.

Fahrlehrer der (PL die **Fahrlehrer**) driving instructor.

Fahrplan der (PL die **Fahrpläne**) timetable.

Fahrpreis der (PL die **Fahrpreise**) fare.

Fahrprüfung die (PL die **Fahrprüfungen**) driving test; **die Fahrprüfung machen** to take your driving test.

Fahrrad das (PL die **Fahrräder**) bicycle.

Fahrradweg der (PL die **Fahrradwege**) cycle lane.

◇ IRREGULAR VERB: See the verb table in the centre of the dictionary

Fahrschein der (PL die Fahrscheine) ticket.

Fahrschule die (PL die Fahrschulen) driving school.

Fahrstuhl der (PL die Fahrstühle) lift.

Fahrt die (PL die Fahrten) 1 journey; **gute Fahrt!** have a good journey!; 2 trip; 3 drive; 4 **in voller Fahrt** at full speed.

Fahrzeug das (PL die Fahrzeuge) vehicle.

fair adjective fair.

Faktor der (PL die Faktoren) factor.

Falke der (PL die Falken) falcon.

Fall der (PL die Fälle) 1 case; **in diesem Fall** in this case; **auf alle Fälle, auf jeden Fall** in any case; **für alle Fälle** just in case; 2 **auf jeden Fall** definitely; 3 **auf keinen Fall** on no account; 4 fall.

Falle die (PL die Fallen) trap.

fallen ◊ verb (PRES **fällt**, IMPERF **fiel**, PERF **ist gefallen**) 1 to fall; 2 **etwas fallen lassen** △ to drop something; **wir haben den Plan fallen lassen** we've dropped the idea; 3 **eine Bemerkung fallen lassen** △ to make a comment.

fallenlassen SEE **fallen**.

fällig adjective due.

falls conjunction 1 if; 2 in case.

Fallschirm der (PL die Fallschirme) parachute.

falsch adjective 1 wrong; **du hast ihn falsch verstanden** you got him

wrong; 2 false (teeth, etc.); 3 forged.

fälschen verb (PERF **hat gefälscht**) to forge.

Fälschung die (PL die Fälschungen) 1 fake; 2 forgery.

Falte die (PL die Falten) 1 fold; 2 crease; 3 pleat; 4 wrinkle.

falten verb (PERF **hat gefaltet**) to fold.

faltig adjective 1 wrinkled; 2 creased.

familiär adjective familiar.

Familie die (PL die Familien) family.

Familienname der (PL die Familiennamen) surname.

Fan der (PL die Fans) fan.

fand SEE **finden**.

fangen ◊ verb (PRES **fängt**, IMPERF **fing**, PERF **hat gefangen**) to catch.

fantastisch adjective fantastic.

Farbe die (PL die Farben) 1 colour; 2 paint; 3 dye; 4 suit (in playing cards).

farbecht adjective colour fast.

färben verb (PERF **hat gefärbt**) 1 to dye; 2 **sich die Haare färben** to dye your hair; 3 **das Sweatshirt färbt** this sweatshirt runs.

Farbfilm der (PL die Farbfilme) colour film.

farbig adjective coloured.

farblos adjective colourless.

Farbstift der (PL die Farbstifte) coloured pencil.

△ NEW SPELLING: See page xii

Farbstoff der (PL die **Farbstoffe**)
1 dye; 2 colouring (for food).

Farbton der (PL die **Farbtöne**) shade.

Fasan der (PL die **Fasane**) pheasant.

Fasching der (PL die **Faschinge**)
carnival.

Faser die (PL die **Fasern**) fibre.

Fass △ das (PL die **Fässer**) barrel; **Bier vom Fass** draught beer.

fassen verb (PERF hat gefasst △) 1 to grasp; 2 einen Dieb fassen to catch a thief; 3 to hold (of a container); 4 to understand; 5 nicht zu fassen unbelievable; 6 sich fassen to compose yourself; 7 einen Entschluss fassen to make a decision; 8 sich kurz fassen to be brief.

Fassung die (PL die **Fassungen**)
1 version; 2 composure; 3 jemanden aus der Fassung bringen to throw somebody, to upset somebody; 4 setting (for gems).

fassungslos adjective speechless.

fast adverb 1 almost; 2 fast nie hardly ever.

Fastenzeit die (PL die **Fastenzeiten**) Lent.

Fastnacht die carnival.

faul adjective 1 lazy; 2 rotten; 3 eine faule Ausrede a lame excuse; 4 an der Sache ist etwas faul (informal) there's something fishy about it.

faulen verb (PERF ist gefault) to rot.

faulenzen verb (PERF hat gefaulenzt) to laze about.

Faust die (PL die **Fäuste**) 1 fist; 2 auf eigene Faust off your own bat.

Fax das (PL die **Fax(e)**) fax.

faxen verb (PERF hat gefaxt) to fax; ich faxe Ihnen die Liste I'll fax you the list.

Februar der February.

fechten ◊ verb (PRES ficht, IMPERF focht, PERF hat gefochten) to fence.

Feder die (PL die **Federn**) 1 feather; 2 spring; 3 nib (of a pen).

Federball der (PL die **Federbälle**)
1 badminton; 2 shuttlecock.

Federmäppchen das (PL die **Federmäppchen**) pencil case.

Fee die (PL die **Feen**) fairy.

fegen verb (PERF hat gefegt) to sweep.

fehl adjective fehl am Platz out of place.

fehlen verb (PERF hat gefehlt) 1 to be missing; 2 to be lacking; 3 to be absent (from school); 4 mir fehlt die Zeit I haven't got the time; es fehlt ihnen einfach das Geld für ein neues Auto they simply haven't got the money for a new car; 5 was fehlt dir? what's the matter?; 6 Rudi fehlt mir I miss Rudi.

Fehler der (PL die **Fehler**) 1 mistake; 2 fault.

Feier die (PL die **Feiern**) 1 party; 2 celebration.

Feierabend der (PL die **Feierabende**) 1 finishing time; 2 nach Feierabend after work.

◊ IRREGULAR VERB: See the verb table in the centre of the dictionary

Feierlichkeiten *plural noun* festivities.

feiern *verb* (PERF hat gefeiert) to celebrate.

Feiertag *der* (PL die Feiertage) 1 holiday; **ein gesetzlicher Feiertag** a public holiday; 2 **am ersten Feiertag** on Christmas Day; **der zweite Feiertag** Boxing Day.

feige *adjective* cowardly; **du bist feige** you're a coward.

Feige *die* (PL die Feigen) fig.

Feigling *der* (PL die Feiglinge) coward.

Feile *die* (PL die Feilen) file.

fein *adjective* 1 fine; 2 delicate; 3 refined; 4 **sich fein machen** △ to dress up.

Feind *der* (PL die Feinde) enemy.

feindlich *adjective* hostile.

Feld *das* (PL die Felder) 1 field; 2 pitch; 3 box (*on a form*); 4 square (*on a board game*).

Fell *das* (PL die Felle) fur, skin.

Fels *der* rock.

Felsen *der* (PL die Felsen) cliff.

feminin *adjective* feminine.

Feminist *der* (PL die Feministen) feminist.

Feministin *die* (PL die Feministinnen) feminist.

Fenster *das* (PL die Fenster) window.

Fensterladen *der* (PL die Fensterläden) shutter.

Ferien *plural noun* holidays; **Ferien haben** to be on holiday.

fern *adjective* 1 distant; 2 **sich fern halten** △ to keep away; **jemanden von etwas fern halten** △ to keep somebody away from something. *adverb* far away.

Fernbedienung *die* remote control.

Ferngespräch *das* (PL die Ferngespräche) long-distance call.

fernhalten SEE **fern.**

Fernglas *das* (PL die Ferngläser) binoculars.

Fernsehapparat *der* (PL die Fernsehapparate) television set.

fernsehen ◇ *verb* (PRES sieht fern, IMPERF sah fern, PERF hat ferngesehen) to watch television.

Fernsehen *das* television; **im Fernsehen** on television.

Fernseher *der* (PL die Fernseher) television (set).

Fernsprecher *der* (PL die Fernsprecher) telephone.

Ferse *die* (PL die Fersen) heel.

fertig *adjective* 1 finished; **mit den Hausaufgaben fertig werden** to finish your homework; **fertig sein** to be finished; 2 **mit jemandem fertig sein** (*informal*) to be through with somebody; 3 **völlig fertig sein** to be completely worn out; 4 **mit etwas fertig werden** to cope with something (*problems, for example*); 5 ready; **das Essen ist fertig** food's ready; 6 **etwas fertig machen** △

△ NEW SPELLING: *See page xii*

(*prepare*) to get something ready; (*complete*) to finish something; **sich fertig machen**△ to get ready; **7 jemanden fertig machen**△ to wear somebody out, to wear somebody down; **der ständige Stress macht mich fertig** this constant stress is wearing me down; **8 es fertig bringen**△, **etwas zu tun** to bring yourself to do something; **ich bringe es einfach nicht fertig** I just can't bring myself to do it. *adverb* **fertig essen** to finish eating.

fertigbringen SEE **fertig.**

Fertiggericht das (PL die **Fertiggerichte**) ready-to-serve meal.

fertigmachen SEE **fertig.**

Fest das (PL die **Feste**) **1** party; **2** celebration; **3** festival.

fest *adjective* **1** firm; **2** fixed (*salary*, *address*); **3** solid; **feste Nahrung** solids; **4** fest werden to harden. *adverb* **1** fest schlafen to be fast asleep; **2** fest befreundet sein to be close friends; **3** fest angestellt sein to be in permanent employment.

festbinden ◇ *verb* (IMPERF **band fest**, PERF **hat festgebunden**) **1** to tie (up).

festhalten ◇ *verb* (PRES **hält fest**, IMPERF **hielt fest**, PERF **hat festgehalten**) **1** to hold on to; **2 sich festhalten** to hold on; **halt dich an mir fest** hold on to me.

Festigkeit die strength.

festlegen *verb* (PERF **hat**

festgelegt) **1** to fix; **2 sich auf etwas festlegen** to commit yourself to something.

festlich *adjective* festive.

festmachen *verb* (PERF **hat festgemacht**) **1** to fix; **ich mache gleich einen Termin fest** I'll fix a date straight away; **2** to fasten.

festnehmen ◇ *verb* (PRES **nimmt fest**, IMPERF **nahm fest**, PERF **hat festgenommen**) to arrest.

feststehen ◇ *verb* (IMPERF **stand fest**, PERF **hat festgestanden**) to be certain; **eins steht fest, Daniel lade ich nicht mehr ein** one thing's certain, I'm not going to invite Daniel again.

feststellen *verb* (PERF **hat festgestellt**) **1** to establish; **2** to notice.

Fett das (PL die **Fette**) **1** fat; **2** grease.

fett *adjective* **1** fat (*person*); **2** greasy, fatty (*food*); **3** bold (*type*).

fettarm *adjective* low-fat.

fettig *adjective* greasy.

Fetzen der (PL die **Fetzen**) **1** scrap; **2** rag.

feucht *adjective* **1** damp; **2** humid.

Feuchtigkeit die **1** moisture; **2** humidity.

Feuer das **1** fire; **2 hast du Feuer?** have you got a light?

Feuerlöscher der (PL die **Feuerlöscher**) fire extinguisher.

Feuermelder der (PL die **Feuermelder**) fire alarm.

◇ IRREGULAR VERB: *See the verb table in the centre of the dictionary*

Feuertreppe die (PL die Feuertreppen) fire escape.

Feuerwehr die (PL die Feuerwehren) fire brigade.

Feuerwehrauto das (PL die Feuerwehrautos) fire engine.

Feuerwehrmann der (PL die Feuerwehrleute) fireman.

Feuerwerk das fireworks.

Feuerzeug das (PL die Feuerzeuge) lighter.

ficht SEE fechten.

Fieber das (high) temperature, fever; **Fieber haben** to have a temperature.

fiel SEE fallen.

fies adjective (informal) nasty.

Figur die (PL die Figuren) 1 figure; 2 character.

Filiale die (PL die Filialen) branch.

Film der (PL die Filme) film.

filmen verb (PERF hat gefilmt) to film.

Filter der (PL die Filter) filter.

Filzstift der (PL die Filzstifte) felt pen.

finanziell adjective financial.

finanzieren verb (PERF hat finanziert) to finance.

finden ◇ verb (IMPERF fand, PERF hat gefunden) 1 to find; 2 to think; **wie findest du das?** what do you think of it?; **findest du?** do you think so?; 3 **ich finde nichts dabei** I don't mind.

fing SEE fangen.

Finger der (PL die Finger) finger.

Fingernagel der (PL die Fingernägel) fingernail.

Finne der (PL die Finnen) Finn.

Finnin die (PL die Finninnen) Finn.

Finnland das Finland.

finster adjective 1 dark; **im Finstern** in the dark; 2 sinister.

Finsternis die darkness.

Firma die (PL die Firmen) firm, company.

Fisch der (PL die Fische) 1 fish; 2 **Fische** Pisces; **Helmut ist Fisch** Helmut is Pisces.

Fischer der (PL die Fischer) fisherman.

fit adjective fit; **er hält sich durch Jogging fit** he keeps fit by jogging.

Fitnesstraining △ das keep fit.

fix adjective 1 quick; 2 **fix und fertig** all finished, all ready; 3 **ich bin fix und fertig** (informal) I'm shattered.

flach adjective 1 flat; 2 low; 3 shallow; **die Erdbeeren kommen in die flache Schüssel** the strawberries go into the shallow bowl.

Fläche die (PL die Flächen) 1 surface; 2 area.

flackern verb (PERF hat geflackert) to flicker.

Flagge die (PL die Flaggen) flag.

Flamme die (PL die Flammen) flame.

Flasche die (PL die Flaschen) bottle.

△ NEW SPELLING: See page xii

Flaschenöffner der (PL die Flaschenöffner) bottle opener.

flauschig adjective 1 fluffy; 2 fleecy.

Fleck der (PL die Flecken) 1 stain; 2 spot; 3 ein blauer Fleck a bruise.

fleckig adjective 1 stained; 2 blotchy (skin).

Fledermaus die (PL die Fledermäuse) bat.

Fleisch das 1 meat; 2 flesh.

Fleischer der (PL die Fleischer) butcher.

Fleischerei die (PL die Fleischereien) butcher's.

Fleiß der hard work.

fleißig adjective hard-working.

flicken verb (PERF hat geflickt) to mend.

Fliege die (PL die Fliegen) 1 fly; 2 bow tie.

fliegen ◇ verb (IMPERF flog, PERF ist geflogen) 1 to fly; 2 ich bin geflogen (informal) I fell; 3 Manfred ist geflogen (informal) Manfred has been fired; 4 (PERF hat geflogen) to fly (a plane).

fliehen ◇ verb (IMPERF floh, PERF ist geflohen) to flee.

Fliese die (PL die Fliesen) tile.

Fließband das (PL die Fließbänder) 1 conveyor belt; 2 assembly line.

fließen ◇ verb (IMPERF floss Δ, PERF ist geflossen) to flow.

fließend adjective 1 running;

2 fluent; fließendes Deutsch fluent German; 3 moving (traffic).

Flitterwochen plural noun honeymoon.

flitzen verb (informal) (PERF ist geflitzt) 1 to dash; 2 to whizz.

Flocke die (PL die Flocken) flake.

flog SEE **fliegen**.

floh SEE **fliehen**.

Floh der (PL die Flöhe) flee.

Flohmarkt der (PL die Flohmärkte) flea market.

floss Δ SEE **fließen**.

Flosse die (PL die Flossen) 1 fin; 2 flipper.

Flöte die (PL die Flöten) flute.

fluchen verb (PERF hat geflucht) to curse.

Flüchtling der (PL die Flüchtlinge) refugee.

Flug der (PL die Flüge) flight.

Flugblatt das (PL die Flugblätter) pamphlet.

Flügel der (PL die Flügel) 1 wing; 2 grand piano.

Fluggast der (PL die Fluggäste) (air) passenger.

Fluggesellschaft die (PL die Fluggesellschaften) airline.

Flughafen der (PL die Flughäfen) airport.

Flugplatz der (PL die Flugplätze) 1 airport; 2 airfield.

◇ IRREGULAR VERB: See the verb table in the centre of the dictionary

Flugzeug das (PL die Flugzeuge) aeroplane.

Fluor das fluoride.

Flur der (PL die Flure) 1 hall; 2 corridor.

Fluss △ der (PL die Flüsse) river.

flüssig adjective liquid.

Flüssigkeit die (PL die Flüssigkeiten) liquid.

flüstern verb (PERF hat geflüstert) to whisper.

Flut die (PL die Fluten) 1 high tide; 2 flood (of letters, complaints).

Flutlicht das floodlight.

focht SEE fechten.

Föhn △ der (PL die Föhne) hair drier.

föhnen △ verb (PERF hat geföhnt) to blow-dry.

Folge die (PL die Folgen) 1 consequence; 2 episode; 3 etwas zur Folge haben to result in something; 4 an den Folgen eines Unfalls sterben to die as the result of an accident.

folgen verb (PERF ist gefolgt) 1 to follow; daraus folgt, dass ... it follows that ...; ich kann dir nicht folgen I can't follow what you're saying; 2 (PERF hat gefolgt) to obey.

folgend adjective 1 following; 2 Folgendes the following.

Folgerung die (PL die Folgerungen) conclusion.

folgsam adjective obedient.

Folie die (PL die Folien) foil.

Fön™ = Föhn.

fönen = föhnen.

fordern verb (PERF hat gefordert) to demand.

fördern verb (PERF hat gefördert) 1 to promote; 2 to sponsor.

Forderung die (PL die Forderungen) 1 demand; 2 claim.

Forelle die (PL die Forellen) trout.

Form die (PL die Formen) 1 shape; 2 form; in Form sein to be on form; 3 tin (for baking).

Format das (PL die Formate) format.

formatieren verb (PERF hat formatiert) to format.

formen verb (PERF hat geformt) 1 to form; 2 sich formen to take shape.

förmlich adjective formal. adverb 1 formally; 2 jemanden förmlich zwingen, etwas zu tun to positively force somebody to do something; ich hätte förmlich schreien können I really could have screamed.

Formular das (PL die Formulare) form.

Forscher der (PL die Forscher) 1 researcher, research scientist; 2 explorer.

Forschung die (PL die Forschungen) research.

Forst der (PL die Forste) forest.

Förster der (PL die Förster) forester.

fort adverb 1 away; 2 fort sein to have gone; 3 und so fort and so on; 4 in einem fort on and on.

fortbewegen verb (PERF hat fortbewegt) 1 to move; 2 sich fortbewegen to move.

fortfahren ◊ verb (PRES fährt fort, IMPERF fuhr fort, PERF ist fortgefahren) 1 to leave; wann fahrt ihr fort? when are you leaving?; 2 to continue.

fortgeschritten adjective advanced.

Fortschritt der (PL die Fortschritte) progress; Fortschritte machen to make progress.

fortsetzen verb (PERF hat fortgesetzt) to continue.

Fortsetzung die (PL die Fortsetzungen) 1 continuation; 2 instalment.

Foto das (PL die Fotos) photo.

Fotoapparat der (PL die Fotoapparate) camera.

Fotograf der (PL die Fotografen) photographer.

Fotografie die (PL die Fotografien) 1 photography; 2 photograph.

fotografieren verb (PERF hat fotografiert) 1 to photograph, to take a photograph of; 2 to take photographs.

Fotografin die (PL die Fotografinnen) photographer.

Fotokopie die (PL die Fotokopien) photocopy.

Fracht die (PL die Frachten) freight, cargo.

Frage die (PL die Fragen) question;

etwas in Frage stellen to question something; das kommt nicht in Frage that's out of the question.

Fragebogen der (PL die Fragebogen) questionnaire.

fragen verb (PERF hat gefragt) 1 to ask; 2 sich fragen to wonder.

Fragezeichen das (PL die Fragezeichen) question mark.

fraglich adjective doubtful.

Franken[1] der (PL die Franken) (Swiss) franc.

Franken[2] das Franconia.

Frankreich das France.

Franzose der (PL die Franzosen) Frenchman.

Französin die (PL die Französinnen) Frenchwoman.

französisch adjective French.

Französisch das French.

fraß SEE fressen.

Frau die (PL die Frauen) 1 woman; 2 wife; 3 Mrs, Ms ('Frau' is usually used to address both married and unmarried women).

Fräulein das (PL die Fräulein) 1 young lady; 2 Miss; Fräulein Schmidt Miss Schmidt.

frech adjective cheeky.

Frechheit die (PL die Frechheiten) 1 cheek; 2 cheeky remark.

frei adjective 1 free; 2 freelance; 3 ist dieser Platz frei? is this seat taken?; 4 ein freier Tag a day off;

◊ IRREGULAR VERB: See the verb table in the centre of the dictionary

sich frei nehmen to take a day off;
5 'Zimmer frei' 'vacancies'.

Freibad das (PL die Freibäder) open-air swimming pool.

Freie das im Freien in the open air.

freigebig adjective generous.

Freiheit die (PL die Freiheiten)
1 freedom; 2 liberty; **sich Freiheiten erlauben** to take liberties.

freimachen verb (PERF hat freigemacht) 1 to take time off;
2 **sich freimachen** to take time off.

Freistoß der (PL die Freistöße) free kick.

Freitag der (PL die Freitage) Friday.

freitags adverb on Fridays.

freiwillig adjective voluntary.

Freizeit die 1 spare time; 2 leisure.

fremd adjective 1 foreign; 2 strange;
fremde Leute strangers; **ich bin hier fremd** I'm a stranger here.

Fremde der/die (PL die Fremden)
1 foreigner; 2 stranger.

Fremdenverkehr der tourism.

Fremdenverkehrsbüro das (PL die Fremdenverkehrsbüros) tourist office.

Fremdenzimmer das (PL die Fremdenzimmer) room (to let).

Fremdsprache die (PL die Fremdsprachen) foreign language.

fressen ◇ verb (PRES frisst △, IMPERF fraß, PERF hat gefressen) to eat.

Freude die (PL die Freuden) 1 joy;
2 pleasure; **mit Freuden** with pleasure; **3 an etwas Freude haben** to be delighted with something;
4 **jemandem eine Freude machen** to please somebody.

freuen verb (PERF hat sich gefreut)
1 **sich freuen** to be pleased; **sich über etwas freuen** to be pleased about something; **2 sich auf etwas freuen** to look forward to something.

Freund der (PL die Freunde)
1 friend; 2 boyfriend.

Freundin die (PL die Freundinnen)
1 friend; 2 girlfriend.

freundlich adjective 1 friendly;
2 kind.

freundlicherweise adverb kindly.

Freundlichkeit die friendliness.

Freundschaft die (PL die Freundschaften) friendship.

Frieden der peace.

Friedhof der (PL die Friedhöfe) cemetery.

friedlich adjective peaceful.

frieren ◇ verb (IMPERF fror, PERF hat gefroren) 1 to be cold; **frierst du?** are you cold?; **2 es friert** it's freezing, it's frosty; **3** (PERF **ist gefroren**) to freeze.

Frikadelle die (PL die Frikadellen) rissole.

frisch adjective fresh; **sich frisch machen** to freshen up.
adverb freshly; '**frisch gestrichen**' 'wet paint'.

Friseur der (PL die Friseure) hairdresser.

Friseuse die (PL die Friseusen) hairdresser.

frisieren verb (PERF hat frisiert)
1 jemanden frisieren to do somebody's hair; 2 sich frisieren to do your hair.

frisst △ SEE fressen.

Frisur die (PL die Frisuren) hairstyle, hairdo.

froh adjective 1 happy; frohe Weihnachten! happy Christmas!; 2 über etwas froh sein to be glad about something.

fröhlich adjective cheerful.

Fröhlichkeit die cheerfulness.

fromm adjective devout.

fror SEE frieren.

Frosch der (PL die Frösche) frog.

Frost der (PL die Fröste) frost.

frostig adjective frosty.

Frottee das (PL die Frottees) towelling.

Frottiertuch das (PL die Frottiertücher) towel.

Frucht die (PL die Früchte) fruit.

fruchtbar adjective fertile.

Fruchtsaft der (PL die Fruchtsäfte) fruit juice.

früh adjective, adverb 1 early; von früh auf from an early age; 2 heute früh this morning.

Frühe die in aller Frühe at the crack of dawn.

früher adjective 1 earlier; 2 former. adverb 1 earlier; 2 formerly; 3 früher war sie ganz anders she used to be quite different; das war früher ein Blumengeschäft it used to be a florist's.

frühestens adverb at the earliest.

Frühjahr das (PL die Frühjahre) spring; im Frühjahr in spring.

Frühling der (PL die Frühlinge) spring; im Frühling in spring.

Frühstück das (PL die Frühstücke) breakfast.

frühstücken verb (PERF hat gefrühstückt) to have breakfast.

frühzeitig adjective early.

Fuchs der (PL die Füchse) fox.

fühlen verb (PERF hat gefühlt) 1 to feel; 2 sich krank fühlen to feel ill.

fuhr SEE fahren.

führen verb (PERF hat geführt) 1 to lead; sie führt mit fünf Punkten she is five points in the lead; unsere Mannschaft führt our team's winning; 2 to run (a shop or business); 3 to show round; 4 to keep (a diary, list); 5 ein Telefongespräch führen to make a phone call.

Führer der (PL die Führer) 1 leader; 2 guide.

Führerschein der (PL die Führerscheine) driving licence; den Führerschein machen to take your driving test.

◇ **IRREGULAR VERB: See the verb table in the centre of the dictionary**

Führung die (PL die Führungen)
1 leadership; 2 guided tour;
3 management (*of a shop*); 4 in
Führung in the lead.

füllen verb (PERF hat gefüllt) 1 to
fill; 2 to stuff (*a turkey, peppers*);
3 sich füllen to fill (up).

Füller der (PL die Füller) fountain
pen.

Füllfederhalter der (PL die
Füllfederhalter) fountain pen.

Füllung die (PL die Füllungen) filling.

Fundament das (PL die
Fundamente) foundations.

Fundbüro das (PL die Fundbüros)
lost property office.

fünf number five.

fünfhundert number five hundred.

Fünftel das (PL die Fünftel) fifth.

fünfter, fünfte, fünftes adjective
fifth.

fünfzehn number fifteen.

fünfzig number fifty.

Funke der (PL die Funken) spark.

funkeln verb (PERF hat gefunkelt)
1 to sparkle; 2 to twinkle (*of a star*).

funktionieren verb (PERF hat
funktioniert) to work.

für preposition ←(+ACC) 1 for; 2 was
für ein ...? what sort of ... ?; 3 für
sich by yourself; jetzt habe ich das
Haus ganz für mich now I've got
the house to myself; 4 das Für und
Wider the pros and cons.

Furcht die fear.

furchtbar adjective terrible.

fürchten verb (PERF hat gefürchtet)
1 to fear; 2 sich fürchten to be
afraid; ich fürchte mich vor ihm I'm
afraid of him; ich fürchte, das geht
nicht I'm afraid that's not possible.

fürchterlich adjective dreadful.

füreinander adverb for each other.

fürs = für das.

Fürsorge die 1 care; 2 welfare;
3 (*informal*) social security.

Fuß der (PL die Füße) 1 foot; zu Fuß
on foot; zu Fuß gehen to walk;
2 base.

Fußball der (PL die Fußbälle)
football.

Fußballplatz der (PL die
Fußballplätze) football pitch.

Fußballspiel das (PL die
Fußballspiele) football match.

Fußballspieler der (PL die
Fußballspieler) footballer.

Fußboden der (PL die Fußböden)
floor.

Fußgänger der (PL die Fußgänger)
pedestrian.

Fußgängerzone die (PL die
Fußgängerzonen) pedestrian
precinct.

Fußweg der (PL die Fußwege)
footpath.

Futter das 1 feed; ich habe dem
Hund schon Futter gegeben I've

△ NEW SPELLING: See page xii

already given the dog his food;
2 lining (*of clothes*).

füttern *verb* (PERF **hat gefüttert**) **1** to feed; **2** to line.

Futur *das* (PL *die* **Future**) future (*tense*).

G g

gab SEE **geben.**

Gabel *die* (PL *die* **Gabeln**) fork.

gähnen *verb* (PERF **hat gegähnt**) to yawn.

Galerie *die* (PL *die* **Galerien**) gallery.

galoppieren *verb* (PERF **ist galoppiert**) to gallop.

Gammler *der* (PL *die* **Gammler**) drop-out.

Gammlerin *die* (PL *die* **Gammlerinnen**) drop-out.

Gang *der* (PL *die* **Gänge**) **1** walk; **2** errand; **3** corridor; **4** ein Platz am Gang an aisle seat; **5** course (*of a meal*); **6** gear (*of a car*); **7** in Gang setzen to get going; **8** im Gange in progress.

gängig *adjective* **1** common; **2** popular (*goods*).

Gans *die* (PL *die* **Gänse**) goose.

Gänseblümchen *das* (PL *die* **Gänseblümchen**) daisy.

Gänsehaut *die* goose pimples.

ganz *adjective* whole; **1** ganz

Deutschland the whole of Germany; **2** im Großen und Ganzen on the whole; **3** eine ganze Menge quite a lot; **4** all; mein ganzes Geld all my money; die ganzen Leute all the people; **5** etwas wieder ganz machen to mend something. *adverb* **1** quite; es war ganz gut it was quite good; **2** ganz und gar completely; **3** ganz und gar nicht not at all.

ganztägig *adjective, adverb* **1** full-time; **2** all-day; ganztägig geöffnet open all day.

ganztags *adverb* **1** full time; **2** all day.

gar *adjective* done, cooked. *adverb* **1** gar nicht not at all; gar nichts nothing; **2** oder gar or even.

Garage *die* (PL *die* **Garagen**) garage.

Garantie *die* (PL *die* **Garantien**) guarantee.

garantieren *verb* (PERF **hat garantiert**) to guarantee.

Garderobe *die* (PL *die* **Garderoben**) cloakroom; wir können die Mäntel an der Garderobe abgeben we can leave the coats in the cloakroom.

Gardine *die* (PL *die* **Gardinen**) curtain.

Garn *das* (PL *die* **Garne**) thread.

Garnele *die* (PL *die* **Garnelen**) **1** shrimp; **2** prawn.

Garten *der* (PL *die* **Gärten**) garden.

Gärtner *der* (PL *die* **Gärtner**) gardener.

◇ **IRREGULAR VERB: See the verb table in the centre of the dictionary**

Gärtnerin die (PL die Gärtnerinnen) gardener.

Gas das (PL die Gase) 1 gas; 2 **Gas geben** to accelerate.

Gasherd der (PL die Gasherde) gas cooker.

Gaspedal das (PL die Gaspedale) accelerator.

Gasse die (PL die Gassen) lane.

Gast der (PL die Gäste) 1 guest; **wir haben heute Abend Gäste** we've got guests tonight; 2 **bei jemandem zu Gast sein** to be staying with somebody.

Gastarbeiter der (PL die Gastarbeiter) foreign worker, guest worker.

Gästezimmer das (PL die Gästezimmer) 1 (hotel) room; 2 spare room.

gastfreundlich adjective hospitable.

Gastfreundschaft die hospitality.

Gastgeber der (PL die Gastgeber) host.

Gastgeberin die (PL die Gastgeberinnen) host.

Gasthaus das (PL die Gasthäuser) inn.

Gasthof der (PL die Gasthöfe) inn.

Gaststätte die (PL die Gaststätten) restaurant.

Gauner der (PL die Gauner) crook.

Gebäck das 1 pastries; 2 biscuits.

gebären ◇ verb (IMPERF gebar, PERF hat geboren) 1 to give birth to; 2 **geboren werden** to be born.

Gebäude das (PL die Gebäude) building.

geben ◇ verb (PRES gibt, IMPERF gab, PERF hat gegeben) 1 to give; 2 to deal (cards); 3 to teach (at school); 4 **geben Sie mir bitte Frau Scheck** please put me through to Mrs Scheck; 5 **es gibt** there is, there are; **es gibt viele gute Restaurants in München** there are lots of good restaurants in Munich; **was gibt's im Kino?** what's on at the cinema?; **was gibt es zum Mittagessen?** what are we having for lunch?; 6 **was gibt's Neues?** what's the news?, what's new?; 7 **sich geschlagen geben** to admit defeat; 8 **das gibt sich wieder** it'll get better; 9 **das gibt's doch nicht!** I don't believe it!

Gebet das (PL die Gebete) prayer.

gebeten SEE bitten.

Gebiet das (PL die Gebiete) 1 area; 2 field.

gebildet adjective educated.

Gebirge das (PL die Gebirge) mountain range; **im Gebirge** in the mountains.

Gebiss △ das (PL die Gebisse) 1 teeth; 2 false teeth, dentures.

gebissen SEE beißen.

geblieben SEE bleiben.

geboren verb SEE gebären.
adjective 1 born; 2 née; **Frau Hahn, geborene Müller** Mrs Hahn, née Müller.

△ NEW SPELLING: See page xii

geborgen *adjective* safe.

geboten SEE **bieten**.

gebracht SEE **bringen**.

gebraten *adjective* fried.

Gebrauch *der* (PL *die* Gebräuche)
1 use; **vor Gebrauch schütteln**
shake before use; 2 custom.

gebrauchen *verb* (PERF **hat**
gebraucht) to use.

Gebrauchsanweisung *die* (PL *die*
Gebrauchsanweisungen)
instructions (for use).

gebraucht *adjective* used, secondhand.

Gebrauchtwagen *der* (PL *die*
Gebrauchtwagen) second-hand
car.

gebrochen SEE **brechen**.

Gebühr *die* (PL *die* Gebühren) fee,
charge.

gebührenfrei *adjective* free (of
charge).

gebührenpflichtig *adjective*
1 subject to a charge; 2 **eine**
gebührenpflichtige Straße a toll
road.

gebunden SLE **binden**.

Geburt *die* (PL *die* Geburten) birth.

Geburtenregelung *die* birth
control.

Geburtsdatum *das* (PL *die*
Geburtsdaten) date of birth.

Geburtsort *der* (PL *die*
Geburtsorte) place of birth.

Geburtstag *der* (PL *die*
Geburtstage) birthday.

Geburtsurkunde *die* (PL *die*
Geburtsurkunden) birth certificate.

gedacht SEE **denken**.

Gedächtnis *das* (PL *die*
Gedächtnisse) memory.

Gedanke *der* (PL *die* Gedanken)
1 thought; **in Gedanken versunken**
sein to be lost in thought; 2 **sich**
Gedanken machen to worry;
3 **jemanden auf andere Gedanken**
bringen to take somebody's mind
off things.

gedankenlos *adjective*
thoughtless.
adverb without thinking.

Gedeck *das* (PL *die* Gedecke)
1 place setting; 2 set meal.

Gedicht *das* (PL *die* Gedichte) poem.

Geduld *die* patience.

geduldig *adjective* patient.

gedurft SEE **dürfen**.

geehrt *adjective* 1 honoured;
2 **Sehr geehrte Frau Ross** Dear
Mrs Ross.

geeignet *adjective* 1 suitable;
2 right.

Gefahr *die* (PL *die* Gefahren)
1 danger; **außer Gefahr** out of
danger; 2 **auf eigene Gefahr** at your
own risk; **Gefahr laufen, etwas zu**
tun to run the risk of doing
something.

gefährlich *adjective* dangerous.

gefallen[1] SEE **fallen**.

✧ IRREGULAR VERB: *See the verb table in the centre of the dictionary*

gefallen² ◇ verb (PRES **gefällt**, IMPERF **gefiel**, PERF **hat gefallen**) 1 es gefällt mir I like it; es hat mir sehr gut gefallen I liked it a lot; 2 sich etwas gefallen lassen to put up with something.

Gefallen¹ der (PL die **Gefallen**) favour.

Gefallen² das pleasure; dir zu Gefallen to please you.

Gefangene der/die (PL die **Gefangenen**) prisoner.

Gefängnis das (PL die **Gefängnisse**) prison.

Gefäß das (PL die **Gefäße**) container.

gefasst Δ adjective 1 calm, composed; 2 auf etwas gefasst sein to be prepared for something.

gefiel SEE **gefallen**.

geflogen SEE **fliegen**.

geflossen SEE **fließen**.

Geflügel das poultry.

gefochten SEE **fechten**.

gefräßig adjective (informal) greedy.

gefrieren ◇ verb (IMPERF **gefror**, PERF **ist gefroren**) to freeze.

Gefrierfach das (PL die **Gefrierfächer**) freezer (compartment).

gefroren adjective frozen.

Gefühl das (PL die **Gefühle**) 1 feeling; 2 etwas im Gefühl haben to have a feel for something.

gefüllt adjective stuffed (peppers, for example).

gefunden SEE **finden**.

gegangen SEE **gehen**.

gegeben SEE **geben**.

gegebenenfalls adverb if need be.

gegen preposition ←(+ACC) 1 against; 2 gegen die Mauer fahren to drive into the wall; 3 ein Mittel gegen Grippe a cure for flu; 4 towards; gegen Abend towards evening; 5 gegen vier Uhr around four o'clock; 6 compared with; 7 versus (in sport).

Gegend die (PL die **Gegenden**) 1 area; 2 neighbourhood.

gegeneinander adverb against each other, against one another.

Gegenmittel das (PL die **Gegenmittel**) 1 remedy; 2 antidote.

Gegensatz der (PL die **Gegensätze**) 1 contrast; 2 opposite; 3 im Gegensatz zu mir unlike me.

gegenseitig adjective mutual. adverb sich gegenseitig helfen to help each other.

Gegenstand der (PL die **Gegenstände**) 1 object; 2 subject (in grammar and of a discussion).

Gegenteil das (PL die **Gegenteile**) 1 opposite; 2 im Gegenteil on the contrary.

gegenüber preposition ←(+DAT) 1 opposite; Susi saß mir gegenüber Susi sat opposite me; 2 compared with; 3 towards; jemandem gegenüber freundlich sein to be friendly towards

Δ NEW SPELLING: See page xii

somebody.

adverb opposite; **meine Freundin wohnt gegenüber** my friend lives opposite.

Gegenwart *die* 1 present; 2 presence.

gegessen SEE **essen**.

Gegner *der* (PL *die* **Gegner**) opponent.

gegrillt *adjective* grilled.

Gehackte *das* mince.

Gehalt *das* (PL *die* **Gehälter**) salary.

gehässig *adjective* spiteful.

geheim *adjective* secret.

Geheimnis *das* (PL *die* **Geheimnisse**) secret.

geheimnisvoll *adjective* mysterious.

gehen ◇ *verb* (IMPERF **ging**, PERF **ist gegangen**) 1 to go; **schlafen gehen** to go to bed; 2 to walk; 3 **über die Straße gehen** to cross the road; 4 **es geht ihr gut** she's well; **wie geht es Ihnen?** how are you?; **es geht** it's not too bad; 5 **das geht nicht** that's impossible; **um etwas gehen** to be about something; **worum geht's hier?** what's it all about?; 7 **die Uhr geht falsch** the clock's wrong.

Gehirn *das* (PL *die* **Gehirne**) brain.

Gehirnerschütterung *die* (PL *die* **Gehirnerschütterungen**) concussion.

gehoben SEE **heben**.

geholfen SEE **helfen**.

Gehör *das* hearing.

gehorchen *verb* (PERF **hat gehorcht**) to obey.

gehören *verb* (PERF **hat gehört**) 1 to belong; **es gehört mir** it belongs to me; 2 **dazu gehört Mut** that takes courage; 3 **es gehört sich nicht** it isn't done.

gehorsam *adjective* obedient.

Gehsteig *der* (PL *die* **Gehsteige**) pavement.

Geige *die* (PL *die* **Geigen**) violin.

Geisel *die* (PL *die* **Geiseln**) hostage.

Geist *der* (PL *die* **Geister**) 1 mind; 2 ghost; 3 wit.

geistesabwesend *adjective* absent-minded.

Geisteskrankheit *die* (PL *die* **Geisteskrankheiten**) mental illness.

Geisteswissenschaften (*plural noun*) arts, humanities.

geistig *adjective* mental.

geizig *adjective* mean.

gekannt SEE **kennen**.

gekonnt SEE **können**.

Gel *das* (PL *die* **Gele**) gel.

Gelächter *das* (PL *die* **Gelächter**) laughter.

geladen SEE **laden**.

gelähmt *adjective* paralysed.

Geländer *das* (PL *die* **Geländer**) 1 banister(s); 2 railing(s).

gelangweilt *adjective* bored.

◇ IRREGULAR VERB: *See the verb table in the centre of the dictionary*

gelassen *verb* SEE **lassen**.
adjective calm.

geläufig *adjective* 1 common; 2 **das ist mir nicht geläufig** I'm not familiar with it.

gelaunt *adjective* **gut gelaunt sein** to be in a good mood.

gelb *adjective* yellow.

Geld *das* (PL die **Gelder**) money.

Geldautomat *der* (PL die **Geldautomaten**) cash dispenser.

Geldbörse *die* (PL die **Geldbörsen**) purse.

Geldschein *der* (PL die **Geldscheine**) banknote.

Geldstrafe *die* (PL die **Geldstrafen**) fine.

Geldwechsel *der* 1 bureau de change; 2 currency exchange.

gelegen SEE **liegen**.

Gelegenheit *die* (PL die **Gelegenheiten**) 1 opportunity; 2 occasion.

gelegentlich *adverb* occasionally.

Gelenk *das* (PL die **Gelenke**) joint.

Geliebte *der/die* (PL die **Geliebten**) lover.

geliehen SEE **leihen**.

gelingen ◇ *verb* (IMPERF **gelang**, PERF **ist gelungen**) to succeed; **es ist mir gelungen, sie zu überreden** I succeeded in persuading her.

gelten ◇ *verb* (PRES **gilt**, IMPERF **galt**, PERF **hat gegolten**) 1 to be valid; 2 to apply (*of a rule*); 3 **jemandem**

gelten to be directed at somebody; 4 **sein Wort gilt viel** his word is worth a lot; 5 **das gilt nicht** that doesn't count; 6 **als etwas gelten** to be regarded as something.

gelungen *verb* SEE **gelingen**.
adjective successful.

Gemälde *das* (PL die **Gemälde**) painting.

gemein *adjective* mean.

Gemeinde *die* (PL die **Gemeinden**) 1 community; 2 congregation.

gemeinsam *adjective* 1 common; 2 joint.
adverb together; **gemeinsam essen** to eat together.

Gemeinschaft *die* (PL die **Gemeinschaften**) community.

gemischt *adjective* mixed.

gemocht SEE **mögen**.

Gemüse *das* (PL die **Gemüse**) vegetables.

Gemüsehändler *der* (PL die **Gemüsehändler**) greengrocer.

gemusst △ SEE **müssen**.

gemustert *adjective* patterned.

gemütlich *adjective* 1 cosy; 2 **mach es dir gemütlich** make yourself comfortable.

genannt SEE **nennen**.

genau *adjective* 1 exact; 2 accurate (*scales, description*); 3 meticulous; 4 **ich weiß nichts Genaues** I don't know any details.
adverb 1 exactly; 2 **genau genommen** △ strictly speaking.

△ NEW SPELLING: *See page xii*

Genauigkeit *die* accuracy.

genauso *adverb* 1 just the same;
2 **genauso gut** just as good;
genauso viel just as much, just as
many; **genauso lange** just as long.

Genehmigung *die* (PL *die*
Genehmigungen) 1 permission;
2 permit; 3 licence.

Generation *die* (PL *die*
Generationen) generation.

generell *adjective* general.

Genetik *die* genetics.

Genf *das* Geneva.

Genfer See *der* Lake Geneva.

genial *adjective* brilliant.

Genick *das* (PL *die* **Genicke**) (back of
the) neck.

Genie *das* (PL *die* **Genies**) genius.

genießbar *adjective* edible.

genießen ✧ *verb* (IMPERF **genoss**△,
PERF **hat genossen**) to enjoy.

genommen SEE **nehmen**.

genug *adverb* enough.

genügen *verb* (PERF **hat genügt**) to
be enough.

genügend *adjective* 1 enough;
2 sufficient.

Genuss△ *der* (PL *die* **Genüsse**)
1 enjoyment; 2 consumption (*of
alcohol*).

geöffnet *adjective* open.

Geometrie *die* geometry.

Gepäck *das* luggage.

Gepäckausgabe *die* left-luggage
office.

Gepäckaufbewahrung *die* left-
luggage office.

Gepäckträger *der* (PL *die*
Gepäckträger) 1 porter; 2 roof
rack; 3 carrier (*on a bike*).

gerade *adjective* 1 straight; 2 **etwas
gerade biegen**△ to straighten
something; 3 upright; 4 **eine
gerade Zahl** an even number.
adverb 1 just; **gerade erst** only
just; 2 **es war nicht gerade billig** it
wasn't exactly cheap.

geradeaus *adverb* straight ahead.

geradebiegen SEE **gerade**.

gerannt SEE **rennen**.

Gerät *das* (PL *die* **Geräte**)
1 appliance; 2 set (*TV or radio*);
3 tool; 4 gadget; 5 **die Geräte**
apparatus (*in gymnastics*).

geraten ✧ *verb* (PRES **gerät**, IMPERF
geriet, PERF **ist geraten**) 1 to get
(*somewhere, the wrong side of the
road etc.*); **in etwas geraten** to get
into something; **in Wut geraten** to
get angry; 2 **an den Richtigen
geraten** to come to the right person;
3 **gut/schlecht geraten** to turn out
well/badly; 4 **nach jemandem
geraten** to take after somebody.

geräuchert *adjective* smoked.

geräumig *adjective* spacious.

Geräusch *das* (PL *die* **Geräusche**)
noise.

gerecht *adjective* 1 just; 2 fair.

✧ IRREGULAR VERB: See the verb table in the centre of the dictionary

Gerechtigkeit *die* justice.

Gerede *das* gossip.

Gericht *das* (PL *die* **Gerichte**)
1 court; 2 dish.

gerieben SEE **reiben**.

gering *adjective* 1 small (*amount*);
2 low (*value*); 3 short (*time, distance*).

Gerippe *das* (PL *die* **Gerippe**)
skeleton.

gerissen *adjective* crafty.

geritten SEE **reiten**.

gern(e) *adverb* 1 gladly;
2 **jemanden gern haben** to like somebody; **etwas gern tun** to like doing something; **ich tanze gern** I like dancing; **ich hätte gerne einen Kaffee** I'd like a coffee; 3 **ja, gern!** yes, I'd love to!; 4 **das glaube ich gern** I can well believe that.

Gerste *die* barley.

Geruch *der* (PL *die* **Gerüche**) smell.

Gerücht *das* (PL *die* **Gerüchte**) rumour.

Gerümpel *das* junk.

gesalzen *verb* SEE **salzen**.
adjective 1 salted; 2 **gesalzene Preise** (*informal*) steep prices.

gesamt *adjective* 1 whole; 2 **die gesamten Kosten** the total cost;
3 **die gesamten Werke** the complete works.

Gesamtschule *die* (PL *die* **Gesamtschulen**) comprehensive school.

gesandt SEE **senden**.

Geschäft *das* (PL *die* **Geschäfte**)
1 shop; 2 business; 3 deal.

Geschäftsführer *der* (PL *die* **Geschäftsführer**) manager.

Geschäftsführerin *die* (PL *die* **Geschäftsführerinnen**) manageress.

Geschäftszeiten *plural noun* business hours.

geschehen ◇ *verb* (PRES **geschieht**, IMPERF **geschah**, PERF **ist geschehen**) to happen.

gescheit *adjective* clever.

Geschenk *das* (PL *die* **Geschenke**)
present, gift.

Geschichte *die* (PL *die* **Geschichten**) 1 story; 2 history;
3 **mach bloß keine große Geschichte daraus** don't make such a thing of it.

Geschick *das* 1 skill; 2 fate.

geschickt *adjective* 1 skilful;
2 clever.

geschieden *verb* SEE **scheiden**.
adjective divorced.

geschienen SEE **scheinen**.

Geschirr *das* 1 crockery; 2 dishes.

Geschirrspülmaschine *die* (PL *die* **Geschirrspülmaschinen**) dishwasher.

Geschirrtuch *das* (PL *die* **Geschirrtücher**) tea towel.

Geschlecht *das* (PL *die* **Geschlechter**) 1 sex; 2 gender.

△ NEW SPELLING: *See page xii*

geschlossen verb SEE **schließen**.
adjective closed.

Geschmack der (PL die Geschmäcke) taste.

geschmacklos *adjective*
1 tasteless; 2 **geschmacklos sein** to be in bad taste.

geschnitten SEE **schneiden**.

geschossen SEE **schießen**.

geschrieben SEE **schreiben**.

geschrien SEE **schreien**.

Geschwätz das talk.

geschwätzig *adjective* talkative.

Geschwindigkeit die (PL die Geschwindigkeiten) speed.

Geschwindigkeits-beschränkung die (PL die Geschwindigkeitsbeschränkungen) speed limit.

Geschwister *plural noun* brothers and sisters, siblings.

geschwommen SEE **schwimmen**.

gesellig *adjective* sociable.

Gesellschaft die (PL die Gesellschaften) 1 society; 2 company; **ich leiste dir Gesellschaft** I'll keep you company; 3 party.

gesessen SEE **sitzen**.

Gesetz das (PL die Gesetze) law.

gesetzlich *adjective* legal; **ein gesetzlicher Feiertag** a public holiday.

Gesicht das (PL die Gesichter) face.

Gesichtsausdruck der (facial) expression.

gesollt SEE **sollen**.

gespannt *adjective* 1 eager; 2 **auf etwas gespannt sein** to look forward eagerly to something; **auf jemanden gespannt sein** to look forward to seeing somebody; 3 **ich bin gespannt, ob …** I wonder whether …; 4 tense; **in Südafrika ist die Lage immer noch gespannt** the situation in South Africa is still tense.

Gespenst das (PL die Gespenster) ghost.

Gespräch das (PL die Gespräche) 1 conversation; 2 call (on the phone).

gesprächig *adjective* talkative.

gesprochen SEE **sprechen**.

gesprungen SEE **springen**.

Gestalt die (PL die Gestalten) 1 figure; 2 form.

gestanden SEE **stehen**, **gestehen**.

Geständnis das (PL die Geständnisse) confession.

gestatten verb (PERF hat gestattet) 1 to permit; 2 **nicht gestattet** prohibited; 3 **gestatten Sie?** may I?

Geste die (PL die Gesten) gesture.

gestehen ◇ *verb* (IMPERF gestand, PERF hat gestanden) to confess.

Gestell das (PL die Gestelle) 1 rack; 2 stand; 3 frame.

gestern *adverb* 1 yesterday; 2 **gestern Nacht** last night.

◇ IRREGULAR VERB: *See the verb table in the centre of the dictionary*

gestohlen SEE **stehlen**.

gestorben SEE **sterben**.

gestreift *adjective* striped.

gesund *adjective* 1 healthy;
2 **wieder gesund werden** to get
well again; 3 **Schwimmen ist
gesund** swimming is good for you.

Gesundheit *die* 1 health;
2 **Gesundheit!** bless you! (*said after
a sneeze*).

gesungen SEE **singen**.

getan SEE **tun**.

Getränk *das* (PL die **Getränke**) drink.

Getränkekarte *die* (PL die
Getränkekarten) wine list.

getrauen *verb* (PERF **hat sich
getraut**) **sich getrauen** to dare.

Getreide *das* grain.

Getriebe *das* (PL die **Getriebe**)
gearbox.

getrieben SEE **treiben**.

getroffen SEE **treffen**.

getrunken SEE **trinken**.

Getue *das* fuss.

geübt *adjective* 1 accomplished;
2 **mit geübtem Auge** with a
practised eye.

Gewalt *die* 1 power; 2 force; **mit
Gewalt** by force; 3 violence.

gewaltig *adjective* enormous.

gewalttätig *adjective* violent.

gewann SEE **gewinnen**.

Gewebe *das* (PL die **Gewebe**)
1 fabric; 2 tissue.

Gewehr *das* (PL die **Gewehre**) rifle,
gun.

Gewerkschaft *die* (PL die
Gewerkschaften) trade union.

gewesen SEE **sein**.

Gewicht *das* (PL die **Gewichte**)
weight.

Gewinn *der* (PL die **Gewinne**)
1 profit; 2 winnings; 3 prize.

gewinnen ◇ *verb* (IMPERF **gewann**,
PERF **hat gewonnen**) 1 to win; 2 to
gain (*time or influence*); **an
Bedeutung gewinnen** to gain in
importance.

Gewinner *der* (PL die **Gewinner**)
winner.

Gewinnerin *die* (PL die
Gewinnerinnen) winner.

gewiss △ *adjective* certain; **ein
gewisser Herr Schmidt möchte Sie
sprechen** a Mr Schmidt would like
to speak to you.
adverb certainly; **'darf ich?' 'aber
gewiss doch'** 'may I?' 'but of
course'.

Gewissen *das* (PL die **Gewissen**)
conscience.

gewissenhaft *adjective*
conscientious.

gewissermaßen *adverb* 1 more or
less; 2 as it were.

Gewitter *das* (PL die **Gewitter**)
thunderstorm.

△ NEW SPELLING: *See page xii*

gewöhnen verb (PERF hat gewöhnt) **1** jemanden an etwas gewöhnen to get somebody used to something; **2** an etwas gewöhnt sein to be used to something; **3** sich an etwas gewöhnen to get used to something.

Gewohnheit die (PL die Gewohnheiten) habit.

gewöhnlich adjective **1** usual; **2** ordinary. adverb usually; **wie gewöhnlich** as usual.

gewohnt adjective **1** usual; **2** etwas gewohnt sein to be used to something; **Renate ist es nicht gewohnt, früh aufzustehen** Renate isn't used to getting up early.

gewollt SEE wollen.

gewonnen SEE gewinnen.

geworden SEE werden.

geworfen SEE werfen.

Gewürz das (PL die Gewürze) spice.

gewusst△ SEE wissen.

Gezeiten plural noun tides.

gezogen SEE ziehen.

gezwungen SEE zwingen.

gibt SEE geben.

gierig adjective greedy.

gießen ◇ verb (IMPERF goss△, PERF hat gegossen) **1** to pour; **es gießt** it's pouring; **2** to water; **vergiss nicht, die Blumen zu gießen** don't forget to water the flowers.

Gießkanne die (PL die Gießkannen) watering can.

Gift das (PL die Gifte) poison.

giftig adjective **1** poisonous; **2** toxic.

ging SEE gehen.

Gipfel der (PL die Gipfel) **1** peak, summit; **2** der Gipfel der Geschmacklosigkeit the height of bad taste.

Gips der plaster.

Girokonto das (PL die Girokonten) current account.

Giraffe die (PL die Giraffen) giraffe.

Gitarre die (PL die Gitarren) guitar.

Gitter das (PL die Gitter) **1** grid; **2** bars.

glänzen verb (PERF hat geglänzt) to shine.

glänzend adjective **1** shining; **2** brilliant; **ein glänzender Erfolg** a brilliant success.

Glas das (PL die Gläser) **1** glass; **2** jar.

Glasscheibe die (PL die Glasscheiben) pane (of glass).

glatt adjective **1** smooth; **2** slippery; **3** eine glatte Absage a flat refusal. adverb **1** smoothly; **2** flatly; **etwas glatt ablehnen** to flatly reject something; **3 das ist glatt gelogen** that's a downright lie; **4 ich habe ihren Geburtstag glatt vergessen** I totally forgot about her birthday.

Glatteis das (black) ice.

Glatze die (PL die Glatzen) eine Glatze haben to be bald; eine Glatze bekommen to go bald.

◇ IRREGULAR VERB: See the verb table in the centre of the dictionary

glauben *verb* (PERF hat geglaubt)
1 to believe; **an Gott glauben** to believe in God; 2 to think; 3 **nicht zu glauben!** incredible!

gleich *adjective* 1 same; 2 identical; 3 **gleich bleibend** ∆ constant; 4 **das ist mir gleich** it's all the same to me; **ganz gleich, wer anruft** no matter who calls.
adverb 1 the same; 2 equally; 3 immediately; 4 **gleich neben** right next to; 5 **er ist gleich fertig** he'll be ready in a minute.

gleichartig *adjective* similar.

gleichberechtigt *adjective* equal.

Gleichberechtigung *die* equality.

gleichbleibend SEE gleich.

gleichen ◇ *verb* (IMPERF glich, PERF hat geglichen) 1 to be like; 2 **sich gleichen** to be alike.

gleichfalls *adverb* 1 also; 2 **danke gleichfalls!** the same to you!

Gleichgewicht *das* balance.

gleichgültig *adjective* indifferent; **das ist doch gleichgültig** it's not important.

gleichzeitig *adverb* at the same time.

Gleis *das* (PL die Gleise) 1 track, line; 2 platform; **Gleis vier** platform four.

glich SEE gleichen.

Glied *das* (PL die Glieder) 1 limb; 2 link.

glitschig *adjective* slippery.

glitzern *verb* (PERF hat geglitzert) to glitter.

Glocke *die* (PL die Glocken) bell.

Glück *das* 1 luck; **viel Glück!** good luck!; **Glück haben** to be lucky; **zum Glück** luckily; 2 happiness.

glücklich *adjective* 1 lucky; **es war ein glücklicher Zufall, dass ich ihn heute in der Stadt getroffen habe** it was a lucky coincidence that I met him in town today; 2 happy.

glücklicherweise *adverb* luckily, fortunately.

Glückwunsch *der* (PL die Glückwünsche) congratulations; **herzlichen Glückwunsch zum Geburtstag!** happy birthday!

Glückwunschkarte *die* (PL die Glückwunschkarten) greetings card.

Glühbirne *die* (PL die Glühbirnen) light bulb.

glühen *verb* (PERF hat geglüht) to glow.

Gold *das* gold.

golden *adjective* 1 gold; 2 golden.

Goldfisch *der* (PL die Goldfische) goldfish.

Golf[1] *der* (PL die Golfe) gulf.

Golf[2] *das* golf.

Golfplatz *der* (PL die Golfplätze) golf course.

Golfschläger *der* (PL die Golfschläger) golf club.

goss ∆ SEE gießen.

Gott *der* (PL die Götter) god.

∆ NEW SPELLING: See page xii

Gottesdienst der (PL die Gottesdienste) service.

Göttin die (PL die Göttinnen) goddess.

Grab das (PL die Gräber) grave.

graben Δ verb (PRES **gräbt**, IMPERF **grub**, PERF **hat gegraben**) to dig.

Grad der (PL die Grade) degree.

Gramm das (PL die Gramme) gram.

Grammatik die (PL die Grammatiken) grammar.

grantig adjective grumpy.

Gras das (PL die Gräser) grass.

grässlich Δ adjective horrible.

Gräte die (PL die Gräten) (fish)bone.

gratis adverb free of charge.

gratulieren verb (PERF **hat gratuliert**) 1 to congratulate; 2 ich habe Gabi zum Geburtstag gratuliert I wished Gabi happy birthday; 3 wir gratulieren! congratulations!

grau adjective grey.

Gräuel Δ der horror.

grauen verb (PERF **hat gegraut**) mir graut es davor I dread it.

grauhaarig adjective grey-haired.

grausam adjective cruel.

Grausamkeit die cruelty.

graziös adjective graceful.

greifen ◇ verb (IMPERF **griff**, PERF **hat gegriffen**) 1 to take hold of; 2 to catch; 3 nach etwas greifen to reach for something; 4 um sich greifen to spread (of fire).

grell adjective 1 glaring; 2 garish; 3 shrill.

Grenze die (PL die Grenzen) 1 border; 2 boundary; 3 limit.

grenzen verb (PERF **hat gegrenzt**) an etwas grenzen to border on something.

Greuel SEE Gräuel.

Grieche der (PL die Griechen) Greek.

Griechenland das Greece.

Griechin die (PL die Griechinnen) Greek.

griechisch adjective Greek.

griff SEE greifen.

Griff der (PL die Griffe) 1 grasp; 2 handle.

griffbereit adjective handy; sie hat den Korkenzieher immer griffbereit she always keeps the corkscrew handy.

Grill der (PL die Grills) 1 grill; 2 barbecue.

Grille die (PL die Grillen) cricket (the insect).

grillen verb (PERF **hat gegrillt**) 1 to grill; 2 to have a barbecue.

Grillfest das (PL die Grillfeste) barbecue.

grinsen verb (PERF **hat gegrinst**) to grin.

Grippe die (PL die Grippen) flu.

grob adjective 1 coarse; 2 rough;

◇ IRREGULAR VERB: See the verb table in the centre of the dictionary

3 rude; 4 **ein grober Fehler** a bad mistake.

Groschen *der* (PL *die* Groschen) 1 (*Austrian money*) groschen; 2 (*informal*) ten-pfennig piece; 3 **der Groschen ist gefallen** the penny's dropped.

groß *adjective* 1 big; 2 great; **Gisela hatte große Angst** Gisela was very frightened; 3 tall; 4 **ein großer Buchstabe** a capital letter; 5 **groß werden** to grow up; 6 **die großen Ferien** the summer holidays; 7 **im Großen und Ganzen** ∆ on the whole; 8 **Groß und Klein** ∆ young and old. *adverb* **was soll man da schon groß machen?** what are you supposed to do?

großartig *adjective* great.

Großbritannien *das* Great Britain.

Großbuchstabe *der* (PL *die* Großbuchstaben) capital (letter).

Größe *die* (PL *die* Größen) 1 size; 2 height; 3 greatness.

Großeltern *plural noun* grandparents.

großenteils *adverb* largely.

Großmarkt *der* (PL *die* Großmärkte) hypermarket.

Großmutter *die* (PL *die* Großmütter) grandmother.

Großstadt *die* (PL *die* Großstädte) city.

großschreiben ◇ *verb* (IMPERF schrieb groß, PERF hat großgeschrieben) **ein Wort**

großschreiben to write a word with a capital.

Großvater *der* (PL *die* Großväter) grandfather.

großzügig *adjective* generous.

grub SEE **graben**.

grün *adjective* 1 green; 2 **im Grünen** in the country; 3 **die Grünen** the Greens.

Grund *der* (PL *die* Gründe) 1 ground; 2 bottom; 3 reason; **aus diesem Grund** for this reason; 4 **im Grunde genommen** basically.

gründen *verb* (PERF hat gegründet) 1 to set up, to found; 2 **sich auf etwas gründen** to be based on something.

Grundlage *die* (PL *die* Grundlagen) basis.

gründlich *adjective* thorough.

grundsätzlich *adjective* 1 fundamental; 2 basic. *adverb* 1 basically; 2 on principle.

Grundschule *die* (PL *die* Grundschulen) primary school.

Grundstück *das* (PL *die* Grundstücke) plot (of land).

Gruppe *die* (PL *die* Gruppen) group.

Gruß *der* (PL *die* Grüße) greeting; **einen schönen Gruß an Lars** give my regards to Lars; **mit herzlichen Grüßen** with best wishes.

grüßen *verb* (PERF hat gegrüßt) 1 to greet; 2 to say hello; 3 **grüß Gott!** hello; 4 **grüße Thomas von mir** give Thomas my regards; **Gisela lässt grüßen** Gisela sends her regards.

∆ NEW SPELLING: *See page xii*

gucken verb (PERF hat geguckt) to look.

gültig adjective valid.

Gummi der (PL die Gummis) rubber.

Gummiband das (PL die Gummibänder) rubber band.

Gummistiefel der (PL die Gummistiefel) wellington (boot).

günstig adjective 1 favourable; 2 convenient.

Gurgel die (PL die Gurgeln) throat.

gurgeln verb (PERF hat gegurgelt) to gargle.

Gurke die (PL die Gurken) 1 cucumber; 2 gherkin.

Gürtel der (PL die Gürtel) belt.

Gürteltasche die (PL die Gürteltaschen) bum bag.

gut adjective 1 good; 2 guten Appetit! enjoy your meal!; 3 schon gut that's all right; also gut all right; 4 im Guten △ amicably; 5 alles Gute! all the best!
adverb 1 well; 2 gut schmecken to taste good; 3 gut zwei Stunden a good two hours; 4 uns geht's gut we're fine; ihm geht es nicht gut he's not well.

Güte die 1 goodness; du meine Güte! my goodness!; 2 quality.

Güterzug der (PL die Güterzüge) goods train.

gutgehen SEE gut.

gutmütig adjective good-natured.

Gutschein der (PL die Gutscheine) 1 voucher; 2 coupon.

Gymnasium das (PL die Gymnasien) grammar school.

Gymnastik die 1 gymnastics; 2 keep-fit (exercises).

H h

Haar das (PL die Haare) 1 hair; sich die Haare waschen to wash your hair; 2 um ein Haar (informal) very nearly.

Haarbürste die (PL die Haarbürsten) hairbrush.

haarig adjective hairy.

Haarschnitt der (PL die Haarschnitte) haircut.

Haarwaschmittel das (PL die Haarwaschmittel) shampoo.

haben ◇ verb (PRES hat, IMPERF hatte, PERF hat gehabt) 1 to have (got); **ich habe ein neues Auto** I have (or I've got) a new car; **etwas gegen jemanden haben** to have something against somebody; 2 (used with another verb, like 'have' in English, to form past tenses) **ich habe Werners Adresse verloren** I've lost Werner's address; **ich habe deine Mutter gestern angerufen** I rang your mother yesterday; 3 **Angst haben** to be frightened; **Hunger haben** to be hungry; 4 **heute haben wir Mittwoch** it's Wednesday today; 5 **die Kinder haben Ferien** the children are on holiday; 6 **was hat sie?** what's the

◇ **IRREGULAR VERB:** *See the verb table in the centre of the dictionary.*

matter with her?; **7 ich hätte gern
... I'd like ...; ich hätte ihr geholfen**
I would have helped her; **8 sich
haben** (*informal*) to make a fuss.

hacken *verb* (PERF **hat gehackt**) **1** to
chop (up); **2** to peck (*of a bird*).

Hackfleisch *das* minced meat.

Hafen *der* (PL *die* **Häfen**) harbour.

Haferflocken *plural noun*
porridge oats.

haftbar *adjective* **für etwas haftbar
sein** to be liable for something.

haften *verb* (PERF **hat gehaftet**) **1** to
stick; **2 für etwas haften** to be
responsible for something.

Hagel *der* hail.

hageln *verb* (PERF **hat gehagelt**) to
hail.

Hagelschauer *der* (PL *die*
Hagelschauer) hailstorm.

Hahn *der* (PL *die* **Hähne**) **1** cock;
2 tap.

Hähnchen *das* (PL *die* **Hähnchen**)
chicken.

Hai *der* (PL *die* **Haie**) shark.

Haken *der* (PL *die* **Haken**) **1** hook;
2 tick; **3** catch; **da muss ein Haken
dran sein** there must be a catch.

halb *adjective* half; **zum halben
Preis** at half price; **halb eins** half
past twelve.

Halbfinale *das* (PL *die* **Halbfinale**)
semi-final.

halbieren *verb* (PERF **hat halbiert**)
to halve.

Halbkreis *der* (PL *die* **Halbkreise**)
semicircle.

Halbpension *die* half board.

halbtags *adverb* part-time.

halbwegs *adverb* **1** half-way;
2 more or less.

Halbzeit *die* (PL *die* **Halbzeiten**)
1 half; **2** half-time; **während der
Halbzeit** during half-time.

half SEE **helfen**.

Hälfte *die* (PL *die* **Hälften**) half; **zur
Hälfte** half.

Halle *die* (PL *die* **Hallen**) **1** hall;
2 foyer.

Hallenbad *das* (PL *die* **Hallenbäder**)
indoor swimming pool.

hallo *exclamation* hello!

Hals *der* (PL *die* **Hälse**) **1** neck;
2 throat; **mir tut der Hals weh** I've
got a sore throat; **3 aus vollem Hals
schreien** to shout at the top of your
voice; **4 Hals über Kopf** in a rush.

Halsband *das* (PL *die* **Halsbänder**)
collar.

Halsschmerzen *plural noun* sore
throat; **Paul hat Halsschmerzen**
Paul's got a sore throat.

Halstuch *das* (PL *die* **Halstücher**)
scarf.

halt *exclamation* stop!

Halt *der* **1** hold; **jetzt hat es einen
besseren Halt** it holds better now;
2 Halt machen △ to stop.

haltbar *adjective* **1** hard-wearing;

2 durable; **3 mindestens haltbar
bis ...** best before ...

halten ◇ *verb* (PRES **hält**, IMPERF
hielt, PERF **hat gehalten**) **1** to hold;
2 to keep; **sein Versprechen halten**
to keep your promise; **warm
halten** ∆ to keep warm; **3** to stop;
**der Bus hält direkt vor seiner
Haustür** the bus stops right outside
his door; **4** to save (*in sport*); **5** to
take (*of milk, magazine*); **6 ich habe
ihn für deinen Bruder gehalten** I
took him for your brother; **7 viel von
jemandem halten** to think a lot of
somebody; **jemanden für ehrlich
halten** to think somebody is
honest; **8 zu jemandem halten** to
stand by somebody; **9 eine Rede
halten** to make a speech; **10 sich
halten** to keep (*of milk, fruit, etc.*);
11 sich links/rechts halten to keep
left/right; **12 sich gut halten** to do
well; **13 sich an etwas halten** to
keep to something.

Haltestelle *die* (PL *die* **Haltestellen**)
stop.

haltmachen SEE Halt.

Haltung *die* (PL *die* **Haltungen**)
1 posture; **2** attitude; **3** composure.

Hammelfleisch *das* mutton.

Hammer *der* (PL *die* **Hämmer**)
hammer.

hämmern *verb* (PERF **hat
gehämmert**) to hammer.

Hamster *der* (PL *die* **Hamster**)
hamster.

Hand *die* (PL *die* **Hände**) hand;

jemandem die Hand geben to
shake hands with somebody.

Handarbeit *die* (PL *die
Handarbeiten*) **1** handicraft;
2 hand-made article.

Handball *der* handball.

Handbremse *die* (PL *die
Handbremsen*) handbrake; **die
Handbremse ziehen** to pull the
handbrake.

Handbuch *das* (PL *die* **Handbücher**)
manual.

Handel *der* **1** trade; **2** deal; **3 in den
Handel kommen** to come on the
market.

handeln *verb* (PERF **hat gehandelt**)
1 to trade, to deal; **2 mit jemandem
handeln** to bargain with somebody;
3 to act; **4 von etwas handeln** to
be about something; **5 es handelt
sich um ...** it's about ...; **worum
handelt es sich?** what's it about?

Handelsschule *die* (PL *die
Handelsschulen*) business school,
vocational college.

Handfläche *die* (PL *die
Handflächen*) palm.

Handgelenk *das* (PL *die
Handgelenke*) wrist.

Handgepäck *das* hand luggage.

handhaben *verb* (PERF **hat
gehandhabt**) to handle.

Händler *der* (PL *die* **Händler**) dealer.

handlich *adjective* handy.

Handlung *die* (PL *die* **Handlungen**)
1 act; **2** action; **3** plot.

◇ IRREGULAR VERB: *See the verb table in the centre of the dictionary*

Handschellen (*plural noun*) handcuffs.

Handschrift *die* (PL *die* **Handschriften**) handwriting.

Handschuh *der* (PL *die* **Handschuhe**) glove.

Handtasche *die* (PL *die* **Handtaschen**) bag.

Handtuch *das* (PL *die* **Handtücher**) towel.

Handwerker *der* (PL *die* **Handwerker**) 1 craftsman; 2 workman.

Handwerkszeug *das* tools.

Handy *das* (PL *die* **Handys**) mobile (phone).

Hang *der* (PL *die* **Hänge**) slope.

Hängematte *die* (PL *die* **Hängematten**) hammock.

hängen[1] *verb* (PERF **hat gehängt**) 1 to hang; **Florian hat das Bild an die Wand gehängt** Florian hung the picture on the wall; **sie hängte ihren Mantel in den Schrank** she hung her coat up in the cupboard; 2 **sie haben den Wohnwagen an das Auto gehängt** they attached the caravan to the car; 3 **sich an jemanden hängen** to latch on to somebody.

hängen[2] ◇ *verb* (IMPERF **hing**, PERF **hat gehangen**) 1 to hang; **mein Bild hat immer hier gehangen** my picture used to hang here; 2 **an seinen Eltern hängen** to be attached to your parents; **sie hängt sehr an ihrer Mutter** she's very attached to her mother; 3 **an etwas**

hängen bleiben △ to catch on something, to stick to something; **ich bin mit dem Ärmel am Zaun hängen geblieben** I got my sleeve caught on the fence.

hängenbleiben SEE **hängen**[2].

Hansaplast™ *das* plaster.

Happen *der* (PL *die* **Happen**) mouthful; **ich habe noch keinen Happen gegessen** I haven't had a bite to eat all day.

Harfe *die* (PL *die* **Harfen**) harp.

Harke *die* (PL *die* **Harken**) rake.

harmlos *adjective* harmless.

hart *adjective* 1 hard; 2 harsh.

hartgekocht *adjective* hard-boiled.

Hase *der* (PL *die* **Hasen**) hare.

Haselnuss △ *die* (PL *die* **Haselnüsse**) hazelnut.

Hass △ *der* hatred.

hassen *verb* (PERF **hat gehasst** △) to hate.

hässlich △ *adjective* 1 ugly; **sie hat ein hässliches Gesicht** she's got an ugly face; 2 nasty; **das war sehr hässlich von dir** that was very nasty of you.

hast SEE **haben**.

hastig *adjective* hasty.

hat, hatte, hatten, hattest, hattet SEE **haben**.

Haube *die* (PL *die* **Hauben**) 1 bonnet; 2 cap.

△ NEW SPELLING: See page xii

hauen ◇ *verb* (PRES **haut**, IMPERF **haute**, PERF **hat gehauen**) **1** to beat; **2** to thump, to bang; **3 sich hauen** to fight; **4 jemanden übers Ohr hauen** (*informal*) to cheat somebody.

Haufen *der* (PL **die Haufen**) **1** heap; **2** crowd (*of people*); **3 ein Haufen** (*informal*) heaps of; **ein Haufen Geld** heaps of money.

haufenweise *adverb* heaps of; **Gabi hat haufenweise CDs** Gabi has heaps of CDs.

häufig *adjective* frequent.

Hauptbahnhof *der* (PL **die Hauptbahnhöfe**) main station.

Hauptrolle *die* (PL **die Hauptrollen**) lead.

Hauptsache *die* (PL **die Hauptsachen**) main thing.

hauptsächlich *adjective* main. *adverb* mainly.

Hauptschule *die* secondary school.

Hauptstadt *die* (PL **die Hauptstädte**) capital.

Hauptstraße *die* (PL **die Hauptstraßen**) main road.

Hauptverkehrszeit *die* (PL **die Hauptverkehrszeiten**) rush hour.

Hauptwort *das* (PL **die Hauptwörter**) noun.

Haus *das* (PL **die Häuser**) **1** house; **2 nach Hause** home; **zu Hause** at home.

Hausarbeit *die* (PL **die Hausarbeiten**) **1** housework; **die Kinder müssen bei der Hausarbeit helfen** the children have to help with the housework; **2** homework.

Hausaufgaben *plural noun* homework; **hast du deine Hausaufgaben gemacht?** have you done your homework?

Hausfrau *die* (PL **die Hausfrauen**) housewife.

Haushalt *der* (PL **die Haushalte**) **1** household; **2 den Haushalt machen** to do the housework; **3** budget.

Haushaltswarengeschäft *das* (PL **die Haushaltswarengeschäfte**) hardware shop.

Hausmeister *der* (PL **die Hausmeister**) caretaker.

Hausnummer *die* house number.

Hausschlüssel *der* (PL **die Hausschlüssel**) front-door key.

Hausschuh *der* (PL **die Hausschuhe**) slipper.

Haustier *das* (PL **die Haustiere**) pet.

Haustür *die* (PL **die Haustüren**) front door.

Haut *die* (PL **die Häute**) skin; **aus der Haut fahren** (*informal*) to go up the wall.

Hebamme *die* (PL **die Hebammen**) midwife.

Hebel *der* (PL **die Hebel**) lever.

heben ◇ *verb* (IMPERF **hob**, PERF **hat gehoben**) **1** to lift; **2 sich heben** to rise.

Hecke *die* (PL **die Hecken**) hedge.

◇ IRREGULAR VERB: *See the verb table in the centre of the dictionary*

Heer das (PL die Heere) army.

Hefe die (PL die Hefen) yeast.

Heft das (PL die Hefte) 1 exercise book; 2 issue (of a magazine).

heften verb (PERF hat geheftet) 1 to pin; 2 to tack (by sewing); 3 to clip; 4 to staple.

heftig adjective 1 violent; 2 heavy (snow, rain).

Heftklammer die (PL die Heftklammern) staple.

Heftpflaster das (PL die Heftpflaster) sticking plaster.

Heftzwecke die (PL die Heftzwecken) drawing pin.

Heide die heath.

Heidekraut das heather.

Heidelbeere die (PL die Heidelbeeren) bilberry.

heilen verb (PERF hat geheilt) 1 to cure; 2 to heal.

heilig adjective 1 holy; 2 heilig halten to hold sacred; 3 der heilige Franz von Assisi Saint Francis of Assisi.

Heiligabend der (PL die Heiligabende) Christmas Eve.

Heilige der/die (PL die Heiligen) saint.

Heilmittel das (PL die Heilmittel) remedy.

heim adverb home.

Heim das (PL die Heime) 1 home; 2 hostel.

Heimat die (PL die Heimaten) 1 home; 2 native land.

Heimatstadt die home town.

Heimfahrt die (PL die Heimfahrten) 1 journey home; 2 way home.

heimgehen ◊ verb (IMPERF ging heim, PERF ist heimgegangen) to go home.

heimlich adjective secret. adverb secretly.

Heimspiel das (PL die Heimspiele) home game.

Heimweg der (PL die Heimwege) way home.

Heimweh das homesickness; Heimweh haben to be homesick.

Heirat die (PL die Heiraten) marriage.

heiraten verb (PERF hat geheiratet) to marry.

heiser adjective hoarse.

heiß adjective hot.

heißen ◊ verb (IMPERF hieß, PERF hat geheißen) 1 to be called; wie heißt du? what's your name?; 2 to mean; 3 das heißt that is; 4 es heißt it is said; 5 wie heißt 'dog' auf Deutsch? what's the German for 'dog'?

heiter adjective 1 bright; 2 cheerful.

heizen verb (PERF hat geheizt) 1 to heat (a room); 2 to put the heating on; 3 to have the heating on.

Heizung die heating.

hektisch adjective hectic.

Held der (PL die Helden) hero.

Δ NEW SPELLING: See page xii

Heldin die (PL die **Heldinnen**)
heroine.

helfen ◇ verb (PRES **hilft**, IMPERF **half**,
PERF **hat geholfen**) 1 to help; **Lisa**
hilft mir Lisa is helping me; 2 **es**
hilft nichts it's no good; 3 **sich zu**
helfen wissen to know what to do;
ich weiß mir nicht zu helfen I don't
know what to do.

Helfer der (PL die **Helfer**) 1 helper;
2 assistant.

Helferin die (PL die **Helferinnen**)
1 helper; 2 assistant.

hell adjective 1 light (colour);
2 bright; 3 **eine helle Stimme** a
clear voice; 4 **helles Bier** lager;
5 **da ist heller Wahnsinn**
(informal) that's sheer madness.

hellwach adjective wide awake.

Helm der (PL die **Helme**) helmet.

Hemd das (PL die **Hemden**) 1 shirt;
2 vest.

Henkel der (PL die **Henkel**) handle.

Henne die (PL die **Hennen**) hen.

her adverb 1 here; **komm her** come
here; 2 **vor jemandem her** in front
of somebody; 3 **hinter etwas her**
sein to be after something; 4 **von**
der Farbe her as far as the colour is
concerned; 5 **wo bist du her?**
where do you come from?; 6 **wo hat**
Klaus das her? where did Klaus get
it from?; 7 **her damit!** (informal)
give it to me!; 8 ago; **das ist schon**
lange her it was a long time ago; **das**
ist drei Tage her it was three days
ago.

herab adverb down.

herablassend adjective
condescending.

herabsetzen verb (PERF **hat**
herabgesetzt) 1 to reduce; 2 to
belittle.

heran adverb 1 **an etwas heran**
close to something, right up to
something; **bis an die Wand heran**
up to the wall; 2 **immer heran!**
come closer!

herankommen ◇ verb (IMPERF
kam heran, PERF **ist**
herangekommen) 1 to come near;
2 **herankommen an** to come up to;
3 **ich komme nicht heran** I can't get
at it.

herauf adverb up.

heraufkommen ◇ verb (IMPERF
kam herauf, PERF **ist**
heraufgekommen) to come up.

heraus adverb out.

herausbekommen ◇ verb (IMPERF
bekam heraus, PERF **hat**
herausbekommen) 1 to get out;
2 to find out; 3 to solve; 4 **Geld**
herausbekommen to get change.

herausfinden ◇ verb (IMPERF **fand**
heraus, PERF **hat herausgefunden**)
1 to find out; 2 to find your way out.

herausgeben ◇ verb (PRES **gibt**
heraus, IMPERF **gab heraus**, PERF **hat**
herausgegeben) 1 to hand over;
2 to bring out.

herauskommen ◇ verb (IMPERF
kam heraus, PERF **ist**
herausgekommen) to come out.

herausnehmen ◇ verb (PRES

◇ IRREGULAR VERB: See the verb table in the centre of the dictionary

nimmt heraus, IMPERF **nahm heraus**, PERF **hat herausgenommen**) 1 to take out; **sie hat ihren Lippenstift aus der Tasche herausgenommen** she took her lipstick out of the bag; 2 **sich die Mandeln herausnehmen lassen** to have your tonsils out; 3 **es sich herausnehmen, etwas zu tun** to have the nerve to do something; **du nimmst dir zu viel heraus** you're going too far.

herausstellen ◊ verb (PERF **hat herausgestellt**) 1 to put out; 2 **sich herausstellen** to turn out; **es stellte sich heraus, dass …** it turned out that …

herausziehen ◊ verb (IMPERF **zog heraus**, PERF **hat herausgezogen**) to pull out.

herb adjective 1 sharp; 2 dry (wine).

herbei adverb over (here); **kommt herbei!** come over here!

Herberge die (PL die **Herbergen**) hostel.

Herbergsmutter die (PL die **Herbergsmütter**) warden (in a youth hostel).

Herbergsvater der (PL die **Herbergsväter**) warden (in a youth hostel).

herbringen ◊ verb (IMPERF **brachte her**, PERF **hat hergebracht**) to bring (here).

Herbst der (PL die **Herbste**) autumn; **im Herbst** in autumn.

Herd der (PL die **Herde**) cooker.

Herde die (PL die **Herden**) 1 herd; 2 flock.

herein adverb in; **herein!** come in!

hereinfallen ◊ verb (PRES **fällt herein**, IMPERF **fiel herein**, PERF **ist hereingefallen**) to be taken in; **auf einen Betrüger hereinfallen** to be taken in by a swindler.

hereinkommen ◊ verb (IMPERF **kam herein**, PERF **ist hereingekommen**) to come in.

hereinlassen ◊ verb (PRES **lässt herein** Δ, IMPERF **ließ herein**, PERF **hat hereingelassen**) to let in; **Max lässt mich nicht ins Zimmer herein** Max won't let me into the room.

Herfahrt die (PL die **Herfahrten**) 1 journey here; 2 way here.

hergeben ◊ verb (PRES **gibt her**, IMPERF **gab her**, PERF **hat hergegeben**) 1 to hand over; **gib die Tasche her!** hand over the bag!; 2 to give away; 3 **sich für etwas hergeben** to get involved in something; **dazu gebe ich mich nicht her** I won't have anything to do with it.

Hering der (PL die **Heringe**) herring.

herkommen ◊ verb (IMPERF **kam her**, PERF **ist hergekommen**) to come (here); **wo kommt das her?** where does it come from?

Herkunft die (PL die **Herkünfte**) 1 origin; 2 background.

Heroin das heroin.

Herr der (PL die **Herren**) 1 gentleman; 2 **Herr Huber** Mr Huber; 3 **Sehr geehrte Herren** Dear Sirs (in a letter); 4 **meine Herren!**

Δ NEW SPELLING: *See page xii*

gentlemen!; **5** master; **6 der Herr** the Lord.

herrichten verb (PERF hat hergerichtet) to get ready, to prepare; **sie richtet die Betten für die Gäste her** she's getting the beds for the guests ready.

herrlich adjective marvellous.

herrschen verb (PERF hat geherrscht) **1** to rule; **2** to be; **es herrschte große Aufregung** there was great excitement.

herstellen verb (PERF hat hergestellt) to manufacture, to make; **in Deutschland hergestellt** made in Germany.

Herstellung die (PL die Herstellungen) manufacture, production.

herüber adverb over (here).

herum adverb um … herum round; **falsch herum** the wrong way round; **im Kreis herum** in a circle.

herumdrehen verb (PERF hat herumgedreht) **1** to turn (over or round); **2 sich herumdrehen** to turn round.

herumführen verb (PERF hat herumgeführt) to show around.

herumgehen verb (IMPERF ging herum, PERF ist herumgegangen) **1** to go round; **2** to walk around; **im Park herumgehen** to walk around the park; **3** to pass (of time).

herunter adverb down; **die Treppe herunter** down the stairs.

herunterfallen ◇ verb (PRES fällt

herunter, IMPERF fiel herunter, PERF ist heruntergefallen) **1** to fall down; **2** to fall off.

herunterkommen ◇ verb (IMPERF kam herunter, PERF ist heruntergekommen) **1** to come down; **2** (informal) to go to rack and ruin.

herunterlassen ◇ verb (PRES lässt herunter △, IMPERF ließ herunter, PERF hat heruntergelassen) to let down, to lower.

hervor adverb out.

hervorragend adjective outstanding.
adverb outstandingly well.

hervorrufen ◇ verb (IMPERF rief hervor, PERF hat hervorgerufen) to cause.

Herz das (PL die Herzen) **1** heart; **2** hearts (in cards).

Herzanfall der (PL die Herzanfälle) heart attack.

herzlich adjective **1** warm; **2** sincere; **3 herzlichen Dank** many thanks; **4 herzliche Grüße** best wishes; **5 herzlichen Glückwunsch!** congratulations!; **6 herzlich willkommen in Passau!** welcome to Passau!

herzlos adjective heartless.

Herzschlag der (PL die Herzschläge) **1** heartbeat; **2** heart failure; **er hat einen Herzschlag bekommen** he had a heart attack.

heterosexuell adjective heterosexual.

◇ IRREGULAR VERB: See the verb table in the centre of the dictionary

Heterosexuelle *der/die* (PL *die* **Heterosexuellen**) heterosexual.

Heu *das* hay.

heulen *verb* (PERF **hat geheult**) 1 to howl; 2 (*informal*) to cry.

Heuschnupfen *der* hay fever.

heute *adverb* today; **heute Abend** this evening; **heute Morgen** this morning.

heutig *adjective* 1 today's; 2 **in der heutigen Zeit** nowadays.

heutzutage nowadays.

Hexe *die* (PL *die* **Hexen**) witch.

Hexenschuss ∆ *der* lumbago.

hielt SEE **halten**.

hier *adverb* here.

hierher *adverb* here; **komm sofort hierher!** come here immediately!

hierin *adverb* here.

hiesig *adjective* local.

hieß SEE **heißen**.

Hilfe *die* (PL *die* **Hilfen**) 1 help; 2 aid.

hilflos *adjective* helpless.

hilfsbereit *adjective* helpful.

hilft SEE **helfen**.

Himbeere *die* (PL *die* **Himbeeren**) raspberry.

Himmel *der* (PL *die* **Himmel**) 1 sky; 2 heaven.

himmlisch *adjective* heavenly.

hin *adverb* 1 there; **hin und zurück** there and back; 2 **hin und wieder** now and again; 3 **hin und her** back

and forth, to and fro; 4 **auf meinen Rat hin** on my advice; **auf Ihren Brief hin** in reply to your letter; 5 **wo ist Dominik hin?** where's Dominik gone?; 6 **es ist nicht mehr lange hin** it's not long to go; 7 **ich bin hin** (*informal*) I'm worn out.

hinauf *adverb* up; **die Straße hinauf** up the road.

hinaufgehen ✧ *verb* (IMPERF **ging hinauf**, PERF **ist hinaufgegangen**) to go up.

hinaus *adverb* 1 out; 2 **auf Jahre hinaus** for years to come.

hinausgehen ✧ *verb* (IMPERF **ging hinaus**, PERF **ist hinausgegangen**) 1 to go out; 2 **über etwas hinausgehen** to exceed something; 3 **das Zimmer geht nach Norden hinaus** the room faces north.

hindern *verb* (PERF **hat gehindert**) to stop; **jemanden daran hindern, etwas zu tun** to stop somebody from doing something.

Hindernis *das* (PL *die* **Hindernisse**) obstacle.

hinduistisch *adjective* Hindu.

hindurch *adverb* 1 through it/them; 2 **das ganze Jahr hindurch** throughout the year.

hinein *adverb* 1 in; 2 **in etwas hinein** into something.

hineingehen ✧ *verb* (IMPERF **ging hinein**, PERF **ist hineingegangen**) 1 to go in; 2 **in etwas hineingehen** to go into something.

∆ NEW SPELLING: *See page xii*

hinfahren ◇ *verb* (PRES **fährt hin**, IMPERF **fuhr hin**, PERF **ist hingefahren**) **1** to go/drive there; **2** (PERF **hat hingefahren**) to take/drive there.

Hinfahrt *die* (PL *die* **Hinfahrten**) **1** journey there, way there; **2** outward journey.

hinfallen ◇ *verb* (PRES **fällt hin**, IMPERF **fiel hin**, PERF **ist hingefallen**) to fall over.

hing SEE **hängen**.

hingehen ◇ *verb* (IMPERF **ging hin**, PERF **ist hingegangen**) **1** to go there; **wo geht ihr hin?** where are you going?; **2** to go by (*of time*).

hinken *verb* (PERF **hat/ist gehinkt**) to limp.

hinkommen ◇ *verb* (IMPERF **kam hin**, PERF **ist hingekommen**) **1** to get there; **2** to go; **wo kommt das Buch hin?** where does the book go?; **3** **mit etwas hinkommen** (*informal*) to manage (with something).

hinlegen *verb* (PERF **hat hingelegt**) **1** to put down; **leg die Zeitung unten hin** put the paper down there; **2** **sich hinlegen** to lie down.

hinsetzen *verb* (PERF **hat sich hingesetzt**) **sich hinsetzen** to sit down; **Petra setzte sich neben ihm hin** Petra sat down next to him.

hinten *adverb* at the back; **von hinten** from behind.

hinter *preposition* ←(+DAT *or* +ACC) **1** behind; **2** **etwas hinter sich bringen** to get something over with.

hintere SEE **hinterer**.

hintereinander *adverb* **1** one behind the other; **2** one after the other; **dreimal hintereinander** three times in a row.

hinterer, hintere, hinteres *adjective* **1** back; **2** **am hinteren Ende** at the far end.

Hintergrund *der* (PL *die* **Hintergründe**) background.

hinterher *adverb* afterwards.

Hintern *der* (PL *die* **Hintern**) bottom.

Hinterrad *das* (PL *die* **Hinterräder**) back wheel.

hinters = hinter das.

hinüber *adverb* **1** over (there), across (there); **2** **das Radio ist hinüber** (*informal*) the radio has had it.

hinübergehen ◇ *verb* (IMPERF **ging hinüber**, PERF **ist hinübergegangen**) to go over, to go across.

hinunter *adverb* down.

Hinweg *der* (PL *die* **Hinwege**) way there; **auf dem Hinweg** on the way there.

Hinweis *der* (PL *die* **Hinweise**) **1** hint; **das war ein deutlicher Hinweis, dass er lieber allein fährt** it was an obvious hint that he prefers to go on his own; **2** reference; **3** **Hinweise zur Bedienung** operating instructions.

hinweisen ◇ *verb* (IMPERF **wies hin**, PERF **hat hingewiesen**) to point; **jemanden auf etwas hinweisen** to point something out to somebody.

Hirn *das* (PL *die* **Hirne**) brain.

◇ IRREGULAR VERB: *See the verb table in the centre of the dictionary*

Hirsch *der* (PL *die* Hirsche) 1 deer; 2 stag; 3 venison.

historisch *adjective* historical.

Hitze *die* heat.

hitzefrei *adjective* **hitzefrei haben** to have the day off school because of hot weather.

Hitzewelle *die* (PL *die* Hitzewellen) heatwave.

Hitzschlag *der* (PL *die* Hitzschläge) heatstroke.

hob SEE **heben**.

Hobby *das* (PL *die* Hobbys) hobby.

hoch *adjective* (*with endings 'hoch' becomes 'hoher/hohe/hohes'*) 1 high; **der Zaun ist zu hoch** the fence is too high; **ein hoher Zaun** a high fence; 2 deep (*snow*); 3 great (*age, weight*).
adverb 1 highly; **hoch begabt** highly gifted; 2 **die Treppe hoch** up the stairs.

Hoch *das* (PL *die* Hochs) 1 cheer; **ein dreifaches Hoch für das Geburtstagskind** three cheers for the birthday girl/boy; 2 high (*pressure*).

hochachtungsvoll *adverb* **Hochachtungsvoll** Yours faithfully.

hochhackig *adjective* high-heeled; **hochhackige Schuhe** high-heeled shoes.

Hochhaus *das* (PL *die* Hochhäuser) high-rise building.

hochheben ◇ *verb* (IMPERF **hob hoch**, PERF **hat hochgehoben**) to lift up; **sie hob das Kind hoch** she lifted up the child.

hochnäsig *adjective* stuck-up.

Hochschule *die* (PL *die* Hochschulen) university, college.

Hochsprung *der* (PL *die* Hochsprünge) high jump.

höchst *adverb* extremely.

höchstens *adverb* 1 at most; 2 except perhaps.

höchster, höchste, höchstes *adjective* highest; **Mount Everest ist der der höchste Berg der Welt** Mount Everest is the highest mountain in the world; **es ist höchste Zeit** it is high time.

Höchstgeschwindigkeit *die* maximum speed.

Höchsttemperatur *die* (PL *die* Höchsttemperaturen) maximum temperature.

Hochzeit *die* (PL *die* Hochzeiten) wedding.

Hochzeitstag *der* (PL *die* Hochzeitstage) 1 wedding day; 2 wedding anniversary.

Hocker *der* (PL *die* Hocker) stool.

Hockey *das* hockey.

Hockeyschläger *der* (PL *die* Hockeyschläger) hockey stick.

Hof *der* (PL *die* Höfe) 1 yard; 2 farm.

hoffen *verb* (PERF **hat gehofft**) to hope; **auf etwas hoffen** to hope for something.

hoffentlich *adverb* hopefully; **hoffentlich nicht** I hope not.

Hoffnung *die* (PL *die* Hoffnungen) hope.

△ NEW SPELLING: *See page xii*

hoffnungslos *adjective* hopeless.

höflich *adjective* polite.

Höflichkeit die (PL die Höflichkeiten) politeness, courtesy.

Höhe die (PL die Höhen) 1 height; **2 das ist die Höhe!** (*informal*) that's the limit!

hoher, hohe, hohes SEE hoch.

höher *adjective* 1 higher; 2 deeper.

hohl *adjective* hollow.

Höhle die (PL die Höhlen) 1 cave; 2 den.

holen *verb* (PERF hat geholt) 1 to get, to fetch; **2 jemanden holen lassen** to send for somebody; **3 sich etwas holen** to get something.

Holland das Holland.

Holländer der (PL die Holländer) Dutchman.

Holländerin die (PL die Holländerinnen) Dutchwoman.

holländisch *adjective* Dutch.

Hölle die (PL die Höllen) hell.

Holz das (PL die Hölzer) wood.

Holzkohle die charcoal.

homöopathisch *adjective* homeopathic.

homosexuell *adjective* homosexual.

Homosexuelle der/die (PL die Homosexuellen) homosexual.

Honig der (PL die Honige) honey.

horchen *verb* (PERF hat gehorcht) 1 to listen; 2 to eavesdrop.

hören *verb* (PERF hat gehört) 1 to hear; 2 to listen (to).

Hörer der (PL die Hörer) 1 listener; 2 receiver (*of a phone*).

Hörerin die (PL die Hörerinnen) listener.

Horizont der (PL die Horizonte) horizon.

Horn das (PL die Hörner) horn.

Horoskop das (PL die Horoskope) horoscope.

Hose die (PL die Hosen) trousers.

Hosenträger *plural noun* braces.

Hotel das (PL die Hotels) hotel.

Hotelverzeichnis das (PL die Hotelverzeichnisse) list of hotels.

hübsch *adjective* 1 pretty; 2 nice.

Hubschrauber der (PL die Hubschrauber) helicopter.

Huf der (PL die Hufe) hoof.

Hufeisen das (PL die Hufeisen) horseshoe.

Hüfte die (PL die Hüften) hip.

Hügel der (PL die Hügel) hill.

Huhn das (PL die Hühner) 1 chicken; 2 hen.

Hummel die (PL die Hummeln) bumble-bee.

Hummer der (PL die Hummer) lobster.

Humor der humour; **Humor haben** to have a sense of humour.

Hund der (PL die Hunde) dog.

✧ IRREGULAR VERB: *See the verb table in the centre of the dictionary*

Hundehütte *die* (PL *die* Hundehütten) kennel.

hundemüde *adjective* (*informal*) dog-tired.

hundert *number* a hundred, one hundred.

Hunger *der* hunger; **Hunger haben** to be hungry.

hungrig *adjective* hungry.

Hupe *die* (PL *die* Hupen) horn.

hurra *exclamation* hooray!

husten *verb* (PERF hat gehustet) to cough.

Husten *der* cough.

Hut *der* (PL *die* Hüte) hat.

hüten *verb* (PERF hat gehütet) **1** to look after (*a child, children*); **2 sich hüten** to be on your guard; **3 sich hüten, etwas zu tun** to take care not to do something.

Hütte *die* (PL *die* Hütten) hut.

hygienisch *adjective* hygienic.

hypnotisieren *verb* (PERF hat hypnotisiert) to hypnotize.

Hypothek *die* (PL *die* Hypotheken) mortgage.

hysterisch *adjective* hysterical.

I i

ich *pronoun* I.

IC-Zug *der* (PL *die* IC-Züge) (*Intercityzug*) intercity train.

ideal *adjective* ideal.

Idee *die* (PL *die* Ideen) idea.

identifizieren *verb* (PERF hat identifiziert) to identify.

identisch *adjective* identical.

Idiot *der* (PL *die* Idioten) idiot.

idiotisch *adjective* idiotic.

idyllisch *adjective* idyllic.

Igel *der* (PL *die* Igel) hedgehog.

ihm *pronoun* **1** him, to him; **2** it, to it.

ihn *pronoun* **1** him; **2** it.

ihnen *pronoun* them, to them.

ihr *pronoun* **1** you (*plural*); **2** her, to her; **3** (*standing for an object*) it, to it.
adjective **1** her; **2** its; **3** their; **sie haben ihr Auto verkauft** they sold their car.

Ihr *adjective* your; **Ihr Sohn hat mir geschrieben** your son wrote to me.

ihrer, ihre, ihr(e)s *pronoun* **1** hers; **mein Rad ist rot, ihrs ist blau** my bike is red, hers is blue; **2** theirs; **das ist nicht ihre Katze, ihre ist**

△ NEW SPELLING: *See page* xii

schwarz that's not their cat, theirs is black.

Ihrer, Ihre, Ihr(e)s pronoun yours; mein Job ist nicht so interessant wie Ihrer my job's not as interesting as yours.

ihretwegen adverb 1 for her sake; 2 for their sake; 3 because of her; 4 because of them.

Ihretwegen adverb 1 for your sake; 2 because of you.

Illusion die (PL die Illusionen) illusion.

Illustration die (PL die Illustrationen) illustration.

Illustrierte die (PL die Illustrierten) magazine.

im = in dem; was läuft im Kino? what's on at the cinema?; im August in August.

Imbiss △ der (PL die Imbisse) 1 snack; 2 snack bar.

Imbissstube △ die (PL die Imbissstuben) snack bar.

imitieren verb (PERF hat imitiert) to imitate.

immer adverb 1 always; 2 immer wieder again and again; 3 immer mehr more and more; immer dunkler darker and darker; 4 immer noch still; 5 immer, wenn er anruft every time he rings; 6 wo/wer/wann immer wherever/whoever/whenever; 7 für immer for ever.

immerhin adverb at least.

immerzu adverb all the time.

impfen verb (PERF hat geimpft) to vaccinate.

Impfung die (PL die Impfungen) vaccination.

imponieren verb (PERF hat imponiert) to impress; jemandem imponieren to impress somebody.

Import der (PL die Importe) import.

importieren verb (PERF hat importiert) to import.

imprägniert adjective waterproof.

imstande adverb imstande sein, etwas zu tun to be able to do something; er ist nicht imstande, seine Hausaufgaben allein zu machen he's not able to do his homework on his own.

in preposition ←(+DAT or +ACC) (the dative is used when talking about position; the accusative shows movement towards something) 1 in; es ist in der Küche it's in the kitchen; 2 into, in; ich habe es in meine Tasche gesteckt I've put it in my bag; 3 in die Schule gehen to go to school; 4 Susi ist in die Schule Susi is at school; 5 in diesem Jahr this year; 6 in sein to be in; der Rap ist in rap is in.

inbegriffen adjective included; Essen ist inbegriffen food is included.

indem conjunction 1 while; 2 by.

Inder der (PL die Inder) Indian.

Inderin die (PL die Inderinnen) Indian.

Indianer der (PL die Indianer)

◇ IRREGULAR VERB: See the verb table in the centre of the dictionary

(American) Indian, native American.

Indianerin die (PL die **Indianerinnen**) (American) Indian, native American.

indianisch adjective (American) Indian, native American.

Indien das India.

indisch adjective Indian.

indiskutabel adjective out of the question.

individuell adjective individual.

Individuum das (PL die **Individuen**) individual.

Industrie die (PL die **Industrien**) industry.

industriell adjective industrial.

Infektion die (PL die **Infektionen**) infection.

Infinitiv der (PL die **Infinitive**) infinitive.

infizieren verb (PERF hat infiziert) 1 to infect; 2 **sich bei jemandem infizieren** to be infected by somebody.

infolge preposition ←(+GEN) as a result of.

infolgedessen adverb consequently.

Informatik die computer science.

Informatiker der (PL die **Informatiker**) computer scientist.

Informatikerin die (PL die **Informatikerinnen**) computer scientist.

Information die (PL die **Informationen**) (piece of) information.

Informationsbüro das (PL die **Informationsbüros**) (tourist) information office.

informieren verb (PERF hat informiert) 1 to inform; 2 **informiert sein** to be aware; **da bist du falsch informiert** you've been wrongly informed; 3 **sich über etwas informieren** to find out about something; **ich habe mich darüber genau informieren lassen** I found out all about it.

Ingenieur der (PL die **Ingenieure**) engineer.

Ingenieurin die (PL die **Ingenieurinnen**) engineer.

Ingwer der ginger.

Inhaber der (PL die **Inhaber**) 1 owner (of a shop); 2 holder (of an office).

Inhaberin die (PL die **Inhaberinnen**) 1 owner (of a shop); 2 holder (of a position).

Inhalt der (PL die **Inhalte**) 1 contents; **den Inhalt der Dose mit etwas Wasser verdünnen** dilute the contents of the tin with a little water; 2 content (of a story, film); **er hat uns eine kurze Zusammenfassung des Inhalts der Geschichte gegeben** he gave us a quick summary of the content of the story; 3 volume; 4 area (of a rectangle, circle, etc.).

△ NEW SPELLING: See page xii

inklusive preposition ←(+GEN)
including.
adverb inclusive.

innen adverb inside; **nach innen**
inwards.

Innenstadt die (PL die Innenstädte)
town centre, city centre.

Innere das 1 interior; 2 inside.

innerer, innere, inneres
adjective 1 inner; 2 inside;
3 internal (injuries).

innerhalb preposition ←(+GEN)
1 within; 2 during.
adverb **innerhalb von** within.

innerlich adjective 1 internal;
2 inner.
adverb 1 internally; 2 inwardly.

ins = in das; **ins Theater gehen** to go
to the theatre.

Insekt das (PL die Insekten) insect.

Insel die (PL die Inseln) island.

Inserat das (PL die Inserate)
advertisement.

inserieren verb (PERF hat inseriert)
to advertise.

insgesamt adverb in all.

Instinkt der (PL die Instinkte)
instinct.

instinktiv adjective instinctive.

Instrument das (PL die
Instrumente) instrument.

intelligent adjective intelligent.

Intelligenz die intelligence.

Intercityzug der (PL die
Intercityzüge) intercity train.

interessant adjective interesting.

Interesse das (PL die Interessen)
interest.

interessieren verb (PERF hat
interessiert) 1 to interest; 2 sich
für etwas interessieren to be
interested in something.

Internat das (PL die Internate)
boarding school.

international adjective
international.

Internet das internet.

Interview das (PL die Interviews)
interview.

inzwischen adverb in the
meantime, meanwhile.

Ire der (PL die Iren) Irishman; **die Iren**
the Irish.

irgend adverb 1 at all; **wenn irgend
möglich** if at all possible; **wenn du
irgend kannst** if you could possibly
manage it; 2 **irgend so ein Idiot**
some such idiot.

irgendein adjective 1 some; 2 any;
3 **irgendein anderer** someone else,
anyone else.

**irgendeiner, irgendeine,
irgendein(e)s** pronoun 1 any
one; **'welche möchten Sie?' –
'irgendeine'** 'which one would you
like?' – 'any one'; 2 somebody,
someone; 3 anybody, anyone; **hat
irgendeiner angerufen?** has
anybody phoned?

◇ IRREGULAR VERB: See the verb table in the centre of the dictionary

irgendetwas ∆ *pronoun*
1 something; 2 anything.

irgendjemand ∆ *pronoun*
1 somebody; 2 anybody, anyone.

irgendwann *adverb* 1 some time, at
some time; 2 any time, at any time.

irgendwas (*informal*) =
irgendetwas.

irgendwie *adverb* somehow.

irgendwo *adverb* 1 somewhere;
2 anywhere.

Irin *die* (PL die **Irinnen**) Irishwoman.

irisch *adjective* Irish.

Irland *das* Ireland.

ironisch *adjective* ironic.

irre *adjective* 1 mad; 2 (*informal*)
incredible, fantastic (*party, song*).
adverb **irre gut** incredibly good.

irren *verb* (PERF **ist geirrt**) 1 to
wander (about) (*when lost*); 2 (PERF
hat sich geirrt) **sich irren** to be
mistaken, to be wrong.

irrsinnig *adjective* 1 mad;
2 (*informal*) incredible.

Irrtum *der* (PL die **Irrtümer**) mistake.

Islam *der* Islam.

isst ∆ SEE essen.

ist SEE sein.

Italien *das* Italy.

Italiener *der* (PL die **Italiener**)
Italian.

Italienerin *die* (PL die
Italienerinnen) Italian.

italienisch *adjective* Italian.

J j

ja *adverb* 1 yes; 2 **ich glaube ja** I
think so; 3 **du kommst doch, ja?**
you'll come, won't you?; **es passt
doch, ja?** it fits, doesn't it?; 4 **sag's
ihm ja nicht!** don't (you dare) tell
him, whatever you do!; **seid ja
vorsichtig!** do be careful!; 5 **es ist
ja noch früh** it's still early; **ich kann
ihn ja mal fragen, ob er mitkommen
will** I could always ask him if he
wants to come.

Jacht *die* (PL die **Jachten**) yacht.

Jacke *die* (PL die **Jacken**) 1 jacket;
2 cardigan.

Jackett *das* (PL die **Jacketts**) jacket.

Jagd *die* (PL die **Jagden**) 1 hunt;
2 hunting.

jagen *verb* (PERF **hat gejagt**) 1 to
hunt; 2 to chase; **drei Polizisten
jagten den Einbrecher, aber er
hängte sie schnell ab** three
policemen chased the burglar, but he
soon shook them off; **meine Mutter
hat mich aus dem Bett gejagt**
(*informal*) my mother chased me
out of bed; 3 **jemanden aus dem
Haus jagen** to throw somebody out
of the house; 4 **damit kannst du
mich jagen** (*informal*) I can't stand
that.

Jahr *das* (PL die **Jahre**) year; **in den
sechziger Jahren** in the sixties;

∆ NEW SPELLING: *See page xii*

Kinder bis zu zwölf Jahren children up to the age of twelve.

jahrelang *adverb* for years.

Jahrestag *der* (PL *die* **Jahrestage**) anniversary.

Jahreszeit *die* (PL *die* **Jahreszeiten**) season.

Jahrgang *der* (PL *die* **Jahrgänge**) 1 year; 2 vintage.

Jahrhundert *das* (PL *die* **Jahrhunderte**) century.

jährlich *adjective, adverb* yearly; zweimal jährlich twice a year.

Jahrmarkt *der* (PL *die* **Jahrmärkte**) fair.

Jahrtausend *das* (PL *die* **Jahrtausende**) millennium.

Jahrzehnt *das* (PL *die* **Jahrzehnte**) decade.

jähzornig *adjective* hot-tempered.

jammern *verb* (PERF **hat gejammert**) to moan.

Januar *der* January.

Japan *das* Japan.

Japaner *der* (PL *die* **Japaner**) Japanese.

/ **Japanerin** *die* (PL *die* **Japanerinnen**) Japanese.

japanisch *adjective* Japanese.

jawohl *adverb* 1 yes; 2 certainly.

je *adverb* 1 ever; besser denn je better than ever; 2 each; sie kosten je zwanzig Mark they are twenty marks each; 3 seit eh und je always; 4 je nach depending on.

preposition ←(+ACC) per.
conjunction 1 je mehr, desto besser the more the better; 2 je nachdem it depends.

Jeans *plural noun* jeans.

jede SEE **jeder**.

jeder, jede, jedes *adjective* 1 every; jedes Mal △ every time; 2 each; 3 any; ohne jeden Grund without any reason. *pronoun* 1 everybody, everyone; 2 each one; 3 anybody, anyone; das kann jeder anybody can do that.

jedermann *pronoun* everybody, everyone.

jederzeit *adverb* at any time.

jedes SEE **jeder**.

jedesmal SEE **jeder**.

jedoch *adverb* however.

jemals *adverb* ever.

jemand *pronoun* 1 somebody, someone; jemand hat das für dich abgegeben sombody left this for you; 2 anybody, anyone; hat jemand angerufen? did anybody call?

jener, jene, jenes *adjective* (used in elevated language and in literature) 1 that; 2 those (*plural*). *pronoun* 1 that one; 2 those (*plural*).

jenseits *preposition* ←(+GEN) (on) the other side of.

jetzt *adverb* now.

◇ IRREGULAR VERB: *See the verb table in the centre of the dictionary*

Job der (PL die Jobs) job.

jobben verb (informal) (PERF hat gejobbt) to work.

joggen verb (PERF ist gejoggt) to jog.

Jogginganzug der (PL die Jogginganzüge) tracksuit.

Joghurt der (PL die Joghurt) yoghurt.

Johannisbeere die (PL die Johannisbeeren) 1 rote Johannisbeeren redcurrants; 2 schwarze Johannisbeeren blackcurrants.

Journalist der (PL die Journalisten) journalist.

Journalistin die (PL die Journalistinnen) journalist.

jubeln verb (PERF hat gejubelt) 1 to cheer; 2 Beifall jubeln to applaud.

Jubiläum das (PL die Jubiläen) 1 anniversary; 2 jubilee.

Jude der (PL die Juden) Jew.

Jüdin die (PL die Jüdinnen) Jew.

jüdisch adjective Jewish.

Jugend die youth.

Jugendherberge die (PL die Jugendherbergen) youth hostel.

Jugendklub der (PL die Jugendklubs) youth club.

Jugendliche der/die (PL die Jugendlichen) 1 young man/woman; 2 die Jugendlichen youth, young people.

Jugoslawien das Yugoslavia.

jugoslawisch adjective Yugoslavian.

Juli der July.

jung adjective 1 young; 2 Jung und Alt△ young and old.

Junge[1] der (PL die Jungen) boy.

Junge[2] das (PL die Jungen) young (animal).

Jungfrau die (PL die Jungfrauen) 1 virgin; 2 Virgo.

jüngster, jüngste, jüngstes adjective 1 youngest; 2 latest (news, developments); 3 in jüngster Zeit recently.

Juni der June.

Jury die (PL die Jurys) 1 jury; 2 judges (in sport).

Juwelier der (PL die Juweliere) jeweller.

Jux der (informal) laugh; aus Jux for a laugh.

K k

Kabel das (PL die Kabel) 1 cable; 2 wire.

Kabelfernsehen das cable television.

Kabeljau der (PL die Kabeljaus) cod.

Kabine die (PL die Kabinen) 1 cabin; 2 cubicle (for changing); 3 car (of a cable car).

Kachel die (PL die Kacheln) tile.

△ NEW SPELLING: See page xii

Käfer der (PL die **Käfer**) beetle.

Kaffee der (PL die **Kaffee(s)**) coffee; **zwei Kaffee mit Milch bitte** two white coffees please.

Kaffeekanne die (PL die **Kaffeekannen**) coffee-pot.

Käfig der (PL die **Käfige**) cage.

kahl adjective 1 bald (head); 2 bare (tree, walls).

Kaiser der (PL die **Kaiser**) emperor.

Kaiserin die (PL die **Kaiserinnen**) empress.

Kakao der (PL die **Kakao(s)**) cocoa; **zwei Kakao bitte** two cups of cocoa please.

Kakerlak der (PL die **Kakerlaken**) cockroach.

Kaktus der (PL die **Kakteen**) cactus.

Kalb das (PL die **Kälber**) 1 calf; 2 veal.

Kalbfleisch das veal.

Kalender der (PL die **Kalender**) 1 calendar; 2 diary.

Kalk der 1 lime; 2 limescale; 3 calcium.

Kalorie die (PL die **Kalorien**) calorie.

kalorienarm adjective low-calorie.

kalt adjective cold; **ist dir kalt?** are you cold?; **stell die Heizung an, den Kindern ist kalt** put on the heating, the children are cold; **abends essen wir kalt** we have a cold meal in the evening; **den Wein kalt stellen** to chill the wine.

Kälte die 1 cold; 2 coldness; 3 **fünf Grad Kälte** five degrees below zero.

kam SEE **kommen**.

Kamel das (PL die **Kamele**) camel.

Kamera die (PL die **Kameras**) camera.

Kamerad der (PL die **Kameraden**) friend.

Kameramann der (PL die **Kameramänner**) cameraman.

Kamin der (PL die **Kamine**) fireplace; **wir saßen am Kamin** we sat by the fire.

Kamm der (PL die **Kämme**) 1 comb; 2 ridge (of a mountain).

kämmen verb (PERF hat **gekämmt**) 1 to comb; 2 **sich kämmen** to comb your hair.

Kammer die (PL die **Kammern**) 1 store room; 2 chamber.

Kampf der (PL die **Kämpfe**) 1 fight; 2 contest; 3 struggle.

kämpfen verb (PERF hat **gekämpft**) to fight.

Kanada das Canada.

Kanadier der (PL die **Kanadier**) Canadian.

Kanadierin die (PL die **Kanadierinnen**) Canadian.

kanadisch adjective Canadian.

Kanal der (PL die **Kanäle**) 1 canal; 2 channel (radio, TV); 3 **der Kanal** the (English) Channel; 4 sewer, drain.

Kanalinseln plural noun Channel Islands.

✧ IRREGULAR VERB: *See the verb table in the centre of the dictionary*

Kanalisation *die* sewers, drains.

Kanarienvogel *der* (PL *die* Kanarienvögel) canary.

Kandidat *der* (PL *die* Kandidaten) candidate.

Kandidatin *die* (PL *die* Kandidatinnen) candidate.

Känguru △ *das* (PL *die* Kängurus) kangaroo.

Kaninchen *das* (PL *die* Kaninchen) rabbit.

kann SEE **können**.

Kännchen *das* (PL *die* Kännchen) 1 pot; **ein Kännchen Kaffee bitte** a pot of coffee please; 2 jug (*of milk*).

Kanne *die* (PL *die* Kannen) 1 pot (*for coffee, tea*); 2 jug (*for water*); 3 can (*for oil*); 4 churn (*for milk*); 5 watering can.

kannst SEE **können**.

kannte SEE **kennen**.

Kante *die* (PL *die* Kanten) edge.

Kantine *die* (PL *die* Kantinen) canteen; **wir essen immer in der Kantine zu Mittag** we always have lunch in the canteen.

Kanu *das* (PL *die* Kanus) canoe; **Kanu fahren** to go canoeing.

Kapelle *die* (PL *die* Kapellen) chapel.

kapieren *verb* (*informal*) (PERF hat kapiert) to understand; **er hat es mir schon dreimal erklärt, aber ich kapier es einfach nicht** he's already explained it to me three times, but I still don't get it.

Kapital *das* capital.

Kapitalismus *der* capitalism.

Kapitän *der* (PL *die* Kapitäne) captain.

Kapitel *das* (PL *die* Kapitel) chapter.

Kappe *die* (PL *die* Kappen) cap.

kaputt *adjective* 1 broken; 2 **an meinem Computer ist etwas kaputt** there's something wrong with my computer; 3 **ich bin kaputt** (*informal*) I'm shattered.

kaputtgehen ✧ *verb* (IMPERF ging kaputt, PERF ist kaputtgegangen) 1 to break; 2 to pack up; **mein Fernseher ist mitten im Fußballspiel kaputtgegangen** the television packed up in the middle of the football match; 3 to wear out (*of clothing*); 4 to break up (*of a marriage or friendship*).

kaputtmachen *verb* (PERF hat kaputtgemacht) 1 to break; **er macht alle seine Spielsachen kaputt** he breaks all his toys; 2 to ruin (*clothes, furniture*); 3 to finish off (*a person*); **die viele Arbeit macht mich ganz kaputt** all this work is wearing me out; 4 **sich kaputtmachen** to wear yourself out.

Kapuze *die* (PL *die* Kapuzen) hood.

Karamell △ *der* (PL *die* Karamells) caramel.

Karfreitag *der* Good Friday.

Karibik *die* **die Karibik** the Caribbean.

karibisch *adjective* Caribbean.

kariert *adjective* 1 check; **ein**

△ NEW SPELLING: *See page xii*

karierter Rock a check skirt;
2 squared (*paper*).

Karneval der (PL die **Karnevale**)
carnival.

Karo das (PL die **Karos**) **1** square;
2 diamonds (*in cards*).

Karotte die (PL die **Karotten**) carrot.

Karriere die (PL die **Karrieren**)
career; **Karriere machen** to get to
the top.

Karte die (PL die **Karten**) **1** card; **ich
schicke euch eine Karte aus
Italien** I'll send you a card from
Italy; **2** card (*for playing*); **wir haben
den ganzen Abend Karten gespielt**
we played cards all evening;
gute/schlechte Karten haben to
have a good/bad hand; **3** ticket; **gibt
es noch Karten für das
Popfestival?** can you still get tickets
for the pop festival?; **4** menu; **5** map;
**ich kann Oberammergau nicht auf
der Karte finden** I can't find
Oberammergau on the map; **6 alles
auf eine Karte setzen** to put all your
eggs in one basket.

Kartenspiel das (PL die
Kartenspiele) **1** card game; **2** pack
of cards.

Kartoffel die (PL die **Kartoffeln**)
potato.

Kartoffelbrei der mashed
potatoes.

Karton der (PL die **Kartons**)
1 cardboard; **2** cardboard box.

Karussell das (PL die **Karussells**)
merry-go-round; **Karussell fahren**
to go on the merry-go-round.

Käse der cheese.

Käsekuchen der (PL die
Käsekuchen) cheesecake.

Kasse die (PL die **Kassen**) **1** till;
2 checkout; **an der Kasse zahlen**
pay at the checkout; **3** cash desk (*in
a bank*); **4** box-office; **Sie können
die Karten an der Kasse abholen**
you can collect the tickets from the
box office; **5** ticket office (*at a sports
stadium*); **Sie müssen sich an der
Kasse anstellen** you have to queue
at the ticket office; **6** health
insurance; **7 knapp bei Kasse sein**
(*informal*) to be short of money; **gut
bei Kasse sein** (*informal*) to be in
the money.

Kassenzettel der (PL die
Kassenzettel) receipt.

Kassette die (PL die **Kassetten**)
1 cassette, tape; **ich habe den neuen
Song auf Kassette aufgenommen**
I've taped the new song; **2** box (*for
money, jewellery*).

Kassettenrekorder der (PL die
Kassettenrekorder) cassette
recorder.

kassieren verb (PERF hat kassiert)
1 to collect the money; **2** to collect
the fares; **3 wie viel hat er kassiert?**
how much did he charge you?;
4 darf ich bei Ihnen kassieren?
would you like to pay now? (*your bill
in a restaurant*); **5** (*informal*) to take
away (*a driving licence, for
example*).

Kassierer der (PL die **Kassierer**)
cashier.

◇ IRREGULAR VERB: *See the verb table in the centre of the dictionary*

Kassiererin die (PL die Kassiererinnen) cashier.

Kastanie die (PL die Kastanien) chestnut.

Kasten der (PL die Kästen) 1 box; 2 crate; **ein Kasten Bier** a crate of beer; 3 bin; 4 letter-box; 5 **was auf dem Kasten haben** (informal) to be brainy.

Katalog der (PL die Kataloge) catalogue.

Katalysator der (PL die Katalysatoren) catalytic converter.

Katastrophe die (PL die Katastrophen) catastrophe.

katastrophal adjective, adverb 1 catastrophic; 2 **sie hat katastrophal schlecht abgeschnitten** she came out terribly badly.

Kategorie die (PL die Kategorien) category.

Kater der (PL die Kater) 1 tom-cat; 2 **einen Kater haben** (informal) to have a hangover.

Kathedrale die (PL die Kathedralen) cathedral.

Katholik der (PL die Katholiken) Catholic.

Katholikin die (PL die Katholikinnen) Catholic.

katholisch adjective Catholic.

Kätzchen das (PL die Kätzchen) kitten.

Katze die (PL die Katzen) cat.

kauen verb (PERF hat gekaut) to chew.

Kauf der (PL die Käufe) 1 purchase; 2 **ein guter Kauf** a bargain; 3 **etwas in Kauf nehmen** to put up with something.

kaufen verb (PERF hat gekauft) to buy.

Käufer der (PL die Käufer) buyer.

Käuferin die (PL die Käuferinnen) buyer.

Kauffrau die (PL die Kauffrauen) businesswoman.

Kaufhaus das (PL die Kaufhäuser) department store.

Kaufmann der (PL die Kaufleute) businessman.

Kaugummi der (PL die Kaugummis) chewing gum.

kaum adverb hardly, scarcely.

kauern verb (PERF hat gekauert) to crouch.

Kaution die (PL die Kautionen) 1 deposit; 2 bail.

Kegel der (PL die Kegel) 1 cone; 2 skittle.

Kegelbahn die skittle alley.

kegeln verb (PERF hat gekegelt) to play skittles.

Kehle die (PL die Kehlen) throat.

Keim der (PL die Keime) 1 shoot; 2 germ.

kein adjective 1 no; **auf keinen Fall** on no account; 2 **ich habe keine Zeit** I haven't got any time; **er hat**

△ NEW SPELLING: See page xii

kein Geld he hasn't got any money;
3 keine zehn Minuten less than ten
minutes.

keiner, keine, kein(e)s *pronoun*
1 nobody, no one; **2** none, not one;
**3 von diesen Kleidern gefällt mir
keins** I don't like any of these
dresses; **4 keiner von beiden**
neither (of them).

keinesfalls *adverb* on no account.

keineswegs *adverb* by no means.

keinmal *adverb* not once.

keins SEE **keiner**.

Keks *der* (PL *die* **Kekse**) biscuit.

Keller *der* (PL *die* **Keller**) cellar.

Kellergeschoss△ *das* (PL *die*
Kellergeschosse) basement.

Kellner *der* (PL *die* **Kellner**) waiter.

Kellnerin *die* (PL *die* **Kellnerinnen**)
waitress.

kennen ◇ *verb* (IMPERF **kannte**, PERF
hat gekannt) **1** to know; **2 kennen
lernen**△ to get to know; **sich kennen
lernen** to get to know each other;
3 kennen lernen△ to meet; **ich habe
Ulrike in London kennen gelernt** I
met Ulrike in London; **wo habt ihr
euch kennen gelernt?** where did
you meet?

kennenlernen SEE **kennen**.

Kenntnis *die* (PL *die* **Kenntnisse**)
1 knowledge; **2 etwas zur Kenntnis
nehmen** to take note of something.

Kennzeichen *das* (PL *die*
Kennzeichen) **1** mark;

2 characteristic; **3** registration
(number) (*of a vehicle*).

Kerl *der* (PL *die* **Kerle**) **1** bloke; **2 Eva
ist ein netter Kerl** Eva's a nice girl.

Kern *der* (PL *die* **Kerne**) **1** pip;
2 stone (*of an apricot, peach*);
3 kernel (*of a nut*).

Kernenergie *die* nuclear power.

Kernkraftwerk *das* (PL *die*
Kernkraftwerke) nuclear power
station.

Kernwaffen *plural noun* nuclear
weapons.

Kerze *die* (PL *die* **Kerzen**) candle.

Kerzenhalter *der* (PL *die*
Kerzenhalter) candlestick.

Kessel *der* (PL *die* **Kessel**) **1** kettle;
2 boiler.

Kette *die* (PL *die* **Ketten**) chain.

Keule *die* (PL *die* **Keulen**) **1** club;
2 leg (*of lamb*); **3** drumstick (*of
chicken*).

kichern *verb* (PERF **hat gekichert**) to
giggle.

Kiefer[1] *der* (PL *die* **Kiefer**) jaw.

Kiefer[2] *die* (PL *die* **Kiefern**) pine tree.

Kieselstein *der* (PL *die*
Kieselsteine) pebble.

Kilo *das* (PL *die* **Kilo(s)**) kilo.

Kilogramm *das* (PL *die*
Kilogramme) kilogram.

Kilometer *der* (PL *die* **Kilometer**)
kilometre.

Kind *das* (PL *die* **Kinder**) child.

◇ IRREGULAR VERB: *See the verb table in the centre of the dictionary*

Kindergarten der (PL die Kindergärten) nursery school.

Kindergeld das child benefit.

kinderleicht adjective very easy; das ist kinderleicht it's child's play.

Kindertagesstätte die (PL die Kindertagesstätten) day nursery.

Kinderwagen der (PL die Kinderwagen) pram.

Kindheit die childhood.

kindisch adjective childish.

Kinn das (PL die Kinne) chin.

Kino das (PL die Kinos) cinema.

kippen verb (PERF hat gekippt) 1 to tip; 2 (PERF ist gekippt) to topple.

Kirche die (PL die Kirchen) church.

Kirsche die (PL die Kirschen) cherry.

Kissen das (PL die Kissen) 1 cushion; 2 pillow.

Kiste die (PL die Kisten) 1 crate; 2 box.

kitzeln verb (PERF hat gekitzelt) to tickle.

kitzlig adjective ticklish.

Kiwi die (PL die Kiwis) kiwi fruit.

klagen verb (PERF hat geklagt) to complain.

Klammer die (PL die Klammern) 1 peg (for washing); 2 grip (for hair); 3 bracket.

klang SEE **klingen**.

Klang der (PL die Klänge) sound.

Klappe die (PL die Klappen) 1 flap;

2 clapperboard; 3 (informal) trap (mouth); halt die Klappe! shut up!

klappen verb (PERF hat geklappt) 1 nach vorne klappen to tilt forward; 2 nach hinten klappen to tip back; 3 nach oben klappen to lift up; 4 nach unten klappen to put down; 5 to work out; hoffentlich klappt es I hope it'll work out.

Klappstuhl der (PL die Klappstühle) folding chair.

klar adjective 1 clear (water, answer); klar werden △ to become clear; 2 jetzt ist mir alles klar now I understand; 3 sich klar werden △ to make up your mind; 4 sich über etwas im Klaren sein △ to realize something.
adverb clearly; na klar! (informal) of course!

klären verb (PERF hat geklärt) 1 to clarify; 2 to sort out; 3 to purify (sewage); 4 sich klären to clear (of the weather or the sky); 5 sich klären to resolve itself, to be settled.

Klarinette die (PL die Klarinetten) clarinet.

klarwerden SEE **klar**.

klasse adjective (informal) great, smashing.

Klasse die (PL die Klassen) 1 class; erster Klasse reisen to travel first class; 2 year; in die sechste Klasse gehen to be in year six.

Klassenarbeit die (PL die Klassenarbeiten) (written) test.

Klassenbuch das register (kept by

the teacher, it also contains notes about students' achievements).

Klassenkamerad der (PL die Klassenkameraden) class-mate.

Klassenkameradin die (PL die Klassenkameradinnen) class-mate.

Klassensprecher der (PL die Klassenprecher) class representative.

Klassensprecherin die (PL die Klassensprecherinnen) class representative.

Klassenzimmer das (PL die Klassenzimmer) classroom.

klassisch adjective classical.

Klatsch der gossip.

klatschen verb (PERF hat geklatscht) 1 to clap; jemandem Beifall klatschen to applaud somebody; 2 to slap; 3 to gossip.

klauen verb (informal) (PERF hat geklaut) to pinch.

Klavier das (PL die Klaviere) piano.

kleben verb (PERF hat geklebt) 1 to stick; 2 to glue; 3 jemandem eine kleben (informal) to belt somebody one.

klebrig adjective sticky.

Klebstoff der (PL die Klebstoffe) glue.

Klebstreifen der (PL die Klebstreifen) sticky tape.

Klecks der (PL die Kleckse) stain.

Kleid das (PL die Kleider) 1 dress;

Uschi hat sich zwei neue Kleider gekauft Uschi bought two new dresses; 2 **Kleider** clothes.

Kleiderbügel der (PL die Kleiderbügel) coat hanger.

Kleiderschrank der (PL die Kleiderschränke) wardrobe.

Kleidung die clothes, clothing.

klein adjective 1 small, little; etwas klein schneiden △ to cut something up small; 2 short; Peter ist kleiner als Klaus Peter is shorter than Klaus.

Kleingeld das change.

Klempner der (PL die Klempner) plumber.

klettern verb (PERF ist geklettert) to climb.

Klima das (PL die Klimas) climate.

Klimaanlage die (PL die Klimaanlagen) air conditioning.

Klinge die (PL die Klingen) blade.

Klingel die (PL die Klingeln) bell.

klingeln verb (PERF hat geklingelt) to ring; es klingelt there's a ring at the door.

klingen ◇ verb (IMPERF klang, PERF hat geklungen) to sound.

Klinik die (PL die Kliniken) clinic.

Klinke die (PL die Klinken) handle.

Klippe die (PL die Klippen) rock.

Klo das (informal) (PL die Klos) loo.

klopfen verb (PERF hat geklopft) 1 to knock; 2 to beat.

◇ IRREGULAR VERB: See the verb table in the centre of the dictionary

Klosett das (PL die Klosetts) lavatory.

Kloster das (PL die Kloster) 1 monastery; 2 convent.

Klotz der (PL die Klötze) block.

Klub der (PL die Klubs) club.

klug adjective 1 clever; 2 **ich werde daraus nicht klug** I don't understand it.

Klugheit die cleverness.

Klumpen der (PL die Klumpen) lump.

knabbern verb (PERF hat geknabbert) to nibble.

Knäckebrot das (PL die Knäckebrote) crispbread.

knacken verb (PERF hat geknackt) to crack.

Knall der (PL die Knalle) bang.

knallen verb (PERF hat geknallt) 1 to go bang; 2 to pop (of a cork); 3 to slam (of a door); 4 to crack (of a whip).

knapp adjective 1 scarce; 2 tight (skirt, top); 3 **knapp bei Kasse sein** to be short of money; 4 **mit knapper Mehrheit** by a narrow majority; 5 just; **eine knappe Stunde** just under an hour; **sie haben knapp verloren** they only just lost; 6 **das war knapp** (informal) that was a close shave.

knarren verb (PERF hat geknarrt) to creak.

Knauf der (PL die Knäufe) knob.

knautschen verb (PERF hat geknautscht) 1 to crumple; 2 to crease.

kneifen ◇ verb (IMPERF kniff, PERF hat gekniffen) 1 to pinch; 2 (informal) to chicken out; **sie hat mal wieder gekniffen und nichts gesagt** she's chickened out yet again and didn't say anything.

Kneipe die (PL die Kneipen) pub.

kneten verb (PERF hat geknetet) to knead.

knicken verb (PERF hat geknickt) 1 to bend; 2 to fold.

Knie das (PL die Knie) knee.

knien verb (PERF hat gekniet) 1 to kneel; 2 **sich knien** to kneel down.

kniff SEE kneifen.

knipsen verb (PERF hat geknipst) (to photograph) to take a snap, to take snaps.

Knoblauch der garlic.

Knoblauchzehe die (PL die Knoblauchzehen) clove of garlic.

Knöchel der (PL die Knöchel) 1 ankle; 2 knuckle; **Mario hat sich beim Jogging den Knöchel verstaucht** Mario sprained his ankle when jogging.

Knochen der (PL die Knochen) bone.

Knopf der (PL die Knöpfe) button.

Knoten der (PL die Knoten) 1 knot; 2 bun (as a hairstyle); 3 lump.

knurren verb (PERF hat geknurrt) 1 to growl; 2 to rumble; 3 to grumble.

knusprig adjective crisp, crusty (bread).

△ NEW SPELLING: See page xii

Koch der (PL die Köche) 1 cook; 2 chef.

Kochbuch das (PL die Kochbücher) cookery book.

kochen verb (PERF hat gekocht) 1 to cook; 2 to boil; **das Wasser kocht** the water's boiling.

Köchin die (PL die Köchinnen) cook.

Kochtopf der (PL die Kochtöpfe) saucepan.

Koffer der (PL die Koffer) suitcase.

Kofferkuli der (PL die Kofferkulis) baggage trolley.

Kofferraum der (PL die Kofferräume) boot.

Kohl der 1 cabbage; 2 (informal) rubbish; **rede keinen Kohl** don't talk rubbish.

Kohle die (PL die Kohlen) coal.

Kokosnuss ∆ die (PL die Kokosnüsse) coconut.

Kollege der (PL die Kollegen) colleague.

Kollegin die (PL die Kolleginnen) colleague.

Köln das Cologne.

Kölnischwasser das eau de cologne.

Kombination die (PL die Kombinationen) combination.

Komfort der comfort.

Komiker der (PL die Komiker) comedian.

komisch adjective funny.

Komma das (PL die Kommas) 1 comma; 2 decimal point; **zwei Komma fünf** two point five.

kommen ◇ verb (IMPERF kam, PERF ist gekommen) 1 to come; 2 to get; **wie komme ich zur U-Bahn?** how do I get to the tube station?; **kommt gut nach Hause!** have a safe journey home!; 3 **etwas kommen lassen** to send for something; 4 **wie kommst du darauf?** what gave you that idea?; 5 **hinter etwas kommen** to find out about something; 6 **zur Schule kommen** to start school; 7 to go; **die Gabeln kommen in die Schublade** the forks go in the drawer; **ins Krankenhaus kommen** to go to hospital; 8 **wer kommt zuerst?** who's first?; **du kommst an die Reihe** it's your turn; 9 **wie kommt das?** why is that?; 10 **zu etwas kommen** to acquire something; 11 **wieder zu sich kommen** to come round (after fainting or anaesthetic); 12 **dazu kommen, etwas zu tun** to get round to doing something; **ich komme einfach nicht zum Einkaufen** I just can't get round to doing the shopping; 13 **das kommt davon!** see what happens!

Kommissar der (PL die Kommissare) superintendent.

Kommode die (PL die Kommoden) chest of drawers.

Kommunismus der communism.

Kommunist der (PL die Kommunisten) communist.

Kommunistin die (PL die Kommunistinnen) communist.

◇ IRREGULAR VERB: See the verb table in the centre of the dictionary

Komödie die (PL die Komödien) comedy.

Kompass△ der (PL die Kompasse) compass.

komplett adjective complete.

Kompliment das (PL die Komplimente) compliment.

kompliziert adjective complicated.

Komponist der (PL die Komponisten) composer.

Komponistin die (PL die Komponistinnen) composer.

Kompott das (PL die Kompotte) stewed fruit.

Kompromiss△ der (PL die Kompromisse) compromise; **einen Kompromiss schließen** to compromise.

Konditorei die (PL die Konditoreien) patisserie, cake shop.

Kondom das (PL die Kondome) condom.

Konfektion die ready-made clothes.

Konferenz die (PL die Konferenzen) conference.

Konflikt der (PL die Konflikte) conflict.

König der (PL die Könige) king.

Königin die (PL die Königinnen) queen.

königlich adjective royal.

Königreich das (PL die Königreiche) kingdom.

Konjunktion die (PL die Konjunktionen) conjunction.

Konkurrent der (PL die Konkurrenten) competitor.

Konkurrentin die (PL die Konkurrentinnen) competitor.

Konkurrenz die competition.

können ◇ verb (PRES **kann**, IMPERF **konnte**, PERF **hat gekonnt**) **1** can; **kann ich Ihnen helfen?** can I help you?; **kannst du Auto fahren?** can you drive?; **kannst du Deutsch?** can you speak German?; **ich konnte nicht früher kommen** I couldn't come any earlier; **das kann ich nicht** I can't do that; **2 etwas können** to be able to do something; **er wird es vor Dienstag nicht machen können** he won't be able to do it before Tuesday; **3 das kann gut sein** that may well be so; **es kann sein, dass …** it may be that …; **4 ich kann nichts dafür** it's not my fault.

Können das ability.

Könner der (PL die Könner) expert.

könnt SEE **können**.

konnte, konnten, konntest, konntet SEE **können**.

Konserven plural noun tinned food.

Konsonant der (PL die Konsonanten) consonant.

Korsika das Corsica.

Kontakt der (PL die Kontakte) contact.

Kontaktlinse die (PL die Kontaktlinsen) contact lens.

△ NEW SPELLING: See page xii

Kontinent der (PL die **Kontinente**) continent.

Konto das (PL die **Konten**) account.

Kontrolle die (PL die **Kontrollen**) 1 check; 2 control.

Kontrolleur der (PL die **Kontrolleure**) inspector.

kontrollieren verb (PERF hat kontrolliert) 1 to check; 2 to control.

konzentrieren verb (PERF hat konzentriert) 1 to concentrate; 2 sich konzentrieren to concentrate.

Konzert das (PL die **Konzerte**) 1 concert; 2 concerto.

Kopf der (PL die **Köpfe**) 1 head; 2 sich den Kopf zerbrechen to rack your brains; 3 seinen Kopf durchsetzen to get your own way; 4 sich den Kopf waschen to wash your hair; 5 auf dem Kopf upside down; 6 ein Kopf Salat a lettuce.

köpfen verb (PERF hat geköpft) 1 to head (in football); 2 to behead.

Kopfhörer der (PL die **Kopfhörer**) headphones.

Kopfkissen das (PL die **Kopfkissen**) pillow.

Kopfsalat der (PL die **Kopfsalate**) lettuce.

Kopfschmerzen plural noun headache.

Kopie die (PL die **Kopien**) copy.

kopieren verb (PERF hat kopiert) to copy.

Kopiergerät das (PL die **Kopiergeräte**) photocopier.

Korb der (PL die **Körbe**) 1 basket; 2 jemandem einen Korb geben to turn somebody down.

Kork der (PL die **Korke**) cork.

Korken der (PL die **Korken**) cork.

Korkenzieher der (PL die **Korkenzieher**) corkscrew.

Korn das (PL die **Körner**) corn.

Körper der (PL die **Körper**) body.

körperbehindert adjective disabled.

körperlich adjective physical.

Korrektur die (PL die **Korrekturen**) correction.

korrigieren verb (PERF hat korrigiert) to correct.

koscher adjective kosher.

Kosmetik die (PL die **Kosmetika**) 1 cosmetics; 2. beauty care.

Kost die food.

kostbar adjective precious.

kosten verb (PERF hat gekostet) 1 to cost; 2 wie viel kostet es? how much is it?; 3 to taste.

Kosten plural noun 1 cost; 2 expenses.

kostenlos adjective free (of charge).

köstlich adjective 1 delicious; 2 funny.

Kostüm das (PL die **Kostüme**) 1 suit; 2 costume.

Kotelett das (PL die **Koteletts**) chop.

◇ IRREGULAR VERB: See the verb table in the centre of the dictionary

Krabbe *die* (PL die **Krabben**) 1 crab; 2 shrimp.

krabbeln *verb* (PERF **ist gekrabbelt**) to crawl.

Krach *der* 1 row; 2 noise; 3 crash.

krachen *verb* (PERF **hat gekracht**) 1 to crash; 2 (PERF **ist gekracht**) to crack; **er ist gegen die Mauer gekracht** he crashed into the wall.

krächzen *verb* (PERF **hat gekrächzt**) to croak.

Kraft *die* (PL die **Kräfte**) 1 strength; **er hat nicht viel Kraft** he's not very strong; 2 force; **in Kraft treten** to come into force; 3 **geistige Kräfte** mental powers; 4 worker.

kräftig *adjective* 1 strong; 2 nourishing.
adverb 1 strongly; 2 hard; **kräftig schütteln** shake hard.

Kraftwerk *das* (PL die **Kraftwerke**) power station.

Kragen *der* (PL die **Kragen**) collar.

Krähe *die* (PL die **Krähen**) crow.

Kralle *die* (PL die **Krallen**) claw.

Kram *der* stuff; **mach deinen Kram allein!** (*informal*) do it yourself!

kramen *verb* (PERF **hat gekramt**) to rummage about.

Krampf *der* (PL die **Krämpfe**) cramp.

Kran *der* (PL die **Kräne**) crane (*machine*).

Kranich *der* (PL die **Kraniche**) crane (*bird*).

krank *adjective* ill, sick; **krank werden** to fall ill.

Kranke *der/die* (PL die **Kranken**) patient.

kränken *verb* (PERF **hat gekränkt**) to hurt.

Krankenhaus *das* (PL die **Krankenhäuser**) hospital; **sie haben ihn gestern ins Krankenhaus eingeliefert** he was taken to hospital yesterday.

Krankenkasse *die* health insurance; **bei welcher Krankenkasse sind Sie versichert?** what health insurance have you got?

Krankenpfleger *der* (PL die **Krankenpfleger**) (male) nurse.

Krankenpflegerin *die* (PL die **Krankenpflegerinnen**) nurse.

Krankenschwester *die* (PL die **Krankenschwestern**) nurse; **Ulrike ist Krankenschwester** Ulrike is a nurse.

Krankenwagen *der* (PL die **Krankenwagen**) ambulance.

Krankheit *die* (PL die **Krankheiten**) illness, disease.

kratzen *verb* (PERF **hat gekratzt**) to scratch.

Kratzer *der* (PL die **Kratzer**) scratch.

kraus *adjective* frizzy.

Kraut *das* (PL die **Kräuter**) 1 herb; 2 sauerkraut; 3 cabbage.

Krawall *der* (PL die **Krawalle**) 1 riot; 2 row.

Krawatte *die* (PL die **Krawatten**) tie.

kreativ *adjective* creative.

△ NEW SPELLING: *See page xii*

Krebs der (PL die Krebse) 1 crab; 2 cancer; 3 Cancer.

Kredit der (PL die Kredite) credit; **auf Kredit** on credit.

Kreditkarte die (PL die Kreditkarten) credit card.

Kreide die (PL die Kreiden) chalk.

kreieren verb (PERF hat kreiert) to create.

Kreis der (PL die Kreise) 1 circle; 2 district.

Kreislauf der 1 cycle; 2 circulation.

Kreuz das (PL die Kreuze) 1 cross; 2 (small of the) back; 3 intersection (of a motorway); 4 clubs (in cards).

kreuzen verb (PERF hat gekreuzt) 1 to cross; 2 sich kreuzen to cross.

Kreuzung die (PL die Kreuzungen) 1 crossroads; 2 cross (of plants, animals).

Kreuzfahrt die (PL die Kreuzfahrten) 1 cruise; **eine Kreuzfahrt machen** to go on a cruise; 2 crusade.

Kreuzworträtsel das (PL die Kreuzworträtsel) crossword (puzzle).

kriechen ◇ verb (IMPERF kroch, PERF ist gekrochen) to crawl.

Krieg der (PL die Kriege) war.

kriegen verb (informal) (PERF hat gekriegt) 1 to get; 2 ein Kind kriegen to have a baby.

Krimi der (PL die Krimis) thriller.

Kriminalroman der (PL die Kriminalromane) crime novel.

kriminell adjective criminal.

Kriminelle der/die (PL die Kriminellen) criminal.

Krippe die (PL die Krippen) 1 manger; 2 crib; 3 crèche.

Krise die (PL die Krisen) crisis.

Kristall[1] der (PL die Kristalle) crystal.

Kristall[2] das (glass) crystal.

kritisch adjective critical.

kritisieren verb (PERF hat kritisiert) 1 to criticize; 2 to review.

kroch SEE kriechen.

Krokodil das (PL die Krokodile) crocodile.

Krone die (PL die Kronen) crown.

Kröte die (PL die Kröten) toad.

Krücke die (PL die Krücken) crutch.

Krug der (PL die Krüge) 1 jug; 2 mug.

Krümel der (PL die Krümel) crumb.

krümelig adjective crumbly.

krumm adjective 1 bent; 2 crooked.

Kruste die (PL die Krusten) crust.

Küche die (PL die Küchen) 1 kitchen; 2 cooking; **die italienische Küche** Italian cooking; 3 warme Küche hot food.

Kuchen der (PL die Kuchen) cake.

Kuckuck der (PL die Kuckucke) cuckoo.

Kugel die (PL die Kugeln) 1 ball; 2 bullet; 3 sphere.

◇ IRREGULAR VERB: *See the verb table in the centre of the dictionary*

Kugelschreiber der (PL die Kugelschreiber) ballpoint pen, biro™.

Kuh die (PL die Kühe) cow.

kühl adjective cool.

kühlen verb (PERF hat gekühlt) 1 to cool, to chill; 2 to refrigerate.

Kühler der (PL die Kühler) radiator.

Kühlerhaube die (PL die Kühlerhauben) bonnet.

Kühlschrank der (PL die Kühlschränke) fridge.

Kühltruhe die (PL die Kühltruhen) freezer.

Küken das (PL die Küken) chick.

Kuli der (PL die Kulis) biro™.

Kultur die (PL die Kulturen) 1 culture; 2 civilization.

Kulturbeutel der (PL die Kulturbeutel) toilet bag.

kulturell adjective cultural.

Kummer der 1 sorrow; 2 worry; 3 trouble.

kümmern verb (PERF hat gekümmert) 1 to concern; 2 sich um jemanden kümmern to look after somebody; sich um den Garten kümmern to look after the garden; 3 sich darum kümmern, dass … to see to it that …; 4 kümmere dich um deine eigenen Angelegenheiten mind your own business.

Kunde der (PL die Kunden) 1 customer; 2 client.

kündigen verb (PERF hat gekündigt) 1 to cancel; 2 to give notice; die Firma hat ihm gekündigt the company gave him his notice; 3 seine Stellung kündigen to hand in your notice.

Kundin die (PL die Kundinnen) 1 customer; 2 client.

Kundschaft die customers.

Kunst die (PL die Künste) 1 art; 2 skill.

Künstler der (PL die Künstler) artist.

Künstlerin die (PL die Künstlerinnen) artist.

künstlerisch adjective artistic.

künstlich adjective artificial.

Kunststoff der (PL die Kunststoffe) plastic.

Kunststück das (PL die Kunststücke) 1 trick; 2 feat.

Kunstwerk das (PL die Kunstwerke) work of art.

Kupfer das copper.

Kupplung die (PL die Kupplungen) 1 clutch (of a car); 2 coupling.

Kürbis der (PL die Kürbisse) pumpkin.

Kurort der (PL die Kurorte) health resort.

Kurs der (PL die Kurse) 1 course; 2 exchange rate; 3 price (of shares).

Kurve die (PL die Kurven) 1 curve; 2 bend.

kurz adjective 1 short; vor kurzem a short time ago; 2 zu kurz kommen to get less than your fair share, to come off badly.

adverb 1 shortly; **2** briefly; **3 kurz gesagt** in a word.

Kurzarbeit *die* short-time working.

kurzärmelig *adjective* short-sleeved.

kürzen *verb* (PERF **hat gekürzt**) **1** to shorten; **2** to cut.

kurzfristig *adjective* short-term.
  adverb at short notice.

kürzlich *adverb* recently.

kurzsichtig *adjective* short-sighted.

Kurzwaren *plural noun* haberdashery.

Kusine *die* (PL *die* **Kusinen**) cousin.

Kuss Δ *der* (PL *die* **Küsse**) kiss.

küssen *verb* (PERF **hat geküsst** Δ) **1** to kiss; **2 sich küssen** to kiss.

Küste *die* (PL *die* **Küsten**) coast.

Kuvert *das* (PL *die* **Kuverts**) envelope.

L l

Labor *das* (PL *die* **Labors**) laboratory.

Lache *die* (PL *die* **Lachen**) pool.

lächeln *verb* (PERF **hat gelächelt**) to smile.

lachen *verb* (PERF **hat gelacht**) to laugh.

lächerlich *adjective* ridiculous.

Lachs *der* (PL *die* **Lachse**) salmon.

Lack *der* (PL *die* **Lacke**) **1** varnish; **2** paint.

lackieren *verb* (PERF **hat lackiert**) **1** to varnish; **2** to spray (*with paint*).

laden ◇ *verb* (PRES **lädt**, IMPERF **lud**, PERF **hat geladen**) **1** to load; **wir haben die Möbel in den Möbelwagen geladen** we loaded the furniture into the removal van; **2 eine Batterie laden** to charge a battery; **3** to summon; **mein Bruder wurde als Zeuge geladen** my brother was summoned as a witness.

Laden *der* (PL *die* **Läden**) **1** shop; **wann macht der Laden zu?** when does the shop close?; **2** shutter; **wenn es heiß ist, lassen wir die Läden den ganzen Tag zu** when it's hot we keep the shutters closed all day.

Ladendieb *der* (PL *die* **Ladendiebe**) shoplifter.

Ladung *die* (PL *die* **Ladungen**) **1** cargo; **2** charge (*of dynamite or shot*); **3** summons; **4** load.

lag SEE **liegen**.

Lage *die* (PL *die* **Lagen**) **1** situation; **nicht in der Lage sein, etwas zu tun** not be in a position to do something; **2** layer.

Lager *das* (PL *die* **Lager**) **1** camp; **2** warehouse; **3** stock; **etwas auf Lager haben** to have something in stock; **4** stock-room; **5** bearing (*in a machine*).

lagern *verb* (PERF **hat gelagert**) **1** to store; **2** to camp.

◇ **IRREGULAR VERB: See the verb table in the centre of the dictionary**

lahm *adjective* lame.

lähmen *verb* (PERF **hat gelähmt**) to paralyse.

Lähmung *die* paralysis.

Laib *der* (PL *die* **Laibe**) loaf.

Laken *das* (PL *die* **Laken**) sheet.

Lakritze *die* liquorice.

Lamm *das* (PL *die* **Lämmer**) lamb.

Lampe *die* (PL *die* **Lampen**) lamp.

Lampenschirm *der* (PL *die* **Lampenschirme**) lampshade.

Land *das* (PL *die* **Länder**) **1** country; **auf dem Land** in the country; **2** land; **3** state (*there are 16 Länder in Germany*).

Landebahn *die* (PL *die* **Landebahnen**) runway.

landen *verb* (PERF **ist gelandet**) **1** to land; **2 im Krankenhaus landen** (*informal*) to end up in hospital.

Landkarte *die* (PL *die* **Landkarten**) map.

Landkreis *der* (PL *die* **Landkreise**) district.

ländlich *adjective* rural.

Landschaft *die* (PL *die* **Landschaften**) **1** countryside; **2** landscape.

Landstraße *die* (PL *die* **Landstraßen**) country road.

Landtag *der* state parliament.

Landwirtschaft *die* agriculture, farming.

lang *adjective* **1** long; **seit langem** for a long time; **2** tall. *adverb* **eine Woche lang** for a week.

langärmelig *adjective* long-sleeved.

lange *adverb* **1** a long time; **lange nicht** not for a long time; **2 so lange wie möglich** as long as possible; **3 er ist lange nicht so reich** he's nowhere near as rich.

Länge *die* (PL *die* **Längen**) **1** length; **2** longitude.

langen *verb* (PERF **hat gelangt**) **1** to be enough; **das Geld langt nicht** it's not enough money; **mir langt's** (*informal*) I've had enough; **2** to reach; **nach etwas langen** to reach for something; **3 jemandem eine langen** (*informal*) to slap somebody's face.

Langlauf *der* cross-country (*in skiing*).

langsam *adjective, adverb* slow; **die Musik geht mir langsam auf die Nerven** the music is slowly getting on my nerves.

längst *adverb* **1** a long time ago; **das habe ich schon längst gemacht** I did it a long time ago; **2** for a long time; **er weiß es schon längst** he's known it for a long time; **3 längst nicht** nowhere near, not nearly.

längster, längste, längstes *adjective* longest; **Marion hat den längsten Aufsatz geschrieben** Marion wrote the longest essay.

langweilen *verb* (PERF **hat gelangweilt**) **1** to bore; **2 sich langweilen** to be bored.

△ NEW SPELLING: *See page xii*

langweilig *adjective* boring.

Lappen *der* (PL *die* Lappen) cloth, rag.

Laptop *der* (PL *die* Laptops) laptop.

Lärm *der* noise.

las SEE **lesen**.

Laser *der* (PL *die* Laser) laser.

Laserdrucker *der* (PL *die* Laserdrucker) laser printer.

lassen ◇ *verb* (PRES **lässt** △, IMPERF **ließ**, PERF **hat gelassen**) 1 to let; **jemanden schlafen lassen** to let somebody sleep; **lass uns jetzt gehen** let's go now; 2 **jemandem etwas lassen** to let somebody have something; 3 to leave; **die Kinder zu Hause lassen** to leave the children at home; **lass mich!** leave me!; 4 **jemanden warten lassen** to keep somebody waiting; 5 **etwas reparieren lassen** to have something repaired; 6 **lass das!** stop it!; 7 **die Tür lässt sich leicht öffnen** the door opens easily; **das lässt sich alles machen** that can all be arranged.

lässig *adjective* casual.

Last *die* (PL *die* Lasten) 1 load; 2 **jemandem zur Last fallen** to be a burden on somebody.

lästig *adjective* troublesome.

Lastwagen *der* (PL *die* Lastwagen) lorry, truck.

Latein *das* Latin.

Laterne *die* (PL *die* Laternen) 1 lantern; 2 street lamp.

Laub *das* leaves.

Lauch *der* leek(s).

Lauf *der* (PL *die* Läufe) 1 run; 2 course; **im Laufe der Zeit** in the course of time; **im Laufe der Jahre** over the years; 3 race; 4 barrel (*of a gun*).

Laufbahn *die* (PL *die* Laufbahnen) career.

laufen ◇ *verb* (PRES **läuft**, IMPERF **lief**, PERF **ist gelaufen**) 1 to run; **sie kann viel schneller laufen als ihr Bruder** she can run much faster than my brother; 2 to walk; **du kannst nach Hause laufen oder mit dem Bus fahren** you can walk home or go on the bus; 3 to be valid; 4 **Ski laufen** to ski; 5 to be on (*of a film, programme, or machine*).

laufend *adjective* 1 running; 2 current (*issue, month*); 3 **auf dem Laufenden sein** △ to be up to date; **Anita hält mich auf dem Laufenden** △ Anita keeps me up to date.
adverb continually, constantly.

Läufer *der* (PL *die* Läufer) 1 runner; 2 rug; 3 bishop (*in chess*).

Läuferin *die* (PL *die* Läuferinnen) runner.

Laufmasche *die* (PL *die* Laufmaschen) ladder (*in your tights*).

Laufwerk *das* (PL *die* Laufwerke) drive (*on a computer*).

Laune *die* (PL *die* Launen) mood.

launisch *adjective* moody.

◇ IRREGULAR VERB: *See the verb table in the centre of the dictionary*

Laus die (PL die Läuse) louse.

laut adjective 1 loud; 2 noisy. adverb 1 loudly; 2 laut lesen to read aloud; 3 lauter stellen to turn up.
preposition ←(+GEN or +DAT) according to.

Laut der (PL die Laute) sound.

lauten verb (PERF hat gelautet) 1 to be; 2 to go.

läuten verb (PERF hat geläutet) to ring.

lauter adjective nothing but.

Lautsprecher der (PL die Lautsprecher) (loud)speaker.

Lautstärke die volume.

lauwarm adjective lukewarm.

Lavendel der lavender.

Lawine die (PL die Lawinen) avalanche.

leben verb (PERF hat gelebt) 1 to live; 2 to be alive; 3 leb wohl! farewell!

Leben das (PL die Leben) life; am Leben sein to be alive; ums Leben kommen to lose your life.

lebend adjective living.

lebendig adjective 1 living; 2 lebendig sein to be alive; 3 lively.

Lebensgefahr die mortal danger; sein Vater ist in Lebensgefahr his father is critically ill.

lebensgefährlich adjective 1 extremely dangerous; 2 critical;

lebensgefährlich verletzt critically injured.

Lebenshaltungskosten plural noun cost of living.

lebenslänglich adjective life. adverb for life.

Lebenslauf der (PL die Lebensläufe) CV.

Lebensmittel plural noun food, groceries.

Lebensmittelgeschäft das (PL die Lebensmittelgeschäfte) grocer's (shop).

Lebensunterhalt der livelihood; seinen Lebensunterhalt verdienen to earn one's living.

Leber die (PL die Lebern) liver.

Leberfleck der (PL die Leberflecke) mole.

Leberwurst die liver sausage.

Lebewesen das (PL die Lebewesen) living being, living thing.

lebhaft adjective 1 lively; 2 vivid (idea, colour).

Lebkuchen der (PL die Lebkuchen) gingerbread.

leblos adjective lifeless.

Leck das (PL die Lecks) leak.

lecken verb (PERF hat geleckt) 1 to lick; die Katze leckte ihre Jungen the cat licked the kittens; an etwas lecken to lick something; 2 to leak.

lecker adjective delicious.

Leder das (PL die Leder) leather.

△ NEW SPELLING: See page xii

ledig *adjective* single.

lediglich *adverb* merely.

leer *adjective* empty; **leer machen** to empty.

leeren *verb* (PERF **hat geleert**) 1 to empty; 2 **ein leeres Blatt Papier** a blank sheet of paper; 3 **sich leeren** to empty.

Leerlauf *der* neutral (*gear*).

Leerung *die* (PL die **Leerungen**) collection.

legal *adjective* legal.

legen *verb* (PERF **hat gelegt**) 1 to put; 2 to lay; 3 **sich legen** to lie down; 4 **sich legen** to die down (*of a storm, noise*); **unsere Begeisterung hat sich gelegt** our enthusiasm has worn off.

leger *adjective, adverb* casual; **leger gekleidet sein** to be casually dressed.

Lehm *der* clay.

Lehne *die* (PL die **Lehnen**) 1 back (*of a chair*); 2 arm (*of a sofa or chair*).

lehnen *verb* (PERF **hat gelehnt**) 1 to lean; 2 **sich an etwas lehnen** to lean against something.

Lehrbuch *das* (PL die **Lehrbücher**) textbook.

lehren *verb* (PERF **hat gelehrt**) to teach.

Lehrer *der* (PL die **Lehrer**) 1 teacher; 2 instructor.

Lehrerin *die* (PL die **Lehrerinnen**) 1 teacher; 2 instructor.

Lehrerzimmer *das* (PL die **Lehrerzimmer**) staffroom.

Lehrling *der* (PL die **Lehrlinge**) 1 apprentice; 2 trainee.

Lehrplan *der* (PL die **Lehrpläne**) syllabus.

Lehrstelle *die* (PL die **Lehrstellen**) apprenticeship.

Leibwächter *der* (PL die **Leibwächter**) bodyguard.

Leiche *die* (PL die **Leichen**) (dead) body, corpse.

leicht *adjective* 1 light; 2 easy; **jemandem leicht fallen** △ to be easy for somebody; **es ist ihm nicht leicht gefallen** it wasn't easy for him; **Markus macht es sich immer leicht** Markus always takes the easy way out; 3 **ein leichter Akzent** a slight accent.

Leichtathletik *die* athletics.

leichtfallen SEE leicht.

Leichtsinn *der* 1 carelessness; 2 recklessness.

leichtsinnig *adjective* 1 careless; 2 reckless.

leid *adjective* **jemanden leid sein** △ to be fed up with somebody; **etwas leid sein** △ to be fed up with something.

Leid *das* 1 sorrow; 2 harm; 3 **es tut mir Leid** △ I'm sorry; **Andreas tut mir Leid** △ I feel sorry for Andreas.

leiden ◇ *verb* (IMPERF **litt**, PERF **hat gelitten**) 1 to suffer; 2 **jemanden gut leiden können** to like

◇ **IRREGULAR VERB: See the verb table in the centre of the dictionary**

somebody; **3 ich kann Erika nicht leiden** I can't stand Erika.

leider *adverb* **1** unfortunately; **2 leider ja** I'm afraid so; **leider nicht** I'm afraid not.

leihen ◇ *verb* (IMPERF **lieh**, PERF **hat geliehen**) **1** to lend; **2 sich etwas leihen** to borrow something; **ich habe mir das Buch von Alex geliehen** I borrowed the book from Alex.

Leihwagen *der* (PL **die Leihwagen**) hire car.

Leim *der* (PL **die Leime**) glue.

Leine *die* (PL **die Leinen**) **1** rope; **2** line (*for washing*); **3** lead (*for a dog*).

Leinen *das* (PL **die Leinen**) linen.

Leinwand *die* screen (*in a cinema*).

leise *adjective* quiet. *adverb* **1** quietly; **2 die Musik leiser stellen** to turn the music down.

leisten *verb* (PERF **hat geleistet**) **1** to achieve; **2 jemandem Hilfe leisten** to help somebody; **3 jemandem Gesellschaft leisten** to keep somebody company; **4 sich etwas leisten** to treat yourself to something; **5 sich etwas leisten können** to be able to afford something; **ich kann mir kein neues Auto leisten** I can't afford a new car.

Leistung *die* (PL **die Leistungen**) **1** achievement; **2** performance; **3 Leistungen** payment.

leiten *verb* (PERF **hat geleitet**) **1** to lead; **2** to direct; **3** to manage, run (*a business*); **4** to conduct.

Leiter[1] *die* (PL **die Leitern**) ladder.

Leiter[2] *der* (PL **die Leiter**) **1** leader; **2** head; **3** manager; **4** director; **5** conductor (*of an orchestra or electricity*).

Leiterin *die* (PL **die Leiterinnen**) **1** leader; **2** head; **3** manageress; **4** director.

Leitung *die* (PL **die Leitungen**) **1** direction; **2** management; **3** (*phone*) line; **4** (*electric*) lead; **5** cable; **6** pipe; **7 unter der Leitung von** conducted by.

Leitungswasser *das* tap water.

Lektion *die* (PL **die Lektionen**) lesson.

lenken *verb* (PERF **hat gelenkt**) **1** to steer; **2** to guide; **3 den Verdacht auf jemanden lenken** to throw suspicion on somebody.

Lenkrad *das* (PL **die Lenkräder**) steering wheel.

Lenkstange *die* (PL **die Lenkstangen**) handlebars.

lernen *verb* (PERF **hat gelernt**) **1** to learn; **schwimmen lernen** to learn to swim; **2** to study.

lesen ◇ *verb* (PRES **liest**, IMPERF **las**, PERF **hat gelesen**) to read.

Leser *der* (PL **die Leser**) reader.

Leserin *die* (PL **die Leserinnen**) reader.

letzte SEE **letzter**.

Letzte △ *der/die/das* (PL **die Letzten**) **1 der/die Letzte** the last (one); **das**

Letzte the last (thing); **2 Boris kam als Letzter** Boris arrived last.

letztens adverb **1** recently; **2** lastly.

letzter, letzte, letztes adjective **1** last; **zum letzten Mal** for the last time; **das letzte Mal** the last time; **2** latest (news, information); **3 in letzter Zeit** recently.

leuchten verb (PERF **hat geleuchtet**) to shine.

Leuchter der (PL die **Leuchter**) candlestick.

Leuchtreklame die neon sign.

Leuchtturm der (PL die **Leuchttürme**) lighthouse.

leugnen verb (PERF **hat geleugnet**) to deny.

Leute plural noun people.

Lexikon das (PL die **Lexika**) **1** encyclopedia; **2** dictionary.

Licht das (PL die **Lichter**) light.

Lichtbild das (PL die **Lichtbilder**) photograph.

Lichtschalter der (PL die **Lichtschalter**) light switch.

Lid das (PL die **Lider**) (eye)lid.

Lidschatten der (PL die **Lidschatten**) eye shadow.

lieb adjective **1** dear; **liebe Gabi** dear Gabi; **2** nice; **das ist lieb von euch** that's nice of you; **3 jemanden lieb haben** △ to be fond of somebody; **4 es wäre mir lieber, wenn ...** I'd prefer it if ...; **5 ihr liebstes Spielzeug** her favourite toy.

Liebe die (PL die **Lieben**) love.

lieben verb (PERF **hat geliebt**) to love.

liebenswürdig adjective kind.

lieber adverb **1** rather; **2 lieber mögen** to like better; **3 lass das lieber** you'd better not do that; **4 ich trinke lieber Kaffee** I prefer coffee.

Liebesbrief der (PL die **Liebesbriefe**) love letter.

Liebeskummer der **Liebeskummer haben** to be lovesick.

liebevoll adjective loving.

liebhaben SEE lieb.

Liebling der (PL die **Lieblinge**) **1** darling; **2** favourite.

Lieblings- prefix favourite.

liebster, liebste, liebstes adjective **1** dearest; **2** favourite. adverb **am liebsten** best (of all); **ich mag Max am liebsten** I like Max best.

Lied das (PL die **Lieder**) song.

lief SEE laufen.

liefern verb (PERF **hat geliefert**) **1** to deliver; **2** to supply.

Lieferung die (PL die **Lieferungen**) delivery.

Lieferwagen der (PL die **Lieferwagen**) (delivery) van.

liegen ◇ verb (IMPERF **lag**, PERF **hat gelegen**) **1** to lie; **der Brief liegt auf dem Tisch** the letter is on the table; **es liegt viel Schnee** there's lots of snow; **2** to be, to be situated; **3 liegen bleiben** △ to stay (in bed); **er ist liegen geblieben** he didn't get

◇ IRREGULAR VERB: See the verb table in the centre of the dictionary

up; **4 etwas bleibt liegen** something is left behind; **die Arbeit ist liegen geblieben** the job was left undone; **5 der Schnee bleibt liegen** the snow is settling; **6 liegen lassen**△ to leave; **7 es liegt mir nicht** it doesn't suit me; **8 an etwas liegen** to be due to something; **9 das liegt an ihm** it's up to him.

liegenbleiben, liegenlassen SEE **liegen**.

Liegestuhl der (PL die **Liegestühle**) deckchair.

Liegewagen der (PL die **Liegewagen**) couchette (car).

ließ SEE **lassen**.

liest SEE **lesen**.

Lift der (PL die **Lifte**) lift.

Liga die (PL die **Ligen**) league.

lila adjective **1** purple; **2** mauve.

Limo die (PL die **Limo(s)**) = **Limonade**.

Limonade die (PL die **Limonaden**) **1** fizzy drink; **2** lemonade.

Limone die (PL die **Limonen**) lime.

Lineal das (PL die **Lineale**) ruler.

Linie die (PL die **Linien**) **1** line; **2** route (of a bus); **Linie 6** number 6.

Linke die **1** left; **zu meiner Linken** on my left; **2** left hand; **3** left side; **4 die Linke** the left (in politics).

linker, linke, linkes adjective **1** left; **2** left-wing.

links adverb **1** on the left; **links fahren** to drive on the left; **links**

abbiegen to turn left; **nach links** left; **von links** from the left; **2 links sein** to be left-wing; **3 zwei links, zwei rechts stricken** to purl two, knit two; **4** (clothing) inside out.

Linkshänder der (PL die **Linkshänder**) left-hander.

Linkshänderin die (PL die **Linkshänderinnen**) left-hander.

Linse die (PL die **Linsen**) **1** lens; **2** lentil.

Lippe die (PL die **Lippen**) lip.

Lippenstift der (PL die **Lippenstifte**) lipstick.

Liste die (PL die **Listen**) list.

listig adjective cunning.

Liter der (PL die **Liter**) litre.

Literatur die literature.

litt SEE **leiden**.

Livesendung△ die (PL die **Livesendungen**) live programme.

Lizenz die (PL die **Lizenzen**) licence.

Lkw der (PL die **Lkws**) (Lastkraftwagen) lorry, truck.

Lob das praise.

loben verb (PERF **hat gelobt**) to praise.

Loch das (PL die **Löcher**) hole.

Locke die (PL die **Locken**) curl.

locken verb (PERF **hat gelockt**) **1** to tempt; **2** to curl.

locker adjective **1** loose; **2** slack (rope); **3** relaxed (atmosphere, person).

△ NEW SPELLING: See page xii

lockerlassen ◇ *verb* (PRES **lässt locker** Δ, IMPERF **ließ locker**, PERF **hat lockergelassen**) **nicht lockerlassen** (*informal*) not to let up.

lockig *adjective* curly.

Löffel *der* (PL *die* **Löffel**) **1** spoon; **2 ein Löffel Mehl** a spoonful of flour.

log SEE **lügen**.

Logik *die* logic.

logisch *adjective* **1** logical; **2 ja, logisch!** yes, of course!

Lohn *der* (PL *die* **Löhne**) **1** wages; **2** reward.

lohnen *verb* (PERF **hat sich gelohnt**) **sich lohnen** to be worth it.

Lokal *das* (PL *die* **Lokale**) **1** bar; **2** restaurant.

Lokomotive *die* (PL *die* **Lokomotiven**) locomotive, engine.

Lorbeerblatt *das* (PL *die* **Lorbeerblätter**) bay leaf.

los *adjective* **1 der Hund ist los** the dog is off the lead; **2 die Schraube ist los** the screw's loose; **3 es ist viel los** there's a lot going on; **4 etwas los sein** to be rid of something; **5 was ist los?** what's the matter?
adverb **1 los!** go on!; **2 Achtung, fertig, los!** ready, steady, go!

Los *das* (PL *die* **Lose**) **1** (lottery) ticket; **2 das große Los ziehen** to hit the jackpot; **3** lot.

losbinden ◇ *verb* (IMPERF **band los**, PERF **hat losgebunden**) to untie.

löschen *verb* (PERF **hat gelöscht**) **1** to put out; **2 seinen Durst löschen** to quench your thirst; **3** to delete, to cancel; **4** to erase.

lose *adjective* loose.

lösen *verb* (PERF **hat gelöst**) **1** to solve; **2** to undo; **3 eine Fahrkarte lösen** to buy a ticket; **4 sich lösen** to come undone; **5 sich lösen** to be solved (*of a puzzle or mystery*); **sich von selbst lösen** to be resolved (*of a problem*); **6 sich in Wasser lösen** to dissolve in water.

losfahren ◇ *verb* (PRES **fährt los**, IMPERF **fuhr los**, PERF **ist losgefahren**) **1** to set off; **2** to drive off.

losgehen ◇ *verb* (IMPERF **ging los**, PERF **ist losgegangen**) **1** to set off; **2** to start; **3** to come off (*of a button*); **4** to go off (*of a bomb*); **5 auf jemanden losgehen** to go for somebody.

loslassen ◇ *verb* (PRES **lässt los** Δ, IMPERF **ließ los**, PERF **hat losgelassen**) **1** to let go of; **2** to let go.

Lösung *die* (PL *die* **Lösungen**) solution.

loswerden ◇ *verb* (PRES **wird los**, IMPERF **wurde los**, PERF **ist losgeworden**) to get rid of.

Lotterie *die* (PL *die* **Lotterien**) lottery.

Lotto *das* (PL *die* **Lottos**) (national) lottery.

Löwe *der* (PL *die* **Löwen**) **1** lion; **2** Leo.

◇ **IRREGULAR VERB: See the verb table in the centre of the dictionary**

Lücke die (PL die Lücken) gap.

Luft die (PL die Lüfte) 1 air; 2 die Luft anhalten to hold your breath; 3 in die Luft gehen (informal) to blow your top; 4 jemanden wie Luft behandeln to ignore somebody.

Luftballon der (PL die Luftballons) balloon.

Luftdruck der air pressure.

Luftmatratze die (PL die Luftmatratzen) air-bed.

Luftpost die airmail; per Luftpost by airmail.

Luftverschmutzung die air pollution.

Luftwaffe die air force.

Lüge die (PL die Lügen) lie.

lügen ◊ verb (IMPERF log, PERF hat gelogen) to lie.

Lügner der (PL die Lügner) liar.

Lügnerin die (PL die Lügnerinnen) liar.

Lunge die (PL die Lungen) lungs.

Lungenentzündung die pneumonia.

Lupe die (PL die Lupen) magnifying glass.

Lust die 1 pleasure; 2 Lust haben, etwas zu tun to feel like doing something; ich habe keine Lust I don't feel like it; Lust auf etwas haben to feel like something.

lustig adjective 1 jolly; 2 funny; 3 Dieter hat sich über mich lustig gemacht Dieter made fun of me.

lutschen verb (PERF hat gelutscht) to suck.

Lutscher der (PL die Lutscher) lollipop.

Luxemburg das Luxembourg.

Luxus der luxury.

M m

machen verb (PERF hat gemacht) 1 to make; 2 to do; was machst du da? what are you doing?; 3 was macht die Arbeit? how's work?; was macht Karin? how's Karin?; 4 sich an die Arbeit machen to get down to work; 5 schnell machen to hurry; 6 das macht nichts it doesn't matter; 7 das macht fünf Mark that's five marks; 8 sich nichts aus etwas machen to not be very keen on something; Roswitha macht sich nichts aus Schokolade Roswitha isn't keen on chocolate.

Macht die (PL die Mächte) power; an die Macht kommen to come to power.

Mädchen das (PL die Mädchen) girl.

Made die (PL die Maden) maggot.

Mädchenname der (PL die Mädchennamen) maiden name.

mag SEE mögen.

Magazin das (PL die Magazine) magazine.

Magen der (PL die Mägen) stomach.

△ NEW SPELLING: See page xii

Magenschmerzen *plural noun* stomach-ache.

mager *adjective* 1 thin; 2 lean; 3 low-fat.

Magie *die* magic.

Magnet *der* (PL die **Magneten**) magnet.

magnetisch *adjective* magnetic.

magst SEE **mögen**.

Mahagoni *das* mahogany.

mähen *verb* (PERF hat **gemäht**) to mow; **den Rasen mähen** to mow the lawn.

mahlen ⬦ *verb* (PERF hat **gemahlen**) to grind.

Mahlzeit *die* (PL die **Mahlzeiten**) meal; **Mahlzeit!** enjoy your meal!

Mai *der* May; **der Erste Mai** May Day.

Maiglöckchen *das* (PL die **Maiglöckchen**) lily of the valley.

Mais *der* maize.

Majonäse ⬠ *die* mayonnaise.

Majoran *der* marjoram.

Makkaroni *(plural noun)* macaroni.

Makler *der* (PL die **Makler**) estate agent.

Makrele *die* (PL die **Makrelen**) mackerel.

mal *adverb* 1 times; **zwei mal drei** two times three; 2 by (*with measurements*); 3 sometime (*in the future*); **ich möchte mal nach Brasilien fahren** I'd like to go to Brazil sometime; 4 **schon mal**

ever; 5 **ich war schon mal da** I've been once before; 6 **nicht mal** not even; 7 **komm mal her!** come here!

Mal *das* (PL die **Male**) 1 time; **nächstes Mal** next time; **zum ersten Mal** for the first time; 2 mark; 3 mole.

malen *verb* (PERF hat **gemalt**) to paint.

Maler *der* (PL die **Maler**) painter.

Malerei *die* painting.

Malerin *die* (PL die **Malerinnen**) painter.

Mallorca *das* Majorca.

Mama *die* (PL die **Mamas**) mum.

Mami *die* (PL die **Mamis**) mummy.

man *pronoun* 1 you, one; **wie macht man das?** how do you do it?; **man kann ja nie wissen** one can never tell; 2 they, people; **man sagt** they say; 3 **man hat mir gesagt** I was told.

mancher, manche, manches *adjective* 1 many a; **so manchen Tag** many a day; 2 **manche** (*plural*) some; **an manchen Tagen** some days. *pronoun* 1 many a person; 2 **manche** (*plural*) some people; 3 **manches** some things.

manchmal *adverb* sometimes.

Mandarine *die* (PL die **Mandarinen**) mandarin.

Mandel *die* (PL die **Mandeln**) 1 almond; 2 tonsil.

⬦ **IRREGULAR VERB: See the verb table in the centre of the dictionary**

Mandelentzündung die tonsillitis.

Mangel der (PL die Mängel) 1 lack; 2 shortage; 3 defect, fault.

mangelhaft adjective 1 faulty; 2 unsatisfactory (school mark).

Manie die (PL die Manien) mania.

Manieren plural noun manners; **er hat keine Manieren** he's got no manners.

Mann der (PL die Männer) 1 man; 2 husband.

Männchen das (PL die Männchen) male (animal).

Mannequin das (PL die Mannequins) model.

männlich adjective 1 male; 2 manly; 3 masculine.

Mannschaft die (PL die Mannschaften) 1 team; 2 crew.

Manschette die (PL die Manschetten) cuff.

Mantel der (PL die Mäntel) coat.

Mappe die (PL die Mappen) 1 folder; 2 briefcase; 3 bag.

Märchen das (PL die Märchen) fairy tale.

Margarine die margarine.

Marienkäfer der (PL die Marienkäfer) ladybird.

Marine die (PL die Marinen) navy.

Mark die (PL die Mark) mark.

Marke die (PL die Marken) 1 make, brand; **meine Mutter fährt seit** Jahren die gleiche Marke my mother has been driving the same make of car for years; **Adidas ist eine führende Marke** Adidas is a leading brand; 2 tag; 3 stamp (for letters); 4 coupon.

markieren verb (PERF hat markiert) 1 to mark; 2 to fake.

Markstück das (PL die Markstücke) one-mark piece.

Markt der (PL die Märkte) market.

Marktplatz der (PL die Marktplätze) market-place.

Marmelade die (PL die Marmeladen) jam.

Marmor der marble.

Marokko das Morocco.

Marsch der (PL die Märsche) march.

März der March.

Masche die (PL die Maschen) 1 stitch; 2 mesh; 3 (informal) trick; **die Masche raushaben** to know how to do it; **das ist die neueste Masche** that's the latest thing.

Maschine die (PL die Maschinen) 1 machine; 2 plane; 3 typewriter; **Maschine schreiben** Δ to type.

Masern plural noun measles.

Maske die (PL die Masken) mask.

maskieren verb (PERF hat sich maskiert) 1 sich maskieren to dress up; 2 sich maskieren to disguise yourself.

maß SEE messen.

Maß[1] das (PL die Maße) 1 measure; 2 measurement; 3 extent; **in hohem**

Maße to a high degree; **4 Maß halten** to show moderation.

Maß[2] die (PL die **Maß**) litre (of beer).

Masse die (PL die **Massen**) 1 mass; **eine Masse Arbeit** masses of work; 2 crowd; 3 mixture (*in cooking*).

massenhaft adjective masses of.

massieren verb (PERF **hat massiert**) to massage.

mäßig adjective moderate.

Maßnahme die (PL die **Maßnahmen**) measure.

Maßstab der (PL die **Maßstäbe**) 1 standard; 2 scale.

Mast der (PL die **Masten**) 1 mast; 2 pole; 3 pylon.

Material das (PL die **Materialien**) 1 material; 2 materials.

Mathe die (*informal*) maths.

Mathematik die mathematics.

Matratze die (PL die **Matratzen**) mattress.

Matrose der (PL die **Matrosen**) sailor.

Matsch der 1 mud; 2 slush.

matschig adjective 1 muddy; 2 slushy.

matt adjective 1 weak; 2 matt; 3 dull; 4 matt! checkmate!

Matte die (PL die **Matten**) mat.

Mauer die (PL die **Mauern**) wall.

Maul das (PL die **Mäuler**) mouth; **halt's Maul!** (*informal*) shut up!

Maulkorb der (PL die **Maulkörbe**) muzzle.

Maulwurf der (PL die **Maulwürfe**) mole.

Maurer der (PL die **Maurer**) bricklayer.

Maus die (PL die **Mäuse**) mouse.

Mayonnaise die mayonnaise.

Mechaniker der (PL die **Mechaniker**) mechanic.

mechanisch adjective mechanical.

meckern verb (PERF **hat gemeckert**) 1 to bleat; 2 to grumble.

Medaille die (PL die **Medaillen**) medal.

Medien plural noun media.

Medikament das (PL die **Medikamente**) medicine, drug.

Medizin die (PL die **Medizinen**) medicine.

Meer das (PL die **Meere**) sea.

Meeresfrüchte plural noun seafood.

Meerschweinchen das (PL die **Meerschweinchen**) guinea pig.

Mehl das flour.

mehr adverb, pronoun more; **nichts mehr** no more; **nie mehr** never again.

mehrere pronoun several.

mehreres pronoun several things.

mehrfach adjective 1 multiple, many; 2 repeated.
adverb several times.

◆ IRREGULAR VERB: *See the verb table in the centre of the dictionary*

Mehrheit die (PL die Mehrheiten) majority.

mehrmalig adjective repeated.

mehrmals adverb several times.

Mehrwertsteuer die value added tax.

Mehrzahl die 1 majority; 2 plural.

meiden ◇ verb (IMPERF mied, PERF hat gemieden) to avoid.

Meile die (PL die Meilen) mile.

mein adjective my.

meine SEE meiner.

meinen verb (PERF hat gemeint) 1 to think; 2 to mean; **es gut meinen** to mean well; 3 to say.

meiner, meine, mein(e)s pronoun mine.

meinetwegen adverb 1 for my sake; 2 because of me; 3 as far as I'm concerned; **'kann ich das Auto haben?'** – **'meinetwegen'** 'can I take the car?' – 'I don't mind'.

meins SEE meiner.

Meinung die (PL die Meinungen) opinion.

meist adverb 1 mostly; 2 usually.

meiste adjective, pronoun **der/die/das meiste** most; **die meisten** most; **am meisten** most, the most.

meistens adverb 1 mostly; 2 usually.

Meister der (PL die Meister) 1 master; 2 champion.

Meisterin die (PL die Meisterinnen) champion.

Meisterschaft die (PL die Meisterschaften) championship.

Meisterwerk das (PL die Meisterwerke) masterpiece.

melden verb (PERF hat gemeldet) 1 to report; 2 to register; 3 **sich melden** to report; (on the phone) to answer; **Luise hat sich gemeldet** (in school) Luise put up her hand; 4 **sich bei jemandem melden** to get in touch with somebody.

Melodie die (PL die Melodien) melody, tune.

Melone die (PL die Melonen) 1 melon; 2 bowler (hat).

Menge die (PL die Mengen) 1 quantity; **eine Menge Geld** a lot of money; 2 crowd; 3 set (in maths).

Mensch der (PL die Menschen) 1 human being; 2 person; **kein Mensch** nobody; **jeder Mensch** everybody; 3 **die Menschen** people; **wie viele Menschen?** how many people?; 4 (as an exclamation) **Mensch!** (informal) wow!, hey!; **Mensch, hab ich mich geärgert!** (informal) I was damn annoyed.

menschenleer adjective deserted.

Menschenverstand der **gesunder Menschenverstand** common sense.

Menschheit die mankind.

menschlich adjective 1 human; 2 humane.

△ NEW SPELLING: **See page xii**

Mentalität die (PL die Mentalitäten) mentality.

Menü das (PL die Menüs) 1 menu; 2 set meal.

merken verb (PERF hat gemerkt) 1 to notice; 2 **sich etwas merken** to remember something.

Merkmal das (PL die Merkmale) feature.

merkwürdig adjective strange, odd.

Messe die (PL die Messen) 1 mass; 2 trade fair.

messen ◇ verb (PRES **misst** Δ, IMPERF **maß**, PERF **hat gemessen**) 1 to measure; (bei jemandem) **Fieber messen** to take somebody's temperature; 2 **sich mit jemandem messen können** to be as good as somebody.

Messer das (PL die Messer) knife.

Messing das brass.

Metall das (PL die Metalle) metal.

Meter der (PL die Meter) metre.

Metermaß das (PL die Metermaße) tape measure.

Methode die (PL die Methoden) method.

metrisch adjective metric.

Metzger der (PL die Metzger) butcher.

Metzgerei die (PL die Metzgereien) butcher's (shop).

Mexiko das Mexico.

miauen verb (PERF hat miaut) to miaow.

mich pronoun 1 me; 2 myself.

mied SEE meiden.

Miete die (PL die Mieten) 1 rent; **zur Miete wohnen** to live in rented accommodation; 2 hire charge.

mieten verb (PERF hat gemietet) 1 to rent; 2 to hire.

Mieter der (PL die Mieter) tenant.

Mieterin die (PL die Mieterinnen) tenant.

Mietshaus das (PL die Mietshäuser) block of rented flats.

Mietvertrag der (PL die Mietverträge) lease.

Mietwagen der (PL die Mietwagen) hire car.

Mikrofon das (PL die Mikrofone) microphone.

Mikroskop das (PL die Mikroskope) microscope.

Mikrowellenherd der (PL die Mikrowellenherde) microwave oven.

Milch die milk.

mild adjective mild.

Militär das army.

militärisch adjective military.

Milliarde die (PL die Milliarden) thousand million, billion.

Millimeter der (PL die Millimeter) millimetre.

Million die (PL die Millionen) million.

◇ IRREGULAR VERB: *See the verb table in the centre of the dictionary*

Millionär *der* (PL *die* **Millionäre**) millionaire.

Millionärin *die* (PL *die* **Millionärinnen**) millionairess.

Minderheit *die* (PL *die* **Minderheiten**) minority.

minderjährig *adjective* under age.

mindestens *adverb* at least.

mindester, mindeste, mindestes *adjective* least. *pronoun* **1 der/die/das Mindeste** △ the least; **zum Mindesten** △ at least; **2 nicht im Mindesten** △ not in the least.

Mine *die* (PL *die* **Minen**) **1** mine; **2** lead (*in a pencil*); **3** refill (*for a ball-point*).

Mineralwasser *das* (PL *die* **Mineralwasser**) mineral water.

Minirock *der* (PL *die* **Miniröcke**) miniskirt.

Minister *der* (PL *die* **Minister**) minister.

Ministerin *die* (PL *die* **Ministerinnen**) minister.

Ministerium *das* (PL *die* **Ministerien**) ministry, department.

minus *adverb* minus.

Minute *die* (PL *die* **Minuten**) minute.

mir *pronoun* **1** me, to me; **2** myself.

mischen *verb* (PERF **hat gemischt**) **1** to mix; **2 die Karten mischen** to shuffle the cards; **3 sich mischen** to mix.

Mischung *die* (PL *die* **Mischungen**) **1** mixture; **2** blend.

miserabel *adjective* (*informal*) **1** hopeless; **2** dreadful.

missbilligen △ *verb* (PERF **hat missbilligt**) to disapprove.

Missbrauch △ *der* abuse.

missbrauchen △ *verb* (PERF **hat missbraucht**) to abuse.

Misserfolg △ *der* (PL *die* **Misserfolge**) failure.

Missgeschick △ *das* (PL *die* **Missgeschicke**) **1** misfortune; **2** mishap.

misshandeln △ *verb* (PRES **misshandelt**) to ill-treat.

misslingen △ ◇ *verb* (IMPERF **misslang**, PERF **ist misslungen**) to fail; **es misslang ihr** she failed.

misst △ SEE **messen**.

Misstrauen △ *das* **1** mistrust; **2** distrust.

misstrauen △ *verb* (PERF **hat misstraut**) **jemandem misstrauen** to mistrust somebody.

misstrauisch △ *adjective* suspicious.

Missverständnis △ *das* (PL *die* **Missverständnisse**) misunderstanding.

missverstehen △ ◇ *verb* (IMPERF **missverstand**, PERF **hat missverstanden**) to misunderstand.

Mist *der* **1** manure; **2** (*informal*) rubbish.

Mistel *die* (PL *die* **Misteln**) mistletoe.

△ NEW SPELLING: See page xii

mit *preposition* ←(+DAT) **1** with; **2 mit der Bahn fahren** to go by train; **3 mit sechs Jahren** at the age of six; **4 mit jemandem sprechen** to speak to somebody; **5 mit Bleistift** in pencil; **6 mit lauter Stimme** in a loud voice. *adverb* as well, too; **warst du mit dabei?** were you there too?

Mitarbeiter *der* (PL die **Mitarbeiter**) **1** colleague; **2** employee.

Mitarbeiterin *die* (PL die **Mitarbeiterinnen**) **1** colleague; **2** employee.

mitbringen ◇ *verb* (IMPERF **brachte mit**, PERF **hat mitgebracht**) to bring, to bring along; **ich bringe den Kindern Schokolade mit** I'm taking the children some chocolate.

miteinander *adverb* with each other, with one another.

Mitesser *der* (PL die **Mitesser**) blackhead.

mitfahren ◇ *verb* (PRES **fährt mit**, IMPERF **fuhr mit**, PERF **ist mitgefahren**) **1 mit jemandem mitfahren** to go with somebody; **die Kinder fahren mit uns mit** the children are coming with us; **2 bei jemandem mitfahren** to get a lift with somebody; **jemanden mitfahren lassen** to give somebody a lift.

mitgeben ◇ *verb* (PRES **gibt mit**, IMPERF **gab mit**, PERF **hat mitgegeben**) to give.

Mitglied *das* (PL die **Mitglieder**) member.

mithalten ◇ *verb* (PRES **hält mit**, IMPERF **hielt mit**, PERF **hat mitgehalten**) to keep up.

mitkommen ◇ *verb* (IMPERF **kam mit**, PERF **ist mitgekommen**) **1** to come too; **2** to keep up.

Mitleid *das* pity; **kein Mitleid mit jemandem haben** not to feel any sympathy for somebody.

mitmachen *verb* (PERF **hat mitgemacht**) **1** to join in; **hast du Lust, bei dem Spiel mitzumachen?** do you want to join in the game?; **2** to take part in; **3** to go through (*experiences, troubles*); **sie hat viel mitgemacht** she's gone through a lot.

mitnehmen ◇ *verb* (PRES **nimmt mit**, IMPERF **nahm mit**, PERF **hat mitgenommen**) **1** to take, to take along; **Anni hat die Kinder auf den Spielplatz mitgenommen** Anni has taken the children to the playground; **2** to give a lift to; **3** to affect (badly); **4 zum Mitnehmen** to take away.

Mitschüler *der* (PL die **Mitschüler**) schoolfriend.

Mitschülerin *die* (PL die **Mitschülerinnen**) schoolfriend.

mitspielen *verb* (PERF **hat mitgespielt**) **1** to play; **wer spielt bei dem Fußballspiel mit?** who's playing in the football match?; **willst du mitspielen?** do you want to join in?; **2 in einem Film mitspielen** to be in a film.

Mittag *der* (PL die **Mittage**) **1** midday; **2** lunch; **zu Mittag essen** to have lunch; **3** lunch-break.

◇ **IRREGULAR VERB: See the verb table in the centre of the dictionary**

Mittagessen das (PL die Mittagessen) lunch; **beim Mittagessen** at lunch.

mittags adverb 1 at lunchtime, at midday; 2 **um zwölf Uhr mittags** at noon.

Mittagspause die (PL die Mittagspausen) lunch-break.

Mitte die (PL die Mitten) 1 middle; 2 centre.

Mitteilung die (PL die Mitteilungen) 1 announcement; 2 communication.

Mittel das (PL die Mittel) 1 means; 2 **ein Mittel gegen Husten** a cough remedy; 3 **öffentliche Mittel** public funds.

Mittelalter das Middle Ages.

mittelgroß adjective medium-sized.

mittelmäßig adjective mediocre.

Mittelmeer das Mediterranean.

Mittelpunkt der (PL die Mittelpunkte) centre; **im Mittelpunkt stehen** to be the centre of attention.

Mittelstand der middle class.

Mittelstürmer der (PL die Mittelstürmer) centre-forward.

mitten adverb **mitten in/auf** in the middle of; **mitten in der Nacht** in the middle of the night.

Mitternacht die midnight.

mittlerer, **mittlere**, **mittleres** adjective 1 middle; 2 medium (quality, size); 3 average.

mittlerweile adverb 1 meanwhile; 2 by now.

Mittwoch der (PL die Mittwoche) Wednesday.

mittwochs adverb on Wednesdays.

Möbel plural noun furniture.

Möbelwagen der (PL die Möbelwagen) removal van.

Mobiltelefon das (PL die Mobiltelefone) mobile phone.

möbliert adjective furnished.

mochte, möchte SEE mögen.

Mode die (PL die Moden) fashion.

Modell das (PL die Modelle) model.

Moderator der (PL die Moderatoren) presenter (on TV).

Moderatorin die (PL die Moderatorinnen) presenter (on TV).

modern adjective modern.

modernisieren verb (PERF hat modernisiert) to modernize.

modisch adjective fashionable.

Mofa das (PL die Mofas) moped.

mogeln verb (PERF hat gemogelt) to cheat.

mögen ◇ verb (PRES mag, IMPERF mochte, PERF hat gemocht) 1 to like; **ich mag ihn nicht** I don't like him; **ich möchte** I'd like; **ich möchte gern wissen** I'd like to know; **möchtest du nach Hause?** would you like to go home?; 2 **lieber mögen** to prefer; **ich möchte lieber Tee** I would prefer tea; 3 **etwas nicht tun mögen** not to want to do

△ NEW SPELLING: See page xii

something; **ich mag nicht fragen** I don't want to ask; **ich mag nicht mehr** I've had enough; **4 das mag sein** maybe; **5 was mag das sein?** whatever can it be?

möglich *adjective* possible; **alles Mögliche** all sorts of things.

möglicherweise *adverb* possibly.

Möglichkeit *die* (PL *die* Möglichkeiten) possibility.

möglichst *adverb* if possible; **möglichst früh** as early as possible.

Möhre *die* (PL *die* Möhren) carrot.

Molekül *das* (PL *die* Moleküle) molecule.

Moment *der* (PL *die* Momente) moment; **im Moment** at the moment; **Moment (mal)!** just a moment!

Monat *der* (PL *die* Monate) month.

monatelang *adverb* for months.

monatlich *adjective, adverb* monthly.

Mönch *der* (PL *die* Mönche) monk.

Mond *der* (PL *die* Monde) moon.

Mondschein *der* moonlight; **im Mondschein** by moonlight.

Montag *der* (PL *die* Montage) Monday.

montags *adverb* on Mondays.

Moped *das* (PL *die* Mopeds) moped.

Moral *die* 1 moral; 2 morale; 3 morals.

moralisch *adjective* moral.

Mord *der* (PL *die* Morde) murder.

Mörder *der* (PL *die* Mörder) murderer.

Mörderin *die* (PL *die* Mörderinnen) murderer.

morgen *adverb* tomorrow; **morgen Abend** tomorrow evening.

Morgen *der* (PL *die* Morgen) morning; **am Morgen** in the morning; **heute Morgen** △ this morning; **guten Morgen!** good morning!

morgens *adverb* in the morning.

Moschee *die* (PL *die* Moscheen) mosque.

Mosel *die* (River) Moselle.

Moslem *der* (PL *die* Moslems) Muslim.

moslemisch *adjective* Muslim.

Moskau *das* Moscow.

Moslime *der* (PL *die* Moslimen) Muslim.

Motiv *das* (PL *die* Motive) 1 motive; 2 motif.

Motor *der* (PL *die* Motoren) engine, motor.

Motorrad *das* (PL *die* Motorräder) motorcycle, motorbike.

Möwe *die* (PL *die* Möwen) seagull.

Mücke *die* (PL *die* Mücken) 1 midge; 2 mosquito.

müde *adjective* tired.

Müdigkeit *die* tiredness.

Mühe *die* (PL *die* Mühen) 1 effort;

◇ IRREGULAR VERB: *See the verb table in the centre of the dictionary*

sich Mühe geben to make an effort; **2** trouble; **machen Sie sich keine Mühe** don't go to any trouble; **3 mit Müh und Not** only just.

Mühle die (PL die **Mühlen**) **1** mill; **2** grinder (for coffee).

mühsam adjective laborious.

Müll der rubbish.

Müllabfuhr die refuse collection.

Mülleimer der (PL die **Mülleimer**) rubbish bin.

Mülltonne die (PL die **Mülltonnen**) dustbin.

Mumps der mumps.

München das Munich.

Mund der (PL die **Münder**) mouth; **halt den Mund!** (informal) shut up!

Mundharmonika die (PL die **Mundharmonikas**) mouth organ.

mündlich adjective oral.

Münster das (PL die **Münster**) cathedral.

Münze die (PL die **Münzen**) coin.

Münzfernsprecher der (PL die **Münzfernsprecher**) payphone.

murmeln verb (PERF hat gemurmelt) to mumble.

mürrisch adjective surly.

Muschel die (PL die **Muscheln**) **1** mussel; **2** (sea) shell; **3** mouthpiece (of a phone).

Museum das (PL die **Museen**) museum.

Musik die music.

musikalisch adjective musical.

Musiker der (PL die **Musiker**) musician.

Musikerin die (PL die **Musikerinnen**) musician.

Muskat der nutmeg.

Muskel der (PL die **Muskeln**) muscle.

Müsli das muesli.

muss △ SEE **müssen**.

müssen ◇ verb (PRES **muss** △, IMPERF **musste** △, PERF **hat gemusst** △) **1 etwas tun müssen** to have to do something; **sie muss es tun** she's got to do it, she must do it; **muss ich?** do I have to?; **muss das sein?** is that necessary?; **2 Sie müssten es mal versuchen** you should try it; **3 sie müssen gleich hier sein** they'll be here at any moment; **4 ich muss mal** (informal) I need (to go to) the loo.

Muster das (PL die **Muster**) **1** pattern; **2** sample.

Mut der courage; **jemandem Mut machen** to encourage somebody.

mutig adjective courageous.

Mutter[1] die (PL die **Mütter**) mother.

Mutter[2] die (PL die **Muttern**) nut.

Muttersprache die (PL die **Muttersprachen**) mother tongue, native language.

Muttertag der (PL die Muttertage)
Mother's Day.

Mutti die (PL die Muttis) mum.

Mütze die (PL die Mützen) cap.

MwSt. (Mehrwertsteuer) VAT.

Mythos der (PL die Mythen) myth.

N n

na exclamation well; **na und?** so
what?; **na gut** all right then.

Nabel der (PL die Nabel) navel.

nach preposition ←(+DAT) **1** to; **nach
Hause gehen** to go home; **nach
oben** up; **nach hinten** back; **nach
rechts abbiegen** to turn right;
2 after; **nach Ihnen** after you; **zehn
nach eins** ten past one; **nach etwas
greifen** to reach for something;
3 according to; **meiner Meinung
nach** in my opinion.
adverb **nach und nach** bit by bit,
gradually; **nach wie vor** still.

nachahmen verb (PERF hat
nachgeahmt) to imitate.

Nachbar der (PL die Nachbarn)
neighbour.

Nachbarin die (PL die
Nachbarinnen) neighbour.

Nachbarschaft die
neighbourhood.

nachdem conjunction **1** after; **2 je
nachdem** it depends; **je nachdem,
wie schnell du damit fertig wirst** it

depends on how quicky you can
finish it.

nachdenken ◇ verb (IMPERF
dachte nach, PERF hat
nachgedacht) to think; **über etwas
nachdenken** to think about
something; **ich lange lange über ihr
Angebot nachgedacht und mich
schließlich dagegen entschieden**
I've thought a long time about her
offer and finally decided against it.

nachdenklich adjective
thoughtful.

nacheinander adverb one after the
other; **die Bewerber kamen
nacheinander herein** the
applicants came in one after the
other.

Nachfrage die (PL die Nachfragen)
demand; **es besteht keine
Nachfrage** there's no demand for it.

nachgehen ◇ verb (IMPERF ging
nach, PERF ist nachgegangen) **1** to
be slow; **meine Uhr geht nach** my
watch is slow; **2 jemandem
nachgehen** to follow somebody;
einer Sache nachgehen to look
into something.

nachher adverb afterwards; **erst
gehen wir ins Kino und nachher
könnten wir essen gehen** we go to
the cinema first and afterwards we
could go for a meal; **bis nachher!**
see you later!

nachholen verb (PERF hat
nachgeholt) **1** to catch up on; **ich
hatte Grippe und muss jetzt viel
Mathe nachholen** I've had flu and
now I've got a lot of maths to catch
up on; **2** to make up for (something

◇ IRREGULAR VERB: See the verb table in the centre of the dictionary

missed); **3 eine Prüfung nachholen** to do an exam at a later date.

Nachtklub *der* (PL *die* **Nachtklubs**) night club.

nachkommen ◊ *verb* (IMPERF **kam nach**, PERF **ist nachgekommen**) **1** to come later, to follow; **2 ich komme nicht nach** I can't keep up; **3 einem Versprechen nachkommen** to carry out a promise; **seinen Verpflichtungen nachkommen** to meet your commitments.

nachlassen ◊ *verb* (PRES **lässt nach**△, IMPERF **ließ nach**, PERF **hat nachgelassen**) **1** to ease; **meine Zahnschmerzen lassen langsam nach** my toothache is getting better; **2** to let up; **sobald die Kälte nachlässt** as soon as it gets warmer; **3** to deteriorate; **4 etwas vom Preis nachlassen** to take something off the price; **jemandem zwanzig Mark nachlassen** to give somebody twenty marks off.

nachlässig *adjective* careless.

nachlaufen ◊ *verb* (PRES **läuft nach**, IMPERF **lief nach**, PERF **ist nachgelaufen**) **jemandem nachlaufen** to run after somebody; **Philipp läuft allen Mädchen nach** (*informal*) Philipp chases all the girls.

nachmachen *verb* (PERF **hat nachgemacht**) to copy.

Nachmittag *der* (PL *die* **Nachmittage**) afternoon.

nachmittags *adverb* in the afternoon.

Nachnahme *die* **per Nachnahme** cash on delivery.

Nachname *der* (PL *die* **Nachnamen**) surname.

nachprüfen *verb* (PERF **hat nachgeprüft**) to check; **er prüft nach, ob es stimmt** he's going to check if it is correct.

Nachricht *die* (PL *die* **Nachrichten**) **1** news; **ich warte noch immer auf eine Nachricht von ihm** I'm still waiting for news of him; **eine Nachricht hinterlassen** to leave a message; **2 die Nachrichten** the news; **das kam in den Nachrichten** it was on the news.

Nachrichtensprecher *der* (PL *die* **Nachrichtensprecher**) newsreader.

Nachrichtensprecherin *der* (PL *die* **Nachrichtensprecherinnen**) newsreader.

nachschlagen ◊ *verb* (PRES **schlägt nach**, IMPERF **schlug nach**, PERF **hat nachgeschlagen**) to look up.

nachsehen ◊ *verb* (PRES **sieht nach**, IMPERF **sah nach**, PERF **hat nachgesehen**) **1** to check; **sieh nach, wer da ist** go and see who's there; **2** to look up; **3 jemandem etwas nachsehen** to let somebody get away with something.

nachsitzen ◊ *verb* (IMPERF **saß nach**, PERF **hat nachgesessen**) to be in detention; **Jan muss nachsitzen** Jan has detention.

Nachspeise *die* (PL *die* **Nachspeisen**) dessert, pudding.

△ NEW SPELLING: *See page xii*

nächste SEE nächster.

nächstens *adverb* shortly.

nächste, nächste, nächstes
adjective 1 next; 2 nearest; **am
nächsten sein** to be nearest; 3 **in
nächster Nähe** close by.
pronoun **der/die/das Nächste** △
(the) next; **als Nächstes** △ next.

Nacht *die* (PL *die* **Nächte**) night.

Nachteil *der* (PL *die* **Nachteile**)
disadvantage.

Nachtfalter *der* (PL *die* **Nachtfalter**)
moth.

Nachthemd *das* (PL *die*
Nachthemden) nightdress,
nightshirt.

Nachtigall *die* (PL *die* **Nachtigallen**)
nightingale.

Nachtisch *der* (PL *die* **Nachtische**)
dessert, pudding.

Nachtleben *das* nightlife.

nachträglich *adjective*
1 subsequent; 2 belated.
adverb 1 later; 2 belatedly.

nachts *adverb* at night; **um zwei Uhr
nachts** at two o'clock in the
morning.

Nacken *der* (PL *die* **Nacken**) neck.

nackt *adjective* 1 naked; 2 bare.

Nadel *die* (PL *die* **Nadeln**) 1 needle;
2 pin.

Nagel *der* (PL *die* **Nägel**) nail.

Nagelbürste *die* (PL *die*
Nagelbürsten) nailbrush.

Nagelfeile *die* (PL *die* **Nagelfeilen**)
nailfile.

Nagellack *der* (PL *die* **Nagellacke**)
nail varnish.

nagelneu *adjective* brand-new.

Nagelschere *die* (PL *die*
Nagelscheren) nail scissors.

nahe, nah *adjective, adverb* 1 near,
nearby; **der Nahe Osten** the Middle
East; **nahe daran sein, etwas zu tun**
to nearly do something; 2 close;
nahe bei close to; **nahe verwandt
sein** to be closely related;
3 **jemandem nahe legen** △, **etwas zu
tun** to urge somebody to do
something; 4 **nahe liegend** △
obvious.
preposition ←(+DAT) near, close to.

Nähe *die* 1 proximity; 2 **in der Nähe
der Kirche** near the church; **ganz
in der Nähe** nearby; 3 **aus der
Nähe** close up.

nahelegen, naheliegend SEE
nahe.

nähen *verb* (PERF **hat genäht**) 1 to
sew; 2 to stitch (*a wound*).

näher *adjective* 1 closer; 2 **nähere
Einzelheiten** further details;
3 shorter (*way, road*).
adverb 1 closer; **näher kommen** to
come closer; 2 more closely;
3 **Näheres** further details.

nähern *verb* (PERF **hat sich
genähert**) **sich nähern** to
approach.

Nähgarn *das* cotton.

nahm SEE nehmen.

◇ IRREGULAR VERB: *See the verb table in the centre of the dictionary*

Nähmaschine die (PL die Nähmaschinen) sewing machine.

Nahrung die food.

Naht die (PL die Nähte) seam.

Nahverkehrszug der (PL die Nahverkehrszüge) local train.

Name der (PL die Namen) name.

nämlich adverb 1 because; 2 namely; 3 das war nämlich ganz anders it was quite different actually.

nannte SEE nennen.

nanu exclamation well, well!

Narbe die (PL die Narben) scar.

Narr der (PL die Narren) fool.

Närrin die (PL die Närrinnen) fool.

Nase die (PL die Nasen) nose; die Nase voll haben (informal) to have had enough.

Nasenbluten das nosebleed.

Nashorn das (PL die Nashörner) rhinoceros.

nass△ adjective wet.

Nation die (PL die Nationen) nation.

Nationalhymne die (PL die Nationalhymnen) national anthem.

Nationalität die (PL die Nationalitäten) nationality.

Natur die 1 nature; von Natur aus by nature; 2 die freie Natur the open countryside.

natürlich adjective natural. adverb of course, naturally.

Naturschutzgebiet das (PL die Naturschutzgebiete) nature reserve.

Naturwissenschaft die natural science.

Nebel der (PL die Nebel) 1 fog; 2 mist.

nebelig adjective = neblig.

neben preposition ←(+DAT, or +ACC with movement towards a place) 1 next to; er hat neben mir gesessen he sat next to me; er hat sich neben mich gesetzt he sat down next to me; 2 apart from.

nebenan adverb next door.

nebenbei adverb 1 as well, at the same time; er liest die Zeitung und hört nebenbei Musik he reads the newspaper and listens to music at the same time; 2 on the side; nebenbei arbeite ich noch in einem Blumengeschäft I work in a florist's on the side; das mache ich so nebenbei (informal) that's just a sideline; 3 in passing; nebenbei bemerkt by the way.

nebeneinander adverb next to each other.

nebenhergehen◇ verb (IMPERF ging nebenher, PERF ist nebenhergegangen) to walk alongside.

neblig adjective 1 foggy; 2 misty.

necken verb (PERF hat geneckt) to tease.

Neffe der (PL die Neffen) nephew.

negativ adjective negative.

△ NEW SPELLING: See page xii

Negativ *das* (PL *die* Negative) negative.

nehmen ◆ *verb* (PRES **nimmt**, IMPERF **nahm**, PERF **hat genommen**) 1 to take; 2 **ich nehme eine Suppe** I'll have soup; 3 **was nehmen Sie dafür?** how much do you want for it?; 4 **jemanden zu sich nehmen** to have somebody live with you; 5 **sich etwas nehmen** to take something; **nimm dir ein Stück Kuchen** help yourself to a piece of cake.

Neid *der* envy, jealousy.

neidisch *adjective* envious, jealous.

nein *adverb* no.

Nelke *die* (PL *die* Nelken) carnation.

nennen ◆ *verb* (IMPERF **nannte**, PERF **hat genannt**) 1 to call; 2 to name; 3 **ihr Name wurde nicht genannt** her name wasn't mentioned; 4 **sich nennen** to call yourself.

Nerv *der* (PL *die* Nerven) nerve; **Gabi geht mir auf die Nerven** Gabi gets on my nerves.

nervös *adjective* nervous.

Nervosität *die* nervousness.

Nessel *die* (PL *die* Nesseln) nettle.

Nest *das* (PL *die* Nester) 1 nest; 2 little place (*a village*).

nett *adjective* nice.

netto *adverb* net.

Netz *das* (PL *die* Netze) 1 net; 2 network; 3 string bag; 4 (*spider's*) web.

neu *adjective* 1 new; **wie neu** as good as new; **neue Sprachen** modern

languages; 2 **seit neuestem** recently; 3 **die neueste Mode** the latest fashion; **das Neueste** the latest news; 4 **das ist mir neu** that's news to me.
adverb 1 newly; 2 only just; **es ist neu eingetroffen** it has only just come in; 3 **etwas neu schreiben** to rewrite something.

neuartig *adjective* new; **ein neuartiger Flaschenöffner** a new kind of bottle opener.

neuerdings *adverb* recently.

Neugier *die* curiosity.

neugierig *adjective* curious, inquisitive.

Neuigkeit *die* (PL *die* Neuigkeiten) piece of news; **gibt es irgendwelche Neuigkeiten?** is there any news?

Neujahr *das* New Year, New Year's Day.

neulich *adverb* the other day.

neun *number* nine.

neunter, neunte, neuntes *adjective* ninth.

neunzehn *number* nineteen.

neunzig *number* ninety.

Neuseeland *das* New Zealand.

nicht *adverb* 1 not; **ich kann nicht** I can't; **Iris hat nicht angerufen** Iris didn't ring; **bitte nicht** please don't; **nicht!** don't!; **nicht berühren!** don't touch!; 2 **'ich mag das nicht' – 'ich auch nicht'** 'I don't like it' – 'neither do I'; 3 **nicht (wahr)?** isn't he/she/it?; **du kennst ihn doch,**

◆ IRREGULAR VERB: *See the verb table in the centre of the dictionary*

nicht? you know him, don't you?;
4 **gar nicht** not at all; 5 **nicht mehr**
no more.

Nichte die (PL die **Nichten**) niece.

Nichtraucher der (PL die
Nichtraucher) non-smoker.

nichts pronoun 1 nothing; 2 **ich
habe nichts gewusst** I didn't know
anything; 3 **nichts mehr** no more;
4 **das macht nichts** it doesn't
matter; 5 **nichts ahnend** △
unsuspecting.

nichtsahnend SEE **nichts**.

nicken verb (PERF hat **genickt**) to
nod.

Nickerchen das (PL die
Nickerchen) nap; **ein Nickerchen
machen** to have a nap.

nie adverb never.

nieder adjective low.
adverb down.

Niederlage die (PL die **Niederlagen**)
defeat.

Niederlande plural noun die
Niederlande the Netherlands.

Niederländer der (PL die
Niederländer) Dutchman; **die
Niederländer** the Dutch.

Niederländerin die (PL die
Niederländerinnen) Dutchwoman.

niederländisch adjective Dutch.

niedlich adjective sweet.

niedrig adjective 1 low; 2 base.

niemals adverb never.

niemand pronoun nobody; **wir**

haben niemand or **niemanden
gesehen** we didn't see anybody.

Niere die (PL die **Nieren**) kidney.

nieseln verb (PERF hat **genieselt**) to
drizzle; **es nieselt** it's drizzling.

niesen verb (PERF hat **geniest**) to
sneeze.

Nilpferd das (PL die **Nilpferde**)
hippopotamus.

nimmt SEE **nehmen**.

nirgends, nirgendwo adverb
nowhere.

Niveau das (PL die **Niveaus**) 1 level;
2 standard.

noch adverb 1 still; **immer noch**
still; 2 even; **noch besser** even
better; 3 **noch nicht** not yet; **noch
nie** never; 4 **gerade noch** only
just; 5 **wer war noch da?** who else
was there?; **was noch?** what else?;
6 **noch einmal** again; 7 **noch ein
Bier** another beer; **noch etwas
Kaffee?** (would you like some) more
coffee?; 8 **noch gestern** only
yesterday; 9 **noch und noch Geld**
loads of money.
conjunction nor; **weder ... noch**
neither ... nor

nochmals adverb again.

Nominativ der (PL die **Nominative**)
nominative.

Nordamerika das North America.

Norden der north.

Nordirland das Northern Ireland.

nördlich adjective 1 northern;
2 northerly (direction).

△ NEW SPELLING: See page xii

adverb, preposition ←(+GEN)
nördlich von Wien to the north of
Vienna; **nördlich der Stadt** north of
the town.

Nordosten der north-east.

Nordpol der North Pole.

Nordsee die North Sea.

Nordwesten der north-west.

nörgeln verb (PERF hat genörgelt) to
grumble.

Norm die (PL die Normen) 1 norm;
2 standard.

normal adjective normal.

normalerweise adverb normally.

Norwegen das Norway.

Norweger der (PL die Norweger)
Norwegian.

Norwegerin die (PL die
Norwegerinnen) Norwegian.

norwegisch adjective Norwegian.

Not die (PL die Nöte) 1 need; **zur Not**
if necessary, at a pinch; **mit knapper
Not** only just; 2 hardship.

Notausgang der (PL die
Notausgänge) emergency exit.

Notdienst der **Notdienst haben** to
be on call.

Note die (PL die Noten) 1 note; **Noten
lesen** to read music; 2 mark.

Notfall der (PL die Notfälle)
emergency.

notfalls adverb if need be.

notieren verb (PERF hat notiert) 1 to
note down; 2 **sich etwas notieren**
to make a note of something.

nötig adjective necessary.
adverb urgently.

Notiz die (PL die Notizen) 1 note;
2 **keine Notiz von etwas nehmen**
to take no notice of something;
3 item (*in a newspaper*).

Notizblock der (PL die Notizblöcke)
notepad.

Notizbuch das (PL die Notizbücher)
notebook.

Notlage die (PL die Notlagen) crisis.

Notruf der (PL die Notrufe)
1 emergency call; 2 emergency
number.

notwendig adjective necessary.

November der November.

nüchtern adjective 1 sober; **wieder
nüchtern werden** to sober up;
2 **auf nüchternen Magen** on an
empty stomach; 3 down-to-earth.

Nudeln plural noun 1 noodles;
2 pasta.

null number 1 nought; **unter null**
below zero; 2 nil; **zwei zu null** two
nil; 3 love (*in tennis*); 4 **null Fehler
haben** to have no mistakes; **ich habe
null Ahnung** (*informal*) I haven't
got a clue; 5 **in null Komma nichts**
(*informal*) in less than no time.

Null die (PL die Nullen) 1 zero,
nought; 2 failure.

numerieren = **nummerieren**.

Nummer die (PL die Nummern)
1 number; 2 issue (*of a magazine*);

✧ **IRREGULAR VERB: See the verb table in the centre of the dictionary**

3 size (*of clothing*); **4** act; **5** auf Nummer sicher gehen to play safe.

nummerieren △ *verb* (PERF hat nummeriert) to number.

Nummernschild das (PL die Nummernschilder) number plate.

nun *adverb* now.
exclamation well; **nun ja …** well, yes …

nur *adverb* **1** only; **2 was sollen wir nur tun?** what on earth are we going to do?; **sie soll es nur versuchen!** just let her try!; **3 nur zu!** go ahead!

Nürnberg das Nuremberg.

Nuss △ die (PL die Nüsse) nut.

Nutzen der benefit; **von Nutzen sein** to be useful.

nutzen, nützen *verb* (PERF hat genutzt/genützt) **1** to use; **etwas nutzen** to take advantage of something; **2** to be useful; **3 nichts nutzen** to be no use; **das nutzt mir nichts** that won't help me; **4 das nutzt ja doch nichts** it's pointless.

nützlich *adjective* useful.

nutzlos *adjective* useless.

O o

ob *conjunction* **1** whether; **wissen Sie, ob heute noch ein Zug nach Freising fährt?** do you know if there is another train to Freising today?; **2 ob Alex noch anruft?** I wonder if Alex will ring; **3 und ob!** you bet!

obdachlos *adjective* homeless.

Obdachlose der/die (PL die Obdachlosen) homeless person; **die Obdachlosen** the homeless.

oben *adverb* **1** on top; **oben auf** on top of; **die Vase steht oben auf dem Schrank** the vase is on top of the cupboard; **2** at the top; **von oben bis unten** from top to bottom; **er hat uns von oben bis unten gemustert** he looked us up and down; **3** upstairs; **4 nach oben** up, upstairs; **er ist nach oben in sein Zimmer gegangen** he went up into his room; **geht der Fahrstuhl nach oben?** is the lift going up?; **hier oben** up here; **da oben** up there; **5 siehe oben** see above (*on a page*); **oben erwähnt** △ above mentioned; **6 oben ohne** (*informal*) topless.

obenerwähnt SEE oben.

Ober der (PL die Ober) waiter; **Herr Ober!** waiter!

oberer, obere, oberes *adjective* upper, top.

Oberfläche die (PL die Oberflächen) surface.

oberflächlich *adjective* superficial.

Oberhaupt das (PL die Oberhäupter) head.

Oberhemd das (PL die Oberhemden) shirt.

Oberschenkel der (PL die Oberschenkel) thigh.

Oberschule die (PL die Oberschulen) secondary school.

oberster, oberste, oberstes
adjective top.

Oberstufe die (PL die **Oberstufen**)
upper school.

Oberweite die (PL die **Oberweiten**)
chest size, bust measurement.

Objekt das (PL die **Objekte**) object.

objektiv *adjective* objective.

Objektiv das (PL die **Objektive**) lens.

Obst das fruit.

Obstbaum der (PL die **Obstbäume**)
fruit tree.

Obstsalat der (PL die **Obstsalate**)
fruit salad.

obszön *adjective* obscene.

obwohl *conjunction* although.

öde *adjective* 1 desolate; 2 dreary;
das ist so ein furchtbar öder Job
it's such terribly dull job.

oder *conjunction* 1 or; 2 **du kennst
sie doch, oder?** you know her, don't
you?

Ofen der (PL die **Öfen**) 1 oven;
2 stove; 3 heater.

offen *adjective* 1 open; **offen haben**
to be open; **Tag der offenen Tür**
open day; 2 frank; 3 vacant; **eine
offene Stelle** a vacancy; 4 **offen
bleiben**△ to stay open; 5 **offen
bleiben**△ to remain open (*of a
question, possibility*).
adverb 1 openly; 2 frankly; **offen
gesagt** frankly.

offenbar *adjective* obvious.
adverb 1 apparently; 2 **da hast du
dich offenbar geirrt** you seem to

have made a mistake; **sie hat
offenbar den Zug verpasst** she
must have missed the train.

offenbleiben SEE **offen**.

offensichtlich *adjective* obvious.

öffentlich *adjective* public.

Öffentlichkeit die public; **in aller
Öffentlichkeit** in public.

offiziell *adjective* official.

Offizier der (PL die **Offiziere**) officer.

öffnen *verb* (PERF **hat geöffnet**) to
open; **jemandem die Tür öffnen** to
open the door for somebody.

Öffner der (PL die **Öffner**) opener.

Öffnung die (PL die **Öffnungen**)
opening.

Öffnungszeiten *plural noun*
opening times.

oft *adverb* often.

öfter, öfters *adverb* quite often; **ich
habe ihn öfters mal getroffen** I
used to meet him quite often.

ohne *preposition* ←(+ACC) 1 without;
ohne mich count me out; 2 **ohne
weiteres** easily; 3 **oben ohne**
(*informal*) topless; 4 **das ist nicht
ohne** (*informal*) it's not bad.
conjunction without; **ohne zu
überlegen** without thinking.

Ohnmacht die **in Ohnmacht fallen**
to faint.

ohnmächtig *adjective*
1 unconscious; 2 **ohnmächtig
werden** to faint; **Roswitha ist
ohnmächtig** Roswitha's fainted.

✧ IRREGULAR VERB: *See the verb table in the centre of the dictionary*

Ohr das (PL die Ohren) ear.

Ohrenschmerzen plural noun earache.

Ohrring der (PL die Ohrringe) earring.

oje exclamation oh dear!

Ökoladen der (PL die Ökoläden) health-food shop.

Ökologie die ecology.

ökologisch adjective ecological.

Oktober der October.

Öl das (PL die Öle) oil.

Ölfarbe die (PL die Ölfarben) oil-paint.

Ölgemälde das (PL die Ölgemälde) oil painting.

ölig adjective oily.

Olive die (PL die Oliven) olive.

Olivenöl das (PL die Olivenöle) olive oil.

Olympiade die (PL die Olympiaden) Olympic Games; **die Olympiade findet alle vier Jahre statt** the Olympic Games take place every four years.

olympisch adjective Olympic.

Oma die (PL die Omas) granny.

Omelett das (PL die Omeletts) omelette.

Omi die (PL die Omis) granny.

Onkel der (PL die Onkel) uncle.

Opa der (PL die Opas) grandpa.

Oper die (PL die Opern) opera.

Operation die (PL die Operationen) operation.

Operationssaal der (PL die Operationssäle) operating theatre.

operieren verb (PERF hat operiert) 1 to operate on; **sich operieren lassen** to have an operation; **sie wurde am Magen operiert** she had a stomach operation; 2 to operate.

Opfer das (PL die Opfer) 1 sacrifice; 2 victim; **das Erdbeben forderte viele Opfer** the earthquake claimed many victims.

Optiker der (PL die Optiker) optician.

Optikerin die (PL die Optikerinnen) optician.

Optimist der (PL die Optimisten) optimist.

optimistisch adjective optimistic.

orange adjective orange.

Orange die (PL die Orangen) orange.

Orangensaft der (PL die Orangensäfte) orange juice.

Orchester das (PL die Orchester) orchestra.

ordentlich adjective 1 tidy; 2 respectable; 3 proper (meal, job, salary); 4 **eine ordentliche Tracht Prügel** (informal) a good hiding. adverb 1 tidily; **ordentlich schreiben** to write neatly; 2 respectably; 3 properly; 4 **ordentlich feiern** (informal) to have a really good celebration; **wir sind ordentlich nass geworden** (informal) we got soaked.

ordinär adjective vulgar.

△ NEW SPELLING: See page xii

ordnen verb (PERF **hat geordnet**)
1 to arrange; 2 to put in order.

Ordner der (PL die **Ordner**) file.

Ordnung die 1 order; **Ordnung
halten** to keep order; 2 **Ordnung
machen** to tidy up; **die Wohnung in
Ordnung bringen** to tidy up the flat;
3 **mit der Waschmaschine ist etwas
nicht in Ordnung** there's something
wrong with the washing machine;
4 **etwas in Ordnung bringen** to put
something right; **die
Waschmaschine in Ordnung
bringen** to repair the washing
machine; 5 **in Ordnung!** okay!;
6 **er ist in Ordnung** he's all right.

Organ das (PL die **Organe**) 1 organ;
2 (informal) voice.

Organisation die (PL die
Organisationen) organization.

organisch adjective organic.

organisieren verb (PERF **hat
organisiert**) 1 to organize;
2 (informal) to get (hold of).

Orgel die (PL die **Orgeln**) organ.

orientieren verb (PERF **hat sich
orientiert**) 1 **sich orientieren** to get
your bearings; 2 **sich über etwas
orientieren** to inform yourself
about something.

Orientierung die 1 orientation;
die Orientierung verlieren to lose
your bearings; 2 **zu Ihrer
Orientierung** for your information.

Orientierungssinn der sense of
direction.

originell adjective original.

Orkan der (PL die **Orkane**) hurricane.

Ort der (PL die **Orte**) 1 place; **an Ort
und Stelle** on the spot; 2 (small)
town.

Orthografie △, **Orthographie**
die spelling.

örtlich adjective local.

Ortschaft die (PL die **Ortschaften**)
village.

Ortsgespräch das (PL die
Ortsgespräche) local call.

Ossi der (informal) (PL die **Ossis**)
East German.

Osten der east.

Osterei das (PL die **Ostereier**) Easter
egg.

Ostern das Easter.

Österreich das Austria.

Österreicher der (PL die
Österreicher) Austrian.

Österreicherin die (PL die
Österreicherinnen) Austrian.

österreichisch adjective Austrian.

östlich adjective 1 eastern;
2 easterly.
adverb, preposition ←(+GEN) **östlich
von Wien** to the east of Vienna;
östlich der Stadt east of the town.

Ostsee die Baltic (Sea).

oval adjective oval.

Ozean der (PL die **Ozeane**) ocean.

Ozon das ozone.

Ozonschicht die ozone layer.

✧ IRREGULAR VERB: *See the verb table in the centre of the dictionary*

P p

paar *pronoun* **ein paar** a few; **ein paar Mal** △ a few times; **alle paar Tage** every few days.

Paar *das* (PL die **Paare**) **1** pair; **ein Paar Schuhe** a pair of shoes; **2** couple.

paarmal SEE **paar**.

paarweise *adjective* in pairs; **die Kinder stellten sich paarweise auf** the children lined up in pairs.

Päckchen *das* (PL die **Päckchen**) **1** package, packet; **2** small parcel.

packen *verb* (PERF **hat gepackt**) **1** to pack; **ich muss jetzt meinen Koffer packen** I must pack my case now; **2** to grab (hold of); **von Furcht gepackt** seized with fear.

Packung *die* (PL die **Packungen**) packet, pack.

Pädagoge *der* (PL die **Pädagogen**) **1** educationalist; **2** teacher.

pädagogisch *adjective* educational.

Paddel *das* (PL die **Paddel**) paddle.

Paket *das* (PL die **Pakete**) **1** parcel; **Gabi hat mir ein Paket geschickt** Gabi sent me a parcel; **2** packet; **kaufe bitte ein Paket Waschpulver für mich** can you please buy a packet of washing powder for me.

Palast *der* (PL die **Paläste**) palace.

Palme *die* (PL die **Palmen**) palm (tree).

Pampelmuse *die* (PL die **Pampelmusen**) grapefruit.

Panik *die* panic; **in Panik geraten** to panic.

Panne *die* (PL die **Pannen**) **1** breakdown; **wir haben auf dem Rückweg eine Panne gehabt** we had a breakdown on the way back; **2** mishap; **uns ist eine Panne passiert** we had a mishap.

Papa *der* (PL die **Papas**) daddy.

Papagei *der* (PL die **Papageien**) parrot.

Papier *das* (PL die **Papiere**) paper.

Papierkorb *der* (PL die **Papierkörbe**) waste-paper basket.

Papiertüte *die* (PL die **Papiertüten**) paper bag.

Pappe *die* (PL die **Pappen**) cardboard.

Paprika *der* (PL die **Paprikas**) **1** pepper; **2** paprika.

Papst *der* (PL die **Päpste**) pope.

Parabolantenne *die* (PL die **Parabolantennen**) satellite dish.

Paradies *das* paradise.

Paragraph *der* (PL die **Paragraphen**) **1** section; **2** clause.

parallel *adjective* parallel.

Pärchen *das* (PL die **Pärchen**) couple.

Parfüm *das* (PL die **Parfüms**) perfume.

△ NEW SPELLING: See page xii

Park der (PL die Parks) park.

Parkanlage die (PL die Parkanlagen) park.

parken verb (PERF hat geparkt) to park.

Parkett das (PL die Parkette) 1 (in a theatre) stalls; 2 parquet floor.

Parkhaus das (PL die Parkhäuser) multi-storey car park.

Parklücke die (PL die Parklücken) parking space.

Parkplatz der (PL die Parkplätze) 1 car park; 2 parking space.

Parkschein der (PL die Parkscheine) car-park ticket.

Parkuhr die (PL die Parkuhren) parking meter.

Parkverbot das 'Parkverbot' 'no parking'; in der Innenstadt ist Parkverbot you can't park in the town centre.

Parlament das (PL die Parlamente) parliament.

Parole die (PL die Parolen) slogan.

Partei die (PL die Parteien) 1 party; 2 für jemanden Partei ergreifen to side with somebody.

Parterre das (PL die Parterres) ground floor.

Partie die (PL die Partien) 1 part; 2 game (of tennis, chess).

Partner der (PL die Partner) partner.

Partnerin die (PL die Partnerinnen) partner.

Partnerstadt die (PL die Partnerstädte) twin town.

Party die (PL die Partys) party.

Pass Δ der (PL die Pässe) 1 passport; 2 pass.

Passagier der (PL die Passagiere) passenger.

Passant der (PL die Passanten) passer-by.

Passantin die (PL die Passantinnen) passer-by.

passen (PERF hat gepasst Δ) 1 to fit; jemandem passen to fit somebody; 2 to suit; jemandem passen to suit somebody; Freitag passt mir nicht Friday doesn't suit me; seine Art passt mir nicht I don't like his manner; 3 zu etwas passen to go with something; zu jemandem passen to be right for somebody.

passend adjective 1 suitable; 2 matching.

passieren verb (PERF ist passiert) to happen.

passiv adjective passive.

Passiv das passive.

Passkontrolle Δ die passport control.

Paste die (PL die Pasten) paste.

Pastete die (PL die Pasteten) pie.

Pate die (PL die Paten) godfather.

Patenkind das (PL die Patenkinder) godchild.

patent adjective capable, clever.

◇ **IRREGULAR VERB:** *See the verb table in the centre of the dictionary*

Patentante der (PL die Patentanten) godmother.

Patient der (PL die Patienten) patient.

Patientin die (PL die Patientinnen) patient.

Patin die (PL die Patinnen) godmother.

patschnass ∆ adjective soaking wet.

pauken verb (informal) (PERF hat gepaukt) to swot.

Pauschalreise die (PL die Pauschalreisen) package tour.

Pause die (PL die Pausen) 1 break; 2 pause; 3 interval.

Pazifik der der Pazifik the Pacific (Ocean).

PC der (PL die PCs) PC.

Pech das 1 bad luck; Pech haben to be unlucky; 2 pitch.

Pedal das (PL die Pedale) pedal.

peinlich adjective 1 embarrassing; es war mir sehr peinlich I felt very embarrassed about it; 2 awkward; 3 meticulous.

Peitsche die (PL die Peitschen) whip.

Pelle die skin.

Pelz der (PL die Pelze) fur.

pendeln verb 1 (PERF ist gependelt) to commute; 2 (PERF hat gependelt) to swing.

Pendler der (PL die Pendler) commuter.

penetrant adjective 1 overpowering (odour, perfume); 2 pushy (person).

Penis der (PL die Penisse) penis.

pennen verb (informal) (PERF hat gepennt) to sleep, to kip.

Pension die (PL die Pensionen) 1 guesthouse; 2 bei voller Pension with full board; 3 pension; eine schöne Pension haben to get a good pension; in Pension gehen to retire.

pensioniert adjective retired.

per preposition ←(+ACC) 1 by; per Luftpost by airmail; 2 per.

perfekt adjective perfect.

Perfekt das (PL die Perfekte) perfect.

Periode die (PL die Perioden) period.

Perle die (PL die Perlen) 1 pearl; 2 bead.

Person die (PL die Personen) person; für vier Personen for four people; ich für meine Person personally.

Personal das staff, personnel.

Personenzug der (PL die Personenzüge) stopping train.

Personalausweis der (PL die Personalausweise) identity card.

persönlich adjective personal. adverb 1 personally; 2 in person.

Perücke die (PL die Perücken) wig.

Pessimist der (PL die Pessimisten) pessimist.

∆ NEW SPELLING: See page xii

pessimistisch *adjective*
pessimistic.

Petersilie *die* parsley.

Petroleum *das* paraffin.

Pfad *der* (PL *die* Pfade) path.

Pfadfinder *der* (PL *die* Pfadfinder)
(Boy) Scout.

Pfadfinderin *die* (PL *die*
Pfadfinderinnen) (Girl) Guide.

Pfand *das* (PL *die* Pfänder) **1** forfeit;
2 deposit (*on a bottle*); **3** pledge.

Pfanne *die* (PL *die* Pfannen) (frying)
pan.

Pfannkuchen *der* (PL *die*
Pfannkuchen) pancake.

Pfarrer *der* (PL *die* Pfarrer) **1** vicar;
2 priest.

Pfau *der* (PL *die* Pfauen) peacock.

Pfeffer *der* pepper.

Pfefferkorn *das* (PL *die*
Pfefferkörner) peppercorn.

Pfefferkuchen *der* gingerbread.

Pfefferminzbonbon *der* (PL *die*
Pfefferminzbonbons) mint.

Pfefferminze *die* peppermint.

Pfeffermühle *die* (PL *die*
Pfeffermühlen) peppermill.

Pfeife *die* (PL *die* Pfeifen) **1** whistle;
2 pipe.

pfeifen ◊ *verb* (IMPERF pfiff, PERF hat
gepfiffen) to whistle.

Pfeil *der* (PL *die* Pfeile) arrow.

Pfeiler *der* (PL *die* Pfeiler) **1** pillar;
2 pier.

Pfennig *der* (PL *die* Pfennige)
pfennig; **ein Kaugummi kostet
zwanzig Pfennig** a chewing gum is
twenty pfennigs; **ich habe keinen
Pfennig mehr** I haven't got a penny
left.

Pferd *das* (PL *die* Pferde) horse.

Pferdeschwanz *der* (PL *die*
Pferdeschwänze) ponytail.

pfiff SEE pfeifen.

Pfingsten *das* (PL *die* Pfingsten)
Whitsun.

Pfirsich *der* (PL *die* Pfirsiche) peach.

Pflanze *die* (PL *die* Pflanzen) plant.

pflanzen *verb* (PERF hat gepflanzt)
to plant.

Pflaster *das* (PL *die* Pflaster)
1 pavement; **2** plaster.

Pflaume *die* (PL *die* Pflaumen) plum.

Pflege *die* **1** care; **2** nursing; **3** ein
Kind in Pflege nehmen to foster a
child.

Pflegeeltern *plural noun* foster
parents.

Pflegeheim *das* (PL *die*
Pflegeheime) nursing home.

Pflegekind *das* (PL *die*
Pflegekinder) foster child.

pflegeleicht *adjective* easy-care
(*fabric*).

pflegen *verb* (PERF hat gepflegt) **1** to
look after, to care for; **eine
Freundschaft pflegen** to foster a
friendship; **2** to nurse.

◊ IRREGULAR VERB: *See the verb table in the centre of the dictionary*

Pfleger der (PL die **Pfleger**) (male) nurse.

Pflicht die (PL die **Pflichten**) duty; **Pflicht sein** to be compulsory.

pflichtbewusst △ adjective conscientious.

Pflichtfach das (PL die **Pflichtfächer**) compulsory subject.

pflücken verb (PERF **hat gepflückt**) to pick.

Pflug der (PL die **Pflüge**) plough.

Pforte die (PL die **Pforten**) gate.

Pförtner der (PL die **Pförtner**) porter.

Pfosten der (PL die **Pfosten**) post.

Pfote die (PL die **Pfoten**) paw.

pfui exclamation ugh!

Pfund das (PL die **Pfund(e)**) pound.

Pfütze die (PL die **Pfützen**) puddle.

Phantasie die 1 imagination; 2 **Phantasien** (plural) fantasies.

phantasievoll adjective imaginative.

phantastisch adjective fantastic.

Philosoph der (PL die **Philosophen**) philosopher.

Philosophie die (PL die **Philosophien**) philosophy.

Photo das (PL die **Photos**) photo.

Physik die physics.

Physiker der (PL die **Physiker**) physicist.

Physikerin die (PL die **Physikerinnen**) physicist.

Pickel der (PL die **Pickel**) spot, pimple.

Picknick das (PL die **Picknicks**) picnic.

Pik das spades (in cards).

pikant adjective spicy.

Pille die (PL die **Pillen**) pill.

Pilot der (PL die **Piloten**) pilot.

Pilz der (PL die **Pilze**) 1 mushroom; 2 fungus.

Pinguin der (PL die **Pinguine**) penguin.

pinkeln verb (informal) (PERF **hat gepinkelt**) to pee.

Pinnwand die (PL die **Pinnwände**) noticeboard.

Pinsel der (PL die **Pinsel**) brush.

Pinzette die (PL die **Pinzetten**) tweezers.

Pirat der (PL die **Piraten**) pirate.

Piste die (PL die **Pisten**) 1 run, piste; 2 track; 3 runway.

Pizza die (PL die **Pizzas**) pizza.

Pkw der (PL die **Pkws**) (Personenkraftwagen) car.

plagen verb (PERF **hat geplagt**) 1 to bother, to torment; 2 to pester; 3 **sich plagen** to struggle; **sich in der Schule plagen** to struggle at school; **er muss sich plagen** he has to work hard.

Plakat das (PL die **Plakate**) poster.

Plan der (PL die **Pläne**) 1 plan; 2 map.

△ NEW SPELLING: See page xii

planen *verb* (PERF hat geplant) to plan.

planmäßig *adjective* scheduled.
adverb **1** according to plan; **alles läuft planmäßig** everything is going according to plan; **2** on schedule; **der Zug ist planmäßig abgefahren** the train left on schedule.

Plastik[1] *das* plastic.

Plastik[2] *die* (PL die **Plastiken**) sculpture.

Plastiktüte *die* (PL die **Plastiktüten**) plastic bag.

platt *adjective* flat; **platt sein** (*informal*) to be flabbergasted.

plattdeutsch *adjective* low German.

Platte *die* (PL die **Platten**) **1** plate; **2** dish; **kalte Platte** cold meats and cheeses; **3** hotplate; **4** record; **5** board (*made of wood*); **6** slab (*made of stone*); **7** sheet (*made of metal or glass*); **8** top (*of a table*).

Plattenspieler *der* (PL die **Plattenspieler**) record player.

Platz *der* (PL die **Plätze**) **1** place; **viel Platz haben** to have a lot of room; **Platz lassen** to leave room; **auf die Plätze, fertig, los!** on your marks, get set, go!; **2** seat; **Platz nehmen** to take a seat; **3** square (*in a town*); **4** ground, pitch; **einen Spieler vom Platz stellen** to send a player off; **5** court (*for tennis*); **6** course (*for golf*).

Plätzchen *das* (PL die **Plätzchen**) **1** biscuit; **2** spot.

platzen *verb* (PERF ist geplatzt) **1** to burst; **2 der Plan ist geplatzt** (*informal*) the plan fell through; **3 vor Neugier platzen** to be bursting with curiosity.

plaudern *verb* (PERF hat geplaudert) to chat.

pleite *adjective* (*informal*) broke.

Plombe *die* (PL die **Plomben**) filling.

plombieren *verb* (PERF hat plombiert) to fill.

plötzlich *adjective* sudden.
adverb suddenly.

plump *adjective* **1** plump; **2** clumsy.

Plural *der* (PL die **Plurale**) plural.

plus *adverb* plus.

Plus *das* **1** plus; **2** profit; **3** advantage.

PLZ = **Postleitzahl**.

Po *der* (*informal*) (PL die **Pos**) bottom.

Poesie *die* poetry.

Pokal *der* (PL die **Pokale**) **1** cup; **2** goblet.

Pokalspiel *das* (PL die **Pokalspiele**) cup-tie.

Pole *der* (PL die **Polen**) Pole.

Polen *das* Poland.

polieren *verb* (PERF hat poliert) to polish.

Polin *die* (PL die **Polinnen**) Pole.

Politik *die* **1** politics; **2** policy.

Politiker *der* (PL die **Politiker**) politician.

✧ IRREGULAR VERB: *See the verb table in the centre of the dictionary*

Politikerin die (PL die Politikerinnen) politician.

politisch adjective political.

Politur die (PL die Polituren) polish.

Polizei die police.

polizeilich adjective police. adverb by the police; **sich polizeilich anmelden** to register with the police.

Polizeiwache die (PL die Polizeiwachen) police station.

Polizist der (PL die Polizisten) policeman.

Polizistin die (PL die Polizistinnen) policewoman.

polnisch adjective Polish.

Pommes frites plural noun chips, French fries.

Pony[1] das (PL die Ponys) pony.

Pony[2] der (PL die Ponys) fringe.

Popmusik die pop music.

poppig adjective bright; **Natalie hat immer poppige Socken an** Natalie always wears bright socks.

Porree der leeks; **eine Stange Porree** a leek.

Portemonnaie das = Portmonee.

Portier der (PL die Portiers) porter.

Portion die (PL die Portionen) portion.

Portmonee△ das (PL die Portmonees) purse.

Porto das postage.

Porträt das (PL die Porträts) portrait.

Portugal das Portugal.

Portugiese der (PL die Portugiesen) Portuguese.

Portugiesin die (PL die Portugiesinnen) Portuguese.

portugiesisch adjective Portuguese.

Posaune die (PL die Posaunen) trombone.

Post die 1 post; **mit der Post** by post; 2 post office.

Postamt das (PL die Postämter) post office.

Postbote der (PL die Postboten) postman.

Poster das (PL die Poster) poster.

Postkarte die (PL die Postkarten) postcard.

Postleitzahl die (PL die Postleitzahlen) postcode.

prächtig adjective splendid.

prahlen verb (PERF hat geprahlt) to boast.

praktisch adjective 1 practical; **praktische Erfahrung** practical experience; 2 handy; 3 **ein praktischer Arzt** a general practitioner. adverb 1 practically; 2 in practice.

Praline die (PL die Pralinen) chocolate.

Präposition die (PL die Präpositionen) preposition.

Präsens das present (tense).

△ NEW SPELLING: See page xii

Präservativ das (PL die
Präservative) condom.

Präsident der (PL die Präsidenten)
president.

Präsidentin die (PL die
Präsidentinnen) president.

Praxis die (PL die Praxen)
1 practice; 2 practical experience;
3 surgery.

Preis der (PL die Preise) 1 price; um
keinen Preis not at any price;
2 prize.

Preisausschreiben das (PL die
Preisausschreiben) competition.

Preiselbeere die (PL die
Preiselbeeren) cranberry.

preiswert adjective reasonable,
cheap.

Prellung die (PL die Prellungen)
bruise.

Premierminister der (PL die
Premierminister) prime minister.

Presse die press.

Priester der (PL die Priester) priest.

prima adjective (informal) brilliant.

Prinz der (PL die Prinzen) prince.

Prinzessin die (PL die
Prinzessinnen) princess.

Prise die (PL die Prisen) pinch; eine
Prise Salz a pinch of salt.

privat adjective private.

Privileg das (PL die Privilegien)
privilege.

pro preposition ←(+ACC) per.

Probe die (PL die Proben) 1 test;
jemanden auf die Probe stellen to
test somebody; ein Auto Probe
fahren △ to test-drive a car;
2 sample; 3 rehearsal.

probefahren SEE Probe.

probieren verb (PERF hat probiert)
1 to try; 2 to taste.

Problem das (PL die Probleme)
problem.

Produkt das (PL die Produkte)
product.

Produzent der (PL die Produzenten)
producer.

produzieren verb (PERF hat
produziert) to produce.

Profi der (PL die Profis) pro.

Profil das (PL die Profile) 1 profile;
2 tread (of a tyre).

Programm das (PL die Programme)
1 programme; 2 program (in
computing); 3 channel (on TV).

programmieren verb (PERF hat
programmiert) to program.

Programmierer der (PL die
Programmierer) programmer.

Projekt das (PL die Projekte) project.

Promille das alcohol level; zuviel
Promille haben to be over the limit.

Pronomen das (PL die Pronomen or
Pronomina) pronoun.

Prospekt der (PL die Prospekte)
brochure.

prost exclamation cheers!

✧ **IRREGULAR VERB:** *See the verb table in the centre of the dictionary*

Protein das (PL die Proteine) protein.

Protest der (PL die Proteste) protest.

protestantisch adjective Protestant.

protestieren verb (PERF hat protestiert) to protest.

Protokoll das (PL die Protokolle) 1 minutes, transcript; 2 record (in court); 3 protocol.

protzen verb (PERF hat geprotzt) to show off; **Klaus protzt mit seinem neuen Auto** Klaus is showing off with his new car.

Proviant der provisions.

Prozent das (PL die Prozente) 1 per cent; **zehn Prozent** ten per cent; **2 Prozente bekommen** (informal) to get a discount.

Prozentsatz der (PL die Prozentsätze) percentage.

Prozess △ der (PL die Prozesse) 1 court case; **einen Prozess gewinnen** to win a case; 2 trial; 3 process.

prüfen verb (PERF hat geprüft) 1 to test, to examine (at school); 2 to check; **hast du die Reifen geprüft?** have you checked the tyres?

Prüfung die (PL die Prüfungen) 1 examination, exam; **eine Prüfung bestehen** to pass an examination; **sie ist durch die Prüfung gefallen** she failed the exam; 2 check.

Prügel der (PL die Prügel) 1 stick; **2 Prügel bekommen** to get a beating.

Prügelei die (PL die Prügeleien) fight.

prügeln verb (PERF hat geprügelt) 1 to beat; **2 sich prügeln** to fight; **sich um etwas prügeln** to fight for something.

Psychiater der (PL die Psychiater) psychiatrist.

Psychiaterin die (PL die Psychiaterinnen) psychiatrist.

psychisch adjective psychological.

Psychologe der (PL die Psychologen) psychologist.

Psychologie die psychology.

Psychologin die (PL die Psychologinnen) psychologist.

Publikum das 1 audience, crowd; 2 public.

Pudding der (PL die Puddings) 1 blancmange; 2 pudding (steamed).

Pudel der (PL die Pudel) poodle.

Puder der (PL die Puder) powder.

Puffmais der popcorn.

Pulli der (PL die Pullis) pullover.

Pullover der (PL die Pullover) pullover.

Puls der (PL die Pulse) pulse.

Pult das (PL die Pulte) desk.

Pulver das (PL die Pulver) powder.

Pulverkaffee der instant coffee.

Pumpe die (PL die Pumpen) pump.

pumpen verb (PERF hat gepumpt) 1 to pump; 2 (informal) to lend;

△ NEW SPELLING: See page xii

jemandem Geld pumpen to lend somebody money; **3** (*informal*) to borrow; **sich etwas pumpen** to borrow something.

Punker *der* (PL *die* **Punker**) punk.

Punkerin *die* (PL *die* **Punkerinnen**) punk.

Punkt *der* (PL *die* **Punkte**) **1** dot, spot; **Punkt sechs Uhr** at six o'clock on the dot; **2** full stop; **3** point; **nach Punkten siegen** to win on points.

pünktlich *adjective* punctual.

Puppe *die* (PL *die* **Puppen**) **1** doll; **2** puppet.

pur *adjective* **1** pure; **2** Whisky pur neat whisky.

Purzelbaum *der* (PL *die* **Purzelbäume**) somersault.

pusten *verb* (PERF **hat gepustet**) to blow.

Pute *die* (PL *die* **Puten**) turkey.

putzen *verb* (PERF **hat geputzt**) **1** to clean; **putz dir die Zähne** clean your teeth; **putzen gehen** to work as a cleaner; **2 sich Nase putzen** to blow your nose.

Putzfrau *die* (PL *die* **Putzfrauen**) cleaning lady, cleaner.

putzig *adjective* cute.

Puzzle *das* (PL *die* **Puzzles**) jigsaw (puzzle).

Pyjama *der* (PL *die* **Pyjamas**) pyjamas.

Pyramide *die* (PL *die* **Pyramiden**) pyramid.

Pyrenäen (*plural noun*) die **Pyrenäen** the Pyrenees.

Q q

Quadrat *das* (PL *die* **Quadrate**) square.

quadratisch *adjective* square.

Quadratmeter *der* (PL *die* **Quadratmeter**) square metre.

quaken *verb* (PERF **hat gequakt**) **1** to quack; **2** to croak (*of a frog*).

Qual *die* (PL *die* **Qualen**) **1** torment; **2** agony; **es war eine Qual, das ansehen zu müssen** it was agony to watch.

quälen *verb* (PERF **hat gequält**) **1** to torment; **2** to torture; **3** to pester; **4 sich quälen** to suffer; **5 sich mit etwas quälen** to struggle with something; **sich durch ein Buch quälen** to struggle (your way) through a book.

Quälgeist *der* (*informal*) (PL *die* **Quälgeister**) pest.

Qualifikation *die* (PL *die* **Qualifikationen**) qualification.

Qualität *die* (PL *die* **Qualitäten**) quality.

Qualle *die* (PL *die* **Quallen**) jellyfish.

Qualm *der* thick smoke.

qualmen *verb* (PERF **hat gequalmt**) to give off clouds of smoke; **sie**

⬦ **IRREGULAR VERB:** *See the verb table in the centre of the dictionary*

qualmt wie ein Schlot (*informal*) she smokes like a chimney.

Quarantäne *die* quarantine.

Quark *der* (*curd cheese*) quark.

Quartett *das* (PL *die* Quartette) quartet.

Quartier *das* (PL *die* Quartiere) 1 accommodation; 2 quarters.

quasseln *verb* (*informal*) (PERF **hat gequasselt**) to natter.

Quatsch *der* (*informal*) rubbish.

quatschen *verb* (*informal*) (PERF **hat gequatscht**) to chat.

Quelle *die* (PL *die* Quellen) 1 source; 2 spring.

quer *adverb* 1 across; 2 crosswise; 3 diagonally; **quer gestreift**△ with diagonal stripes; 4 **quer durch** straight through.

quergestreift SEE **quer**.

Querstraße *die* (PL *die* Querstraßen) side street; **die erste Querstraße rechts** the first turning on the right.

quetschen *verb* (PERF **hat gequetscht**) 1 to crush; 2 to squash; 3 **ich habe mich in meine Jeans gequetscht** I squeezed into my jeans.

Quetschung *die* (PL *die* Quetschungen) bruise.

quietschen *verb* (PERF **hat gequietscht**) to squeak.

quitt *adjective* quits.

Quittung *die* (PL *die* Quittungen) receipt.

Quiz *das* (PL *die* Quiz) quiz.

R r

Rabatt *der* (PL *die* Rabatte) discount.

Rache *die* revenge.

rächen *verb* (PERF **hat gerächt**) 1 to avenge; 2 **sich an jemandem rächen** to take revenge on somebody; 3 **das wird sich rächen** you'll have to pay for it.

Rad *das* (PL *die* Räder) 1 wheel; 2 bike; **Julia ist mit dem Rad gekommen** Julia came by bike; 3 **Rad fahren**△ to cycle.

Radar *der* radar.

Radarschirm *der* (PL *die* Radarschirme) radar screen.

radfahren SEE **Rad**.

Radfahrer *der* (PL *die* Radfahrer) cyclist.

Radfahrerin *die* (PL *die* Radfahrerinnen) cyclist.

Radfahrweg *der* (PL *die* Radfahrwege) cycle lane.

radeln *verb* (PERF **ist geradelt**) to cycle; **Max ist ins Dorf geradelt** Max cycled into the village.

Radiergummi *der* (PL *die* Radiergummis) rubber.

Radieschen *das* (PL *die* Radieschen) radish.

△ NEW SPELLING: *See page xii*

Radio das (PL die Radios) radio.

radioaktiv adjective radioactive.

Radler der (PL die Radler) cyclist.

Radlerin die (PL die Radlerinnen) cyclist.

Radrennen das 1 cycle race; **Maria hat das Radrennen gewonnen** Maria won the cycle race; 2 cycle racing.

raffiniert adjective crafty.

Rahm der cream.

Rahmen der (PL die Rahmen) 1 frame; 2 framework; 3 limits; **im Rahmen des Möglichen** within the bounds of possibility.

rahmen verb (PERF hat gerahmt) to frame (a picture).

Rakete die (PL die Raketen) rocket.

ran (informal) SEE heran.

Rand der (PL die Ränder) 1 edge; 2 rim; **der Rand der Tasse war angeschlagen** the rim of the cup was chipped; 3 ring, mark; 4 margin (of a page); **du musst einen Rand für die Korrekturen lassen** you must leave a margin for the corrections; 5 outskirts (of a town); 6 **etwas am Rande erwähnen** to mention something in passing; 7 **am Rande der Pleite sein** to be on the verge of bankruptcy; 8 **außer Rand und Band geraten** (informal) to go wild.

Randstreifen der (PL die Randstreifen) hard shoulder.

Rang der (PL die Ränge) 1 rank; 2 (in a theatre) circle.

rannte SEE rennen.

rasch adjective quick.

Rasen der (PL die Rasen) lawn, grass.

rasen verb (PERF ist gerast) to tear along, to rush; **gegen eine Mauer rasen** to career into a wall.

Rasenmäher der (PL die Rasenmäher) lawnmower.

Rasierapparat der (PL die Rasierapparate) 1 shaver; 2 razor.

Rasiercreme die (PL die Rasiercremes) shaving cream.

rasieren verb (PERF hat rasiert) 1 to shave; 2 **sich rasieren** to shave.

Rasierklinge die (PL die Rasierklingen) razor blade.

Rasierwasser das aftershave.

Rasse die (PL die Rassen) 1 race; 2 breed; **ich weiß nicht, was für eine Rasse unser Hund ist** I don't know what breed our dog is.

Rassenhass △ der racial hatred.

rassisch adjective racial.

Rassismus der racism.

Rassist der (PL die Rassisten) racist.

Rassistin die (PL die Rassistinnen) racist.

rassistisch adjective racist.

rasten verb (PERF hat gerastet) to rest.

Rastplatz der (PL die Rastplätze) picnic area (on a motorway).

Raststätte die (PL die Raststätten) services (on a motorway).

⬦ IRREGULAR VERB: See the verb table in the centre of the dictionary

Rat der 1 advice; ein Rat a piece of advice; jemanden zu Rate ziehen to ask somebody's advice; 2 sich keinen Rat wissen not to know what to do; 3 council.

Rate die (PL die Raten) instalment; in monatlichen Raten abzahlen to pay in monthly instalments.

raten ◇ verb (PRES rät, IMPERF riet, PERF hat geraten) 1 jemandem raten to advise somebody; was rätst du mir? what do you advise me to do? 2 to guess; richtig raten to guess right.

Rathaus das (PL die Rathäuser) town hall.

rationell adjective efficient.

ratlos adjective helpless; Emma hat mich ratlos angesehen Emma gave me a helpless look; ratlos sein not to know what to do.

ratsam adjective advisable; es wäre ratsam, früher zu fahren it would be advisable to leave earlier.

Ratschlag der (PL die Ratschläge) piece of advice, advice; deine klugen Ratschläge kannst du dir sparen you can keep your advice to yourself.

Rätsel das (PL die Rätsel) 1 puzzle; 2 mystery.

rätselhaft adjective mysterious.

Ratte die (PL die Ratten) rat.

rau△ adjective 1 rough; 2 harsh; 3 eine raue Stimme a husky voice; 4 einen rauen Hals haben to have a sore throat.

Raub der robbery.

Räuber der (PL die Räuber) robber.

Rauch der smoke.

rauchen verb (PERF hat geraucht) to smoke; 'Rauchen verboten' 'no smoking'.

Raucher der (PL die Raucher) smoker.

Raucherin die (PL die Raucherinnen) smoker.

räuchern verb (PERF hat geräuchert) to smoke (fish, meat).

rauf (informal) SEE herauf, hinauf.

rauh adjective = rau.

Raum der (PL die Räume) 1 room; das Haus hat sehr große Räume the house has very big rooms; 2 space; wir brauchen mehr Raum we need more space; 3 die Rakete ist im Raum explodiert the rocket exploded in space; 4 area; im Raum Berlin in the area of Berlin.

räumen verb (PERF hat geräumt) 1 to clear; das Geschirr vom Tisch räumen to clear away the dishes; 2 die Hemden in den Schrank räumen to put the shirts in the cupboard; seine Sachen beiseite räumen to put your things to one side; die Akten aus dem Schrank räumen to take the files out of the cabinet; 3 to vacate.

Raumfahrt die space travel.

Raumschiff das (PL die Raumschiffe) space ship.

Raupe die (PL die Raupen) caterpillar.

△ NEW SPELLING: See page xii

raus (*informal*) SEE **heraus, hinaus**.

Rauschgift *das* (PL *die* Rauschgifte) drug; **Rauschgift nehmen** to take drugs.

Rauschgiftsüchtige *der/die* (PL *die* Rauschgiftsüchtigen) drug addict.

rauskriegen *verb* (*informal*) (PERF hat rausgekriegt) **1** to get out; **2 ein Geheimnis rauskriegen** to find out a secret; **3 ich kann die Aufgabe nicht rauskriegen** I can't do the exercise.

räuspern *verb* (PERF hat sich geräuspert) **sich räuspern** to clear your throat.

reagieren *verb* (PERF hat reagiert) to react.

Reaktion *die* (PL *die* Reaktionen) reaction.

realisieren *verb* (PERF hat realisiert) **1** to realize; **2** to implement.

Realschule *die* (PL *die* Realschulen) secondary school.

rebellieren *verb* (PERF hat rebelliert) to rebel.

rechnen *verb* (PERF hat gerechnet) **1** to do arithmetic; **Peter kann gut rechnen** Peter's good at arithmetic, Peter's good at figures; **2** to reckon; **mit etwas rechnen** to reckon with something; **3 er wird zu den besten Schauspielern gerechnet** he's reckoned to be one of the best actors; **4** to count; **jemanden zu seinen Freunden rechnen** to count somebody as a friend; **5 mit etwas**

rechnen to expect something; **6 auf jemanden rechnen** to count on somebody.

Rechner *der* (PL *die* Rechner) **1** calculator; **2** computer.

Rechnung *die* (PL *die* Rechnungen) **1** bill; **2** invoice; **die Rechnung liegt bei** the invoice is enclosed; **3** calculation.

recht *adjective* **1** right; **jemandem recht sein** to be all right with somebody; **wenn es dir recht ist** if it's all right with you; **2** *der/die* Rechte the right man/woman; **3 das Rechte** the right thing; **etwas Rechtes** something proper; **ich habe nichts Rechtes gegessen** I haven't had a proper meal; **etwas Rechtes lernen** to learn something useful; **4** real; **ich habe keine rechte Lust** I don't really feel like it. *adverb* **1** correctly; **2** quite; **recht einfach** quite simple; **3** really; **4 recht vielen Dank** many thanks; **5 das geschieht dir recht!** (it) serves you right!; **6 man kann es nicht allen recht machen** you can't please everyone.

Recht *das* (PL *die* Rechte) **1** law; **nach deutschem Recht** under German law; **2** right; **Recht haben** △ to be right; **im Recht sein** to be in the right; **Recht bekommen** △ to be proved right; **3 jemandem Recht geben** △ to agree with somebody; **4 mit Recht** rightly; **du hast dich mit Recht beschwert** you were right to complain.

rechte SEE **rechter**.

Rechte *die* **1** right (side); **zu meiner**

◇ IRREGULAR VERB: *See the verb table in the centre of the dictionary*

Rechten on my right; **2** right hand; **3** die **Rechte** the right (*in politics*).

rechteckig *adjective* rectangular.

Rechteck das (PL die **Rechtecke**) rectangle.

rechter, rechte, rechtes *adjective* **1** right; **auf der rechten Seite** on the right; **2** right-wing.

rechtfertigen *verb* **1** (PERF hat **gerechtfertigt**) to justify; **2 sich rechtfertigen** to justify yourself.

rechtlich *adjective* legal.

rechts *adverb* **1** on the right; **von rechts** from the right; **rechts abbiegen** to turn right; **2 rechts sein** to be right-wing; **3 zwei rechts, zwei links stricken** to knit two, purl two.

Rechtsanwalt der (PL die **Rechtsanwälte**) lawyer.

Rechtsanwältin die (PL die **Rechtsanwältinnen**) lawyer.

Rechtschreibung die spelling.

Rechtshänder der (PL die **Rechtshänder**) **Klaus ist Rechtshänder** Klaus is right-handed.

Rechtshänderin die (PL die **Rechtshänderinnen**) **Beate ist Rechtshänderin** Beate is right-handed.

rechtzeitig *adjective* timely. *adverb* in time; **wir sind gerade noch rechtzeitig angekommen** we got there just in time.

Redakteur der (PL die **Redakteure**) editor.

Redakteurin die (PL die **Redakteurinnen**) editor.

Rede die (PL die **Reden**) **1** speech; **eine Rede halten** to make a speech; **2 nicht der Rede wert** not worth mentioning; **davon kann keine Rede sein** it's out of the question; **jemanden zur Rede stellen** to take somebody to task.

reden *verb* (PERF hat **geredet**) **1** to talk; **2** to speak; **mit jemandem reden** to speak to somebody; **3 sie hat kein Wort geredet** she didn't say a word; **4 mir ist egal, was über mich geredet wird** I don't care what people say about me.

reduzieren *verb* (PERF hat **reduziert**) to reduce.

reflexiv *adjective* reflexive.

Reformhaus das (PL die **Reformhäuser**) health-food shop.

Regal das (PL die **Regale**) **1** shelf; **2** shelves, bookcase.

Regel die (PL die **Regeln**) **1** rule; **in der Regel** as a rule; **2** period (*menstruation*).

regelmäßig *adjective* regular.

regeln *verb* (PERF hat **geregelt**) **1** to regulate; **2** to direct (*the traffic*); **3** to settle (*a matter*); **wir haben die Sache so geregelt, dass …** we've arranged things so that …; **4 sich von selbst regeln** to sort itself out.

Regelung die (PL die **Regelungen**) **1** regulation; **2** settlement.

Regen der rain.

△ NEW SPELLING: See page xii

Regenbogen der (PL die Regenbogen) rainbow.

Regenmantel der (PL die Regenmäntel) raincoat.

Regenschirm der (PL die Regenschirme) umbrella.

Regenwurm der (PL die Regenwürmer) earthworm.

regieren verb (PERF hat regiert) 1 to govern; 2 to rule, to reign.

Regierung die (PL die Regierungen) 1 government; 2 reign.

Regisseur der (PL die Regisseure) director.

Regisseurin die (PL die Regisseurinnen) director.

regnen verb (PERF hat geregnet) to rain.

regnerisch adjective rainy.

Reh das (PL die Rehe) deer.

reiben ◇ verb (IMPERF rieb, PERF hat gerieben) 1 to rub; 2 to grate.

reibungslos adjective smooth.

reich adjective rich.

Reich das (PL die Reiche) 1 empire; 2 kingdom, realm.

reichen verb (PERF hat gereicht) 1 to hand, to pass; 2 to be enough; **mit dem Geld reichen** to have enough money; 3 **bis zu etwas reichen** to reach up to something; **er reicht seinem Vater bis zur Schulter** he comes up to his father's shoulder; **die Felder reichen bis zum Wald** the fields extend as far as or go right up to the forest; 4 **mir reicht's!** (informal) I've had enough!

reichlich adjective 1 large; 2 ample (space). adverb plenty of.

Reichtum der (PL die Reichtümer) wealth.

Reichweite die 1 reach; **außer Reichweite** out of reach; 2 range.

reif adjective 1 ripe; 2 mature.

Reifen der (PL die Reifen) 1 tyre; 2 hoop.

Reifenpanne die (PL die Reifenpannen) puncture.

Reifendruck der tyre pressure.

Reihe die (PL die Reihen) 1 row; 2 series; 3 **der Reihe nach** in turn; **außer der Reihe** out of turn; **du bist an der Reihe** it's your turn.

Reihenfolge die (PL die Reihenfolgen) order.

Reihenhaus das (PL die Reihenhäuser) terraced house.

Reim der (PL die Reime) rhyme.

reimen verb (PERF hat gereimt) 1 to rhyme; 2 **sich reimen** to rhyme.

rein[1] adjective 1 pure; 2 clean; 3 sheer (madness); 4 **etwas ins Reine schreiben** △ to make a fair copy of something; **etwas ins Reine bringen** △ to sort something out. adverb 1 purely; 2 absolutely; **rein gar nichts** absolutely nothing.

rein[2] (informal) SEE **herein**, **hinein**.

◇ IRREGULAR VERB: See the verb table in the centre of the dictionary

reinigen *verb* (PERF hat gereinigt) to clean.

Reinigung *die* (PL die **Reinigungen**) 1 cleaning; 2 cleaner's.

Reis *der* rice.

Reise *die* (PL die **Reisen**) 1 journey, trip; **gute Reise!** have a good journey!; **auf meinen Reisen** on my travels; 2 voyage.

Reiseandenken *das* (PL die **Reiseandenken**) souvenir.

Reisebüro *das* (PL die **Reisebüros**) travel agency.

Reisebus *der* (PL die **Reisebusse**) coach.

Reiseführer *der* (PL die **Reiseführer**) 1 guidebook; 2 (travel) guide.

Reiseleiter *der* (PL die **Reiseleiter**) (travel) guide.

reisen *verb* (PERF ist gereist) to travel.

Reisende *der/die* (PL die **Reisenden**) traveller.

Reisepass △ *der* (PL die **Reisepässe**) passport.

Reisescheck *der* (PL die **Reiseschecks**) traveller's cheque.

Reiseziel *das* (PL die **Reiseziele**) destination.

reißen ◇ *verb* (IMPERF **riss** △, PERF hat **gerissen**) 1 to tear; 2 to snatch; 3 to pull; **an etwas reißen** to pull at something; 4 **mit sich reißen** to sweep away; 5 **etwas an sich reißen** to snatch something; **die Macht an** sich reißen to seize power; 6 **Witze reißen** to crack jokes; 7 **sich um etwas reißen** to fight for something; 8 **hin und her gerissen sein** to be torn; 9 (PERF ist gerissen) to tear, to break.

Reißverschluss △ *der* (PL die **Reißverschlüsse**) zip.

Reißzwecke *die* (PL die **Reißzwecken**) drawing pin.

reiten ◇ *verb* (IMPERF **ritt**, PERF hat/ist geritten) to ride.

Reiter *der* (PL die **Reiter**) rider.

Reiterin *die* (PL die **Reiterinnen**) rider.

Reitschule *die* (PL die **Reitschulen**) riding school.

Reiz *der* (PL die **Reize**) 1 attraction, appeal; 2 charm.

reizen *verb* (PERF hat gereizt) 1 to appeal to, to tempt; **das reizt mich sehr** it's very tempting; 2 to annoy; **jemanden zum Zorn reizen** to provoke somebody to anger; 3 to irritate (*the skin, eyes*); 4 to bid (*when playing cards*).

reizend *adjective* charming.

reizvoll *adjective* attractive.

Reklame *die* (PL die **Reklamen**) 1 advertisement, advert; **für etwas Reklame machen** to advertise something; 2 commercial (*on TV*).

Rekord *der* (PL die **Rekorde**) record.

Rektor *der* (PL die **Rektoren**) 1 head (*of a school*); 2 vice-chancellor (*of a university*).

△ NEW SPELLING: *See page xii*

Religion *die* (PL *die* **Religionen**) religion.

religiös *adjective* religious.

Rendezvous *das* (PL *die* **Rendezvous**) date.

Rennbahn *die* (PL *die* **Rennbahnen**) racetrack.

rennen ◇ *verb* (IMPERF **rannte**, PERF **ist gerannt**) to run.

Rennen *das* (PL *die* **Rennen**) race.

Rennfahrer *der* (PL *die* **Rennfahrer**) racing driver.

Rennwagen *der* (PL *die* **Rennwagen**) racing car.

renovieren *verb* (PERF **hat renoviert**) to renovate, to redecorate.

rentabel *adjective* profitable.

Rente *die* (PL *die* **Renten**) pension; **in Rente gehen** to retire.

Rentner *der* (PL *die* **Rentner**) pensioner.

Rentnerin *die* (PL *die* **Rentnerinnen**) pensioner.

Reparatur *die* (PL *die* **Reparaturen**) repair.

reparieren *verb* (PERF **hat repariert**) to repair.

Reportage *die* (PL *die* **Reportagen**) 1 report; 2 live commentary.

Reporter *der* (PL *die* **Reporter**) reporter.

Reporterin *die* (PL *die* **Reporterinnen**) reporter.

Reptil *das* (PL *die* **Reptile**) reptile.

Republik *die* (PL *die* **Republiken**) republic.

Reservat *das* (PL *die* **Reservate**) reservation.

Reserverad *das* (PL *die* **Reserveräder**) spare wheel.

reservieren *verb* (PERF **hat reserviert**) to reserve.

Reservierung *die* (PL *die* **Reservierungen**) reservation.

Respekt *der* respect.

respektieren *verb* (PERF **hat respektiert**) to respect.

Rest *der* (PL *die* **Reste**) 1 rest, remainder; 2 left-over; **zum Mittagessen gibt's die Reste** we're having the leftovers for lunch; 3 **die Reste** the remains.

Restaurant *das* (PL *die* **Restaurants**) restaurant.

restlich *adjective* remaining.

restlos *adjective* complete.

Resultat *das* (PL *die* **Resultate**) result.

retten *verb* (PERF **hat gerettet**) 1 to save, to rescue; **jemandem das Leben retten** to save somebody's life; 2 **sich retten** to escape.

Rettich *der* (PL *die* **Rettiche**) radish.

Rettung *die* rescue.

Rettungsring *der* (PL *die* **Rettungsringe**) lifebelt.

Rettungswagen *der* (PL *die* **Rettungswagen**) ambulance.

◇ IRREGULAR VERB: *See the verb table in the centre of the dictionary*

Rezept das (PL die Rezepte)
1 prescription; 2 recipe.

Rezeption die (PL die Rezeptionen)
reception; **bitte geben Sie Ihren
Schlüssel an der Rezeption ab**
please leave your key at reception.

R-Gespräch das (PL die R-
Gespräche) reverse-charge call.

Rhabarber der rhubarb.

Rhein der Rhine.

Rheuma das rheumatism.

Rhythmus der (PL die Rhythmen)
rhythm.

richten verb (PERF hat gerichtet)
1 to direct, to point (a torch,
telescope, gun); 2 **eine Frage an
jemanden richten** to put a question
to somebody; 3 to address (a letter,
remarks); 4 to prepare (a meal,
room); 5 **sich auf etwas richten** to
be directed towards something;
6 **sich nach jemandem richten** to
fit in with somebody's wishes; **sich
nach den Vorschriften richten** to
follow the rules; 7 **sich nach etwas
richten** to depend on something.

Richter der (PL die Richter) judge.

richtig adjective 1 right; 2 **das
Richtige** the right thing; **der/die
Richtige** the right man/woman;
3 real, proper.
adverb 1 correctly; 2 really;
3 **richtig stellen**△ to put right; **die
Uhr geht richtig** the clock is right.

Richtung die (PL die Richtungen)
1 direction; 2 trend.

rieb SEE **reiben**.

riechen ◇ verb (IMPERF roch, PERF
hat gerochen) 1 to smell; 2 **ich
kann ihn nicht riechen** (informal)
I can't stand him.

rief SEE **rufen**.

Riegel der (PL die Riegel) 1 bolt;
2 **ein Riegel Schokolade** a bar of
chocolate.

Riemen der (PL die Riemen) strap.

Riese der (PL die Riesen) giant.

riesengroß adjective gigantic.

riesig adjective huge.

riet SEE **raten**.

Rind das (PL die Rinder) 1 ox; 2 cow;
Rinder cattle; 3 beef.

Rinde die (PL die Rinden) 1 bark;
2 rind; 3 crust.

Rindfleisch das beef.

Ring der (PL die Ringe) ring.

Ringbuch das (PL die Ringbücher)
ring binder.

Ringen das wrestling.

Rippe die (PL die Rippen) rib.

Risiko das (PL die Risiken) risk.

riskant adjective risky.

riskieren verb (PERF hat riskiert) to
risk.

riss△ SEE **reißen**.

Riss△ der (PL die Risse) 1 tear;
2 crack.

ritt SEE **reiten**.

Rivale der (PL die Rivalen) rival.

Rivalin die (PL die Rivalinnen) rival.

△ NEW SPELLING: See page xii

Robbe die (PL die Robben) seal.

Roboter der (PL die Roboter) robot.

roch SEE riechen.

Rock der (PL die Röcke) skirt.

Roggen der rye.

roh adjective 1 raw; 2 rough; 3 brutal.

Rohr das (PL die Rohre) 1 pipe; 2 reed; 3 cane.

Rolladen = Rollladen.

Rolle die (PL die Rollen) 1 roll; 2 reel; 3 role, part; 4 es spielt keine Rolle it doesn't matter.

rollen verb (PERF hat gerollt) 1 to roll; 2 (PERF ist gerollt) to roll.

Roller der (PL die Roller) scooter.

Rollkragen der (PL die Rollkrägen) polo neck.

Rollladen △ der (PL die Rollläden) shutter.

Rollschuh der (PL die Rollschuhe) roller-skate.

Rollschuhlaufen das roller-skating.

Rollstuhl der (PL die Rollstühle) wheelchair.

Rolltreppe die (PL die Rolltreppen) escalator.

Rom das Rome.

Roman der (PL die Romane) novel.

romantisch adjective romantic.

röntgen verb (PERF hat geröntgt) to X-ray.

rosa adjective pink.

Rose die (PL die Rosen) rose.

Rosenkohl der (Brussels) sprouts.

Rosine die (PL die Rosinen) raisin.

Rosmarin der rosemary.

Rosskastanie △ die (PL die Rosskastanien) horse-chestnut.

Rost der (PL die Roste) 1 rust; 2 grate, grill.

rosten verb (PERF ist gerostet) to rust.

rösten (PERF hat geröstet) 1 to roast; 2 to toast.

rostig adjective rusty.

rot adjective red.

Röteln plural noun German measles.

rothaarig adjective red-haired.

Rotkehlchen das (PL die Rotkehlchen) robin.

Rotwein der (PL die Rotweine) red wine.

rüber adverb (informal) over; komm zu uns rüber come over to us.

rücken verb (PERF hat gerückt) to move; kannst du ein wenig rücken? can you move over a bit?

Rücken der (PL die Rücken) 1 back; 2 spine (of a book).

Rückfahrkarte die (PL die Rückfahrkarten) return ticket; eine Rückfahrkarte nach München a return ticket to Munich.

✧ IRREGULAR VERB: *See the verb table in the centre of the dictionary*

Rückfahrt die return journey; **auf der Rückfahrt** on the way back.

Rückgabe die (PL die Rückgaben) return.

rückgängig adjective **etwas rückgängig machen** to cancel something.

Rückkehr die return.

Rückreise die return journey.

Rucksack der (PL die Rucksäcke) rucksack.

Rückseite die (PL die Rückseiten) back.

Rücksicht die consideration.

rücksichtslos adjective 1 inconsiderate; **ein rücksichtsloser Fahrer** a reckless driver; 2 ruthless.

rücksichtsvoll adjective considerate.

Rücksitz der (PL die Rücksitze) back seat.

rückwärts adverb backwards.

Rückwärtsgang der (PL die Rückwärtsgänge) reverse (gear).

Rückweg der (PL die Rückwege) 1 way back; 2 return journey.

Rückzahlung die (PL die Rückzahlungen) refund, repayment.

Ruder das (PL die Ruder) 1 oar; 2 rudder.

Ruderboot das (PL die Ruderboote) rowing boat.

rudern verb (PERF ist gerudert) 1 to row; **ich bin über den See gerudert** I rowed across the lake; 2 (PERF hat gerudert) to row; **ich habe Monika über den See gerudert** I rowed Monika across the lake.

Ruf der (PL die Rufe) 1 call, shout; 2 reputation; 3 phone number.

rufen ◇ verb (IMPERF rief, PERF hat gerufen) to call; **den Arzt rufen** to send for the doctor.

Rufnummer die (PL die Rufnummern) phone number.

Ruhe die 1 silence; **Ruhe bitte !** quiet please !; 2 rest; 3 peace; **jemanden in Ruhe lassen** to leave somebody in peace; **in aller Ruhe** calmly; 4 **sich nicht aus der Ruhe bringen lassen** to not get worked up; 5 **sich zur Ruhe setzen** to retire.

ruhen verb (PERF hat geruht) to rest; **hier ruht ...** here lies ...

Ruhestand der im Ruhestand retired.

Ruhetag der (PL die Ruhetage) closing day; **'Dienstag Ruhetag'** 'closed on Tuesdays'.

ruhig adjective 1 quiet; 2 peaceful; 3 calm.
adverb 1 quietly; **sich ruhig verhalten** to keep quiet; 2 calmly; **ruhig bleiben** to remain calm; 3 **sehen Sie sich ruhig um** you're welcome to look around; **du kannst es ihm ruhig sagen** it's OK, you can tell him.

Ruhm der fame.

Rührei das scrambled eggs.

△ NEW SPELLING: See page xii

rühren verb (PERF hat gerührt) 1 to move; 2 to stir; 3 sich rühren to move; 4 an etwas rühren to touch, to touch on.

Ruine die (PL die Ruinen) ruin.

ruinieren verb (PERF hat ruiniert) to ruin.

rülpsen verb (PERF hat gerülpst) to belch.

Rumänien das Romania.

rumänisch adjective Romanian.

Rummel der 1 hustle and bustle; 2 fuss; 3 fair.

Rummelplatz der (PL die Rummelplätze) fairground.

rund adjective round. adverb about; rund um around.

Runde die (PL die Runden) 1 round; 2 lap; 3 circle, group; 4 über die Runden kommen (informal) to get by.

Rundfahrt die (PL die Rundfahrten) tour.

Rundfrage die (PL die Rundfragen) poll.

Rundfunk der radio; im Rundfunk on the radio.

rundherum adverb all around.

runter adverb (informal) SEE herunter, hinunter; runter da! get off!

runzlig adjective wrinkled.

Rüsche die (PL die Rüschen) frill.

Russe der (PL die Russen) Russian.

Rüssel der (PL die Rüssel) trunk.

Russin die (PL die Russinnen) Russian.

russisch adjective Russian.

Russland△ das Russia.

Rüstung die (PL die Rüstungen) 1 armament; 2 arms; 3 (suit of) armour.

Rutschbahn die (PL die Rutschbahnen) slide.

rutschen verb (PERF ist gerutscht) 1 to slide; 2 to slip; 3 rutsch mal! move over!

rutschig adjective slippery.

rütteln verb (PERF hat gerüttelt) to shake; an der Tür rütteln to rattle at the door.

S s

Saal der (PL die Säle) hall.

Sabbat der (PL die Sabbate) Sabbath.

Sache die (PL die Sachen) 1 matter; das ist eine andere Sache that's a different matter; 2 business; das ist seine Sache that's his business; 3 thing; meine Sachen my things (clothing); sie räumt nie ihre Sachen weg she never puts away her things; 4 zur Sache kommen to get to the point; 5 das ist so'ne Sache (informal) it's a bit tricky.

Sachgebiet das (PL die Sachgebiete) field, area.

◆ IRREGULAR VERB: See the verb table in the centre of the dictionary

sachlich *adjective* 1 objective; 2 factual.

sächlich *adjective* neuter.

Sachsen *das* Saxony.

Sack *der* (PL die Säcke) 1 sack; 2 bag.

Sackgasse *die* (PL die Sackgassen) cul-de-sac.

Saft *der* (PL die Säfte) 1 juice; 2 sap.

saftig *adjective* juicy.

Säge *die* (PL die Sägen) saw.

Sägemehl *das* sawdust.

sagen *verb* (PERF hat gesagt) 1 to say; **man sagt, dass** ... it's said that ...; 2 **was ich noch sagen wollte** by the way; **unter uns gesagt** between you and me; 3 to tell; **jemandem etwas sagen** to tell somebody something; **sag mal** tell me; **was sagen Sie dazu?** what do you think about it? 4 to mean; **das hat nichts zu sagen** it doesn't mean anything; 5 **zu jemandem Tante sagen** to call somebody aunt; 6 **ihr Gesicht sagte alles** it was written all over her face.

sägen *verb* (PERF hat gesägt) to saw.

sagenhaft *adjective* 1 legendary; 2 (*informal*) brilliant.

sah SEE sehen.

Sahne *die* cream.

Saison *die* (PL die Saisons) season.

Saite *die* (PL die Saiten) string.

Sakko *das* (PL die Sakkos) jacket.

Salat *der* (PL die Salate) 1 lettuce; 2 salad.

Salatsoße *die* (PL die Salatsoßen) salad dressing.

Salbe *die* (PL die Salben) ointment.

Salbei *der* sage.

salopp *adjective* casual, informal.

Salz *das* salt.

salzen *verb* (PERF hat gesalzen) to salt.

salzig *adjective* salty.

Salzkartoffeln *plural noun* boiled potatoes.

Salzwasser *das* 1 salt water; 2 salted water (*for cooking*).

Samen *der* (PL die Samen) 1 seed; 2 sperm, semen.

sammeln *verb* (PERF hat gesammelt) 1 to collect; **Martin sammelt Briefmarken** Martin collects stamps; 2 to gather; 3 **sich sammeln** to gather; **seine Gedanken sammeln** to gather your thoughts.

Sammlung *die* (PL die Sammlungen) collection; **eine Sammlung für einen guten Zweck** a collection for charity.

Samstag *der* (PL die Samstage) Saturday.

samstags *adverb* on Saturdays.

samt *preposition* ←(+DAT) (together) with; **Mimi kam samt Puppen und Katze** Mimi arrived with her dolls and cat.

△ NEW SPELLING: See page xii

Samt der (PL die Samte) velvet.

sämtlicher, sämtliche, sämtliches adjective all the; **meine sämtlichen Bücher** all my books.

Sand der sand.

Sandale die (PL die Sandalen) sandal.

sandig adjective sandy.

sandte SEE senden.

sanft adjective gentle; **eine sanfte Stimme** a soft voice.

sang SEE singen.

Sänger der (PL die Sänger) singer.

Sängerin die (PL die Sängerinnen) singer.

sank SEE sinken.

Sardelle die (PL die Sardellen) anchovy.

Sardine die (PL die Sardinen) sardine.

Sarg der (PL die Särge) coffin.

Sarkasmus der sarcasm.

sarkastisch adjective sarcastic.

saß SEE sitzen.

Satellit der (PL die Satelliten) satellite.

Satellitenfernsehen das satellite television.

satt adjective 1 full (up); **bist du satt geworden?** have you had enough to eat?; **sich satt essen** to eat as much as one wants; **satt machen** to be filling; 2 **etwas satt haben** (informal) to be fed up with something.

Sattel der (PL die Sättel) saddle.

Satz der (PL die Sätze) 1 sentence; 2 set (of things in tennis); **ein Satz Reifen** a set of tyres; 3 movement (in music); 4 rate (of tax, interest); 5 leap.

sauber adjective 1 clean; 2 neat; 3 (informal) fine (expressing irony); 4 **sauber machen**△ to clean.

Sauberkeit die cleanliness, cleanness.

saubermachen SEE sauber.

Sauce die (PL die Saucen) = Soße.

sauer adjective 1 sour; 2 pickled; 3 acid; **saurer Regen** acid rain; 4 **sauer sein** (informal) to be annoyed; **ich bin sauer auf Eva** I'm annoyed with Eva.

Sauerei die (informal) (PL die Sauereien) 1 mess; 2 disgrace, scandal; 3 obscenity.

Sauerstoff der oxygen.

saufen ◇ verb (informal) (PRES **säuft**, IMPERF **soff**, PERF **hat gesoffen**) to drink, to booze.

saugen verb (PERF **hat gesaugt**) 1 to suck; 2 to vacuum, to hoover.

Säugetier das (PL die Säugetiere) mammal.

Säugling der (PL die Säuglinge) baby, infant.

Säule die (PL die Säulen) column.

Säure die (PL die Säuren) acid.

◇ IRREGULAR VERB: See the verb table in the centre of the dictionary

Saxofon △ *das* (PL *die* **Saxofone**) saxophone.

S-Bahn *die* (PL *die* **S-Bahnen**) city and suburban railway.

schäbig *adjective* shabby.

Schach *das* chess; **Schach!** check!

Schachbrett *das* (PL *die* **Schachbretter**) chessboard.

Schachfigur *die* (PL *die* **Schachfiguren**) chess piece.

Schachtel *die* (PL *die* **Schachteln**) box.

schade *adjective* 1 schade sein to be a pity; **schade!** (what a) pity!; 2 zu schade für jemanden sein to be too good for somebody.

schaden *verb* (PERF hat geschadet) 1 to damage; das hat seinem Ruf geschadet it damaged his reputation; 2 jemandem schaden to harm somebody; 3 das schadet nichts it doesn't matter.

Schaden *der* (PL *die* **Schäden**) 1 damage; 2 disadvantage.

schädlich *adjective* harmful.

Schaf *das* (PL *die* **Schafe**) sheep.

Schäfer *der* (PL *die* **Schäfer**) shepherd.

Schäferhund *der* (PL *die* **Schäferhunde**) sheepdog.

schaffen¹ ◇ *verb* (IMPERF schuf, PERF hat geschaffen) to create; wie geschaffen für made for.

schaffen² *verb* (PERF hat geschafft) 1 to manage; es schaffen, etwas zu tun to manage to do something; 2 eine Prüfung schaffen to pass an exam; 3 jemandem zu schaffen machen to cause somebody trouble; 4 geschafft sein (*informal*) to be worn out.

Schaffner *der* (PL *die* **Schaffner**) 1 conductor; 2 (ticket) inspector.

Schaffnerin *die* (PL *die* **Schaffnerinnen**) 1 conductress; 2 (ticket) inspector.

Schal *der* (PL *die* **Schals**) scarf.

Schale *die* (PL *die* **Schalen**) 1 skin; 2 peel; 3 shell; 4 dish, bowl; eine Schale Obst a bowl of fruit.

schälen *verb* (PERF hat geschält) 1 to peel; er hat ihr eine Orange geschält he peeled an orange for her; 2 sich schälen to peel; mein Rücken schält sich my back's peeling.

Schall *der* sound.

Schallplatte *die* (PL *die* **Schallplatten**) record.

schalten *verb* (PERF hat geschaltet) 1 to switch; auf etwas schalten to turn to something; 2 to change gear; 3 schnell schalten (*informal*) to catch on quickly.

Schalter *der* (PL *die* **Schalter**) 1 switch; 2 counter.

Schaltjahr *das* (PL *die* **Schaltjahre**) leap year.

schämen *verb* (PERF hat sich geschämt) sich schämen to be ashamed.

Schampon *das* (PL *die* **Schampons**) shampoo.

△ NEW SPELLING: *See page xii*

Schande die 1 disgrace; 2 shame.

scharf adjective 1 sharp; 2 hot (food); **ein scharfer Wind** a biting wind; 3 fierce (dog, frost); 4 **scharf nachdenken** to think hard; 5 (in photography) **scharf sein** to be in focus; **scharf einstellen** to focus; 6 **scharf schießen** to fire live ammunition; 7 **scharf auf etwas sein** (informal) to be really keen on something; **sie ist scharf auf Bernd** (informal) she fancies Bernd.

Schaschlik der (PL die Schaschliks) kebab.

Schatten der (PL die Schatten) 1 shadow; 2 shade.

schattig adjective shady.

Schatz der (PL die Schätze) 1 treasure; 2 darling.

Schätzchen das (PL die Schätzchen) darling.

schätzen verb (PERF hat geschätzt) 1 to estimate; 2 to value; 3 to reckon, to guess; **schätz mal!** guess!; 4 **etwas zu schätzen wissen** to appreciate something.

Schau die (PL die Schauen) show.

schauen verb (PERF hat geschaut) to look.

Schauer der (PL die Schauer) shower.

Schauergeschichte die (PL die Schauergeschichten) horror story.

Schaufel die (PL die Schaufeln) 1 shovel; 2 dustpan.

Schaufenster das (PL die Schaufenster) shop window.

Schaukel die (PL die Schaukeln) swing.

schaukeln verb (PERF hat geschaukelt) to swing.

Schaukelstuhl der (PL die Schaukelstühle) rocking chair.

Schaum der 1 foam; 2 froth; 3 lather.

schäumen verb (PERF hat geschäumt) 1 to foam; 2 to froth (up).

Schauplatz der (PL die Schauplätze) scene.

Schauspiel das (PL die Schauspiele) 1 play; 2 spectacle.

Schauspieler der (PL die Schauspieler) actor.

Schauspielerin die (PL die Schauspielerinnen) actress.

Scheck der (PL die Schecks) cheque.

Scheckbuch das (PL die Scheckbücher) chequebook.

Scheckkarte die (PL die Scheckkarten) cheque card.

Scheibe die (PL die Scheiben) 1 pane (of a window, car); 2 slice; **eine Scheibe Schinken** a slice of ham; **die Salami in Scheiben schneiden** to slice the salami; **du könntest dir eine Scheibe von ihr abschneiden** (informal) you could take a leaf out of her book; 3 disc.

Scheibenwischer der (PL die

◇ **IRREGULAR VERB: See the verb table in the centre of the dictionary**

Scheibenwischer) windscreen
wiper.

scheiden ◇ verb (IMPERF schied,
PERF hat geschieden) 1 to separate;
sich scheiden lassen to get
divorced; 2 geschieden sein to be
divorced.

Scheidung die (PL die
Scheidungen) divorce.

Schein der (PL die Scheine) 1 light;
2 appearance; etwas nur zum
Schein machen to only pretend to
do something; 3 certificate; 4 note
(money).

scheinbar adverb apparently.

scheinen ◇ verb (IMPERF schien,
PERF hat geschienen) 1 to shine;
2 to seem; mir scheint it seems to
me.

Scheinwerfer der (PL die
Scheinwerfer) 1 headlamp,
headlight; 2 floodlight, spotlight.

scheitern verb (PERF ist
gescheitert) to fail.

Schenkel der (PL die Schenkel)
thigh.

schenken verb (PERF hat
geschenkt) 1 to give; etwas
geschenkt bekommen to be given
something; 2 sich etwas schenken
to give something a miss; 3 das ist
ja geschenkt! (informal) it's a gift!

Schere die (PL die Scheren) 1 (pair
of) scissors; 2 shears; 3 claw (of a
crab).

scheren verb (informal) (PERF hat
geschert) to bother; sich nicht um
etwas scheren not to care about

something; scher dich um deine
eigenen Angelegenheiten! mind
your own business!; scher dich zum
Teufel! go to hell!

Scherz der (PL die Scherze) joke.

scheu adjective shy.

scheuern verb (PERF hat
gescheuert) 1 to scrub; 2 to rub.

Scheune die (PL die Scheunen)
barn.

scheußlich adjective horrible.

Schi der (PL die Schi(er)) = Ski.

Schicht die (PL die Schichten)
1 layer; 2 class; 3 shift.

schick adjective 1 stylish, smart;
2 (informal) great.

schicken verb (PERF hat geschickt)
to send.

Schicksal das (PL die Schicksale)
fate.

schieben ◇ verb (IMPERF schob,
PERF hat geschoben) 1 to push;
2 etwas auf etwas schieben to
blame something for something; die
Schuld auf jemanden schieben to
put the blame on somebody.

schied SEE scheiden.

Schiedsrichter der (PL die
Schiedsrichter) referee, umpire.

schief adjective crooked; ein
schiefer Blick a funny look.
adverb 1 das Bild hängt schief the
picture is not straight; 2 schief
gehen △ to go wrong.

Schiefer der slate.

schiefgehen SEE schief.

△ NEW SPELLING: See page xii

schielen verb (PERF **hat geschielt**)
to squint.

schien SEE **scheinen**

Schienbein das (PL die
Schienbeine) shin.

Schiene die (PL die **Schienen**)
1 rail; 2 splint.

schießen ◊ verb (IMPERF **schoss** △,
PERF **hat geschossen**) 1 to shoot;
auf jemanden schießen to shoot at
somebody; **ein Tor schießen** to
score a goal; 2 (PERF **ist geschossen**)
to shoot (along); **Andrea ist in die
Höhe geschossen** Andrea's shot up .
(*has grown a lot taller*).

Schiff das (PL die **Schiffe**) ship.

schikanieren verb (PERF **hat
schikaniert**) to bully.

Schikoree △ der chicory.

Schild das (PL die **Schilder**) 1 sign;
2 badge; 3 label.

Schildkröte die (PL die
Schildkröten) 1 tortoise; 2 turtle.

Schilling der (PL die **Schilling(e)**)
Schilling.

Schimmel der (PL die **Schimmel**)
1 mould; 2 white horse.

Schimpanse der (PL die
Schimpansen) chimpanzee.

schimpfen verb (PERF **hat
geschimpft**) 1 to tell off; 2 to
grumble.

Schinken der (PL die **Schinken**)
ham.

Schirm der (PL die **Schirme**)

1 umbrella; 2 sunshade; 3 shade (*of
a lamp*); 4 peak (*of a cap*).

Schlaf der sleep.

Schlafanzug der (PL die
Schlafanzüge) pyjamas.

schlafen ◊ verb (PRES **schläft**,
IMPERF **schlief**, PERF **hat geschlafen**)
1 to sleep; 2 to be asleep; 3 **schlafen
gehen** to go to bed.

Schlafcouch die (PL die
Schlafcouchs) sofa bed.

schlaff adjective 1 slack (*rope*);
2 limp (*handshake, body*);
3 lethargic.

Schlafsaal der (PL die **Schlafsäle**)
dormitory.

Schlafsack der (PL die
Schlafsäcke) sleeping bag.

Schlafzimmer das (PL die
Schlafzimmer) bedroom.

Schlafwagen der (PL die
Schlafwagen) sleeper.

Schlag der (PL die **Schläge**) 1 blow,
punch; **Schläge kriegen** to get a
beating; 2 stroke; 3 (*electric*) shock;
4 **Schlag auf Schlag** in quick
succession; **auf einen Schlag** all at
once.

schlagen ◊ verb (PRES **schlägt**,
IMPERF **schlug**, PERF **hat geschlagen**)
1 to hit; **einen Nagel in die Wand
schlagen** to knock a nail into the
wall; 2 to beat; 3 to bang; **mit dem
Kopf gegen etwas schlagen** to
bang your head against something;
4 to strike (*of a clock*); 5 to whip
(*cream*); 6 **sich schlagen** to fight;

◊ IRREGULAR VERB: *See the verb table in the centre of the dictionary*

7 sich geschlagen geben to admit defeat.

Schlager der (PL die **Schlager**) hit.

Schläger der (PL die **Schläger**)
1 racket (in tennis); 2 bat (in baseball); 3 club (in golf); 4 stick (in hockey); 5 thug.

Schlägerei die (PL die **Schlägereien**) fight.

Schlagsahne die 1 whipping cream; 2 whipped cream.

Schlagzeile die (PL die **Schlagzeilen**) headline.

Schlagzeug das (PL die **Schlagzeuge**) drums.

Schlagzeuger der (PL die **Schlagzeuger**) drummer.

Schlamm der mud.

schlampen verb (PERF hat **geschlampt**) to be sloppy.

Schlamperei die (PL die **Schlampereien**) 1 sloppiness; 2 mess.

schlampig adjective sloppy.

Schlange die (PL die **Schlangen**) 1 snake; 2 queue; **Schlange stehen** to queue.

schlank adjective slim.

Schlankheitskur die (PL die **Schlankheitskuren**) diet; **eine Schlankheitskur machen** to be on a diet.

schlapp adjective worn out, tired out.

schlau adjective 1 crafty; 2 clever;

ich werde nicht schlau daraus I can't make head nor tail of it.

Schlauch der (PL die **Schläuche**) hose.

schlecht adjective 1 bad; **schlecht werden** to go bad; **2 mir ist schlecht** I feel sick; **3 jemanden schlecht machen** △ to run somebody down.
adverb 1 badly; **schlecht gelaunt** in a bad mood; **2 es geht ihm schlecht** he's not well.

schleichen ◇ verb (IMPERF schlich, PERF ist geschlichen) 1 to creep; 2 to crawl (in traffic); 3 **sich schleichen** to creep.

Schleife die (PL die **Schleifen**) 1 bow; 2 loop.

Schleuder die (PL die **Schleudern**) 1 catapult; 2 spin-dryer.

schleudern verb (PERF hat **geschleudert**) 1 to hurl; 2 to spin (washing); 3 (PERF ist geschleudert) to skid.

schlich SEE **schleichen**.

schlicht adjective plain, simple.

schlief SEE **schlafen**.

schließen ◇ verb (IMPERF schloss △, PERF hat geschlossen) 1 to close, to shut; 2 to close down; 3 to lock; 4 to conclude; **aus etwas schließen, dass ...** to conclude from something that ...; 5 **einen Vertrag schließen** to enter into a contract; **6 Freundschaft mit jemandem schließen** to make friends with somebody; 7 **sich schließen** to close.

△ NEW SPELLING: See page xii

Schließfach das (PL die Schließfächer) locker.

schließlich adverb 1 finally; 2 after all; er hat sie schließlich doch eingeladen he's invited her after all.

schlimm adjective bad.

schlimmstenfalls adverb if the worst comes to the worst.

Schlips der (PL die Schlipse) tie.

Schlitten der (PL die Schlitten) sledge; **Schlitten fahren gehen** to go sledging.

Schlittschuh der (PL die Schlittschuhe) skate; **Schlittschuh laufen** to skate.

Schlittschuhlaufen das ice-skating.

Schlitz der (PL die Schlitze) 1 slit; 2 flies (in trousers); 3 slot.

schloss △ SEE **schließen**.

Schloss △ das (PL die Schlösser) 1 lock; 2 castle.

Schluck der (PL die Schlucke) 1 mouthful; 2 gulp.

Schluckauf der hiccups.

schlucken verb (PERF hat geschluckt) to swallow.

schlug SEE **schlagen**.

Schlüpfer der (PL die Schlüpfer) knickers.

Schluss △ der (PL die Schlüsse) 1 end, ending; **zum Schluss** in the end; **Schluss machen** to stop; **mit jemandem Schluss machen** to finish with somebody; 2 conclusion.

Schlüssel der (PL die Schlüssel) 1 key; 2 spanner.

Schlussverkauf △ der sales.

schmal adjective 1 narrow; 2 thin (face, nose); 3 **sie ist schmäler geworden** she's lost weight.

schmecken verb (PERF hat geschmeckt) to taste; **die Suppe schmeckt gut** the soup tastes good; **das schmeckt mir nicht** I don't like it; **das Eis schmeckt nacht Zitrone** the ice cream tastes of lemon.

schmeicheln verb (PERF hat geschmeichelt) to flatter; **jemandem schmeicheln** to flatter somebody.

schmeißen ✧ verb (informal) (IMPERF schmiss △, PERF hat geschmissen) to chuck; **mit etwas schmeißen** to chuck something.

schmelzen ✧ verb (PRES schmilzt, IMPERF schmolz, PERF ist geschmolzen) 1 to melt; **der Schnee ist geschmolzen** the snow has melted; 2 (PERF hat geschmolzen) to melt (snow, ice); 3 (PERF hat geschmolzen) to smelt (ore).

Schmerz der (PL die Schmerzen) 1 pain; 2 grief.

schmerzen verb (PERF hat geschmerzt) to hurt.

schmerzhaft adjective painful.

Schmerzmittel das (PL die Schmerzmittel) painkiller.

Schmetterling der (PL die Schmetterlinge) butterfly.

✧ IRREGULAR VERB: See the verb table in the centre of the dictionary

schmieren verb (PERF hat geschmiert) 1 to lubricate; 2 to spread (butter, jam); **Brote schmieren** to spread slices of bread; **jemandem eine schmieren** (informal) to clout somebody; 3 to scrawl; 4 to smudge.

schmilzt SEE **schmelzen**.

Schminke die make-up.

schminken verb (PERF hat geschminkt) 1 to make up; 2 **sich schminken** to put on make-up.

schmiss △ SEE **schmeißen**.

schmolz SEE **schmelzen**.

Schmuck der 1 jewellery; 2 decoration.

schmücken verb (PERF hat geschmückt) to decorate.

schmuggeln verb (PERF hat geschmuggelt) to smuggle.

schmusen verb (PERF hat geschmust) to cuddle; **Gabi hat mit Max geschmust** Gabi cuddled Max.

Schmutz der dirt.

schmutzig adjective dirty.

Schnabel der (PL die Schnäbel) beak.

Schnalle die (PL die Schnallen) buckle.

schnarchen verb (PERF hat geschnarcht) to snore.

Schnauze die (PL die Schnauzen) 1 muzzle; **eine kalte Schnauze** a cold nose; 2 **die Schnauze halten** (informal) to keep your mouth shut.

schnäuzen △ (PERF hat sich geschnäuzt) **sich schnäuzen** to blow your nose.

Schnecke die (PL die Schnecken) snail.

Schnee der snow.

Schneeregen der sleet.

schneiden ◇ verb (IMPERF schnitt, PERF hat geschnitten) 1 to cut; **ich kann dir die Haare schneiden** I can cut your hair; **Evi hat sich die Haare kurz schneiden lassen** Evi had her hair cut short; **in Scheiben schneiden** to slice; 2 **sich schneiden** to cut yourself; **ich habe mich in den Finger geschnitten** I've cut my finger; 3 **sich schneiden** to intersect; 4 **Gesichter schneiden** to pull faces.

Schneider der (PL die Schneider) tailor.

Schneiderin die (PL die Schneiderinnen) dressmaker.

schneien verb (PERF hat geschneit) to snow; **es schneit** it's snowing.

schnell adjective quick, fast. adverb quickly; **mach schnell!** hurry up!

Schnelligkeit die speed.

Schnellimbiss △ der (PL die Schnellimbisse) snack bar.

schnellstens adverb as quickly as possible.

Schnellzug der (PL die Schnellzüge) express (train).

schneuzen = **schnäuzen**.

schnitt SEE **schneiden**.

Schnitt der (PL die **Schnitte**) 1 cut; **er hat einen tiefen Schnitt im Finger** he's got a deep cut in his finger; **das Kostüm hat einen sehr guten Schnitt** the suit is well cut; 2 cutting (*of a film*); 3 **im Schnitt** on average; 4 pattern.

Schnittlauch der chives.

Schnitzel das (PL die **Schnitzel**) 1 escalope; 2 scrap.

schnitzen verb (PERF hat **geschnitzt**) to carve.

Schnorchel der (PL die **Schnorchel**) snorkel.

schnüffeln verb (PERF hat **geschnüffelt**) 1 to sniff; 2 to snoop around.

Schnuller der (PL die **Schnuller**) dummy.

Schnupfen der (PL die **Schnupfen**) cold.

Schnur die (PL die **Schnüre**) 1 (piece of) string; 2 flex; 3 cord.

Schnurrbart der (PL die **Schnurrbärte**) moustache.

schnurren verb (PERF hat **geschnurrt**) to purr.

Schnürsenkel der (PL die **Schnürsenkel**) shoelace.

schob SEE **schieben**.

Schock der (PL die **Schocks**) shock.

schockieren verb (PERF hat **schockiert**) to shock.

Schokolade die (PL die **Schokoladen**) chocolate.

schon adverb 1 already (*'schon' is often not translated*); **schon wieder** again; **schon oft** often; **du wirst schon sehen** you'll see; **ja schon, aber …** well yes, but …; **nun geh schon!** go on then!; 2 yet; **hast du sie schon gesehen?** have you seen her yet?; **du weißt schon** you know; 3 even; 4 **komm schon!** come on!; 5 **schon deshalb** for that reason alone; 6 **das ist schon möglich** that's quite possible; 7 **er war schon mal da** he's been there before.

schön adjective 1 beautiful; 2 nice; **schönes Wochenende!** have a nice weekend!; 3 good; **na schön** all right then; 4 **schönen Dank** thank you very much; **schöne Grüße** best wishes.

schonen verb (PERF hat **geschont**) 1 to look after; 2 **sich schonen** to take things easy.

Schönheit die (PL die **Schönheiten**) beauty.

Schornstein der (PL die **Schornsteine**) chimney, funnel.

schoss △ SEE **schießen**.

Schoß der (PL die **Schöße**) lap.

Schotte der (PL die **Schotten**) Scot, Scotsman.

Schottin die (PL die **Schottinnen**) Scot, Scotswoman.

schottisch adjective Scottish.

Schottland das Scotland.

schräg adjective 1 diagonal;

2 sloping.
adverb etwas schräg halten to tilt
something; etwas schräg stellen
to put something at an angle.

Schrank *der* (PL die Schränke)
1 cupboard; 2 wardrobe.

Schranke *die* (PL die Schranken)
barrier.

Schraube *die* (PL die Schrauben)
screw.

schrauben *verb* (PERF hat
geschraubt) to screw.

Schraubenschlüssel *der* (PL die
Schraubenschlüssel) spanner.

Schraubenzieher *der* (PL die
Schraubenzieher) screwdriver.

Schreck *der* fright; jemandem
einen Schreck einjagen to give
somebody a fright; ich habe einen
Schreck bekommen I got a fright.

schrecklich *adjective* terrible.

Schrei *der* (PL die Schreie) 1 cry,
shout; 2 scream; 3 der letzte
Schrei (*informal*) the latest thing.

Schreibblock *der* (PL die
Schreibblöcke) writing pad.

schreiben ◇ *verb* (IMPERF schrieb,
PERF hat geschrieben) 1 to write;
David hat mir einen Brief
geschrieben David wrote a letter to
me; einen Test schreiben to do a
test; 2 to spell; wie schreibt man
das? how is it spelt?; 3 to type.

Schreibmaschine *die* (PL die
Schreibmaschinen) typewriter.

Schreibpapier *das* writing paper.

Schreibtisch *der* (PL die
Schreibtische) desk.

Schreibwaren *plural noun*
stationery.

schreien ◇ *verb* (IMPERF schrie, PERF
hat geschrien) 1 to cry, to shout;
das Baby schreit the baby's crying;
2 to scream; vor Lachen schreien to
scream with laughter; zum Schreien
sein (*informal*) to be a scream.

Schreiner *der* (PL die Schreiner)
joiner.

schrie SEE schreien.

schrieb SEE schreiben.

Schrift *die* (PL die Schriften)
1 writing; 2 type; 3 script.

schriftlich *adjective* written.
adverb in writing; das lasse ich mir
schriftlich geben I'll get that in
writing; jemanden schriftlich
einladen to send somebody a
written invitation.

Schriftsteller *der* (PL die
Schriftsteller) writer.

Schriftstellerin *die* (PL die
Schriftstellerinnen) writer.

Schritt *der* (PL die Schritte) step.

schrumpfen *verb* (PERF ist
geschrumpft) 1 to shrink; 2 to
shrivel.

Schublade *die* (PL die Schubladen)
drawer.

schubsen *verb* (PERF hat
geschubst) to shove.

schüchtern *adjective* shy.

schuf SEE schaffen.

△ NEW SPELLING: See page xii

Schuh der (PL die Schuhe) shoe.

Schuhgröße die (PL die Schuhgrößen) shoe size.

Schularbeiten plural noun homework.

Schulaufgaben plural noun homework.

Schulbuch das (PL die Schulbücher) schoolbook.

Schuld die (PL die Schulden)
1 blame; **Schuld haben** △ to be to blame; **jemandem Schuld geben** to blame somebody; **2** fault; **es war seine Schuld** it was his fault; **3** guilt; **4** debt; **Schulden haben** to be in debt; **Schulden machen** to get into debt.

schuld adjective **schuld sein** to be to blame; **du bist schuld daran** it's your fault.

schulden verb (PERF **hat geschuldet**) to owe.

schuldig adjective **1** guilty; **2 jemandem etwas schuldig sein** to owe somebody something.

Schule die (PL die Schulen) school.

schulen verb (PERF **hat geschult**) to train.

Schüler der (PL die Schüler) pupil, student.

Schülerin die (PL die Schülerinnen) pupil, student.

Schulferien plural noun school holidays.

schulfrei adjective **ein schulfreier Tag** a day off school; **wir haben heute schulfrei** there's no school today.

Schulfreund der (PL die Schulfreunde) schoolfriend.

Schulfreundin die (PL die Schulfreundinnen) schoolfriend.

Schulhof der (PL die Schulhöfe) playground.

Schulstunde die (PL die Schulstunden) period.

Schultasche die (PL die Schultaschen) schoolbag.

Schulter die (PL die Schultern) shoulder.

schummeln verb (PERF **hat geschummelt**) to cheat.

Schuppe die (PL die Schuppen)
1 scale; **2 Schuppen** dandruff.

Schuppen der (PL die Schuppen) shed.

Schürze die (PL die Schürzen) apron.

Schuss △ der (PL die Schüsse)
1 shot; **2** dash (of brandy, vinegar); **3** schuss (in skiing).

Schüssel die (PL die Schüsseln) bowl, dish.

Schuster der (PL die Schuster) shoemaker.

schütten verb (PERF **hat geschüttet**) **1** to pour; **es schüttet** (informal) it's pouring (down); **2** to tip; **3** to spill.

schütteln verb (PERF **hat geschüttelt**) **1** to shake; **2 sich**

⬦ **IRREGULAR VERB: See the verb table in the centre of the dictionary**

schütteln to shake yourself; **sich vor Ekel schütteln** to shudder.

Schutz der 1 protection; 2 shelter.

Schütze der (PL die Schützen) 1 marksman; 2 Sagittarius; **Daniel ist Schütze** Daniel's Sagittarius.

schützen verb (PERF hat geschützt) 1 to protect; **die meisten Cremes schützen die Haut gegen Sonnenbrand** most creams protect the skin from sunburn; 2 **gesetzlich geschützt** registered (as a trademark).

schwach adjective 1 weak; 2 poor (performance, memory).

Schwäche die (PL die Schwächen) weakness.

schwachsinnig adjective idiotic.

Schwager der (PL die Schwäger) brother-in-law.

Schwägerin die (PL die Schwägerinnen) sister-in-law.

Schwalbe die (PL die Schwalben) swallow.

schwamm SEE schwimmen.

Schwamm der (PL die Schwämme) sponge.

Schwan der (PL die Schwäne) swan.

schwanger adjective pregnant.

schwanken verb (PERF hat geschwankt) 1 to sway; 2 to fluctuate; 3 to waver; 4 (PERF ist geschwankt) to stagger.

Schwanz der (PL die Schwänze) tail.

schwänzen verb (PERF hat geschwänzt) to skip, to skive off; **die Schule schwänzen** to play truant.

Schwarm der (PL die Schwärme) swarm.

schwarz adjective, adverb 1 black; **schwarz gekleidet** dressed in black; **ein schwarz gestreiftes Kleid** a dress with black stripes; **das habe ich schwarz auf weiß** I have it in black and white; 2 **ins Schwarze treffen** to hit the nail on the head, to score a bull's eye; 3 **schwarz sehen**△ to be pessimistic; 4 **etwas schwarz machen** to do something illegally.

Schwarze der/die (PL die Schwarzen) black.

schwarzsehen SEE schwarz.

Schwarzwald der Black Forest.

schwätzen verb (PERF hat geschwätzt) to chatter.

Schwede der (PL die Schweden) Swede.

Schweden das Sweden.

Schwedin die (PL die Schwedinnen) Swede.

schwedisch adjective Swedish.

schweigen ◆ verb (IMPERF schwieg, PERF hat geschwiegen) to be silent; **ganz zu schweigen von ...** not to mention ...

Schwein das (PL die Schweine) 1 pig; 2 pork; 3 **du Schwein!** (informal) you swine!; **Schwein haben** (informal) to be lucky.

Schweinefleisch das pork.

△ NEW SPELLING: See page xii

Schweiß *der* sweat.

Schweiz *die* die Schweiz Switzerland.

Schweizer *der* (PL die Schweizer) Swiss.

Schweizerin *die* (PL die Schweizerinnen) Swiss.

schweizerisch *adjective* Swiss.

schwer *adjective* 1 heavy; **zwei Pfund schwer sein** to weigh two pounds; 2 difficult; 3 serious. *adverb* 1 heavily; 2 seriously; **schwer krank** seriously ill; **3 schwer arbeiten** to work hard; **jemandem schwer fallen** △ to be hard for somebody; **4 sich mit etwas schwer tun** △ to have difficulty with something.

schwerfallen SEE schwer.

schwerhörig *adjective* hard of hearing.

Schwert *das* (PL die Schwerter) sword.

schwertun SEE schwer.

Schwester *die* (PL die Schwestern) sister.

schwieg SEE schweigen.

Schwiegereltern *plural noun* parents-in-law.

Schwiegermutter *die* (PL die Schwiegermütter) mother-in-law.

Schwiegersohn *der* (PL die Schwiegersöhne) son-in-law.

Schwiegertochter *die* (PL die Schwiegertöchter) daughter-in-law.

Schwiegervater *der* (PL die Schwiegerväter) father-in-law.

schwierig *adjective* difficult.

Schwierigkeit *die* (PL die Schwierigkeiten) difficulty.

Schwimmbad *das* (PL die Schwimmbäder) swimming baths.

Schwimmbecken *das* (PL die Schwimmbecken) swimming pool.

schwimmen ◇ (IMPERF schwamm, PERF ist/hat geschwommen) 1 to swim; 2 to float.

Schwimmweste *die* (PL die Schwimmwesten) life-jacket.

schwindlig *adjective* dizzy; **mir ist schwindlig** I feel dizzy.

Schwips *der* (PL die Schwipse) **einen Schwips haben** to be tipsy.

schwitzen *verb* (PERF hat geschwitzt) to sweat.

schwören ◇ *verb* (IMPERF schwor, PERF hat geschworen) to swear.

schwul *adjective* gay.

schwül *adjective* close.

Schwule *der* (PL die Schwulen) gay.

Schwung *der* (PL die Schwünge) 1 swing; 2 drive; **die Party in Schwung bringen** to get the party going.

sechs *number* six.

sechster, sechste, sechstes *adjective* sixth.

sechzehn *number* sixteen.

sechzig *number* sixty.

◇ IRREGULAR VERB: *See the verb table in the centre of the dictionary*

See[1] der (PL die Seen) lake.

See[2] die die sea.

Seehund der (PL die Seehunde) seal.

seekrank adjective seasick.

Seele die (PL die Seelen) soul.

Seemann der (PL die Seeleute) seaman, sailor.

Seetang der seaweed.

Segel das (PL die Segel) sail.

Segelboot das (PL die Segelboote) sailing boat.

Segelfliegen das gliding.

Segelflugzeug das (PL die Segelflugzeuge) glider.

segeln verb (PERF ist gesegelt) to sail.

sehen ◇ verb (PRES sieht, IMPERF sah, PERF hat gesehen) 1 to see; jemanden wieder sehen △ to see somebody again; mal sehen, ob ... let's see if ...; 2 to look; 3 eine Fernsehsendung sehen to watch a television programme; 4 gut/schlecht sehen to have good/bad eyesight; 5 nach jemandem sehen to look after somebody.

sehenswert adjective worth seeing.

Sehenswürdigkeiten plural noun sights.

Sehnsucht die longing; Sehnsucht nach jemandem haben to long to see somebody.

sehr adverb 1 very; sehr gut very good; 2 danke sehr thank you very much; 3 ich habe Karin sehr gern I like Karin a lot; 4 Sehr geehrte Frau Huber Dear Mrs Huber.

seid SEE sein.

Seide die (PL die Seiden) silk.

Seife die (PL die Seifen) soap.

Seil das (PL die Seile) 1 rope; 2 cable.

Seilbahn die (PL die Seilbahnen) cable railway.

sein[1] ◇ verb (PRES ist, IMPERF war, PERF ist gewesen) 1 to be; wir sind in der Küche we're in the kitchen; Rosi ist krank Rosi is ill; mir ist schlecht I feel sick; mir ist kalt I'm cold; 2 sie ist Lehrerin she's a teacher; 3 es ist drei Uhr it's three o'clock; Karl ist aus München Karl's from Munich; es war viel zu tun there was a lot to be done; 4 aus Seide sein to be made of silk; 5 etwas sein lassen △ to stop something; lass das sein! stop it!; 6 es sei denn, dass ... unless ...; 7 (used with certain verbs to form past tenses) ich bin nach Berlin gefahren I went to Berlin; wir sind kurz vor acht nach Hause gekommen we got home shortly before eight o'clock; er ist abgeholt worden he's been collected.

sein[2] adjective 1 his; 2 (of a thing or animal) its; der Hund ist in seiner Hütte the dog is in its kennel; 3 (after the pronoun 'man') your, one's; wenn man sich seine Eltern aussuchen könnte if you could choose your parents.

△ NEW SPELLING: See page xii

seiner, seine, sein(e)s pronoun
1 his; **das ist nicht meine CD, das
ist seine** it's not my CD, it's his; **du
kannst seins nehmen** you can take
his; 2 (after the pronoun 'man') your
own, one's own; **das Seine tun** to
do one's share.

seinetwegen adverb 1 for his sake;
2 because of him; 3 on his account.

seinlassen SEE sein.

seins SEE seiner.

seit preposition ←(+DAT),
conjunction 1 since; **seit etwa einer
Woche** since about a week; **seit du
hier wohnst** since you've been
living here; **seit wann?** since
when?; 2 **ich bin seit zwei Wochen
hier** I've been here for two weeks;
seit einiger Zeit for some time.

seitdem adverb since then; **ich
habe sie seitdem nicht mehr
gesehen** I haven't seen her since.
conjunction since.

Seite die (PL die Seiten) 1 side; **auf
der einen Seite** on the one hand;
2 page; **das steht auf Seite zwanzig**
it's on page twenty.

Seitenstechen das stich; **ich habe
Seitenstechen** I've got a stitch.

Seitenstraße die (PL die
Seitenstraßen) side street.

seither adverb since then.

Sekretärin die (PL die
Sekretärinnen) secretary.

Sekt der (PL die Sekte) sparkling
wine.

Sekte die (PL die Sekten) sect.

Sekunde die (PL die Sekunden)
second.

selbst pronoun 1 **ich selbst** I
myself; **er selbst** he himself; **wir
selbst** we ourselves; **Sie selbst** you
yourself, you yourselves; 2 **von
selbst** by itself; 3 **sie schneidet
sich die Haare selbst** she cuts her
own hair; 4 on one's own; **ich kann
es selbst machen** I can do it on my
own; 5 **selbst gemacht** △ homemade.
adverb even; **selbst wenn** even if.

selbständig = **selbstständig**.

Selbstbedienung die self-service.

selbstbewusst △ adjective self-
confident.

Selbstbewusstsein △ das
self-confidence.

selbstgemacht SEE selbst.

Selbstmord der (PL die
Selbstmorde) suicide; **Selbstmord
begehen** to commit suicide.

selbstständig △ adjective
1 independent; 2 self-employed;
sich selbstständig machen to set
up on your own.

selbstverständlich adjective
natural; **etwas für
selbstverständlich halten** to take
something for granted; **das ist
selbstverständlich** it goes without
saying.
adverb naturally, of course; **wir
haben ihn selbstverständlich auf
die Party eingeladen** of course we
invited him to the party.

✧ IRREGULAR VERB: *See the verb table in the centre of the dictionary*

selten *adjective* rare.
adverb rarely.

seltsam *adjective* strange, odd.

Semester *das* (PL *die* **Semester**)
semester, term.

Semikolon *das* (PL *die* **Semikolons**)
semicolon.

Semmel *die* (PL *die* **Semmeln**) roll.

senden *verb* (PERF **hat gesendet**)
1 to send; **etwas an jemanden
senden** to send something to
somebody; 2 to broadcast; **seine
Rede wird im ersten Programm
gesendet** his speech will be
broadcast on channel one; 3 to
transmit.

Sendung *die* (PL *die* **Sendungen**)
1 programme; 2 consignment.

Senf *der* (PL *die* **Senfe**) mustard.

Senior *der* (PL *die* **Senioren**)
1 senior; 2 **Senioren** senior
citizens.

sensationell *adjective* sensational.

sensibel *adjective* sensitive.

September *der* September.

Serie *die* (PL *die* **Serien**) 1 series;
2 serial.

Service[1] *das* (PL *die* **Service**) set (*of
china, for example*).

Service[2] *der* service; **das Essen im
Hotel ist gut, aber der Service ist
furchtbar** the food in the hotel is
good but the service is appalling.

servieren *verb* (PERF **hat serviert**) to
serve.

Serviette *die* (PL *die* **Servietten**)
napkin.

Sessel *der* (PL *die* **Sessel**) armchair.

Sessellift *der* (PL *die* **Sessellifte**)
chair-lift.

setzen *verb* (PERF **hat gesetzt**) 1 to
put; **ein Komma setzen** to put a
comma; **vergiss nicht, deinen
Namen auf die Liste zu setzen**
don't forget to put your name on the
list; 2 to move (*a counter in games*);
3 **auf etwas setzen** to bet on
something; **auf ein Pferd setzen** to
back a horse; 4 **sich setzen** to sit
down; **sich auf einen Stuhl setzen**
to sit down on a chair.

seufzen *verb* (PERF **hat geseufzt**) to
sigh.

Seufzer *der* (PL *die* **Seufzer**) sigh.

Sex *der* sex.

Sexismus *der* sexism.

sexistisch *adjective* sexist.

sexuell *adjective* sexual.

Shampoo *das* (PL *die* **Shampoos**)
shampoo.

sich *pronoun* 1 (*with 'er/sie/es'*)
himself/herself/itself; **sie hat sich
eingeschlossen** she locked herself
in; 2 (*with plural 'sie'*)
themselves; 3 (*with 'Sie'*) yourself, yourselves
(*plural*); 4 each other, one another;
sich kennen to know each other;
Petra und Werner lieben sich Petra
and Werner love each other; 5 (*not
translated with certain verbs*) **sich
freuen** to be pleased; **sich wundern**
to be surprised; 6 **Anita wäscht sich**

△ NEW SPELLING: *See page xii*

die Haare Anita is washing her hair; **sich den Arm brechen** to break your arm; **7 sich gut verkaufen** to sell well; **8 von sich aus** of your own accord.

sicher *adjective* 1 safe; 2 certain; **bist du sicher?** are you sure? *adverb* 1 safely; 2 certainly, surely; **sicher!** certainly!

Sicherheit *die* 1 safety; **zur Sicherheit** for safety's sake; **schnallen Sie sich zur Ihrer eigenen Sicherheit an** fasten your seat belt for your own safety; **etwas in Sicherheit bringen** to rescue something; **in Sicherheit sein** to be safe; 2 security; **die Sicherheit der Arbeitsplätze** job security; 3 certainty; **mit Sicherheit!** certainly! (*as a reply*).

Sicherheitsgurt *der* (PL die **Sicherheitsgurte**) seatbelt.

Sicherheitsnadel *die* (PL die **Sicherheitsnadeln**) safety pin.

sicherlich *adverb* certainly.

sichern *verb* (PERF **hat gesichert**) to secure; **jemandem etwas sichern** to secure something for somebody.

Sicherung *die* (PL die **Sicherungen**) 1 fuse; **die Sicherung ist durchgebrannt** the fuse has blown; 2 safeguard; **die Sicherung der Arbeitsplätze** safeguarding jobs; 3 safety catch.

Sicht *die* 1 view; **ich hatte eine gute Sicht auf den See** I had a good view of the lake; **auf lange Sicht** in the long term; 2 **aus meiner Sicht** as I

see it; 3 visibility; **gute/schlechte Sicht** good/poor visibility.

sichtbar *adjective* visible.

sie *pronoun* 1 she; 2 her; **ich kenne sie** I know her; 3 it; **so eine hübsche Bluse, war sie teuer?** what a pretty blouse, was it expensive?; 4 they; **sie sind in der Küche** they're in the kitchen; 5 them; **ich habe sie gestern abgeschickt** I posted them yesterday.

Sie *pronoun* you; **kommen Sie herein!** come in!

Sieb *das* (PL die **Siebe**) 1 sieve; 2 strainer.

sieben *number* seven.

siebter, siebte, siebtes *adjective* seventh.

siebzehn *number* seventeen.

siebzig *number* seventy.

Siedlung *die* (PL die **Siedlungen**) 1 (housing) estate; 2 settlement.

Sieg *der* (PL die **Siege**) victory, win.

Siegel *das* (PL die **Siegel**) seal.

siegen *verb* (PERF **hat gesiegt**) to win.

Sieger *der* (PL die **Sieger**) winner.

Siegerin *die* (PL die **Siegerinnen**) winner.

sieht SEE **sehen**.

Silbe *die* (PL die **Silben**) syllable.

Silber *das* silver.

silbern *adjective* silver.

◆ **IRREGULAR VERB: See the verb table in the centre of the dictionary**

Silvester *das* New Year's Eve.

sind SEE **sein.**

Sinfonie *die* (PL *die* Sinfonien) symphony.

singen ◇ *verb* (IMPERF **sang,** PERF **hat gesungen**) to sing.

sinken ◇ *verb* (IMPERF **sank,** PERF **ist gesunken**) **1** to sink; **2** to go down.

Sinn *der* (PL *die* Sinne) **1** sense; **2** meaning; **3** point; **das hat keinen Sinn** there's no point.

sinnlos *adjective* pointless.

sinnvoll *adjective* **1** sensible; **2** meaningful.

Situation *die* (PL *die* Situationen) situation.

Sitz *der* (PL *die* Sitze) **1** seat; **2** fit (*of clothes*).

sitzen ◇ *verb* (IMPERF **saß,** PERF **hat gesessen**) **1** to sit; **sitzen bleiben** ∆ to remain seated; **2** **sitzen bleiben** ∆ to have to repeat a year, to stay down (*at school*); **3** **er sitzt** (*informal*) he's in jail; **4** **jemanden sitzen lassen** ∆ to leave somebody in the lurch; **5** to fit (*of clothes*); **der Mantel sitzt gut** the coat fits well.

Sitzplatz *der* (PL *die* Sitzplätze) seat.

Sitzung *die* (PL *die* Sitzungen) **1** meeting; **2** session.

Sizilien *das* Sicily.

Skandal *der* (PL *die* Skandale) scandal.

Skandinavien *das* Scandinavia.

skandinavisch *adjective* Scandinavian.

Skelett *das* (PL *die* Skelette) skeleton.

Ski *der* (PL *die* Ski(er)) ski; **Ski fahren/laufen** to ski.

Skifahren *das* skiing.

Skifahrer *der* (PL *die* Skifahrer) skier.

Skifahrerin *die* (PL *die* Skifahrerinnen) skier.

Skilaufen *das* skiing.

Skiläufer *der* (PL *die* Skiläufer) skier.

Skiläuferin *die* (PL *die* Skiläuferinnen) skier.

Skilehrer *der* (PL *die* Skilehrer) ski instructor.

Skizze *die* (PL *die* Skizzen) sketch.

Skorpion *der* (PL *die* Skorpione) **1** scorpion; **2** Scorpio.

Skulptur *die* (PL *die* Skulpturen) sculpture.

Slip *der* (PL *die* Slips) briefs, pants.

Slowake *der* (PL *die* Slowaken) Slovak.

Slowakei *die* Slovakia.

Slowakin *die* (PL *die* Slowakinnen) Slovak.

slowakisch *adjective* Slovak.

Smoking *der* (PL *die* Smokings) dinner jacket.

so *adverb* **1** so; **nicht so viel** not so much; **und so weiter** and so on; **2** like this, like that; **so nicht** not like

that; 3 as; **so bald wie** as soon as; 4 such; **so ein Zufall!** what a coincidence!; 5 **das kriegst du so** (*informal*) you get it for nothing; 6 **so um zwanzig Mark** (*informal*) about twenty marks.
▸ *conjunction* **so dass** so that.
▸ *exclamation* right!, well!; **so?** really?

sobald *conjunction* as soon as.

Socke *die* (PL **die Socken**) sock.

Sofa *das* (PL **die Sofas**) sofa.

sofort *adverb* immediately.

sogar *adverb* even.

sogleich *adverb* at once.

Sohle *die* (PL **die Sohlen**) sole.

Sohn *der* (PL **die Söhne**) son.

solange *conjunction* as long as.

solch *pronoun* such; **solch einer/eine/eins** one like that, somebody like that.

solcher, solche, solches *adjective, pronoun* 1 such; **ich habe solche Angst** I'm so frightened; 2 **ein solcher Mann** a man like that; **eine solche Frage** a question like that; **ein solches Haus** a house like that; 3 **solche** (*plural*) those; **solche wie die** people like that.

Soldat *der* (PL **die Soldaten**) soldier.

solide *adjective* 1 solid; 2 respectable.

Solist *der* (PL **die Solisten**) soloist.

Solistin *die* (PL **die Solistinnen**) soloist.

sollen ◇ *verb* (PRES **soll**, IMPERF **sollte**, PERF **hat gesollt**) 1 should; **sollte es regnen** if it should rain; 2 to be supposed to; **was soll das heißen?** what's that supposed to mean?; 3 **sagen Sie ihr, sie soll anrufen** tell her to ring; 4 **was soll ich machen?** what shall I do?; **soll ich?** shall I?; 5 **was soll's!** so what!

sollte, sollten, solltest, solltet
SEE **sollen**.

Sommer *der* (PL **die Sommer**) summer.

sommerlich *adjective* summery, summer.

Sommersprossen *plural noun* freckles.

Sonderangebot *das* (PL **die Sonderangebote**) special offer; **im Sonderangebot** on special offer.

sonderbar *adjective* strange, odd.

sondern *conjunction* but; **nicht nur ..., sondern auch ...** not only ..., but also ...

Song *der* (PL **die Songs**) song.

Sonnabend *der* (PL **die Sonnabende**) Saturday.

sonnabends *adverb* on Saturdays.

Sonne *die* (PL **die Sonnen**) sun.

sonnen *verb* (PERF **hat sich gesonnt**) **sich sonnen** to sun yourself.

Sonnenaufgang *der* sunrise.

Sonnenbrand *der* sunburn.

Sonnenbrille *die* (PL **die Sonnenbrillen**) sunglasses.

◇ IRREGULAR VERB: *See the verb table in the centre of the dictionary*

sozusagen

Sonnencreme die (PL die Sonnencremes) suntan lotion.

Sonnenenergie die solar energy.

Sonnenmilch die suntan lotion.

Sonnenöl das suntan oil.

Sonnenschein der sunshine.

Sonnenstich der sunstroke.

sonnig adjective sunny.

Sonntag der (PL die Sonntage) Sunday.

sonntags adverb on Sundays.

sonst adverb 1 usually; 2 else; wer sonst? who else?; was sonst? what else?; 3 sonst noch etwas? anything else?; sonst noch jemand? anybody else?; 4 sonst wo △ somewhere; es kann sonst wo sein it could be anywhere; 5 otherwise; geh jetzt, sonst verpasst du den Bus go now, otherwise you'll miss the bus.

sonstwo SEE sonst.

sooft conjunction whenever.

Sorge die (PL die Sorgen) worry; sich Sorgen machen to worry.

sorgen verb (PERF hat gesorgt) 1 für etwas sorgen to take care of something; für die Musik sorgen to see to the music; für jemanden sorgen to look after somebody; 2 dafür sorgen, dass ... to make sure that ...; 3 sich sorgen to worry; ich sorge mich um meine Eltern I worry about my parents.

sorgfältig adjective careful.

Sorte die (PL die Sorten) 1 kind; 2 brand.

Soße die (PL die Soßen) 1 sauce; 2 gravy; 3 dressing.

Souvenir das (PL die Souvenirs) souvenir.

soviel conjunction as far as; soviel ich weiß as far as I know. adverb SEE viel.

soweit conjunction as far as; soweit ich weiß, ist er in Ferien as far as I know, he's on holiday. adverb SEE weit.

sowenig SEE wenig.

sowie conjunction 1 as well as; 2 as soon as.

sowieso adverb anyway.

sowohl adverb sowohl ... als auch ... both ... and ...; sowohl er wie auch sein Freund both he and his friend.

sozial adjective social.

Sozialarbeiter der (PL die Sozialarbeiter) social worker.

Sozialarbeiterin die (PL die Sozialarbeiterinnen) social worker.

Sozialhilfe die social security.

Sozialismus der socialism.

sozialistisch adjective socialist.

Sozialkunde die social studies.

Sozialwohnung die (PL die Sozialwohnungen) council flat.

Soziologie die sociology.

sozusagen adverb so to speak.

Spalte die (PL die Spalten) 1 crack;
2 column (in text).

spalten verb (PERF hat gespalten) to
split.

Spanien das Spain.

Spanier der (PL die Spanier)
Spaniard.

Spanierin die (PL die Spanierinnen)
Spaniard.

spanisch adjective Spanish.

spann SEE **spinnen**.

spannend adjective exciting.

Spannung die (PL die Spannungen)
1 tension; 2 suspense (in a film or
novel, for example); **ich erwarte
seine Antwort mit Spannung** I can't
wait for his answer; 3 voltage.

sparen verb (PERF hat gespart) 1 to
save; **auf etwas sparen** to save up
for something; 2 **sich etwas sparen**
not to bother with something; **sich
die Mühe sparen** to save yourself
the trouble; 3 **an etwas sparen** to
economize on something.

Spargel der asparagus.

Sparkasse die savings bank.

sparsam adjective 1 economical;
2 thrifty.

Spaß der (PL die Späße) 1 fun;
zum/aus Spaß for fun; **das macht
Spaß** it's fun; **Segeln macht mir
keinen Spaß** I don't like sailing;
2 **viel Spaß !** have a good time!;
3 joke; **er macht nur Spaß** he's only
joking.

spät adjective, adverb late; **zu spät**

kommen to be late; **wie spät ist
es?** what time is it?

Spaten der (PL die Spaten) spade.

später adjective later.

spätestens adverb at the latest.

Spatz der (PL die Spatzen) sparrow.

spazieren verb (PERF ist spaziert)
1 to stroll; 2 **spazieren gehen** △ to
go for a walk; **hast du Lust,
spazieren zu gehen?** would you
like to go for a walk?

spazierengehen SEE **spazieren**.

Spaziergang der (PL die
Spaziergänge) walk; **einen
Spaziergang machen** to go for a
walk.

Speck der bacon.

Speiche die (PL die Speichen) spoke.

Speicher der (PL die Speicher)
1 loft, attic; 2 memory (in
computing).

speichern verb (PERF hat
gespeichert) 1 to store; 2 to save
(in computing).

Speise die (PL die Speisen) 1 food;
2 dish.

Speisekarte die (PL die
Speisekarten) menu.

Speisesaal der (PL die Speisesäle)
1 dining hall; 2 dining room.

Speisewagen der (PL die
Speisewagen) dining car.

Spende die (PL die Spenden)
donation.

◇ IRREGULAR VERB: *See the verb table in the centre of the dictionary*

spenden *verb* (PERF **hat gespendet**)
1 to donate; 2 to give.

spendieren *verb* (PERF **hat spendiert**) **jemandem etwas spendieren** to treat somebody to something.

Sperre *die* (PL *die* **Sperren**)
1 barrier; 2 ban.

sperren *verb* (PERF **hat gesperrt**)
1 to close; 2 to block (*an entrance, access*); 3 **den Strom sperren** to cut off the electricity; 4 **einen Scheck sperren** to stop a cheque; 5 **ein Tier in einen Käfig sperren** to shut an animal (up) in a cage.

Spezialität *die* (PL *die* **Spezialitäten**) speciality.

speziell *adjective* special.

Spiegel *der* (PL *die* **Spiegel**) mirror.

Spiegelbild *das* (PL *die* **Spiegelbilder**) reflection.

Spiegelei *das* (PL *die* **Spiegeleier**) fried egg.

spiegeln *verb* (PERF **hat gespiegelt**)
1 to reflect; 2 **sich spiegeln** to be reflected.

Spiel *das* (PL *die* **Spiele**) 1 game;
2 **ein Spiel Karten** a pack of cards;
3 **es steht viel auf dem Spiel** there's a lot at stake.

spielen *verb* (PERF **hat gespielt**) 1 to play; **wir spielen morgen Tennis** we're going to play tennis tomorrow;
2 to gamble; 3 to act; **das Stück war gut gespielt** the play was well acted; 4 **der Film spielt in Rom** the film is set in Rome.

spielend *adverb* easily.

Spieler *der* (PL *die* **Spieler**) 1 player;
2 gambler.

Spielerin *die* (PL *die* **Spielerinnen**)
1 player; 2 gambler.

Spielfeld *das* (PL *die* **Spielfelder**) pitch, field.

Spielhalle *die* (PL *die* **Spielhallen**) amusement arcade.

Spielplatz *der* (PL *die* **Spielplätze**) playground.

Spielverderber *der* (PL *die* **Spielverderber**) spoilsport.

Spielverderberin *die* (PL *die* **Spielverderberinnen**) spoilsport.

Spielwaren *plural noun* toys.

Spielzeug *das* 1 toy; 2 toys.

Spinat *der* spinach.

Spinne *die* (PL *die* **Spinnen**) spider.

spinnen ◇ *verb* (IMPERF **spann**, PERF **hat gesponnen**) 1 to spin; 2 **du spinnst!** (*informal*) you're mad!

Spinnennetz *das* (PL *die* **Spinnennetze**) cobweb.

Spion *der* (PL *die* **Spione**) spy.

Spionage *die* spying, espionage.

spionieren *verb* (PERF **hat spioniert**) to spy.

Spirituosen *plural noun* spirits (*alcohol*).

spitz *adjective* pointed.

Spitze *die* (PL *die* **Spitzen**) 1 point;
2 top; **Schalke liegt jetzt an der Spitze** Schalke is top of the league

at the moment; **3** peak; **von hier kann man die schneebedeckten Spitzen sehen** you can see the snow-covered peaks from here; **4** front; **an der Spitze liegen** to be in the lead; **5** lace; **6 Spitze sein** (*informal*) to be great.

spitzen verb (PERF **hat gespitzt**) **1** to sharpen; **2 sich auf etwas spitzen** (*informal*) to look forward to something.

Spitzname der (PL die **Spitznamen**) nickname.

Splitter der (PL die **Splitter**) splinter.

sponsern verb (PERF **hat gesponsert**) to sponsor.

Sport der sport.

Sporthalle die (PL die **Sporthallen**) sports hall.

Sportler der (PL die **Sportler**) sportsman.

Sportlerin die (PL die **Sportlerinnen**) sportswoman.

sportlich adjective **1** sporting; **2** sporty.

Sportplatz der (PL die **Sportplätze**) sports field, sports ground.

Sportschuh der (PL die **Sportschuhe**) trainer.

Sportverein der (PL die **Sportvereine**) sports club.

Sportwagen der (PL die **Sportwagen**) **1** sports car; **2** pushchair.

Sportzentrum das (PL die **Sportzentren**) sports centre.

spotten verb (PERF **hat gespottet**) to mock.

sprach SEE **sprechen**.

Sprache die (PL die **Sprachen**) **1** language; **2** speech; **etwas zur Sprache bringen** to bring something up.

sprachlos adjective speechless.

sprang SEE **springen**.

sprechen ✧ verb (PRES **spricht**, IMPERF **sprach**, PERF **hat gesprochen**) **1** to speak; **Deutsch sprechen** to speak German; **mit wem spreche ich?** who's speaking? (*on the phone*); **jemanden sprechen** to speak to somebody; **2 Frau Hahn ist nicht zu sprechen** Mrs Hahn is not available; **3** to talk; **mit jemandem über etwas sprechen** to talk to somebody about something; **4** to say (*a word, sentence*).

Sprecher der (PL die **Sprecher**) **1** spokesman; **2** (*on TV*) announcer; **3** (*in a film*) narrator; **4** speaker.

Sprecherin die (PL die **Sprecherinnen**) **1** spokeswoman; **2** (*on TV*) announcer; **3** (*in a film*) narrator; **4** speaker.

Sprechstunde die (PL die **Sprechstunden**) surgery.

spricht SEE **sprechen**.

Sprichwort das (PL die **Sprichwörter**) proverb.

springen ✧ verb (IMPERF **sprang**, PERF **ist gesprungen**) **1** to jump;

✧ **IRREGULAR VERB: See the verb table in the centre of the dictionary**

2 to bounce (*of a ball*); 3 to dive;
4 to crack.

Spritze die (PL die Spritzen)
1 syringe; 2 injection; 3 hose.

spritzen verb (PERF hat gespritzt)
1 to inject; 2 to splash; **du hast mich
nass gespritzt** you've splashed me;
3 to spray; 4 to spit (*of fat*); 5 (PERF
ist gespritzt) to splash up.

Sprudel der (PL die Sprudel)
sparkling mineral water.

sprühen verb (PERF hat gesprüht)
1 to spray; 2 to sparkle (*of eyes*);
3 (PERF **ist gesprüht**) to fly (*of
sparks*); **die Funken sind in alle
Richtungen gesprüht** sparks flew in
all directions.

Sprung der (PL die Sprünge)
1 jump; 2 dive; 3 crack (*in china,
glass*).

Sprungbrett das (PL die
Sprungbretter) diving board.

spucken verb (PERF hat gespuckt)
to spit.

Spülbecken das (PL die
Spülbecken) sink.

spülen verb (PERF hat gespült) 1 to
rinse; 2 to wash up; 3 to flush.

Spülmaschine die (PL die
Spülmaschinen) dishwasher.

Spülmittel das (PL die Spülmittel)
washing-up liquid.

Spur die (PL die Spuren) 1 track; **auf
der falschen Spur sein** to be on the
wrong track; **jemandem auf die Spur
kommen** to get on to somebody;

2 lane; **in der Spur bleiben** to keep
in lane; 3 trail; 4 trace.

spüren verb (PERF hat gespürt) 1 to
feel; 2 to sense.

Staat der (PL die Staaten) state.

staatlich adjective state; **eine
staatliche Schule** a state school.
adverb by the state.

Staatsangehörigkeit die (PL die
Staatsangehörigkeiten) nationality.

stabil adjective 1 stable; 2 sturdy.

stach SEE **stechen**.

Stachel der (PL die Stacheln)
1 spine; 2 spike; 3 sting.

Stachelbeere die (PL die
Stachelbeeren) gooseberry.

Stacheldraht der barbed wire.

Stadion das (PL die Stadien)
stadium.

Stadium das (PL die Stadien) stage.

Stadt die (PL die Städte) town, city.

städtisch adjective 1 urban;
2 municipal.

Stadtmitte die town centre.

Stadtplan der (PL die Stadtpläne)
street map.

Stadtrand der outskirts (of town);
am Stadtrand on the outskirts.

Stadtrundfahrt die (PL die
Stadtrundfahrten) sightseeing tour
(*of a town*).

Stadtteil der (PL die Stadtteile)
district.

stahl SEE **stehlen**.

△ NEW SPELLING: *See page xii*

Stahl der steel.

Stall der (PL die Ställe) 1 stable;
2 cowshed; 3 pigsty.

Stamm der (PL die Stämme)
1 trunk; 2 tribe; 3 stem (of a word).

stammen verb (PERF hat gestammt)
aus Deutschland stammen to
come from Germany.

Stammgast der (PL die
Stammgäste) regular customer (in
a pub or restaurant).

stand SEE stehen.

Stand der (PL die Stände) 1 state;
etwas auf den neuesten Stand
bringen to bring something up to
date; 2 score (in a game); 3 stall;
4 level.

ständig adjective constant.

Standort der (PL die Standorte)
position, location; von ihrem
Standort aus konnte sie nichts
sehen she couldn't see anything
from where she was standing.

Stange die (PL die Stangen) 1 bar;
2 pole.

stank SEE stinken.

starb SEE sterben.

stark adjective 1 strong; 2 heavy
(rain, traffic); 3 severe (frost, pain);
4 (informal) great; das ist stark!
that's great!

Stärke die (PL die Stärken)
1 strength; 2 starch.

starrsinnig adjective obstinate.

Start der (PL die Starts) 1 start;
2 take-off.

Startbahn die (PL die Startbahnen)
runway.

starten verb (PERF ist gestartet)
1 (of a plane) to take off; 2 (PERF hat
gestartet) to start, to launch (a
campaign).

Station die (PL die Stationen)
1 station; 2 stop; Station machen
to stop over; 3 ward.

statt conjunction, preposition
←(+GEN) instead of; statt zu
arbeiten instead of working; sie
ging statt ihrer Schwester she went
instead of her sister.

stattdessen Δ conjunction instead.

stattfinden ◇ verb (IMPERF fand
statt, PERF hat stattgefunden) to
take place.

Stau der (PL die Staus) 1 congestion;
2 traffic jam.

Staub der dust.

staubig adjective dusty.

staubsaugen verb (PERF hat
staubgesaugt) to vacuum.

Staubsauger der (PL die
Staubsauger) vacuum cleaner.

staunen verb (PERF hat gestaunt) to
be amazed.

stechen ◇ verb (PRES sticht, IMPERF
stach, PERF hat gestochen) 1 to
prick; sich in den Finger stechen to
prick your finger; 2 to sting, to bite
(of an insect); 3 mit etwas in etwas
stechen to jab something into
something.

◇ IRREGULAR VERB: See the verb table in the centre of the dictionary

Stereoanlage

Steckdose die (PL die Steckdosen) socket.

stecken verb (PERF hat gesteckt) 1 to put; du musst die Münze in den Schlitz stecken put the coin into the slot; 2 to pin; 3 wo steckt er? where is he? 4 stecken bleiben △ to get stuck; den Schlüssel stecken lassen △ to leave the key in the lock.

Stecker der (PL die Stecker) plug.

Stecknadel die (PL die Stecknadeln).

stehen ◇ verb (IMPERF stand, PERF hat gestanden) 1 to stand; 2 to be; es steht zwei zu zwei the score is two all; wie steht's? what's the score? 3 to have stopped (of a clock or a machine); 4 es steht schlecht um ihn he's in a bad way; na, wie steht's? how are you? 5 stehen bleiben △ to stop; die Uhr ist stehen geblieben the clock has stopped; 6 in der Zeitung steht, dass ... it says in the paper that ...; 7 jemandem stehen to suit somebody; 8 zu jemandem stehen to stand by somebody; 9 sich gut stehen to be on good terms; 10 zum Stehen kommen to come to a standstill.

stehenbleiben SEE stehen.

stehlen ◇ verb (PRES stiehlt, IMPERF stahl, PERF hat gestohlen) to steal.

steif adjective stiff.

steigen verb (IMPERF stieg, PERF ist gestiegen) 1 to climb; auf eine Leiter steigen to climb up a ladder; auf ein Fahrrad steigen to get on a bike; in den Bus steigen to get on the bus; 2 to rise.

steil adjective steep.

Stein der (PL die Steine) stone.

Steinbock der (PL die Steinböcke) 1 ibex; 2 Capricorn; Petra ist Steinbock Petra's Capricorn.

Stelle die (PL die Stellen) 1 place; an deiner Stelle in your place; 2 job; 3 authority; 4 auf der Stelle immediately.

stellen verb (PERF hat gestellt) 1 to put; 2 to set (a watch, task); 3 zur Verfügung stellen to provide; 4 lauter stellen to turn up; leiser stellen to turn down; die Heizung höher stellen to turn the heating up; 5 sich krank stellen to pretend to be ill; 6 sich stellen to give yourself up; 7 die Kinder stellten sich an die Wand the children stood against the wall.

Stellenanzeige die (PL die Stellenanzeigen) job advertisement.

Stellung die (PL die Stellungen) position.

Stempel der (PL die Stempel) 1 stamp; 2 postmark.

stempeln verb (PERF hat gestempelt) to stamp.

Steppdecke die (PL die Steppdecken) quilt.

sterben ◇ verb (PRES stirbt, IMPERF starb, PERF ist gestorben) to die.

Stereoanlage die (PL die Stereoanlagen) stereo (system).

△ NEW SPELLING: See page xii

Stern der (PL die Sterne) star.

Sternzeichen das (PL die Sternzeichen) star sign; **was ist dein Sternzeichen?** what star sign are you?

Steuer[1] das (PL die Steuer) 1 (steering) wheel; 2 helm.

Steuer[2] die (PL die Steuern) tax.

steuern verb (PERF hat gesteuert) 1 to steer; 2 to control; 3 (PERF ist gesteuert) to head.

Stewardess△ die (PL die Stewardessen) stewardess, air hostess.

Stich der (PL die Stiche) 1 prick; 2 stab; 3 sting, bite (of an insect); 4 stitch; 5 trick (when playing cards); 6 engraving; 7 **jemanden im Stich lassen** to leave somebody in the lurch.

sticht SEE stechen.

sticken verb (PERF hat gestickt) to embroider.

Stickstoff der nitrogen.

Stiefbruder der (PL die Stiefbrüder) stepbrother.

Stiefel der (PL die Stiefel) boot.

Stiefkind das (PL die Stiefkinder) stepchild.

Stiefmutter die (PL die Stiefmütter) stepmother.

Stiefschwester die (PL die Stiefschwestern) stepsister.

Stiefvater der (PL die Stiefväter) stepfather.

stieg SEE steigen.

stiehlt SEE stehlen.

Stiel der (PL die Stiele) 1 handle; 2 stem.

Stier der (PL die Stiere) 1 bull; 2 Taurus; **Andrea ist Stier** Andrea's Taurus.

stieß SEE stoßen.

Stift der (PL die Stifte) 1 pencil; 2 crayon; 3 tack (nail).

Stil der (PL die Stile) style.

still adjective 1 quiet; 2 still.

stillen verb (PERF hat gestillt) 1 to quench; 2 to breast-feed.

stillhalten ◇ verb (PRES hält still, IMPERF hielt still, PERF hat stillgehalten) to keep still.

Stimme die (PL die Stimmen) 1 voice; 2 vote.

stimmen verb (PERF hat gestimmt) 1 to be right; **stimmt das?** is that right?; 2 to vote; 3 to tune.

Stimmung die (PL die Stimmungen) 1 mood; 2 atmosphere.

stinken ◇ verb (IMPERF stank, PERF hat gestunken) to smell, to stink.

Stipendium das (PL die Stipendien) 1 scholarship; 2 grant.

stirbt SEE sterben.

Stirn die (PL die Stirnen) forehead.

Stock[1] der (PL die Stöcke) stick.

Stock[2] der (PL die Stock) floor.

Stockwerk das (PL die Stockwerke) floor.

◇ **IRREGULAR VERB:** See the verb table in the centre of the dictionary

Stoff der (PL die Stoffe) 1 material, fabric; 2 substance.

stöhnen verb (PERF hat gestöhnt) to groan.

stolpern verb (PERF ist gestolpert) 1 to stumble; 2 to trip; **ich bin über einen Stein gestolpert** I tripped on a stone.

stolz adjective proud.

stoppen verb (PERF hat gestoppt) to stop.

Stöpsel der (PL die Stöpsel) 1 plug; 2 stopper.

stören verb (PERF hat gestört) 1 to disturb; 2 to bother; **das stört mich nicht** that doesn't bother me; 3 **stört es Sie, wenn ich das Fenster aufmache?** do you mind if I open the window?; **der Empfang ist gestört** there's interference (on a TV).

Störung die (PL die Störungen) 1 disturbance, interruption; **entschuldigen Sie die Störung** I'm sorry to bother you; 2 interference; **eine technische Störung** a technical fault.

Stoß der (PL die Stöße) 1 push; 2 pile; **ein Stoß Handtücher** a pile of towels.

stoßen ◇ verb (PRES stößt, IMPERF stieß, PERF hat gestoßen) 1 to push; 2 to kick; 3 **sich den Kopf stoßen** to hit your head; **ich habe mir den Kopf am Balken gestoßen** I hit my head on the beam; **sich stoßen** to bump yourself; 4 **sich an etwas stoßen** to object to something;

5 (PERF **ist gestoßen) gegen etwas stoßen** to bump into something; 6 (PERF **ist gestoßen) auf etwas stoßen** to come across something.

Stoßstange die (PL die Stoßstangen) bumper.

Stoßzeit die (PL die Stoßzeiten) rush hour.

stottern verb (PERF hat gestottert) to stutter.

Strafe die (PL die Strafen) 1 punishment; 2 fine; 3 penalty.

Straftat die (PL die Straftaten) crime.

Strahl der (PL die Strahlen) 1 ray, beam; 2 jet.

strahlen verb (PERF hat gestrahlt) 1 to shine; 2 to beam.

Strand der (PL die Strände) beach.

Straße die (PL die Straßen) street, road; **in welcher Straße ist der Supermarkt?** which street is the supermarket in?; **über die Straße gehen** to cross the road; **jemanden auf die Straße setzen** (informal) to give somebody the sack; **mein Wirt hat mich einfach auf die Straße gesetzt** (informal) my landlord just turned me out (of a flat or room).

Straßenbahn die (PL die Straßenbahnen) tram; **mit der Straßenbahn fahren** to go by tram.

Strauch der (PL die Sträucher) bush.

Strauß[1] der (PL die Sträuße) bunch of flowers, bouquet.

Strauß[2] der (PL die Strauße) ostrich.

△ NEW SPELLING: *See page xii*

Streber der (PL die Streber) swot.

Strecke die (PL die Strecken)
1 distance; 2 route; 3 line (rail).

strecken verb (PERF hat gestreckt)
1 to stretch (your arms, legs); 2 sich
strecken to stretch.

Streich der (PL die Streiche) trick.

streicheln verb (PERF hat
gestreichelt) to stroke.

streichen ◇ verb (IMPERF strich,
PERF hat gestrichen) 1 to paint;
'frisch gestrichen' 'wet paint'; 2 to
spread (with butter); 3 to delete;
4 to cancel (a flight); 5 jemandem
über den Kopf streichen to stroke
somebody's head.

Streichholz das (PL die
Streichhölzer) match.

Streifen der (PL die Streifen)
1 stripe; 2 strip.

Streik der (PL die Streiks) strike.

streiken verb (PERF hat gestreikt) to
strike.

Streit der (PL die Streite) quarrel,
argument.

streiten ◇ verb (IMPERF stritt, PERF
hat gestritten) 1 to quarrel, to
argue; 2 sich streiten to quarrel, to
argue.

streng adjective strict.

Stress △ der stress.

stressig adjective stressful.

streuen verb (PERF hat gestreut)
1 to spread; die Straßen streuen to
grit the roads; 2 to sprinkle.

strich SEE streichen.

Strich der (PL die Striche) 1 line;
2 stroke.

Strichpunkt der (PL die
Strichpunkte) semicolon.

stricken verb (PERF hat gestrickt) to
knit.

Strickjacke die (PL die
Strickjacken) cardigan.

stritt SEE streiten.

Stroh das straw.

Strohhalm der (PL die Strohhalme)
straw (for drinking).

Strom der (PL die Ströme) 1 river;
2 stream (of people or blood); es
regnet in Strömen it's pouring with
rain; 3 current.

strömen verb (PERF ist geströmt) to
stream.

Strömung die (PL die Strömungen)
current.

Strumpf der (PL die Strümpfe)
1 stocking; 2 sock.

Strumpfhose die (PL die
Strumpfhosen) tights.

Stube die (PL die Stuben) room.

Stück das (PL die Stücke) 1 piece;
2 item; eine Mark das Stück one
mark each; 3 play.

Stückchen das (PL die Stückchen)
little piece.

Student der (PL die Studenten)
student.

Studentin die (PL die Studentinnen)
student.

◇ IRREGULAR VERB: See the verb table in the centre of the dictionary

studieren verb (PERF hat studiert) to study; **Horst studiert Mathematik** Horst is studying mathematics.

Studium das (PL die Studien) studies.

Stufe die (PL die Stufen) 1 step; **'Vorsicht Stufe'** 'mind the step'; 2 stage (of development).

Stuhl der (PL die Stühle) chair.

stumm adjective 1 dumb; 2 silent.

stumpf adjective 1 blunt; 2 dull; 3 **ein stumpfer Winkel** an obtuse angle.

Stunde die (PL die Stunden) 1 hour; 2 lesson.

stundenlang adverb for hours.

Stundenplan der (PL die Stundenpläne) timetable.

stündlich adjective hourly.

stur adjective stubborn.

Sturm der (PL die Stürme) storm.

stürmisch adjective stormy.

Sturz der (PL die Stürze) 1 fall; 2 overthrow.

stürzen verb (PERF ist gestürzt) 1 to fall; 2 to rush (into a room); 3 (PERF hat gestürzt) to overthrow; 4 (PERF hat sich gestürzt) **er hat sich aus dem Fenster gestürzt** he threw himself out of the window; **sich auf jemanden stürzen** to pounce on somebody.

Sturzhelm der (PL die Sturzhelme) crash helmet.

stützen verb (PERF hat gestützt) to support; **sich auf jemanden stützen** to lean on somebody.

Subjekt das (PL die Subjekte) subject.

Substantiv das (PL die Substantive) noun.

subventionieren verb (PERF hat subventioniert) to subsidize.

Suche die (PL die Suchen) search.

suchen verb (PERF hat gesucht) 1 to look for; **'Zimmer gesucht'** 'room wanted'; 2 to search.

süchtig adjective addicted.

Süchtige der/die (PL die Süchtigen) addict.

Südafrika das South Africa.

Südamerika das South America.

Süden der south.

südlich adjective 1 southern; 2 southerly.
adverb, preposition ←(+GEN) **südlich von Wien** south of Vienna; **südlich der Stadt** to the south of the town.

Südosten der south-east.

Südpol der South Pole.

Südwesten der south-west.

Summe die (PL die Summen) sum.

summen verb (PERF hat gesummt) 1 to hum; 2 to buzz.

super adjective (informal) great.

Supermarkt der (PL die Supermärkte) supermarket.

Suppe die (PL die Suppen) soup.

△ NEW SPELLING: See page xii

surfen *verb* (PERF **hat gesurft**) to surf.

süß *adjective* sweet.

Süßigkeit *die* (PL *die* **Süßigkeiten**) sweet.

sympathisch *adjective* likeable.

Synagoge *die* (PL *die* **Synagogen**) synagogue.

synthetisch *adjective* synthetic.

System *das* (PL *die* **Systeme**) system.

Szene *die* (PL *die* **Szenen**) scene.

T t

Tabak *der* (PL *die* **Tabake**) tobacco.

Tabelle *die* (PL *die* **Tabellen**) table.

Tablett *das* (PL *die* **Tabletts**) tray.

Tablette *die* (PL *die* **Tabletten**) tablet.

Tafel *die* (PL *die* **Tafeln**) 1 board, blackboard; **ein Wort an die Tafel schreiben** to write a word on the blackboard; 2 **eine Tafel Schokolade** a bar of chocolate.

Tag *der* (PL *die* **Tage**) day; **guten Tag** hello; **am Tag** in the daytime.

Tagebuch *das* (PL *die* **Tagebücher**) diary.

tagelang *adverb* for days.

Tagesanbruch *der* dawn.

Tageskarte *die* (PL *die* **Tageskarten**) 1 today's menu; 2 day ticket.

Tageslicht *das* daylight.

Tageslichtprojektor *der* (PL *die* **Tageslichtprojektoren**) overhead projector.

Tagesmutter *die* (PL *die* **Tagesmütter**) childminder.

Tagesschau *die* (PL *die* **Tagesschauen**) news (*on television*).

Tageszeitung *die* (PL *die* **Tageszeitungen**) daily paper.

täglich *adverb, adjective* daily; **zweimal täglich** twice a day.

tagsüber *adverb* during the day.

Taille *die* (PL *die* **Taillen**) waist.

Takt *der* (PL *die* **Takte**) 1 tact; 2 time; **im Takt** in time to the music; 3 rhythm.

taktlos *adjective* tactless.

taktvoll *adjective* tactful.

Tal *das* (PL *die* **Täler**) valley.

Talent *das* (PL *die* **Talente**) talent.

Tampon *der* (PL *die* **Tampons**) tampon.

Tank *der* (PL *die* **Tanks**) tank.

tanken *verb* (PERF **hat getankt**) to fill up (*with petrol*), to get petrol.

Tankstelle *die* (PL *die* **Tankstellen**) petrol station.

Tankwart *der* (PL *die* **Tankwarte**) petrol-pump attendant.

Tanne *die* (PL *die* **Tannen**) fir.

Tannenbaum *der* (PL *die* **Tannenbäume**) 1 fir tree; 2 Christmas tree.

◆ IRREGULAR VERB: *See the verb table in the centre of the dictionary*

Tante die (PL die Tanten) aunt.

Tanz der (PL die Tänze) dance.

tanzen verb (PERF hat getanzt) to dance.

Tänzer der (PL die Tänzer) dancer.

Tänzerin die (PL die Tänzerinnen) dancer.

Tapete die (PL die Tapeten) wallpaper.

tapezieren verb (PERF hat tapeziert) to (wall)paper.

tapfer adjective brave.

Tarif der (PL die Tarife) 1 tariff; 2 rate.

Tasche die (PL die Taschen) 1 bag; 2 pocket; **er hat es aus eigener Tasche bezahlt** he paid for it out of his own pocket; **Max hat mir fünf Mark aus der Tasche gezogen** (informal) Max wangled five marks out of me.

Taschenbuch das (PL die Taschenbücher) paperback.

Taschendieb der (PL die Taschendiebe) pickpocket.

Taschengeld das pocket money.

Taschenlampe die (PL die Taschenlampen) torch.

Taschenmesser das (PL die Taschenmesser) penknife.

Taschenrechner der (PL die Taschenrechner) pocket calculator.

Taschentuch das (PL die Taschentücher) handkerchief.

Tasse die (PL die Tassen) cup.

Tastatur die (PL die Tastaturen) keyboard.

Taste die (PL die Tasten) 1 key; 2 button (on a phone or a machine).

tasten verb (PERF hat getastet) 1 to feel; 2 **sich tasten** to feel your way.

tat SEE tun.

Tat die (PL die Taten) 1 action; 2 **eine gute Tat** a good deed; 3 crime; 4 **in der Tat** indeed.

Täter der (PL die Täter) 1 culprit; 2 offender.

Täterin die (PL die Täterinnen) 1 culprit; 2 offender.

Tätigkeit die (PL die Tätigkeiten) 1 activity; 2 job.

Tätowierung die (PL die Tätowierungen) tattoo.

Tatsache die (PL die Tatsachen) fact.

tatsächlich adjective actual. adverb 1 actually; 2 really.

Tau[1] der dew.

Tau[2] das (PL die Taue) rope.

taub adjective deaf.

Taube die (PL die Tauben) 1 pigeon; 2 dove.

tauchen verb (PERF hat getaucht) 1 to dip; 2 (PERF hat/ist getaucht) ('ist getaucht' is used when movement is described) to dive.

Taucher der (PL die Taucher) diver.

Taucherin die (PL die Taucherinnen) diver.

tauen verb (PERF **ist getaut**) **1** to melt; **2 es taut** it's thawing.

Taufe die (PL die **Taufen**) christening.

taufen verb (PERF **hat getauft**) **1** to christen; **2** to baptize.

taugen verb (PERF **hat getaugt**) **nichts taugen** to be no good.

tauschen verb (PERF **hat getauscht**) to exchange, to swap.

tausend number a thousand.

Taxi das (PL die **Taxis**) taxi.

Taxifahrer der (PL die **Taxifahrer**) taxi driver.

Taxifahrerin die (PL die **Taxifahrerinnen**) taxi driver.

Taxistand der (PL die **Taxistände**) taxi rank.

Technik die (PL die **Techniken**) **1** technology; **2** technique.

Techniker der (PL die **Techniker**) technician.

Technikerin die (PL die **Technikerinnen**) technician.

technisch adjective **1** technical; **2** technological.

Technologie die technology.

technologisch adjective technological.

Teddybär der (PL die **Teddybären**) teddy bear.

Tee der (PL die **Tee(s)**) tea; **Tee mit Zitrone** lemon tea.

Teebeutel der (PL die **Teebeutel**) tea bag.

Teekanne die (PL die **Teekannen**) teapot.

Teelöffel der (PL die **Teelöffel**) teaspoon.

Teenager der (PL die **Teenager**) teenager.

Teich der (PL die **Teiche**) pond.

Teig der (PL die **Teige**) **1** dough; **2** pastry; **3** mixture.

Teigwaren plural noun pasta.

Teil[1] der (PL die **Teile**) **1** part; **der zweite Teil** the second part; **zum größten Teil** for the most part; **zum 2 um Teil** partly; **3** share; **mein Teil am Gewinn** my share of the profit.

Teil[2] das (PL die **Teile**) **1** spare part; **2** part (of a car, machine); **3** unit (of furniture).

teilen verb (PERF **hat geteilt**) **1** to divide; **2 sich etwas mit jemandem teilen** to share something with somebody.

teilnehmen ◇ verb (PRES **nimmt teil**, IMPERF **nahm teil**, PERF **hat teilgenommen**) **an etwas teilnehmen** to take part in something.

Teilnehmer der (PL die **Teilnehmer**) **1** participant; **2** competitor.

Teilnehmerin die (PL die **Teilnehmerinnen**) **1** participant; **2** competitor.

teils adverb partly.

Teilung die (PL die **Teilungen**) division.

◇ IRREGULAR VERB: See the verb table in the centre of the dictionary

Teilzeitarbeit die part-time work.

Telefax das (PL die Telefax(e)) fax.

Telefon das (PL die Telefone) telephone.

Telefonanruf der (PL die Telefonanrufe) phone call.

Telefonbuch das (PL die Telefonbücher) telephone directory, phone book.

Telefongespräch das (PL die Telefongespräche) telephone call.

Telefonhörer der (PL die Telefonhörer) receiver.

telefonieren verb (PERF hat telefoniert) to telephone, to make a phone call.

telefonisch adjective telephone. adverb by telephone; **er ist telefonisch nicht erreichbar** he can't be contacted by phone.

Telefonkarte die (PL die Telefonkarten) phone card.

Telefonnummer die (PL die Telefonnummern) telephone number.

Telefonzelle die (PL die Telefonzellen) phone box, call box.

Teller der (PL die Teller) plate.

Temperatur die (PL die Temperaturen) temperature.

Tempo das (PL die Tempos) speed; **Tempo Tempo!** (informal) hurry up!

Tendenz die (PL die Tendenzen) 1 trend; 2 tendency.

tendieren verb (PERF hat tendiert) **zu etwas tendieren** to tend towards something.

Tennis das tennis.

Tennisplatz der (PL die Tennisplätze) tennis court.

Tennisschläger der (PL die Tennisschläger) tennis racket.

Tennisspieler der (PL die Tennisspieler) tennis player.

Tennisspielerin die (PL die Tennisspielerinnen) tennis player.

Teppich der (PL die Teppiche) 1 carpet; 2 rug.

Termin der (PL die Termine) 1 date; **einen Termin vereinbaren** to fix a date; 2 appointment; 3 **der letzte Termin** the deadline.

Terminal[1] der (PL die Terminals) terminal.

Terminal[2] das (PL die Terminals) (computer) terminal.

Terrasse die (PL die Terrassen) terrace.

Terror der terror.

Terrorismus der terrorism.

Terrorist der (PL die Terroristen) terrorist.

Terroristin die (PL die Terroristinnen) terrorist.

Tesafilm™ der Sellotape™.

Test der (PL die Tests) test.

testen verb (PERF hat getestet) to test.

△ NEW SPELLING: See page xii

teuer *adjective* expensive; **wie teuer?** how much?

Teufel *der* (PL *die* Teufel) devil.

Text *der* (PL *die* Texte) **1** text; **2** lyrics; **3** caption.

Textverarbeitung *die* word processing.

Theater *das* (PL *die* Theater) **1** theatre; **2** (*informal*) fuss.

Theaterstück *das* (PL *die* Theaterstücke) play.

Theke *die* (PL *die* Theken) **1** bar; **2** counter.

Thema *das* (PL *die* Themen) subject, topic.

Themse *die* Thames.

theoretisch *adjective* theoretical. *adverb* in theory.

Theorie *die* (PL *die* Theorien) theory.

Therapie *die* (PL *die* Therapien) therapy.

Thermometer *das* (PL *die* Thermometer) thermometer.

Thron *der* (PL *die* Throne) throne.

Thunfisch *der* (PL *die* Thunfische) tuna.

Thymian *der* thyme.

tief *adjective* **1** deep; **2** low.

Tiefe *die* (PL *die* Tiefen) depth.

Tiefgarage *die* (PL *die* Tiefgaragen) underground car park.

Tiefkühlfach *das* (PL *die* Tiefkühlfächer) freezer compartment.

Tiefkühlkost *die* frozen food.

Tiefkühltruhe *die* (PL *die* Tiefkühltruhen) freezer.

Tiefsttemperatur *die* (PL *die* Tiefsttemperaturen) minimum temperature.

Tier *das* (PL *die* Tiere) animal.

Tierarzt *der* (PL *die* Tierärzte) vet.

Tierärztin *die* (PL *die* Tierärztinnen) vet.

Tiergarten *der* (PL *die* Tiergärten) zoo.

Tierkreis *der* zodiac.

Tiger *der* (PL *die* Tiger) tiger.

Tinte *die* (PL *die* Tinten) ink.

Tintenfisch *der* (PL *die* Tintenfische) **1** octopus; **2** squid.

Tipp △ *der* (PL *die* Tipps) tip.

tippen *verb* (PERF hat getippt) **1** to type; **2** to tap; **3** **auf etwas tippen** to bet on something; **ich tippe auf ihn** I'm tipping him to win; **im Lotto tippen** to do the lottery.

Tisch *der* (PL *die* Tische) **1** table; **2** **nach Tisch** after the meal.

Tischdecke *die* (PL *die* Tischdecken) tablecloth.

Tischler *der* (PL *die* Tischler) joiner, carpenter.

Tischtennis *das* table tennis.

Tischtuch *das* (PL *die* Tischtücher) tablecloth.

Titel *der* (PL *die* Titel) title.

Toast *der* (PL *die* Toasts) toast.

✧ IRREGULAR VERB: *See the verb table in the centre of the dictionary*

toben *verb* (PERF hat getobt) 1 to rage; 2 to go mad; 3 to charge about.

Tochter *die* (PL die Töchter) daughter.

Tod *der* (PL die Tode) death.

Todesstrafe *die* death penalty.

tödlich *adjective* 1 fatal; 2 deadly.

todmüde *adjective* dead tired.

todschick *adjective* trendy.

Toilette *die* (PL die Toiletten) toilet; **auf die Toilette gehen** to go to the toilet.

Toilettenpapier *das* toilet paper.

toll *adjective* (*informal*) brilliant.

Tollwut *die* rabies.

Tomate *die* (PL die Tomaten) tomato.

Tomatenmark *das* tomato purée.

Ton¹ *der* (PL die Töne) 1 sound; **er hat keinen Ton gesagt** he didn't make a sound; 2 **große Töne spucken** (*informal*) to talk big; 3 tone; **einen frechen Ton anschlagen** to adopt a cheeky tone; 4 note; 5 shade (*of colour*); 6 stress (*in pronunciation*).

Ton² *der* clay.

Tonband *das* (PL die Tonbänder) tape.

Tonbandgerät *das* (PL die Tonbandgeräte) tape recorder.

Tonne *die* (PL die Tonnen) 1 barrel; 2 bin (*for rubbish*); 3 tonne, ton.

Topf *der* (PL die Töpfe) 1 pot; 2 pan.

Töpferei *die* (PL die Töpfereien) pottery.

Tor *das* (PL die Tore) 1 gate; 2 goal.

Torte *die* (PL die Torten) 1 gateau; 2 cake.

Torwart *der* (PL die Torwarte) goalkeeper.

tot *adjective* dead.

total *adjective* complete.
adverb completely; **du bist total verrückt** you're totally mad.

Tote *der/die* (PL die Toten) 1 dead man/woman; **die Toten** the dead; 2 fatality.

töten *verb* (PERF hat getötet) to kill.

totlachen *verb* (*informal*) (PERF hat sich totgelacht) **sich totlachen** to laugh your head off.

Tour *die* (PL die Touren) 1 tour; 2 trip; 3 **auf diese Tour** (*informal*) in this way.

Tourismus *der* tourism.

Tourist *der* (PL die Touristen) tourist.

Touristin *die* (PL die Touristinnen) tourist.

Tournee *die* (PL die Tournees) tour.

traben *verb* (PERF ist getrabt) to trot.

Tradition *die* (PL die Traditionen) tradition.

traditionell *adjective* traditional.

traf SEE **treffen**.

tragbar *adjective* 1 portable; 2 wearable.

tragen ◇ *verb* (PRES trägt, IMPERF trug, PERF hat getragen) 1 to carry; 2 to wear; **sie trug ein weißes Kleid** she wore a white dress; **man trägt**

△ NEW SPELLING: *See page xii*

wieder kurz short skirts are in fashion again; **3** to bear; **die Verantwortung für etwas tragen** to be responsible for something; **4** to support; **die Organisation trägt sich selbst** the organization is self-supporting.

Träger der (PL die **Träger**) **1** porter; **2** bearer (of a name, title); **3** strap (of a dress); **4** girder.

Tragetasche die (PL die **Tragetaschen**) carrier bag.

tragisch adjective tragic.

Tragödie die (PL die **Tragödien**) tragedy.

Trainer der (PL die **Trainer**) coach, trainer.

trainieren verb (PERF hat trainiert) **1** to coach; **2** to train.

Training das training.

Trainingsanzug der (PL die **Trainingsanzüge**) tracksuit.

Traktor der (PL die **Traktoren**) tractor.

trampen verb (PERF ist getrampt) to hitchhike.

Tramper der (PL die **Tramper**) hitchhiker.

Tramperin die (PL die **Tramperinnen**) hitchhiker.

Träne die (PL die **Tränen**) tear.

trank SEE trinken.

Transport der (PL die **Transporte**) **1** transport; **2** consignment.

transportieren verb (PERF hat transportiert) to transport.

trat SEE treten.

Traube die (PL die **Trauben**) grape.

trauen verb (PERF hat getraut) **1** to trust; **jemandem trauen** to trust somebody; **2 sich trauen** to dare; **ich trau mich nicht** I don't dare; **3** to marry.

Trauer die **1** grief; **2** mourning.

Traum der (PL die **Träume**) dream.

träumen verb (PERF hat geträumt) to dream.

traumhaft adjective fabulous.

traurig adjective sad.

Traurigkeit die sadness.

Trauung die (PL die **Trauungen**) wedding.

treffen ◇ verb (PRES trifft, IMPERF traf, PERF hat getroffen) **1** to hit; **2** to meet; **3** to make (arrangements, a decision); **4 sich mit jemandem treffen** to meet somebody; **5 sich gut treffen** to be convenient; **6 sich ist getroffen) auf etwas treffen** to meet with (resistance, difficulties).

Treffen das (PL die **Treffen**) meeting.

Treffer der (PL die **Treffer**) **1** hit; **2** winner; **3** goal.

Treffpunkt der (PL die **Treffpunkte**) meeting place.

treiben ◇ verb (IMPERF trieb, PERF hat getrieben) **1** to drive; **2** to do; **viel Sport treiben** to do a lot of sport;

◇ IRREGULAR VERB: See the verb table in the centre of the dictionary

Handel treiben to trade;
3 jemanden zur Eile treiben to
hurry somebody up; **4 Unsinn
treiben** to mess about; **5** (PERF **ist
getrieben**) to drift.

Treibhaus das (PL die **Treibhäuser**)
hothouse.

Treibhauseffekt der greenhouse
effect.

Treibstoff der fuel.

trennen verb (PERF **hat getrennt**)
1 to separate; **2** to divide (words,
parts of a room); **3** to
separate; **wir haben uns getrennt**
we've separated; **Jutta hat sich von
ihm getrennt** Jutta has left him;
4 sich von etwas trennen to part
with something.

Trennung die (PL die **Trennungen**)
1 separation; **2** division.

Treppe die (PL die **Treppen**) stairs;
eine Treppe a flight of stairs.

Treppenhaus das stairwell; **im
Treppenhaus** on the stairs.

treten ◇ verb (PRES **tritt**, IMPERF **trat**,
PERF **ist getreten**) **1** to step; **2** to
tread; **3** to kick; **4 mit jemandem in
Verbindung treten** to get in touch
with somebody.

treu adjective faithful.

Tribüne die (PL die **Tribünen**)
1 stand (in a stadium); **2** platform.

Trick der (PL die **Tricks**) trick.

Trickfilm der (PL die **Trickfilme**)
cartoon.

trieb SEE **treiben**.

trifft SEE **treffen**.

Trimm-dich-Pfad der (PL die
Trimm-dich-Pfade) keep-fit trail.

trimmen verb (PERF **hat getrimmt**)
1 to trim; **2 sich trimmen** to keep
fit.

trinken ◇ verb (IMPERF **trank**, PERF
hat getrunken) to drink.

Trinkgeld das (PL die **Trinkgelder**)
tip.

Trinkwasser das drinking water.

tritt SEE **treten**.

Tritt der (PL die **Tritte**) **1** step; **2** kick.

Triumph der (PL die **Triumphe**)
triumph.

trocken adjective dry.

trocknen verb (PERF **hat
getrocknet**) to dry.

Trockner der (PL die **Trockner**) drier.

Trödel der (informal) junk.

Trödelmarkt der (PL die
Trödelmärkte) flea market.

Trommel die (PL die **Trommeln**)
drum.

trommeln verb (PERF **hat
getrommelt**) to drum.

Trompete die (PL die **Trompeten**)
trumpet.

Tropen (plural noun) die **Tropen**
the tropics.

tropfen verb (PERF **hat getropft**) to
drip.

Tropfen der (PL die **Tropfen**) drop.

△ NEW SPELLING: See page xii

Trophäe die (PL die Trophäen) trophy.

tropisch adjective tropical.

trösten verb (PERF hat getröstet) to console, to comfort.

trotz preposition ←(+GEN) despite, in spite of.

trotzdem adverb nevertheless.

trüb adjective 1 dull, dismal; 2 cloudy (liquid).

trübsinnig adjective gloomy.

trug SEE **tragen**.

Truhe die (PL die Truhen) chest.

Trümmer plural noun ruins.

Trumpf der (PL die Trümpfe) 1 trump (card); 2 trumps.

Trunkenheit die drunkenness; **Trunkenheit am Steuer** drink-driving.

Truppen plural noun troops.

Truthahn der (PL die Truthähne) turkey.

Tscheche der (PL die Tschechen) Czech.

Tschechin die (PL die Tschechinnen) Czech.

tschechisch adjective Czech.

Tschechische Republik die Czech Republic.

tschüss △ exclamation bye!

T-Shirt das (PL die T-Shirts) T-shirt.

Tube die (PL die Tuben) tube.

Tuberkulose die tuberculosis.

Tuch das (PL die Tücher) 1 cloth; 2 scarf.

tüchtig adjective 1 competent; 2 big.

Tulpe die (PL die Tulpen) tulip.

Tumor der (PL die Tumoren) tumour.

tun ◇ verb (PRES tut, IMPERF tat, PERF hat getan) 1 to do; **das tut man nicht** it isn't done; **das tut's** (informal) that'll do; 2 to put; **die Butter in den Kühlschrank tun** to put the butter in the fridge; 3 to pretend; **er tut nur so** he's only pretending; 4 to act; **freundlich tun** to act friendly; 5 **jemandem etwas tun** to hurt somebody; 6 **mit jemandem etwas zu tun haben** to have dealings with somebody; **das hat nichts damit zu tun** it's got nothing to do with it; 7 **das tut nichts** it doesn't matter; **es hat sich viel getan** lots has happened.

Tunfisch △ der (PL die Tunfische) tuna.

Tunesien das Tunisia.

Tunesier der (PL die Tunesier) Tunisian.

Tunesierin die (PL die Tunesierinnen) Tunisian.

tunesisch adjective Tunisian.

Tunnel der (PL die Tunnel) tunnel.

tupfen verb (PERF hat getupft) to dab.

Tupfen der (PL die Tupfen) dot.

Tür die (PL die Türen) door.

Türke der (PL die Türken) Turk.

◇ IRREGULAR VERB: See the verb table in the centre of the dictionary

Türkei *die* Turkey.

Türkin *die* (PL *die* **Türkinnen**) Turk.

türkis *adjective* turquoise.

türkisch *adjective* Turkish.

Turm *der* (PL *die* **Türme**) 1 tower;
2 steeple; 3 rook, castle (*in chess*).

turnen *verb* (PERF **hat geturnt**) to do gymnastics.

Turnen *das* 1 gymnastics;
2 physical education, PE.

Turnhalle *die* (PL *die* **Turnhallen**)
gymnasium, gym.

Turnier *das* (PL *die* **Turniere**)
tournament.

Turnschuh *der* (PL *die* **Turnschuhe**)
1 trainer; 2 gym shoe.

Turnverein *der* (PL *die* **Turnvereine**)
gymnastics club.

tuscheln *verb* (PERF **hat getuschelt**)
to whisper.

tut SEE **tun**.

Tüte *die* (PL *die* **Tüten**) bag.

Typ *der* (PL *die* **Typen**) 1 type;
2 (*informal*) bloke.

typisch *adjective* typical.

U u

U-Bahn *die* (PL *die* **U-Bahnen**)
underground.

übel *adjective* 1 bad; 2 **mir ist übel**
I feel sick; 3 **etwas übel nehmen** △
to take offence at something;
jemandem etwas übel nehmen △ to
hold something against somebody.

Übelkeit *die* nausea.

übelnehmen SEE **übel**.

üben *verb* (PERF **hat geübt**) to
practise.

über *preposition* ←(+DAT, *or* +ACC *with
movement towards a place*) 1 over;
über Weihnachten over Christmas;
2 above; **er wohnt über uns** he lives
above us; **fünf Grad über Null** five
degrees above zero; 3 about; **über
etwas schreiben** to write about
something; 4 for; **ein Scheck über
hundert Mark** a cheque for one
hundred marks; 5 across (*a field, the
street*); 6 **über Frankfurt fahren** to
go via Frankfurt; 7 **über die Straße
gehen** to cross the road.
adverb 1 **über und über** over and
over; 2 **jemandem über sein** to be
better than somebody; 3 **über sein**
(*informal*) to be left over;
4 **jemandem ist etwas über**
(*informal*) somebody is fed up with
something; 5 **etwas über haben** △
(*informal*) to be fed up with
something; **Nudeln habe ich über**
I'm getting fed up with pasta.

△ NEW SPELLING: *See page xii*

überall *adverb* everywhere.

Überblick *der* (PL die Überblicke)
1 einen guten Überblick über
etwas haben to have a good view of
something; 2 overall view; den
Überblick verlieren to lose track of
things; 3 summary.

überblicken *verb* (PERF hat
überblickt) 1 to overlook; 2 to
assess.

Überdruss △ *der* bis zum
Überdruss ad nauseam.

übereinander *adverb* 1 one on top
of the other; 2 übereinander
sprechen to talk about each other.

übereinstimmen *verb* (PERF hat
übereingestimmt) to agree.

überempfindlich *adjective*
hypersensitive.

überfahren ⬦ *verb* (PRES
überfährt, IMPERF überfuhr, PERF hat
überfahren) to run over; das Kind ist
von einem Auto überfahren
worden the child was run over by a
car.

Überfahrt *die* (PL die Überfahrten)
crossing.

Überfall *der* (PL die Überfälle)
1 attack; 2 raid.

überfallen ⬦ *verb* (PRES überfällt,
IMPERF überfiel, PERF hat überfallen)
1 to attack, to mug; 2 to raid;
3 jemanden mit Fragen überfallen
to bombard somebody with
questions.

überfällig *adjective* overdue.

überflüssig *adjective* superfluous.

Überführung *die* (PL die
Überführungen) 1 transfer;
2 flyover; 3 footbridge.

überfüllt *adjective* 1 crowded;
2 oversubscribed.

Übergang *der* (PL die Übergänge)
1 crossing; 2 transition.

übergeben ⬦ *verb* (PRES übergibt,
IMPERF übergab, PERF hat
übergeben) 1 to hand over; 2 sich
übergeben to be sick.

überhaben SEE über.

überhaupt *adverb* 1 in general;
2 anyway; was will er überhaupt?
what does he want anyway?;
3 überhaupt nicht not at all;
überhaupt nichts nothing at all;
überhaupt keine Zeit haben to
have no time at all.

überholen *verb* (PERF hat überholt)
1 to overtake; 2 to overhaul.

überholt *adjective* out-of-date.

überlassen ⬦ *verb* (PRES
überlässt △, IMPERF überließ, PERF
hat überlassen) 1 jemandem etwas
überlassen to let somebody have
something; 2 etwas jemandem
überlassen to leave something up
to somebody (*a decision, for
example*); das bleibt dir
überlassen it's up to you.

überlaufen ⬦ *verb* (PRES läuft über,
IMPERF lief über, PERF ist
übergelaufen) to overflow.

überleben *verb* (PERF hat überlebt)
to survive.

überlegen[1] *verb* (PERF hat

⬦ IRREGULAR VERB: See the verb table in the centre of the dictionary

überlegt 1 to think; **sich etwas überlegen** to think something over; **ohne zu überlegen** without thinking; 2 **ich habe es mir anders überlegt** I've changed my mind.

überlegen[2] *adjective* 1 superior; **jemandem überlegen sein** to be superior to somebody; 2 convincing (*victory*).

überm = über dem.

übermäßig *adjective* excessive.

übermorgen *adverb* the day after tomorrow.

übernächster, übernächste, übernächstes *adjective* next but one; **übernächstes Jahr** the year after next.

übernachten *verb* (PERF hat übernachtet) to stay the night; **bei jemandem übernachten** to stay the night at somebody's house.

übernehmen ◇ *verb* (PRES übernimmt, IMPERF übernahm, PERF hat übernommen) 1 to take over; 2 to take on; 3 **sich übernehmen** to take on too much.

überqueren *verb* (PERF hat überquert) to cross.

überraschen *verb* (PERF hat überrascht) to surprise.

Überraschung *die* (PL die Überraschungen) surprise.

überreden *verb* (PERF hat überredet) to persuade.

übers = über das.

Überschrift *die* (PL die Überschriften) heading.

überschüssig *adjective* surplus.

überschütten *verb* (PERF hat überschüttet) **jemanden mit etwas überschütten** to shower somebody with something.

Überschwemmung *die* (PL die Überschwemmungen) flood.

übersehen[1] ◇ *verb* (PRES übersieht, IMPERF übersah, PERF hat übersehen) 1 to overlook; **einen Fehler übersehen** to overlook a mistake; 2 to assess (*consequences, damages*).

übersehen[2] ◇ *verb* (PRES sieht sich über, IMPERF sah sich über, PERF hat sich übergesehen) **sich etwas übersehen** to get fed up of seeing something.

übersetzen *verb* (PERF hat übersetzt) to translate.

Übersetzer *der* (PL die Übersetzer) translator.

Übersetzerin *die* (PL die Übersetzerinnen) translator.

Übersetzung *die* (PL die Übersetzungen) translation.

Übersicht *die* 1 overall view; 2 summary.

überspringen ◇ *verb* (IMPERF übersprang, PERF hat übersprungen) 1 to jump (over); 2 to skip (*a chapter*).

überstehen ◇ *verb* (IMPERF überstand, PERF hat überstanden) 1 to get over; 2 to survive.

△ NEW SPELLING: *See page xii*

Überstunden *plural noun*
overtime; **Überstunden machen** to work overtime.

übertragen ◇ *verb* (PRES **überträgt**, IMPERF **übertrug**, PERF **hat übertragen**) 1 to transfer; 2 to transmit; 3 to broadcast; 4 **etwas ins Reine übertragen** to make a fair copy of something; 5 **sich auf jemanden übertragen** to communicate it to somebody (*of enthusiasm or nervousness*).

Übertragung *die* (PL *die* **Übertragungen**) 1 broadcast; 2 transmission.

übertreiben ◇ *verb* (IMPERF **übertrieb**, PERF **hat übertrieben**) 1 to exaggerate; 2 to overdo.

Übertreibung *die* (PL *die* **Übertreibungen**) exaggeration.

überwältigend *adjective* overwhelming.

überweisen ◇ *verb* (IMPERF **überwies**, PERF **hat überwiesen**) 1 to transfer; 2 to refer (*a patient*).

überzeugen *verb* (PERF **hat überzeugt**) 1 to convince; 2 **sich selbst überzeugen** to satisfy yourself.

überzeugend *adjective* convincing.

Überzeugung *die* (PL *die* **Überzeugungen**) conviction.

überziehen[1] ◇ *verb* (IMPERF **zog über**, PERF **hat übergezogen**) to put on (*a cardigan, jacket*).

überziehen[2] ◇ *verb* (IMPERF

überzog, PERF **hat überzogen**) 1 to overdraw; 2 to cover (*with icing, for example*).

üblich *adjective* usual.

übrig *adjective* 1 remaining; 2 **übrig sein** to be left over; 3 **etwas übrig lassen** △ to leave something (over); 4 **uns blieb nichts anderes übrig** we had no other choice; 5 **alles Übrige** the rest; **die Übrigen** the others; 6 **im Übrigen** besides.

übrigens *adverb* by the way.

übriglassen SEE **übrig**.

Übung *die* (PL *die* **Übungen**) 1 exercise; 2 practice; **aus der Übung sein** to be out of practice.

Ufer *das* (PL *die* **Ufer**) 1 bank (*of a river*); 2 shore.

Uhr *die* (PL *die* **Uhren**) 1 clock; 2 watch; 3 (*in time phrases*) **es ist ein Uhr** it's one o'clock; **wie viel Uhr ist es?** what's the time?; **um sechzehn Uhr** at four o'clock (in the afternoon).

Uhrzeiger *der* (PL *die* **Uhrzeiger**) hand (*of a clock or watch*).

Uhrzeigersinn *der* im **Uhrzeigersinn** clockwise; **entgegen dem Uhrzeigersinn** anti-clockwise.

Uhrzeit *die* time; **jemanden nach der Uhrzeit fragen** to ask somebody the time.

ulkig *adjective* funny.

um *preposition* ←(+ACC) 1 round, around; **um das Haus herum** around the house; 2 at; **um fünf Uhr**

◇ IRREGULAR VERB: *See the verb table in the centre of the dictionary*

at five o'clock; **3** around (about);
4 for; **um etwas bitten** to ask for
something; **um seinetwillen** for his
sake; **5 sich um jemanden sorgen**
to worry about somebody; **6** by
(*indicating difference*); **um vieles
besser** better by far; **um so besser**
so much the better.
adverb **1** about, around; **um die
dreihundert Mark herum** about
three hundred marks; **um
Weihnachten** around Christmas;
2 um sein (*informal*) to be over.
conjunction **um zu** (in order) to; **er
ist noch zu klein, um in die Schule
zu gehen** he's too young to go to
school.

umarmen *verb* (PERF **hat umarmt**)
to hug.

Umbau *der* (PL *die* **Umbauten**)
1 renovation; **2** conversion.

umbinden ◇ *verb* (IMPERF **band um**,
PERF **hat umgebunden**) to put on.

umblättern *verb* (PERF **hat
umgeblättert**) to turn over.

umbringen ◇ *verb* (IMPERF **brachte
um**, PERF **hat umgebracht**) to kill.

umdrehen *verb* (PERF **hat
umgedreht**) **1** to turn (round);
2 sich umdrehen to turn round, to
turn over.

umfallen ◇ *verb* (PRES **fällt um**,
IMPERF **fiel um**, PERF **ist umgefallen**)
to fall down.

Umfrage *die* (PL *die* **Umfragen**)
survey.

umgänglich *adjective* sociable.

Umgangsformen *plural noun*
manners.

Umgangssprache *die* slang,
colloquial language.

umgeben ◇ *verb* (PRES **umgibt**,
IMPERF **umgab**, PERF **hat umgeben**)
to surround.

Umgebung *die* (PL *die*
Umgebungen) **1** surroundings;
2 neighbourhood.

umgehen[1] ◇ *verb* (IMPERF **ging um**,
PERF **ist umgegangen**) **1** to go round
(*of a rumour, an illness*); **2 mit
jemandem streng umgehen** to
treat somebody strictly; **3 er kann
mit Geld nicht umgehen** he can't
handle money; **mit seinen Sachen
sorgfältig umgehen** to handle one's
things carefully.

umgehen[2] ◇ *verb* (IMPERF **umging**,
PERF **hat umgangen**) to avoid.

umgekehrt *adjective* **1** opposite;
2 reverse (*order*); **3 es war
umgekehrt** it was the other way
round.
adverb **1 und umgekehrt** and vice
versa; **2** the other way round;
**warum machst du es nicht
umgekehrt?** why don't you do it the
other way round?

umkehren *verb* (PERF **ist
umgekehrt**) **1** to turn back; **nach
zehn Minuten sind wir wieder
umgekehrt** ten minutes later we
turned back again; **2** to turn round
(*a picture, book*); **3** to turn inside
out (*a bag, for example*); **4 sie hat
das ganze Zimmer umgekehrt**

△ NEW SPELLING: *See page xii*

(*informal*) she turned the whole room upside down.

Umkleidekabine *die* (PL *die* **Umkleidekabinen**) changing cubicle.

Umkleideraum *der* (PL *die* **Umkleideräume**) changing room.

umkommen ✧ *verb* (IMPERF **kam um**, PERF **ist umgekommen**) to be killed.

Umlaut *der* (PL *die* **Umlaute**) umlaut.

umlegen *verb* (PERF **hat umgelegt**) 1 to put on (*a scarf*); 2 to transfer (*a patient, call*); 3 jemanden umlegen (*informal*) to bump somebody off.

Umleitung *die* (PL *die* **Umleitungen**) diversion.

umrechnen *verb* (PERF **hat umgerechnet**) to convert.

Umrechnung *die* conversion.

Umrechnungskurs *der* exchange rate.

Umriss △ *der* (PL *die* **Umrisse**) outline.

umrühren *verb* (PERF **hat umgerührt**) to stir.

ums = um das.

umschalten *verb* (PERF **hat umgeschaltet**) 1 to turn over; vom ersten aufs zweite Programm umschalten to change from channel one to channel two; 2 auf Rot umschalten to change to red.

Umschlag *der* (PL *die* **Umschläge**) 1 envelope; 2 cover.

umsehen ✧ *verb* (PRES **sieht sich um**, IMPERF **sah sich um**, PERF **hat sich umgesehen**) sich umsehen to look round.

umso △ *adverb* umso besser all the better; je mehr, umso besser the more the better.

umsonst *adverb* 1 in vain; 2 free, for nothing.

Umstand *der* (PL *die* **Umstände**) 1 circumstance; 2 unter Umständen possibly; 3 jemandem Umstände machen to put somebody to trouble; das macht gar keine Umstände it's no trouble at all; 4 in anderen Umständen sein to be pregnant.

umständlich *adjective* 1 laborious; 2 complicated.

umsteigen ✧ *verb* (IMPERF **stieg um**, PERF **ist umgestiegen**) to change.

umstellen[1] *verb* (PERF **hat umgestellt**) 1 to rearrange; 2 to reset; 3 to change over; 4 sich umstellen to adjust.

umstellen[2] *verb* (PERF **hat umstellt**) to surround.

Umtausch *der* exchange.

umtauschen *verb* (PERF **hat umgetauscht**) to change, to exchange.

Umweg *der* (PL *die* **Umwege**) detour.

Umwelt *die* environment.

umweltfreundlich *adjective* environmentally friendly.

Umweltschützer *der* (PL *die* **Umweltschützer**) environmentalist.

✧ IRREGULAR VERB: *See the verb table in the centre of the dictionary*

Umweltverschmutzung *die* pollution.

umwerfen ✧ *verb* (PRES **wirft um**, IMPERF **warf um**, PERF **hat umgeworfen**) 1 to knock over; 2 to upset (*a plan*); **das hat mich umgeworfen** it's thrown me.

umwerfend *adjective* fantastic.

umziehen ✧ *verb* (IMPERF **zog um**, PERF **ist umgezogen**) 1 to move; **sie ziehen nächste Woche um** they're moving next week; 2 (PERF **hat umgezogen**) to change; 3 (PERF **hat sich umgezogen**) **sich umziehen** to get changed.

Umzug *der* (PL **die Umzüge**) move.

unabhängig *adjective* independent.

Unabhängigkeit *die* independence.

unangenehm *adjective* 1 unpleasant; 2 embarrassing (*question, situation*).

unartig *adjective* naughty.

unbedeutend *adjective* insignificant. *adverb* slightly.

unbedingt *adjective* absolute. *adverb* really; **ich muss ihn unbedingt sprechen** I really must talk to him; **nicht unbedingt** not necessarily.

unbefriedigend *adjective* unsatisfactory.

unbefriedigt *adjective* unsatisfied.

unbehaglich *adjective* 1 uncomfortable; 2 uneasy.

unbekannt *adjective* unknown.

unbeliebt *adjective* unpopular.

unbequem *adjective* uncomfortable.

unbestimmt *adjective* 1 indefinite; **auf unbestimmte Zeit** for an indefinite period; 2 uncertain. *adverb* vaguely; **etwas unbestimmt lassen** to leave something open.

unbewusst △ *adjective* unconscious.

und *conjunction* and; **und so weiter** and so on; **na und?** so what?

undankbar *adjective* ungrateful.

undeutlich *adjective* unclear.

undicht *adjective* leaking, leaky; **eine undichte Stelle** a leak.

uneben *adjective* uneven.

unempfindlich *adjective* 1 hard-wearing, easy-care; 2 immune; **gegen Kälte unempfindlich sein** not to feel the cold.

unentbehrlich *adjective* indispensable.

unentschieden *adjective* undecided; **unentschieden spielen** to draw.

unerträglich *adjective* unbearable.

unerwartet *adjective* unexpected.

unfähig *adjective* 1 incompetent; 2 **unfähig sein, etwas zu tun** to be incapable of doing something.

△ NEW SPELLING: *See page xii*

unfair *adjective* unfair.

Unfall *der* (PL *die* **Unfälle**) accident.

unfreundlich *adjective* unfriendly.

Unfug *der* 1 nonsense; 2 mischief; **Unfug machen** to get up to mischief.

Ungar *der* (PL *die* **Ungarn**) Hungarian.

Ungarin *die* (PL *die* **Ungarinnen**) Hungarian.

ungarisch *adjective* Hungarian.

Ungarn *das* Hungary.

Ungeduld *die* impatience.

ungeduldig *adjective* impatient.

ungeeignet *adjective* unsuitable.

ungefähr *adjective* approximate. *adverb* approximately, about.

ungefährlich *adjective* safe, harmless.

ungeheuer *adjective* enormous.

Ungeheuer *das* (PL *die* **Ungeheuer**) monster.

ungehorsam *adjective* disobedient.

ungelegen *adjective* inconvenient.

ungemütlich *adjective* uncomfortable.

ungenau *adjective* 1 inaccurate; 2 vague.

ungenießbar *adjective* 1 inedible; 2 undrinkable; 3 **Bernd ist heute aber ungenießbar** (*informal*) Bernd is quite unbearable today.

ungenügend *adjective* 1 insufficient; 2 unsatisfactory (*mark at school*).

ungerade *adjective* **eine ungerade Zahl** an odd number.

ungerecht *adjective* unjust.

ungern *adverb* reluctantly.

ungeschickt *adjective* clumsy.

ungesund *adjective* unhealthy.

ungewöhnlich *adjective* unusual.

Ungeziefer *das* vermin.

ungezwungen *adjective* 1 informal; 2 natural.

unglaublich *adjective* incredible.

Unglück *das* (PL *die* **Unglücke**) 1 accident; 2 misfortune; 3 bad luck; **das bringt Unglück** that's unlucky.

unglücklich *adjective* 1 unhappy; 2 unfortunate.

unglücklicherweise *adverb* unfortunately.

unheilbar *adjective* incurable.

unheimlich *adjective* eerie. *adverb* 1 eerily; 2 (*informal*) incredibly; **unheimlich viel** an incredible amount.

unhöflich *adjective* impolite.

Uniform *die* (PL *die* **Uniformen**) uniform.

uninteressant *adjective* uninteresting.

Universität *die* (PL *die* **Universitäten**) university.

Unkenntnis *die* ignorance.

◇ IRREGULAR VERB: *See the verb table in the centre of the dictionary*

unklar *adjective* unclear.

Unkosten *plural noun* expenses.

Unkraut *das* weed.

unmodern *adjective* old-fashioned.

unleserlich *adjective* illegible.

unlogisch *adjective* illogical.

unmittelbar *adjective* immediate, direct.

unmöglich *adjective* impossible.

Unmöglichkeit *die* impossibility.

unnötig *adjective* unnecessary.

unordentlich *adjective* untidy.

Unordnung *die* 1 disorder; 2 mess.

unpraktisch *adjective* impractical.

unpünktlich *adjective* unpunctual; **unpünktlich sein** to be late.

unrecht *adjective* wrong; **jemandem unrecht tun** to do somebody an injustice.

Unrecht *das* 1 wrong; **zu Unrecht** wrongly; **Unrecht haben** △ to be wrong; **Unrecht geben** △ to disagree with somebody.

unregelmäßig *adjective* irregular.

unreif *adjective* 1 unripe; 2 immature.

Unruhe *die* (PL **die Unruhen**) 1 restlessness; 2 agitation; 3 **Unruhen** unrest.

Unruhestifter *der* (PL **die Unruhestifter**) troublemaker.

unruhig *adjective* restless.

uns *pronoun* 1 us; **gib es uns** give it

to us; **sie kommen mit uns** they're coming with us; 2 ourselves; **wir waschen uns die Hände** we are washing our hands; 3 each other; **wir kennen uns** we know each other.

unschuldig *adjective* innocent.

unser our.

unserer, unsere, unser(e)s *pronoun* ours.

unsertwegen *adverb* 1 for our sake; 2 because of us; 3 as far as we're concerned.

unsicher *adjective* 1 uncertain; 2 insecure. *adverb* unsteadily.

unsichtbar *adjective* invisible.

Unsinn *der* nonsense.

unsrer SEE **unserer**.

unsympathisch *adjective* unpleasant; **Tobias ist mir unsympathisch** I don't like Tobias.

unten *adverb* 1 at the bottom; 2 underneath; 3 downstairs; **hier unten** down here; **nach unten** down.

unter *preposition* ←(+DAT *or* +ACC *with movement towards a place*) 1 under, below; 2 among; **unter anderem** among other things; 3 **unter sich** by themselves; **unter uns gesagt** between ourselves; 4 **unter der Woche** during the week.

Unterbewusstsein △ *das* subconscious.

unterbrechen ◇ *verb* (PRES **unterbricht**, IMPERF **unterbrach**, PERF **hat unterbrochen**) to interrupt.

△ NEW SPELLING: See page xii

Unterbrechung die (PL die Unterbrechungen) interruption.

unterbringen ◇ verb (IMPERF brachte unter, PERF hat untergebracht) 1 to put; 2 to put up (a guest).

untere SEE unterer.

untereinander adverb 1 among ourselves/yourselves/themselves; 2 one below the other.

unterer, untere, unteres adjective lower.

Unterführung die (PL die Unterführungen) subway.

untergehen ◇ verb (IMPERF ging unter, PERF ist untergegangen) 1 to set (of the sun); 2 to sink, to drown; 3 to come to an end.

Untergrundbahn die (PL die Untergrundbahnen) underground.

unterhalb preposition ←(+GEN) below.

unterhalten ◇ verb (PRES unterhält, IMPERF unterhielt, PERF hat unterhalten) 1 to support; 2 to run (a hotel, leisure centre); 3 to entertain; 4 sich über etwas unterhalten to talk about something; 5 sich unterhalten to enjoy yourself.

unterhaltsam adjective entertaining.

Unterhaltung die (PL die Unterhaltungen) 1 conversation; 2 entertainment.

Unterhemd das (PL die Unterhemden) vest.

Unterhose die (PL die Unterhosen) underpants.

Unterkunft die (PL die Unterkünfte) accommodation.

Unterlagen plural noun documents, papers.

Untermieter der (PL die Untermieter) lodger.

Untermieterin die (PL die Untermieterinnen) lodger.

unternehmen ◇ verb (PRES unternimmt, IMPERF unternahm, PERF hat unternommen) 1 to undertake; 2 nichts unternehmen to do nothing; was unternehmt ihr heute? what are you doing today?

Unternehmen das (PL die Unternehmen) 1 enterprise; 2 concern.

Unterricht der 1 lessons; heute haben wir keinen Unterricht we've got no lessons today; 2 teaching.

unterrichten verb (PERF hat unterrichtet) 1 to teach; 2 to inform; 3 sich unterrichten to inform yourself.

Unterrichtsfach das (PL die Unterrichtsfächer) subject.

Unterrock der (PL die Unterröcke) slip.

unterscheiden ◇ verb (IMPERF unterschied, PERF hat unterschieden) 1 to distinguish, to tell apart; 2 sich unterscheiden to differ.

Unterschied der (PL die Unterschiede) difference.

◇ IRREGULAR VERB: See the verb table in the centre of the dictionary

unterschiedlich *adjective* different; **das ist unterschiedlich** it varies.

unterschreiben ◇ *verb* (IMPERF **unterschrieb**, PERF **hat unterschrieben**) to sign.

Unterschrift *die* (PL *die* **Unterschriften**) signature.

unterster, unterste, unterstes *adjective* bottom, lowest.

unterstreichen ◇ *verb* (IMPERF **unterstrich**, PERF **hat unterstrichen**) to underline.

unterstützen *verb* (PERF **hat unterstützt**) to support.

Unterstützung *die* support.

untersuchen *verb* (PERF **hat untersucht**) 1 to examine; 2 to investigate.

Untersuchung *die* (PL *die* **Untersuchungen**) 1 examination, check-up; 2 investigation.

Untertasse *die* (PL *die* **Untertassen**) saucer.

Untertitel *der* (PL *die* **Untertitel**) subtitle.

Unterwäsche *die* underwear.

unterwegs *adverb* on the way; **den ganzen Tag unterwegs sein** to be out all day.

untreu *adjective* 1 unfaithful; 2 disloyal.

ununterbrochen *adjective* uninterrupted.

unverbleit *adjective* unleaded.

unvergleichlich *adjective* incomparable.

unverheiratet *adjective* unmarried.

unverkäuflich *adjective* not for sale; **ein unverkäufliches Muster** a free sample.

unverschämt *adjective* impertinent.

unverständlich *adjective* incomprehensible.

unvorsichtig *adjective* careless.

unwahr *adjective* untrue.

unwahrscheinlich *adjective* 1 unlikely; 2 incredible. *adverb* (*informal*) incredibly; **unwahrscheinlich schön** incredibly beautiful.

Unwetter *das* storm.

unwichtig *adjective* unimportant.

unzählig *adjective* countless.

unzerbrechlich *adjective* unbreakable.

unzertrennlich *adjective* inseparable.

unzufrieden *adjective* dissatisfied.

üppig *adjective* lavish.

uralt *adjective* ancient.

Urenkel *der* (PL *die* **Urenkel**) great-grandson; **die Urenkel** the great-grandchildren.

Urenkelin *die* (PL *die* **Urenkelinnen**) great-granddaughter.

△ NEW SPELLING: *See page xii*

Urkunde die (PL die Urkunden) certificate.

Urlaub der (PL die Urlaube) holiday; **Urlaub haben** to be on holiday; **auf/im Urlaub** on holiday.

Urlauber der (PL die Urlauber) holidaymaker.

Ursache die (PL die Ursachen) cause; **keine Ursache!** don't mention it!

Urprung der (PL die Ursprünge) origin.

ursprünglich adjective original. adverb originally.

Urteil das (PL die Urteile) 1 judgement; 2 opinion; 3 verdict.

urteilen verb (PERF hat geurteilt) to judge.

Urwald der (PL die Urwälder) jungle.

USA plural noun USA.

usw. (und so weiter) etc.

V v

vage adjective vague.

Vagina die (PL die Vaginen) vagina.

Valentinstag der Valentine's Day.

Vanille die vanilla.

Vase die (PL die Vasen) vase.

Vater der (PL die Väter) father.

Vaterunser das Lord's Prayer.

Vati der (PL die Vatis) dad.

Veganer der (PL die Veganer) vegan.

Vegetarier der (PL die Vegetarier) vegetarian.

Vegetarierin die (PL die Vegetarierinnen) vegetarian.

vegetarisch adjective vegetarian.

Veilchen das (PL die Veilchen) violet.

Vene die (PL die Venen) vein.

Ventil das (PL die Ventile) valve.

Ventilator der (PL die Ventilatoren) fan.

verabreden verb (PERF hat verabredet) 1 to arrange; **was habt ihr verabredet?** what did you arrange?; **mit jemandem verabredet sein** to have arranged to meet somebody; 2 **sich mit jemandem verabreden** to arrange to meet somebody; **ich habe mich mit Oliver zum Tennis verabredet** I've arranged to play tennis with Oliver.

Verabredung die (PL die Verabredungen) 1 appointment; 2 date; 3 arrangement.

verabschieden verb (PERF hat verabschiedet) 1 to say goodbye to; 2 **sich verabschieden** to say goodbye.

Verachtung die contempt.

verallgemeinern verb (PERF hat verallgemeinert) to generalize.

veralten verb (PERF ist veraltet) to become obsolete.

veränderlich adjective changeable.

♦ IRREGULAR VERB: See the verb table in the centre of the dictionary

verändern verb (PERF hat verändert) 1 to change; 2 sich verändern to change.

Veränderung die (PL die Veränderungen) change.

veranstalten verb (PERF hat veranstaltet) to organize.

Veranstalter der (PL die Veranstalter) organizer.

Veranstaltung die (PL die Veranstaltungen) event.

verantwortlich adjective responsible.

Verantwortung die responsibility.

verantwortungsbewusst Δ adjective responsible.

verantwortungslos adjective irresponsible.

verarbeiten verb (PERF hat verarbeitet) 1 to process; etwas zu etwas verarbeiten to make something into something; 2 to digest (food, information).

verärgern verb (PERF hat verärgert) to annoy.

Verb das (PL die Verben) verb.

verband SEE verbinden.

Verband der (PL die Verbände) 1 association; sich zu einem Verband zusammenschließen to form an associaton; 2 bandage, dressing; einen Verband anlegen to apply a dressing.

verbergen ◇ verb (PRES verbirgt, IMPERF verbarg, PERF hat verborgen) 1 to hide; 2 sich verbergen to hide.

verbessern verb (PERF hat verbessert) 1 to improve; 2 to correct; 3 sich verbessern to improve.

Verbesserung die (PL die Verbesserungen) 1 improvement; 2 correction.

verbiegen ◇ verb (IMPERF verbog, PERF hat verbogen) 1 to bend; 2 sich verbiegen to bend.

verbieten ◇ verb (IMPERF verbot, PERF hat verboten) 1 to forbid; sie hat ihm verboten, das Haus zu betreten she forbade him to enter the house; meine Eltern verbieten mir, am Abend wegzugehen my parents don't allow me to go out in the evening; 2 to ban.

verbilligt adjective reduced.

verbinden ◇ verb (IMPERF verband, PERF hat verbunden) 1 to connect, to join; 2 to combine; 3 to bandage, to dress (a wound); jemandem die Augen verbinden to blindfold somebody; 4 jemanden verbinden to put somebody through (on the phone); ich verbinde I'm putting you through.

verbindlich adjective 1 friendly; 2 binding (agreement, decision).

Verbindung die (PL die Verbindungen) 1 connection; 2 gute Verbindungen haben to have good contacts; sich mit jemandem in Verbindung setzen to get in touch with somebody; 3 combination; 4 eine chemische Verbindung a chemical compound.

verbirgt SEE verbergen.

verbleit adjective leaded.

verblüffen verb (PERF hat verblüfft) to amaze.

verbog SEE **verbiegen**.

verbogen adjective hidden.

verbot SEE **verbieten**.

Verbot das (PL die Verbote) ban.

verboten adjective forbidden; 'Rauchen verboten' 'no smoking'.

verbracht, verbrachte SEE **verbringen**.

verbrannt, verbrannte SEE **verbrennen**.

Verbrauch der consumption.

verbrauchen verb (PERF hat verbraucht) to use, to use up; die Waschmaschine verbraucht nicht viel Strom the washing machine doesn't use up much electricity.

Verbraucher der (PL die Verbraucher) consumer.

Verbrechen das (PL die Verbrechen) crime.

Verbrecher der (PL die Verbrecher) criminal.

verbreiten verb (PERF hat verbreitet) 1 to spread; eine Krankheit verbreiten to spread an illness; 2 eine Meldung über den Rundfunk verbreiten to broadcast a message; 3 sich verbreiten to spread; die Neuigkeit hat sich schnell verbreitet the news spread quickly.

verbreitet adjective widespread.

verbrennen ✧ verb (IMPERF verbrannte, PERF ist verbrannt) 1 to burn; 2 (PERF hat verbrannt) to burn (rubbish, leaves); 3 to cremate; 4 sich die Hand verbrennen to burn your hand.

verbringen ✧ verb (IMPERF verbrachte, PERF hat verbracht) to spend; wir haben schöne Ferien in Bayern verbracht we spent a nice holiday in Bavaria.

verbunden SEE **verbinden**.

Verdacht der suspicion.

verdächtig adjective suspicious.

verdächtigen verb (PERF hat verdächtigt) to suspect.

verdammt adjective, adverb (informal) damned; verdammt! damn!

verdarb SEE **verderben**.

Verdauung die digestion.

verderben ✧ verb (PRES verdirbt, IMPERF verdarb, PERF hat verdorben) 1 to spoil, to ruin; das hat mir den Abend verdorben it ruined the evening for me; ich habe mir den Magen verdorben I have an upset stomach; 2 es sich mit jemandem verderben to get into somebody's bad books; 3 (PERF ist verdorben) to go off; die Milch verdirbt, wenn du sie nicht in den Kühlschrank stellst the milk will go off if you don't put it in the fridge.

verdienen verb (PERF hat verdient) 1 to earn; 2 to deserve.

✧ IRREGULAR VERB: See the verb table in the centre of the dictionary

Verdienst *der* (PL *die* Verdienste)
1 salary; 2 achievement.

verdirbt SEE **verderben**.

verdoppeln *verb* (PERF hat
verdoppelt) 1 to double; 2 sich
verdoppeln to double.

verdorben SEE **verderben**.

verdünnen *verb* (PERF hat
verdünnt) to dilute.

verehren *verb* (PERF hat verehrt) to
worship.

Verehrer *der* (PL *die* Verehrer)
admirer.

Verehrerin *die* (PL *die*
Verehrerinnen) admirer.

Verein *der* (PL *die* Vereine) 1 society;
2 organization; 3 club.

vereinbaren *verb* (PERF hat
vereinbart) to arrange.

Vereinbarung *die* (PL *die*
Vereinbarungen) 1 agreement;
2 arrangement.

vereinfachen *verb* (PERF hat
vereinfacht) to simplify.

vereinigen *verb* (PERF hat vereinigt)
to unite; ein Land wieder
vereinigen △ to reunify a country.

Vereinigte Staaten *plural noun*
United States.

Vereinigung *die* (PL *die*
Vereinigungen) organization.

verfahren ◇ *verb* (PRES verfährt,
IMPERF verfuhr, PERF ist verfahren)
1 to proceed; 2 ich habe mich
verfahren I've lost my way.

verfallen ◇ *verb* (PRES verfällt,
IMPERF verfiel, PERF ist verfallen) 1 to
decay; 2 to expire (*of a passport or
ticket*).

Verfassung *die* (PL *die*
Verfassungen) 1 constitution;
2 state (*of a person*).

verfaulen *verb* (PERF ist verfault) to
rot.

verfiel SEE **verfallen**.

verfolgen *verb* (PERF hat verfolgt)
1 to follow; 2 to persecute.

Verfolgung *die* (PL *die*
Verfolgungen) 1 pursuit, hunt;
2 persecution.

verfügbar *adjective* available.

Verfügung *die* jemandem etwas
zur Verfügung stellen to put
something at somebody's disposal;
jemandem zur Verfügung stehen
to be at somebody's disposal.

verfuhr SEE **verfahren**.

verführen *verb* (PERF hat verführt)
1 to tempt; 2 to seduce.

Verführung *die* (PL *die*
Verführungen) 1 temptation;
2 seduction.

vergab SEE **vergeben**.

vergangen *verb* SEE **vergehen**.
adjective last.

Vergangenheit *die* 1 past; 2 past
tense.

vergaß SEE **vergessen**.

vergeben ◇ *verb* (PRES vergibt,
IMPERF vergab, PERF hat vergeben)
1 to forgive; jemandem etwas
vergeben to forgive somebody for

△ NEW SPELLING: *See page xii*

something; **2** to give away, to award; **3 vergeben sein** to be taken; **das Zimmer ist schon vergeben** the room's already taken.

vergeblich adverb in vain.

vergehen ◇ verb (IMPERF **verging**, PERF **ist vergangen**) to pass.

vergessen ◇ verb (PRES **vergisst** Δ, IMPERF **vergaß**, PERF **hat vergessen**) to forget.

vergesslich Δ adjective forgetful.

vergewaltigen verb (PERF **hat vergewaltigt**) to rape.

Vergewaltigung die (PL die **Vergewaltigungen**) rape.

vergibt SEE **vergeben**.

vergiften verb (PERF **hat vergiftet**) to poison.

verging SEE **vergehen**.

vergisst Δ SEE **vergessen**.

Vergleich der (PL die **Vergleiche**) comparison.

vergleichen ◇ verb (IMPERF **verglich**, PERF **hat verglichen**) to compare.

Vergnügen das (PL die **Vergnügen**) pleasure; **viel Vergnügen!** have fun!

vergnügt adjective cheerful.

vergrößern verb (PERF **hat vergrößert**) **1** to enlarge; **2** to increase; **3** to magnify; **4** to extend (*a room, building*); **5 sich vergrößern** to expand, to grow.

Vergrößerung die (PL die **Vergrößerungen**) **1** expansion; **2** enlargement (*of a photograph*).

verhaften verb (PERF **hat verhaftet**) to arrest; **er ist verhaftet worden** he was arrested.

verhalten ◇ verb (PRES **verhält sich**, IMPERF **verhielt sich**, PERF **hat sich verhalten**) **sich verhalten** to behave.

Verhalten das behaviour.

Verhältnis das (PL die **Verhältnisse**) **1** relationship; **sie hat ein gutes Verhältnis zu ihren Eltern** she has a good relationship with her parents; **2** affair; **Gabi hat ein Verhältnis mit einem verheirateten Mann** Gabi is having an affair with a married man; **3** ratio (*in maths*); **4 in keinem Verhältnis zu etwas stehen** to be out of all proportion to something; **5 Verhältnisse** conditions; **über seine Verhältnisse leben** to live beyond your means.

verhältnismäßig adverb relatively.

verhandeln verb (PERF **hat verhandelt**) to negotiate; **über etwas verhandeln** to negotiate something.

Verhandlung die (PL die **Verhandlungen**) **1** negotiation; **2** hearing; **3** trial.

verhauen verb (PERF **hat verhauen**) **1** to beat up; **2 die Prüfung verhauen** (*informal*) to make a mess of the exam.

verheimlichen verb (PERF **hat verheimlicht**) to keep secret.

◇ IRREGULAR VERB: *See the verb table in the centre of the dictionary*

verheiratet *adjective* married.

verhielt SEE **verhalten**.

verhindern *verb* (PERF hat verhindert) 1 to prevent; 2 verhindert sein to be unable to make it; **Petra ist verhindert** Petra won't be able to make it.

verhungern *verb* (PERF ist verhungert) to starve.

Verhütungsmittel *das* (PL die Verhütungsmittel) contraceptive.

verirren *verb* (PERF hat sich verirrt) sich verirren to get lost.

verkam SEE **verkommen**.

Verkauf *der* (PL die Verkäufe) sale; **zum Verkauf** for sale.

verkaufen *verb* (PERF hat verkauft) to sell; **zu verkaufen** for sale.

Verkäufer *der* (PL die Verkäufer) 1 seller; 2 sales assistant.

Verkäuferin *die* (PL die Verkäuferinnen) 1 seller; 2 sales assistant.

Verkehr *der* traffic.

Verkehrsampel *die* (PL die Verkehrsampeln) traffic lights.

Verkehrsamt *das* (PL die Verkehrsämter) tourist office.

Verkehrsunfall *der* (PL die Verkehrsunfälle) road accident.

Verkehrszeichen *das* (PL die Verkehrszeichen) traffic sign, road sign.

verkehrt *adjective* 1 wrong;

2 **verkehrt herum** inside out, the wrong way round.

verklagen *verb* (PERF hat verklagt) to sue.

verkleiden *verb* (PERF hat sich verkleidet) sich verkleiden to dress up.

Verkleidung *die* (PL die Verkleidungen) disguise, fancy dress.

verkommen ◇ *verb* (IMPERF verkam, PERF ist verkommen) 1 to go off (*of food*); 2 to become dilapidated (*of a house*); 3 to go to the bad.

verkratzt *adjective* scratched.

Verlag *der* (PL die Verlage) publisher's.

verlangen *verb* (PERF hat verlangt) 1 to ask for, to require; am Telefon verlangt werden to be wanted on the phone; 2 to demand; 3 to charge.

verlängern *verb* (PERF hat verlängert) 1 to extend; 2 to lengthen; 3 to renew (*a passport, driving licence*).

Verlängerung *die* (PL die Verlängerungen) 1 extension; 2 renewal; 3 extra time (*in sport*).

verlassen[1] ◇ *verb* (PRES verlässt △, IMPERF verließ, PERF hat verlassen) 1 to leave; jemanden verlassen to leave somebody; 2 sich auf etwas verlassen to rely on something; du kannst dich auf ihn verlassen you can rely on him.

verlassen[2] *adjective* deserted.

△ NEW SPELLING: See page xii

verlaufen ◇ verb (PRES **verläuft**, IMPERF **verlief**, PERF **ist verlaufen**) 1 to go; **es ist gut verlaufen** it went well; 2 **sich verlaufen** to lose your way; 3 **die Menge verlief sich schnell** the crowd quickly dispersed.

verlegen[1] adjective embarrassed.

verlegen[2] verb (PERF **hat verlegt**) 1 to mislay; 2 to postpone; 3 to publish; 4 to lay (a carpet, cable).

Verlegenheit die embarrassment.

Verleih der (PL die **Verleihe**) 1 renting out, hiring out; 2 rental firm, hire shop.

verleihen ◇ verb (IMPERF **verlieh**, PERF **hat verliehen**) 1 to hire out; 2 to lend; 3 to award.

verlernen verb (PERF **hat verlernt**) to forget.

verletzen verb (PERF **hat verletzt**) 1 to injure; 2 to hurt; 3 to violate (a law); 4 **sich verletzen** to hurt yourself.

Verletzte der/die (PL die **Verletzten**) 1 injured person; 2 casualty.

Verletzung die (PL die **Verletzungen**) injury.

verlieben verb (PERF **hat sich verliebt**) **sich verlieben** to fall in love.

verlief SEE **verlaufen**.

verlieh SEE **verleihen**.

verlieren ◇ verb (IMPERF **verlor**, PERF **hat verloren**) to lose.

verließ SEE **verlassen**.

verloben verb (PERF **hat sich verlobt**) **sich verloben** to get engaged.

Verlobte der/die (PL die **Verlobten**) fiancé, fiancée.

Verlobung die (PL die **Verlobungen**) engagement.

verlor, verloren SEE **verlieren**.

Verlosung die (PL die **Verlosungen**) prize draw.

Verlust der (PL die **Verluste**) loss.

vermeiden ◇ verb (IMPERF **vermied**, PERF **hat vermieden**) to avoid.

vermieten verb (PERF **hat vermietet**) 1 to rent out, to hire out; 2 to let; **Zimmer zu vermieten** rooms to let.

Vermieter der (PL die **Vermieter**) landlord.

Vermieterin die (PL die **Vermieterinnen**) landlady.

vermissen verb (PERF **hat vermisst** Δ) to miss.

Vermittlung die (PL die **Vermittlungen**) 1 arrangement; 2 agency; 3 switchboard; 4 telephone exchange; 5 mediation.

Vermögen das (PL die **Vermögen**) fortune.

vermuten verb (PERF **hat vermutet**) to suspect.

vermutlich adjective probable. adverb probably.

vernichten verb (PERF **hat vernichtet**) 1 to destroy; 2 to exterminate.

◇ IRREGULAR VERB: See the verb table in the centre of the dictionary

Vernunft *die* reason.

vernünftig *adjective* sensible.

verpacken *verb* (PERF hat verpackt) 1 to pack; 2 to wrap up.

Verpackung *die* (PL *die* Verpackungen) packaging.

verpassen *verb* (PERF hat verpasst Δ) to miss.

Verpflegung *die* food; Unterkunft und Verpflegung board and lodging.

verpflichten *verb* (PERF hat verpflichtet) 1 sich verpflichten to promise; 2 sich vertraglich verpflichten to sign a contract; 3 verpflichtet sein, etwas zu tun to be obliged to do something; jemandem zu Dank verpflichtet sein to be obliged to somebody; 4 verpflichtend binding.

Verpflichtung *die* (PL *die* Verpflichtungen) 1 obligation; 2 commitment.

verprügeln *verb* (PERF hat verprügelt) to beat up.

verraten ◊ *verb* (PRES verrät, IMPERF verriet, PERF hat verraten) 1 to betray; 2 to give away; 3 to tell; 4 sich verraten to give yourself away.

verrechnen *verb* (PERF hat sich verrechnet) sich verrechnen to make a mistake.

verregnet *adjective* rainy.

verreisen *verb* (PERF ist verreist) to go away; verreist sein to be away.

verriet SEE verraten.

verrosten *verb* (PERF ist verrostet) to rust.

verrostet *adjective* rusty.

verrückt *adjective* mad, crazy.

Verrückte *der/die* (PL *die* Verrückten) maniac.

versagen *verb* (PERF hat versagt) to fail.

versammeln *verb* (PERF hat versammelt) 1 to assemble; 2 sich versammeln to assemble.

Versammlung *die* (PL *die* Versammlungen) meeting.

versäumen *verb* (PERF hat versäumt) to miss; es versäumen, etwas zu tun to fail to do something.

verschenken *verb* (PERF hat verschenkt) to give away.

verschieben ◊ *verb* (IMPERF verschob, PERF hat verschoben) to postpone.

verschieden *adjective* 1 different; 2 various.

verschlafen ◊ *verb* (PRES verschläft, IMPERF verschlief, PERF hat verschlafen) 1 to oversleep; 2 to sleep through (*the day*); 3 to miss (*a date, the train*).

verschlechtern *verb* (PERF hat verschlechtert) 1 to make worse; 2 sich verschlechtern to get worse.

verschlief SEE verschlafen.

verschließen ◊ *verb* (IMPERF verschloss Δ, PERF hat verschlossen) 1 to close (*a tin,*

Δ NEW SPELLING: See page xii

package); **2** to lock (*a door, drawer).*

verschlimmern *verb* (PERF hat
verschlimmert) **1** to make worse;
2 sich verschlimmern to get worse.

verschloss △ SEE **verschließen.**

verschlucken *verb* (PERF hat
verschluckt) **1** to swallow; **2 sich
verschlucken** to choke.

Verschluss △ *der* (PL *die*
Verschlüsse) **1** fastener, clasp;
2 top (*of a bottle).*

verschmutzen *verb* (PERF hat
verschmutzt) to soil; **die Umwelt
verschmutzen** to pollute the
environment.

Verschmutzung *die* pollution.

verschob SEE **verschieben.**

verschreiben ◇ *verb* (IMPERF
verschrieb, PERF hat verschrieben)
1 to prescribe; **2 sich verschreiben**
to make a mistake.

verschütten *verb* (PERF hat
verschüttet) to spill.

verschwand SEE **verschwinden.**

verschwenden *verb* (PERF hat
verschwendet) to waste.

Verschwendung *die* waste.

verschwinden ◇ *verb* (IMPERF
verschwand, PERF ist
verschwunden) to disappear.

Versehen *das* (PL *die* Versehen)
oversight; **aus Versehen** by mistake.

versehentlich *adverb* by mistake.

versetzen *verb* (PERF hat versetzt)
1 to move, to transfer (*a person);*

2 to move up (*into the next class at
school);* **3 jemanden versetzen** to
stand somebody up; **4 jemandem
einen Schreck versetzen** to give
somebody a fright; **jemandem einen
Tritt versetzen** to kick somebody;
5 sich in jemandes Lage versetzen
to put yourself in somebody's
position.

versichern *verb* (PERF hat
versichert) **1** to insure; **2** to assert;
jemandem versichern, dass ... to
assure somebody that ...

Versicherung *die* (PL *die*
Versicherungen) **1** insurance;
2 assurance.

versöhnen *verb* (PERF hat sich
versöhnt) **sich versöhnen** to make
up; **sich mit jemandem versöhnen**
to make it up with somebody.

versorgen *verb* (PERF hat versorgt)
1 to supply; **2** to provide for; **3** to
look after.

verspäten *verb* (PERF hat sich
verspätet) **sich verspäten** to be
late.

Verspätung *die* lateness, delay;
Verspätung haben to be late.

versprechen ◇ *verb* (PRES
verspricht, IMPERF versprach, PERF
hat versprochen) **1** to promise;
2 sich viel von etwas versprechen
to have high hopes of something;
3 sich versprechen to make a slip
of the tongue.

Versprechen *das* (PL *die*
Versprechen) promise.

verstand SEE **verstehen.**

◇ IRREGULAR VERB: *See the verb table in the centre of the dictionary*

Verstand der 1 mind; **den Verstand
verlieren** to go out of your mind;
2 reason.

verstanden SEE **verstehen**.

verständigen verb (PERF hat
verständigt) 1 to notify; 2 **sich
verständigen** to communicate, to
make yourself understood; 3 **sich
über etwas verständigen** to agree
on something.

verständlich adjective
1 understandable; **jemandem
etwas verständlich machen** to
make something clear to somebody;
2 comprehensible.

Verständigung die
1 communication; 2 notification.

Verstärker der (PL die **Verstärker**)
amplifier.

verstauchen verb (PERF hat
verstaucht) to sprain; **sich den Fuß
verstauchen** to sprain your ankle.

Versteck das (PL die **Verstecke**)
hiding place.

verstecken verb (PERF hat
versteckt) 1 to hide; 2 **sich
verstecken** to hide.

verstehen ◇ verb (IMPERF verstand,
PERF hat verstanden) 1 to
understand; **etwas falsch
verstehen** to misunderstand
something; 2 **sich gut verstehen** to
get on well; 3 **das versteht sich von
selbst** that goes without saying.

verstellbar adjective adjustable.

verstellen verb (PERF hat verstellt)
1 to adjust; 2 to block; 3 to disguise;
4 **sich verstellen** to pretend.

verstimmt adjective 1 out of tune;
2 peeved; 3 **ein verstimmter
Magen** an upset stomach.

Versuch der (PL die **Versuche**)
1 attempt; 2 experiment.

versuchen verb (PERF hat versucht)
to try.

verteidigen verb (PERF hat
verteidigt) to defend.

Verteidiger der (PL die **Verteidiger**)
1 defender; 2 defence counsel.

Verteidigung die defence.

verteilen verb (PERF hat verteilt) to
distribute.

Vertrag der (PL die **Verträge**)
1 contract; 2 treaty.

vertragen ◇ verb (PRES verträgt,
IMPERF vertrug, PERF hat vertragen)
1 to stand, to take; 2 **ich vertrage
keinen Kaffee** coffee disagrees with
me; 3 **sich vertragen** to get on; **sich
wieder vertragen** to make it up.

vertrat SEE **vertreten**.

vertrauen verb (PERF hat vertraut)
to trust.

Vertrauen das trust; **im Vertrauen**
in confidence.

vertraulich adjective
1 confidential; 2 familiar.

vertreten ◇ verb (PRES vertritt,
IMPERF vertrat, PERF hat vertreten)
1 to stand in for; 2 to represent;
3 **eine Meinung vertreten** to hold
an opinion; 4 **sich die Beine
vertreten** to stretch your legs.

△ NEW SPELLING: See page xii

Vertreter der (PL die Vertreter)
1 representative; 2 deputy.

Vertreterin die (PL die
Vertreterinnen) 1 representative;
2 deputy.

vertritt SEE vertreten.

vertrug SEE vertragen.

verunglücken verb (PERF ist
verunglückt) to have an accident.

verursachen verb (PERF hat
verursacht) to cause.

verurteilen verb (PERF hat
verurteilt) 1 to sentence; 2 to
condemn.

Verwaltung die (PL die
Verwaltungen) administration.

verwandt adjective related.

Verwandte der/die (PL die
Verwandten) relative.

Verwandtschaft die relatives.

verwechseln verb (PERF hat
verwechselt) to mix up, to confuse;
jemanden mit jemandem
verwechseln to mistake somebody
for somebody.

verwenden verb (PERF hat
verwendet) to use.

Verwendung die use.

verwickelt adjective complicated.

verwirren verb (PERF hat verwirrt)
1 to confuse; 2 to tangle up.

verwirrt adjective confused.

verwöhnen verb (PERF hat
verwöhnt) to spoil.

verwunden verb (PERF hat
verwundet) to wound.

Verwundete der/die (PL die
Verwundeten) casualty, injured
person.

Verwundung die (PL die
Verwundungen) injury, wound.

verzählen verb (PERF hat sich
verzählt) sich verzählen to
miscount.

Verzeichnis das (PL die
Verzeichnisse) 1 list; 2 index.

verzeihen verb (IMPERF verzieh, PERF
hat verziehen) to forgive; verzeihen
Sie, können Sie mir sagen ...?
excuse me, could you tell me ...?

Verzeihung die forgiveness;
jemanden um Verzeihung bitten to
apologize to somebody;
Verzeihung! sorry!

verzieh, verziehen SEE verzeihen.

verzichten verb (PERF hat
verzichtet) 1 to do without; ich
verzichte auf deine Hilfe I can do
without your help; 2 auf etwas
verzichten to give up something
(smoking or your share of
something); to relinquish something
(a right or privilege).

verzögern verb (PERF hat
verzögert) 1 to delay; 2 sich
verzögern to be delayed.

Verzögerung die (PL die
Verzögerungen) delay.

verzollen verb (PERF hat verzollt) to
pay duty on; haben Sie etwas zu

⬧ IRREGULAR VERB: See the verb table in the centre of the dictionary

verzollen? have you anything to declare?

verzweifeln verb (PERF **ist verzweifelt**) to despair.

verzweifelt adjective desperate.

Verzweiflung die despair.

Vetter der (PL die **Vettern**) cousin.

Video das (PL die **Videos**) video.

Videokamera die (PL die **Videokameras**) video camera.

Videokassette die (PL die **Videokassetten**) video cassette.

Videorekorder der (PL die **Videorekorder**) video recorder.

Videospiel das (PL die **Videospiele**) video game.

Videothek die (PL die **Videotheken**) video shop.

Vieh das cattle.

viel adjective, pronoun **1** a lot of; Erika hat viel Arbeit Erika's got a lot of work; **2** viele (plural) many, a lot of; viele Leute many people; **3** much, a lot; wie viel? how much?, how many?; zu viel too much; vielen Dank thank you very much; viel Spaß! have fun!; viel Glück! good luck!; **4** das viele Geld all that money.
adverb **1** much, a lot; viel weniger much less; so viel wie möglich as much as possible; sie redet viel she talks a lot; **2** viel zu groß far too big, much too big; das dauert viel zu lange it'll take far too long.

vielleicht adverb perhaps.

vielmals adverb danke vielmals thanks a lot.

vier number four.

Viereck das (PL die **Vierecke**) **1** rectangle; **2** square.

viereckig adjective **1** rectangular; **2** square.

vierte SEE vierter.

Viertel das (PL die **Viertel**) quarter; es ist Viertel vor acht it's quarter to eight.

viertel adjective quarter; wir treffen uns um viertel acht△ we'll meet at quarter past seven; um drei viertel acht△ at quarter to eight.

Viertelstunde die (PL die **Viertelstunden**) quarter of an hour.

vierter, vierte, viertes adjective fourth.

vierzehn number fourteen.

vierzig number forty.

Villa die (PL die **Villen**) villa.

virtuell adjective virtual; virtuelle Realität virtual reality.

Virus das (PL die **Viren**) virus.

visuell adjective visual.

Visum das (PL die **Visa**) visa.

Vitamin das (PL die **Vitamine**) vitamin.

Vogel der (PL die **Vögel**) bird.

Vokabel die (PL die **Vokabeln**) word; Vokabeln vocabulary.

Vokal der (PL die **Vokale**) vowel.

Volk das (PL die **Völker**) people.

△ NEW SPELLING: See page xii

Volkshochschule *die* adult education centre; **ein Kurs an der Volkshochschule** an adult education class.

Volkslied *das* (PL *die* **Volkslieder**) folk song.

Volkswirtschaft *die* economics.

voll *adjective* 1 full; **ein Korb voll Äpfel** a basket full of apples; **die volle Wahrheit** the whole truth; 2 **etwas voll machen** △ to fill something up; **voll tanken** △ to fill up with petrol.
adverb 1 fully, completely; **voll und ganz** completely; 2 **jemanden nicht für voll nehmen** (*informal*) not to take somebody seriously.

völlig *adjective* complete.
adverb completely.

vollkommen *adjective* 1 perfect; 2 complete.
adverb completely.

Vollkornbrot *das* wholemeal bread.

vollmachen SEE **voll**.

Vollpension *die* full board.

vollständig *adjective* complete.

volltanken SEE **voll**.

vom = **von dem**.

von *preposition* ←(+DAT) 1 from; **von heute an** from today; **von hier bis ...** from here to ...; 2 of; **eine Freundin von mir** a friend of mine; 3 about; **Peter hat mir von dem neuen Haus erzählt** Peter told me about the new house; 4 by; **ein**

Theaterstück von Brecht a play by Brecht; 5 **von mir aus** I don't mind.

voneinander *adverb* from each other; **sie sind voneinander abhängig** they depend on each other.

vor *preposition* ←(+DAT or +ACC *with movement towards a place*) 1 in front of; 2 before; **Manfred war vor euch da** Manfred arrived before you; **kurz vor der Ampel** shortly before the lights; 3 with; **vor Angst zittern** to tremble with fear; 4 (*with clock time*) **zehn vor fünf** ten to five; 5 ago; **vor zwei Jahren** two years ago; 6 **sich vor jemandem fürchten** to be frightened of somebody; 7 **vor allen Dingen** above all; 8 **vor sich hin summen** to hum to yourself.
adverb forward; **vor und zurück** backwards and forwards.

voraus *adverb* 1 ahead; 2 **im Voraus** △ in advance.

vorausgehen ◇ *verb* (IMPERF **ging voraus**, PERF **ist vorausgegangen**) 1 to go on ahead; 2 to precede.

voraussetzen *verb* (PERF **hat vorausgesetzt**) 1 to take for granted; 2 to require; 3 **vorausgesetzt, dass ...** provided that ...

Voraussetzung *die* (PL *die* **Voraussetzungen**) 1 condition; 2 assumption.

vorbei *adverb* 1 past; 2 over; **vorbei sein** to be over.

vorbeifahren ◇ *verb* (PRES **fährt vorbei**, IMPERF **fuhr vorbei**, PERF **ist**

◇ IRREGULAR VERB: *See the verb table in the centre of the dictionary*

vorbeigefahren) to drive past, to pass.

vorbeigehen ◇ verb (IMPERF **ging vorbei**, PERF **ist vorbeigegangen**) 1 to go past, to pass; 2 to drop in; **ich gehe bei Anne vorbei** I'll drop in on Anne.

vorbeikommen ◇ verb (IMPERF **kam vorbei**, PERF **ist vorbeigekommen**) 1 to pass; 2 to get past; 3 to drop in.

vorbereiten verb (PERF **hat vorbereitet**) 1 to prepare; 2 **sich vorbereiten** to prepare.

Vorbereitung die (PL die **Vorbereitungen**) preparation.

vorbeugen verb (PERF **hat vorgebeugt**) 1 to prevent; 2 **sich vorbeugen** to lean forward.

Vorbild das (PL die **Vorbilder**) example.

vorderer, vordere, vorderes adjective front.

Vorderseite die front.

vorderster, vorderste, vorderstes adjective front.

Vorfahrt die right of way; '**Vorfahrt beachten/gewähren**' 'give way'.

Vorfall der (PL die **Vorfälle**) incident.

Vorführung die (PL die **Vorführungen**) 1 performance; 2 demonstration.

Vorgänger der (PL die **Vorgänger**) predecessor.

Vorgängerin die (PL die **Vorgängerinnen**) predecessor.

vorgehen ◇ verb (IMPERF **ging vor**, PERF **ist vorgegangen**) 1 to go on ahead; 2 to go forward; 3 to proceed; 4 **die Uhr geht vor** the clock is fast; 5 **was geht hier vor?** what's going on here?

vorgestern adverb the day before yesterday.

vorhaben ◇ verb (PRES **hat vor**, IMPERF **hatte vor**, PERF **hat vorgehabt**) 1 to intend; 2 **etwas vorhaben** to have something planned.

Vorhang der (PL die **Vorhänge**) curtain.

vorher adverb beforehand, before.

Vorhersage die (PL die **Vorhersagen**) 1 forecast; 2 prediction.

vorhin adverb just now.

voriger, vorige, voriges adjective last.

vorkommen ◇ verb (IMPERF **kam vor**, PERF **ist vorgekommen**) 1 to happen; 2 to occur; 3 to come forward; 4 to come out (from behind somewhere); 5 to seem; **jemandem bekannt vorkommen** to seem familiar to somebody; 6 **sich alt vorkommen** to feel old.

vorlesen ◇ verb (PRES **liest vor**, IMPERF **las vor**, PERF **hat vorgelesen**) 1 to read (out); 2 **jemandem vorlesen** to read to somebody.

vorletzter, vorletzte, vorletztes adjective last but one; **vorletztes Jahr** the year before last.

△ NEW SPELLING: See page xii

Vormittag der (PL die Vormittage) morning.

vormittags adverb in the morning.

vorn adverb 1 at the front; **nach vorn** to the front; 2 **von vorn** from the beginning; **wieder von vorn anfangen** to start again at the beginning; **da vorn** over there.

Vorname der (PL die Vornamen) first name.

vorne = vorn.

vornehm adjective 1 elegant; 2 distinguished.

vornehmen ◇ verb (PRES **nimmt vor**, IMPERF **nahm vor**, PERF **hat vorgenommen**) 1 to carry out; 2 **sich vornehmen, etwas zu tun** to plan to do something.

Vorort der (PL die Vororte) suburb.

Vorrat der (PL die Vorräte) supply, stock.

Vorsatz der (PL die Vorsätze) intention.

Vorschau die 1 preview; 2 trailer (of a film).

Vorschlag der (PL die Vorschläge) suggestion.

vorschlagen ◇ verb (PRES **schlägt vor**, IMPERF **schlug vor**, PERF **hat vorgeschlagen**) to suggest.

Vorschrift die (PL die Vorschriften) 1 regulation; 2 instruction.

Vorschule die (PL die Vorschulen) infant school.

vorsehen ◇ verb (PRES **sieht sich vor**, IMPERF **sah sich vor**, PERF **hat**

sich vorgesehen) **sich vorsehen** to be careful.

Vorsicht die care; **Vorsicht!** careful!; (on a sign) caution!

vorsichtig adjective careful.

vorsichtshalber adverb to be on the safe side.

Vorspeise die (PL die Vorspeisen) starter.

Vorsprung der (PL die Vorsprünge) 1 ledge (of a rock); 2 lead (over somebody).

vorstellen verb (PERF **hat vorgestellt**) 1 to introduce; **darf ich Ihnen Herrn Schulz vorstellen?** may I introduce Mr Schulz?; 2 **die Uhr vorstellen** to put the clock forward; 3 **sich vorstellen** to introduce yourself; 4 **sich beim Personalchef vorstellen** to go for an interview with the personnel manager; 5 **sich etwas vorstellen** to imagine something; **stell dir vor!** can you imagine?

Vorstellung die (PL die Vorstellungen) 1 performance; 2 introduction; 3 interview (for a job); 4 idea; 5 imagination.

Vorteil der (PL die Vorteile) advantage.

Vortrag der (PL die Vorträge) talk.

vorüber adverb **vorüber sein** to be over.

vorübergehend adjective temporary.
adverb temporarily.

◇ IRREGULAR VERB: See the verb table in the centre of the dictionary

Vorurteil das (PL die Vorurteile) prejudice.

Vorwahl die (PL die Vorwahlen) dialling code.

vorwärts adverb forward(s).

vorwiegend adverb predominantly.

Vorwurf der (PL die Vorwürfe) reproach; **jemandem Vorwürfe machen** to reproach somebody.

vorzeigen verb (PERF hat vorgezeigt) to show.

vorziehen ◇ verb (PRES zieht vor, IMPERF zog vor, PERF hat vorgezogen) 1 to prefer; 2 to pull up (a chair); 3 **den Vorhang vorziehen** to draw the curtain.

vorzüglich adjective excellent.

vulgär adjective vulgar.

Vulkan der (PL die Vulkane) volcano.

W w

Waage die (PL die Waagen) 1 scales; 2 Libra; **Gabi ist Waage** Gabi's Libra.

waagerecht adjective horizontal.

wach adjective awake; **wach sein** to be awake; **wach werden** to wake up.

Wache die (PL die Wachen) 1 guard; 2 (police) station.

Wachhund der (PL die Wachhunde) guard dog.

Wachs das wax.

wachsen ◇ verb (PRES wächst, IMPERF wuchs, PERF ist gewachsen) to grow.

Wachstum das growth.

wackelig adjective wobbly.

wackeln verb (PERF hat gewackelt) to wobble.

Wade die (PL die Waden) calf.

Waffe die (PL die Waffen) weapon.

Waffel die (PL die Waffeln) waffle.

wagen verb (PERF hat gewagt) 1 to risk; 2 **es wagen, etwas zu tun** to dare to do something; **sich nicht irgendwohin wagen** not dare to go somewhere.

Wagen der (PL die Wagen) 1 car; **nimmst du den Wagen?** are you going by car?; 2 carriage (of a train); 3 cart.

Wagenheber der (PL die Wagenheber) jack.

Wahl die (PL die Wahlen) 1 choice; **er hat die Wahl** it's his choice; 2 election; **die nächsten Wahlen sind im Herbst** the next election is in autumn.

wählen verb (PERF hat gewählt) 1 to choose; **zwischen zwei Möglichkeiten wählen** to choose between two possibilities; 2 **haben Sie schon gewählt?** are you ready to order? (in a restaurant); 3 to elect; 4 to vote; **wählt Schröder!** vote for Schröder; 5 to dial; **ich muss die falsche Nummer gewählt**

△ NEW SPELLING: See page xii

haben I must have dialled the wrong number.

Wahlfach das (PL die **Wahlfächer**) optional subject, option.

Wahnsinn der madness.

wahnsinnig adjective 1 mad; **wahnsinnig werden** to go mad; 2 **wahnsinnigen Durst haben** to be terribly thirsty; **der Film war wahnsinnig gut** the film was incredibly good.

wahr adjective 1 true; 2 **du kommst doch, nicht wahr?** you're coming, aren't you?

während preposition ←(+GEN) during.
conjunction 1 while; 2 whereas.

Wahrheit die (PL die **Wahrheiten**) truth.

Wahrsager der (PL die **Wahrsager**) fortune-teller.

Wahrsagerin die (PL die **Wahrsagerinnen**) fortune-teller.

wahrscheinlich adjective probable, likely.
adverb probably.

Währung die (PL die **Währungen**) currency.

Waise die (PL die **Waisen**) orphan.

Wal der (PL die **Wale**) whale.

Wald der (PL die **Wälder**) wood, forest.

Waliser der (PL die **Waliser**) Welshman.

Waliserin die (PL die **Waliserinnen**) Welshwoman.

walisisch adjective Welsh.

Walkman™ der (PL die **Walkmen**) walkman™.

Walnuss △ die (PL die **Walnüsse**) walnut.

Wand die (PL die **Wände**) wall.

wandern verb (PERF **ist gewandert**) 1 to hike; 2 to go walking.

Wanderung die (PL die **Wanderungen**) 1 hike; 2 walking tour.

wann adverb when.

Wanne die (PL die **Wannen**) 1 tub; 2 bath.

war SEE **sein**.

warb SEE **werben**.

Ware die (PL die **Waren**) 1 article; 2 **Waren** goods.

waren SEE **sein**.

Warenhaus das (PL die **Warenhäuser**) department store.

warf SEE **werfen**.

warm adjective warm; **eine warme Mahlzeit** a hot meal; **das Essen warm machen** to heat up the food.

Wärme die warmth.

wärmen verb (PERF **hat gewärmt**) to warm, to heat.

Warndreieck das (PL die **Warndreiecke**) warning triangle.

warnen verb (PERF **hat gewarnt**) to warn; **jemanden vor etwas warnen** to warn somebody of something.

✧ IRREGULAR VERB: *See the verb table in the centre of the dictionary*

Warnung die (PL die Warnungen) warning.

varst, wart SEE **sein**.

Warteliste die (PL die Wartelisten) waiting list.

warten verb (PERF hat gewartet) 1 to wait; **auf jemanden warten** to wait for somebody; 2 **auf sich warten lassen** to take your time.

Wärter der (PL die Wärter) 1 keeper; 2 attendant; 3 warder.

Warteraum der (PL die Warteräume) waiting room.

Wärterin die (PL die Wärterinnen) 1 keeper; 2 attendant; 3 warder.

Wartezeit die wait; **eine Stunde Wartezeit** an hour's wait.

Wartezimmer das (PL die Wartezimmer) waiting room.

warum adverb why.

was pronoun 1 what; **was für ein/eine ...?** what kind of ...?; **was für ein Fahrrad hast du?** what kind of bike do you have?; **was für ein Glück!** what luck!; **was kostet das?** how much is it?; 2 that; **alles, was wir brauchen** all (that) we need; **alles, was du willst** all (that) you want; 3 (short for 'etwas') something; **heute gibt's was Gutes im Fernsehen** there's something good on television today; 4 (short for 'etwas' in questions and negatives) anything; **hast du was für mich?** have you got anything for me?

Waschbecken das (PL die Waschbecken) washbasin.

Wäsche die 1 washing; 2 underwear.

waschen ◇ verb (PRES wäscht, IMPERF wusch, PERF hat gewaschen) 1 to wash; 2 **sich waschen** to have a wash; **sich die Hände waschen** to wash your hands.

Wäscherei die (PL die Wäschereien) laundry.

Waschlappen der (PL die Waschlappen) flannel.

Waschmaschine die (PL die Waschmaschinen) washing machine.

Waschsalon der (PL die Waschsalons) launderette.

Waschpulver das (PL die Waschpulver) washing powder.

Wasser das water.

wasserdicht adjective waterproof.

Wasserfall der (PL die Wasserfälle) waterfall.

Wasserfarbe die (PL die Wasserfarben) watercolour.

Wasserhahn der (PL die Wasserhähne) tap.

Wassermann der Aquarius; **Lisa ist Wassermann** Lisa's Aquarius.

Wasserskifahren das water-skiing.

Watte die cotton wool.

wattiert adjective padded.

WC das (PL die WCs) WC, toilet.

weben verb (PERF hat gewebt) to weave.

△ NEW SPELLING: See page xii

Wechselkurs der (PL die Wechselkurse) exchange rate.

wechseln verb (PERF hat gewechselt) 1 to change; kannst du mir zehn Mark wechseln? have you got change for ten marks?; 2 to exchange (glances, letters).

Wechselstube die (PL die Wechselstuben) bureau de change.

wecken verb (PERF hat geweckt) to wake (up).

Wecker der (PL die Wecker) alarm clock; Max geht mir auf den Wecker (informal) Max gets on my nerves.

weder conjunction weder ... noch neither ... nor.

weg adverb 1 away; geh weg! go away!; Hände weg! hands off!; 2 gone; der Ring ist weg the ring's gone; Heidi ist schon weg Heidi's already gone.

Weg der (PL die Wege) 1 way; auf dem Weg nach Hause on the way home; 2 path; 3 sich auf den Weg machen to set off; 4 im Weg sein to be in the way.

wegen preposition ←(+GEN) because of.

wegfahren ◊ verb (PRES fährt weg, IMPERF fuhr weg, PERF ist weggefahren) 1 to leave; sie fahren gerade weg they are leaving just now; 2 (PERF hat weggefahren) to drive away (a car or things).

weggehen ◊ verb (IMPERF ging weg, PERF ist weggegangen) 1 to go away; 2 to leave; 3 to go out; wir gehen heute Abend weg we're going out tonight; 4 to come out (of a stain).

weglassen ◊ verb (PRES lässt weg △, IMPERF ließ weg, PERF hat weggelassen) 1 to let go; 2 to leave out.

weglaufen ◊ verb (PRES läuft weg, IMPERF lief weg, PERF ist weggelaufen) to run away.

weglegen verb (PERF hat weggelegt) 1 to put down; 2 to put away.

wegmachen verb (PERF hat weggemacht) to get rid of (a stain or wart, for example).

wegmüssen ◊ verb (informal) (PRES muss weg △, IMPERF musste weg △, PERF hat weggemusst △) to have to go.

wegnehmen ◊ verb (PRES nimmt weg, IMPERF nahm weg, PERF hat weggenommen) to take away.

wegräumen verb (PERF hat weggeräumt) to clear away.

wegschicken verb (PERF hat weggeschickt) 1 to send away; 2 to send off.

wegtun ◊ verb (IMPERF tat weg, PERF hat weggetan) to put away.

Wegweiser der (PL die Wegweiser) signpost.

wegwerfen ◊ verb (PRES wirft weg, IMPERF warf weg, PERF hat weggeworfen) to throw away.

◊ IRREGULAR VERB: See the verb table in the centre of the dictionary

weh *adjective* 1 sore; 2 **oh weh!** oh dear!; 3 **es tut weh** it hurts.

wehen *verb* (PERF **hat geweht**) to blow.

Wehrdienst *der* military service.

wehren *verb* (PERF **hat sich gewehrt**) **sich wehren** to defend yourself.

wehrlos *adjective* defenceless.

wehtun △ ◇ *verb* (PRES **tut weh**, IMPERF **tat weh**, PERF **hat wehgetan**) 1 to hurt; **mein Arm tut weh** my arm hurts; **jemandem wehtun** to hurt somebody; 2 **sich wehtun** to hurt yourself.

Weibchen *das* (PL *die* **Weibchen**) female.

weiblich *adjective* 1 female; 2 feminine (*noun*).

weich *adjective* soft.

Weide *die* (PL *die* **Weiden**) 1 willow; 2 pasture.

weigern *verb* (PERF **hat sich geweigert**) **sich weigern** to refuse.

Weihnachten *das* (PL *die* **Weihnachten**) Christmas; **Frohe Weihnachten!** Merry Christmas!

Weihnachtslied *das* (PL *die* **Weihnachtslieder**) Christmas carol.

Weihnachtsmann *der* (PL *die* **Weihnachtsmänner**) Father Christmas.

Weihnachtstag *der* (PL *die* **Weihnachtstage**) Christmas Day; **zweiter Weihnachtstag** Boxing Day.

weil *conjunction* because.

Weile *die* while.

Wein *der* (PL *die* **Weine**) wine.

Weinberg *der* (PL *die* **Weinberge**) vineyard.

Weinbergschnecke *die* (PL *die* **Weinbergschnecken**) snail.

Weinbrand *der* brandy.

weinen *verb* (PERF **hat geweint**) to cry.

Weinkarte *die* (PL *die* **Weinkarten**) wine list.

Weinkeller *der* (PL *die* **Weinkeller**) wine cellar.

Weinstube *die* (PL *die* **Weinstuben**) wine bar.

Weintraube *die* (PL *die* **Weintrauben**) grape.

weise *adjective* wise.

Weise *die* (PL *die* **Weisen**) way; **auf diese Weise** in this way.

Weisheit *die* (PL *die* **Weisheiten**) wisdom.

weiß[1] SEE **wissen**.

weiß[2] *adjective* white.

Weißwein *der* (PL *die* **Weißweine**) white wine.

weit *adjective, adverb* 1 wide, loose (*clothes*); 2 long; **eine weite Reise** a long journey; 3 far; **wie weit ist es?** how far is it?; **ist es noch weit?** is it much further?; **so weit wie möglich** as far as possible; **bei weitem** by far; 4 **von weitem** from a distance; 5 **ich bin so weit** I'm ready; 6 **weit verbreitet**

△ NEW SPELLING: *See page xii*

widespread; **7 zu weit gehen** . to go too far.

weiten verb (PERF **hat sich geweitet**) **sich weiten** to stretch.

weiter adjective, adverb **1** further; **2** in addition; **3 etwas weiter tun** to go on doing something; **weiter nichts** nothing else; **weiter niemand** nobody else; **4 und so weiter** and so on.

weiterer, weitere, weiteres adjective **1** further; **2 ohne weiteres** just like that, easily; **3 bis auf weiteres** for the time being.

weiterfahren ◇ verb (PRES **fährt weiter**, IMPERF **fuhr weiter**, PERF **ist weitergefahren**) to go on.

weitergehen ◇ verb (IMPERF **ging weiter**, PERF **ist weitergegangen**) to go on.

weiterhin adverb **1** still; **2** in future; **3 etwas weiterhin tun** to go on doing something.

weitermachen verb (PERF **hat weitergemacht**) to carry on.

Weitsprung der long jump.

Weizen der wheat.

welcher, welche, welches adjective which; **welches Kleid?** which dress?; **um welche Zeit?** at what time? pronoun **1** which (one); **2** some; **brauchst du Briefmarken? ich habe welche** do you need stamps? I've got some; **3** any; **hast du welche?** have you got any?

Welle die (PL die **Wellen**) wave.

Wellensittich der (PL die **Wellensittiche**) budgerigar.

wellig adjective wavy.

Welt die (PL die **Welten**) world; **auf der ganzen Welt** in the whole world.

Weltall das universe.

Weltkrieg der (PL die **Weltkriege**) world war.

Weltmeister der (PL die **Weltmeister**) world champion.

Weltmeisterin die (PL die **Weltmeisterinnen**) world champion.

Weltmeisterschaft die (PL die **Weltmeisterschaften**) **1** world championship; **2 die Weltmeisterschaft** (football) the World Cup.

Weltraum der space.

wem pronoun to whom; **wem hat er das Geld gegeben?** who did he give the money to?

wen pronoun whom, who; **wen hast du eingeladen?** who did you invite?

Wende die **1** change; **2** reunification (of Germany).

wenig pronoun, adjective **1** little; **zu wenig** too little, not enough; **2 wenige** few; **in wenigen Wochen** in a few weeks. adverb little; **so wenig wie möglich** as little as possible.

weniger pronoun, adjective less, fewer; **sie hat weniger Geschenke bekommen** she got fewer presents;

◇ IRREGULAR VERB: See the verb table in the centre of the dictionary

immer weniger Geld less and less money; **immer weniger Häuser** fewer and fewer houses.
adverb, conjunction less; **zehn weniger fünf** ten minus five.

wenigste SEE **wenigster**.

wenigstens *adverb* at least.

wenigster, wenigste, wenigstes *adjective, pronoun* least; **am wenigsten** least; **sein Geschenk hat mir am wenigsten gefallen** I liked his present least.

wenn *conjunction* 1 when; **wenn ich in München bin, schreibe ich dir** I'll write to you when I'm in Munich; **immer, wenn** whenever; 2 if; **wenn es regnet** if it rains; 3 **außer wenn** unless.

wer *pronoun* who.

werben ◇ *verb* (PRES **wirbt**, IMPERF **warb**, PERF **hat geworben**) 1 to advertise; 2 to recruit (*members*).

Werbespot *der* (PL die **Werbespots**) advert, commercial.

Werbung *die* 1 advertising; **in der Werbung arbeiten** to work in advertising; 2 advert; **im Fernsehen kommt viel Werbung** there are many adverts on television; **Werbung für etwas machen** to advertise something.

werden ◇ *verb* (PRES **wird**, IMPERF **wurde**, PERF **ist geworden**) 1 to become; **Arzt werden** to become a doctor; 2 **müde werden** to get tired; **alt werden** to get old; **mir wird kalt** I'm getting cold; 3 **mir wurde schlecht** I felt sick; **blass werden**

to turn pale; 4 **wach werden** to wake up; 5 (*used to form the future tense*) will, shall; **sie wird anrufen** she'll ring; **sie wird gleich da sein** she'll be here in a minute; 6 (*used to form the passive*) to be; **gerufen werden** to be called; **er wurde gefragt** he was asked; 7 (*used to form the conditional*) **sie würde kommen** she would come; **ich würde gern kommen, aber ...** I'd like to come but ...

werfen ◇ *verb* (PRES **wirft**, IMPERF **warf**, PERF **hat geworfen**) to throw.

Werk *das* (PL die **Werke**) 1 work; 2 works (*a factory*).

Werken *das* handicraft.

Werkstatt *die* (PL die **Werkstätten**) workshop.

Werktag *der* (PL die **Werktage**) weekday.

werktags *adverb* on weekdays.

Werkzeug *das* (PL die **Werkzeuge**) tool.

wert *adjective* **viel wert sein** to be worth a lot; **nichts wert sein** to be worthless.

Wert *der* (PL die **Werte**) 1 value; **im Wert von hundert Mark** worth one hundred marks; 2 **auf etwas Wert legen** to attach importance to something; 3 **es hat doch keinen Wert** there's no point.

wertlos *adjective* worthless.

wertvoll *adjective* valuable.

Wesen *das* (PL die **Wesen**) 1 nature, manner; 2 creature.

△ NEW SPELLING: *See page xii*

wesentlich adjective essential; **im Wesentlichen**△ essentially.
adverb considerably.

weshalb adverb why.

Wespe die (PL die **Wespen**) wasp.

wessen pronoun whose.

Wessi der (informal) (PL die **Wessis**) West German.

Weste die (PL die **Westen**) waistcoat.

Westen der west.

Westinder der (PL die **Westinder**) West Indian.

Westinderin die (PL die **Westinderinnen**) West Indian.

westlich adjective 1 western; 2 westerly.
adverb, preposition ←(+GEN)
westlich von Wien west of Vienna; **westlich der Stadt** to the west of the town.

weswegen adverb why.

Wettbewerb der (PL die **Wettbewerbe**) competition, contest.

Wette die (PL die **Wetten**) bet; **mit jemandem um die Wette laufen** to race somebody.

wetten verb (PERF hat **gewettet**) to bet; **mit jemandem um etwas wetten** to bet somebody something.

Wetter das weather.

Wetterbericht der (PL die **Wetterberichte**) weather report.

Wettervorhersage die weather forecast.

Wettkampf der (PL die **Wettkämpfe**) contest.

Wettlauf der race.

wichtig adjective important.

wickeln verb (PERF hat **gewickelt**) 1 to wind; 2 **ein Kind wickeln** to change a baby.

Widder der (PL die **Widder**) 1 ram; 2 Aries; **Jan ist Widder** Jan's Aries.

widerlic· adjective disgusting.

widersprechen ✧ verb (PRES **widerspricht**, IMPERF **widersprach**, PERF **hat widersprochen**) to contradict.

Widerspruch der (PL die **Widersprüche**) contradiction.

Widerstand der resistance.

widerstehen ✧ verb (IMPERF **widerstand**, PERF **hat widerstanden**) to resist.

widmen verb (PERF hat **gewidmet**) 1 to dedicate; 2 to devote; 3 **sich einer Sache widmen** to devote yourself to something.

wie adverb 1 how; **wie geht's?** how are you?; **wie viel?**△ how much?, how many?; **um wie viel**△ **Uhr kommst du?** (at) what time are you coming?; 2 **wie ist Ihr Name?** what is your name?; **wie ist das Wetter?** what's the weather like?; 3 **wie bitte?** sorry?
conjunction 1 as; **so schnell wie möglich** as quickly as possible; 2 like; **wie du** like you; 3 **wie zum Beispiel** such as.

wieder adverb 1 again; **sie ist**

wieder da she's back again;
2 jemanden wieder erkennen △ to
recognize somebody; **etwas wieder
finden** △ to find something (again);
etwas wieder verwerten △ to
recycle something.

wiederbekommen ◇ *verb* (IMPERF
bekam wieder, PERF **hat
wiederbekommen**) to get back.

wiedererkennen SEE **wieder**.

wiederfinden SEE **wieder**.

wiederholen *verb* (PERF **hat
wiederholt**) **1** to repeat; **2** to revise
(*work at school*); **3 sich
wiederholen** to recur; **er hat sich
wiederholt** he's repeated himself.

Wiederholung *die* (PL *die*
Wiederholungen) **1** repetition;
2 repeat; **3** revision (*at school*).

Wiederhören *das* **auf
Wiederhören!** (*said on the phone*)
goodbye!

wiederkommen ◇ *verb* (IMPERF
kam wieder, PERF **ist
wiedergekommen**) **1** to come back;
2 to come again.

wiedersehen SEE **sehen**.

Wiedersehen *das* (PL *die*
Wiedersehen) **1** reunion; **2 auf
Wiedersehen!** goodbye!

wiedervereinigen SEE **vereinigen**.

Wiedervereinigung *die*
reunification.

wiederverwerten SEE **wieder**.

Wiege *die* (PL *die* **Wiegen**) cradle.

wiegen ◇ *verb* (IMPERF **wog**, PERF **hat
gewogen**) to weigh.

Wiegenlied *das* (PL *die*
Wiegenlieder) lullaby.

Wien *das* Vienna.

Wiese *die* (PL *die* **Wiesen**) meadow.

wieso *adverb* why.

wieviel SEE **wie**.

wievielmal *adverb* how often.

**wievielter, wievielte,
wievieltes** *adjective* **1** which;
**2 die wievielte Querstraße ist das
von hier aus?** how many roads is
that from here?; **der Wievielte ist
heute?** what's the date today?

wild *adjective* wild.

Wildleder *das* suede.

Wildpark *der* (PL *die* **Wildparks**)
wildlife park.

will SEE **wollen**.

Wille *der* will; **seinen Willen
durchsetzen** to get your own way.

willkommen *adjective* welcome.

willst SEE **wollen**.

Wimper *die* (PL *die* **Wimpern**)
eyelash.

Wimperntusche *die* (PL *die*
Wimperntuschen) mascara.

Wind *der* (PL *die* **Winde**) wind.

Windel *die* (PL *die* **Windeln**) nappy.

Windhund *der* (PL *die* **Windhunde**)
greyhound.

windig *adjective* windy.

△ NEW SPELLING: *See page xii*

Windmühle die (PL die Windmühlen) windmill.

Windpocken plural noun chickenpox.

Windschutzscheibe die (PL die Windschutzscheiben) windscreen.

Winkel der (PL die Winkel) 1 angle; 2 corner.

winken verb (PERF hat gewinkt) to wave.

Winter der (PL die Winter) winter.

winzig adjective tiny.

wir pronoun we; **wir sind es** it's us; **wir alle** all of us.

Wirbelsäule die (PL die Wirbelsäulen) spine.

wirbt SEE werben.

wird SEE werden.

wirft SEE werfen.

wirken verb (PERF hat gewirkt) 1 to have an effect; 2 **gegen etwas wirken** to be effective against something; 3 to seem (sad, happy).

wirklich adjective real. adverb really.

Wirklichkeit die reality.

wirksam adjective effective.

Wirkung die (PL die Wirkungen) effect.

wirst SEE werden.

Wirt der (PL die Wirte) landlord.

Wirtin die (PL die Wirtinnen) landlady.

Wirtschaft die (PL die Wirtschaften) 1 economy; 2 pub.

wirtschaftlich adjective economic.

Wirtshaus das (PL die Wirtshäuser) pub.

wischen verb (PERF hat gewischt) to wipe.

wissen ◇ verb (PRES weiß, IMPERF wusste △, PERF hat gewusst △) to know; **ich weiß, dass er in London wohnt** I know he lives in London; **ich wüsste gern …** I'd like to know …; **von etwas wissen** to know about something; **weißt du was?** you know what?

Wissen das knowledge.

Wissenschaft die (PL die Wissenschaften) science.

Wissenschaftler der (PL die Wissenschaftler) scientist.

Wissenschaftlerin die (PL die Wissenschaftlerinnen) scientist.

wissenschaftlich adjective scientific.

Witwe die (PL die Witwen) widow.

Witwer der (PL die Witwer) widower.

Witz der (PL die Witze) joke.

witzig adjective funny.

wo adverb where; **wo seid ihr gewesen?** where have you been?; **in München, wo Markus seit einem Jahr lebt** in Munich, where Markus has been living for a year; **wo immer** wherever. conjunction 1 seeing that;

◇ IRREGULAR VERB: See the verb table in the centre of the dictionary

2 although; **jetzt ist sie mir böse, wo ich doch so nett zu ihr war** now she's angry with me, although I've been so nice to her.

woanders *adverb* elsewhere.

Woche *die* (PL *die* **Wochen**) week.

Wochenende *das* (PL *die* **Wochenenden**) weekend.

wochenlang *adverb* for weeks.

Wochentag *der* (PL *die* **Wochentage**) weekday.

wochentags *adverb* on weekdays.

wöchentlich *adjective* weekly.

wofür *adverb* what ... for; **wofür brauchst du das Geld?** what do you need the money for?

wog SEE **wiegen**.

woher *adverb* where ... from; **woher ist er?** where does he come from?; **woher weißt du das?** how do you know?

wohin *adverb* where ... (to); **wohin geht ihr?** where are you going?

wohl *adverb* **1** well; **sich wohl fühlen** to feel well; **ich fühle mich heute nicht wohl** I don't feel well today; **2 sich wohl fühlen** to be happy; **Anni fühlt sich in London wohl** Anni is happy in London; **3** jemandem **wohl tun** △ to do somebody good; **4** probably; **er hat den Zug wohl verpasst** he probably missed the train; **du bist wohl verrückt!** you must be mad!; **5 wohl kaum** hardly.

Wohl *das* **1** welfare, well-being; **2 zu** seinem **Wohl** for his benefit; **3 zum Wohl!** cheers!

wohlhabend *adjective* well-off.

wohltun SEE **wohl**.

wohnen *verb* (PERF **hat gewohnt**) **1** to live; **2** to stay (*for a short time*).

Wohngemeinschaft *die* (PL *die* **Wohngemeinschaften**) people sharing a flat/house; **wir wohnen in einer Wohngemeinschaft** we share a flat.

wohnhaft *adjective* resident.

Wohnheim *das* (PL *die* **Wohnheime**) **1** hostel; **2** home (*for old people*).

Wohnort *der* (PL *die* **Wohnorte**) place of residence.

Wohnsitz *der* (PL *die* **Wohnsitze**) place of residence.

Wohnung *die* (PL *die* **Wohnungen**) flat.

Wohnwagen *der* (PL *die* **Wohnwagen**) caravan.

Wohnzimmer *das* (PL *die* **Wohnzimmer**) living room.

Wolf *der* (PL *die* **Wölfe**) wolf.

Wolke *die* (PL *die* **Wolken**) cloud.

Wolkenkratzer *der* (PL *die* **Wolkenkratzer**) skyscraper.

wolkig *adjective* cloudy.

Wolldecke *die* (PL *die* **Wolldecken**) blanket.

Wolle *die* wool.

wollen ◇ *verb* (PRES **will**, IMPERF **wollte**, PERF **hat gewollt**) **1** to want; **Anne will einen Hund** Anne wants a

△ NEW SPELLING: *See page xii*

dog; **ich will nach Hause** I want to go home; **2 sie wollte gerade gehen** she was just about to go; **3 ganz wie du willst** as you like.

womit *adverb* **1** what ... with; **womit hast du das gewaschen?** what did you wash it with?; **2** with which.

womöglich *adverb* possibly.

wonach *adverb* **1** what ... for; **wonach suchst du?** what are you looking for?; **wonach riecht es?** what does it smell of?; **2** after which, according to which; **eine Regelung, wonach wir eine Stunde mehr arbeiten müssen** a rule according to which we have to work an extra hour.

woran *adverb* what ... of; **1 woran denkst du?** what are you thinking of?; **woran hast du ihn erkannt?** how did you recognize him?; **2** on which, of which; **nichts, woran man sich verletzen könnte** nothing you could hurt yourself on.

worauf *adverb* **1** what ... on, what ... for; **worauf hast du die Vase gestellt?** what did you put the vase on?; **worauf wartet ihr?** what are you waiting for?; **2** on which, for which; **das Regal, worauf das Radio steht** the shelf the radio is on; **das Einzige, worauf ich mich freue** the only thing I'm looking forward to.

woraus *adverb* **1** what ... from, what ... of; **woraus ist das?** what's it made of?; **2** from which; **es gibt nichts, woraus wir trinken können** there isn't anything we can drink out of.

worin *adverb* **1** what ... in, in what; **2** in which; **die Punkte, worin ich mit dir übereinstimme** the points I agree with you on.

Wort *das* (PL *die* **Worte/Wörter**) word; **mir fehlen die Worte** I'm lost for words; **ich habe heute zwanzig neue Wörter gelernt** I've learnt twenty new words today.

Wörterbuch *das* (PL *die* **Wörterbücher**) dictionary.

wörtlich *adjective* word for word.

Wortschatz *der* vocabulary.

Wortspiel *das* (PL *die* **Wortspiele**) pun.

worüber *adverb* **1** what ... over, what ... about; **worüber lacht ihr?** what are you laughing about?; **2** over which, about which.

worum *adverb* **1** about what; **worum geht es?** what's it about?; **worum hat sie dich gebeten?** what did she ask you for?; **2** for which; **3** about which.

wovon *adverb* **1** what ... from, what ... about; **wovon redet ihr?** what are you talking about?; **2** from which, about which; **der Geruch, wovon mir schlecht geworden ist** the smell which made me feel sick.

wovor *adverb* **1** what ... of; **wovor hast du Angst?** what are you frightened of?; **2** in front of what; **3** of which; **4** in front of which; **der Turm, wovor wir stehen** the tower we are standing in front of.

wozu *adverb* **1** what ... for, why; **wozu brauchst du das?** what do you need it for?; **wozu?** what for?; **2** to which, for which; **wozu ich dir raten würde** which I would advise.

Wrack das (PL die Wracks) wreck.

wuchs SEE **wachsen**.

Wuchs der growth.

wund adjective sore.

Wunde die (PL die Wunden) wound.

Wunder das (PL die Wunder) miracle; **kein Wunder!** no wonder!

wunderbar adjective wonderful.

wundern verb (PERF hat sich gewundert) **sich wundern** to be surprised.

wunderschön adjective beautiful.

wundervoll adjective wonderful.

Wunsch der (PL die Wünsche) wish; **auf Wunsch** on request; **haben Sie sonst noch einen Wunsch?** will there be anything else?

wünschen verb (PERF hat gewünscht) **1** to wish; **ich wünsche dir alles Gute zum Geburtstag** I wish you a happy birthday; **ich wünschte, ich könnte …** I wish I could …; **was wünschen Sie?** can I help you?; **2 sich etwas wünschen** to want something.

wünschenswert adjective desirable.

wurde, würde, wurden, würden, wurdest, würdest, wurdet, würdet SEE **werden**.

Wurf der (PL die Würfe) throw.

Würfel der (PL die Würfel) **1** dice (in games); **2** cube.

würfeln verb (PERF hat gewürfelt) to throw the dice.

Wurm der (PL die Würmer) worm.

Wurst die (PL die Würste) **1** sausage; **2 das ist mir Wurst** (informal) I couldn't care less.

Würstchen das (PL die Würstchen) (little) sausage.

Wurzel die (PL die Wurzeln) root.

würzen verb (PERF hat gewürzt) to season.

würzig adjective spicy.

wusch SEE **waschen**.

wusste Δ SEE **wissen**.

Wüste die (PL die Wüsten) desert.

Wut die rage; **eine Wut auf jemanden haben** to be furious with somebody.

wütend adjective furious.

X x

x-beliebig adjective (informal) any; **eine x-beliebige Zahl** any number (you like).

x-mal adverb (informal) umpteen times; **zum x-ten Mal** for the umpteenth time.

Xylophon das (PL die Xylophone) xylophone.

Δ NEW SPELLING: See page xii

Y y

Yoga *das* yoga.

Ypsilon *das* (PL *die* Ypsilons) Y.

Z z

zaghaft *adjective* 1 timid;
2 tentative.

zäh *adjective* tough.

Zahl *die* (PL *die* Zahlen) 1 number;
2 figure.

zahlen *verb* (PERF hat gezahlt) 1 to
pay; **hast du schon gezahlt?** have
you paid?; 2 to pay for; **bitte zahlen!**
the bill please!

zählen *verb* (PERF hat gezählt) 1 to
count; **auf jemanden zählen** to
count on somebody; **jemanden zu
seinen Freunden zählen** to count
somebody among your friends;
2 **zählen zu** to be one of.

Zähler *der* (PL *die* Zähler) meter.

zahlreich *adjective* numerous.

Zahlung *die* (PL *die* Zahlungen)
payment.

Zählung *die* (PL *die* Zählungen)
1 count; 2 census.

zahm *adjective* tame.

Zahn *der* (PL *die* Zähne) tooth.

Zahnarzt *der* (PL *die* Zahnärzte)
dentist.

Zahnärztin *die* (PL *die*
Zahnärztinnen) dentist.

Zahnbürste *die* (PL *die*
Zahnbürsten) toothbrush.

Zahnfleisch *das* gums.

Zahnpasta *die* (PL *die* Zahnpasten)
toothpaste.

Zahnschmerzen *plural noun*
toothache.

Zange *die* (PL *die* Zangen) pliers.

zanken *verb* (PERF hat sich gezankt)
sich zanken to squabble.

zappeln *verb* (PERF hat gezappelt)
1 to wriggle; 2 to fidget.

zart *adjective* 1 delicate, soft;
2 gentle; 3 tender.

zärtlich *adjective* affectionate.

Zauber *der* 1 magic; 2 spell.

Zauberer *der* (PL *die* Zauberer)
magician, conjurer.

zauberhaft *adjective* enchanting.

zaubern *verb* (PERF hat gezaubert)
to do magic.

Zaun *der* (PL *die* Zäune) fence.

z.B. (*zum Beispiel*) e.g.

Zebra *das* (PL *die* Zebras) zebra.

Zebrastreifen *der* (PL *die*
Zebrastreifen) zebra crossing.

Zeh *der* (PL *die* Zehen) toe.

Zehe *die* (PL *die* Zehen) 1 toe;
2 clove (*of garlic*).

◇ IRREGULAR VERB: *See the verb table in the centre of the dictionary*

zehn *number* ten.

Zehntel *das* (PL *die* Zehntel) tenth.

zehnter, zehnte, zehntes *adjective* tenth.

Zeichen *das* (PL *die* Zeichen) 1 sign; 2 signal.

zeichnen *verb* (PERF *hat* gezeichnet) to draw.

Zeichnung *die* (PL *die* Zeichnungen) drawing.

Zeigefinger *der* (PL *die* Zeigefinger) index finger.

zeigen *verb* (PERF hat gezeigt) 1 to show; **Peter hat uns sein neues Auto gezeigt** Peter showed us his new car; 2 to point; **auf jemanden zeigen** to point at somebody; 3 **sich zeigen** to appear; 4 **es hat sich gezeigt, dass ...** it has become clear that ...; **es wird sich zeigen** time will tell.

Zeiger *der* (PL *die* Zeiger) hand.

Zeile *die* (PL *die* Zeilen) line.

Zeit *die* (PL *die* Zeiten) 1 time; **sich Zeit lassen** to take your time; **ich habe keine Zeit mehr** I haven't got any more time; **eine Zeit lang** for a time; 2 **es hat Zeit** there's no hurry; **die erste Zeit** at first; **in nächster Zeit** in the near future.

Zeitalter *das* (PL *die* Zeitalter) age.

Zeitlang *die* SEE Zeit.

Zeitlupe *die* slow motion; **in Zeitlupe** in slow motion.

Zeitraum *der* (PL *die* Zeiträume) period.

Zeitschrift *die* (PL *die* Zeitschriften) magazine.

Zeitung *die* (PL *die* Zeitungen) newspaper.

Zeitverschwendung *die* waste of time.

zeitweise *adverb* at times.

Zeitungshändler *der* (PL *die* Zeitungshändler) newsagent.

Zelle *die* (PL *die* Zellen) 1 cell; 2 booth.

Zelt *das* (PL *die* Zelte) tent.

zelten *verb* (PERF hat gezeltet) to camp.

Zeltplatz *der* (PL *die* Zeltplätze) campsite.

Zement *der* cement.

Zentimeter *der* (PL *die* Zentimeter) centimetre.

Zentimetermaß *das* (PL *die* Zentimetermaße) tape measure.

zentral *adjective* central.

Zentrale *die* (PL *die* Zentralen) 1 central office, head office; 2 headquarters; 3 (telephone) exchange, switchboard.

Zentralheizung *die* central heating.

Zentrum *das* (PL *die* Zentren) centre.

zerbrechen ◊ *verb* (PRES **zerbricht**, IMPERF **zerbrach**, PERF **hat zerbrochen**) 1 to break; **Irene hat meine Vase zerbrochen** Irene broke my vase; 2 (PERF **ist zerbrochen**) to break; spelling

△ NEW SPELLING: *See page xii*

Untertasse ist zerbrochen the saucer broke.

zerbrechlich *adjective* fragile.

Zeremonie *die* (PL *die* Zeremonien) ceremony.

zerreißen ◇ *verb* (IMPERF zerriss △, PERF hat zerrissen) 1 to tear; **sie hat sich das Kleid zerrissen** she tore her dress; 2 to tear up; **Anna hat seinen Brief zerrissen** Anna tore up his letter; 3 (PERF ist zerrissen) to tear; **das Hemd ist in der Wäsche zerrissen** the shirt got torn in the washing.

zerschlagen ◇ *verb* (PRES zerschlägt, IMPERF zerschlug, PERF hat zerschlagen) 1 to smash, to smash up; 2 **sich zerschlagen** to fall through (*of plans*); **meine Hoffnungen haben sich zerschlagen** my hopes were dashed.

zerschneiden ◇ *verb* (IMPERF zerschnitt, PERF hat zerschnitten) to cut, to cut up.

zerstören *verb* (PERF hat zerstört) to destroy.

Zerstörung *die* destruction.

zerstreuen *verb* (PERF hat zerstreut) 1 to scatter; 2 **jemanden zerstreuen** to entertain somebody; 3 **sich zerstreuen** to take your mind off things; 4 **die Menge hat sich zerstreut** the crowd's dispersed.

zerstreut *adjective* absent-minded.

Zettel *der* (PL *die* Zettel) 1 piece of paper; 2 note; 3 leaflet.

Zeug *das* (*informal*) 1 stuff; 2 things, gear; 3 **dummes Zeug** nonsense.

Zeuge *der* (PL *die* Zeugen) witness.

Zeugin *die* (PL *die* Zeuginnen) witness.

Zeugnis *das* (PL *die* Zeugnisse) 1 certificate; 2 report (*at school*).

Zickzack *der* (PL *die* Zickzacke) zigzag; **im Zickzack laufen** to zigzag.

Ziege *die* (PL *die* Ziegen) goat.

Ziegel *der* (PL *die* Ziegel) 1 brick; 2 tile.

ziehen ◇ *verb* (IMPERF zog, PERF hat gezogen) 1 to pull; **an etwas ziehen** to pull on something; **einen Zahn ziehen** to pull out a tooth; 2 to draw; **einen Strich ziehen** to draw a line; **eine Niete ziehen** to draw a blank; 3 **die Bremse ziehen** to put on the brakes; 4 to grow (*vegetables, flowers*); 5 **sich ziehen** to run (*of a path, road*); 6 (PERF ist gezogen) to move; **sie sind nach Berlin gezogen** they've moved to Berlin.

Ziel *das* (PL *die* Ziele) 1 destination; 2 goal, aim; 3 finish (*in sport*).

zielen *verb* (PERF hat gezielt) to aim; **auf etwas zielen** to aim at something.

Zielscheibe *die* (PL *die* Zielscheiben) target.

ziemlich *adjective* fair. *adverb* 1 quite; **ziemlich viel** quite a lot; 2 fairly; **ihre Eltern haben ein**

◇ **IRREGULAR VERB: See the verb table in the centre of the dictionary**

ziemlich großes Haus her parents have a fairly large house.

zierlich adjective dainty.

Ziffer die (PL die **Ziffern**) figure.

Zifferblatt das (PL die **Zifferblätter**) face, dial.

zig adjective (informal) umpteen.

Zigarette die (PL die **Zigaretten**) cigarette.

Zigarre die (PL die **Zigarren**) cigar.

Zigeuner der (PL die **Zigeuner**) gypsy.

Zigeunerin die (PL die **Zigeunerinnen**) gypsy.

Zimmer das (PL die **Zimmer**) room; **Zimmer mit Frühstück** bed and breakfast; **'Zimmer frei'** 'vacancies'.

Zimmermädchen das (PL die **Zimmermädchen**) chambermaid.

Zimt der cinnamon.

Zink das zinc.

zirka adverb about.

Zirkel der (PL die **Zirkel**) pair of compasses.

Zirkus der (PL die **Zirkusse**) circus.

zischen verb (PERF hat gezischt) to hiss.

Zitat das (PL die **Zitate**) quotation.

zitieren verb (PERF hat zitiert) to quote.

Zitrone die (PL die **Zitronen**) lemon.

Zitronensaft der (PL die **Zitronensäfte**) lemon juice.

zittern verb (PERF hat gezittert) to tremble; **vor Kälte zittern** to shiver.

Zivildienst der community service.

Zivilisation die (PL die **Zivilisationen**) civilization.

zog SEE **ziehen**.

zögern verb (PERF hat gezögert) to hesitate.

Zoll der (PL die **Zölle**) 1 customs; **am Zoll** at customs; 2 duty; **Zoll auf etwas bezahlen** to pay duty on something.

Zollbeamte der (PL die **Zollbeamten**) customs officer.

Zollbeamtin die (PL die **Zollbeamtinnen**) customs officer.

zollfrei adjective duty-free.

Zollkontrolle die (PL die **Zollkontrollen**) customs check.

Zone die (PL die **Zonen**) zone.

Zoo der (PL die **Zoos**) Zoo.

Zoomobjektiv das (PL die **Zoomobjektive**) zoom lens.

Zopf der (PL die **Zöpfe**) plait.

Zorn der anger.

zornig adjective angry.

zu preposition ←(+DAT) 1 to; **ich gehe zum Arzt** I'm going to the doctor's; **zu einer Party eingeladen sein** to be invited to a party; **2 zu ... hin** towards; **zum Fenster hin** towards the window; **er kam in through this door; 3 with; das passt nicht zu meinem Mantel** it doesn't go with my coat; **es gab Wein zum Käse** there was wine with the cheese; **4** at; **zu Weihnachten** at Christmas; **zu Hause** at home; **5 zu etwas werden** to turn into something; **6 zu diesem Zweck** for this purpose; **was schenkst du Karin zum Geburtstag?** what are you giving Karin for her birthday?; **zum Spaß** for fun; **zum ersten Mal** for the first time; **7 sich zu etwas äußern** to comment on something; **Papier zum Schreiben** paper to write on; **8 nett zu jemandem sein** to be nice to somebody; **9 sie waren zu zweit** there were two of them; **eine Marke zu achtzig Pfennig** an 80-pfennig stamp; **es steht drei zu zwei** the score is 3–2; **10 zu Fuß** on foot.

adverb **1** too; **zu groß** too big; **2** closed; **zu haben** △ to be closed; **Tür zu!** (*informal*) shut the door!; **3 zu sein** △ to be closed; **alle Läden sind zu gewesen** the shops were all closed; **4** towards (*indicating direction*); **5 mach zu!** (*informal*) hurry up!

conjunction to; **nichts zu essen** nothing to eat; **zu verkaufen** for sale.

zuallererst *adverb* first of all.

zuallerletzt *adverb* last of all.

Zubehör *das* accessories.

zubereiten *verb* (PERF **hat zubereitet**) to prepare; **sie bereitet das Essen zu** she's preparing the meal.

zubinden ◇ *verb* (IMPERF **band zu**, PERF **hat zugebunden**) to tie, to tie up.

zubringen ◇ *verb* (IMPERF **brachte zu**, PERF **hat zugebracht**) to spend; **sie bringt viel Zeit bei ihrem Freund zu** she spends a lot of time with her boyfriend.

Zucchini *plural noun* courgettes.

züchten *verb* (PERF **hat gezüchtet**) to breed.

zucken *verb* (PERF **hat gezuckt**) to twitch.

Zucker *der* sugar.

Zuckerguss △ *der* icing.

zuckerkrank *adjective* diabetic.

zudecken *verb* (PERF **hat zugedeckt**) **1** to cover up, to cover; **2** to tuck up (*in bed*).

zueinander *adverb* **1** to one another; **lieb zueinander sein** to be nice to one another; **2** together; **zueinander passen** to go together; **zueinander halten** △ to stick together.

zuerst *adverb* **1** first; **2** at first.

Zufahrt *die* (PL *die* **Zufahrten**) **1** access; **2** drive(way).

Zufall *der* (PL *die* **Zufälle**) **1** chance; **durch Zufall** by chance; **2** coincidence; **so ein komischer Zufall** such a strange coincidence; **per Zufall traf ich ihn in der U-Bahn** I happened to meet him on the tube.

zufällig *adjective* chance; **das war rein zufällig** it was purely by chance; *adverb* by chance; **kannst du mir zufällig zehn Mark leihen?** could

◇ **IRREGULAR VERB: See the verb table in the centre of the dictionary**

you lend me ten marks by any chance?

zufrieden *adjective* 1 content; 2 satisfied; **mit etwas zufrieden sein** to be satisfied with something. *adverb* **jemanden zufrieden lassen**△ to leave somebody in peace; **jemanden zufrieden stellen**△ to satisfy somebody.

zufriedenlassen, zufriedenstellen SEE zufrieden.

Zug *der* (PL *die* Züge) 1 train; 2 procession; 3 characteristic, trait; 4 move (*in games*); 5 swig (*when drinking*); 6 drag (*when smoking*); 7 **in einem Zug** in one go.

Zugabe *die* (PL *die* Zugaben) 1 free gift; 2 encore.

Zugang *der* (PL *die* Zugänge) access.

zugeben ◇ *verb* (PRES **gibt zu**, IMPERF **gab zu**, PERF **hat zugegeben**) 1 to add; 2 to admit.

zugehen ◇ *verb* (IMPERF **ging zu**, PERF **ist zugegangen**) 1 to close, to shut; **die Tür geht nicht zu** the door won't shut; 2 **auf etwas zugehen** to go towards something; **auf jemanden zugehen** to walk up to somebody; 3 **jemandem zugehen** to be sent to somebody; 4 **auf der Party ging es lustig zu** the party was good fun; 5 **dem Ende zugehen** to be nearing the end.

zügig *adjective* quick.

zugreifen ◇ *verb* (IMPERF **griff zu**, PERF **hat zugegriffen**) 1 to grab it/them; 2 to help yourself; 3 to lend a hand.

zugunsten *preposition* ←(+GEN) in favour of.

zuhaben SEE zu.

Zuhause *das* home.

zuhören *verb* (PERF **hat zugehört**) to listen.

Zuhörer *der* (PL *die* Zuhörer) listener.

Zuhörerin *die* (PL *die* Zuhörerinnen) listener.

zukommen ◇ *verb* (IMPERF **kam zu**, PERF **ist zugekommen**) 1 **auf jemanden zukommen** to come up to somebody; **nächstes Jahr kommt eine Menge Arbeit auf mich zu** I'm in for a lot of work next year; 2 **jemandem etwas zukommen lassen** to give somebody something; 3 **etwas auf sich zukommen lassen** to take things as they come.

Zukunft *die* future.

zukünftig *adjective* future.

zulassen ◇ *verb* (PRES **lässt zu**△, IMPERF **ließ zu**, PERF **hat zugelassen**) 1 to allow; 2 to register (*a car*); 3 to leave closed.

Zulassung *die* (PL *die* Zulassungen) 1 registration; 2 admission.

zuletzt *adverb* 1 last; 2 in the end.

zum = zu dem; 1 **etwas zum Lesen** something to read; 2 **spätestens zum fünften März** by 5 March at the latest; 3 **er hat es zum Fenster hinausgeworfen** he threw it out of the window.

△ NEW SPELLING: See page xii

zumachen verb (PERF hat zugemacht) 1 to close, to shut; 2 to fasten.

zumindest adverb at least.

zunächst adverb 1 first (of all); 2 at first.

Zuname der (PL die Zunamen) surname.

zunehmen ◇ verb (PRES nimmt zu, IMPERF nahm zu, PERF hat zugenommen) 1 to increase; 2 to put on weight.

Zunge die (PL die Zungen) tongue.

zur = zu der.

zurechtkommen ◇ verb (IMPERF kam zurecht, PERF ist zurechtgekommen) to cope, to manage.

zurechtlegen verb (PERF hat zurechtgelegt) 1 to put out ready; 2 sich eine Ausrede zurechtlegen to think up an excuse.

zurück adverb 1 back; 2 Hamburg, hin und zurück a return to Hamburg.

zurückbekommen ◇ verb (IMPERF bekam zurück, PERF hat zurückbekommen) to get back; zehn Pfennig zurückbekommen to get 10 pfennig change.

zurückbringen ◇ verb (IMPERF brachte zurück, PERF hat zurückgebracht) 1 to bring back; 2 to take back.

zurückfahren ◇ verb (PRES fährt zurück, IMPERF fuhr zurück, PERF ist zurückgefahren) 1 to go back; 2 to

drive back; 3 (PERF hat zurückgefahren) to drive back; jemanden zurückfahren to drive somebody back.

zurückgeben ◇ verb (PRES gibt zurück, IMPERF gab zurück, PERF hat zurückgegeben) to give back.

zurückgehen ◇ verb (IMPERF ging zurück, PERF ist zurückgegangen) 1 to go back; zurückgehen auf to go back to; 2 to go down; 3 to decrease.

zurückhalten ◇ verb (PRES hält zurück, IMPERF hielt zurück, PERF zurückgehalten) 1 to hold back; 2 sich zurückhalten to restrain yourself.

zurückkommen ◇ verb (IMPERF kam zurück, PERF ist zurückgekommen) 1 to come back; 2 to get back.

zurücklassen ◇ verb (PRES lässt zurück △, IMPERF ließ zurück, PERF zurückgelassen) to leave behind.

zurücklegen verb (PERF hat zurückgelegt) 1 to put back; 2 to keep, to put aside; 3 Geld für etwas zurücklegen to put money by for something; 4 to cover (a distance); 5 sich zurücklegen to lie back.

zurücknehmen ◇ verb (PRES nimmt zurück, IMPERF nahm zurück, PERF hat zurückgenommen) to take back.

zurückrufen ◇ verb (IMPERF rief zurück, PERF hat zurückgerufen) to call back.

zurücktreten ◇ verb (PRES tritt zurück, IMPERF trat zurück, PERF ist

◇ IRREGULAR VERB: *See the verb table in the centre of the dictionary*

zurückgetreten 1 to step back; 2 to resign.

zurückzahlen verb (PERF hat zurückgezahlt) to pay back.

zurückziehen ◇ verb (IMPERF zog zurück, PERF hat zurückgezogen) 1 to draw back; 2 to withdraw (*an offer*); 3 sich zurückziehen to withdraw, to retire.

zurzeit △ adverb at the moment.

Zusage die (PL die Zusagen) acceptance.

zusammen adverb 1 together; zusammen sein to be together; 2 altogether.

Zusammenarbeit die co-operation.

zusammenarbeiten verb (PERF hat zusammengearbeitet) to co-operate.

zusammenbleiben ◇ verb (IMPERF blieb zusammen, PERF ist zusammengeblieben) to stay together.

zusammenbrechen ◇ verb (PRES bricht zusammen, IMPERF brach zusammen, PERF ist zusammengebrochen) to collapse.

zusammenfassen verb (PERF hat zusammengefasst △) to summarize.

Zusammenfassung die (PL die Zusammenfassungen) summary.

zusammenhalten ◇ verb (PRES hält zusammen, IMPERF hielt zusammen, PERF hat zusammengehalten) 1 to hold together; 2 to keep together; 3 die

Kinder haben zusammengehalten the children stuck together.

Zusammenhang der (PL die Zusammenhänge) 1 context; 2 connection.

zusammenkommen ◇ verb (IMPERF kam zusammen, PERF ist zusammengekommen) 1 to meet; 2 to accumulate.

Zusammenkunft die (PL die Zusammenkünfte) meeting.

zusammenlegen verb (PERF hat zusammengelegt) 1 to put together; 2 to fold up; 3 to club together.

zusammennehmen ◇ verb (PRES nimmt zusammen, IMPERF nahm zusammen, PERF hat zusammengenommen) 1 to gather up; 2 to summon up, to collect; 3 sich zusammennehmen to pull yourself together.

zusammenpassen verb (PERF hat zusammengepasst △) 1 to match; 2 to be well matched (*of people*); 3 to fit together.

Zusammensein das get-together.

Zusammenstoß der (PL die Zusammenstöße) collision, crash.

zusammenstoßen ◇ verb (PRES stößt zusammen, IMPERF stieß zusammen, PERF ist zusammengestoßen) to collide, to crash.

zusammenzählen verb (PERF hat zusammengezählt) to add up.

△ NEW SPELLING: See page xii

zusätzlich *adjective* additional, extra.
adverb in addition, extra.

zuschauen *verb* (PERF hat zugeschaut) to watch.

Zuschauer *der* (PL die Zuschauer) 1 spectator; 2 viewer; 3 die Zuschauer the audience.

Zuschauerin *die* (PL die Zuschauerinnen) 1 spectator; 2 viewer.

Zuschlag *der* (PL die Zuschläge) 1 surcharge; 2 supplement.

Zuschuss△ *der* (PL die Zuschüsse) 1 contribution; 2 grant.

zusehen ◇ *verb* (PRES sieht zu, IMPERF sah zu, PERF hat zugesehen) 1 to watch; 2 zusehen, dass ... to see (to it) that ...

zusein SEE zu.

zusenden *verb* (PERF hat zugesendet) to send; jemandem etwas zusenden to send something to somebody.

Zustand *der* (PL die Zustände) 1 condition; 2 state.

zustande *adverb* zustande bringen to bring about; zustande kommen to come about.

zuständig *adjective* responsible.

Zustellung *die* (PL die Zustellungen) delivery.

zustimmen *verb* (PERF hat zugestimmt) to agree.

Zustimmung *die* (PL die

Zustimmungen) 1 agreement; 2 approval.

zustoßen ◇ *verb* (PRES stößt zu, IMPERF stieß zu, PERF ist zugestoßen) to happen.

Zutat *die* (PL die Zutaten) ingredient.

zutreffen ◇ *verb* (PRES trifft zu, IMPERF traf zu, PERF hat zugetroffen) auf etwas zutreffen to apply to something.

Zutritt *der* entry; Zutritt haben to have access.

zuverlässig *adjective* reliable.

zuviel SEE viel.

zuvor *adverb* 1 before; der Tag zuvor the day before; 2 first.

zuwenig SEE wenig.

zuzahlen *verb* (PERF hat zugezahlt) to pay extra.

zuziehen ◇ *verb* (IMPERF zog zu, PERF hat zugezogen) 1 to pull tight; 2 to draw (curtains); 3 to call in (an expert etc.); 4 (PERF ist zugezogen) to move into an area; 5 sich eine Verletzung zuziehen to sustain an injury; sich eine Erkältung zuziehen to catch a cold.

zuzüglich *preposition* ←(+GEN) plus.

zwang SEE zwingen.

Zwang *der* (PL die Zwänge) 1 compulsion; 2 urge; 3 obligation.

zwängen *verb* (PERF hat gezwängt) to squeeze.

zwanglos *adjective* casual, informal.

◇ IRREGULAR VERB: *See the verb table in the centre of the dictionary*

zwar *adverb* 1 admittedly; 2 ich war zwar dabei, habe aber nichts gesehen I was there, but I didn't see anything; 3 und zwar to be exact.

Zweck *der* (PL *die* Zwecke) 1 purpose; 2 point; es hat keinen Zweck there's no point.

zwecklos *adjective* pointless.

zwei *number* two.

zweideutig *adjective* ambiguous.

zweifach *adjective* twice.

Zweifel *der* (PL *die* Zweifel) doubt.

zweifelhaft *adjective* 1 doubtful; 2 dubious.

zweifellos *adverb* undoubtedly.

zweifeln *verb* (PERF hat gezweifelt) to doubt; an etwas zweifeln to doubt something.

Zweig *der* (PL *die* Zweige) branch.

zweihundert *number* two hundred.

zweimal *adverb* twice.

zweisprachig *adjective* bilingual.

zweit *adverb* zu zweit in twos; wir sind zu zweit there are two of us.

zweite SEE **zweiter**.

zweitens *adverb* secondly.

zweiter, zweite, zweites *adjective* second; Mario kam als Zweiter Mario was the second to arrive.

Zwerg *der* (PL *die* Zwerge) dwarf.

Zwiebel *die* (PL *die* Zwiebeln) 1 onion; 2 bulb.

Zwilling *der* (PL *die* Zwillinge) 1 twin; 2 Zwillinge Gemini; Markus ist Zwilling Markus is Gemini.

zwingen ◇ *verb* (IMPERF zwang, PERF hat gezwungen) 1 to force; 2 sich zwingen to force yourself.

zwinkern *verb* (PERF hat gezwinkert) to wink.

zwischen *preposition* ←(+DAT, *or* +ACC *with movement towards a place*) 1 between; 2 among (*a crowd*).

zwischendurch *adverb* 1 in between; 2 now and again.

Zwischenfall *der* (PL *die* Zwischenfälle) incident.

Zwischenlandung *die* (PL *die* Zwischenlandungen) stop-over.

Zwischenraum *der* (PL *die* Zwischenräume) gap, space.

Zwischenzeit *die* in der Zwischenzeit in the meantime.

zwo *number* two.

zwölf *number* twelve.

zwoter, zwote, zwotes *adjective* second.

△ NEW SPELLING: See page xii

VERB TABLES
AND FORMS

On the following pages you will find forms for a regular German verb **machen** followed by the forms for a reflexive verb **sich waschen** and then the forms for the twelve most important irregular verbs in alphabetical order: **dürfen, essen, fahren, gehen, haben, kommen, können, müssen, sein, sollen, werden, wissen**.

After these are given the main forms for other irregular verbs. Note that the forms for separable verbs such as **aufstehen** are not given as they can be looked up under the base form (**stehen**).

machen
to do *or* to make

Imperative	Past participle
mach!	hat gemacht
macht!	
machen Sie!	

Present
ich mache
du machst
er* macht
wir machen
ihr macht
sie machen

Present subjunctive
ich mache
du machest
er mache
wir machen
ihr machet
sie machen

Perfect
ich habe gemacht
du hast gemacht
er hat gemacht
wir haben gemacht
ihr habt gemacht
sie haben gemacht

Imperfect
ich machte
du machtest
er machte
wir machten
ihr machtet
sie machten

Future
ich werde machen
du wirst machen
er wird machen
wir werden machen
ihr werdet machen
sie werden machen

Conditional
ich würde machen
du würdest machen
er würde machen
wir würden machen
ihr würdet machen
sie würden machen

* er *should be read as* er/sie/es

2

sich waschen
to wash (oneself)

Imperative
wasch dich!
wascht euch!
waschen Sie sich!

Past participle
hat sich
gewaschen

Present
ich wasche mich
du wäschst dich
er wäscht sich
wir waschen uns
ihr wascht euch
sie waschen sich

Present subjunctive
ich wasche mich
du waschest dich
er wasche sich
wir waschen uns
ihr waschet euch
sie waschen sich

Perfect
ich habe mich gewaschen
du hast dich gewaschen
er hat sich gewaschen
wir haben uns gewaschen
ihr habt euch gewaschen
sie haben sich gewaschen

Imperfect
ich wusch mich
du wuschst dich
er wusch sich
wir wuschen uns
ihr wuscht euch
sie wuschen sich

Future
ich werde mich waschen
du wirst dich waschen
er wird sich waschen
wir werden uns waschen
ihr werdet euch waschen
sie werden sich waschen

Conditional
ich würde mich waschen
du würdest dich waschen
er würde sich waschen
wir würden uns waschen
ihr würdet euch waschen
sie würden sich waschen

Note: New German spellings are
used throughout this verb table.
For a general note on the
German spelling reform see
page xii.

dürfen
to be allowed

Imperative
—

Past participle
hat gedurft

Present	**Present subjunctive**
ich darf	ich dürfe
du darfst	du dürfest
er darf	er dürfe
wir dürfen	wir dürfen
ihr dürft	ihr dürfet
sie dürfen	sie dürfen

Perfect	**Imperfect**
ich habe gedurft	ich durfte
du hast gedurft	du durftest
er hat gedurft	er durfte
wir haben gedurft	wir durften
ihr habt gedurft	ihr durftet
sie haben gedurft	sie durften

Future	**Conditional**
ich werde dürfen	ich würde dürfen
du wirst dürfen	du würdest dürfen
er wird dürfen	er würde dürfen
wir werden dürfen	wir würden dürfen
ihr werdet dürfen	ihr würdet dürfen
sie werden dürfen	sie würden dürfen

4

Imperative	Past participle	**essen**
iss!	hat gegessen	to eat
esst!		
essen Sie!		

Present	**Present subjunctive**
ich esse	ich esse
du isst	du essest
er isst	er esse
wir essen	wir essen
ihr esst	ihr esset
sie essen	sie essen

Perfect	**Imperfect**
ich habe gegessen	ich aß
du hast gegessen	du aßest
er hat gegessen	er aß
wir haben gegessen	wir aßen
ihr habt gegessen	ihr aßt
sie haben gegessen	sie aßen

Future	**Conditional**
ich werde essen	ich würde essen
du wirst essen	du würdest essen
er wird essen	er würde essen
wir werden essen	wir würden essen
ihr werdet essen	ihr würdet essen
sie werden essen	sie würden essen

fahren
to drive *or* to go

Imperative	Past participle
fahr! fahrt! fahren Sie!	ist gefahren

Present
ich fahre
du fährst
er fährt
wir fahren
ihr fahrt
sie fahren

Present subjunctive
ich fahre
du fahrest
er fahre
wir fahren
ihr fahret
sie fahren

Perfect
ich bin gefahren
du bist gefahren
er ist gefahren
wir sind gefahren
ihr seid gefahren
sie sind gefahren

Imperfect
ich fuhr
du fuhrst
er fuhr
wir fuhren
ihr fuhrt
sie fuhren

Future
ich werde fahren
du wirst fahren
er wird fahren
wir werden fahren
ihr werdet fahren
sie werden fahren

Conditional
ich würde fahren
du würdest fahren
er würde fahren
wir würden fahren
ihr würdet fahren
sie würden fahren

6

Imperative	Past participle	**gehen**
geh!	ist gegangen	to go
geht!		
gehen Sie!		

Present

ich gehe
du gehst
er geht
wir gehen
ihr geht
sie gehen

Present subjunctive

ich gehe
du gehest
er gehe
wir gehen
ihr gehet
sie gehen

Perfect

ich bin gegangen
du bist gegangen
er ist gegangen
wir sind gegangen
ihr seid gegangen
sie sind gegangen

Imperfect

ich ging
du gingst
er ging
wir gingen
ihr gingt
sie gingen

Future

ich werde gehen
du wirst gehen
er wird gehen
wir werden gehen
ihr werdet gehen
sie werden gehen

Conditional

ich würde gehen
du würdest gehen
er würde gehen
wir würden gehen
ihr würdet gehen
sie würden gehen

haben
to have

Imperative	Past participle
hab!	hat gehabt
habt!	
haben Sie!	

Present	Present subjunctive
ich habe	ich habe
du hast	du habest
er hat	er habe
wir haben	wir haben
ihr habt	ihr habet
sie haben	sie haben

Perfect	Imperfect
ich habe gehabt	ich hatte
du hast gehabt	du hattest
er hat gehabt	er hatte
wir haben gehabt	wir hatten
ihr habt gehabt	ihr hattet
sie haben gehabt	sie hatten

Future	Imperfect subjunctive
ich werde haben	ich hätte
du wirst haben	du hättest
er wird haben	er hätte
wir werden haben	wir hätten
ihr werdet haben	ihr hättet
sie werden haben	sie hätten

Conditional

ich würde haben
du würdest haben
er würde haben
wir würden haben
ihr würdet haben
sie würden haben

8

Imperative	Past participle	**kommen**
komm!	ist gekommen	to come
kommt!		
kommen Sie!		

Present
ich komme
du kommst
er kommt
wir kommen
ihr kommt
sie kommen

Perfect
ich bin gekommen
du bist gekommen
er ist gekommen
wir sind gekommen
ihr seid gekommen
sie sind gekommen

Future
ich werde kommen
du wirst kommen
er wird kommen
wir werden kommen
ihr werdet kommen
sie werden kommen

Present subjunctive
ich komme
du kommest
er komme
wir kommen
ihr kommet
sie kommen

Imperfect
ich kam
du kamst
er kam
wir kamen
ihr kamt
sie kamen

Conditional
ich würde kommen
du würdest kommen
er würde kommen
wir würden kommen
ihr würdet kommen
sie würden kommen

können
can *or* to be able to

Imperative	Past participle
—	hat gekonnt *or* hätte können

Present
ich kann
du kannst
er kann
wir können
ihr könnt
sie können

Present subjunctive
ich könne
du könnest
er könne
wir können
ihr könnet
sie können

Perfect
ich habe gekonnt
du hast gekonnt
er hat gekonnt
wir haben gekonnt
ihr habt gekonnt
sie haben gekonnt

Imperfect
ich konnte
du konntest
er konnte
wir konnten
ihr konntet
sie konnten

Future
ich werde können
du wirst können
er wird können
wir werden können
ihr werdet können
sie werden können

Imperfect subjunctive
ich könnte
du könntest
er könnte
wir könnten
ihr könntet
sie könnten

Conditional
ich würde können
du würdest können
er würde können
wir würden können
ihr würdet können
sie würden können

10

Imperative	Past participle	**müssen**
—	hat gemusst *or* hätte müssen	must *or* to have to

Present
ich muss
du musst
er muss
wir müssen
ihr müsst
sie müssen

Present subjunctive
ich müsse
du müssest
er müsse
wir müssen
ihr müsset
sie müssen

Perfect
ich habe gemusst
du hast gemusst
er hat gemusst
wir haben gemusst
ihr habt gemusst
sie haben gemusst

Imperfect
ich musste
du musstest
er musste
wir mussten
ihr musstet
sie mussten

Future
ich werde müssen
du wirst müssen
er wird müssen
wir werden müssen
ihr werdet müssen
sie werden müssen

Imperfect subjunctive
ich müsste
du müsstest
er müsste
wir müssten
ihr müsstet
sie müssten

Conditional
ich würde müssen
du würdest müssen
er würde müssen
wir würden müssen
ihr würdet müssen
sie würden müssen

sein
to be

Imperative	Past participle
sei!	ist gewesen
seid!	
seien Sie!	

Present
ich bin
du bist
er ist
wir sind
ihr seid
sie sind

Present subjunctive
ich sei
du sei(e)st
er sei
wir seien
ihr seiet
sie seien

Perfect
ich bin gewesen
du bist gewesen
er ist gewesen
wir sind gewesen
ihr seid gewesen
sie sind gewesen

Imperfect
ich war
du warst
er war
wir waren
ihr wart
sie waren

Future
ich werde sein
du wirst sein
er wird sein
wir werden sein
ihr werdet sein
sie werden sein

Imperfect subjunctive
ich wäre
du wär(e)st
er wäre
wir wären
ihr wär(e)t
sie wären

Conditional
ich würde sein
du würdest sein
er würde sein
wir würden sein
ihr würdet sein
sie würden sein

Imperative	Past participle	**sollen**
—	hat gesollt	should

Present

ich soll
du sollst
er soll
wir sollen
ihr sollt
sie sollen

Perfect

ich habe gesollt
du hast gesollt
er hat gesollt
wir haben gesollt
ihr habt gesollt
sie haben gesollt

Future

ich werde sollen
du wirst sollen
er wird sollen
wir werden sollen
ihr werdet sollen
sie werden sollen

Present subjunctive

ich solle
du sollest
er solle
wir sollen
ihr sollet
sie sollen

Imperfect

ich sollte
du solltest
er sollte
wir sollten
ihr solltet
sie sollten

Imperfect subjunctive

ich sollte
du solltest
er sollte
wir sollten
ihr solltet
sie sollten

Conditional

ich würde sollen
du würdest sollen
er würde sollen
wir würden sollen
ihr würdet sollen
sie würden sollen

werden
to become *or* to get

Imperative

werde!
werdet!
werden Sie!

Past participle

ist geworden

Present

ich werde
du wirst
er wird
wir we...en
ihr werdet
sie werden

Present subjunctive

ich werde
du werdest
er werde
wir werden
ihr werdet
sie werden

Perfect

ich bin geworden
du bist geworden
er ist geworden
wir sind geworden
ihr seid geworden
sie sind geworden

Imperfect

ich wurde
du wurdest
er wurde
wir wurden
ihr wurdet
sie wurden

Future

ich werde werden
du wirst werden
er wird werden
wir werden werden
ihr werdet werden
sie werden werden

Conditional

ich würde werden
du würdest werden
er würde werden
wir würden werden
ihr würdet werden
sie würden werden

14

Imperative	Past participle	**wissen**
wisse!	hat gewusst	to know
wisst!		
wissen Sie!		

Present

ich weiß
du weißt
er weiß
wir wissen
ihr wisst
sie wissen

Present subjunctive

ich wisse
du wissest
er wisse
wir wissen
ihr wisset
sie wissen

Perfect

ich habe gewusst
du hast gewusst
er hat gewusst
wir haben gewusst
ihr habt gewusst
sie haben gewusst

Imperfect

ich wusste
du wusstest
er wusste
wir wussten
ihr wusstet
sie wussten

Future

ich werde wissen
du wirst wissen
er wird wissen
wir werden wissen
ihr werdet wissen
sie werden wissen

Conditional

ich würde wissen
du würdest wissen
er würde wissen
wir würden wissen
ihr würdet wissen
sie würden wissen

German irregular verb forms

This list shows the main forms of other irregular verbs.

Infinitive	Present ich, du, er/sie/es	Imperfect er/sie/es	Perfect er/sie/es
bekommen	bekomme, bekommst, bekommt	bekam	hat bekommen
bergen	berge, birgst, birgt	barg	hat geborgen
besitzen	besitze, besitzt, besitzt	besaß	hat besessen
betrügen	betrüge, betrügst, betrügt	betrog	hat betrogen
biegen	biege, biegst, biegt	bog	hat or ist gebogen
bieten	biete, bietest, bietet	bot	hat geboten
binden	binde, bindest, bindet	band	hat gebunden
bitten	bitte, bittest, bittet	bat	hat gebeten
blasen	blase, bläst, bläst	blies	hat geblasen
bleiben	bleibe, bleibst, bleibt	blieb	ist geblieben
braten	brate, brätst, brät	briet	hat gebraten
brechen	breche, brichst, bricht	brach	hat or ist gebrochen
brennen	brenne, brennst, brennt	brannte	hat gebrannt
bringen	bringe, bringst, bringt	brachte	hat gebracht
denken	denke, denkst, denkt	dachte	hat gedacht
dürfen	darf, darfst, darf	durfte	hat gedurft
einladen	lade ein, lädst ein, lädt ein	lud ein	hat eingeladen
empfangen	empfange, empfängst, empfängt	empfing	hat empfangen
empfehlen	empfehle, empfiehlst, empfiehlt	empfahl	hat empfohlen
entscheiden	entscheide, entscheidest, entscheidet	entschied	hat entschieden

Infinitive	Present ich, du, er/sie/es	Imperfect er/sie/es	Perfect er/sie/es
erfahren	erfahre, erfährst, erfährt	erfuhr	hat erfahren
erfinden	erfinde, erfindest, erfindet	erfand	hat erfunden
erschrecken	erschrecke, erschrickst, erschrickt	erschrak	ist erschrocken
ertrinken	ertrinke, ertrinkst, ertrinkt	ertrank	ist ertrunken
essen	esse, isst, isst	aß	hat gegessen
fahren	fahre, fährst, fährt	fuhr	ist or hat gefahren
fallen	falle, fällst, fällt	fiel	ist gefallen
fangen	fange, fängst, fängt	fing	hat gefangen
fechten	fechte, fichtst, ficht	focht	hat gefochten
finden	finde, findest, findet	fand	hat gefunden
fliegen	fliege, fliegst, fliegt	flog	ist or hat geflogen
fliehen	fliehe, fliehst, flieht	floh	ist geflohen
fließen	fließe, fließt, fließt	floss	ist geflossen
fressen	fresse, frisst, frisst	fraß	hat gefressen
frieren	friere, frierst, friert	fror	hat or ist gefroren
geben	gebe, gibst, gibt	gab	hat gegeben
gefallen	gefalle, gefällst, gefällt	gefiel	hat gefallen
gehen	gehe, gehst, geht	ging	ist gegangen
gelingen	es gelingt mir/dir/ihm/ ihr/ihm	gelang	ist gelungen
gelten	gelte, giltst, gilt	galt	hat gegolten
genießen	genieße, genießt, genießt	genoss	hat genossen
geraten	gerate, gerätst, gerät	geriet	ist geraten
geschehen	es geschieht	geschah	ist geschehen
gewinnen	gewinne, gewinnst, gewinnt	gewann	hat gewonnen
gießen	gieße, gießt, gießt	goss	hat gegossen
gleichen	gleiche, gleichst, gleicht	glich	hat geglichen
graben	grabe, gräbst, gräbt	grub	hat gegraben
greifen	greife, greifst, greift	griff	hat gegriffen

Infinitive	Present ich, du, er/sie/es	Imperfect er/sie/es	Perfect er/sie/es
haben	habe, hast, hat	hatte	hat gehabt
halten	halte, hältst, hält	hielt	hat gehalten
hängen	hänge, hängst, hängt	hing	hat gehangen
heben	hebe, hebst, hebt	hob	hat gehoben
heißen	heiße, heißt, heißt	hieß	hat geheißen
helfen	helfe, hilfst, hilft	half	hat geholfen
hinweisen	weise hin, weist hin, weist hin	wies hin	hat hingewiesen
kennen	kenne, kennst, kennt	kannte	hat gekannt
klingen	klinge, klingst, klingt	klang	hat geklungen
kneifen	kneife, kneifst, kneift	kniff	hat gekniffen
kommen	komme, kommst, kommt	kam	ist gekommen
können	kann, kannst, kann	konnte	hat gekonnt
kriechen	krieche, kriechst, kriecht	kroch	ist gekrochen
lassen	lasse, lässt, lässt	ließ	hat gelassen
laufen	laufe, läufst, läuft	lief	ist gelaufen
leiden	leide, leidest, leidet	litt	hat gelitten
leihen	leihe, leihst, leiht	lieh	hat geliehen
lesen	lese, liest, liest	las	hat gelesen
liegen	liege, liegst, liegt	lag	hat gelegen
lügen	lüge, lügst, lügt	log	hat gelogen
mahlen	mahle, mahlst, mahlt	mahlte	hat gemahlen
meiden	meide, meidest, meidet	mied	hat gemieden
messen	messe, mißt, mißt	maß	hat gemessen
misslingen Δ	misslinge, misslingst, misslingt	misslang	ist misslungen
mögen	mag, magst, mag	mochte	hat gemocht
müssen	muss, musst, muss	musste	hat gemusst

Infinitive	Present ich, du, er/sie/es	Imperfect er/sie/es	Perfect er/sie/es
nehmen	nehme, nimmst, nimmt	nahm	hat genommen
nennen	nenne, nennst, nennt	nannte	hat genannt
pfeifen	pfeife, pfeifst, pfeift	pfiff	hat gepfiffen
raten	rate, rätst, rät	riet	hat geraten
reiben	reibe, reibst, reibt	rieb	hat gerieben
reißen	reiße, reißt, reißt	riss	hat or ist gerissen
reiten	reite, reitest, reitet	ritt	hat or ist geritten
rennen	renne, rennst, rennt	rannte	ist gerannt
riechen	rieche, riechst, riecht	roch	hat gerochen
rufen	rufe, rufst, ruft	rief	hat gerufen
saufen	saufe, säufst, säuft	soff	hat gesoffen
schaffen	schaffe, schaffst, schafft	schuf	hat geschaffen
scheiden	scheide, scheidest, scheidet	schied	hat or ist geschieden
scheinen	scheine, scheinst, scheint	schien	hat geschienen
schieben	schiebe, schiebst, schiebt	schob	hat geschoben
schießen	schieße, schießt, schießt	schoss	hat or ist geschossen
schlafen	schlafe, schläfst, schläft	schlief	hat geschlafen
schlagen	schlage, schlägst, schlägt	schlug	hat geschlagen
schleichen	schleiche, schleichst, schleicht	schlich	ist geschlichen
schließen	schließe, schließt, schließt	schloss	hat geschlossen
schmeißen	schmeiße, schmeißt, schmeißt	schmiss	hat geschmissen
schmelzen	schmelze, schmilzt, schmilzt	schmolz	ist geschmolzen
schneiden	schneide, schneidest, schneidet	schnitt	hat geschnitten

Infinitive	Present ich, du, er/sie/es	Imperfect er/sie/es	Perfect er/sie/es
schreiben	schreibe, schreibst, schreibt	schrieb	hat geschrieben
schreien	schreie, schreist, schreit	schrie	hat geschrien
schweigen	schweige, schweigst, schweigt	schwieg	hat geschwiegen
schwimmen	schwimme, schwimmst, schwimmt	schwamm	ist or hat geschwommen
schwören	schwöre, schwörst, schwört	schwor	hat geschworen
sehen	sehe, siehst, sieht	sah	hat gesehen
sein	bin, bist, ist	war	ist gewesen
singen	singe, singst, singt	sang	hat gesungen
sinken	sinke, sinkst, sinkt	sank	ist gesunken
sitzen	sitze, sitzt, sitzt	saß	hat gesessen
sollen	soll, sollst, soll	sollte	hat gesollt
spinnen	spinne, spinnst, spinnt	spann	hat gesponnen
sprechen	spreche, sprichst, spricht	sprach	hat gesprochen
springen	springe, springst, springt	sprang	ist gesprungen
stechen	steche, stichst, sticht	stach	hat gestochen
stehen	stehe, stehst, steht	stand	hat gestanden
stehlen	stehle, stiehlst, stiehlt	stahl	hat gestohlen
steigen	steige, steigst, steigt	stieg	ist gestiegen
sterben	sterbe, stirbst, stirbt	starb	ist gestorben
stinken	stinke, stinkst, stinkt	stank	hat gestunken
stoßen	stoße, stößt, stößt	stieß	hat or ist gestoßen
streichen	streiche, streichst, streicht	strich	hat gestrichen
streiten	streite, streitest, streitet	stritt	hat gestritten
tragen	trage, trägst, trägt	trug	hat getragen
treffen	treffe, triffst, trifft	traf	hat getroffen
treiben	treibe, treibst, treibt	trieb	hat getrieben
treten	trete, trittst, tritt	trat	hat or ist getreten
trinken	trinke, trinkst, trinkt	trank	hat getrunken
tun	tue, tust, tut	tat	hat getan

Infinitive	Present ich, du, er/sie/es	Imperfect er/sie/es	Perfect er/sie/es
überweisen	überweise, überweist, überweist	überwies	hat überwiesen
umziehen	ziehe um, ziehst um, zieht um	zog um	ist or hat umgezogen
verbieten	verbiete, verbietest, verbietet	verbot	hat verboten
verderben	verderbe, verdirbst, verdirbt	verdarb	hat or ist verdorben
vergessen	vergesse, vergißt, vergißt	vergaß	hat vergessen
verlieren	verliere, verlierst, verliert	verlor	hat verloren
verschwinden	verschwinde, verschwindest, verschwindet	verschwand	ist verschwunden
verstehen	verstehe, verstehst, versteht	verstand	hat verstanden
verzeihen	verzeihe, verzeihst, verzeiht	verzieh	hat verziehen
wachsen	wachse, wächst, wächst	wuchs	ist gewachsen
waschen	wasche, wäscht, wäscht	wusch	hat gewaschen
werben	werbe, wirbst, wirbt	warb	hat geworben
werden	werde, wirst, wird	wurde	ist geworden
werfen	werfe, wirfst, wirft	warf	hat geworfen
wiegen	wiege, wiegst, wiegt	wog	hat gewogen
wissen	weiß, weißt, weiß	wusste	hat gewusst
wollen	will, willst, will	wollte	hat gewollt
ziehen	ziehe, ziehst, zieht	zog	hat or ist gezogen
zwingen	zwinge, zwingst, zwingt	zwang	hat gezwungen

Note: New German spellings are used throughout this verb table. For a general note on the German spelling reform see page xii.

A a

a *indefinite article* 1 (*before a noun which is masculine in German*) ein; **a tree** ein Baum; 2 (*before a noun which is feminine in German*) eine; **a story** eine Geschichte; 3 (*before a noun which is neuter in German*) ein; **a dress** ein Kleid; 4 **not a** kein; **the party was not a success** die Party war kein Erfolg; **he didn't say a word** er hat kein Wort gesagt; 5 **six marks a kilo** sechs Mark das Kilo; 6 **fifty kilometres an hour** fünfzig Stundenkilometer; 7 **three times a day** dreimal täglich.

abandon *verb* 1 aufgeben ◇ SEP; **they abandoned the plan** sie gaben den Plan auf; 2 verlassen ◇; **they abandoned the city** sie verließen die Stadt.

abbey *noun* Abtei *die* (PL *die* Abteien).

abbreviation *noun* Abkürzung *die* (PL *die* Abkürzungen).

ability *noun* Fähigkeit *die* (PL *die* Fähigkeiten); **to have the ability to do something** etwas tun können.

about *preposition* 1 über (+ACC); **a film about space** ein Film über den Weltraum; **to talk about something/somebody** über etwas/jemanden reden; **what is she talking about?** worüber redet sie?; 2 um (+ACC); **to be about something**

um etwas gehen; **what's it about?** worum geht es?; 3 **to know about something** wissen ←(DAT); **she didn't know about the party** sie wusste nichts von der Party; **he knows nothing about it** er weiß nichts davon; 4 **to think about something/somebody** an etwas/jemanden ←(ACC) denken; **I'm thinking about you** ich denke an dich.
adverb 1 (*approximately*) ungefähr; **about sixty people** ungefähr sechzig Leute; **in about a week** in ungefähr einer Woche; 2 (*when talking about time*) gegen; **about three o'clock** gegen drei Uhr; 3 **to be about to do something** gerade etwas tun wollen; **I was (just) about to leave** ich wollte gerade gehen.

above *preposition* 1 über (+DAT); **the lamp above the table** die Lampe über dem Tisch; 2 **above all** vor allem.

abroad *adverb* im Ausland; **to live abroad** im Ausland leben; **to go abroad** ins Ausland fahren.

absent *adjective* abwesend; **to be absent from school** in der Schule fehlen.

absent-minded *adjective* zerstreut.

absolute *adjective* absolut; **an absolute disaster** eine absolute Katastrophe.

absolutely *adverb* 1 wirklich; **it's absolutely dreadful** das ist wirklich furchtbar; 2 völlig; **you're**

absolutely right du hast völlig recht.

abuse noun 1 Missbrauch △ der; **drug abuse** Missbrauch von Drogen; 2 (insults) Beschimpfungen (plural). verb 1 **to abuse somebody** jemanden missbrauchen; 2 (to insult) beschimpfen.

accelerator noun Gaspedal das (PL die Gaspedale).

accent noun Akzent der (PL die Akzente); **to speak with a German accent** mit deutschem Akzent sprechen.

accept verb annehmen ◇ SEP; **he accepted the invitation** er nahm die Einladung an.

acceptable adjective annehmbar.

access noun Zugang der. verb **to access data** auf Daten zugreifen.

accessory noun 1 Zubehörteil das; **accessories** Zubehör das; 2 **accessories** (fashion items) Accessoires (plural).

accident noun 1 Unfall der (PL die Unfälle); **to have an accident** einen Unfall haben; **road accident** der Verkehrsunfall; **car accident** der Autounfall; 2 Zufall der (PL die Zufälle); **by accident** zufällig; **I found it by accident** ich habe es zufällig gefunden.

accidental adjective zufällig; **an accidental discovery** eine zufällige Entdeckung.

accidentally adverb 1 (without meaning to) versehentlich; **I accidentally threw it away** ich habe es versehentlich weggeworfen; 2 (by chance) zufällig; **I accidentally discovered that ...** ich habe zufällig herausgefunden, dass ...

accommodation noun Unterkunft die; **accommodation is free** Unterkunft ist kostenlos; **I'm looking for accommodation** (when looking for a room) ich suche ein Zimmer.

according in phrase **according to** laut (+DAT); **according to Sophie** laut Sophie.

accordion noun Akkordeon das (PL die Akkordeons).

account noun 1 (in a bank, shop, or post office) Konto das (PL die Konten); **bank account** das Bankkonto; **to open an account** ein Konto eröffnen; **I have fifty pounds in my account** ich habe fünfzig Pfund auf meinem Konto; 2 (an explanation) Darstellung die (PL die Darstellungen); **I want to hear his account of what happened** ich möchte seine Darstellung der Ereignisse hören; 3 **on account of** wegen (+GEN); 4 **to take something into account** etwas berücksichtigen.

accountant noun Buchhalter der (PL die Buchhalter), Buchhalterin die (PL die Buchhalterinnen); **she's an accountant** sie ist Buchhalterin.

accurate adjective genau.

accurately adverb genau.

◇ IRREGULAR VERB: See the verb table in the centre of the dictionary

accuse *verb* beschuldigen; **she accused me of stealing her pen** sie beschuldigte mich, ihren Kugelschreiber gestohlen zu haben.

ace *noun* Ass ∆ *das* (PL die Asse); **the ace of hearts** das Herzass.
adjective klasse (*informal*); **he's an ace drummer** er spielt klasse Schlagzeug.

achieve *verb* **1** leisten; **she's achieved a great deal** sie hat eine Menge geleistet; **2** erreichen (*an aim*); **he achieved what he wanted** er hat erreicht, was er wollte.

achievement *noun* Leistung *die* (PL die Leistungen); **it's a great achievement** das ist eine große Leistung.

acid *noun* Säure *die* (PL die Säuren).

acne *noun* Akne *die*.

across *preposition* **1** (*over to the other side of*) über (+ACC); **to run across the road** über die Straße laufen; **we walked across the park** wir sind durch den Park gegangen; **2** (*on the other side of*) auf der anderen Seite (+GEN); **he lives across the river** er wohnt auf der anderen Seite des Flusses; **3** **they live across the street** sie wohnen gegenüber.

act *noun* (*deed*) Tat *die* (PL die Taten).
verb (*in a play or film*) spielen; **to act the part of the hero** die Rolle des Helden spielen.

action *noun* **1** Handlung *die* (PL die Handlungen); **2** **to take action** etwas unternehmen.

active *adjective* aktiv.

activity *noun* Aktivität *die* (PL die Aktivitäten).

actor *noun* Schauspieler *der* (PL die Schauspieler).

actress *noun* Schauspielerin *die* (PL die Schauspielerinnen).

actual *adjective* **what were his actual words?** was genau hat er gesagt?; **in actual fact** eigentlich.

actually *adverb* **1** (*in fact, as it happens*) eigentlich; **actually, I've changed my mind** ich habe mich eigentlich anders entschlossen; **2** (*really and truly*) wirklich; **did she actually say that?** hat sie das wirklich gesagt?

ad *noun* **1** (*on TV*) Werbespot *der* (PL die Werbespots); **2** (*in a newspaper*) Anzeige *die* (PL die Anzeigen); **to put an ad in the paper** eine Anzeige in die Zeitung setzen; **the small ads** die Kleinanzeigen.

AD (*Anno Domini*) n.Chr. (*nach Christus*); **in 400 AD** 400 n.Chr.

adapt *verb* **1** **to adapt something** (*a book or film*) etwas bearbeiten; **2** **to adapt to** sich anpassen SEP (+DAT); **she's adapted to her new surroundings** sie hat sich der neuen Umgebung angepasst.

adaptor *noun* **1** Adapter *der* (PL die Adapter); **2** (*for two plugs*) Doppelstecker *der* (PL die Doppelstecker).

add *verb* **1** hinzufügen SEP; **to add an introduction to something** etwas ←(DAT) eine Einleitung hinzufügen; **2** dazugeben ◇ SEP; **add three eggs** geben Sie drei Eier dazu.
● **to add up** zusammenzählen SEP.

∆ NEW SPELLING: See page xii

addict noun 1 (drug addict) Süchtige der/die (PL die Süchtigen); 2 she's a telly addict sie ist fernsehsüchtig; he's a football addict er hat die Fußballsucht.

addicted adjective 1 to become addicted to drugs drogensüchtig werden; 2 he's addicted to football Fußball ist bei ihm zur Sucht geworden; 3 I'm addicted to sweets ich bin nach Süßigkeiten süchtig.

addition noun 1 (adding up) Addition die; 2 in addition außerdem; 3 in addition to zusätzlich zu (+DAT).

additional adjective zusätzlich.

additive noun Zusatz der (PL die Zusätze).

address noun Adresse die (PL die Adressen); do you know his address? weißt du seine Adresse?; to change address die Adresse wechseln.

address book noun Adressbuch △ das (PL die Adressbücher).

adhesive noun Klebstoff der. adjective adhesive tape der Klebstreifen.

adjective noun Adjektiv das (PL die Adjektive).

adjust verb 1 to adjust something etwas einstellen SEP; he adjusted the set er stellte das Gerät ein; to adjust the distance auf die richtige Entfernung einstellen; 2 to adjust

to something sich an etwas ←(ACC) gewöhnen.

adjustable adjective verstellbar.

administration noun Verwaltung die.

admiration noun Bewunderung die.

admire verb bewundern.

admission noun Eintritt der; 'admission free' 'Eintritt frei'.

admit verb 1 (confess, concede) zugeben ◇ SEP; she admits she lied sie gibt zu, dass sie gelogen hat; 2 (allow to enter) hereinlassen ◇ SEP; to admit somebody to a restaurant jemanden in ein Restaurant hereinlassen; 3 to be admitted to hospital ins Krankenhaus eingeliefert werden.

adolescence noun Jugend die.

adolescent noun Jugendliche der/die (PL die Jugendlichen).

adopt verb adoptieren.

adopted adjective adoptiert.

adoption noun Adoption die (PL die Adoptionen).

adore verb lieben.

adult noun Erwachsene der/die (PL die Erwachsenen). adjective the adult population Erwachsene (plural).

Adult Education noun Erwachsenenbildung die.

advance noun Fortschritt der (PL die Fortschritte); advances in

◇ IRREGULAR VERB: See the verb table in the centre of the dictionary

technology technologische Fortschritte.
verb 1 (*make progress*) Fortschritte machen; **2** (*move forward*) (*of a group or an army*) vorrücken SEP (PERF sein).

advanced *adjective* fortgeschritten (*student, age*).

advantage *noun* **1** Vorteil der (PL die Vorteile); **there are several advantages** es gibt verschiedene Vorteile; **2** **to take advantage of something** etwas ausnutzen SEP; **I always take advantage of the sales to buy myself some shoes** ich nutze immer den Ausverkauf aus, um mir Schuhe zu kaufen; **3** **to take advantage of somebody** (*unfairly*) jemanden ausnutzen SEP.

Advent *noun* Advent der.

adventure *noun* Abenteuer das (PL die Abenteuer).

adverb *noun* Adverb das (PL die Adverbien).

advert, advertisement *noun* **1** (*at the cinema or on television*) Werbespot der (PL die Werbespots); **2** (*in a newspaper for a job, article for sale, etc.*) Anzeige die (PL die Anzeigen); **she answered a job advertisement** sie meldete sich auf eine Stellenanzeige.

advertise *verb* **to advertise something in the newspaper** (*in the small ads*) etwas in der Zeitung inserieren; **I saw a bike advertised in the paper** ich habe ein Rad in der Zeitung inseriert gesehen.

advertising *noun* Werbung die.

advice *noun* Rat der; **to ask somebody's advice** jemanden um Rat fragen; **a piece of advice** ein Ratschlag.

advise *verb* raten ◇ (+DAT); **to advise somebody to do something** jemandem raten, etwas zu tun; **I advised him to stop** ich riet ihm anzuhalten; **I advised her not to buy the car** ich habe ihr geraten, das Auto nicht zu kaufen.

aerial *noun* Antenne die (PL die Antennen).

aerobics *noun* Aerobic das; **to do aerobics** Aerobic machen.

aeroplane *noun* Flugzeug das (PL die Flugzeuge).

aerosol *noun* **an aerosol can** eine Spraydose.

affair *noun* **1** Angelegenheit die (PL die Angelegenheiten); **international affairs** internationale Angelegenheiten; **current affairs** die Tagespolitik; **2** **love affair** das Liebesverhältnis.

affect *verb* beeinflussen.

affectionate *adjective* liebevoll.

afford *verb* **to be able to afford something** sich ← (+DAT) etwas leisten können; **we can't afford to go out much** wir können es uns nicht leisten, oft auszugehen; **I can't afford a new bike** ich kann mir kein neues Rad leisten.

afraid *adjective* **1** **to be afraid of something** Angst vor etwas ← (+DAT) haben; **she's afraid of dogs** sie hat vor Hunden Angst; **2** **I'm afraid I**

△ NEW SPELLING: See page xii

can't help you ich kann dir leider nicht helfen; **I'm afraid so** leider ja; **I'm afraid not** leider nicht.

Africa noun Afrika das; **to Africa** nach Afrika.

African noun Afrikaner der (PL die Afrikaner), Afrikanerin die (PL die Afrikanerinnen).
adjective afrikanisch; **she is African** sie ist Afrikanerin.

after preposition, adverb **1** nach (+DAT); **after 10 o'clock** nach zehn Uhr; **after lunch** nach dem Mittagessen; **after school** nach der Schule; **2 the day after tomorrow** übermorgen; **soon after** kurz danach; **3 to run after somebody** jemandem hinterherlaufen ◇ SEP.
conjunction nachdem; **after I'd finished my homework** nachdem ich meine Hausaufgaben gemacht hatte.

after all adverb schließlich; **after all, she's only six** sie ist schließlich erst sechs.

afternoon noun **1** Nachmittag der (PL die Nachmittage); **in the afternoon** am Nachmittag; **every afternoon** jeden Nachmittag; **2 this afternoon** heute Nachmittag; **on Sunday afternoon** am Sonntagnachmittag; **3 on Saturday afternoons** samstagsnachmittags; **at four o' clock in the afternoon** um vier Uhr nachmittags.

after-shave noun Rasierwasser das.

afterwards adverb danach; **shortly afterwards** kurz danach.

again adverb **1** wieder; **she's ill again** sie ist wieder krank; **2 I saw her again yesterday** ich habe sie gestern wieder gesehen; **3 never again!** nie wieder!; **again and again** immer wieder; **4** (one more time) noch einmal; **try again** versuche es noch einmal; **you should ask her again** du solltest sie noch einmal fragen.

against preposition gegen (+ACC); **against the wall** gegen die Wand; **to lean against the wall** sich gegen die Wand lehnen; **I'm against the idea** ich bin gegen die Idee.

age noun **1** Alter das; **at the age of fifty** im Alter von fünfzig; **she's the same age as me** sie ist genauso alt wie ich; **to be under age** minderjährig sein; **2 I haven't seen Johnny for ages** ich habe Johnny schon ewig nicht mehr gesehen; **I haven't been to London for ages** ich bin schon ewig nicht mehr in London gewesen.

agent noun Vertreter der (PL die Vertreter); **an estate agent** ein Immobilienmakler; **a travel agent's** ein Reisebüro.

aggressive adjective aggressiv.

ago adverb vor (+DAT); **an hour ago** vor einer Stunde; **three days ago** vor drei Tagen; **a long time ago** vor langer Zeit; **not long ago** vor kurzem; **how long ago was it?** wie lange ist das her?

agree verb **1 to agree with somebody** mit jemandem übereinstimmen SEP; **I agree with**

◇ **IRREGULAR VERB:** See the verb table in the centre of the dictionary

Laura ich stimme mit Laura überein; **2 I agree** ich bin der gleichen Meinung; **I don't agree** ich bin anderer Meinung; **3 to agree that …** zugeben ◇ SEP, dass …; **I agree that it's too late now** ich gebe zu, dass es jetzt zu spät ist; **4 to agree to something** mit etwas einverstanden sein; **Steve's agreed to help me** Steve war damit einverstanden, mir zu helfen; **5 coffee doesn't agree with me** Kaffee bekommt mir nicht.

agreement noun **1** (*when sharing an opinion*) Übereinstimmung die; **2** (*contract*) Abkommen das (PL die Abkommen).

agriculture noun Landwirtschaft die.

ahead adverb **1 go ahead!** bitte!; **2 straight ahead** geradeaus; **keep going straight ahead until you get to the crossroads** gehen Sie immer geradeaus bis zur Kreuzung; **3 our team was ten points ahead** unsere Mannschaft hatte zehn Punkte Vorsprung; **4 ahead of time** früher als geplant; **5 the people ahead of me** die Leute vor mir.

aid noun **1** Hilfe die; **aid to developing countries** die Entwicklungshilfe; **2 in aid of** zugunsten (+GEN); **in aid of the homeless** zugunsten der Obdachlosen.

Aids noun Aids das; **to have Aids** Aids haben.

aim noun Ziel das (PL die Ziele); **their aim is to control pollution** ihr Ziel ist es, die Verschmutzung unter Kontrolle zu bringen.
verb **1 to aim to do something** beabsichtigen, etwas zu tun; **we're aiming to finish it today** wir beabsichtigen, es heute fertig zu machen; **2 the campaign is aimed at young people** die Kampagne ist auf junge Leute abgezielt.

air noun **1** Luft die; **in the open air** im Freien; **to go out for a breath of air** frische Luft schöpfen gehen; **2 to travel by air** fliegen ◇ (PERF sein).

air-conditioned adjective klimatisiert.

air conditioning noun Klimaanlage die.

Air Force noun Luftwaffe die.

air hostess noun Stewardess △ die (PL die Stewardessen); **she's an air hostess** sie ist Stewardess.

airline noun Fluggesellschaft die (PL die Fluggesellschaften).

airmail noun **by airmail** per Luftpost.

airport noun Flughafen der (PL die Flughäfen).

alarm noun Alarm der (PL die Alarme); **fire alarm** der Feuermelder; **burglar alarm** die Alarmanlage.

alarm clock noun Wecker der (PL die Wecker).

album noun Album das (PL die Alben).

alcohol noun Alkohol der.

△ NEW SPELLING: *See page xii*

alcoholic noun Alkoholiker der (PL die Alkoholiker), Alkoholikerin die (PL die Alkoholikerinnen).
adjective alkoholisch.

A levels noun Abitur das (Students who want to go to university do Abitur at the end of secondary school; they are examined in four subjects).

alike adjective 1 gleich; 2 they're all alike sie sind alle gleich; 3 to look alike sich ←(DAT) ähnlich sehen; the two brothers look alike die beiden Brüder sehen sich ähnlich.

alive adjective 1 to be alive leben; to stay alive am Leben bleiben; 2 (lively) lebendig.

all adjective 1 (with a singular noun) ganz; all the time die ganze Zeit; all day den ganzen Tag; 2 (with a plural noun) alle; all the knives die Messer; all our friends alle unsere Freunde.
pronoun 1 (everything) alles; they've eaten it all sie haben alles aufgegessen; 2 (everybody) alle; all of us wir alle; they're all there sie sind alle da; 3 not at all gar nicht.
adverb 1 ganz; all alone ganz allein; 2 three all drei zu drei.

all along adverb die ganze Zeit; I knew it all along ich habe es die ganze Zeit gewusst.

allergic adjective allergisch; to be allergic to something gegen etwas ←(ACC) allergisch sein.

allow verb 1 to allow somebody to do something jemandem erlauben, etwas zu tun; the teacher allowed them to go home der Lehrer

erlaubten ihnen, nach Hause zu gehen; 2 to be allowed to dürfen ◇; I'm not allowed to go to the cinema during the week ich darf während der Woche nicht ins Kino gehen.

all right adverb 1 (yes) ist gut, okay (informal); 'come round to my house around six' – 'all right' 'komm um sechs bei mir vorbei' – 'okay'; 2 (fine) in Ordnung, okay (informal); is everything all right? ist alles okay?; she's all right now sie ist jetzt okay; it's all right by me das geht in Ordnung; is it all right if I come later? geht es in Ordnung, wenn ich später komme?; 3 (not bad) gut, okay (informal); the meal was all right das Essen war okay; 4 'how are you?' – 'I'm all right' 'wie geht's dir?' – 'mir geht's gut'.

almost adverb fast; almost every day fast jeden Tag; almost everybody fast alle.

alone adjective 1 allein; he lives alone er lebt allein; 2 leave me alone! lass mich in Ruhe!

along preposition 1 entlang (+ACC, or +DAT); there are trees all along the river den ganzen Fluss entlang stehen Bäume; to go for a walk along the beach am Strand entlang spazieren gehen; 2 (there is often no direct translation for 'along', so the sentence has to be expressed differently) she lives along the road from me sie wohnt in der gleichen Straße wie ich; I'll bring it along ich bringe es mit.

◇ IRREGULAR VERB: See the verb table in the centre of the dictionary

loud *adverb* laut; **to read something aloud** etwas vorlesen ◇ SEP.

lphabet *noun* Alphabet *das* (PL die Alphabete).

Alps *plural noun* **the Alps** die Alpen.

lready *adverb* schon; **they've already left** sie sind schon weggefahren; **it's six o'clock already** es ist schon sechs Uhr.

Alsatian *noun* Schäferhund *der* (PL die Schäferhunde).

lso *adverb* auch; **I've also invited Karen** ich habe Karen auch eingeladen.

lternative *noun* 1 Alternative *die* (PL die Alternativen); **there are several alternatives** es gibt mehrere Alternativen; **2 we have no alternative** wir haben keine andere Wahl.
adjective anderer/andere/anderes (*masculine/feminine/neuter*); **to find an alternative solution** eine andere Lösung finden.

lternative medicine *noun* Alternativmedizin *die*.

lthough *conjunction* obwohl; **although she's ill, she wants to help us** obwohl sie krank ist, will sie uns helfen.

ltogether *adverb* 1 insgesamt; **I've spent thirty pounds altogether** insgesamt habe ich dreißig Pfund ausgegeben; **2** (*completely*) ganz; **I'm not altogether convinced** ich bin nicht ganz überzeugt.

always *adverb* immer; **I always leave at five** ich gehe immer um fünf weg.

am *verb* SEE be.

a.m. *abbreviation* vormittags; **at 8 a.m.** um acht Uhr morgens.

amateur *noun* 1 Amateur *der* (PL die Amateure); **2 amateur dramatics** das Laientheater.

amaze *verb* erstaunen; **what amazes me is...** was mich erstaunt, ist...

amazed *adjective* erstaunt; **I was amazed to see her** ich war erstaunt, sie zu sehen.

amazing *adjective* 1 (*terrific*) fantastisch △; **they've got an amazing house** sie haben ein fantastisches Haus; **2** (*extraordinary*) erstaunlich; **she has an amazing number of friends** sie hat erstaunlich viele Freunde.

ambition *noun* Ehrgeiz *der*.

ambitious *adjective* ehrgeizig.

ambulance *noun* Krankenwagen *der* (PL die Krankenwagen).

America *noun* Amerika *das*; **in America** in Amerika; **to America** nach Amerika.

American *noun* Amerikaner *der* (PL die Amerikaner), Amerikanerin *die* (PL die Amerikanerinnen).
adjective amerikanisch; **she's American** sie ist Amerikanerin.

among, amongst *preposition* 1 unter (+DAT); **I found it amongst my books** ich habe das unter

△ NEW SPELLING: *See page xii*

meinen Büchern gefunden;
amongst other things unter
anderem; **2** (*between*) **among
yourselves** untereinander.

amount noun **1** Menge die (PL die
Mengen); **a huge amount of work**
eine Menge Arbeit; **2** (*of money*)
Betrag der (PL die Beträge); **a large
amount of money** ein sehr hoher
Betrag.

amp noun (*amplifier*)
Verstärker der (PL die Verstärker).

amplifier noun Verstärker der (PL
die Verstärker).

amuse verb amüsieren.

amusement arcade noun
Spielhalle die (PL die Spielhallen).

amusing adjective amüsant.

an article SEE **a**.

anchovy noun Sardelle die (PL die
Sardellen).

ancient adjective **1** alt; **ancient
Greece** das alte Griechenland;
2 (*very old*) uralt; **an ancient pair of
jeans** uralte Jeans.

and conjunction **1** und; **Rosie and I**
Rosie und ich; **girls and boys**
Mädchen und Jungen; **2 louder and
louder** immer lauter; **3 try and
come** versuche zu kommen.

angel noun Engel der (PL die Engel).

anger noun Zorn der.

angle noun Winkel der (PL die
Winkel).

angrily adverb wütend.

angry adjective **to be angry** böse
sein; **she was angry with me** sie
war böse auf mich; **to get angry**
böse werden.

animal noun Tier das (PL die Tiere).

ankle noun Knöchel der (PL die
Knöchel).

anniversary noun **1** Jahrestag der
(PL die Jahrestage); **2 our wedding
anniversary** unser Hochzeitstag.

annoy verb **to be annoyed** verärgert
sein; **to get annoyed with
somebody** sich über jemanden
ärgern; **she got annoyed about it**
sie hat sich darüber geärgert.

annoying adjective ärgerlich.

annual adjective jährlich.

anorak noun Anorak der (PL die
Anoraks).

anorexia noun Magersucht die.

another adjective **1** (*additional*)
noch ein/noch eine/noch ein;
would you like another cup of tea?
möchtest du noch eine Tasse Tee?;
we need another three chairs wir
brauchen noch drei Stühle;
2 (*different*) ein anderer/eine
andere/ein anderes; **we saw
another film** wir haben einen
anderen Film gesehen; **3 in another
two years** in zwei weiteren Jahren.

answer noun **1** Antwort die (PL die
Antworten); **the right answer** die
richtige Antwort; **the wrong answer**
die falsche Antwort; **2 the answer
to a problem** die Lösung eines
Problems.
verb **1** antworten (+DAT); **why don't
you answer him?** warum

◇ IRREGULAR VERB: *See the verb table in the centre of the dictionary*

antwortest du ihm nicht?;
2 beantworten (*a letter, a question*);
he hasn't answered our letter er
hat unseren Brief nicht beantwortet.

answering machine *noun*
Anrufbeantworter *der* (PL *die*
Anrufbeantworter).

anthem *noun* **the national anthem**
die Nationalhymne.

antibiotic *noun* Antibiotikum *das*
(PL *die* Antibiotika).

antique *noun* **antiques**
Antiquitäten (*plural*).
adjective antik; **an antique table**
ein antiker Tisch.

antique shop *noun*
Antiquitätengeschäft *das* (PL *die*
Antiquitätengeschäfte).

anxious *adjective* **1** (*worried*)
besorgt; **2** (*keen*) **she was anxious
to see him** sie wollte ihn unbedingt
sehen.

anxiously *adverb* ängstlich.

any *adjective* **1** irgendein; **if they had
any plan** wenn sie irgendeinen Plan
hätten; **2** (*with plural nouns*)
irgendwelche; **if they had any plans**
wenn sie irgendwelche Pläne hätten;
3 (*in questions 'any' is often not
translated*) **have you got any
stamps?** haben Sie Briefmarken?;
have we got any milk? haben wir
Milch?; **4 not any** kein; **they
haven't made any plans** sie haben
keine Pläne gemacht; **we haven't
got any milk** wir haben keine Milch;
5 (*no matter which*) jeder
beliebige/jede beliebige/jedes

beliebige; **you can have any colour**
du kannst jede beliebige Farbe
haben.
pronoun **1** (*in questions, replacing
the noun*) welcher/welche/welches;
(*replacing a plural noun*) welche;
**I need some flour, have you got
any?** ich brauche Mehl, hast du
welches?; **2 not any** keiner/keine/
keins; (*replacing a plural noun*)
keine; **I don't want any** ich will
keins haben; **there aren't any** es gibt
keine; **3** (*no matter which one*)
irgendein; **'which chair can I take?'
– 'take any of them'** 'welchen
Stuhl kann ich nehmen?' – 'nimm
irgendeinen'.
adverb **1** (*in questions*) noch; **would
you like any more?** möchtest du
noch etwas?; **2** (*with negatives*) **I
can't see him any more** ich kann
ihn nicht mehr sehen.

anybody, anyone *pronoun* **1** (*in
questions*) jemand; **does anybody
want some tea?** möchte jemand
Tee?; **is anybody in?** ist
irgendjemand da?; **2 not anybody**
niemand; **there isn't anybody in the
office** niemand ist im Büro;
3 (*absolutely anybody*) jeder;
anybody can do it das kann jeder.

anyhow *adverb* SEE **anyway**.

anyone *pronoun* SEE **anybody**.

anything *pronoun* **1** (*in questions*)
irgendetwas △; **is there anything I
can do to help?** kann ich irgendwie
helfen?; **2 not anything** nichts;
there isn't anything on the table
auf dem Tisch liegt nichts;
3 (*anything at all*) alles; **I'll do**

△ NEW SPELLING: *See page xii*

anything to help him ich werde alles tun, um ihm zu helfen.

anyway, anyhow *adverb*
1 *jedenfalls*; **anyway, I'll ring you before I leave** jedenfalls ruf ich dich an, bevor ich fahre; 2 *sowieso*.

anywhere *adverb* 1 (*in questions*) *irgendwo*; **have you seen my keys anywhere?** hast du meine Schlüssel irgendwo gesehen?; 2 **not anywhere** *nirgends*; **I can't find my keys anywhere** ich kann meine Schlüssel nirgends finden; 3 (*to any place*) *irgendwohin*; **are you going anywhere tomorrow?** fahrt ihr morgen irgendwohin?; **put your cases down anywhere** stell deine Koffer irgendwohin; 4 (*in any place*) *überall*; **you can get that anywhere** das kann man überall kriegen.

apart *adjective, adverb* 1 (*separate*) *auseinander*; **they've been apart for some time** sie sind schon lange auseinander; 2 **to be two metres apart** zwei Meter auseinander liegen; 3 **apart from** außer (+DAT); **apart from my brother everybody was there** außer meinem Bruder waren alle da.

apologize *verb* sich entschuldigen; **he apologized for his mistake** er enschuldigte sich für seinen Fehler; **he apologized to Sam** er hat sich bei Sam entschuldigt.

apology *noun* Entschuldigung *die* (PL *die* Entschuldigungen).

apostrophe *noun* Apostroph *der* (PL *die* Apostrophe).

apparent *adjective* offensichtlich.

apparently *adverb* offensichtlich.

appeal *noun* Appell *der* (PL *die* Appelle).
verb 1 **to appeal for something** um etwas ←(ACC) bitten ◇; 2 **to appeal to somebody** sich an jemanden wenden ◇; **horror films don't appeal to me** Horrorfilme sind nicht mein Geschmack.

appear *verb* 1 erscheinen ◇ (PERF *sein*); **Mick appeared at breakfast** Mick erschien zum Frühstück; 2 **to appear on television** im Fernsehen auftreten ◇ SEP (PERF *sein*); 3 (*seem*) scheinen ◇; **it appears that somebody has stolen the key** es scheint, dass jemand den Schlüssel gestohlen hat.

appendicitis *noun* Blinddarmentzündung *die*.

appetite *noun* Appetit *der*; **it'll spoil your appetite** das verdirbt dir den Appetit.

applaud *verb* Beifall klatschen.

applause *noun* Beifall *der*.

apple *noun* Apfel *der* (PL *die* Äpfel).

apple tree *noun* Apfelbaum *der* (PL *die* Apfelbäume).

applicant *noun* Bewerber *der* (PL *die* Bewerber), Bewerberin *die* (PL *die* Bewerberinnen).

application *noun* Bewerbung *die* (PL *die* Bewerbungen).

application form *noun* (*for a job*) Bewerbungsformular *das* (PL *die* Bewerbungsformulare).

◇ IRREGULAR VERB: *See the verb table in the centre of the dictionary*

apply verb 1 to apply for a job sich um eine Stellung bewerben ◇; 2 to apply for university sich um einen Studienplatz bewerben ◇; 3 to apply for a passport einen Pass beantragen; 4 to apply to zutreffen ◇ SEP auf (+ACC); that doesn't apply to students das trifft nicht auf Studenten zu.

appointment noun Termin der (PL die Termine); to make a dental appointment einen Termin mit dem Zahnarzt vereinbaren; I've got a hair appointment at four ich bin um vier beim Friseur angemeldet.

appreciate verb I appreciate your advice ich bin dir für deinen Rat dankbar; I'd appreciate it if you could tidy up afterwards es wäre nett von dir, wenn du danach aufräumen würdest.

apprentice noun Lehrling der (PL die Lehrlinge).

apprenticeship noun Lehre die (PL die Lehren).

approve verb to approve of something mit etwas ←(DAT) einverstanden sein; they don't approve of her friends sie sind nicht mit ihren Freunden einverstanden.

approximate adjective ungefähr.

approximately adverb ungefähr; approximately fifty people ungefähr fünfzig Personen.

apricot noun Aprikose die (PL die Aprikosen).

April noun April der; in April im April.

April Fool noun (trick) Aprilscherz der (PL die Aprilscherze); April fool! April, April!

April Fool's Day noun der erste April.

apron noun Schürze die (PL die Schürzen).

Aquarius noun Wassermann der; Sharon's Aquarius Sharon ist Wassermann.

archaeologist noun Archäologe der (PL die Archäologen), Archäologin die (PL die Archäologinnen); she's an archaeologist sie ist Archäologin.

archaeology noun Archäologie die.

architect noun Architekt der (PL die Architekten), Architektin die (PL die Architektinnen); he's an architect er ist Architekt.

architecture noun Architektur die.

are verb SEE be.

area noun 1 (part of a town, a region) Gegend die (PL die Gegenden); a nice area eine nette Gegend; in the Leeds area in der Gegend von Leeds; 2 picnic area der Picknickplatz.

argue verb sich streiten ◇; to argue about something sich über etwas ←(ACC) streiten; they're arguing about the result sie streiten sich über das Ergebnis.

argument noun Streit der (PL die Streite); to get into an argument with somebody mit jemandem in

△ NEW SPELLING: See page xii

Streit geraten ◇; **to have an argument** sich streiten ◇.

Aries noun Widder der; **Pauline's Aries** Pauline ist Widder.

arm noun Arm der (PL die Arme); **arm in arm** Arm in Arm; **to break your arm** sich ←(DAT) den Arm brechen.

armchair noun Sessel der (PL die Sessel).

armed adjective bewaffnet.

army noun 1 Heer das (PL die Heere); 2 (profession) Militär das; **to join the army** zum Militär gehen.

around preposition, adverb 1 (with time of day) gegen (+ACC); **we'll be there around ten** wir werden gegen zehn da sein; 2 (with ages or amounts) she's around fifteen sie ist etwa fünfzehn; **we need around six kilos** wir brauchen etwa sechs Kilo; 3 (with dates) um (+ACC); **around 10 August** um den 10. August; 4 (surrounding) um ... herum; **the countryside around Edinburgh** die Landschaft um Edinburgh herum; 5 (near) **is there a post office around here?** gibt es hier in der Gegend eine Post?; **is Phil around?** ist Phil da?

arrange verb **to arrange something** etwas vereinbaren; **we've arranged to go to the cinema on Saturday** wir haben vereinbart, am Samstag ins Kino zu gehen.

arrest noun **to be under arrest** verhaftet sein.
verb verhaften.

arrival noun Ankunft die (PL die Ankünfte).

arrive verb ankommen ◇ SEP (PERF sein); **they arrived at 3 p.m.** sie kamen um fünfzehn Uhr an.

art noun 1 Kunst die (PL die Künste); **modern art** moderne Kunst; 2 (school subject) Kunsterziehung die.

art gallery noun Kunstgalerie die (PL die Kunstgalerien).

article noun 1 (in a newspaper or magazine) Artikel der (PL die Artikel); 2 (object) Stück das (PL die Stücke).

artificial adjective künstlich.

artist noun Künstler der (PL die Künstler), Künstlerin die (PL die Künstlerinnen); **he's an artist** er ist Künstler.

artistic adjective künstlerisch.

art school noun Kunsthochschule die (PL die Kunsthochschulen).

as conjunction, adverb 1 wie; **as you know** wie du weißt; **as usual** wie üblich; **as I told you** wie ich dir gesagt habe; 2 (because) da; **as there was no bus, we took a taxi** da es keinen Bus gab, nahmen wir ein Taxi; 3 **as ... as** so ... wie; **he's as tall as his brother** er ist so groß wie sein Bruder; **come as quickly as possible** komm so schnell wie möglich; 4 **as much ... as** so viel ... wie; **you have as much time as I do** du hast so viel Zeit wie ich; 5 **as many ... as** so viele ... wie; **we have**

◇ IRREGULAR VERB: See the verb table in the centre of the dictionary

as many problems as he does wir haben so viele Probleme wie er; **6 as long as** vorausgesetzt; **we'll go tomorrow, as long as it's a nice day** wir gehen morgen, vorausgesetzt es ist schönes Wetter; **7 for as long as** solange; **you can stay for as long as you like** du kannst bleiben, solange du willst; **8 as soon as possible** so bald wie möglich; **9 to work as** arbeiten als; **he works as a waiter in the evenings** abends arbeitet er als Kellner; **as well** auch.

ash noun **1** Asche die (PL die Aschen); **2** (tree) Esche die (PL die Eschen).

ashamed adjective **to be ashamed of something** sich über etwas ←(ACC) schämen; **you should be ashamed of yourself!** du solltest dich schämen!

ashtray noun Aschenbecher der (PL die Aschenbecher).

Asia noun Asien das; **in Asia** in Asien.

ask verb **1** fragen; **to ask somebody something** jemanden nach etwas ←(DAT) fragen; **I asked him the way** ich fragte ihn nach dem Weg; **2 to ask something** um etwas ←(ACC) bitten; **to ask somebody a favour** jemanden um einen Gefallen bitten; **to ask somebody to do something** jemanden bitten, etwas zu tun; **ask Danny to give you a hand** bitte Danny, dir zu helfen; **3 to ask somebody a question** jemandem eine Frage stellen; **I asked him a few questions** ich habe ihm ein paar Fragen gestellt; **4** einladen ◇ SEP;

they've asked us to a party sie haben uns auf eine Party eingeladen; **Paul's asked Janie out on Friday** Paul hat Janie Freitag eingeladen; **5 to ask for** verlangen; **how much are they asking for the car?** wieviel verlangen sie für das Auto?

asparagus noun Spargel der (PL die Spargel).

aspirin noun Aspirin das.

assembly noun (at school) Morgenandacht die (PL die Morgenandachten).

assignment noun (at school) Aufgabe die (PL die Aufgaben).

assistance noun Hilfe die.

assistant noun **1** Helfer der (PL die Helfer), Helferin die (PL die Helferinnen); **2** (in school) Assistent der (PL die Assistenten), Assistentin die (PL die Assistentinnen); **3 shop assistant** der Verkäufer, die Verkäuferin.

association noun Verband der (PL die Verbände).

assorted adjective gemischt.

assortment noun Auswahl die.

assume verb annehmen ◇ SEP; **I assume** ich nehme an.

asthma noun Asthma das.

astrology noun Astrologie die.

astronaut noun Astronaut der (PL die Astronauten), Astronautin die (PL die Astronautinnen).

astronomy noun Astronomie die.

△ NEW SPELLING: See page xii

at *preposition* **1** in (+DAT); **at school** in der Schule; **at my office** in meinem Büro; **at the supermarket** im Supermarkt; **2** an (+DAT); **at the station** am Bahnhof; **at the bus stop** an der Bushaltestelle; **3** bei (+DAT); **at the dentist** beim Zahnarzt; **at discussions** bei Besprechungen; **at Emma's** bei Emma; **she's at her brother's this evening** sie ist heute Abend bei ihrem Bruder; **at the hairdresser's** beim Friseur; **4 at a party** auf einer Party; **5 at home** zu Hause; **6** (*talking about the time*) um; **at eight o'clock** um acht Uhr; **7 at night** nachts; **at Christmas** zu Weihnachten; **at the weekend** am Wochenende; **8 at last** endlich; **she's found a job at last** sie hat endlich einen Job gefunden.

athlete *noun* Athlet *der* (PL *die* Athleten), Athletin *die* (PL *die* Athletinnen).

athletic *adjective* sportlich.

athletics *noun* Leichtathletik *die*.

Atlantic *noun* **the Atlantic (Ocean)** der Atlantik.

atlas *noun* Atlas *der* (PL *die* Atlanten).

atmosphere *noun* Atmosphäre *die* (PL *die* Atmosphären).

attach *verb* befestigen.

attached *adjective* (*emotionally*) **to be attached to somebody/ something** an jemandem/ etwas ←(DAT) hängen ◇.

attack *noun* Angriff *der* (PL *die* Angriffe).
verb **1** angreifen ◇ SEP; **2** (*mug or raid*) überfallen ◇.

attempt *noun* Versuch *der* (PL *die* Versuche); **at the first attempt** beim ersten Versuch.
verb **to attempt to do something** versuchen, etwas zu tun.

attend *verb* teilnehmen ◇ SEP an (+DAT); **to attend a meeting** an einer Besprechung teilnehmen; **to attend an evening class** einen Abendkurs besuchen.

attention *noun* **1** Aufmerksamkeit *die*; **to pay attention** aufpassen SEP; **I wasn't paying attention** ich habe nicht aufgepasst; **2 he wasn't paying attention to the teacher** er hörte dem Lehrer nicht zu.

attic *noun* Dachboden *der* (PL *die* Dachböden); **in the attic** auf dem Dachboden.

attitude *noun* **1** (*way of thinking*) Einstellung *die*; **2** (*way of acting*) Haltung *die*.

attract *verb* anziehen ◇ SEP.

attraction *noun* **1** Anziehung *die*; **2** (*a thing that attracts*) Attraktion *die* (PL *die* Attraktionen); **the whale was a big attraction** der Wal war eine große Attraktion.

attractive *adjective* attraktiv.

aubergine *noun* Aubergine *die* (PL *die* Auberginen).

audience *noun* Publikum *das*; **the television audience** die Fernsehzuschauer (*plural*).

◇ IRREGULAR VERB: *See the verb table in the centre of the dictionary*

August noun August der; **in August** im August.

aunt, auntie noun Tante die (PL die Tanten).

au pair noun Aupairmädchen ∆ das (PL die Aupairmädchen); **I'm looking for a job as an au pair** ich suche eine Aupair-Stelle.

Australia noun Australien das; **to Australia** nach Australien.

Australian noun Australier der (PL die Australier), Australierin die (PL die Australierinnen). adjective australisch; **she's Australian** sie ist Australierin.

Austria noun Österreich das; **in Austria** in Österreich.

Austrian noun Österreicher der (PL die Österreicher), Österreicherin die (PL die Österreicherinnen). adjective österreichisch; **he's Austrian** er ist Österreicher.

author noun Autor der (PL die Autoren), Autorin die (PL die Autorinnen).

autograph noun Autogramm das (PL die Autogramme).

automatic adjective automatisch.

automatically adverb automatisch.

autumn noun Herbst der (PL die Herbste); **in autumn** im Herbst.

available adjective (on sale) erhältlich.

average noun Durchschnitt der (PL die Durchschnitte); **on average** im Durchschnitt; **above average** über dem Durchschnitt. adjective durchschnittlich; **the average height** die durchschnittliche Größe.

avocado noun Avocado die (PL die Avocados).

avoid verb 1 vermeiden ◇; **to avoid doing something** es vermeiden, etwas zu tun; **I avoid speaking to him** ich vermeide es, mit ihm zu reden; 2 (keep away from somebody or a place) meiden ◇; **she avoids me** sie meidet mich.

awake adjective **to be awake** wach sein; **are you still awake?** bist du noch wach?

award noun Preis der (PL die Preise); **to win an award** einen Preis gewinnen.

aware adjective **to be aware of a problem** sich ←(DAT) eines Problems bewusst ∆ sein; **I'm aware of the danger** ich bin mir der Gefahr bewusst; **as far as I'm aware** soweit ich weiß.

away adverb 1 **to be away** nicht da sein; **I'll be away next week** ich bin nächste Woche nicht da; 2 **to go away** verreisen (PERF sein); **Laura's gone away for a week** Laura ist auf eine Woche verreist; **go away!** geh weg!; 3 **to run away** weglaufen ◇ SEP (PERF sein); **the thieves ran away** die Diebe liefen weg; **the school is two kilometres away** die Schule ist zwei Kilometer entfernt; **how far away is it?** wie weit entfernt ist es?; **not far away** nicht weit entfernt; 5 **to put something away** etwas wegräumen SEP; **I'm just putting my**

∆ NEW SPELLING: See page xii

books away ich räume gerade
meine Bücher weg; **6 to give
something away** etwas
weggeben ◇ SEP; (*as a present*) etwas
verschenken; **she's given away all
her cassettes** sie hat alle ihre
Kassetten verschenkt.

awful *adjective* furchtbar; **the film
was awful** der Film war furchtbar; **I
feel awful** (*ill*) ich fühle mich
furchtbar; **I feel awful about it** es
ist mir furchtbar unangenehm; **an
awful lot of mistakes** furchtbar
viele Fehler.

awkward *adjective* **1** schwierig; **it's
an awkward situation** das ist eine
schwierige Situation; **it's a bit
awkward** das ist ein bisschen
schwierig; **an awkward child** ein
schwieriges Kind; **2 an awkward
question** eine peinliche Frage.

B b

baby *noun* Baby *das* (PL *die* Babys).

babysit *verb* babysitten.

babysitter *noun* Babysitter *der* (PL
die Babysitter).

babysitting *noun* Babysitten *das*.

back *noun* **1** (*of a person or animal*)
Rücken *der* (PL *die* Rücken); **he did
it behind my back** er hat es hinter
meinem Rücken getan; **2** (*of a piece
of paper, cheque, or building*)
Rückseite *die* (PL *die* Rückseiten); **on
the back** auf der Rückseite; **3 the**

back of your hand der
Handrücken; **4 at the back** hinten;
at the back of the room hinten im
Zimmer; **we sat at the back** wir
saßen hinten; **a garden at the back
of the house** ein Garten hinter dem
Haus; **5** (*of a chair or sofa*)
Rückenlehne *die* (PL *die*
Rückenlehnen); **6** (*in football or
hockey*) Verteidiger *der* (PL *die*
Verteidiger); **left back** *der*
Linksverteidiger.
adjective **1 the back seat** (*of a car*)
der Rücksitz; **2 the back door** die
Hintertür; **the back garden** der
Garten hinter dem Haus.
adverb **1** zurück; **there and back**
hin und zurück; **to go back** (*on
foot*) zurückgehen ◇ SEP (PERF *sein*);
(*in a vehicle*) zurückfahren ◇ SEP
(PERF *sein*); **2 to come back**
zurückkommen ◇ SEP (PERF *sein*);
they've come back from Italy sie
sind aus Italien zurückgekommen;
I'll be back at 8 o'clock ich bin um
acht Uhr zurück; **Sue's not back yet**
Sue ist noch nicht zurück; **3 to
phone back** zurückrufen ◇ SEP; **I'll
ring back later** ich rufe dich später
zurück; **4 to give something back
to somebody** jemandem etwas
zurückgeben ◇ SEP; **give it back!**
gib es zurück!
verb (*bet on*) setzen auf (+ACC).
● **to back up** (*computing*) sichern; **to
back up a file** eine Sicherungsdatei
machen.
● **to back somebody up** jemanden
unterstützen.

backache *noun* Rückenschmerzen
(*plural*).

◇ **IRREGULAR VERB: See the verb table in the centre of the dictionary**

background noun 1 (of a person)
Verhältnisse (plural); she comes
from a poor background sie kommt
aus ärmlichen Verhältnissen;
2 (in a picture, view, or situation)
Hintergrund der (PL die
Hintergründe); background noise
Hintergrundgeräusche (plural);
3 (to events or problems)
Hintergründe (plural).

backing noun 1 (on sticky-back
plastic, for example)
Verstärkung die (PL die
Verstärkungen); 2 (moral support)
Unterstützung die; 3 (in music)
Begleitung die; a backing group
eine Begleitband.

backpack noun Rucksack der (PL
die Rucksäcke).
verb to go backpacking trampen
(PERF sein).

back seat noun Rücksitz der (PL die
Rücksitze).

backstroke noun
Rückenschwimmen das.

back to front adverb verkehrt
herum; your jumper's back to front
du hast deinen Pullover verkehrt
herum an.

backup noun 1 (support)
Unterstützung die; 2 (in
computing) Sicherungskopie die (PL
die Sicherungskopien); a backup
disk eine Sicherungsdiskette.

backwards adverb 1 rückwärts;
2 to lean backwards sich nach
hinten lehnen; to fall backwards
nach hinten fallen.

bacon noun Speck der; bacon and
eggs Eier mit Speck.

bad adjective 1 (not good) schlecht;
a bad idea eine schlechte Idee; a
bad meal ein schlechtes Essen; his
new film's not bad sein neuer Film
ist nicht schlecht; it's bad for your
health das ist ungesund; I'm bad at
physics ich bin schlecht in Physik;
2 (serious) schlimm; a bad mistake
ein schlimmer Fehler; a bad cold
eine schlimme Erkältung; 3 a bad
accident ein schwerer Unfall;
4 (rotten) schlecht; to go bad
schlecht werden; 5 a bad apple ein
fauler Apfel; 6 bad language
Kraftausdrücke (plural); ★ too
bad! schade!, so ein Pech!

badge noun Abzeichen das (PL die
Abzeichen).

badly adverb 1 (poorly) schlecht; he
writes badly er schreibt schlecht; I
slept badly ich habe schlecht
geschlafen; 2 (seriously) schwer;
they were badly injured sie waren
schwer verletzt; 3 (very much)
dringend; to need something badly
etwas dringend brauchen.

bad-mannered adjective to be
bad-mannered schlechte
Manieren haben.

badminton noun Badminton das.

bad-tempered adjective schlecht
gelaunt △; a bad-tempered old man
ein schlecht gelaunter alter Mann.

bag noun 1 Tasche die (PL die
Taschen); 2 (made of paper or
plastic) Tüte die (PL die Tüten).

△ NEW SPELLING: See page xii

baggage noun Gepäck das.

bagpipes plural noun
Dudelsack der.

bags plural noun Gepäck das; **to
pack your bags** sein Gepäck
packen; ★ **to have bags under your
eyes** Ringe unter den Augen haben
(informal).

bake verb 1 backen; **to bake a cake**
einen Kuchen backen; 2 **to bake
vegetables** Gemüse backen.

baked adjective 1 (fish or fruit)
überbacken; **baked apples**
Bratäpfel; 2 **a baked potato** eine
(in der Schale) gebackene Kartoffel.

baked beans plural noun Bohnen
in Tomatensoße.

baker noun 1 Gleichgewicht das;
to lose your balance das
Gleichgewicht verlieren; 2 (in a
bank account) Kontostand der.

baker noun Bäcker der (PL die
Bäcker); **to go to the baker's** zum
Bäcker gehen.

balance noun 1 Gleichgewicht das;
to lose your balance das
Gleichgewicht verlieren; 2 (in a
bank account) Kontostand der.

balanced adjective ausgeglichen.

balcony noun Balkon der (PL die
Balkons).

bald adjective 1 kahl; 2 (of a person)
kahlköpfig; **to go bald** eine Glatze
bekommen.

ball noun 1 (for tennis, football, or
golf) Ball der (PL die Bälle); 2 (for
billiards, croquet) Kugel die (PL die
Kugeln); 3 (of string or wool)
Knäuel das (PL die Knäuel).

ballet noun Ballett das (PL die
Ballette).

ballet dancer noun
Balletttänzer△ der (PL die
Balletttänzer), Balletttänzerin△ die
(PL die Balletttänzerinnen).

balloon noun 1 Luftballon der (PL
die Luftballons); 2 (hot-air)
Ballon der (PL die Ballons).

ballpoint (pen) noun
Kugelschreiber der (PL die
Kugelschreiber).

ban noun Verbot das (PL die
Verbote); **a ban on smoking** ein
Rauchverbot.
verb verbieten ◇; **to ban someone
from smoking** jemandem verbieten
zu rauchen.

banana noun 1 Banane die (PL die
Bananen); 2 **a banana yoghurt** ein
Bananenjoghurt.

band noun 1 (playing music)
Band die (PL die Bands); **rock band**
die Rockband; **brass band** die
Blaskapelle; 2 **rubber band** das
Gummiband.

bandage noun Verband der (PL die
Verbände).
verb verbinden ◇.

bang noun (noise) Knall der (PL die
Knalle).
verb 1 (hit, knock) schlagen ◇; **he
banged his fist on the table** er hat
mit der Faust auf den Tisch
geschlagen; **to bang on the door**
gegen die Tür schlagen; 2 **I banged
my head on the door** ich habe mir
den Kopf an der Tür gestoßen; 3 **to
bang into something** gegen etwas
←(ACC) knallen; 4 (shut loudly)
zuknallen SEP; **he banged the door**

◇ IRREGULAR VERB: See the verb table in the centre of the dictionary

er knallte die Tür zu.
exclamation peng!

bank *noun* 1 *(for money)* Bank *die*
(PL *die* Banken); **I'm going to the
bank** ich gehe auf die Bank; 2 *(of a
river or lake)* Ufer *das* (PL *die* Ufer).

bank account *noun*
Bankkonto *das* (PL *die* Bankkonten).

bank balance *noun*
Kontostand *der* (PL *die*
Kontostände).

bank card *noun* Scheckkarte *die*
(PL *die* Scheckkarten).

bank holiday *noun* gesetzliche
Feiertag *der* (PL *die* gesetzlichen
Feiertage).

banknote *noun* Geldschein *der* (PL
die Geldscheine).

bank statement *noun*
Kontoauszug *der* (PL *die*
Kontoauszüge).

bar *noun* 1 *(selling drinks)* Bar *die*
(PL *die* Bars); **Janet works in a bar**
Janet arbeitet in einer Bar;
2 *(counter)* Theke *die* (PL *die*
Theken); **on the bar** auf der Theke;
3 **a bar of chocolate** eine Tafel
Schokolade; 4 **a bar of soap** ein
Stück Seife; 5 *(made of wood or
metal)* Stange *die* (PL *die* Stangen);
an iron bar eine Eisenstange;
6 *(in music)* Takt *der* (PL *die* Takte).

barbecue *noun* 1 *(apparatus)*
Grill *der* (PL *die* Grills); 2 *(party)*
Grillfest *das* (PL *die* Grillfeste).
verb **to barbecue a chicken** ein
Hühnchen grillen; **barbecued
chicken** gegrilltes Hühnchen.

bare *adjective* nackt.

barefoot *adjective* **to be barefoot**
barfuß sein; **to walk barefoot**
barfuß gehen.

bargain *noun* *(a good buy)* gute
Kauf *der* (PL *die* guten Käufe); **I got
a bargain** ich habe einen guten Kauf
gemacht; **it's a bargain!** ein guter
Kauf!

bark *noun* 1 *(of a tree)* Rinde *die* (PL
die Rinden); 2 *(of a dog)* Bellen *das*.
verb bellen.

barmaid *noun* Bardame *die* (PL *die*
Bardamen).

barman *noun* Barkeeper *der* (PL *die*
Barkeeper).

barn *noun* Scheune *die* (PL *die*
Scheunen).

barrel *noun* Fass △ *das* (PL *die*
Fässer).

barrier *noun* Absperrung *die* (PL *die*
Absperrungen).

base *noun* *(bottom part)* Fuß *der*
(PL *die* Füße).

baseball *noun* Baseball *der*.

based *adjective* 1 **to be based on**
basieren auf (+DAT); **the film is
based on a true story** der Film
basiert auf einer wahren
Geschichte; 2 **to be based in**
wohnen in (+DAT); **he's based in
Bristol** er wohnt in Bristol.

basement *noun*
Kellergeschoss △ *das* (PL *die*
Kellergeschosse).

△ NEW SPELLING: *See page xii*

bash noun 1 Schlag der (PL die Schläge); 2 I'll have a bash ich probier's mal.
verb I bashed my head ich habe mir den Kopf angehauen.

basic adjective 1 grundlegend, Grund-; basic knowledge Grundkenntnisse (plural); her basic salary ihr Grundgehalt; 2 the basic problem das Hauptproblem; 3 (not luxurious) einfach.

basically adverb 1 grundsätzlich; it's basically all right grundsätzlich ist es okay; 2 basically, I don't want to come eigentlich will ich nicht kommen.

basics plural noun the basics das Wesentliche.

basin noun Becken das (PL die Becken).

basis noun 1 Basis die; 2 on a regular basis regelmäßig.

basket noun Korb der (PL die Körbe); a basket of apples ein Korb Äpfel; waste-paper basket der Papierkorb.

basketball noun Basketball der.

bass noun 1 Bass △ der (PL die Bässe); 2 double bass der Kontrabass △.

bass guitar noun Bassgitarre △ die (PL die Bassgitarren).

bassoon noun Fagott das (PL die Fagotte).

bat noun 1 (for games) Schläger der (PL die Schläger); 2 (animal) Fledermaus die (PL die Fledermäuse).

bath noun 1 Bad das (PL die Bäder); to have a bath baden; 2 (tub) Badewanne die (PL die Badewannen).

bathroom noun Badezimmer das (PL die Badezimmer).

baths plural noun Badeanstalt die (PL die Badeanstalten).

bath towel noun Badetuch das (PL die Badetücher).

batter noun Teig der (PL die Teige); fish in batter ausgebackener Fisch.

battery noun Batterie die (PL die Batterien).

battle noun 1 (in war) Schlacht die (PL die Schlachten); 2 (contest) Kampf der (PL die Kämpfe).

Bavaria noun Bayern das.

bay noun Bucht die (PL die Buchten).

BC (before Christ) v.Chr. (vor Christus).

be verb 1 sein ✧ (PERF sein); Melanie is in the kitchen Melanie ist in der Küche; where is the butter? wo ist die Butter?; I'm tired ich bin müde; when we were in Germany als wir in Deutschland waren; sein ✧ (PERF sein); she's a teacher sie ist Lehrerin; he's a taxi driver er ist Taxifahrer; 3 (in clock times, days of the week, dates, and age) sein ✧ (PERF sein); it's three o'clock es ist drei Uhr; it's half past five es ist halb sechs; what day is it today? welcher Tag ist heute?; it's Tuesday today heute ist Dienstag; it's the twentieth of May heute ist der zwanzigste Mai; what's

✧ IRREGULAR VERB: See the verb table in the centre of the dictionary

the date today? der Wievielte ist heute?; **how old are you?** wie alt bist du?; **I'm fifteen** ich bin fünfzehn; 4 (*cold, hot, ill*) sein ◇ (PERF *sein*); **I'm hot** mir ist heiß; **I'm cold** mir ist kalt; **to be ill** krank sein; 5 (*weather*) sein ◇ (PERF *sein*); **it's cold today** heute ist es kalt; **it's a nice day** es ist schönes Wetter; **it's raining** es regnet; 6 **I'm hungry** ich habe Hunger; **she's thirsty** sie hat Durst; 7 (*saying how much something costs*) kosten; **how much are the bananas?** wie viel kosten die Bananen?; 8 (*go, come, or visit*) sein ◇ (PERF *sein*); **I've never been to Berlin** ich bin noch nie in Berlin gewesen; **have you been to England before?** bist du schon einmal in England gewesen?; **has the postman been?** war der Briefträger schon da?; 9 (*forming the passive*) werden ◇ (PERF *sein*); **to be loved** geliebt werden; **he has been promoted** er ist befördert worden; 10 **there is/are** es gibt; **are there any shops near here?** gibt es hier in der Nähe Geschäfte?

beach *noun* Strand der (PL die Strände); **to go to the beach** zum Strand gehen; **on the beach** am Strand.

bead *noun* Perle die (PL die Perlen).

beam *noun* 1 (*of light*) Strahl der (PL die Strahlen); 2 (*for a roof*) Balken der (PL die Balken).

bean *noun* Bohne die (PL die Bohnen); **green beans** grüne Bohnen.

bear *noun* Bär der (PL die Bären). *verb* 1 ertragen ◇; **I can't bear the idea** ich kann den Gedanken nicht ertragen; 2 **to bear something in mind** an etwas ←(ACC) denken; **I'll bear it in mind** ich denke daran.

beard *noun* Bart der (PL die Bärte).

bearded *adjective* bärtig.

bearings *plural noun* **to get one's bearings** sich orientieren.

beast *noun* 1 (*animal*) Tier das (PL die Tiere); 2 **you beast!** du Biest!

beat *noun* (*in music*) Takt der. *verb* 1 schlagen ◇; (*defeat*) **we beat them!** wir haben sie geschlagen; 2 **you can't beat a good meal** es geht doch nichts über ein gutes Essen.
- **to beat somebody up** jemanden verprügeln.

beautiful *adjective* schön.

beauty *noun* 1 Schönheit die (PL die Schönheiten); 2 **the beauty of it is that** ... das Schöne daran ist, dass ...

because *conjunction* 1 weil; **because it's cold** weil es kalt ist; 2 **because of** wegen (+GEN); **because of the accident** wegen des Unfalls; **because of you** deinetwegen.

become *verb* werden ◇ (PERF *sein*); **she's become a painter** sie ist Malerin geworden.

bed *noun* 1 Bett das (PL die Betten); **double bed** das Doppelbett; **in bed** im Bett; **to go to bed** ins Bett gehen; 2 (*flower bed*) Beet das (PL die Beete).

△ NEW SPELLING: See page xii

bedclothes *plural noun*
Bettwäsche *die.*

bedding *noun* Bettzeug *das.*

bedroom *noun* Schlafzimmer *das*
(PL *die* Schlafzimmer); **bedroom
furniture** Schlafzimmermöbel
(*plural*); **my bedroom window**
mein Schlafzimmerfenster.

bedside table *noun* Nachttisch
der.

bedsit, bedsitter *noun* möblierte
Zimmer *das* (PL *die* möblierten
Zimmer).

bedspread *noun* Tagesdecke *die*
(PL *die* Tagesdecken).

bedtime *noun* Schlafenszeit *die;* **at
bedtime** vor dem Schlafengehen.

bee *noun* Biene *die* (PL *die* Bienen).

beech *noun* Buche *die* (PL *die*
Buchen).

beef *noun* Rindfleisch *das;* **we had
roast beef** wir haben Rinderbraten
gegessen.

beefburger *noun* Hamburger *der*
(PL *die* Hamburger).

beer *noun* Bier *das* (PL *die* Biere);
two beers please zwei Bier bitte;
beer can die Bierdose.

beetle *noun* Käfer *der* (PL *die* Käfer).

beetroot *noun* Rote Bete Δ *die.*

before *preposition* 1 vor (+DAT);
before Monday vor Montag; **he left
before me** er ist vor mir gegangen;
the day before the wedding am Tag
vor der Hochzeit; 2 **the day before**
am Tag zuvor; **the day before**

yesterday vorgestern; **the week
before** in der Woche zuvor;
3 (*already*) schon einmal; **I've seen
him before somewhere** ich habe
ihn schon einmal irgendwo gesehen;
I had seen the film before ich hatte
den Film schon einmal gesehen.
conjunction bevor; **I closed the
windows before leaving** (*or* **before
I left**) ich habe die Fenster
zugemacht, bevor ich wegging;
before the train leaves bevor der
Zug abfährt; **oh, before I forget ...**
bevor ich es vergesse ...

beforehand *adverb* (*ahead of time*)
vorher; **phone beforehand** rufe
vorher an.

beg *verb* 1 betteln; **to beg for money**
um Geld betteln; 2 (*ask*) bitten ◇;
he begged her not to say anything
er bat sie, nichts zu sagen; 3 **I beg
your pardon** entschuldigen Sie
bitte.

begin *verb* anfangen ◇ SEP,
beginnen ◇; **the meeting begins at
ten** die Besprechung fängt um zehn
an; **the words beginning with P** die
Wörter, die mit P anfangen; **to begin
to do something** anfangen, etwas
zu tun; beginnen, etwas zu tun; **I'm
beginning to understand why ...**
ich beginne zu verstehen, warum ...

beginner *noun* Anfänger *der* (PL *die*
Anfänger), Anfängerin *die* (PL *die*
Anfängerinnen).

beginning *noun* Anfang *der* (PL *die*
Anfänge); **at the beginning** am
Anfang; **at the beginning of the
holidays** am Anfang der Ferien.

behave verb 1 sich benehmen ◇; he behaved badly er hat sich schlecht benommen; 2 to behave oneself sich benehmen ◇; behave yourself! benimm dich!

behaviour noun Benehmen das.

behind noun Hintern der (informal) (PL die Hintern). preposition, adverb hinter (+DAT, or +ACC when there is movement towards a place); behind the sofa hinter dem Sofa; behind them hinter ihnen; the car behind das Auto hinter ihnen/uns; 2 to leave something behind (belongings) etwas vergessen.

beige adjective beige.

Belgian noun Belgier der (PL die Belgier), Belgierin die (PL die Belgierinnen). adjective belgisch; he's Belgian er ist Belgier.

Belgium noun Belgien das; to Belgium nach Belgien.

belief noun Glaube der (PL Glauben); his political beliefs seine politische Überzeugung.

believe verb 1 glauben; I believe so ich glaube schon; they believed what I said sie glaubten, was ich sagte; I don't believe you das glaube ich dir nicht; 2 to believe in something an etwas ←(ACC) glauben; to believe in God an Gott glauben.

bell noun 1 (in a church) Glocke die (PL die Glocken); 2 (on a door) Klingel die (PL die Klingeln); to ring the bell klingeln; 3 (for a cat or toy) Glöckchen das (PL die Glöckchen); ★ that name rings a bell der Name sagt mir etwas (literally: says something to me).

belong verb 1 to belong to gehören (+DAT); that belongs to my mother das gehört meiner Mutter; 2 to belong to a club einem Klub angehören; 3 (go) gehören; where does this vase belong? wo gehört diese Vase hin?

belongings plural noun Sachen (plural); all my belongings alle meine Sachen.

below preposition unter (+DAT, or +ACC when there is movement towards a place); below the window unter dem Fenster; the flat below yours die Wohnung unter dir. adverb 1 (further down) unten; he called from below er rief von unten; 2 the flat below die Wohnung darunter.

belt noun Gürtel der (PL die Gürtel).

bench noun Bank die (PL die Bänke).

bend noun 1 (in a road) Kurve die (PL die Kurven); 2 (in a river) Biegung die (PL die Biegungen). verb 1 (make a bend in) biegen ◇ (a pipe or wire), beugen (your knee, arm, or head); 2 (curve) eine Biegung machen; 3 to bend down sich bücken.

beneath preposition unter (+DAT).

benefit noun 1 Vorteil der (PL die Vorteile); 2 unemployment benefit die Arbeitslosenunterstützung.

bent adjective verbogen.

△ NEW SPELLING: See page xii

beret noun Baskenmütze die (PL die Baskenmützen).

beside preposition (next to) neben (+DAT, or +ACC when there is movement towards a place); **she was sitting beside me** sie saß neben mir; **she sat down beside me** sie hat sich neben mich gesetzt; ★ **that's beside the point** das hat nichts damit zu tun.

besides adverb (anyway) außerdem; **besides, it's too late** außerdem ist es zu spät; (as well) **four dogs, and six cats besides** vier Hunde und außerdem sechs Katzen.

best adjective 1 bester/beste/bestes; **she's my best friend** sie ist meine beste Freundin; **she's the best at tennis** im Tennis ist sie die Beste; **it's best to wait** das Beste ist zu warten.
adverb am besten; **he plays best** er spielt am besten; **I like Munich best** München gefällt mir am besten; **best of all** am allerbesten; **I like grapes best** ich mag Weintrauben am liebsten; ★ **all the best!** alles Gute!; ★ **to make the best of it** das Beste daraus machen; ★ **to do your best** sein Bestes tun; **I did my best to help her** ich habe mein Bestes getan, um ihr zu helfen.

bet noun Wette die (PL die Wetten).
verb wetten; **to bet on a horse** auf ein Pferd wetten; **I bet you'll forget it** ich wette mit dir, dass er es vergisst.

better adjective, adverb 1 besser; **she's found a better flat** sie hat eine bessere Wohnung gefunden; 2 **it works better than the other one** dieser geht besser als der andere; **even better** noch besser; **it's even better than before** das ist noch besser als vorher; 3 (less ill) **I'm better** es geht mir besser; **he's a bit better today** es geht ihm heute ein bisschen besser; **I feel better** ich fühle mich besser; 4 **to get better** besser werden; **my German is getting better** mein Deutsch wird besser; 5 **so much the better** umso besser; **the sooner the better** je eher, desto besser.
adverb **it's better to phone at once** es wäre besser, sofort anzurufen; **he'd better not go** er sollte besser nicht gehen; **I'd better go now** ich gehe jetzt besser.

better off adjective 1 (richer) besser gestellt; **they're better off than us** sie sind besser gestellt als wir; 2 (more comfortable) **to be better off** besser dran sein; **you'd be better off in bed** du wärst im Bett besser dran.

between preposition 1 zwischen (+DAT, or +ACC when there is movement towards a place); **between London and Dover** zwischen London und Dover; **between Monday and Friday** zwischen Montag und Freitag; 2 (sharing) unter (+DAT); **between ourselves** unter uns; **between the two of them** unter sich.

beyond preposition 1 (in space)

✧ **IRREGULAR VERB: See the verb table in the centre of the dictionary**

jenseits (+GEN); **beyond the border** jenseits der Grenze; **2** (*in time*) nach (+DAT); **beyond midnight** nach Mitternacht; **3 it's beyond me!** das ist mir unverständlich.

bicycle *noun* Fahrrad *das* (PL *die* Fahrräder); **she rides a bicycle** sie fährt Rad.

big *adjective* groß; **a big house** ein großes Haus; **my big sister** meine große Schwester; **a big mistake** ein großer Fehler; **it's too big for me** das ist mir zu groß.

big toe *noun* große Zehe *die* (PL *die* großen Zehen).

bike *noun* Rad *das* (PL *die* Räder); **by bike** mit dem Rad.

bilingual *adjective* zweisprachig.

bill *noun* Rechnung *die* (PL *die* Rechnungen); **can we have the bill, please?** die Rechnung bitte.

billiards *noun* Billard *das*; **to play billiards** Billard spielen.

bin *noun* Mülleimer *der* (PL *die* Mülleimer).

biochemistry *noun* Biochemie *die*.

biology *noun* Biologie *die*.

bird *noun* Vogel *der* (PL *die* Vögel).

bird sanctuary *noun* Vogelschutzgebiet *das* (PL *die* Vogelschutzgebiete).

Biro™ *noun* Kugelschreiber *der* (PL *die* Kugelschreiber).

birth *noun* Geburt *die* (PL *die* Geburten).

birth certificate *noun* Geburtsurkunde *die* (PL *die* Geburtsurkunden).

birthday *noun* Geburtstag *der* (PL *die* Geburtstage); **happy birthday!** herzlichen Glückwunsch zum Geburtstag!

birthday party *noun* Geburtstagsfeier *die* (PL *die* Geburtstagsfeiern).

biscuit *noun* Keks *der* (PL *die* Kekse).

bit *noun* **1** (*piece*) Stückchen *das*; **a bit of chocolate** ein Stückchen Schokolade; **2** (*a small amount*) **a bit of** ein bisschen △; **a bit of sugar** ein bisschen Zucker; **3** (*in a book, film, etc.*) Teil *der* (PL *die* Teile); **this bit is brilliant** dieser Teil ist glänzend; **4 a bit** ein bisschen △; **a bit too early** ein bisschen zu früh; **wait a bit!** warte ein bisschen!; **5 he's a bit of a show-off** er ist ein ziemlicher Angeber; **6 bit by bit** nach und nach.

bite *noun* **1** (*snack*) Happen *der* (PL *die* Happen); **we'll just have a bite before we go** wir essen noch einen kleinen Happen, bevor wir gehen; **2** (*from an insect*) Stich *der* (PL *die* Stiche); **mosquito bite** *der* Mückenstich; **3** (*from a dog*) Biss △ *der* (PL *die* Bisse). *verb* **1** (*person or dog*) beißen ♦; **2** (*insect*) stechen ♦.

bitter *adjective* (*taste*) bitter.

black *adjective* **1** schwarz; **my black jacket** meine schwarze Jacke; **2 a black man** ein Schwarzer; **a black woman** eine Schwarze.

△ NEW SPELLING: See page xii

blackberry *noun* Brombeere *die* (PL *die* Brombeeren).

blackbird *noun* Amsel *die* (PL *die* Amseln).

blackboard *noun* Tafel *die* (PL *die* Tafeln).

blackcurrant *noun* schwarze Johannisbeere *die* (PL *die* schwarzen Johannisbeeren).

blame *noun* Schuld *die*; **to take the blame for something** die Schuld für etwas ←(ACC) auf sich ←(ACC) nehmen; **to put the blame on somebody** die Schuld auf jemanden schieben; *verb* **to blame somebody for something** jemandem die Schuld an etwas ←(DAT) geben; **they blamed him for the accident** sie haben ihm die Schuld an dem Unfall gegeben; **she is to blame for it** sie ist daran schuld; **I blame the parents** ich gebe den Eltern Schuld; **I don't blame you** ich kann es dir nicht verdenken.

blank *noun* Lücke *die* (PL *die* Lücken). *adjective* **1** (*page*) leer; (*tape or disk*) unbespielt; **2 blank cheque** der Blankoscheck.

blanket *noun* Decke *die* (PL *die* Decken).

blaze *noun* Feuer *das* (PL *die* Feuer). *verb* brennen ◇.

bleach *noun* Bleichmittel *das* (PL *die* Bleichmittel).

bleed *verb* bluten; **my nose is bleeding** meine Nase blutet.

blend *verb* mischen.

blender *noun* Mixer *der* (PL *die* Mixer).

bless *verb* segnen; **bless you!** (*after a sneeze*) Gesundheit!

blind *noun* (*in a window*) Rollo *das* (PL *die* Rollos). *adjective* blind.

blister *noun* Blase *die* (PL *die* Blasen).

block *noun* (*a building or buildings*) Block *der* (PL *die* Blocks); **block of flats** der Wohnblock; **office block** das Bürohaus; **to drive round the block** um den Block fahren. *verb* **1** sperren (*an exit or a road*); **2 the sink's blocked** das Spülbecken ist verstopft.

blonde *adjective* blond.

blood *noun* Blut *das*.

blood test *noun* Blutprobe *die* (PL *die* Blutproben).

blouse *noun* Bluse *die* (PL *die* Blusen).

blow *noun* Schlag *der* (PL *die* Schläge). *verb* **1** (*a person*) blasen ◇; **2** (*the wind*) wehen; **3 the bomb blew the bridge to pieces** die Bombe hat die Brücke in die Luft gesprengt; **4 to blow your nose** sich ←(DAT) die Nase putzen.

- **to blow something out** etwas ausblasen ◇ SEP.
- **to blow up** (*explode*) explodieren (PERF sein).
- **to blow something up** (*a tyre or balloon*) etwas aufblasen ◇ SEP; (*with explosives*) etwas sprengen.

◇ IRREGULAR VERB: *See the verb table in the centre of the dictionary*

blow-dry noun Föhnen△ das; a cut and blow-dry Schneiden und Föhnen.

blue adjective blau; blue eyes blaue Augen.

blunder noun Fehler der (PL die Fehler).

blunt adjective 1 (a knife, pencil, or scissors) stumpf; 2 (a person or question) direkt.

blush verb erröten (PERF sein).

board noun 1 (plank, notice board, game) Brett das (PL die Bretter); chess board das Schachbrett; 2 (blackboard) Tafel die (PL die Tafeln); 3 (accommodation in a hotel) full board die Vollpension; half board die Halbpension; board and lodging Unterkunft und Verpflegung.

boarder noun (in a school) Internatsschüler der (PL die Internatsschüler), Internatsschülerin die (PL die Internatsschülerinnen).

board game noun Brettspiel das (PL die Brettspiele).

boarding noun (on a plane, train) Einsteigen das.

boarding card noun Bordkarte die (PL die Bordkarten).

boarding school noun Internat das (PL die Internate).

boast verb prahlen; he was boasting about his new bike er prahlte mit seinem neuen Rad.

boat noun 1 Boot das (PL die Boote); rowing boat das Ruderboot; 2 (larger boat) Schiff das (PL die Schiffe); to go by boat mit dem Schiff fahren.

body noun 1 Körper der (PL die Körper); 2 (corpse) Leiche die (PL die Leichen).

bodybuilding noun Bodybuilding das.

bodyguard noun Leibwächter der (PL die Leibwächter).

boil noun 1 to bring the water to the boil das Wasser zum Kochen bringen; 2 (swelling) Furunkel der (PL die Furunkel).
verb 1 kochen; the water's boiling das Wasser kocht; to boil vegetables Gemüse kochen; 2 (put the kettle on) to boil some water Wasser aufsetzen SEP.

● to boil over überkochen SEP (PERF sein).

boiled egg noun gekochte Ei das (PL die gekochten Eier).

boiled potato noun Salzkartoffel die (PL die Salzkartoffeln).

boiler noun (for central heating) Heizkessel der (PL die Heizkessel).

boiling adjective 1 (water) kochend; 2 it's boiling hot today heute ist es wahnsinnig heiß.

bolt noun (on a door) Riegel der (PL die Riegel).
verb 1 (lock) verriegeln; 2 (gobble down) runterschlingen ◆ SEP (informal).

△ NEW SPELLING: See page xii

bomb noun Bombe die (PL die Bomben).
verb bombardieren.

bombing noun 1 (in war) Bombardierung die (PL die Bombardierungen); 2 (a terrorist attack) Bombenattentat das (PL die Bombenattentate).

bone noun 1 Knochen der (PL die Knochen); 2 (of a fish) Gräte die (PL die Gräten).

bonfire noun Feuer das (PL die Feuer).

book noun 1 Buch das (PL die Bücher); **a book about dinosaurs** ein Buch über Dinosaurier; **my biology book** mein Biologiebuch; 2 (of stamps, tickets) Heft das (PL die Hefte); 3 **exercise book** das Heft; **cheque book** das Scheckbuch.
verb 1 buchen (holiday, flight); 2 bestellen (a table, theatre, or cinema tickets); **I booked a table for 8 p.m.** ich habe einen Tisch für zwanzig Uhr bestellt.

bookcase noun Bücherregal das (PL die Bücherregale).

booking noun (for a flight or a holiday, for example) Buchung die (PL die Buchungen).

booking office noun 1 (at a train station) Fahrkartenschalter der (PL die Fahrkartenschalter); 2 (in a theatre or cinema) Kasse die (PL die Kassen).

booklet noun Broschüre die (PL die Broschüren).

bookshelf noun Bücherregal das (PL die Bücherregale).

bookshop noun Buchhandlung die (PL die Buchhandlungen).

boot noun 1 Stiefel der (PL die Stiefel); 2 (for football, walking, climbing, or skiing) Schuh der (PL die Schuhe); **football boots** Fußballschuhe; 3 (of a car) Kofferraum der (PL die Kofferräume).

border noun (between countries) Grenze die (PL die Grenzen); **at the border** an der Grenze.

bore noun 1 (a boring person) langweilige Mensch der (PL die langweiligen Menschen); 2 (a nuisance) **what a bore!** wie ärgerlich!

bored adjective **to be bored** sich langweilen; **I'm bored** ich langweile mich.

boring adjective langweilig.

born adjective geboren; **to be born** geboren werden; **she was born in Germany** sie ist in Deutschland geboren.

borrow verb sich ←(DAT) borgen; **can I borrow your bike?** kann ich mir dein Rad borgen?; **to borrow something from somebody** sich etwas von jemandem borgen; **I borrowed some money from Dad** ich habe mir Geld von Vati geborgt.

boss noun Chef der (PL die Chefs), Chefin die (PL die Chefinnen).

bossy adjective herrisch.

◇ **IRREGULAR VERB:** See the verb table in the centre of the dictionary

both *pronoun* beide; **they both came** sie kamen beide; **both my sisters were there** meine beiden Schwestern waren da; **both of us** wir beide; **they are both sold** beide sind verkauft.
adverb both at home and at school sowohl zu Hause als auch in der Schule; **both in summer and in winter** sowohl im Sommer als auch im Winter.

bother *noun* 1 (*minor trouble*) Ärger *der*; **I've had a lot of bother with the car** ich hatte viel Ärger mit dem Auto; 2 **if it isn't too much bother** wenn es nicht zuviel Mühe macht; **it's no bother** das ist kein Problem; **the children were no bother** die Kinder waren kein Problem; **without any bother** ohne irgendwelche Schwierigkeiten.
verb 1 (*disturb*) stören; **I'm sorry to bother you** es tut mir leid, dich zu stören; 2 (*worry*) stören; **what's bothering you?** was stört dich?; **it doesn't bother me at all** das stört mich überhaupt nicht; 3 (*take trouble*) **don't bother to write** du brauchst nicht zu schreiben; **she didn't even bother to wait** sie hat nicht einmal gewartet; **don't bother!** lass es! (*informal*); **I can't be bothered** ich habe keine Lust.

bottle *noun* Flasche *die* (PL die Flaschen).

bottle bank *noun* Altglascontainer *der* (PL die Altglascontainer).

bottle opener *noun* Flaschenöffner *der* (PL die Flaschenöffner).

bottom *noun* 1 (*of a bag, bottle, hole, or stretch of water*) Boden *der* (PL die Böden); **at the bottom of the lake** am Boden des Sees; 2 (*of a hill or building*) Fuß *der* (PL die Füße); **at the bottom of the tower** am Fuß des Turms; 3 (*of a garden, street, list*) Ende *das* (PL die Enden); **at the bottom of the street** am Ende der Straße; 4 **at the bottom of the page** unten auf der Seite; 5 (*buttocks*) Hintern *der* (*informal*) (PL die Hintern).
adjective 1 unterster/unterste/unterstes; **the bottom shelf** das unterste Regal; **the bottom flat** die Wohnung im Erdgeschoss.

bounce *verb* (*jump*) springen ◇ (PERF sein).

bouncer *noun* Rausschmeißer *der* (PL die Rausschmeißer).

bound *adjective* (*certain*) **he's bound to be late** er kommt ganz bestimmt zu spät; **that was bound to happen** das musste ja kommen.

bow *noun* 1 (*in a shoelace or ribbon*) Schleife *die* (PL die Schleifen); 2 (*for a violin or with arrows*) Bogen *der* (PL die Bogen); **with bow and arrow** mit Pfeil und Bogen.

bowl *noun* 1 (*large, for salad, mixing, or washing up*) Schüssel *die* (PL die Schüsseln); 2 (*smaller*) Schale *die* (PL die Schalen).

bowler *noun* (*in cricket*) Werfer *der* (PL die Werfer), Werferin *die* (PL die Werferinnen).

bowling *noun* (*tenpin*) Bowling *das*; **to go bowling** bowlen gehen.

△ NEW SPELLING: See page xii

bow tie noun Fliege die (PL die Fliegen).

box noun 1 Schachtel die (PL die Schachteln); **a box of chocolates** eine Schachtel Pralinen; **2 cardboard box** der Karton; **3** (on a form) Kästchen das (PL die Kästchen).

boxer noun Boxer der (PL die Boxer).

boxing noun 1 Boxen das; **2 boxing match** der Boxkampf.

Boxing Day noun zweite Weihnachtsfeiertag der.

boy noun Junge der (PL die Jungen); **a little boy** ein kleiner Junge.

boyfriend noun Freund der (PL die Freunde).

bra noun BH der (PL die BHs).

brace noun (for teeth) Spange die (PL die Spangen).

bracelet noun Armband das (PL die Armbänder).

bracket noun Klammer die (PL die Klammern); **in brackets** in Klammern.

brain noun Gehirn das (PL die Gehirne).

brainwave noun Geistesblitz der (PL die Geistesblitze).

brake noun Bremse die (PL die Bremsen).
verb bremsen.

branch noun 1 (of a tree) Ast der (PL die Äste); **2** (of a shop) Filiale die (PL die Filialen); **3** (of a bank) Zweigstelle die (PL die Zweigstellen).

brand noun Marke die (PL die Marken).

brand new adjective nagelneu.

brass noun 1 (metal) Messing das; **2** (in an orchestra) **the brass** das Blech.

brass band noun Blaskapelle die (PL die Blaskapellen).

brave adjective tapfer.

bread noun Brot das (PL die Brote); **a slice of bread** eine Scheibe Brot; **a piece of bread and butter** ein Butterbrot.

break noun 1 (a short rest or at school) Pause die (PL die Pausen); **ten minutes' break** eine Pause von zehn Minuten; **to take a break** Pause machen; **at break** in der Pause; **2 the Christmas break** die Weihnachtsferien (plural).
verb 1 zerbrechen ✧, kaputtmachen SEP (informal); **he broke a glass** er hat ein Glas zerbrochen; **don't break the doll** mach die Puppe nicht kaputt; **2** (get damaged) zerbrechen ✧ (PERF sein), kaputtgehen ✧ SEP (informal) (PERF sein); **the glass broke** das Glas zerbrach; **the eggs broke** die Eier sind kaputtgegangen; **3 to break your arm** sich ←(DAT) den Arm brechen; **4** brechen ✧ (rules, promise); **to break one's promise** sein Versprechen brechen; **5 to break the record** den Rekord brechen ✧; **6 to break the news that ...** melden, dass ...
● **to break down** (car) eine Panne haben; **the car broke down** das

Auto hatte eine Panne; **2** (*talks, negotiations*) scheitern (PERF *sein*).

● **to break in** einbrechen ◇ SEP (PERF *sein*).

● **to break up 1** (*couple*) sich trennen; **2** (*crowd*) sich auflösen SEP; **3 we break up on Thursday** die Ferien fangen Donnerstag an.

breakdown *noun* **1** (*of a vehicle*) Panne *die* (PL *die* Pannen); **we had a breakdown on the motorway** wir hatten eine Panne auf der Autobahn; **2** (*in talks or negotiations*) Scheitern *das*; **3** (*a nervous collapse*) Zusammenbruch *der* (PL *die* Zusammenbrüche); **to have a nervous breakdown** einen Nervenzusammenbruch haben.

breakfast *noun* Frühstück *das* (PL *die* Frühstücke); **we have breakfast at eight** wir frühstücken um acht Uhr.

break-in *noun* Einbruch *der* (PL *die* Einbrüche).

breast *noun* Brust *die* (PL *die* Brüste).

breath *noun* Atem *der*; **out of breath** außer Atem; **to hold your breath** den Atem anhalten; **to get your breath back** wieder zu Atem kommen; **to take a deep breath** tief einatmen.

breathe *verb* atmen.

breed *noun* (*of animal*) Rasse *die* (PL *die* Rassen).

breeze *noun* Brise *die* (PL *die* Brisen).

brew *verb* **1** brauen (*beer*); **2** aufbrühen SEP (*tea*); **the tea's brewing** der Tee zieht noch.

brick *noun* Ziegel *der* (PL *die* Ziegel); **a brick wall** eine Ziegelmauer.

bride *noun* Braut *die* (PL *die* Bräute; **the bride and groom** das Brautpaar.

bridegroom *noun* Bräutigam *der* (PL *die* Bräutigame).

bridesmaid *noun* Brautjungfer *die* (PL *die* Brautjungfern).

bridge *noun* **1** (*over a river*) Brücke *die* (PL *die* Brücken); **2** (*card game*) Bridge *das*.

brief *adjective* kurz.

briefcase *noun* Aktentasche *die* (PL *die* Aktentaschen).

briefly *adverb* kurz.

briefs *plural noun* Slip *der* (PL *die* Slips).

bright *adjective* **1** (*colour*) leuchtend; **bright green socks** leuchtend grüne Socken; **2** (*eyes, sunshine*) strahlend; **3** (*light*) hell; **4** (*clever*) intelligent; **she's not very bright** sie ist nicht sehr intelligent; ★ **to look on the bright side** die Sache positiv sehen (*literally: to see things positively*).

brilliant *adjective* **1** (*very clever*) glänzend; **he's a brilliant surgeon** er ist ein glänzender Chirurg; **2** (*wonderful*) toll; **the party was brilliant!** die Party war toll!

bring *verb* **1** mitbringen ◇ SEP; **he brought a present** er brachte ein Geschenk mit; **bring your camera**

△ NEW SPELLING: See page xii

bring deinen Fotoapparat mit; **2** (*to a place*) bringen ◇; **she's bringing the children home** sie bringt die Kinder nach Hause.

● **to bring somebody up** jemanden großziehen ◇ SEP; **he was brought up by his aunt** er wurde von seiner Tante großgezogen.

Britain noun Großbritannien *das*; **to Britain** nach Großbritannien.

British *plural noun* the British die Briten.
adjective **1** britisch; **the British Isles** die Britischen Inseln; **2** he's **British** er ist Brite; **she's British** sie ist Britin.

broad *adjective* **1** (*wide*) breit; **2** (*extensive*) weit.

broad bean noun dicke Bohne *die* (PL die dicken Bohnen).

broadcast noun Sendung *die* (PL die Sendungen).
verb senden.

broccoli noun Brokkoli *der* (PL die Brokkoli).

brochure noun Broschüre *die* (PL die Broschüren).

broke *adjective* to be broke pleite sein (*informal*).

broken *adjective* zerbrochen, kaputt (*informal*); **the window's broken** das Fenster ist kaputt; **to have a broken leg** ein gebrochenes Bein haben.

bronchitis noun Bronchitis *die*.

brooch noun Brosche *die* (PL die Broschen).

brother noun Bruder *der* (PL die Brüder); **my mother's brother** der Bruder meiner Mutter.

brother-in-law noun Schwager *der* (PL die Schwäger).

brown *adjective* braun; **my brown shoes** meine braunen Schuhe; **light brown** hellbraun; **dark brown** dunkelbraun; **to go brown** (*suntanned*) braun werden.

brown bread noun Mischbrot *das* (PL die Mischbrote).

bruise noun **1** (*on a person*) blaue Fleck *der* (PL die blauen Flecken); **2** (*on fruit*) Druckstelle *die* (PL die Druckstellen).

brush noun **1** (*for your hair, clothes, nails, or shoes*) Bürste *die* (PL die Bürsten); **my hair brush** meine Haarbürste; **2** (*for sweeping*) Besen *der* (PL die Besen); **3** (*for paint*) Pinsel *der* (PL die Pinsel).
verb **1** bürsten; **to brush your hair** sich ←(DAT) die Haare bürsten; **I brushed my hair** ich habe mir die Haare gebürstet; **2** to brush your teeth sich ←(DAT) die Zähne putzen.

Brussels noun Brüssel *das*.

Brussels sprout noun Rosenkohl *der*; **he likes Brussels sprouts** er mag Rosenkohl.

bubble noun Blase *die* (PL die Blasen).

bubble bath noun Badeschaum *der*.

bucket noun Eimer *der* (PL die Eimer).

◇ IRREGULAR VERB: *See the verb table in the centre of the dictionary*

buckle noun Schnalle die (PL die Schnallen).

Buddhism noun Buddhismus der.

Buddhist noun Buddhist der (PL die Buddhisten), Buddhistin die (PL die Buddhistinnen).

budget noun Budget das (PL die Budgets).

buffet car noun Speisewagen der (PL die Speisewagen).

bug noun 1 (insect) Wanze die (PL die Wanzen); 2 (germ) Bazillus der (PL die Bazillen); a stomach bug eine Magengrippe; 3 a computer bug ein Programmierfehler.

build verb bauen.

builder noun Bauarbeiter der (PL die Bauarbeiter).

building noun Gebäude das (PL die Gebäude).

building site noun Baustelle die (PL die Baustellen).

built-up adjective 1 bebaut; 2 built-up area das Wohngebiet.

bulb noun 1 (lightbulb) Birne die (PL die Birnen); 2 (flower bulb) Zwiebel die (PL die Zwiebeln).

bull noun Bulle der (PL die Bullen).

bullet noun Kugel die (PL die Kugeln).

bulletin noun 1 (written) Bulletin das (PL die Bulletins); 2 (on TV, radio) news bulletin die Kurzmeldung.

bully noun 1 (in school) Rabauke der (PL die Rabauken); 2 (adult) Tyrann der (PL die Tyrannen).
verb schikanieren.

bum noun Hintern der (informal) (PL die Hintern).

bump noun 1 (on a surface) Unebenheit die (PL die Unebenheiten); there are lots of bumps in the road die Straße hat viele Unebenheiten; 2 (swelling) Beule die (PL die Beulen); a bump on the head eine Beule am Kopf; 3 (jolt) Stoß der (PL die Stöße); 4 (noise) Bums der (PL die Bumse). verb 1 (bang) stoßen ◇; I bumped my head ich habe mir den Kopf gestoßen; to bump into something gegen etwas ←(ACC) stoßen ◇; 2 to bump into somebody (meet by chance) jemanden zufällig treffen.

bumper noun Stoßstange die (PL die Stoßstangen).

bumpy adjective holperig.

bun noun 1 (for a burger) Brötchen das (PL die Brötchen), Semmel die (PL die Semmeln); 2 (sweet) süße Brötchen das (PL die süßen Brötchen), süße Semmel die (PL die süßen Semmeln).

bunch noun 1 (of flowers) Strauß der (PL die Sträuße); 2 (of carrots, radishes, or keys) Bund das (PL die Bunde); 3 a bunch of grapes eine ganze Weintraube.

bundle noun Bündel das (PL die Bündel).

bunk noun 1 (on a boat) Koje die (PL die Kojen); 2 (on a train) Bett das (PL die Betten).

bunk beds plural noun
Etagenbett das (singular).

burger noun Hamburger der (PL die Hamburger).

burglar noun Einbrecher der (PL die Einbrecher).

burglar alarm noun
Alarmanlage die (PL die Alarmanlagen).

burglary noun Einbruch der (PL die Einbrüche).

burn noun 1 (on the skin)
Verbrennung die (PL die Verbrennungen); 2 (on fabric, object) Brandstelle die (PL die Brandstellen).
verb 1 verbrennen ✧; **she burnt his letters** sie hat seine Briefe verbrannt; 2 (fire, candle) brennen ✧; 3 (injure) verbrennen ✧; **to burn yourself** sich verbrennen; **you'll burn your fingers!** du verbrennst dir die Finger!; 4 (cake, meat, etc.) anbrennen ✧ SEP; **Mum's burnt the cake** Mutti hat den Kuchen anbrennen lassen.

burnt adjective 1 (papers, rubbish) verbrannt; 2 (cake, meat, etc.) angebrannt.

burst verb 1 platzen lassen (a balloon); **the tyre has burst** der Reifen ist geplatzt; 2 **to burst out laughing** in Lachen ausbrechen ✧ SEP (PERF sein); **to burst into tears** in Tränen ausbrechen ✧ SEP (PERF sein); 3 **to burst into flames** in Flammen aufgehen ✧ SEP (PERF sein).

bury verb 1 begraben ✧ (a dead person); 2 vergraben ✧ (a treasure or a bone).

bus noun Bus der (PL die Busse); **on the bus** im Bus; **by bus** mit dem Bus.

bus driver noun Busfahrer der (PL die Busfahrer), Busfahrerin die (PL die Busfahrerinnen).

bush noun Busch der (PL die Büsche).

business noun 1 (commercial dealings) Geschäfte (plural); **business is bad** die Geschäfte gehen schlecht; **he's in Leeds on business** er ist geschäftlich in Leeds; 2 (a line of business or profession) Branche die (PL die Branchen); **he's in the insurance business** er ist in der Versicherungsbranche; 3 (firm or company) Betrieb der (PL die Betriebe); **small businesses** kleine Betriebe; 4 (personal concern) Angelegenheit die (PL die Angelegenheiten); **mind your own business!** kümmere dich um deine eigenen Angelegenheiten!

businessman noun
Geschäftsmann der (PL die Geschäftsleute).

business trip noun
Geschäftsreise die (PL die Geschäftsreisen).

businesswoman noun
Geschäftsfrau die (PL die Geschäftsfrauen).

bus pass noun Zeitkarte die (PL die Zeitkarten).

✧ IRREGULAR VERB: See the verb table in the centre of the dictionary

bus route noun Buslinie die (PL die Buslinien).

bus shelter noun Wartehäuschen das (PL die Wartehäuschen).

bus station noun Busbahnhof der (PL die Busbahnhöfe).

bus stop noun Bushaltestelle die (PL die Bushaltestellen).

bus ticket noun Busfahrkarte die (PL die Busfahrkarten).

busy adjective 1 beschäftigt; **he's busy** er ist beschäftigt; **she was busy packing** sie war mit Packen beschäftigt; 2 **to have a busy day** viel zu tun haben; 3 **the shops were busy** die Läden waren sehr voll; 4 (phone) besetzt.

but conjunction 1 aber; **small but strong** klein aber stark; 2 (after a negative statement) sondern; **not Thursday but Friday** nicht Donnerstag, sondern Freitag; **not only ... but also** nicht nur ... sondern auch.
preposition 1 außer (+DAT); **everyone but Winston** alle außer Winston; **anything but that!** nur das nicht!; 2 **the last but one** der/die/das Vorletzte.

butcher noun 1 Fleischer der (PL die Fleischer), Metzger der (PL die Metzger); **he's a butcher** er ist Fleischer, er ist Metzger; 2 **the butcher's** die Fleischerei, die Metzgerei.

butter noun Butter die.
verb buttern.

butterfly noun Schmetterling der (PL die Schmetterlinge).

button noun Knopf der (PL die Knöpfe).

buttonhole noun Knopfloch das (PL die Knopflöcher).

buy noun Kauf der (PL die Käufe); **a bad buy** ein schlechter Kauf.
verb kaufen; **I bought the tickets** ich habe die Karten gekauft; **to buy something for somebody** jemandem etwas kaufen; **Sarah bought him a sweater** Sarah hat ihm einen Pullover gekauft.

buzz verb (a fly or bee) summen.

buzzer noun Summer der (PL die Summer).

by preposition 1 von (+DAT); **I was bitten by a dog** ich bin von einem Hund gebissen worden; **by Mozart** von Mozart; 2 **by mistake** versehentlich; 3 (travel) mit (+DAT); **to come by bus** mit dem Bus kommen; **to go by train** mit dem Zug fahren; **by bike** mit dem Rad; 4 (near) an (+DAT); **by the sea** am Meer; **the stop by the school** die Haltestelle an der Schule; 5 (before) bis; **it'll be ready by Monday** es wird bis Montag fertig sein; **I'll be back by four** ich bin bis vier Uhr zurück; 6 **by now** inzwischen; 7 **by yourself** ganz allein; **I was by myself in the house** ich war ganz allein im Haus; **she did it by herself** sie hat es ganz allein gemacht; 8 **by the way** übrigens; 9 **to go by** vorbeigehen ✧ SEP (PERF sein).

bye exclamation tschüs! (informal).

C c

cab noun 1 Taxi das (PL die Taxis); **to call a cab** ein Taxi rufen; 2 (on a lorry) Führerhaus das (PL die Führerhäuser).

cabbage noun Kohl der.

café noun Café das (PL die Cafés).

cage noun Käfig der (PL die Käfige).

cake noun Kuchen der (PL die Kuchen); **would you like a piece of cake?** möchtest du ein Stück Kuchen?

calculate verb berechnen.

calculation noun Rechnung die (PL die Rechnungen).

calculator noun Taschenrechner der (PL die Taschenrechner).

calendar noun Kalender der (PL die Kalender).

calf noun 1 (animal) Kalb das (PL die Kälber); 2 (of your leg) Wade die (PL die Waden).

call noun 1 (telephone) Anruf der (PL die Anrufe); **I had several calls this morning** ich erhielt heute Morgen mehrere Anrufe; **thank you for your call** danke für deinen Anruf; **a phone call** ein Telefonanruf.
verb 1 rufen ◇; **to call a taxi** ein Taxi rufen; **to call the doctor** einen Arzt rufen; **they called the police** sie riefen die Polizei; 2 (phone)

anrufen ◇ sep; **call me later** ruf mich später an; **thank you for calling** danke für deinen Anruf; **I'll call you back later** ich rufe dich später zurück; 3 nennen ◇; **they've called the baby Julie** sie haben das Baby Julie genannt; 4 **to be called** heißen ◇; **her brother is called Dan** ihr Bruder heißt Dan; **what's he called?** wie heißt er?

call box noun Telefonzelle die (PL die Telefonzellen).

calm adjective ruhig.
verb beruhigen.
• **to calm down** sich beruhigen; **he's calmed down a bit** er hat sich etwas beruhigt.
• **to calm somebody down** jemanden beruhigen; **I tried to calm her down** ich habe versucht, sie zu beruhigen.

calmly adverb ruhig.

camcorder noun Camcorder der (PL die Camcorder).

camera noun 1 Fotoapparat der (PL die Fotoapparate); 2 (film or video camera) Kamera die (PL die Kameras).

camp noun Lager das (PL die Lager).
verb campen, zelten.

camper van noun Camper der (PL die Camper).

camping noun Camping das; **to go camping** zelten; **we're going camping in Bavaria this summer** diesen Sommer zelten wir in Bayern.

campsite noun Campingplatz der (PL die Campingplätze).

can[1] noun 1 Dose die (PL die Dosen);

◇ IRREGULAR VERB: See the verb table in the centre of the dictionary

a can of tomatoes eine Dose Tomaten; **2** (for petrol or oil) Kanister der (PL die Kanister).

can² verb **1** können ◇; **I can't be there before ten** ich kann vor zehn Uhr nicht da sein; **can you open the door, please?** kannst du die Tür bitte aufmachen?; **can I help you?** kann ich Ihnen helfen?; **they couldn't come** sie konnten nicht kommen; **you could have told me** das hättest du mir wirklich sagen können; **I can't see him** ich kann ihn nicht sehen; **I can't remember it** ich kann mich nicht daran erinnern; **she can't drive** sich kann nicht Auto fahren; **2** (be allowed) dürfen ◇; **you can't smoke here** Sie dürfen hier nicht rauchen.

Canada noun Kanada das; **to Canada** nach Kanada.

Canadian noun Kanadier der (PL die Kanadier), Kanadierin die (PL die Kanadierinnen).
adjective kanadisch; **he is Canadian** er ist Kanadier.

canal noun Kanal der (PL die Kanäle).

cancel verb absagen SEP; **the concert's been cancelled** das Konzert ist abgesagt worden.

cancer noun Krebs der; **to have lung cancer** Lungenkrebs haben.

Cancer noun Krebs der (PL die Krebse); **I'm Cancer** ich bin Krebs.

candidate noun Kandidat der (PL die Kandidaten), Kandidatin die (PL die Kandidatinnen).

candle noun Kerze die (PL die Kerzen).

candlestick noun Kerzenhalter der (PL die Kerzenhalter).

canned adjective in Dosen; **canned tomatoes** Tomaten in Dosen.

canoe noun Kanu das (PL die Kanus).

canoeing noun **to go canoeing** Kanu fahren ◇ (PERF sein); **I like canoeing** ich fahre gerne Kanu.

can-opener noun Dosenöffner der (PL die Dosenöffner).

canteen noun Kantine die (PL die Kantinen).

canvas noun **1** (of a tent or bag) Segeltuch das; **2** (for painting on) Leinwand die.

cap noun **1** (hat) Kappe die (PL die Kappen); **baseball cap** die Baseballkappe; **2** (on a bottle or tube) Verschluss △ der (PL die Verschlüsse).

capable adjective fähig.

capital noun **1** (city) Hauptstadt die (PL die Hauptstädte); **Berlin is the capital of Germany** Berlin ist die Hauptstadt von Deutschland; **2** (letter) Großbuchstabe der (PL die Großbuchstaben); **in capitals** mit Großbuchstaben.

capitalism noun Kapitalismus der.

△ NEW SPELLING: See page xii

Capricorn noun Steinbock der (PL die Steinböcke); Linda's Capricorn Linda ist Steinbock.

captain noun Kapitän der (PL die Kapitäne).

car noun Auto das (PL die Autos); **to park the car** das Auto einparken; **we're going by car** wir fahren mit dem Auto; **car crash** der Autounfall.

caramel noun Karamell △ der (PL die Karamells).

caravan noun Wohnwagen der (PL die Wohnwagen).

card noun Karte die (PL die Karten); **card game** das Kartenspiel; **to have a game of cards** Karten spielen.

cardboard noun Pappe die.

cardigan noun Strickjacke die (PL die Strickjacken).

cardphone noun Kartentelefon das (PL die Kartentelefone).

care noun 1 Vorsicht die; **to take care crossing the road** vorsichtig beim Überqueren der Straße sein; **take care!** (be careful) sei vorsichtig!; (when saying goodbye) mach's gut!; 2 **to take care to do something** aufpassen SEP, dass man etwas tut; **to take care of somebody** auf jemanden aufpassen.
verb 1 **to care about something** sich um etwas ←(ACC) kümmern; **she cares about the environment** sie kümmert sich um die Umwelt; 2 **she doesn't care** es ist ihr egal; **I couldn't care less!** das ist mir völlig egal!

careful adjective vorsichtig; **a careful driver** ein vorsichtiger Fahrer, eine vorsichtige Fahrerin; **be careful!** sei vorsichtig!

carefully adverb 1 sorgfältig; **to read the instructions carefully** die Anweisungen sorgfältig lesen; 2 vorsichtig; **she put the vase down carefully** sie stellte die Vase vorsichtig hin; **drive carefully!** fahr vorsichtig!; 3 **listen carefully!** hören Sie gut zu!

careless adjective 1 **he's very careless** er ist sehr nachlässig; **this is careless work** das ist eine nachlässige Arbeit; 2 **a careless mistake** ein Flüchtigkeitsfehler; 3 **a careless driver** ein leichtsinniger Fahrer.

car ferry noun Autofähre die (PL die Autofähren).

car hire noun Autovermietung die.

Caribbean noun **the Caribbean (islands)** die Karibik (singular).

carnation noun Nelke die (PL die Nelken).

carnival noun Karneval der (PL die Karnevale).

car park noun Parkplatz der (PL die Parkplätze); (multi-storey) Parkhaus das (PL die Parkhäuser).

carpenter noun Tischler der (PL die Tischler).

carpentry noun Tischlerhandwerk das.

carpet noun Teppich der (PL die Teppiche).

◈ IRREGULAR VERB: See the verb table in the centre of the dictionary

car phone noun Autotelefon das (PL die Autotelefone).

car radio noun Autoradio das (PL die Autoradios).

carriage noun (of a train) Abteil das (PL die Abteile).

carrier bag noun Tragetasche die (PL die Tragetaschen).

carrot noun 1 Karotte die (PL Karotten), Möhre die (PL die Möhren).

carry verb tragen; **she was carrying a case** sie trug einen Koffer.
● **to carry on** weitermachen SEP; **they carried on working** sie machten ihre Arbeit weiter.

carrycot noun Babytragetasche die (PL die Babytragetaschen).

carsick adjective **he gets carsick** ihm wird beim Autofahren schlecht.

carton noun 1 (of cream or yoghurt) Becher der (PL die Becher); 2 (of milk or orange) Tüte die (PL die Tüten).

cartoon noun 1 (a film) Zeichentrickfilm der (PL die Zeichentrickfilme); 2 (a comic strip) Cartoon der (PL die Cartoons); 3 (a drawing) Karikatur die (PL die Karikaturen).

cartridge noun (for a pen) Patrone die (PL die Patronen).

case[1] noun 1 (suitcase) Koffer der (PL die Koffer); **to pack a case** einen Koffer packen; 2 (a large wooden box) Kiste die (PL die Kisten); 3 (for spectacles or small things) Etui die (PL die Etuis).

case[2] noun 1 Fall der (PL die Fälle); **in that case** in dem Fall; **that's not the case** das ist nicht der Fall; **in case of fire** bei Feuer; 2 **in case** falls; **in case he comes** falls er kommt; 3 **just in case** für alle Fälle; 4 **in any case** sowieso; **in any case, it's too late** es ist sowieso zu spät.

cash noun 1 (money in general) Geld das; **I haven't any cash on me** ich habe kein Geld dabei; 2 (money rather than a cheque) Bargeld das; **to pay in cash** bar zahlen; **£50 in cash** fünfzig Pfund in bar.

cash card noun Bankkarte die (PL die Bankkarten).

cash desk noun Kasse die (PL die Kassen); **to pay at the cash desk** an der Kasse zahlen.

cash dispenser noun Geldautomat der (PL die Geldautomaten).

cashier noun Kassierer der (PL die Kassierer), Kassiererin die (PL die Kassiererinnen).

cash point noun Geldautomat der (PL die Geldautomaten).

cassette noun Kassette die (PL die Kassetten).

cassette recorder noun Kassettenrekorder der (PL die Kassettenrekorder).

cast noun (of a play) Besetzung die.

castle noun 1 Burg die (PL die Burgen); 2 (in chess) Turm der (PL die Türme).

casual adjective zwanglos.

△ NEW SPELLING: See page xii

casualty noun 1 (in an accident)
Verletzte der/die (PL die Verletzten);
2 (hospital department)
Unfallstation die (PL die
Unfallstationen); **he's in casualty** er
ist auf der Unfallstation.

cat noun Katze die (PL die Katzen);
(tomcat) Kater der (PL die Kater);
★ **it's raining cats and dogs** es
regnet in Strömen (literally: it's
raining in streams).

catalogue noun Katalog der (PL die
Kataloge).

catastrophe noun
Katastrophe die (PL die
Katastrophen).

catch noun 1 (on a door)
Schnapper der (PL die Schnapper);
2 (a drawback) Haken der (PL die
Haken); **where's the catch?** wo ist
der Haken?
verb 1 fangen ◇; **Tom caught the
ball** Tom hat den Ball gefangen; **she
caught a fish** sie hat einen Fisch
gefangen; **catch me!** fang mich!;
2 **to catch somebody doing
something** jemanden bei etwas
←(DAT) erwischen; **he was caught
stealing money** er wurde beim
Geldstehlen erwischt; 3 (be in time
for) noch erreichen; **did Tim catch
his plane?** hat Tim sein Flugzeug
noch erreicht? 4 (become ill with)
bekommen ◇; **she's caught
chickenpox** sie hat die
Windpocken bekommen;
5 verstehen ◇ (what somebody
says); **I didn't catch your name** ich
habe Ihren Namen nicht verstanden.
● **to catch up with somebody**
jemanden einholen SEP.

catering noun 1 (trade)
Gastronomie die; 2 **who's doing the
catering?** wer liefert das Essen und
die Getränke?

cathedral noun Kathedrale die (PL
die Kathedralen); **Cologne
cathedral** der Kölner Dom.

Catholic noun Katholik der (PL die
Katholiken), Katholikin die (PL die
Katholikinnen).
adjective katholisch.

cattle plural noun Vieh das.

cauliflower noun Blumenkohl der;
cauliflower cheese der
Blumenkohlauflauf.

cause noun 1 Ursache die (PL die
Ursachen); **the cause of the
accident** die Unfallursache; 2 **for a
good cause** für eine gute Sache.
verb verursachen; **to cause
difficulties** Schwierigkeiten
verursachen.

cave noun Höhle die (PL die
Höhlen).

caving noun Höhlenforschung die,
to go caving auf Höhlenforschung
gehen.

CD noun CD die (PL die CDs).

CD player noun CD-Spieler der (PL
die CD-Spieler).

CD-ROM noun CD-ROM die (PL die
CD-ROMs).

ceiling noun Decke die (PL die
Decken); **on the ceiling** an der
Decke.

◇ IRREGULAR VERB: See the verb table in the centre of the dictionary

celebrate verb feiern; he's celebrating his birthday er feiert seinen Geburtstag.

celebrity noun Berühmtheit die (PL die Berühmtheiten).

celery noun Sellerie die (PL die Sellerie).

cell noun Zelle die (PL die Zellen).

cellar noun Keller der (PL die Keller).

cello noun Cello das (PL die Cellos); to play the cello Cello spielen.

cement noun Zement der.

cemetery noun Friedhof der (PL die Friedhöfe).

centigrade adjective Celsius; ten degrees centigrade zehn Grad Celsius.

centimetre noun Zentimeter der (PL die Zentimeter).

central adjective 1 zentral; the office is very central das Büro ist sehr zentral gelegen; 2 in central London im Zentrum von London.

central heating noun Zentralheizung die.

centre noun Zentrum das (PL die Zentren); in the centre of im Zentrum von (+DAT); in the town centre im Stadtzentrum; a shopping centre ein Einkaufszentrum.

century noun Jahrhundert das (PL die Jahrhunderte); in the twentieth century im zwanzigsten Jahrhundert.

cereal noun breakfast cereal Frühstücksflocken (plural).

certain adjective 1 (definite) bestimmt; a certain number eine bestimmte Zahl von (+DAT); 2 (confident) sicher; to be certain sich ←(DAT) sicher sein; are you certain of the address? bist du dir der Adresse sicher?; I'm absolutely certain ich bin mir ganz sicher; to be certain that … sicher sein, dass …; 3 nobody knows for certain niemand weiß es genau.

certainly adverb bestimmt; certainly not bestimmt nicht.

certificate noun 1 Bescheinigung die (PL die Bescheinigungen); 2 birth certificate die Geburtsurkunde; 3 (at school) Zeugnis das (PL die Zeugnisse).

chain Kette die (PL die Ketten).

chair noun 1 (upright) Stuhl der (PL die Stühle); a kitchen chair ein Küchenstuhl; 2 (with arms) Sessel der (PL die Sessel).

chair lift noun Sessellift der (PL die Sessellifte).

chalet noun 1 (in the mountains) Chalet das (PL die Chalets); 2 (in a holiday camp) Ferienhaus das (PL die Ferienhäuser).

challenge noun Herausforderung die (PL die Herausforderungen).

champion noun Meister der (PL die Meister), Meisterin die (PL die Meisterinnen); the world slalom champion der Weltmeister im Slalom, die Weltmeisterin im Slalom.

△ NEW SPELLING: See page xii

chance noun 1 (*opportunity*)
Gelegenheit *die* (PL *die*
Gelegenheiten); **to have the chance
to do something** die Gelegenheit
haben, etwas zu tun; **if you have the
chance to go to New York** wenn
du die Gelegenheit hast, nach New
York zu fahren; **I had no chance to
speak to him** ich hatte keine
Gelegenheit, mit ihm zu reden;
2 (*likelihood*) Aussicht *die* (PL *die*
Aussichten); **he's got no chance of
winning** er hat keine Aussicht zu
gewinnen; 3 (*luck*) by chance
zufällig; **do you have her address,
by any chance?** hast du zufällig ihre
Adresse?

change noun 1 (*from one thing to
another*) Änderung *die* (PL *die*
Änderungen); **a change of address**
eine Adressenänderung; **there's
been a change of plan** der Plan ist
geändert worden; 2 (*alteration*)
Veränderung *die* (PL *die*
Veränderungen); **they've made
some changes to the house** sie
haben im Haus ein paar
Veränderungen vorgenommen; **a
change in the weather** eine
Wetterveränderung; 3 (*for the sake
of variety*) **for a change, we could
go to a restaurant** zur Abwechslung
könnten wir in ein Restaurant gehen;
**it makes a change from
hamburgers** das ist mal etwas
anderes als Hamburger; **a change of
clothes** etwas anderes zum
Anziehen; 4 (*cash*)
Wechselgeld *das*; **I haven't any
change** ich habe kein Wechselgeld.
verb 1 (*make different*) ändern; **you
can't change her** du kannst sie nicht

ändern; **to change your address**
seine Adresse ändern; 2 (*become
different*) sich verändern; **Liz has
changed a lot** Liz hat sich sehr
verändert; 3 (*transform completely*)
verwandeln; **the prince changed
into a frog** der Prinz hat sich in
einen Frosch verwandelt;
4 (*exchange in a shop*) umtauschen
SEP; **just change it for a larger size**
tauschen Sie es einfach gegen eine
größere Größe um; 5 (*change
clothes*) sich umziehen ◇ SEP;
Mike's just changing Mike zieht
sich gerade um; 6 (*switch from one
train or bus to another*)
umsteigen ◇ SEP (PERF *sein*); **we
changed trains at Crewe** wir sind
in Crewe umgestiegen; 7 (*switch one
thing for another*) wechseln; **I want
to change my job** ich möchte meine
Stellung wechseln; **they changed
places** sie haben die Plätze
gewechselt; 8 **to change your mind**
sich anders entschließen ◇.

changing room noun (*for sport or
swimming*) Umkleideraum *der* (PL
die Umkleideräume).

channel noun 1 (*on TV*) Kanal *der*
(PL *die* Kanäle); **to change channels**
auf einen anderen Kanal schalten;
2 **the Channel** der Kanal.

Channel Tunnel noun
Eurotunnel *der*.

chaos noun Chaos *das*; **it was
chaos!** das war ein Chaos!

chapel noun Kapelle *die* (PL *die*
Kapellen).

◇ IRREGULAR VERB: See the verb table in the centre of the dictionary

chapter noun Kapitel das (PL die Kapitel); **in chapter two** im zweiten Kapitel.

character noun 1 (personality) Charakter der; 2 (somebody in a book) Charakter der (PL die Charaktere); 3 (part in a play or film) Rolle die (PL die Rollen); **the main character** die Hauptrolle.

charcoal noun 1 (for burning) Holzkohle die; 2 (for drawing) Kohlestift der (PL die Kohlestifte).

charge noun 1 (what you pay) Gebühr die (PL die Gebühren); **a booking charge** Buchungskosten (plural); **an extra or additional charge** eine zusätzliche Gebühr; **there's no charge** das ist kostenlos; **2 to be in charge** für etwas ←(ACC) verantwortlich sein; **who's in charge of the children?** wer ist für die Kinder verantwortlich?; **3 to be on a charge of theft** wegen Diebstahls angeklagt sein.
verb 1 (ask to pay) berechnen; **they charge us fifteen pounds an hour** sie berechnen uns fünfzehn Pfund pro Stunde; **they didn't charge for delivery** sie haben die Lieferung nicht berechnet; **we won't charge you for it** wir berechnen Ihnen nichts dafür; **2 to charge somebody with something** jemanden wegen etwas ←(GEN) anklagen SEP.

charity noun Wohltätigkeitsverein der (PL die Wohltätigkeitsvereine).

charming adjective reizend.

chart noun 1 (table) Tabelle die (PL die Tabellen); **2 the weather chart** die Wetterkarte; **3 the charts** die Hitparade.

charter flight noun Charterflug der (PL die Charterflüge).

chase noun Verfolgungsjagd die (PL die Verfolgungsjagden); **a car chase** eine Verfolgungsjagd im Auto.
verb jagen.

chat noun Plauderei die (PL die Plaudereien); **to have a chat with somebody** mit jemandem plaudern.

chat show noun Talkshow die (PL die Talkshows).

chatter verb 1 (talk) schwatzen; **2 my teeth were chattering** ich habe mit den Zähnen geklappert.

cheap adjective billig; **cheap shoes** billige Schuhe; **that's very cheap** das ist sehr billig.

cheaply adverb billig; **to eat cheaply** billig essen.

cheap-rate adjective verbilligt; **a cheap-rate phone call** ein Gespräch zum Spartarif.

cheat noun 1 Betrüger der (PL die Betrüger), Betrügerin die (PL die Betrügerinnen); 2 (in games) Mogler der (PL die Mogler), Moglerin die (PL die Moglerinnen).
verb 1 betrügen ◆; 2 (in games) mogeln.

check noun 1 (in a factory or at a border control) Kontrolle die (PL die Kontrollen); **passport check** die

△ NEW SPELLING: See page xii

Passkontrolle; 2 (*in chess*) **check!** Schach!

verb 1 (*make sure*) prüfen; **he checked their statements** er prüfte ihre Aussage; 2 (*make sure by looking*) nachsehen ◊ SEP; **to check the time** nachsehen, wie viel Uhr es ist; **check they're all back** sieh nach, ob alle wieder da sind; 3 (*inspect*) kontrollieren; **to check the tickets** die Fahrkarten kontrollieren.

check in *verb* (*for a flight*) einchecken SEP.

check-in *noun* Abfertigungsschalter *der* (PL *die* Abfertigungsschalter).

checkout *noun* Kasse *die* (PL *die* Kassen); **at the checkout** an der Kasse.

check-up *noun* Untersuchung *die* (PL *die* Untersuchungen).

cheek *noun* 1 (*part of face*) Backe *die* (PL *die* Backen); 2 (*nerve*) Frechheit *die*; **what a cheek!** so eine Frechheit!

cheer *noun* 1 **three cheers for Tom!** ein dreifaches Hurra für Tom!; 2 (*when drinking*) **cheers!** prost!

verb (*shout hurray*) Hurra schreien ◊.

- **to cheer somebody up** jemanden aufmuntern SEP; **your visits always cheer me up** dein Besuch muntert mich immer auf; **cheer up!** Kopf hoch!

cheerful *adjective* fröhlich.

cheese *noun* Käse *der*; **a cheese sandwich** ein Käsebrot.

chef *noun* Koch *der* (PL *die* Köche), Köchin *die* (PL *die* Köchinnen).

chemist *noun* 1 (*in a pharmacy*) Apotheker *der* (PL *die* Apotheker), Apothekerin *die* (PL *die* Apothekerinnen); 2 (*chemist's (dispensing*) Apotheke *die* (PL *die* Apotheken); **at the chemist's** in der Apotheke; 3 (*scientist*) Chemiker *der* (PL *die* Chemiker), Chemikerin *die* (PL *die* Chemikerinnen).

chemistry *noun* Chemie *die*.

cheque *noun* Scheck *der* (PL *die* Schecks); **to pay by cheque** mit Scheck bezahlen; **to write a cheque** einen Scheck austellen.

cheque book *noun* Scheckbuch *das* (PL *die* Scheckbücher).

cherry *noun* Kirsche *die* (PL *die* Kirschen).

chess *noun* Schach *das*; **to play chess** Schach spielen.

chessboard *noun* Schachbrett *das* (PL *die* Schachbretter).

chest *noun* 1 (*part of the body*) Brust *die* (PL *die* Brüste); 2 (*box*) Truhe *die* (PL *die* Truhen); 3 **a chest of drawers** eine Kommode.

chestnut *noun* Esskastanie △ *die* (PL *die* Esskastanien).

chestnut tree *noun* 1 (*horse-chestnut*) Rosskastanie △ *die* (PL *die* Rosskastanien); 2 (*sweet chestnut*)

◊ IRREGULAR VERB: See the verb table in the centre of the dictionary

Edelkastanie *die* (PL *die* Edelkastanien).

chew *verb* kauen.

chewing gum *noun* Kaugummi *der* (PL *die* Kaugummis).

chicken *noun* Huhn *das* (PL *die* Hühner); **roast chicken** *das* Brathähnchen; **chicken breast** *die* Hühnerbrust.

chickenpox *noun* Windpocken (*plural*).

child *noun* Kind *das* (PL *die* Kinder); **when I was a child ...** als Kind ...

childish *adjective* kindisch.

childminder *noun* Tagesmutter *die* (PL *die* Tagesmütter).

chill *noun* 1 Kälte *die*; 2 **to have a chill** eine Erkältung haben.

chilled *adjective* gekühlt.

chilli *noun* Chili *der*.

chimney *noun* Schornstein *der* (PL *die* Schornsteine).

chimpanzee *noun* Schimpanse *der* (PL *die* Schimpansen).

chin *noun* Kinn *das* (PL *die* Kinne).

china *noun* Porzellan *das*; **china bowl** die Porzellanschüssel.

China *noun* China *das*.

Chinese *noun* 1 **the Chinese** (*people*) die Chinesen; 2 (*language*) Chinesisch *das*. *adjective* 1 chinesisch; **a Chinese man** ein Chinese; **a Chinese**

woman eine Chinesin; 2 **to have a Chinese meal** chinesisch essen.

chip *noun* 1 (*fried potato*) **chips** Pommes frites (*plural*); **fish and chips** ausgebackener Fisch mit Pommes frites; 2 (*microchip*) Chip *der* (PL *die* Chips); 3 (*in glass or china*) angeschlagene Stelle *die* (PL *die* angeschlagenen Stellen).

chipped *adjective* angeschlagen.

chocolate *noun* 1 Schokolade *die*; **a box of chocolates** eine Schachtel Pralinen; 2 **chocolate ice cream** *das* Schokoladeneis; **a cup of hot chocolate** eine Tasse Kakao.

choice *noun* 1 Wahl *die* (PL *die* Wahlen); **to make a good choice** eine gute Wahl treffen; 2 (*variety*) Auswahl *die*; **you have a choice of two flights** du hast zwei Flüge zur Auswahl.

choir *noun* Chor *der* (PL *die* Chöre).

choke *noun* (*on a car*) Choke *der* (PL *die* Chokes). *verb* (*by yourself*) sich verschlucken; **she choked on a bone** sie hat sich an einer Gräte verschluckt.

choose *verb* 1 wählen; **you chose well** du hast gut gewählt; **it's hard to choose from all these colours** es ist schwer, unter allen diesen Farben zu wählen; 2 (*select from a group of things*) sich ←(DAT) aussuchen SEP; **Cathy chose the red skirt** Cathy suchte sich den roten Rock aus.

chop *noun* Kotelett *das* (PL *die* Koteletts); **a pork chop** ein

△ **NEW SPELLING: See page xi**

Schweinekotelett.
verb hacken.

chord *noun* Akkord *der* (PL *die*
Akkorde).

chorus *noun* 1 (*when you all join in
the song*) Refrain *der* (PL *die*
Refrains); 2 (*a group of singers*)
Chor *der* (PL *die* Chöre).

Christ *noun* Christus *der*.

christening *noun* Taufe *die* (PL *die*
Taufen).

Christian *noun* Christ *der* (PL *die*
Christen), Christin *die* (PL *die*
Christinnen).
adjective christlich.

Christian name *noun*
Vorname *der* (PL *die* Vornamen).

Christmas *noun* Weihnachten *das*
(PL *die* Weihnachten); **at Christmas**
zu Weihnachten; **what did you get
for Christmas?** was hast du zu
Weihnachten bekommen?; **Happy
Christmas!** Frohe Weihnachten!

Christmas card *noun*
Weihnachtskarte *die* (PL *die*
Weihnachtskarten).

Christmas carol *noun*
Weihnachtslied *das* (PL *die*
Weihnachtslieder).

Christmas cracker *noun*
Knallbonbon *der* (PL *die*
Knallbonbons).

Christmas Day *noun* erste
Weihnachtstag *der*.

Christmas Eve *noun*
Heiligabend; **on Christmas Eve**
Heiligabend.

Christmas present *noun*
Weihnachtsgeschenk *das* (PL *die*
Weihnachtsgeschenke).

Christmas tree *noun*
Weihnachtsbaum *der* (PL *die*
Weihnachtsbäume).

church *noun* Kirche *die* (PL *die*
Kirchen); **to go to church** in die
Kirche gehen.

chute *noun* (*in a swimming pool or
playground*) Rutsche *die* (PL *die*
Rutschen).

cider *noun* Apfelwein *der* (PL *die*
Apfelweine).

cigar *noun* Zigarre *die* (PL *die*
Zigarren).

cigarette *noun* Zigarette *die* (PL *die*
Zigaretten).

cinema *noun* Kino *das* (PL *die*
Kinos); **to go to the cinema** ins
Kino gehen.

circle *noun* Kreis *der* (PL *die* Kreise);
to sit in a circle im Kreis sitzen; **to
go round in circles** sich im Kreis
drehen.

circus *noun* Zirkus *der* (PL *die*
Zirkusse).

citizen *noun* Bürger *der* (PL *die*
Bürger), Bürgerin *die* (PL *die*
Bürgerinnen).

city *noun* Stadt *die* (PL *die* Städte);
the city of Berlin die Stadt Berlin.

city centre *noun*
Stadtzentrum *das* (PL *die*
Stadtzentren); **in the city centre** im
Stadtzentrum.

◇ IRREGULAR VERB: See the verb table in the centre of the dictionary

civilization noun Zivilisation die (PL die Zivilisationen).

civil servant noun Beamte der (PL die Beamten), Beamtin die (PL die Beamtinnen); **she's a civil servant** sie ist Beamtin.

claim verb behaupten; **he claims to know who ...** er behauptet zu wissen, wer ...

clap verb 1 klatschen; **everyone clapped** alle klatschten; 2 **to clap your hands** in die Hände klatschen.

clarinet noun Klarinette die (PL die Klarinetten); **to play the clarinet** Klarinette spielen.

clash noun (between two groups) Zusammenstoß der (PL die Zusammenstöße).
verb 1 (rival groups) zusammenstoßen ✧ SEP; 2 (colours) sich beißen ✧; **the curtains clash with the wallpaper** die Vorhänge beißen sich mit der Tapete.

class noun 1 (a group of students or pupils) Klasse die (PL die Klassen); **she's in my class** sie geht in meine Klasse; 2 (a lesson) Stunde die (PL die Stunden); **history class** die Geschichtsstunde; **in class** im Unterricht; 3 (category) Klasse die (PL die Klassen); **social class** die gesellschaftliche Klasse.

classical adjective klassisch; **classical music** die klassische Musik.

classroom noun Klassenzimmer das (PL die Klassenzimmer).

clay noun Ton der.

clean adjective sauber; **a clean shirt** ein sauberes Hemd; **my hands are clean** ich habe saubere Hände.
verb 1 putzen; **I cleaned the windows** ich habe die Fenster geputzt; 2 **to clean your teeth** sich ←(DAT) die Zähne putzen; **I'm going to clean my teeth** ich putze mir jetzt die Zähne.

cleaner noun 1 (cleaning lady) Putzfrau die (PL die Putzfrauen); 2 (in a public place) Reinigungskraft die (PL die Reinigungskräfte); 3 **dry cleaner's** die chemische Reinigung.

cleaning noun **to do the cleaning** putzen.

cleanser noun 1 (for the house) Reinigungsmittel das (PL die Reinigungsmittel); 2 (for your face) Reinigungsmilch die.

clear adjective 1 (that you can see through) klar; **clear water** klares Wasser; 2 (cloudless) klar; 3 (easy to understand) klar; **clear instructions** klare Anweisungen; **is that clear?** ist das klar? (informal); **to make something clear** etwas klarmachen.
verb 1 räumen; **have you cleared your stuff out of your room?** hast du deine Sachen aus deinem Zimmer geräumt?; 2 **can I clear the table?** kann ich den Tisch abräumen?; 3 **to clear your throat** sich räuspern.
● **clear up** 1 (tidy up) aufräumen SEP; 2 (the weather) sich aufklären SEP; **the weather's clearing up a bit**

△ NEW SPELLING: See page xii

das Wetter klärt sich ein bisschen auf.

clearly adverb 1 (to think, speak, or hear) deutlich; 2 (obviously) eindeutig; **she was clearly better** sie war eindeutig besser.

clementine noun Klementine die (PL die Klementinen).

clever adjective 1 klug; **their children are all very clever** ihre Kinder sind alle sehr klug; 2 (ingenious) clever; **a clever idea** eine clevere Idee.

cliff noun Klippe die (PL die Klippen).

climate noun Klima das (PL die Klimas).

climb verb 1 (the stairs, a hill) hinaufgehen ✧ SEP (PERF sein); **to climb a mountain** auf einen Berg steigen ✧ (PERF sein); 2 (a wall, tree, or rock) klettern (PERF sein) auf (+ACC); **to climb a tree** auf einen Baum klettern.

climber noun Bergsteiger der (PL die Bergsteiger), Bergsteigerin die (PL die Bergsteigerinnen).

climbing noun Bergsteigen das; **they go climbing in Italy** sie gehen in Italien bergsteigen.

clinic noun Klinik die (PL die Kliniken).

clip noun 1 (from a film) Ausschnitt der (PL die Ausschnitte); 2 (for your hair) Klammer die (PL die Klammern).

cloakroom noun (for coats) Garderobe die (PL die Garderoben).

clock noun 1 Uhr die (PL die Uhren); **to put the clocks forward an hour** die Uhr eine Stunde vorstellen; **to put the clocks back** die Uhr zurückstellen; 2 **an alarm clock** ein Wecker.

close¹ adjective, adverb 1 (result) knapp; 2 (friend, connection) eng; 3 (relation or acquaintance) nahe; 4 (near) in der Nähe; **the station's very close** der Bahnhof ist ganz in der Nähe; **she lives close by** sie wohnt in der Nähe; **to be close to** nahe, nah (informal) (+DAT); **close to the cinema** nahe am Kino; **not very close** nicht sehr nah.

close² noun Ende das; **at the close** am Ende.
verb zumachen SEP, schließen ✧; **close your eyes!** mach die Augen zu!; **she closed the door** sie machte die Tür zu; **the post office closes at six** die Post macht um sechs zu, die Post schließt um sechs.

closed adjective geschlossen; **'closed on Mondays'** 'Montags geschlossen'.

closing date noun **the closing date for entries** (for a competition) der Einsendeschluss △; (for a sporting event) der Meldeschluss △.

closing time noun 1 Ladenschluss △ der; 2 (of a pub) Polizeistunde die.

cloth noun 1 (for drying up and polishing) Tuch das (PL die Tücher); 2 (for the floor) Lappen der (PL die

---

✧ IRREGULAR VERB: See the verb table in the centre of the dictionary

Lappen); 3 (fabric) Stoff der (PL die Stoffe).

clothes plural noun 1 Kleider (plural); 2 to put your clothes on sich anziehen ◇ SEP; to take your clothes off sich ausziehen ◇ SEP; to change your clothes sich umziehen ◇ SEP.

clothes peg noun Wäscheklammer die (PL die Wäscheklammern).

clothing noun Kleidung die.

cloud noun Wolke die (PL die Wolken).

cloudy adjective bewölkt.

clown noun Clown der (PL die Clowns).

club noun 1 (association, for tennis-players, golfers) Klub der (PL die Klubs); (for footballers) Verein der (PL die Vereine); a football club ein Fußballverein; 2 (in cards) Kreuz das (PL die Kreuze); the four of clubs die Kreuz-Vier; 3 (golfing iron) Schläger der (PL die Schläger).

clue noun 1 Anhaltspunkt der (PL die Anhaltspunkte); they have a few clues sie haben ein paar Anhaltspunkte; 2 (in a crossword) Frage die (PL die Fragen). ★ I haven't a clue ich habe keine Ahnung.

clumsy adjective ungeschickt.

clutch noun (in a car) Kupplung die (PL die Kupplungen). verb to clutch something etwas festhalten ◇ SEP.

coach noun 1 (bus) Bus der (PL die Busse); on the coach im Bus; to travel by coach mit dem Bus fahren; 2 (sports trainer) Trainer der (PL die Trainer), Trainerin die (PL die Trainerinnen); 3 (railway carriage) Wagen der (PL die Wagen).

coach station noun Busbahnhof der (PL die Busbahnhöfe).

coach trip noun Busausflug der (PL die Busausflüge); to go on a coach trip einen Busausflug machen.

coal noun Kohle die (PL die Kohlen).

coarse adjective grob.

coast noun Küste die (PL die Küsten); on the east coast an der Ostküste.

coat noun 1 Mantel der (PL die Mäntel); 2 coat of paint der Anstrich.

coat hanger noun Kleiderbügel der (PL die Kleiderbügel).

cock noun Hahn der (PL die Hähne).

cocoa noun Kakao der.

coconut noun Kokosnuss △ die (PL die Kokosnüsse).

cod noun Kabeljau der (PL die Kabeljaue).

code noun 1 (in law) Gesetzbuch das; the highway code die Straßenverkehrsordnung; 2 the dialling code for Hull die Vorwahl für Hull.

coffee noun Kaffee der (PL die Kaffees); a cup of coffee eine Tasse

coffee break noun
Kaffeepause die (PL die
Kaffeepausen).

coffee cup noun Kaffeetasse die
(PL die Kaffeetassen).

coffee machine noun
Kaffeemaschine die (PL die
Kaffeemaschinen).

coin noun 1 Münze die (PL die
Münzen); **he collects old coins** er
sammelt alte Münzen; **2 a pound
coin** ein Einpfundstück.

coincidence noun Zufall der (PL
die Zufälle).

Coke™ noun Cola die; **two
Cokes™ please** zwei Cola bitte.

cold noun 1 (cold weather)
Kälte die; **to be out in the cold**
draußen in der Kälte sein; **2** (illness)
Schnupfen der (PL die Schnupfen),
Erkältung die (PL die Erkältungen);
to have a cold Schnupfen haben;
Carol's got a cold Carol hat
Schnupfen; **a bad cold** eine
schlimme Erkältung.
adjective 1 kalt; **your hands are
cold** du hast kalte Hände; **cold milk**
kalte Milch; **2** (weather,
temperature) **it's cold today** heute
ist es kalt; **3** (feeling) **I'm cold** mir
ist kalt.

collapse verb 1 (a roof or wall)
einstürzen SEP (PERF sein); **2** (a
person) zusammenbrechen ◊ SEP
(PERF sein); **he collapsed in his**

office er brach in seinem Büro
zusammen.

collar noun 1 (on a garment)
Kragen der (PL die Kragen); **2** (for an
animal) Halsband das (PL die
Halsbänder).

colleague noun Kollege der (PL die
Kollegen), Kollegin die (PL die
Kolleginnen).

collect verb 1 (as a hobby)
sammeln; **do you collect stamps?**
sammelst du Briefmarken?; **2** (fetch)
abholen SEP; **she collects the
children from school** sie holt die
Kinder von der Schule ab; **3 to
collect up the exercise books** die
Hefte einsammeln SEP.

collection noun (of stamps, CDs,
money, etc.) Sammlung die (PL die
Sammlungen).

college noun 1 (for higher
education) Hochschule die (PL die
Hochschulen); **to go to college**
studieren; **2** (a school) College das
(PL die Colleges).

Cologne noun Köln das.

colour noun Farbe die (PL die
Farben); **what colour is it?** welche
Farbe hat es?; **do you have it in a
different colour?** haben Sie es in
einer anderen Farbe?
verb 1 (with paints or crayons)
anmalen SEP; **to colour something
red** etwas rot anmalen; **2** (with dye)
färben.

colour film noun Farbfilm der (PL
die Farbfilme).

colourful adjective bunt.

◊ IRREGULAR VERB: See the verb table in the centre of the dictionary

column noun 1 (of a building) Säule die (PL die Säulen); 2 (on a page) Spalte die (PL die Spalten).

comb noun Kamm der (PL die Kämme).
verb kämmen; **to comb your hair** sich ←(DAT) die Haare kämmen; **I'll just comb my hair** ich kämme mir nur die Haare.

come verb 1 kommen ◇ (PERF sein); **come quick!** komm schnell!; **come here!** komm her!; **Nick came by car** Nick kam mit dem Auto; **can you come over for a coffee?** kannst du auf eine Tasse Kaffe kommen?; **did Jess come to school yesterday?** war Jess gestern in der Schule?; 2 (arrive) **coming!** ich komme schon!; **the bus is coming** der Bus kommt gerade; **come along!** komm schon!

• to come back zurückkommen ◇ SEP (PERF sein); **he's coming back to collect us** er kommt zurück, um uns abzuholen.

• to come down herunterkommen ◇ SEP (PERF sein).

• to come for (collect) abholen SEP; **my father's coming for me** mein Vater holt mich ab.

• to come in hereinkommen ◇ SEP (PERF sein); **come in!** herein!; **she came into the kitchen** sie kam in die Küche.

• to come off (a button) abgehen ◇ SEP (PERF sein).

• to come out herauskommen ◇ SEP (PERF sein); **they came out when I called** als ich rief, kamen sie heraus; **the new CD's coming out soon** die neue CD kommt bald heraus.

• to come up heraufkommen ◇ SEP (PERF sein); **can you come up a moment?** kannst du eine Sekunde heraufkommen?

• to come up to somebody auf jemanden zukommen ◇ SEP (PERF sein).

comedian noun Komiker der (PL die Komiker), Komikerin die (PL die Komikerinnen).

comedy noun Komödie die (PL die Komödien), Komikerin die (PL die Komikerinnen).

comfortable adjective 1 bequem; **this chair's really comfortable** dieser Sessel ist wirklich bequem; 2 **to feel comfortable** (a person) sich wohl fühlen.

comfortably adverb bequem.

comic noun (magazine) Comic-Heft das (PL die Comic-Hefte).

comic strip noun Comic der (PL die Comics).

comma noun Komma das (PL die Kommas).

comment noun (remark) Bemerkung die (PL die Bemerkungen); **he made some rude comments about my friends** er hat ein paar unhöfliche Bemerkungen über meine Freunde gemacht.

commentary noun Reportage die (PL die Reportagen); **the commentary on the soccer match** die Reportage über das Fußballspiel.

commentator noun Reporter der (PL die Reporter), Reporterin die (PL *die* Reporterinnen); **sports commentator** *der* Sportreporter.

commercial *noun* Werbespot *der* (PL *die* Werbespots).
adjective kommerziell.

committee *noun* Ausschuss △ *der* (PL *die* Ausschüsse).

common *adjective* 1 häufig; **it's a common problem** das Problem kommt häufig vor; 2 (*group*) gemeinsam; **they have nothing in common** sie haben nichts gemeinsam.

common sense *noun* gesunde Menschenverstand *der*.

communication *noun* Verständigung *die*.

communion *noun* (*in a Catholic church*) Kommunion *die*; (*in a Protestant church*) Abendmahl *das*.

communism *noun* Kommunismus *der*.

community *noun* Gemeinschaft *die* (PL *die* Gemeinschaften); **the European Community** die Europäische Gemeinschaft.

commute *verb* **to commute between Oxford and London** zwischen Oxford und London pendeln (PERF *sein*).

commuter *noun* Pendler *der* (PL *die* Pendler), Pendlerin *die* (PL *die* Pendlerinnen).

compact disc *noun* Compactdisc △ *die* (PL *die* Compactdiscs).

compact disc player *noun* Compactdisc Spieler △ *der* (PL *die* Compactdisc Spieler).

company *noun* 1 (*business*) Gesellschaft *die* (PL *die* Gesellschaften); **an airline company** eine Fluggesellschaft; **she's set up a company** sie hat eine Firma gegründet; 2 (*group*) Truppe *die* (PL *die* Truppen); **a theatre company** eine Theatertruppe; 3 **to keep somebody company** jemandem Gesellschaft leisten; **the dog keeps me company** der Hund leistet mir Gesellschaft.

compare *verb* vergleichen ◇; **if you compare the German phrase with the English** wenn man den deutschen mit dem englischen Ausdruck vergleicht; **our house is small compared with yours** unser Haus ist klein verglichen mit eurem.

compass *noun* Kompass △ *der* (PL *die* Kompasse).

compatible *adjective* 1 zueinander passend; 2 (*in computing*) kompatibel.

compete *verb* 1 **to compete in something** (*race, event*) an etwas ←(DAT) teilnehmen ◇ SEP; 2 **to compete with each other** miteinander konkurrieren; 3 **to compete for something** um etwas ←(ACC) kämpfen; **thirty people are competing for one job** dreißig Leute kämpfen um eine Stelle.

competent *adjective* fähig.

◇ IRREGULAR VERB: *See the verb table in the centre of the dictionary*

seinem Brief und meiner Entscheidung; 2 (*between trains, planes, on phone, and electrical*) Anschluss △ der (PL die Anschlüsse); **Sally missed her connection** Sally hat ihren Anschluss verpasst.

conscience noun Gewissen das; **to have a guilty conscience** ein schlechtes Gewissen haben.

conservation noun (*of nature*) Schutz der; **environmental conservation** der Umweltschutz.

conservative noun Konservative der/die (PL die Konservativen). adjective konservativ.

conservatory noun Wintergarten der (PL die Wintergärten).

consider verb 1 sich ←(DAT) überlegen; (*a suggestion or idea*) **all things considered** alles in allem; 2 (*think about (doing)*) erwägen ✧; **we are considering buying a flat** wir erwägen, eine Wohnung zu kaufen.

considerate adjective rücksichtsvoll.

considering preposition wenn man bedenkt; **considering her age** wenn man ihr Alter bedenkt; **considering he did it all himself** wenn man bedenkt, dass er es ganz allein gemacht hat.

consist verb **to consist of** bestehen ✧ aus (+DAT).

constant adjective ständig.

construct verb bauen.

consumer noun Verbraucher der (PL die Verbraucher), Verbraucherin die (PL die Verbraucherinnen).

contact noun Kontakt der (PL die Kontakte); **to be in contact with somebody** mit jemandem in Kontakt sein; **we've lost contact** wir haben den Kontakt verloren; **Rob has contacts in the music business** Rob hat Kontakte zur Musikindustrie. verb sich in Verbindung setzen mit (+DAT); **I'll contact you tomorrow** ich setze mich morgen mit dir in Verbindung.

contact lens noun Kontaktlinse die (PL die Kontaktlinsen).

contain verb enthalten ✧.

container noun Behälter der (PL die Behälter).

contemporary adjective 1 (*around today*) zeitgenössisch; 2 (*modern*) modern.

contents plural noun Inhalt der; **the contents of my suitcase** der Inhalt meines Koffers.

contest noun Wettbewerb der (PL die Wettbewerbe).

contestant noun Teilnehmer der (PL die Teilnehmer), Teilnehmerin die (PL die Teilnehmerinnen).

continent noun Kontinent der (PL die Kontinente).

continue verb 1 fortsetzen SEP; **we continued (with) our journey** wir setzten unsere Reise fort; 2 **to**

continue to do something etwas weiter tun; **Jill continued talking** Jill redete weiter; **3 'to be continued'** 'Fortsetzung folgt'.

continuous *adjective* ununterbrochen.

contraceptive *noun* Verhütungsmittel *das* (PL die Verhütungsmittel).

contract *noun* Vertrag *der* (PL die Verträge).

contradict *verb* widersprechen ✧ (+DAT).

contradiction *noun* Widerspruch *der* (PL die Widersprüche).

contrary *noun* Gegenteil *das*; **on the contrary** im Gegenteil.

contrast *noun* Kontrast *der* (PL die Kontraste).

contribute *verb* beisteuern SEP (money).

contribution *noun* (to charity or an appeal) Spende *die* (PL die Spenden).

control *noun* (of a crowd or animals) Kontrolle *die*; **the police are in control of the situation** die Polizei hat die Situation unter Kontrolle; **keep your dogs under control** halten Sie Ihre Hunde unter Kontrolle; **everything's under control** alles ist unter Kontrolle; **to get out of control** außer Kontrolle geraten.
verb **to control yourself** sich beherrschen.

convenient *adjective* **1** praktisch; **frozen food is very convenient** Tiefkühlkost ist sehr praktisch; **2** **to be convenient for somebody** jemandem passen; **whenever's convenient for you** wann immer es dir passt.

conventional *adjective* konventionell.

conversation *noun* Gespräch *das* (PL die Gespräche).

convert *verb* **1** umwandeln SEP; **2** (adapt a building) umbauen SEP; **we're going to convert the garage into a workshop** wir wollen die Garage zu einer Werkstatt umbauen.

convince *verb* überzeugen; **I'm convinced he's wrong** ich bin davon überzeugt, dass er sich irrt.

convincing *adjective* überzeugend.

cook *noun* Koch *der* (PL die Köche), Köchin *die* (PL die Köchinnen).
verb **1** kochen; **who's cooking tonight?** wer kocht heute Abend?; **I like cooking** ich koche gern; **to cook vegetables and pasta** Gemüse und Nudeln kochen; **cook the cabbage for five minutes** lass den Kohl fünf Minuten kochen; **2** (prepare food or a meal) machen; **Fran's busy cooking supper** Fran macht gerade Abendessen; **how do you cook duck?** wie macht man Ente?; **3** (boil) kochen; (fry or roast) braten ✧; **the potatoes are cooking** die Kartoffeln kochen; **the sausages are cooking** die Würstchen braten.

cooker *noun* Herd *der* (PL die Herde); **electric cooker** *der*

✧ **IRREGULAR VERB: See the verb table in the centre of the dictionary**

Elektroherd; **gas cooker** *der* Gasherd.

cookery *noun* Kochen *das*.

cookery book *noun* Kochbuch *das* (PL *die* Kochbücher).

cooking *noun* **1** (*preparing food*) Kochen *das*; **cooking is fun** Kochen macht Spaß; **who's doing the cooking?** wer kocht?; **2** (*food*) Küche *die*; **Italian cooking die** italienische Küche.

cool *noun* **1** (*coldness*) Kühle *die*; **2** (*calm*) **to lose one's cool** durchdrehen SEP (PERF *sein*) (*informal*); **don't lose your cool!** dreh nicht durch!; **he kept his cool** er blieb gelassen.
adjective **1** (*cold*) kühl; **it's cool inside** es ist kühl drinnen; **2** (*laid back*) gelassen; **to stay cool** gelassen bleiben (PERF *sein*).
verb abkühlen SEP (PERF *sein*).

cop *noun* Polizist *der* (PL *die* Polizisten).

cope *verb* zurechtkommen ◆ SEP (PERF *sein*); **she copes well** sie kommt gut zurecht; **to cope with the children** mit den Kindern zurechtkommen; **she's had a lot to cope with** sie musste mit viel zurechtkommen.

copy *noun* **1** (*photocopy*) Kopie *die* (PL *die* Kopien); **2** (*of a book*) Exemplar *das* (PL *die* Exemplare).
verb **1** (*imitate*) kopieren; **2** (*make a copy of*) abschreiben ◆ SEP; **I copied (down) the address** ich habe die Adresse abgeschrieben; (*in*

an exam) **to copy from somebody** bei jemandem abschreiben.

cord *noun* (*for a blind, for example*) Schnur *die* (PL *die* Schnüre).

cordless telephone *noun* schnurlose Telefon *das* (PL *die* schnurlosen Telefone).

core *noun* (*of an apple or a pear*) Kerngehäuse *das* (PL *die* Kerngehäuse).

cork *noun* **1** (*in a bottle*) Korken *der* (PL *die* Korken); **2** (*material*) Kork *der*.

corkscrew *noun* Korkenzieher *der* (PL *die* Korkenzieher).

corn *noun* **1** (*wheat*) Korn *das*; **2** (*sweetcorn*) Mais *der*.

corner *noun* **1** Ecke *die* (PL *die* Ecken); **at the corner of the street** an der Straßenecke; **it's just round the corner** es ist gleich um die Ecke; **2** (*of mouth, eye*) Winkel *der* (PL *die* Winkel); **out of the corner of your eye** aus dem Augenwinkel heraus; **3** (*bend in the road*) Kurve *die* (PL *die* Kurven); **4** (*in football*) Eckball *der* (PL *die* Eckbälle).

corpse *noun* Leiche *die* (PL *die* Leichen).

correct *adjective* **1** richtig; **the correct answer** die richtige Antwort; **2** **yes, that's correct** ja, das stimmt.
verb **1** verbessern; **2** (*teacher*) korrigieren; **the teacher has already corrected our homework**

△ NEW SPELLING: See page xii

der Lehrer hat unsere Hausaufgaben schon korrigiert.

correction noun Verbesserung *die* (PL die Verbesserungen).

corridor noun Korridor *der* (PL die Korridore).

cosmetics plural noun Kosmetik *die*.

cost noun 1 Kosten (*plural*); **the cost of living** die Lebenshaltungskosten (*plural*); 2 **the cost of a new computer** der Preis für einen neuen Computer. verb kosten; **how much does it cost?** was kostet es?; **the tickets cost £10** die Karten kosten zehn Pfund; **it costs too much** das ist zu teuer.

costume noun Kostüm *das* (PL die Kostüme).

cosy adjective (*a room*) gemütlich.

cot noun Kinderbett *das* (PL die Kinderbetten).

cottage noun Häuschen *das* (PL die Häuschen).

cotton noun 1 (*fabric*) Baumwolle *die*; **cotton shirt** das Baumwollhemd; 2 (*thread*) Nähgarn *das* (PL die Nähgarne).

cotton wool noun Watte *die*.

couch noun Couch *die* (PL die Couchs).

cough noun Husten *der*; **a nasty cough** ein schlimmer Husten; **to have a cough** Husten haben. verb husten.

could verb 1 (*the past tense of können is used to translate 'was able to'*) **I couldn't open it** ich konnte es nicht aufmachen; **they couldn't come** sie konnten nicht kommen; **she did all she could** sie hat getan, was sie konnte; **he couldn't drive** er konnte nicht Auto fahren; **she couldn't see anything** sie konnte überhaupt nichts sehen; 2 (*the past tense of dürfen is used to translate 'was allowed to'*) **they couldn't smoke there** sie durften da nicht rauchen; 3 (*might*) (*the subjunctive of können is used to translate a wish or suggestion*) **could I speak to David?** könnte ich David sprechen?; **you could try phoning** du könntest versuchen anzurufen; **if he could pay** wenn er zahlen könnte; **he could be right** er könnte recht haben.

count verb 1 (*reckon up*) zählen; **I counted my money** ich habe mein Geld gezählt; 2 (*include*) mitzählen SEP; **thirty-five not counting the children** fünfunddreißig, die Kinder nicht mitgezählt.

counter noun 1 (*in a shop*) Ladentisch *der* (PL die Ladentische); 2 (*in a post office or bank*) Schalter *der* (PL die Schalter); 3 (*in a bar or café*) Theke *die* (PL die Theken); 4 (*for board games*) Spielmarke *die* (PL die Spielmarken).

country noun 1 (*Germany, England, etc.*) Land *das* (PL die Länder); **a foreign country** ein fremdes Land; **from another country** aus einem anderen Land; 2 (*not town*)

◈ **IRREGULAR VERB: See the verb table in the centre of the dictionary**

Land *das*; **in the country** auf dem Land; **country road** die Landstraße.

country dancing *noun*
Volkstanz *der*.

countryside *noun* 1 (*not town*) Land *das*; 2 (*scenery*) Landschaft *die*.

county *noun* Grafschaft *die* (PL die Grafschaften).

couple *noun* 1 (*a pair*) Paar *das* (PL die Paare); 2 **a couple of** ein paar; **a couple of times** ein paar Mal; **I've got a couple of things to do** ich habe ein paar Sachen zu tun.

courage *noun* Mut *der*.

course *noun* 1 (*lessons*) Kurs *der* (PL die Kurse); **computer course** der Computerkurs; **to go on a course** einen Kurs machen; 2 (*part of a meal*) Gang *der* (PL die Gänge); **the main course** der Hauptgang; 3 **golf course** der Golfplatz; 4 **of course** natürlich; **yes, of course!** ja, natürlich!; **he's forgotten, of course** er hat es natürlich vergessen.

court *noun* 1 (*for playing sports*) Platz *der* (PL die Plätze); 2 (*lawcourt*) Gericht *das*; **to go to court** vor Gericht gehen.

cousin *noun* Vetter *der* (PL die Vettern), Kusine *die* (PL die Kusinen); **my cousin Sonia** meine Kusine Sonia.

cover *noun* 1 (*of a book*) Einband *der* (PL die Einbände); 2 (*for a duvet or cushion*) Bezug *der* (PL die Bezüge).

verb 1 (*to cover up*) zudecken SEP; **he covered her with a blanket** er hat sie mit einer Decke zugedeckt; 2 **he was covered in spots** er war völlig verpickelt; **the room was covered in dust** das Zimmer war völlig verstaubt; 3 (*with leaves, snow, for protection*) bedecken; **the ground was covered with snow** der Boden war mit Schnee bedeckt; 4 (*with fabric*) beziehen ◊.

cow *noun* Kuh *die* (PL die Kühe); **mad cow disease** der Rinderwahn.

coward *noun* Feigling *der* (PL die Feiglinge).

cowboy *noun* Cowboy *der* (PL die Cowboys).

crack *noun* 1 (*in a glass or cup*) Sprung *der* (PL die Sprünge); 2 (*in wood or a wall*) Riss *der* (PL die Risse); 3 (*a cracking noise*) Knack *der* (PL die Knacke).
verb 1 (*to make a crack in*) anschlagen ◊ SEP; 2 (*to break*) zerbrechen ◊; 3 (*to make a noise*) (*a twig*) knacken.

cracker *noun* 1 (*biscuit*) Cracker *der* (PL die Cracker); 2 (*Christmas cracker*) Knallbonbon *der* (PL die Knallbonbons).

craft *noun* (*at school*) Werken *das*.

cramp *noun* Krampf *der* (PL die Krämpfe); **to have cramp in your leg** einen Krampf im Bein haben.

crash *noun* 1 (*an accident*) Unfall *der* (PL die Unfälle); **car crash** der Autounfall; 2 (*a noise*) Krachen *das*.

△ NEW SPELLING: *See page xii*

crash verb 1 (*a plane*) abstürzen SEP (PERF sein); **the plane crashed** das Flugzeug ist abgestürzt; 2 (*have a collision in a car*) einen Unfall haben; 3 **to crash into something** gegen etwas ←(ACC) krachen (PERF sein); **the car crashed into a tree** das Auto krachte gegen einen Baum.

crash course noun Schnellkurs der (PL die Schnellkurse).

crash helmet noun Sturzhelm der (PL die Sturzhelme).

crate noun Kiste die (PL die Kisten).

crawl noun (*in swimming*) Kraul das.
verb 1 (*a person*) kriechen ◇ (PERF sein); (*a baby*) krabbeln (PERF sein); 2 (*cars in a jam*) im Schneckentempo fahren ◇ (PERF sein); **we were crawling along** wir fuhren im Schneckentempo.

crayon noun 1 (*wax*) Wachsstift der (PL die Wachsstifte); 2 (*coloured pencil*) Buntstift der (PL die Buntstifte).

craze noun Mode die; **the craze for rollerblades** die Inlinermode.

crazy adjective verrückt; **to be crazy for something** verrückt auf etwas ←(ACC) sein.

cream noun Sahne die; **strawberries and cream** Erdbeeren mit Sahne.

cream cheese noun Frischkäse der.

creased adjective zerknittert.

creative adjective kreativ.

creature noun Geschöpf das (PL die Geschöpfe).

credit noun Kredit der; **to buy something on credit** etwas auf Kredit kaufen.

credit card noun Kreditkarte die (PL die Kreditkarten).

cress noun Kresse die.

crew noun 1 (*on a ship or plane*) Besatzung die; 2 **camera crew** das Kamerateam; 3 (*in water sports*) Mannschaft die (PL die Mannschaften).

crew cut noun Bürstenschnitt der (PL die Bürstenschnitte).

cricket noun 1 (*game*) Kricket das; **to play cricket** Kricket spielen; 2 (*insect*) Grille die (PL die Grillen).

cricket bat noun Kricketschläger der.

crime noun 1 Verbrechen das (PL die Verbrechen); **theft is a crime** Diebstahl ist ein Verbrechen; 2 (*criminality*) Kriminalität die; **to fight crime** die Kriminalität bekämpfen.

criminal noun Kriminelle der/die (PL die Kriminellen).
adjective kriminell.

crisis noun Krise die (PL die Krisen).

crisp noun Chip der (PL die Chips); **a packet of potato crisps** eine Tüte Kartoffelchips.
adjective 1 (*biscuit*) knusprig; 2 (*apple*) knackig.

◇ IRREGULAR VERB: See the verb table in the centre of the dictionary

criticism noun Kritik die (PL die Kritiken).

criticize verb kritisieren.

crocodile noun Krokodil das (PL die Krokodile).

crook noun (criminal) Schwindler der (PL die Schwindler).

crop noun Ernte die.

cross noun Kreuz das (PL die Kreuze).
adjective ärgerlich; **she was very cross** sie war sehr ärgerlich; **I'm cross with you** ich bin sehr ärgerlich auf dich.
verb 1 (to cross over) überqueren; **to cross the road** die Straße überqueren; 2 **to cross your legs** die Beine übereinanderschlagen ◇ SEP; 3 (to cross each other) sich kreuzen; **the two roads cross here** die beiden Straßen kreuzen sich hier.
● **to cross out** ausstreichen ◇ SEP.

cross-Channel adjective **a cross-Channel ferry** eine Fähre über den Kanal.

cross-country noun 1 Cross der; 2 **cross-country skiing** der Langlauf.

crossing noun 1 (from one place to another) Überquerung die (PL die Überquerungen); 2 (a sea journey) Überfahrt die (PL die Überfahrten); **Channel crossing** die Überfahrt über den Kanal; 3 **pedestrian crossing** der Fußgängerübergang; **level crossing** der Bahnübergang.

crossroads noun Kreuzung die (PL die Kreuzungen); **at the crossroads** an der Kreuzung.

crossword noun Kreuzworträtsel das (PL die Kreuzworträtsel); **to do the crossword** ein Kreuzworträtsel machen.

crow noun Krähe die (PL die Krähen).
verb (a cock) krähen.

crowd noun 1 Menschenmenge die (PL die Menschenmengen); **in the crowd** in der Menschenmenge; 2 (spectators) **a crowd of five thousand** fünftausend Zuschauer (plural).
verb **to crowd into** or **onto something** sich in etwas ←(ACC) drängen; **we all crowded into the train** wir drängten uns alle in den Zug.

crowded adjective überfüllt.

crown noun Krone die (PL die Kronen).

crude adjective 1 (rough and ready) primitiv; 2 (vulgar) ordinär.

cruel adjective grausam.

crumb noun Krümel der (PL die Krümel).

crumpled adjective zerknittert.

crunchy adjective knusprig.

crush verb zerquetschen.

crust noun Kruste die (PL die Krusten).

crusty adjective knusprig.

△ NEW SPELLING: *See page xii*

crutch noun Krücke die (PL die Krücken); **to be on crutches** an Krücken gehen.

cry noun Schrei der (PL die Schreie). verb 1 (weep) weinen; 2 (call out) schreien ✧.

cub noun 1 (animal) Junge das (PL die Jungen); 2 (boy scout) Wölfling der (PL die Wölflinge).

cube noun Würfel der (PL die Würfel); **ice cube** der Eiswürfel.

cubic adjective (in measurements) Kubik-; **three cubic metres** drei Kubikmeter.

cubicle noun 1 (in a changing room) Kabine die; 2 (in a pub 'lavatory') Toilette die (PL die Toiletten).

cuckoo noun Kuckuck der (PL die Kuckucke).

cucumber noun Gurke die (PL die Gurken).

cuddle noun **to give somebody a cuddle** jemanden in den Arm nehmen. verb schmusen.

cue noun (billiards, pool, snooker) Queue das (PL die Queues).

cuff noun (on a shirt) Manschette die (PL die Manschetten).

cul-de-sac noun Sackgasse die (PL die Sackgassen).

culture noun Kultur die (PL die Kulturen).

cunning adjective listig.

cup noun 1 (for drinking) Tasse die (PL die Tassen); **a cup of tea** eine

Tasse Tee; 2 (a trophy) Pokal der (PL die Pokale).

cupboard noun Schrank der (PL die Schränke); **in the kitchen cupboard** im Küchenschrank.

cup tie noun Pokalspiel das (PL die Pokalspiele).

cure noun Heilmittel das (PL die Heilmittel). verb heilen.

curiosity noun Neugier die.

curious adjective neugierig.

curl noun Locke die (PL die Locken). verb 1 locken (hair); 2 (of hair) sich locken.

currant noun Korinthe die (PL die Korinthen).

currency noun Währung die (PL die Währungen); **the Japanese currency** die japanische Währung; **foreign currencies** Devisen (plural).

current noun 1 (electricity) Strom der; 2 (in water or air) Strömung die (PL die Strömungen). adjective aktuell.

current affairs noun Tagespolitik die.

curriculum noun Lehrplan der (PL die Lehrpläne).

curry noun Curry das; **vegetable curry** das Gemüse in Currysoße.

curtain noun Vorhang der (PL die Vorhänge).

cushion noun Kissen das (PL die Kissen).

✧ IRREGULAR VERB: See the verb table in the centre of the dictionary

custard *noun* Vanillesoße *die* (PL *die* Vanillesoßen).

custom *noun* Brauch *der* (PL *die* Bräuche).

customer *noun* Kunde *der* (PL *die* Kunden), Kundin *die* (PL *die* Kundinnen).

customs plural *noun* Zoll *der*; **to go through customs** durch den Zoll gehen.

customs hall *noun* Zollabfertigung *die*.

customs officer *noun* Zollbeamte *der* (PL *die* Zollbeamten), Zollbeamtin *die* (PL *die* Zollbeamtinnen).

cut *noun* 1 (*injury*) Schnittwunde *die* (PL *die* Schnittwunden); 2 (*haircut*) Schnitt *der* (PL *die* Schnitte). *verb* 1 schneiden ◇; **can you cut the bread please?** kannst du bitte Brot schneiden?; **you'll cut yourself!** du schneidest dich!; **Kevin's cut his finger** Kevin hat sich in den Finger geschnitten; 2 **to cut the grass** den Rasen mähen; 3 **to get your hair cut** sich ←(DAT) die Haare schneiden lassen; **I had my hair cut** ich habe mir die Haare schneiden lassen; 4 **to cut prices** die Preise senken.

● **to cut down** 1 fällen (*a tree*); 2 **to cut down on cigarettes** seinen Zigarettenkonsum einschränken SEP

● **to cut out something** 1 etwas ausschneiden ◇ SEP (*a shape, a newspaper article*); 2 etwas streichen ◇ (*sugar, fatty food, holidays, for example*).

● **to cut something up** etwas zerschneiden ◇ (*food*).

cutlery *noun* Besteck *das* (PL *die* Bestecke).

CV *noun* Lebenslauf *der* (PL *die* Lebensläufe).

cycle *noun* (*bike*) Rad *das* (PL *die* Räder). *verb* Rad fahren ◇ △ (PERF *sein*); **do you like cycling?** fährst du gerne Rad?; **we cycle to school** wir fahren mit dem Rad zur Schule.

cycle lane *noun* Fahrradspur *die* (PL *die* Fahrradspuren).

cycle race *noun* Radrennen *das* (PL *die* Radrennen).

cycling *noun* Radfahren *das*.

cycling shorts *noun* Radlerhose *die* (PL *die* Radlerhosen).

cyclist *noun* Radfahrer *der* (PL *die* Radfahrer), Radfahrerin *die* (PL *die* Radfahrerinnen).

D d

dad *noun* Vati *der* (PL *die* Vatis).

daffodil *noun* Osterglocke *die* (PL *die* Osterglocken).

daily *adjective* täglich.

dairy products plural *noun* Milchprodukte (*plural*).

daisy *noun* Gänseblümchen *das* (PL *die* Gänseblümchen).

△ NEW SPELLING: See page xii

damage *noun* Schaden *der* (PL *die* Schäden); **to do a lot of damage** großen Schaden anrichten. *verb* beschädigen.

damn *noun* **I don't give a damn** das ist mir piepegal (*informal*). *exclamation* **damn!** verdammt!

damp *adjective* feucht. *noun* Feuchtigkeit *die*.

dance *noun* Tanz *der* (PL *die* Tänze); **a folk dance** ein Volkstanz. *verb* tanzen; **I like dancing** ich tanze gerne.

dancer *noun* Tänzer *der* (PL *die* Tänzer), Tänzerin *die* (PL *die* Tänzerinnen).

dancing *noun* Tanzen *das*.

dancing class *noun* Tanzstunde *die* (PL *die* Tanzstunden); **to go to dancing classes** in die Tanzstunde gehen.

dandruff *noun* Schuppen (*plural*).

danger *noun* Gefahr *die* (PL *die* Gefahren); **to be in danger** in Gefahr sein.

dangerous *adjective* gefährlich; **it's dangerous to drive too fast** es ist gefährlich, zu schnell zu fahren.

Danish *noun* Dänisch *das*. *adjective* dänisch; **he's Danish** er ist Däne; **she's Danish** sie ist Dänin.

dare *verb* **1** wagen; **to dare to do something** es wagen, etwas zu tun; **I didn't dare suggest it** ich habe es nicht gewagt, das vorzuschlagen; **2 don't you dare tell her I'm here!** untersteh dich, ihr zu sagen, dass ich da bin!; **3 I dare you!** trau dich!; **I**

dare you to tell him! sag's ihm, trau dich doch!

daring *adjective* gewagt; **that was a bit daring** das war etwas gewagt.

dark *noun* **in the dark** im Dunkeln; **after dark** nach Einbruch der Dunkelheit; **to be afraid of the dark** Angst im Dunkeln haben. *adjective* **1** (*colour*) dunkel (*adjectives ending in* -el *drop the* e *when followed by a vowel, which means that* dunkel *becomes* dunkler/dunkle/dunkles); **a dark colour** eine dunkle Farbe; **it gets dark around five** es wird gegen fünf dunkel; **2 a dark blue skirt** ein dunkelblauer Rock; **she has dark brown hair** sie hat dunkelbraune Haare.

darkness *noun* Dunkelheit *die*; **in darkness** .in der Dunkelheit.

darling *noun* Liebling *der* (PL *die* Lieblinge); **see you later, darling!** bis später, Liebling!

dart *noun* **1** Wurfpfeil *der* (PL *die* Wurfpfeile); **2** (*game*) **darts** Darts *das*; **to play darts** Darts spielen.

data *plural noun* Daten (*plural*).

database *noun* Datenbank *die* (PL *die* Datenbanken).

date *noun* **1** Datum *das* (PL *die* Daten); **what's the date today?** welches Datum haben wir heute?; **the date of the meeting** das Datum für das Treffen; **what date is he coming?** wann kommt er?; **2** Termin *der* (PL *die* Termine); **the**

◈ **IRREGULAR VERB: See the verb table in the centre of the dictionary**

last date for payment der letzte
Zahlungstermin; **3 out of date**
ungültig; **my passport's out of date**
mein Pass ist ungültig; **4** (fruit)
Dattel die (PL die Datteln).

date of birth noun
Geburtsdatum das (PL die
Geburtsdaten).

daughter noun Tochter die (PL die
Töchter); **Tina's daughter** Tinas
Tochter.

daughter-in-law noun
Schwiegertochter die (PL die
Schwiegertöchter).

dawn noun Morgendämmerung die
(PL die Morgendämmerungen).

day noun Tag der (PL die Tage);
three days later drei Tage später; **a
few days ago** vor ein paar Tagen;
the day I went to London den
Tag, an dem ich nach London
gefahren bin; **we spent the day in
London** wir haben den Tag in
London verbracht; **it rained all day**
es hat den ganzen Tag geregnet; **the
day after** am Tag danach; **the day
after the wedding** am Tag nach der
Hochzeit; **the day before** am Tag
davor; **the day before the wedding**
am Tag vor der Hochzeit; **2 the day
after tomorrow** übermorgen; **my
sister's arriving the day after
tomorrow** meine Schwester kommt
übermorgen an; **3 the day before
yesterday** vorgestern; **my brother
arrived the day before yesterday**
mein Bruder kam vorgestern an; **4
during the day** tagsüber.

dead adjective tot; **her father's
dead** ihr Vater ist tot.

adverb (really) irre (informal); **he's
dead nice** er ist irre nett; **it was
dead good** es war irre gut; **it was
dead easy** es war kinderleicht;
you're dead right du hast völlig
Recht; **she arrived dead on time** sie
kam auf die Minute pünktlich an.

deadline noun letzte Termin der
(PL die letzten Termine).

deaf adjective taub.

deafening adjective
ohrenbetäubend.

deal noun **1** (involving money)
Geschäft das (PL die Geschäfte); **it's
a good deal** das ist ein gutes
Geschäft; **2** (agreement)
Vereinbarung die (PL die
Vereinbarungen); **to make a deal
with somebody** mit jemandem eine
Vereinbarung treffen; **it's a deal!**
abgemacht!; **3 a great deal of** viel;
I don't have a great deal of time
ich habe nicht viel Zeit.

verb (in cards) geben; **it's you to
deal** du gibst.

● **to deal with something** sich um
etwas ←(ACC) kümmern; **Linda deals
with the accounts** Linda kümmert
sich um die Buchführung; **I'll deal
with it as soon as possible** ich
kümmere mich so schnell wie
möglich darum.

dear adjective **1** lieb; **Dear Franz**
Lieber Franz; **Dear Mr Smith** Sehr
geehrter Herr Smith; **2** (expensive)
teuer.

death noun Tod der; **after his
father's death** nach dem Tod seines
Vaters; **three deaths** drei

△ NEW SPELLING: See page xii

Todesfälle; ★ **I was bored to death** ich habe mich zu Tode gelangweilt; ★ **I'm sick to death of it** ich habe es gründlich satt.

death penalty noun Todesstrafe die.

debate noun Debatte die (PL die Debatten).
verb debattieren.

debt noun (money owed) Schulden (plural); **to get into debt** in Schulden geraten.

decaffeinated adjective koffeinfrei.

deceive verb betrügen ✧.

December noun Dezember der (PL die Dezember); **in December** im Dezember.

decent adjective anständig; **a decent salary** ein anständiges Gehalt; **a decent meal** ein anständiges Essen.

decide verb 1 entscheiden ✧; **to decide on something** sich für etwas ←(ACC) entscheiden; **he's decided against buying a new car** er hat sich entschieden, kein neues Auto zu kaufen; 2 **to decide to do something** sich entschließen ✧, etwas zu tun; **they've decided to buy a house** sie haben sich entschlossen, ein Haus zu kaufen.

decimal adjective Dezimal-; **decimal number** die Dezimalzahl.

decimal point noun Komma das (PL die Kommas).

decision noun Entscheidung die (PL die Entscheidungen); **to make a decision** eine Entscheidung treffen.

deckchair noun Liegestuhl der (PL die Liegestühle).

declare verb 1 erklären; 2 (at customs) **nothing to declare** nichts zu verzollen.

decorate verb 1 schmücken; **to decorate the Christmas tree** den Weihnachtsbaum schmücken; 2 (with paint) streichen ✧; (with wallpaper) tapezieren; **we're decorating the kitchen this weekend** wir streichen dieses Wochenende die Küche.

decoration noun Verzierung die (PL die Verzierungen); **Christmas decorations** der Weihnachtsschmuck.

deep adjective tief; **a deep feeling of gratitude** ein tiefes Dankbarkeitsgefühl; **how deep is the swimming pool?** wie tief ist das Schwimmbecken?; **a hole two metres deep** ein zwei Meter tiefes Loch.

deep freeze noun Tiefkühltruhe die (PL die Tiefkühltruhen); (upright) Tiefkühlschrank der (PL die Tiefkühlschränke).

deeply adverb tief.

deer noun 1 Hirsch der (PL die Hirsche); 2 (roe deer) Reh das (PL die Rehe).

defeat noun Niederlage die (PL die Niederlagen).
verb schlagen ✧.

defence noun Verteidigung die.

✧ IRREGULAR VERB: See the verb table in the centre of the dictionary

defend verb verteidigen.

defender noun Verteidiger der (PL die Verteidiger), Verteidigerin die (PL die Verteidigerinnen).

definite adjective 1 eindeutig; a definite improvement eine eindeutige Besserung; 2 (certain) sicher; it's not definite yet es ist noch nicht sicher; 3 (exact) klar; a definite answer eine klare Antwort.

definitely adverb 1 (when giving your opinion about something) eindeutig; your German is definitely better than mine dein Deutsch ist eindeutig besser als meins; 2 (without doubt) bestimmt; she's definitely going to be there sie wird bestimmt dort sein; I'm definitely not coming ich komme ganz bestimmt nicht; 3 'are you sure you like this one better?' – 'definitely!' 'gefällt dir diese wirklich besser?' – 'klar!' (informal).

degree noun 1 Grad der (PL die Grade); thirty degrees dreißig Grad; 2 a university degree ein akademischer Grad.

delay noun Verspätung die (PL die Verspätungen); a two-hour delay eine zweistündige Verspätung. verb 1 (hold up) aufhalten ◇ SEP; she was delayed in the office sie ist im Büro aufgehalten worden; 2 (train, plane) to be delayed Verspätung haben; the flight was delayed by bad weather der Flug hatte wegen des schlechten Wetters Verspätung; 3 (postpone) aufschieben ◇ SEP; the decision has been delayed until Thursday die Entscheidung wurde bis Donnerstag aufgeschoben.

delete verb 1 streichen ◇; 2 (in computing) löschen.

deliberate adjective absichtlich.

deliberately adverb absichtlich; she did it deliberately sie hat das absichtlich getan.

delicate adjective 1 (fabric, health) zart; 2 (situation, question) heikel; 3 (taste, smell) fein.

delicatessen noun Feinkostgeschäft das (PL die Feinkostgeschäfte).

delicious adjective köstlich.

delighted adjective hocherfreut; to be delighted begeistert sein; they're delighted with their new flat sie sind von ihrer neuen Wohnung begeistert; I'm delighted that you can come ich freue mich sehr, dass ihr kommen könnt.

deliver verb 1 liefern; they're delivering the washing machine tomorrow die Waschmaschine wird morgen geliefert; 2 (mail, newspapers) zustellen SEP.

delivery noun 1 Lieferung die (PL die Lieferungen); 2 (of mail, newspapers) Zustellung die (PL die Zustellungen).

demand noun Nachfrage die (PL die Nachfragen); much in demand sehr gefragt. verb verlangen.

demo noun (protest) Demo die (informal) (PL die Demos).

democracy noun Demokratie die (PL die Demokratien).

democratic adjective demokratisch.

demonstrate verb 1 (a machine, product, or technique) vorführen SEP; 2 (protest) demonstrieren; to demonstrate against something gegen etwas ←(ACC) demonstrieren.

demonstration noun 1 (of a machine, product, or technique) Vorführung die (PL die Vorführungen); 2 (protest) Demonstration die (PL die Demonstrationen).

demonstrator noun Demonstrant der (PL die Demonstranten), Demonstrantin die (PL die Demonstrantinnen).

denim noun Jeansstoff der (PL die Jeansstoffe); a denim jacket eine Jeansjacke.

Denmark noun Dänemark das.

dental adjective 1 Zahn-; dental floss die Zahnseide; dental hygiene die Zahnpflege; 2 to have a dental appointment beim Zahnarzt angemeldet sein.

dentist noun Zahnarzt der (PL die Zahnärzte), Zahnärztin die (PL die Zahnärztinnen); my mum's a dentist meine Mutter ist Zahnärztin.

deny verb bestreiten ◇.

deodorant noun Deodorant das (PL die Deodorants).

depart verb 1 (set out on a journey) abreisen SEP (PERF sein); 2 (train, coach) abfahren ◇ SEP (PERF sein); 3 (plane) abfliegen ◇ SEP (PERF sein).

department noun 1 (in a shop, firm, or hospital) Abteilung die (PL die Abteilungen); the men's department die Herrenabteilung; 2 (of a university) Seminar das (PL die Seminare); the history department das Seminar für Geschichte; 3 (in school) Fachbereich der (PL die Fachbereiche).

department store noun Kaufhaus das (PL die Kaufhäuser).

departure noun 1 (of a person) Abreise die; 2 (of a car, train) Abfahrt die; 3 (of a plane) Abflug der.

departure lounge noun Abflughalle die (PL die Abflughallen).

depend verb 1 to depend on abhängen ◇ SEP von (+DAT); it depends on the price das hängt vom Preis ab; it depends on what you want das hängt davon ab, was du willst; 2 it depends es kommt darauf an.

deposit noun 1 (when renting or hiring) Kaution die (PL die Kautionen); 2 (when booking a holiday or hotel room) Anzahlung die (PL die Anzahlungen); to pay a deposit eine Anzahlung leisten; 3 (on a bottle) Pfand das.

depressed adjective deprimiert.

depressing adjective deprimierend.

◇ IRREGULAR VERB: See the verb table in the centre of the dictionary

depth noun Tiefe die.

deputy noun Stellvertreter der (PL die Stellvertreter), Stellvertreterin die (PL die Stellvertreterinnen).

describe verb beschreiben ◇.

description noun Beschreibung die (PL die Beschreibungen).

desert noun Wüste die (PL die Wüsten).

desert island noun verlassene Insel die (PL die verlassenen Inseln).

deserve verb verdienen.

design noun 1 Konstruktion die (PL die Konstruktionen); **the design of the plane** die Flugzeugkonstruktion; 2 (artistic design) Design das (PL die Designs); **modern design** modernes Design; 3 (pattern) Muster das (PL die Muster); **a floral design** ein Blumenmuster; 4 (sketch) Entwurf der (PL die Entwürfe).
verb 1 konstruieren (a machine, plane, system); 2 entwerfen ◇ (costumes, fabric, scenery).

designer noun Designer der (PL die Designer), Designerin die (PL die Designerinnen).

desk noun 1 (in an office or at home) Schreibtisch der (PL die Schreibtische); 2 (pupil's) Pult das (PL die Pulte); 3 **the reception desk** die Rezeption; **the information desk** die Auskunft.

despair noun Verzweiflung die.
verb **to despair of doing**

something alle Hoffnung aufgeben ◇ SEP, etwas zu tun.

desperate adjective 1 verzweifelt; **a desperate attempt** ein verzweifelter Versuch; 2 **to be desperate to do something** etwas dringend tun müssen; **I'm desperate to speak to you** ich muss dich dringend sprechen; **to be desperate for something** etwas dringend brauchen.

dessert noun Nachtisch der (PL die Nachtische); **what's for dessert?** was gibt's zum Nachtisch?

destination noun Ziel das (PL die Ziele).

destroy verb zerstören.

destruction noun Zerstörung die.

detached house noun Einzelhaus das (PL die Einzelhäuser).

detail noun Einzelheit die (PL die Einzelheiten).

detailed adjective ausführlich.

detective noun 1 (in the police) Kriminalbeamte der (PL die Kriminalbeamten), Kriminalbeamtin die (PL die Kriminalbeamtinnen); 2 **private detective** der Detektiv, die Detektivin.

detective story noun Detektivgeschichte die (PL die Detektivgeschichten).

detention noun 1 (at school) Nachsitzen das; 2 (in prison) Haft die.

△ NEW SPELLING: See page xii

detergent noun Waschmittel das (PL die Waschmittel).

determined entschlossen; **he's determined to leave** er ist fest entschlossen zu gehen.

detour noun Umweg der (PL die Umwege).

develop verb 1 entwickeln; **to get a film developed** einen Film entwickeln lassen; 2 sich entwickeln; **how children develop** wie Kinder sich entwickeln.

developing country noun Entwicklungsland das (PL die Entwicklungsländer).

development noun Entwicklung die (PL die Entwicklungen).

devil noun Teufel der (PL die Teufel).

devoted adjective treu.

diabetes noun Zuckerkrankheit die.

diabetic noun Diabetiker der (PL die Diabetiker), Diabetikerin die (PL die Diabetikerinnen).
adjective zuckerkrank; **to be diabetic** zuckerkrank sein.

diagonal adjective diagonal.

diagram noun Diagramm das (PL die Diagramme).

dial verb wählen; **I dialled the wrong number** ich habe die falsche Nummer gewählt.

dialling tone noun Freizeichen das.

dialogue noun Dialog der (PL die Dialoge).

diamond noun 1 Diamant der (PL die Diamanten); (gemstone) Brillant der (PL die Brillanten); 2 (in cards) Karo das; **the jack of diamonds** der Karobube; 3 (shape) Raute die (PL die Rauten).

diarrhoea noun Durchfall der.

diary noun 1 (for appointments) Terminkalender der (PL die Terminkalender); 2 Tagebuch das (PL die Tagebücher); **to keep a diary** ein Tagebuch führen.

dice noun Würfel der (PL die Würfel); **to throw the dice** würfeln.

dictation noun Diktat das (PL die Diktate).

dictionary noun Wörterbuch das (PL die Wörterbücher).

did verb SEE do.

die verb 1 sterben ◇ (PERF sein); **my grannie died in January** meine Oma starb im Januar; 2 **to be dying to do something** darauf brennen, etwas zu tun; **I'm dying to meet her** ich brenne darauf, sie kennen zu lernen.

diesel noun 1 Dieselöl das; 2 **diesel engine** der Dieselmotor; **diesel car** der Diesel.

diet noun 1 Ernährung die; **a healthy diet** eine gesunde Ernährung; 2 (slimming or special) Diät die (PL die Diäten); **to be on a diet** Diät machen.

◇ IRREGULAR VERB: See the verb table in the centre of the dictionary

difference noun 1 Unterschied der (PL die Unterschiede); **I can't see any difference between the two** ich finde, es besteht kein Unterschied zwischen den beiden; **what's the difference between …?** was ist der Unterschied zwischen …?; 2 **it makes a difference** es ist ein Unterschied; **it makes no difference** es ist egal; **it makes no difference what I say** es ist egal, was ich sage.

different adjective 1 verschieden; **the two sisters are very different** die beiden Schwestern sind sehr verschieden; 2 **to be different from** anders sein als; **she's very different from her sister** sie ist ganz anders als ihre Schwester; 3 (separate) anderer/andere/anderes; **she reads a different book every day** sie liest jeden Tag ein anderes Buch.

difficult adjective schwer; **it's really difficult** es ist sehr schwer; **he finds it difficult** es fällt ihm schwer.

difficulty noun Schwierigkeit die (PL die Schwierigkeiten); **to have difficulty doing something** Schwierigkeiten haben, etwas zu tun; **I had difficulty finding your house** ich hatte Schwierigkeiten, dein Haus zu finden.

dig verb graben ♦; **to dig a hole** ein Loch graben.

digital adjective digital; **digital watch** die Digitaluhr; **digital recording** die Digitalaufnahme.

din noun Lärm der; **stop making such a din!** hör auf, so einen Lärm zu machen!

dinghy noun 1 **sailing dinghy** das Dingi; 2 **rubber dinghy** das Schlauchboot.

dining room noun Esszimmer △ das (PL die Esszimmer); **in the dining room** im Esszimmer.

dinner noun 1 (evening) Abendessen das (PL die Abendessen); **to invite somebody to dinner** jemanden zum Abendessen einladen; 2 (midday) Mittagessen das (PL die Mittagessen); **to have school dinner** in der Schulkantine zu Mittag essen.

dinner party noun Abendessen das (PL die Abendessen).

dinner time noun Essenszeit die.

dinosaur noun Dinosaurier der (PL die Dinosaurier).

diploma noun Diplom das (PL die Diplome).

direct adjective direkt.
verb 1 **to direct a film or a play** bei einem Film oder einem Theaterstück Regie führen; 2 regeln (traffic).

direction noun 1 Richtung die (PL die Richtungen); **to go in the other direction** in die andere Richtung gehen; 2 **to ask somebody for directions** jemanden nach dem Weg fragen; 3 **directions for use** die Gebrauchsanweisung (singular).

director noun 1 (of a company) Direktor der (PL die Direktoren), Direktorin die (PL die Direktorinnen); 2 (of a programme,

△ NEW SPELLING: See page xii

play, or film) Regisseur *der* (PL *die* Regisseure), Regisseurin *die* (PL *die* Regisseurinnen).

directory *noun* Telefonbuch *das* (PL *die* Telefonbücher); **he's ex-directory** seine Nummer steht nicht im Telefonbuch.

dirt *noun* Schmutz *der*.

dirty *adjective* schmutzig; **my hands are dirty** ich habe schmutzige Hände; **to get something dirty** etwas schmutzig machen; **you'll get your dress dirty** du machst dir das Kleid schmutzig; **to get dirty** schmutzig werden; **the curtains get dirty quickly** die Vorhänge werden sehr schnell schmutzig.

disabled *adjective* behindert; **disabled people** Behinderte (*plural*).

disadvantage *noun* 1 Nachteil *der* (PL *die* Nachteile); 2 **to be at a disadvantage** im Nachteil sein.

disagree *verb* 1 **I disagree** ich bin anderer Meinung; 2 **to disagree with somebody** mit jemandem nicht übereinstimmen SEP; **I disagree with James** ich stimme mit James nicht überein.

disappear *verb* verschwinden ◊ (PERF *sein*).

disappearance *noun* Verschwinden *das*.

disappointed *adjective* enttäuscht; **I'm disappointed with my marks** ich bin über meine Noten enttäuscht.

disappointment *noun* Enttäuschung *die* (PL *die* Enttäuschungen).

disaster *noun* Katastrophe *die* (PL *die* Katastrophen); **it was a complete disaster** es war eine komplette Katastrophe.

disastrous *adjective* katastrophal.

disc *noun* 1 **compact disc** die Compact disc; 2 **tax disc** (*for a vehicle*) die Steuerplakette; 3 **slipped disc** *der* Bandscheibenvorfall.

discipline *noun* Disziplin *die*.

disc-jockey *noun* Diskjockey *der* (PL *die* Diskjockeys).

disco *noun* 1 Diskoparty *die* (PL *die* Diskopartys); **they're having a disco** sie machen eine Diskoparty; 2 (*club*) Disko *die* (PL *die* Diskos); **to go to a disco** in eine Disko gehen.

discount *noun* Rabatt *der* (PL *die* Rabatte).

discover *verb* entdecken.

discovery *noun* Entdeckung *die* (PL *die* Entdeckungen).

discreet *adjective* diskret.

discrimination *noun* Diskriminierung *die*; **discrimination against women** die Diskriminierung von Frauen; **racial discrimination** die Rassendiskriminierung.

discuss *verb* **to discuss something** etwas besprechen ◊; **we'll discuss the problem tomorrow** wir besprechen das Problem morgen;

◊ IRREGULAR VERB: *See the verb table in the centre of the dictionary*

I'm going to discuss it with Phil ich werde es mit Phil besprechen.

discussion *noun* Gespräch *das* (PL die Gespräche).

disease *noun* Krankheit *die* (PL die Krankheiten).

disguise *noun* Verkleidung *die* (PL die Verkleidungen); **to be in disguise** verkleidet sein. *verb* verkleiden; **disguised as a woman** als Frau verkleidet.

disgust *noun* Ekel *der*.

disgusted *adjective* 1 (*filled with indignation*) empört; 2 (*nauseated*) angeekelt.

disgusting *adjective* eklig.

dish *noun* 1 Schüssel *die* (PL die Schüsseln); **a large white dish** eine große weiße Schüssel; **satellite dish** die Satellitenschüssel; 2 (*type of food*) Gericht *das* (PL die Gerichte); **risotto is my favourite dish** Risotto ist mein Lieblingsgericht; 3 (*crockery*) **the dishes** das Geschirr; **to do the dishes** Geschirr spülen.

dishonest *adjective* unehrlich.

dishonesty *noun* Unehrlichkeit *die*.

dishwasher *noun* Geschirrspülmaschine *die* (PL die Geschirrspülmaschinen).

disinfectant *noun* Desinfektionsmittel *das*.

disk *noun* Diskette *die* (PL die Disketten); **floppy disk** die Diskette; **hard disk** die Festplatte.

diskette *noun* Diskette *die* (PL die Disketten).

dismiss *verb* entlassen ◇ (*an employee*).

disobedient *adjective* ungehorsam.

display *noun* 1 Ausstellung *die* (PL die Ausstellungen); **handicrafts display** die Handarbeitsausstellung; **to be on display** ausgestellt sein; 2 **window display** die Auslage; 3 **firework display** das Feuerwerk. *verb* ausstellen SEP.

disposable *adjective* Wegwerf-; **disposable towel** das Wegwerfhandtuch.

disqualify *verb* disqualifizieren.

dissolve *verb* auflösen SEP.

distance *noun* Entfernung *die* (PL die Entfernungen); **from this distance** aus dieser Entfernung; **from a distance** von weitem; **in the distance** in der Ferne; **it's within walking distance** es ist zu Fuß erreichbar.

distant *adjective* fern.

distinct *adjective* deutlich.

distinctly *adverb* 1 deutlich; 2 **it's distinctly odd** es ist äußerst komisch.

distract *verb* ablenken SEP.

distribute *verb* verteilen.

district *noun* 1 (*of a town*) Stadtteil *der* (PL die Stadtteile); **a poor district of Berlin** ein ärmlicher Stadtteil von Berlin; 2 (*in the country*) Gebiet *das* (PL die Gebiete).

△ NEW SPELLING: *See page xii*

disturb verb stören; **sorry to disturb you** Entschuldigung, dass ich störe.

dive noun Kopfsprung der (PL die Kopfsprünge).
verb 1 einen Kopfsprung machen; 2 (swim underwater) tauchen (PERF sein).

diver noun 1 (underwater) Taucher der (PL die Taucher), Taucherin die (PL die Taucherinnen); 2 (from a diving board) Springer der (PL die Springer), Springerin die (PL die Springerinnen).

diversion noun (of traffic) Umleitung die (PL die Umleitungen).

divide verb teilen.

diving noun 1 (underwater) Tauchen das; 2 (from a diving board) Kopfspringen das.

diving board noun Sprungbrett das (PL die Sprungbretter).

division noun 1 Teilung die (PL die Teilungen); 2 (in maths) Division die (PL die Divisionen); 3 (sports league) Liga die (PL die Ligen).

divorce noun Scheidung die (PL die Scheidungen).

divorced adjective geschieden.

DIY noun 1 Heimwerken das; 2 to do DIY heimwerken; 3 DIY shop der Baumarkt (PL die Baumärkte).

dizzy adjective I feel dizzy mir ist schwindlig.

DJ noun DJ der (PL die DJs).

do verb 1 tun ✧, machen; **what are you doing?** was machst du?; **I'm doing my homework** ich mache meine Hausaufgaben; **what have you done with the hammer?** was hast du mit dem Hammer gemacht?; **can you do me a favour?** kannst du mir einen Gefallen tun?; **do as I say** tu was ich sage; **she's doing the cleaning** sie putzt; **I'll do the washing up** ich wasche ab; **I must do the shopping** ich muss einkaufen gehen; 3 (in questions) **do you like it?** gefällt es dir?; **when does the film start?** wann fängt der Film an?; **how do you open the door?** wie macht man die Tür auf?; **do you know him?** kennst du ihn?; 4 (in negative sentences) **I don't like mushrooms** ich mag keine Pilze; **Rosie doesn't like spinach** Rosie mag keinen Spinat; **you didn't shut the door** du hast die Tür nicht zugemacht; **it doesn't matter** das macht nichts; 5 (when it refers back to another verb, 'do' is not translated) **'do you live here?'** – **'yes, I do'** 'wohnst du hier?' -'ja'; **she has more money than I do** sie hat mehr Geld als ich; **'I live in Oxford'** – **'so do I'** 'ich wohne in Oxford' – 'ich auch'; **'I didn't phone Gemma'** – **'neither did I'** 'ich habe Gemma nicht angerufen' – 'ich auch nicht'; 6 **don't you?, doesn't he?, etc.** nicht wahr?; **you know Helen, don't you?** du kennst Helen, nicht wahr?; **she left on Thursday, didn't she?** sie ist Donnerstag abgefahren, nicht

✧ **IRREGULAR VERB: See the verb table in the centre of the dictionary**

wahr?; **7 that'll do** das reicht; **it'll do like that** das geht so.

● **to do something up 1** etwas zubinden ◇ SEP (*shoes*); **2** etwas zumachen SEP (*a cardigan, jacket*); **3** etwas renovieren (*a house*).

● **to do without something** ohne etwas ←(ACC) auskommen ◇ SEP (PERF *sein*); **we can do without knives** wir können ohne Messer auskommen.

doctor *noun* Arzt *der* (PL *die* Ärzte), Ärztin *die* (PL *die* Ärztinnen); **her mother's a doctor** ihre Mutter ist Ärztin.

documentary *noun* Dokumentarfilm *der* (PL *die* Dokumentarfilme).

dog *noun* Hund *der* (PL *die* Hunde).

do-it-yourself *noun* Heimwerken *das*.

dole *noun* Stempelgeld *das*; **to be on the dole** stempeln gehen (*informal*).

doll *noun* Puppe *die* (PL *die* Puppen).

dollar *noun* Dollar *der* (PL *die* Dollars).

domino *noun* **1** Dominostein *der* (PL *die* Dominosteine); **2** (*game*) **dominoes** Domino *das*; **to play dominoes** Domino spielen.

donkey *noun* Esel *der* (PL *die* Esel).

don't SEE do.

door *noun* Tür *die* (PL *die* Türen); **to open the door** die Tür aufmachen; **to shut the door** die Tür zumachen.

doorbell *noun* Türklingel *die* (PL *die* Türklingeln); **to ring the doorbell** klingeln.

dot *noun* **1** Punkt *der* (PL *die* Punkte); **at ten on the dot** Punkt zehn Uhr; **2** (*small dot on fabric*) Pünktchen *das* (PL *die* Pünktchen).

double *adjective, adverb* **1** doppelt; **a double helping** eine doppelte Portion; **double the size** doppelt so groß; **double the time** doppelt so viel Zeit; **at double the price** zum doppelten Preis; **2 double room** *das* Doppelzimmer; **3 double bed** *das* Doppelbett.

double bass *noun* Kontrabass △ *der* (PL *die* Kontrabässe).

double-decker bus *noun* Doppeldeckerbus *der* (PL *die* Doppeldeckerbusse).

doubles *noun* (*in tennis*) Doppel *das* (PL *die* Doppel).

doubt *noun* Zweifel *der* (PL *die* Zweifel); **there's no doubt about it** es besteht kein Zweifel daran; **I have my doubts** ich habe gewisse Zweifel.
verb **to doubt something** etwas bezweifeln; **I doubt it** das bezweifle ich; **I doubt that …** ich bezweifle, dass …; **I doubt they'll buy it** ich bezweifle, dass sie es kaufen.

doubtful *adjective* **1** fraglich; **it's doubtful** es ist fraglich; **2 to be doubtful about doing something** Bedenken haben, ob man etwas tun soll; **I'm doubtful about inviting them together** ich habe Bedenken, ob ich sie zusammen einladen soll.

△ NEW SPELLING: *See page xii*

dough noun Teig der.

doughnut noun Krapfen der (PL die Krapfen).

down adverb, preposition 1 unten; he's down in the cellar er ist unten im Keller; it's down there er ist da unten; 2 down the road (nearby) in der Nähe; there's a chemist's just down the road eine Apotheke ist ganz in der Nähe; 3 to go down nach unten gehen; I went down to open the door ich bin nach unten gegangen, um die Tür aufzumachen; to walk down the street die Straße entlanggehen ◇ SEP; to run down the stairs die Treppe runterrennen SEP (PERF sein) (informal); 4 to come down herunterkommen ◇ SEP (PERF sein); she came down into the kitchen sie kam in die Küche herunter; 5 to sit down sich setzen; she sat down on the chair sie setzte sich auf den Stuhl; 6 to write something down etwas aufschreiben ◇ SEP.

downstairs adverb 1 unten; she's downstairs sie ist unten; 2 (with movement) nach unten; to go downstairs nach unten gehen; 3 im Erdgeschoss Δ; the flat downstairs die Wohnung im Erdgeschoss.

dozen noun Dutzend das (PL die Dutzende).

drag noun 1 what a drag! so'n Mist! (informal); 2 what a drag she is! Mann, ist die langweilig! (informal). verb schleppen.

drama noun 1 (play) Drama das (PL die Dramen); he made a big drama out of it er hat ein großes Drama daraus gemacht (informal); 2 (dramatic nature) Dramatik die.

dramatic adjective dramatisch.

draught noun Luftzug der; there's a draught in here hier zieht es.

draughts noun Damespiel das; to play draughts Dame spielen.

draw noun 1 (in a match) Unentschieden das; to end in a draw mit einem Unentschieden enden; 2 (lottery) Ziehung die (PL die Ziehungen).
verb 1 zeichnen; she can draw really well sie kann wirklich sehr gut zeichnen; 2 to draw the curtains (open) die Vorhänge aufziehen ◇ SEP; (close) die Vorhänge zuziehen ◇ SEP; 3 (in a match) unentschieden spielen; we drew three all wir haben drei zu drei unentschieden gespielt.

drawer noun Schublade die (PL die Schubladen).

drawing noun Zeichnung die (PL die Zeichnungen).

drawing pin noun Reißzwecke die (PL die Reißzwecken).

dreadful adjective furchtbar.

dreadfully adverb furchtbar; I'm dreadfully late ich habe mich furchtbar verspätet; I'm dreadfully sorry es tut mir furchtbar Leid.

dream noun Traum der (PL die Träume); to have a dream einen Traum haben.
verb träumen; to dream about something von etwas ←(DAT) träumen.

◇ IRREGULAR VERB: See the verb table in the centre of the dictionary

dress noun Kleid das (PL die Kleider).
verb to dress a child ein Kind anziehen ◇ SEP.
● to dress up sich verkleiden; to dress up as a vampire sich als Vampir verkleiden.

dressed adjective 1 angezogen; is Tom dressed yet? ist Tom schon angezogen?; 2 she was dressed in black trousers and a yellow shirt sie trug schwarze Hosen und ein gelbes Hemd; 3 to get dressed sich anziehen ◇ SEP; I got dressed quickly ich zog mich schnell an.

dressing gown noun Morgenrock der (PL die Morgenröcke).

dressing table noun Frisierkommode die (PL die Frisierkommoden).

drier noun hair drier der Föhn △; tumble drier der Wäschetrockner.

drill noun Bohrer der (PL die Bohrer).

drink noun Getränk das (PL die Getränke); 1 to have a drink etwas trinken; would you like a drink of water? möchtest du etwas Wasser trinken?; 2 (an alcoholic drink) Drink der (PL die Drinks); they've invited us round for drinks sie haben uns auf einen Drink eingeladen; let's have a drink! trinken wir einen! (informal).
verb trinken ◇; he drank a glass of water er trank ein Glas Wasser.

drive noun 1 to go for a drive eine Autofahrt machen; 2 (in front of a house) Einfahrt die (PL die Einfahrten).

verb 1 fahren ◇ (PERF sein); she drives very fast sie fährt sehr schnell; to drive a car Auto fahren; I'd like to learn to drive ich möchte Autofahren lernen; can you drive? kannst du Auto fahren?; 2 we drove to Berlin wir sind mit dem Auto nach Berlin gefahren; 3 to drive somebody (to a place) jemanden (irgendwohin) fahren (PERF haben); Mum drove me to the station Mutti hat mich zum Bahnhof gefahren; to drive somebody home jemanden nach Hause fahren; ★ she drives me mad! sie macht mich verrückt!

driver noun 1 Fahrer der (PL die Fahrer), Fahrerin die (PL die Fahrerinnen); 2 (of a locomotive) Führer der (PL die Führer), Führerin die (PL die Führerinnen).

driving instructor noun Fahrlehrer der (PL die Fahrlehrer), Fahrlehrerin die (PL die Fahrlehrerinnen).

driving lesson noun Fahrstunde die (PL die Fahrstunden).

driving licence noun Führerschein der.

driving test noun Fahrprüfung die; to take your driving test die Fahrprüfung machen; Jenny's passed her driving test Jenny hat den Führerschein gemacht.

drop noun Tropfen der (PL die Tropfen).
verb 1 to drop something etwas fallen lassen; I dropped my glasses

△ NEW SPELLING: See page xii

ich habe meine Brille fallen lassen;
2 drop it! lass das!; **3 I'm going to
drop history next year** nächstes
Jahr lege ich Geschichte ab;
4 absetzen SEP (*a person*); **could you
drop me at the station?** könntest
du mich am Bahnhof absetzen?

drug noun **1** (*medicine*)
Medikament *das* (PL die
Medikamente); **2** (*illegal*) **drugs**
Drogen (*plural*).

drug abuse noun
Drogenmissbrauch △ der.

drug addict noun
Drogenabhängige der/die (PL die
Drogenabhängigen).

drug addiction noun
Drogenabhängigkeit die.

drum noun **1** Trommel die (PL die
Trommeln); **2 drums** das
Schlagzeug; **to play drums**
Schlagzeug spielen.

drummer noun Schlagzeuger der
(PL die Schlagzeuger).

drunk noun Betrunkene der/die (PL
die Betrunkenen).
adjective betrunken; **to get drunk**
sich betrinken ◇.

dry adjective trocken.
verb **1** trocknen; **to let something
dry** etwas trocknen lassen; **to dry
your hair** sich ←(DAT) die Haare
trocknen; **to dry the washing** die
Wäsche trocknen; **2 to dry your
hands** sich ←(DAT) die Hände
abtrocknen SEP; **I dried my feet** ich
trocknete mir die Füße ab; **to dry the
dishes** das Geschirr abtrocknen .

dry cleaner's noun chemische
Reinigung die.

dryer noun SEE drier.

dubbed adjective **a dubbed film** ein
synchronisierter Film.

duck noun Ente die (PL die Enten).

due adjective, adverb **1 to be due to
do something** etwas tun müssen;
Paul's due back soon Paul muss
bald zurück sein; **we're due to leave
on Thursday** wir müssen
Donnerstag abfahren; **2 due to**
wegen (+GEN); **due to bad weather**
wegen schlechten Wetters.

dull adjective **1 dull weather** trübes
Wetter; **it's a dull day today** heute
ist ein trüber Tag; **2** (*boring*)
langweilig.

dumb adjective **1** stumm; **2** (*stupid*)
dumm; **he asked some dumb
questions** er hat ein paar dumme
Fragen gestellt.

dump verb **1** abladen ◇ SEP
(*rubbish*); **2** (*put down*)
hinwerfen ◇ SEP; **he dumped it in the
rubbish** er hat es in den Müll
geworfen; **3** abschieben ◇ SEP (*a
person*) (*informal*); **she's dumped
her boyfriend** sie hat ihren Freund
abgeschoben.

dungarees plural noun
Latzhose die (PL die Latzhosen).

during preposition während (+GEN);
during the night während der
Nacht; **I saw her during the
holidays** ich habe sie während der
Ferien gesehen.

◇ IRREGULAR VERB: *See the verb table in the centre of the dictionary*

dust noun Staub der.
verb 1 abstauben SEP (furniture, objects); 2 (in a room) Staub wischen; **she's dusting** sie wischt Staub.

dustbin noun Mülltonne die (PL die Mülltonnen).

dustman noun Müllmann der (PL die Müllmänner).

dusty adjective staubig.

Dutch noun 1 (language) Holländisch das; 2 **the Dutch** (people) die Holländer.
adjective holländisch; **he's Dutch** er ist Holländer; **she's Dutch** sie ist Holländerin.

duty noun 1 Pflicht die (PL die Pflichten); **to have a duty to do something** die Pflicht haben, etwas zu tun; **you have a duty to inform us** du hast die Pflicht, uns zu benachrichtigen; 2 **to be on duty** Dienst haben; **to be on night duty** Nachtdienst haben; **I'm off duty tonight** ich habe heute Abend keinen Dienst.

duty-free adjective zollfrei; **duty-free shop** der Dutyfreeshop; **duty-free goods** zollfreie Waren (plural).

duvet noun Federbett das (PL die Federbetten).

duvet cover noun Bettbezug der (PL die Bettbezüge).

dye noun Farbe die (PL die Farben).
verb färben; **to dye your hair** sich ←(DAT) die Haare färben; **I'm going to have my hair dyed pink** ich lasse mir die Haare rosa färben.

dynamic adjective dynamisch.

dyslexia noun Legasthenie die.

dyslexic adjective legasthenisch; **to be dyslexic** Legastheniker sein, Legasthenikerin sein.

E e

each adjective, pronoun
1 jeder/jede/jedes; **each Sunday** jeden Sonntag; **each time** jedes Mal; **at the beginning of each year** am Anfang jedes Jahres; **we each have an invitation** jeder von uns hat eine Einladung; **my sisters each have a computer** meine Schwestern haben alle einen Computer; **she gave us an apple each** sie hat jedem von uns einen Apfel gegeben; **each of you** jeder von euch/jede von euch; **we each got a present** jeder Einzelne hat ein Geschenk bekommen; 2 **the tickets cost ten pounds each** die Karten kosten je zehn Pfund; **£5 each** (per person) fünf Pfund pro Person; (per item) fünf Pfund pro Stück.

each other pronoun ('each other' is usually translated using a reflexive pronoun) **they love each other** sie lieben sich; **we know each other** wir kennen uns; **do you see each other often?** seht ihr euch oft?

ear noun Ohr das (PL die Ohren).

earache noun **to have earache** Ohrenschmerzen haben.

△ NEW SPELLING: See page xii

earlier adverb 1 (a while ago) vor kurzem; **your brother phoned earlier** dein Bruder hat vor kurzem angerufen; 2 (not as late) früher; **we should have started earlier** wir hätten früher anfangen sollen.

early adverb 1 (in the morning) früh; **to get up early** es ist zu früh aufstehen; **it's too early** es ist zu früh; 2 (for an appointment) **to be early** früh dran sein; **we're early, the train doesn't leave until ten** wir sind früh dran, der Zug fährt erst um zehn Uhr ab. adjective 1 (one of the first) **in the early months** während der ersten Monate; **I'm getting the early train** ich nehme den früheren Zug; 2 **to have an early lunch** früh zu Mittag essen; **Jan's having an early night** Jan geht früh zu Bett; 3 **in the early afternoon** am frühen Nachmittag; **in the early hours** in den frühen Morgenstunden.

earn verb verdienen; **Richard earns four pounds an hour** Richard verdient vier Pfund die Stunde.

earring noun Ohrring der (PL die Ohrringe).

earth noun Erde die; **life on earth** das Leben auf der Erde; ★ **what on earth are you doing?** was in aller Welt machst du da?

easily adverb leicht; **he's easily the best** er ist mit Abstand der Beste.

east noun Osten der; **in the east** im Osten. adjective, adverb östlich, Ost-; **the east side** die Ostseite; **an east**

wind ein Ostwind; **east of Munich** östlich von München.

Easter noun Ostern das (PL die Ostern); **they're coming at Easter** sie kommen zu Ostern; **Happy Easter** Frohe Ostern.

Easter Day noun Ostersonntag der (PL die Ostersonntage).

Easter egg noun Osterei das (PL die Ostereier).

Eastern Europe noun Osteuropa das.

easy adjective leicht; **it's easy!** das ist leicht!; **it was easy to decide** es war leicht zu entscheiden.

eat verb 1 essen ✧; **he was eating a banana** er aß eine Banane; **we're going to have something to eat** wir essen jetzt etwas; 2 **to eat your breakfast** frühstücken.

EC noun EG die (Europäische Gemeinschaft).

ecological adjective ökologisch.

ecology noun Ökologie die.

economical adjective sparsam.

economics noun Wirtschaftswissenschaften (plural).

economy noun Wirtschaft die.

edge noun 1 Kante die (PL die Kanten); **the edge of the table** die Tischkante; 2 (of a road, sheet of paper, or cliff) Rand der (PL die Ränder); **at the edge of the forest** am Waldrand.

editor noun 1 (of a newspaper or magazine) Chefredakteur der (PL

die Chefredakteure),
Chefredakteurin die (PL die
Chefredakteurinnen); 2 (of a book)
Redakteur der (PL die Redakteure),
Redakteurin die (PL die
Redakteurinnen).

educate verb erziehen ◇.

education noun Ausbildung die.

effect noun 1 Wirkung die (PL die
Wirkungen); the effect of the
explosion was horrific die Wirkung
der Explosion war entsetzlich; 2 to
have an effect on something eine
Auswirkung auf etwas ←(ACC) haben;
it had a good effect on the whole
family es hatte eine gute
Auswirkung auf die ganze Familie;
3 (in a film) Effekt der (PL die
Effekte); special effects besondere
Effekte.

efficient adjective 1 (person)
tüchtig; 2 (machine or
organization) leistungsfähig.

effort noun 1 Mühe die (PL die
Mühen); 2 to make an effort sich
bemühen; Toya made an effort to
help us Toya hat sich bemüht, uns
zu helfen; he didn't even make the
effort to apologize er hat sich nicht
einmal die Mühe gemacht, sich zu
entschuldigen.

e.g. abbreviation z.B. (zum Beispiel).

egg noun Ei das (PL die Eier); a fried
egg ein Spiegelei; a hard-boiled
egg ein hart gekochtes Ei.

egg-cup noun Eierbecher der (PL
die Eierbecher).

eggshell noun Eierschale die (PL die
Eierschalen).

egg-white noun Eiweiß das (PL die
Eiweiße).

egg-yolk noun Eigelb das (PL die
Eigelbe).

eight number acht; Maya's eight
Maya ist acht; at eight o'clock um
acht Uhr.

eighteen number achtzehn;
Jason's eighteen Jason ist
achtzehn.

eighth number achter/achte/
achtes; on the eighth of July am
achten Juli.

eighty number achtzig; eighty-five
fünfundachtzig.

either pronoun 1 (one or the other)
einer von beiden/eine von
beiden/eins von beiden; take either
(of them) nimm einen von
beiden/eine von beiden/eins von
beiden; I don't like either (of them)
ich mag keinen von beiden/keine
von beiden/keins von beiden;
2 (both) beide (plural); either is
possible beide sind möglich; on
either side auf beiden Seiten.
conjunction 1 either ... or entweder
... oder; either Susie or Judy
entweder Susie oder Judy; 2 either
... or (with a negative) weder ...
noch; he didn't ring either Sam or
Emma er hat weder Sam noch
Emma angerufen; 3 I don't know
them either ich kenne sie auch
nicht.

elastic noun Gummiband das (PL
die Gummibänder).

elastic band noun
Gummiband das (PL die
Gummibänder).

△ NEW SPELLING: See page xii

elbow noun Ellbogen der (PL die Ellbogen).

elder adjective älterer/ältere/älteres; **her elder brother** ihr älterer Bruder.

elderly adjective alt; **the elderly** ältere Menschen (plural).

eldest adjective ältester/älteste/ältestes; **her eldest brother** ihr ältester Bruder.

elect verb wählen; **she has been elected** sie ist gewählt worden.

election noun Wahl die (PL die Wahlen); **in the election** bei den Wahlen.

electric adjective elektrisch.

electrical adjective elektrisch, Elektro-; **electrical equipment** Elektrogeräte (plural).

electrician noun Elektriker der (PL die Elektriker), Elektrikerin die (PL die Elektrikerinnen).

electricity noun Strom der.

electronic adjective elektronisch.

electronics noun Elektronik die.

elephant noun Elefant der (PL die Elefanten).

eleven number elf; **Josh is eleven** Josh ist elf; **at eleven o'clock** um elf Uhr; **a football eleven** eine Fußballelf.

eleventh number elfter/elfte/elftes; **the eleventh of May** der elfte Mai; **on the eleventh floor** im elften Stock.

else adverb 1 (in addition) sonst; **who else?** wer sonst?; **did you see anyone else?** hast du sonst noch jemanden gesehen?; **nothing else** sonst nichts; **I don't want anything else** ich will sonst nichts; 2 **would you like something else?** möchten Sie sonst noch etwas?; 3 (instead or different) anderer/andere/anderes; **somewhere else** irgendwo anders; **everyone else** alle anderen; **somebody else** jemand anders; **something else** etwas anderes; 4 **or else** sonst; **hurry up, or else we'll be late** beeil dich, sonst kommen wir zu spät.

E-mail noun E-Mail die (PL die E-Mails).

embarrassed adjective verlegen; **he was very embarrassed** er war ganz verlegen.

embarrassing adjective peinlich.

emergency noun Notfall der (PL die Notfälle).

emergency exit noun Notausgang der (PL die Notausgänge).

emotion noun Gefühl das (PL die Gefühle).

emotional adjective 1 (person) empfindsam; 2 (speech or occasion) emotionsgeladen.

emphasize verb betonen; **he emphasized that it was voluntary** er betonte, dass es freiwillig war.

employ verb 1 (have working for you) beschäftigen; 2 (take on a worker) einstellen SEP.

✧ IRREGULAR VERB: *See the verb table in the centre of the dictionary*

employee *noun* Angestellte *der/die* (PL *die* Angestellten).

employer *noun* Arbeitgeber *der* (PL *die* Arbeitgeber), Arbeitgeberin *die* (PL *die* Arbeitgeberinnen).

employment *noun* Arbeit *die*.

empty *adjective* leer; **an empty bottle** eine leere Flasche. *verb* **1** (*empty out*) ausleeren SEP; **2** (*pour*) schütten.

enclose *verb* (*in a letter*) beilegen SEP; **please find enclosed a cheque** ein Scheck liegt bei.

encourage *verb* ermutigen; **to encourage somebody to do something** jemanden dazu ermutigen, etwas zu tun; **Mum encouraged me to try again** Mutti hat mich dazu ermutigt, es noch einmal zu versuchen.

encouragement *noun* Ermutigung *die* (PL *die* Ermutigungen).

encouraging *adjective* ermutigend.

encyclopedia *noun* Lexikon *das* (PL *die* Lexika).

end *noun* **1** Ende *das* (PL *die* Enden); **'The End'** 'Ende'; **at the end of the film** am Ende des Films; **by the end of the lesson** als die Stunde zu Ende war; **in the end I went home** schließlich bin ich nach Hause gegangen; **Sally's coming at the end of June** Sally kommt Ende Juni; **I read to the end of the page** ich habe die Seite zu Ende gelesen; **hold the other end** halte das andere Ende fest; **at the end of the street** am Ende der Straße; **2** (*in sports*) Spielfeldhälfte *die* (PL *die* Spielfeldhälften); **to change ends** die Seiten wechseln. *verb* **1** (*to put an end to*) beenden; **they've ended the strike** sie haben den Streik beendet; **2** (*to come to an end*) enden; **the day ended with a meal** der Tag endete mit einem Essen.

● **to end up 1 to end up doing something** am Ende etwas tun; **we ended up taking a taxi** am Ende haben wir ein Taxi genommen; **2 to end up somewhere** irgendwo landen (PERF *sein*) (*informal*); **Rob ended up in Berlin** Rob ist in Berlin gelandet.

ending *noun* **1** Ende *das* (PL *die* Enden); **2** (*in grammar*) Endung *die* (PL *die* Endungen).

endless *adjective* endlos (*day or journey, for example*).

enemy *noun* Feind *der* (PL *die* Feinde); **to make enemies** sich ←(DAT) Feinde machen.

energetic *adjective* energiegeladen.

energy *noun* Energie *die*.

engaged *adjective* **1** (*to be married*) verlobt; **they're engaged** sie sind verlobt; **to get engaged** sich verloben; **2** (*a phone or toilet*) besetzt; **it's engaged, I'll ring later** es ist besetzt, ich rufe später an.

engagement *noun* (*to marry*) Verlobung *die* (PL *die* Verlobungen).

△ NEW SPELLING: *See page xii*

engagement ring *noun*
Verlobungsring *der* (PL *die*
Verlobungsringe).

engine *noun* 1 (*in a car*) Motor *der*
(PL *die* Motoren); 2 (*pulling a train*)
Lokomotive *die* (PL *die*
Lokomotiven).

engineer *noun* 1 (*who comes for
repairs*) Techniker *der* (PL *die*
Techniker), Technikerin *die* (PL *die*
Technikerinnen); 2 (*who builds
roads and bridges*) Ingenieur *der* (PL
die Ingenieure), Ingenieurin *die* (PL
die Ingenieurinnen).

England *noun* England *das*; **I'm
from England** ich bin Engländer,
ich bin Engländerin.

English *noun* 1 (*the language*)
Englisch *das*; **do you speak
English?** sprechen Sie Englisch?; **he
answered in English** er hat auf
Englisch geantwortet; 2 (*the people*)
the English die Engländer.
adjective 1 (*of or from England*)
englisch; **the English team** die
englische Mannschaft; **he's English**
er ist Engländer; **she's English** sie
ist Engländerin; 2 **an English
lesson** eine Englischstunde; **our
English teacher** unser
Englischlehrer.

English Channel *noun* **the
English Channel** der Ärmelkanal.

Englishman *noun* Engländer *der*
(PL *die* Engländer).

Englishwoman *noun*
Engländerin *die* (PL *die*
Engländerinnen).

enjoy *verb* 1 **did you enjoy the
party?** hat dir die Party gefallen?; **we**

really enjoyed the concert das
Konzert hat uns wirklich gut
gefallen; 2 **to enjoy doing
something** etwas gerne tun ◇; **I
enjoy reading** ich lese gerne; **do you
enjoy living in York?** wohnst du
gerne in York?; 3 **to enjoy oneself**
sich gut amüsieren; **we really
enjoyed ourselves** wir haben uns
richtig gut amüsiert; **enjoy
yourselves!** viel Vergnügen !; **did
you enjoy yourself?** hast du dich
gut amüsiert?

enjoyable *adjective* nett.

enormous *adjective* riesig.

enough *adverb, adjective, pronoun*
1 genug; **there's enough for
everyone** es gibt genug für alle; **big
enough** groß genug; **have we got
enough bread?** haben wir genug
Brot?; 2 **that's enough** das reicht.

enrol *verb* sich anmelden SEP; **I want
to enrol on the course** ich möchte
mich zu dem Kurs anmelden.

enter *verb* 1 (*to go inside*) gehen ◇
(PERF *sein*) (in (+ACC) *a room or a
building*); **we all entered the
church** wir gingen alle in die
Kirche; 2 (*in computing*)
eingeben ◇ SEP; 3 **to enter for** sich
anmelden SEP zu (+DAT) (*an exam or
a race*); **to enter for a competition**
an einem Preisausschreiben
teilnehmen ◇ SEP.

entertain *verb* 1 (*to keep amused*)
unterhalten ◇; 2 (*to have people
round*) Gäste haben ◇; **they don't
entertain much** sie haben selten
Gäste.

◇ IRREGULAR VERB: *See the verb table in the centre of the dictionary*

entertainment noun (fun)
Unterhaltung die; **there wasn't
much entertainment in the
evenings** abends wurde wenig
Unterhaltung geboten.

enthusiasm noun
Begeisterung die.

enthusiast noun 1 Enthusiast der
(PL die Enthusiasten), Enthusiastin
die (PL die Enthusiastinnen); 2 (for
sports) Fan der (PL die Fans); **he's a
rugby enthusiast** er ist ein
Rugbyfan.

enthusiastic adjective begeistert.

entire adjective ganz; **the entire
class** die ganze Klasse.

entirely adverb ganz.

entrance noun 1 (fee) Eintritt der;
2 (way in) Eingang der (PL die
Eingänge).

entry noun 1 (way in) Eingang der
(PL die Eingänge); (for cars)
Einfahrt die (PL die Einfahrten);
2 **'no entry'** 'Zutritt verboten'; (to
cars) 'Einfahrt verboten'.

entry phone noun
Sprechanlage die (PL die
Sprechanlagen).

envelope noun Briefumschlag der
(PL die Briefumschläge).

environment noun Umwelt die.

environmental adjective Umwelt-;
environmental pollution die
Umweltverschmutzung.

environment-friendly adjective
umweltfreundlich.

epidemic noun Epidemie die (PL
die Epidemien).

epileptic adjective epileptisch.

episode noun 1 (an event)
Episode die (PL die Episoden);
2 (on TV or radio) Folge die (PL die
Folgen).

equal adjective gleich; **milk and
water in equal quantities** gleich
viel Milch und Wasser.
verb gleichen ◇ (+DAT).

equality noun
Gleichberechtigung die.

equally adverb (to share)
gleichmäßig; **we divided it equally**
wir haben es gleichmäßig verteilt.

equator noun Äquator der.

equip verb ausrüsten SEP; **well
equipped for the hike** für die
Wanderung gut ausgerüstet;
equipped with rucksacks mit
Rucksäcken ausgerüstet.

equipment noun 1 (for sport)
Ausrüstung die (PL die
Ausrüstungen); 2 Ausstattung die
(PL die Ausstattungen); **laboratory
equipment** die Laborausstattung;
3 (something needed for an activity)
Geräte (plural); **recording
equipment** Aufnahmegeräte.

error noun 1 (in spelling, typing, on
a computer, or in maths) Fehler der
(PL die Fehler); **spelling error** der
Schreibfehler; 2 (wrong opinion)
Irrtum der (PL die Irrtümer).

error message noun
Fehlermeldung die (PL die
Fehlermeldungen).

△ NEW SPELLING: See page xii

escalator noun Rolltreppe die (PL die Rolltreppen).

escape noun (from prison) Ausbruch der (PL die Ausbrüche). verb 1 (from prison) ausbrechen ◇ SEP (PERF sein); 2 entkommen ◇ (PERF sein); **to escape from somebody** jemandem entkommen.

especially adverb besonders.

essay noun Aufsatz der (PL die Aufsätze); **an essay on German reunification** ein Aufsatz über die deutsche Wiedervereinigung.

essential adjective unbedingt erforderlich; **it's essential to reply quickly** es ist unbedingt erforderlich, sofort zu antworten.

estate noun 1 (a housing estate) Wohnsiedlung die (PL die Wohnsiedlungen); 2 (a big house and grounds) Landsitz der (PL die Landsitze).

estate agent noun Immobilienmakler der (PL die Immobilienmakler).

estate car noun Kombiwagen der (PL die Kombiwagen).

estimate noun 1 (a quote for work) Kostenvoranschlag der (PL die Kostenvoranschläge); 2 (a rough guess) Schätzung die (PL die Schätzungen). verb schätzen.

etc. abbreviation usw. (und so weiter).

ethnic adjective ethnisch; **an ethnic minority** eine ethnische Minderheit.

EU noun EU die (Europäische Union).

Europe noun Europa das.

European noun Europäer der (PL die Europäer), Europäerin die (PL die Europäerinnen). adjective europäisch.

European Union noun Europäische Union die.

even[1] adverb 1 sogar; **even Lisa is coming** sogar Lisa kommt; 2 **not even** nicht einmal; **I don't like animals, not even dogs** ich mag keine Tiere, nicht einmal Hunde; 3 **without even asking** ohne wenigstens zu fragen; 4 **even if** selbst wenn; **even if they arrive late** selbst wenn sie spät ankommen; 5 (with a comparison) (sogar) noch; **even bigger** sogar noch größer; **even faster** noch schneller; **even better than** sogar noch besser als; **the song is even better than their last one** das Lied ist sogar noch besser als ihr letztes; 6 **even so** trotzdem; **even so, we had a good time** trotzdem haben wir uns amüsiert.

even[2] adjective 1 (surface or layer) eben; 2 (number) gerade; **six is an even number** sechs ist eine gerade Zahl; 3 (equal) gleich (distance, value); **the score is even** die Punktzahl ist gleich; 4 **to get even with somebody** es jemandem heimzahlen.

evening noun 1 Abend der (PL die Abende); **in the evening** am Abend; **this evening** heute Abend;

◇ IRREGULAR VERB: See the verb table in the centre of the dictionary

tomorrow evening morgen Abend;
on Monday evening am
Montagabend; **every Thursday
evening** jeden Donnerstagabend;
the evening before am Abend
zuvor; **the evening meal** das
Abendessen; **2 at six o'clock in the
evening** um sechs Uhr abends; **the
other evening** neulich abends; **I
work in the evening(s)** ich arbeite
abends.

evening class noun
Abendkurs der (PL die Abendkurse).

event noun **1** (a happening)
Ereignis das (PL die Ereignisse).
2 (in athletics) Disziplin die (PL die
Disziplinen).

eventually adverb schließlich.

ever adverb **1** (at any time) je; **have
you ever noticed that?** hast du das
je bemerkt?; **more than ever** mehr
denn je; **colder than ever** kälter
denn je; **he drove more slowly than
ever** er fuhr langsamer als je zuvor;
2 not ever nie; **nobody ever came**
es kam nie jemand; **hardly ever** fast
nie; **3** (always) immer; **as cheerful
as ever** so vergnügt wie immer; **the
same as ever** so wie immer; **4 ever
since** seitdem; **and it's been
raining ever since** und seitdem
regnet es.

every adjective **1** jeder/jede/jedes;
every house has a garden jedes
Haus hat einen Garten; **every day**
jeden Tag; **every Monday** jeden
Montag; **every time** jedes Mal;
2 every few days alle paar Tage;
every ten kilometres alle zehn
Kilometer; **3 every one** jeder

Einzelne/jede Einzelne/jedes
Einzelne △; **I've seen every one of**
his films ich habe jeden Einzelnen
seiner Filme gesehen; **4 every now
and then** ab und zu.

everybody, everyone pronoun
1 alle (plural); **everybody knows
that …** alle wissen, dass …;
everyone else alle anderen;
2 (each one) jeder; **not everybody
can afford it** das kann sich nicht
jeder leisten.

everything pronoun alles;
everything is ready es ist alles
fertig; **everything's fine** alles ist
okay (informal); **everything else**
alles andere; **he gets everything
he wants** er bekommt alles, was
er will.

everywhere adverb **1** überall; **there
was dirt everywhere** überall war
Dreck; **she went everywhere** sie ist
überall hingegangen; **everywhere
else** sonst überall; **2 everywhere
she went** wohin sie auch ging.

evidently adverb offensichtlich.

exact adjective genau; **the exact
fare** das genaue Fahrgeld; **it 's the
exact opposite** das ist genau das
Gegenteil.

exactly adverb genau; **they're
exactly the right age** sie sind genau
im richtigen Alter; **yes, exactly!** ja,
genau!

exaggerate verb übertreiben ✦.

exaggeration noun
Übertreibung die (PL die
Übertreibungen).

△ NEW SPELLING: See page xii

exam noun Prüfung die (PL die Prüfungen); **history exam** die Geschichtsprüfung; **to sit an exam** eine Prüfung machen; **to pass an exam** eine Prüfung bestehen; **to fail an exam** durch eine Prüfung fallen.

examination noun Prüfung die (PL die Prüfungen).

examine verb 1 (at school or university) prüfen; 2 (at the doctor's) untersuchen.

examiner noun Prüfer der (PL die Prüfer), Prüferin die (PL die Prüferinnen).

example noun Beispiel das (PL die Beispiele); **for example** zum Beispiel; **to set a good example** ein gutes Beispiel geben.

excellent adjective ausgezeichnet.

except preposition 1 außer (+DAT); **every day except Tuesday** täglich außer Dienstag; **we play except when it rains** wir spielen, außer wenn es regnet; **except in March** außer März; 2 **except for** außer (+DAT); **except for the children** außer den Kindern.

exception noun Ausnahme die (PL die Ausnahmen); **without exception** ohne Ausnahme; **with the exception of** mit Ausnahme von (+DAT).

exchange noun 1 Austausch der; **the students are coming to London on an exchange** die Studenten kommen im Austausch nach London; **exchange student** der Austauschstudent, die Austauschstudentin; **an exchange of** pupils ein Schüleraustausch; 2 **in exchange for his help** für seine Hilfe.
verb umtauschen SEP; **can I exchange this shirt for a smaller one?** kann ich dieses Hemd gegen ein kleineres umtauschen?

exchange rate noun Wechselkurs der (PL die Wechselkurse).

excite verb 1 (thrill) begeistern; 2 (agitate) aufregen SEP.

excited adjective 1 aufgeregt; **the children are excited** die Kinder sind aufgeregt; **the dogs get excited when they hear the car** die Hunde sind aufgeregt, wenn sie das Auto hören; 2 (annoyed or angry) **to get excited** sich aufregen SEP.

exciting adjective aufregend; **a very exciting film** ein sehr aufregender Film.

exclamation mark noun Ausrufezeichen das (PL die Ausrufezeichen).

excursion noun Ausflug der (PL die Ausflüge).

excuse noun Entschuldigung die (PL die Entschuldigungen).
verb (apologizing) **excuse me!** Entschuldigung!

exercise noun 1 Übung die (PL die Übungen); **a maths exercise** eine Übung in Mathe; 2 physical exercise körperliche Bewegung; **to get exercise** Bewegung haben.

exercise bike noun Heimtrainer der (PL die Heimtrainer).

◇ **IRREGULAR VERB: See the verb table in the centre of the dictionary**

exercise book noun Heft das (PL die Hefte); **my German exercise book** mein Deutschheft.

exhausted adjective erschöpft.

exhaust fumes noun Abgase (plural).

exhaust (pipe) noun Auspuff der (PL die Auspuffe).

exhibition noun Ausstellung die (PL die Ausstellungen); **the Dürer exhibition** die Dürer-Ausstellung.

exist verb existieren.

exit noun 1 Ausgang der (PL die Ausgänge); 2 (from a motorway) Ausfahrt die (PL die Ausfahrten).

expect verb 1 erwarten (guests or a baby); **we're expecting thirty visitors** wir erwarten dreißig Besucher; 2 (require something) **to expect somebody to do something** von jemandem erwarten, dass er etwas tut; 3 rechnen mit (+DAT) (something to happen); **I didn't expect that** damit habe ich nicht gerechnet; **I didn't expect it at all** damit habe ich überhaupt nicht gerechnet; 4 (suppose) glauben; **I expect she'll bring her boyfriend** ich glaube, sie bringt ihren Freund mit; **yes, I expect so** ich glaube ja.

expel verb **to be expelled** (from school) von der Schule verwiesen werden.

expensive adjective teuer; **those shoes are too expensive for me** diese Schuhe sind mir zu teuer; **the most expensive CDs** die teuersten CDs.

experience noun 1 Erfahrung die (PL die Erfahrungen); 2 (an event) Erlebnis das (PL die Erlebnisse).

experienced adjective erfahren.

experiment noun Experiment das (PL die Experimente); **to do an experiment** ein Experiment machen.

expert noun Experte der (PL die Experten), Expertin die (PL die Expertinnen); **he's a computer expert** er ist ein Computerexperte.

expire verb ablaufen ◇ SEP (PERF sein).

explain verb erklären.

explanation noun Erklärung die (PL die Erklärungen).

explode verb explodieren (PERF sein).

explore verb erforschen.

explosion noun Explosion die (PL die Explosionen).

exposure noun (of a film) Belichtung die; **a 24-exposure film** ein Film mit 24 Aufnahmen.

express noun (train) Schnellzug der (PL die Schnellzüge). verb 1 ausdrücken SEP; 2 **to express yourself** sich ausdrücken.

expression noun Ausdruck der (PL die Ausdrücke).

extension noun 1 (to a house) Anbau der (PL die Anbauten); 2 (telephone) Apparat der (PL die Apparate); **can I have extension 2347 please?** bitte verbinden Sie mich mit Apparat 2347 (note that in

△ NEW SPELLING: See page xii

spoken German telephone numbers are usually broken down into groups of two figures; **3** (*electrical*) Verlängerung *die* (PL *die* Verlängerungen).

extension number *noun* Apparatnummer *die* (PL *die* Apparatnummern).

exterior *adjective* äußerer/äußere/äußeres.

extinguish *verb* **1** löschen (*a fire*); **2** to extinguish a cigarette eine Zigarette ausmachen SEP.

extinguisher *noun* Feuerlöscher *der* (PL *die* Feuerlöscher).

extra *adjective* **1** zusätzlich, extra (*informal*) (*extra never has an ending*); **extra homework** zusätzliche Hausaufgaben; **wine is extra** Wein ist extra; **you have to pay extra** das wird extra berechnet; **2** at no extra charge ohne Aufschlag.
adverb **1** besonders; **he was extra careful** er war besonders vorsichtig; **2** extra large extragroß.

extraordinary *adjective* außerordentlich.

extra time *noun* (*in football*) Verlängerung *die* (PL *die* Verlängerungen); **to go into extra time** in die Verlängerung gehen.

extravagant *adjective* verschwenderisch (*person*).

extreme *noun* Extrem *das* (PL *die* Extreme); **to go from one extreme to another** von einem Extrem ins

andere fallen.
adjective extrem.

extremely *adverb* äußerst; **extremely fast** äußerst schnell.

eye *noun* Auge *das* (PL *die* Augen); **a girl with blue eyes** ein Mädchen mit blauen Augen; **shut your eyes!** mach die Augen zu!; ★ to keep an eye on something auf etwas ←(ACC) aufpassen SEP.

eyebrow *noun* Augenbraue *die* (PL *die* Augenbrauen).

eyelash *noun* Augenwimper *die* (PL *die* Augenwimpern).

eyelid *noun* Augenlid *das* (PL *die* Augenlider).

eyeliner *noun* Eyeliner *der* (PL *die* Eyeliner).

eye shadow *noun* Lidschatten *der* (PL *die* Lidschatten).

eyesight *noun* to have good eyesight gute Augen haben; **to have bad eyesight** schlechte Augen haben.

F f

fabric *noun* (*cloth*) Stoff *der* (PL *die* Stoffe).

fabulous *adjective* phantastisch.

face *noun* **1** (*of a person*) Gesicht *das* (PL *die* Gesichter); **to pull a face** ein Gesicht machen; **2** (*of a clock or watch*) Zifferblatt *das* (PL *die* Zifferblätter).

verb 1 gegenüberstehen ✧ SEP (PERF *sein*) (+DAT); **she was facing him** sie stand ihm gegenüber; **2 the house faces the park** das Haus ist gegenüber dem Park; **3** (*to stand the idea of*) verkraften; **I can't face going back** ich kann es nicht verkraften zurückzugehen; **4** to face up to something sich etwas ←(DAT) stellen.

facilities *plural noun* **1 the school has good sports facilities** die Schule hat gute Sportanlagen; **2 the flat has no cooking facilities** die Wohnung hat keine Kochgelegenheit.

fact *noun* Tatsache die (PL die Tatsachen); **the fact is that ...** Tatsache ist, dass ...; **in fact** tatsächlich; **is that a fact?** Tatsache?

factory *noun* Fabrik die (PL die Fabriken).

fade *verb* **1** (*fabric*) verbleichen ✧ (PERF *sein*); **faded jeans** ausgeblichene Jeans; **2** (*a colour or memory*) verblassen (PERF *sein*); **the colours have faded** die Farben sind verblasst.

fail *verb* **1** nicht bestehen ✧ (*a test or an exam*); **I failed my driving test** ich habe meine Fahrprüfung nicht bestanden; **2** (*in a test or an exam*) durchfallen ✧ SEP (PERF *sein*); **three students failed** drei Studenten sind durchgefallen; **3** to fail to do something etwas nicht tun; **he failed to inform us** er hat uns nicht benachrichtigt; ★ **without fail** auf jeden Fall; **ring me without fail** ruf mich auf jeden Fall an.

faint *adjective* **1** (*slight*) leicht; **a faint smell of gas** ein leichter Gasgeruch; **I haven't the faintest idea** ich habe keine blasse Ahnung (*informal*); **2** (*voice or sound*) leise. *verb* ohnmächtig werden; **Lisa fainted** Lisa wurde ohnmächtig.

fair *noun* Jahrmarkt der (PL die Jahrmärkte). *adjective* **1** (*not unfair*) gerecht; **2** (*hair*) blond; **he's fair-haired** er ist blond; **3** (*skin*) hell; **fair-skinned** hellhäutig; **4** (*fairly good*) ganz gut (*chance, condition, or performance*); **5** (*weather*) schön; **if it's fair tomorrow** wenn es morgen schön ist.

fairground *noun* Jahrmarkt der (PL die Jahrmärkte).

fairly *adverb* (*quite*) ziemlich.

fairy *noun* Fee die (PL die Feen).

fairy tale *noun* Märchen das (PL die Märchen).

faith *noun* **1** (*trust*) Vertrauen das; **to have faith in somebody** Vertrauen zu jemandem haben; **2** (*religious belief*) Glaube der (PL die Glauben).

faithful *adjective* treu; **to be faithful to somebody** jemandem treu sein.

faithfully *adverb* **Yours faithfully** Hochachtungsvoll.

fake *noun* Imitation die (PL die Imitationen); **the diamonds were fakes** die Brillanten waren eine Imitation (*a painting or money*)

△ NEW SPELLING: *See page xii*

Fälschung die (PL die Fälschungen).
adjective gefälscht; **a fake passport**
ein gefälschter Pass.

fall noun Fall der (PL die Fälle); **to
have a fall** stürzen (PERF sein).
verb 1 fallen ◇ (PERF sein); **mind,
you'll fall** pass auf, dass du nicht
hinfällst; **Tony fell off his bike** Tony
ist vom Rad gefallen; **she fell down
the stairs** sie ist die Treppe
heruntergefallen; 2 (of temperature,
prices) sinken ◇ (PERF sein).

false adjective falsch; **a false alarm**
ein falscher Alarm.

fame noun Ruhm der.

familiar adjective bekannt; **his face
is familiar** sein Gesicht kommt mir
bekannt vor.

family noun Familie die (PL die
Familien); **a family of six** eine
sechsköpfige Familie; **Ben's one of
the family** Ben gehört zur Familie;
the Morris family Familie Morris.

famous adjective berühmt.

fan noun 1 (a supporter) Fan der (PL
die Fans); **Will's a Chelsea fan** Will
ist ein Fan von Chelsea; 2 (electric,
for cooling) Ventilator der (PL die
Ventilatoren); 3 (hand-held)
Fächer der (PL die Fächer).

fanatic noun Fanatiker der (PL die
Fanatiker), Fanatikerin die (PL die
Fanatikerinnen).

fancy noun **to take somebody's
fancy** jemandem gefallen ◇; **the
picture took his fancy** das Bild hat
es ihm angetan.
adjective (equipment) ausgefallen.

verb 1 (to want) **(do) you fancy a
coffee?** hast du Lust auf einen
Kaffee?; **do you fancy going to the
cinema?** hast du Lust, ins Kino zu
gehen?; 2 **I really fancy him** ich mag
ihn wirklich sehr gern; 3 (just) **fancy
that!** stell dir vor!; **fancy you being
here!** na so was, dich hier zu
treffen!

fancy dress noun **in fancy dress**
verkleidet; **fancy-dress party** das
Kostümfest.

fantastic adjective fantastisch △;
really? that's fantastic! wirklich?
das ist ja fantastisch!; **a fantastic
holiday** fantastische Ferien.

far adverb, adjective 1 weit; **it's not
far** es ist nicht weit; **is it far to
Carlisle?** ist Carlisle weit von hier?;
how far is it to Bristol? wie weit ist
es bis nach Bristol?; 2 **he took us as
far as Newport** er hat uns bis
Newport mitgenommen; 3 **by far**
bei weitem; **the prettiest by far** bei
weitem die hübscheste; 4 (much)
viel; **far better** viel besser; **far
faster** viel schneller; **far too many
people** viel zu viele Leute; 5 **so far**
bis jetzt; **so far everything's going
well** bis jetzt läuft alles gut; 6 **as far
as I know** soweit ich weiß.

fare noun 1 (on a bus, train, or the
underground) Fahrpreis der (PL
die Fahrpreise); 2 (on a plane)
Flugpreis der (PL die Flugpreise);
half fare der halbe Fahrpreis; **full
fare** der volle Fahrpreis.

farm noun Bauernhof der (PL die
Bauernhöfe).

◇ IRREGULAR VERB: See the verb table in the centre of the dictionary

farmer noun Bauer der (PL die Bauern), Bäuerin die (PL die Bäuerinnen).

fascinating adjective faszinierend.

fashion noun Mode die (PL die Moden); **in fashion** in Mode; **to go out of fashion** aus der Mode kommen.

fashionable adjective modisch.

fashion model noun Mannequin das (PL die Mannequins).

fashion show noun Modenschau die (PL die Modenschauen).

fast adjective 1 schnell; **a fast car** ein schnelles Auto; 2 (of a clock or watch) **to be fast** vorgehen ◇ SEP (PERF sein); **my watch is fast** meine Uhr geht vor; **you're ten minutes fast** deine Uhr geht zehn Minuten vor.
adverb 1 schnell; **he swims fast** er schwimmt schnell; 2 **to be fast asleep** fest schlafen.

fat noun Fett das (PL die Fette).
adjective 1 (meat) fett; 2 (person) dick, fett (informal); **a fat man** ein dicker Mann; **to get fat** fett werden (informal).

father noun Vater der (PL die Väter); **my father's office** das Büro von meinem Vater.

Father Christmas noun der Weihnachtsmann.

father-in-law noun Schwiegervater der (PL die Schwiegerväter).

fault noun 1 (when you are responsible) Schuld die; **it's Stephen's fault** Stephen ist Schuld; **it's not my fault** es ist nicht meine Schuld; 2 (in tennis) **double fault** der Doppelfehler.

favour noun 1 (a kindness) Gefallen der (PL die Gefallen); **to do somebody a favour** jemandem einen Gefallen tun; **can you do me a favour?** kannst du mir einen Gefallen tun?; **to ask a favour of somebody** jemanden um einen Gefallen bitten; 2 **to be in favour of something** für etwas ←(ACC) sein.

favourite adjective Lieblings-; **my favourite band** meine Lieblingsband.

fax noun Fax das (PL die Faxe).
verb faxen.

fear noun Angst die (PL die Ängste).
verb fürchten.

feather noun Feder die (PL die Federn).

feature noun 1 (of your face) Gesichtszug der (PL die Gesichtszüge); **to have delicate features** feine Gesichtszüge haben; 2 (of a car or a machine) Merkmal das (PL die Merkmale).

February noun Februar der; **in February** im Februar.

fed up adjective 1 **I'm fed up** ich habe die Nase voll (informal); **he's fed up with her** er hat die Nase voll von ihr; 2 **to be fed up with something** etwas ←(ACC) satt haben (informal); **I'm fed up with working**

△NEW SPELLING: See page xii

every day ich habe es satt, jeden Tag zu arbeiten.

feed verb füttern; **have you fed the dog?** hast du den Hund gefüttert?

feel verb 1 sich fühlen; **I don't feel well** ich fühle mich nicht gut; 2 spüren; **I didn't feel a thing** ich habe nichts gespürt; 3 **I feel tired** ich bin müde; **I feel cold** mir ist kalt; 4 **to feel afraid** Angst haben; **to feel thirsty** Durst haben; 5 **to feel like doing something** Lust haben, etwas zu tun; **I feel like going to the cinema** ich habe Lust, ins Kino zu gehen; 6 (touch) fühlen; 7 (to the touch) sich anfühlen SEP; **to feel soft** sich weich anfühlen.

feeling noun 1 Gefühl das (PL die Gefühle); **to show your feelings** seine Gefühle zeigen; **a dizzy feeling** ein Schwindelgefühl; **I have the feeling James doesn't like me** ich habe das Gefühl, dass James mich nicht mag; 2 **to hurt somebody's feelings** jemanden verletzen.

felt-tip (pen) noun Filzstift der (PL die Filzstifte).

female noun (animal) Weibchen das (PL die Weibchen). adjective weiblich.

feminine adjective weiblich.

feminist noun Feministin die (PL die Feministinnen), Feminist der (PL die Feministen). adjective feministisch.

fence noun Zaun der (PL die Zäune).

ferry noun Fähre die (PL die Fähren).

festival noun (of films, art, or music) Festspiele (plural).

fetch verb 1 (collect) abholen SEP; **Tom's fetching the children** Tom holt die Kinder ab; 2 holen; **fetch me the other knife** hol mir das andere Messer.

fever noun Fieber das.

few adjective, pronoun 1 wenige; **few people know that** ... wenige Leute wissen, dass ...; 2 **a few** (several) ein paar (ein paar never changes); **a few weeks** ein paar Wochen; **in a few minutes** in ein paar Minuten; **have you got any tomatoes? we want a few for the salad** haben Sie Tomaten? wir brauchen ein paar für den Salat; 3 **quite a few** eine ganze Menge; **there were quite a few questions** es gab eine ganze Menge Fragen.

fewer adjective weniger; **there are fewer mosquitoes this year** dieses Jahr gibt es weniger Mücken.

field noun 1 (with grass or crops) Feld das (PL die Felder); **a field of wheat** ein Kornfeld; 2 (for sport) Spielfeld das (PL die Spielfelder).

fierce adjective 1 wild (animal or person); 2 heftig (storm or battle).

fifteen number fünfzehn.

fifth number fünfter/fünfte/fünftes; **the fifth of January** der fünfte Januar; **on the fifth floor** im fünften Stock.

fifty number fünfzig.

fight noun 1 (a scuffle) Schlägerei die (PL die Schlägereien); 2 (in boxing or against illness) Kampf der (PL die Kämpfe).

verb 1 (to have a fight) sich prügeln; **they were fighting** sie haben sich geprügelt; 2 (to quarrel) sich streiten ◇; **they're always fighting** sie streiten sich immer; 3 (struggle against) kämpfen gegen (+ACC) (poverty or a disease).

figure noun 1 (number) Zahl die (PL die Zahlen); **a four-figure number** eine vierstellige Zahl; 2 (body shape) Figur die; **good for your figure** gut für die Figur; 3 (a person) Gestalt die (PL die Gestalten).

verb **to figure something out** etwas herausfinden ◇ SEP (the answer or reason).

file noun 1 (for records of a person or case) Akte die (PL die Akten); 2 (ring binder or folder) Ordner der (PL die Ordner); 3 (on a computer) Datei die (PL die Dateien); 4 **a nail file** eine Nagelfeile.

verb 1 ablegen SEP (documents); 2 **to file your nails** sich ← (DAT) die Nägel feilen.

fill verb 1 füllen (a container); **she filled my glass** sie füllte mein Glas; 2 **to be filled with people** voller Menschen sein; **filled with smoke** voller Rauch.

• **to fill in** ausfüllen SEP (a form).

film noun (in a cinema and for a camera) Film der (PL die Filme); **shall we go and see the new film about Freud?** wollen wir uns den neuen Film über Freud ansehen?; **to make a film** einen Film drehen; a

24-exposure colour film ein Farbfilm mit 24 Aufnahmen.

film star noun Filmstar der (PL die Filmstars).

filter noun Filter der (PL die Filter).

filthy adjective dreckig.

final noun (in sport) Endspiel das (PL die Endspiele).

adjective letzter/letzte/letztes; **the final instalment** die letzte Folge; **the final result** das Endergebnis.

finally adverb schließlich.

find verb finden ◇; **did you find your passport?** hast du deinen Pass gefunden?; **I can't find my keys** ich kann meine Schlüssel nicht finden.

• **to find out** 1 (to enquire) sich informieren; **I don't know, I'll find out** das weiß ich nicht, ich werde mich informieren; 2 **to find something out** etwas ← (ACC) herausfinden ◇ SEP (the facts or an answer); **when she found out the truth** als sie die Wahrheit herausfand.

fine noun Bußgeld das (PL die Bußgelder) (for parking or speeding).

adjective 1 (in good health) gut; **'how are you?' – 'fine, thanks'** 'wie geht's?' – 'danke, gut'; **I'm fine** mir geht es gut; 2 (convenient) in Ordnung; **ten o'clock? yes, that's fine** zehn Uhr? ja, in Ordnung!; **Friday will be fine** Freitag geht in Ordnung; 3 (sunny) schön; (weather or day) **if it's fine** wenn es schön ist; **in fine weather** bei schönem Wetter; 4 (not coarse or thick) fein.

△ NEW SPELLING: See page xii

finely adverb fein (chopped or grated).

finger noun Finger der (PL die Finger); ★ **I'll keep my fingers crossed for you** ich drücke dir den Daumen.

fingernail noun Fingernagel der (PL die Fingernägel).

finish noun 1 (end) Schluss △ der (PL die Schlüsse); 2 (in a race) Ziel das (PL die Ziele).

verb 1 beenden (a conversation or quarrel); **to finish a discussion** ein Gespräch beenden; **to be finished with something** mit etwas ←(DAT) fertig sein (work or a project); **have you finished your homework?** bist du mit den Hausaufgaben fertig?; **wait, I haven't finished!** warte, ich bin noch nicht fertig!; 2 (to finish off) **to finish doing something** etwas zu Ende tun; **have you finished (reading) the letter?** hast du den Brief zu Ende gelesen?; **he hasn't yet finished (writing) the report** er hat den Bericht noch nicht zu Ende geschrieben; 3 (come to an end) zu Ende sein, aus sein △ (informal) (a meeting or performance); **the film finishes at ten o'clock** der Film ist um zehn Uhr zu Ende; **when does school finish?** wann ist die Schule aus?

• **to finish with** (complete your use of) nicht mehr brauchen; **when you've finished with these clothes, give them back to me** wenn du die Sachen nicht mehr brauchst, gib sie mir zurück; **have you finished with**

the computer? brauchen Sie den Computer noch?

Finland noun Finnland das.

Finnish noun (the language) Finnisch das.
adjective finnisch; **he's Finnish** er ist Finne; **she's Finnish** sie ist Finnin.

fire noun 1 (in a grate) Kaminfeuer das (PL die Kaminfeuer); **to light the fire** das Feuer im Kamin anmachen; 2 (accidental) Feuer das (PL die Feuer); **to catch fire** (fabric, furnishings) Feuer fangen; 3 (in a building or forest) Brand der (PL die Brände); **to set fire to a factory** eine Fabrik in Brand stecken; 4 **to be on fire** brennen ◇.
verb 1 (with a gun) schießen ◇; **to fire at somebody** auf jemanden schießen; 2 abfeuern SEP (a gun).

fire alarm noun Feuermelder der (PL die Feuermelder).

fire brigade noun Feuerwehr die.

fire engine noun Feuerwehrauto das (PL die Feuerwehrautos).

fire escape noun Feuertreppe die (PL die Feuertreppen).

fire extinguisher noun Feuerlöscher der (PL die Feuerlöscher).

firefighter noun Feuerwehrmann der (PL die Feuerwehrleute).

fireplace noun Kamin der (PL die Kamine).

fire station noun Feuerwache die (PL die Feuerwachen).

firework noun Feuerwerkskörper der (PL die Feuerwerkskörper); **firework display** das Feuerwerk.

firm noun (business) Firma die (PL die Firmen).
adjective **1** fest; **2** (strict) streng.

first adjective erster/erste/erstes; **the first of May** der erste Mai; **for the first time** zum ersten Mal; **I was the first to arrive** ich kam als Erster/Erste an; **Susan was first** Susan war die Erste; **to come first in the 100 metres** beim Hundertmeterlauf Erster/Erste werden.
adverb **1** (to begin with) zuerst; **first, I'm going to make some tea** zuerst mache ich Tee; **2** at first zuerst; **at first he was shy** er war zuerst schüchtern.

first aid noun erste Hilfe Δ die.

first class adjective (ticket, carriage, or hotel) erster Klasse (goes after the noun); **a first-class hotel** ein Hotel erster Klasse; **he always travels first class** er reist immer erster Klasse; **a first-class compartment** ein Erste-Klasse-Abteil.

first floor noun erste Stock der; **on the first floor** im ersten Stock.

first name noun Vorname der (PL die Vornamen).

fir tree noun Tanne die (PL die Tannen).

fish noun Fisch der (PL die Fische).
verb fischen; (with a rod) angeln.

fish and chips noun ausgebackener Fisch mit Pommes frites.

fishing noun Fischen das; (with a rod) Angeln das; **to go fishing** fischen/angeln gehen.

fishing rod noun Angel die (PL die Angeln).

fishing tackle noun Angelgeräte (plural).

fist noun Faust die (PL die Fäuste).

fit noun **1** (of rage) Anfall der (PL die Anfälle); **your dad'll have a fit when he sees your hair** dein Vater kriegt bestimmt einen Anfall, wenn er deine Haare sieht; **2** an epileptic fit ein epileptischer Anfall.
adjective (healthy) fit; **I feel really fit** ich fühle mich richtig fit; **to keep fit** fit bleiben.
verb **1** (be the right size for) (of shoes or a garment) passen (+DAT); **this skirt doesn't fit me** der Rock passt mir nicht; **2** (be able to be put into) passen in (+ACC); **will my cases all fit in the car?** passen meine Koffer alle in das Auto?; **3** (install) einbauen SEP.

fitted carpet noun Teppichboden der (PL die Teppichböden).

fitted kitchen noun Einbauküche die (PL die Einbauküchen).

Δ **NEW SPELLING: See page xii**

five *number* fünf; **it's five o'clock** es ist fünf Uhr.

fix *verb* **1** (*repair*) reparieren; **Mum's fixed the computer** Mutti hat den Computer repariert; **2** (*decide on*) festlegen ◇ SEP; **to fix a date** einen Termin festlegen; **3** machen (*a meal*); **I'll fix supper** ich mache Abendessen.

fizzy *adjective* sprudelnd; **fizzy water** *das* Sprudelwasser.

flag *noun* Fahne *die* (PL *die* Fahnen).

flame *noun* Flamme *die* (PL *die* Flammen).

flan *noun* Torte *die* (PL *die* Torten); **fruit flan** *die* Obsttorte.

flap *verb* (*of a bird*) **to flap its wings** mit den Flügeln schlagen ◇.

flash *noun* (*on a camera*) Blitz *der* (PL *die* Blitze); **flash of lightning** *der* Blitz.
verb **1** (*a light*) aufleuchten SEP; (*repeatedly*) blinken; **2 to flash by** or **past** vorbeiflitzen SEP (*informal*).

flat *noun* Wohnung *die* (PL *die* Wohnungen); **a third-floor flat** eine Wohnung im dritten Stock.
adjective **1** flach; **flat shoes** flache Schuhe; **a flat landscape** eine flache Landschaft; **2 a flat tyre** ein platter Reifen.

flatmate *noun* Mitbewohner *der* (PL *die* Mitbewohner), Mitbewohnerin *die* (PL *die* Mitbewohnerinnen).

flavour *noun* **1** Geschmack *der* (PL *die* Geschmäcke); **the sauce has a bitter flavour** die Soße hat einen

bitteren Geschmack; **strawberry flavour** Erdbeergeschmack; **2** (*of drinks, coffee, or tea*) Aroma *das* (PL *die* Aromen).
verb abschmecken SEP; **vanilla-flavoured** mit Vanillegeschmack.

flea *noun* Floh *der* (PL *die* Flöhe).

flight *noun* **1** Flug *der* (PL *die* Flüge); **the flight was delayed** der Flug hatte Verspätung; **charter flight** *der* Charterflug; **the flight from Munich to London takes an hour and a half** die Flugzeit von München nach London beträgt eineinhalb Stunden; **2 flight of stairs** die Treppe.

flipper *noun* Flosse *die* (PL *die* Flossen).

flirt *verb* flirten.

float *verb* **1** (*on water*) treiben ◇; **2** (*in the air*) schweben ◇.

flood *noun* **1** (*of water*) Überschwemmung *die* (PL *die* Überschwemmungen); **2 to be in floods of tears** in Tränen aufgelöst sein; **3** (*of letters or complaints*) Flut *die*.
verb überschwemmen.

floodlight *noun* Flutlicht *das*.

floor *noun* **1** Boden *der* (PL *die* Böden); **your glasses are on the floor** deine Brille liegt auf dem Boden; **2 to sweep the floor** ausfegen SEP; **to sweep the kitchen floor** die Küche ausfegen; **3** (*a storey*) Stock *der* (PL *die* Stock); **on the second floor** im zweiten Stock.

floppy disk *noun* Diskette *die* (PL *die* Disketten).

◇ **IRREGULAR VERB:** *See the verb table in the centre of the dictionary*

florist *noun* Blumenhändler *der* (PL die Blumenhändler), Blumenhändlerin *die* (PL die Blumenhändlerinnen).

flour *noun* Mehl *das*.

flower *noun* Blume *die* (PL die Blumen); **bunch of flowers** *der* Blumenstrauß.
verb blühen.

flu *noun* Grippe *die* (PL die Grippen); **to have flu** die Grippe haben.

fluent *adjective* **she speaks fluent Italian** sie spricht fließend Italienisch.

fluently *adverb* fließend.

flute *noun* Flöte *die* (PL die Flöten); **to play the flute** Flöte spielen.

fly *noun* Fliege *die* (PL die Fliegen).
verb **1** fliegen ◇ (PERF *sein*); **we flew to Berlin** wir sind nach Berlin geflogen; **2** steigen lassen (*a kite*); **3** fliegen ◇ (PERF *haben*) (*a plane or helicopter*); **4** (*to pass quickly*) schnell vergehen ◇ (PERF *sein*).

foam *noun* **1** (*foam rubber*) Schaumgummi *der*; **foam mattress** *die* Schaumgummimatratze; **2** (*on a drink*) Schaum *der*.

fog *noun* Nebel *der*.

foggy *adjective* neblig.

foil *noun* (*kitchen foil*) Alufolie *die*.

fold *noun* **1** (*in fabric or skin*) Falte *die* (PL die Falten); **2** (*in paper*) Kniff *der* (PL die Kniffe).
verb falten; **to fold something up** etwas zusammenfalten SEP.

folder *noun* Mappe *die* (PL die Mappen).

follow *verb* **1** folgen (PERF *sein*) (+DAT); **follow me!** folgen Sie mir!; **2 do you follow me?** verstehst du, was ich meine?

following *adjective* folgend; **the following evening** am folgenden Abend.

fond *adjective* **to be fond of somebody** jemanden gern haben; **I'm very fond of him** ich habe ihn sehr gern.

food *noun* **1** Essen *das*; **I have to buy some food** ich muss noch etwas zu essen einkaufen; **2 I like German food** ich mag die deutsche Küche; **3** (*stocks*) Lebensmittel (*plural*); **we bought food for the holiday** wir haben Lebensmittel für die Ferien eingekauft.

fool *noun* Dummkopf *der* (PL die Dummköpfe).

foot *noun* Fuß *der* (PL die Füße); **Lucy came on foot** Lucy ist zu Fuß gekommen.

football *noun* Fußball *der* (PL die Fußbälle); **to play football** Fußball spielen.

footballer *noun* Fußballspieler *der* (PL die Fußballspieler), Fußballspielerin *die* (PL die Fußballspielerinnen).

footpath *noun* Fußweg *der* (PL die Fußwege).

for *preposition* **1** für (+ACC); **a present for my mother** ein Geschenk für

△ NEW SPELLING: See page xii

meine Mutter; **what's it for?** wofür ist das?; **2** (*for a particular occasion or event*) zu (+DAT); **sausages for lunch** Würstchen zum Mittagessen; **Sam got a bike for Christmas** Sam hat ein Rad zu Weihnachten bekommen; **what for?** wozu?; **3** (*time expressions in the past but continuing in the present*) seit (+DAT); **I've been waiting here for an hour** (*and I'm still waiting*) ich warte hier seit einer Stunde; **my brother's been living in Berlin for three years** (*and he still lives there*) mein Bruder wohnt seit drei Jahren in Berlin; **4** (*time expressions in the past or the future*) für (+ACC); **I studied French for six years** (*but I no longer do*) ich habe sechs Jahre lang Französisch gelernt; **I'll be away for four days** ich werde vier Tage nicht da sein; **5** (*with a price*) für (+ACC); **I sold my bike for fifty pounds** ich habe mein Rad für fünfzig Pfund verkauft; **6 what's the German for 'bee'?** wie heißt 'bee' auf Deutsch?

forbid *verb* verbieten ◇; **to forbid somebody to do something** jemanden verbieten, etwas zu tun.

forbidden *adjective* verboten.

force *noun* Kraft *die* (PL die Kräfte). *verb* zwingen ◇; **to force somebody to do something** jemanden zwingen, etwas zu tun.

forecast *noun* Vorhersage *die* (PL die Vorhersagen).

forehead *noun* Stirn *die* (PL die Stirnen).

foreign *adjective* **1** ausländisch; **in a**

foreign country im Ausland; **from a foreign country** aus dem Ausland; **2 foreign language** *die* Fremdsprache.

foreigner *noun* Ausländer *der* (PL die Ausländer), Ausländerin *die* (PL die Ausländerinnen).

forest *noun* Wald *der* (PL die Wälder).

forever *adverb* **1** immer; **I'd like to stay here forever** ich möchte immer hier bleiben; **2** (*non-stop*) ständig; **he's forever asking questions** er fragt ständig.

forget *verb* vergessen ◇; **to forget about something** etwas vergessen; **we've forgotten the bread** wir haben Brot vergessen; **to forget to do something** vergessen, etwas zu tun; **I forgot to phone** ich habe vergessen anzurufen.

forgive *verb* verzeihen ◇ (+DAT); **to forgive somebody** jemandem verzeihen; **I forgave him** ich habe ihm verziehen; **to forgive somebody for doing something** jemandem verzeihen, dass er/sie etwas getan hat; **I forgave her for losing my ring** ich habe ihr verziehen, dass sie meinen Ring verloren hat.

fork *noun* Gabel *die* (PL die Gabeln).

form *noun* **1** Formular *das* (PL die Formulare); **to fill in a form** ein Formular ausfüllen; **2** (*shape or kind*) Form *die* (PL die Formen); **in the form of** in Form von; **to be on form** gut in Form sein; **3** (*in school*)

◇ IRREGULAR VERB: *See the verb table in the centre of the dictionary*

Klasse *die* (PL *die* Klassen).
verb bilden.

formal *adjective* formell (*invitation, event*).

format *noun* Format *das* (PL *die* Formate).

former *adjective* ehemalig; **a former pupil** ein ehemaliger Schüler, eine ehemalige Schülerin.

fortnight *noun* vierzehn Tage (*plural*); **we're going to Spain for a fortnight** wir fahren vierzehn Tage nach Spanien.

fortunately *adverb* glücklicherweise.

forty *number* vierzig.

forward *noun* (*in sport*) Stürmer *der* (PL *die* Stürmer). *adverb* (*to the front*) nach vorn; **to move forward** vorrücken SEP (PERF sein); **a seat further forward** ein Platz weiter vorn.

foster child *noun* Pflegekind *das* (PL *die* Pflegekinder).

foul *noun* (*in sport*) Foul *das* (PL *die* Fouls). *adjective* scheußlich; **the weather's foul** das Wetter ist scheußlich.

fountain *noun* Brunnen *der* (PL *die* Brunnen).

fountain pen *noun* Füllfederhalter *der* (PL *die* Füllfederhalter).

four *number* vier; **it's four o'clock** es ist vier Uhr; ★ **on all fours** auf allen vieren.

fourteen *number* vierzehn.

fourth *number* vierter/vierte/viertes; **the fourth of July** der vierte Juli; **on the fourth floor** im vierten Stock.

fox *noun* Fuchs *der* (PL *die* Füchse).

frame *noun* **1** Rahmen *der* (PL *die* Rahmen); **2** (*of spectacles*) Gestell *das* (PL *die* Gestelle).

franc *noun* **1** Franc *der* (PL *die* Francs); **a fifty-franc note** ein Fünfzig-Franc-Schein; **2** (*Swiss*) Franken *der* (PL *die* Franken).

France *noun* Frankreich *das*; **to France** nach Frankreich.

frantic *adjective* **1** (*very upset*) **to be frantic** außer sich ←(DAT) sein; **I was frantic with worry** ich war außer mir vor Sorge; **2** (*desperate*) hektisch (*effort or search*).

freckle *noun* Sommersprosse *die* (PL *die* Sommersprossen).

free *adjective* **1** (*when you don't pay*) kostenlos; **a free ride** eine kostenlose Fahrt; **a free ticket** eine Freikarte; **2** (*without charge*) umsonst; **to do something for free** etwas umsonst machen; **3** (*not occupied*) frei; **are you free on Thursday?** sind Sie am Donnerstag frei?; **4** sugar-free ohne Zucker; lead-free bleifrei. *verb* befreien.

freedom *noun* Freiheit *die*.

free gift *noun* Werbegeschenk *das* (PL *die* Werbegeschenke).

freeze *verb* **1** (*in a freezer*) einfrieren ✧ SEP; **to freeze raspberries** Himbeeren einfrieren;

△ NEW SPELLING: **See page xii**

2 (*in cold weather*) frieren ✧; **it's freezing** es friert; **3** (*become covered with ice*) zufrieren ✧ SEP (PERF *sein*); **the pond is frozen** der Teich ist zugefroren.

freezer *noun* Gefrierschrank *der* (PL *die* Gefrierschränke).

freezing *noun* **below freezing** unter Null; **three degrees above freezing** drei Grad über Null. *adjective* **1** I'm freezing ich friere sehr; **2** it's freezing outside es ist eiskalt draußen.

French *noun* **1** (*the language*) Französisch *das*; **2** (*the people*) **the French** die Franzosen. *adjective* **1** französisch; **Jean-Marc is French** Jean-Marc ist Franzose; **2** (*teacher or lesson*) Französisch-; **the French class** der Französischunterricht.

French bean *noun* grüne Bohne *die* (PL *die* grünen Bohnen).

French dressing *noun* Vinaigrette *die*.

French fries *plural noun* Pommes frites (*plural*).

Frenchman *noun* Franzose *der* (PL *die* Franzosen).

French window *noun* Verandatür *die* (PL *die* Verandatüren).

Frenchwoman *noun* Französin *die* (PL *die* Französinnen).

fresh *adjective* frisch; **fresh eggs** frische Eier; **I'm going out for some fresh air** ich gehe ein bisschen frische Luft schnappen.

Friday *noun* **1** Freitag *der* (PL *die* Freitage); **next Friday** nächsten Freitag; **last Friday** letzten Freitag; **on Friday** (am) Freitag; **I'll phone you on Friday evening** ich rufe dich Freitagabend an; **every Friday** jeden Freitag; **Good Friday** Karfreitag; **2 on Fridays** freitags; **closed on Fridays** freitags geschlossen.

fridge *noun* Kühlschrank *der* (PL *die* Kühlschränke); **put it in the fridge** stell es in den Kühlschrank.

friend *noun* **1** Freund *der* (PL *die* Freunde), Freundin *die* (PL *die* Freundinnen); **a friend of mine** ein Freund von mir; **2 to make friends** sich anfreunden; **he made friends with Danny** er hat sich mit Danny angefreundet; **he is friends with Danny** er ist mit Danny befreundet.

friendly *adjective* freundlich.

fries *plural noun* Pommes frites (*plural*).

fright *noun* **1** Schreck *der* (PL *die* Schrecke); **to have** or **get a fright** einen Schreck bekommen; **2 you gave me a fright!** du hast mich erschreckt!

frighten *verb* **1** (*of an explosion or shot*) erschrecken; **2** (*scare or threaten*) **to frighten somebody** jemandem Angst machen.

frightened *adjective* **to be frightened** Angst haben; **Martin's frightened of snakes** Martin hat Angst vor Schlangen.

frightening *adjective* beängstigend.

✧ IRREGULAR VERB: *See the verb table in the centre of the dictionary*

fringe noun 1 (*hairstyle*) Pony der (PL die Ponys); 2 (*on clothes or a curtain*) Fransen (*plural*).

frog noun Frosch der (PL die Frösche).

from preposition 1 von (+DAT); **ten metres from the cinema** zehn Meter vom Kino; **a letter from Tom** ein Brief von Tom; **from Monday to Friday** von Montag bis Freitag; **from now on** von jetzt an; 2 aus (+DAT); **he comes from Dublin** er kommt aus Dublin; **the train from London** der Zug aus London; 3 **from seven o'clock onwards** ab sieben Uhr; **from then on** von da ab.

front noun 1 (*of a building*) Vorderfront die (PL die Vorderfronten); (*of a cupboard, card, or envelope*) Vorderseite die (PL die Vorderseiten); 2 (*of a garment or in an interior*) Vorderteil das (PL die Vorderteile); 3 (*at the seaside*) Strandpromenade die (PL die Strandpromenaden); 4 (*of a car*) **to sit in (the) front** vorne sitzen; 5 (*of a train or queue*) vordere Ende das; 6 (*of a procession or in a race*) Spitze die; 7 **in/at the front** vorne; **in/at the front of** vorne in (+DAT, or +ACC with movement towards a place); **there are still seats at the front of the train** es gibt noch Plätze vorne im Zug; **we got on at the front of the train** wir sind vorne in den Zug eingestiegen; 8 **in front of** vor (+DAT, or +ACC with movement towards a place); **in front of the TV** vor dem Fernseher; **in front of me** vor mir. adjective 1 vorderer/vordere/

vorderes; **in the front rows** in den vorderen Reihen; 2 Vorder-; **front seat** (*of a car*) der Vordersitz; **front wheel** das Vorderrad.

front door noun Haustür die (PL die Haustüren).

frontier noun Grenze die (PL die Grenzen).

frost noun Frost der.

frosty adjective frostig.

frown verb die Stirn runzeln; **he frowned at us** er runzelte die Stirn.

frozen adjective (*in a freezer*) tiefgekühlt; **a frozen pizza** eine tiefgekühlte Pizza.

fruit noun 1 (*a single fruit or type of fruit*) Frucht die (PL die Früchte); 2 (*various fruits*) Obst das; **we bought cheese and fruit** wir haben Käse und Obst gekauft.

fruit juice noun Fruchtsaft der (PL die Fruchtsäfte).

fruit machine noun Spielautomat der (PL die Spielautomaten).

fruit salad noun Obstsalat der (PL die Obstsalate).

frustrated adjective frustriert.

fry verb braten✧; **we fried fish** wir haben Fisch gebraten; **fried potatoes** Bratkartoffeln; **fried egg** das Spiegelei.

frying pan noun Bratpfanne die (PL die Bratpfannen).

fuel noun (*for a car*) Kraftstoff der.

△ NEW SPELLING: *See page xii*

full *adjective* 1 voll; **the glass is full** das Glas ist voll; **I'm full** ich bin voll (*informal*); 2 **full of** voller (+GEN); **the train was full of tourists** der Zug war voll Touristen; 3 **at full speed** in voller Fahrt; 4 **to write something out in full** etwas voll ausschreiben.

full stop *noun* Punkt *der* (PL *die* Punkte).

full-time *adjective* **a full-time job** eine Ganztagsstelle.

fully *adverb* voll.

fun *noun* 1 Spaß *der*; **have fun!** viel Spaß!; **we had fun catching the ponies** wir hatten Spaß daran, die Ponys einzufangen; **skiing is fun** Skifahren macht Spaß; **I do it for fun** ich mache es aus Spaß; 2 **to have fun** sich amüsieren; ★ **to make fun of somebody** sich über jemanden lustig machen.

funds *plural noun* Geldmittel (*plural*).

funeral *noun* Beerdigung *die* (PL *die* Beerdigungen).

funfair *noun* Jahrmarkt *der* (PL *die* Jahrmärkte).

funny *adjective* 1 (*amusing*) lustig; **he's so funny** er ist so lustig; **a funny story** eine lustige Geschichte; 2 (*strange*) komisch; **a funny noise** ein komisches Geräusch; **that's funny, I'm sure I paid** das ist komisch, ich bin mir sicher, dass ich gezahlt habe.

fur *noun* 1 (*on an animal*) Fell *das* (PL *die* Felle); 2 (*for a coat*) Pelz *der*

(PL *die* Pelze); **fur coat** *der* Pelzmantel.

furious *adjective* wütend; **she was furious with Steve** sie war wütend auf Steve.

furniture *noun* Möbel (*plural*); **to buy some furniture** Möbel kaufen; **piece of furniture** *das* Möbelstück.

further *adverb* weiter; **further than the station** weiter als der Bahnhof; **ten kilometres further on** zehn Kilometer weiter; **further off** weiter entfernt; **further forward** weiter vorn; **further back** weiter hinten.

fuse *noun* Sicherung *die* (PL *die* Sicherungen).

fuss *noun* Theater *das*; **to make a fuss** ein Theater machen; **to make a big fuss about the bill** ein großes Theater um die Rechnung machen.

fussy *adjective* **to be fussy about something** wählerisch in etwas ←(DAT) sein (*food, for example*).

future *noun* Zukunft *die*; **in future** in Zukunft.

G g

gadget *noun* Gerät *das* (PL *die* Geräte).

gain *verb* 1 gewinnen ◇; **in order to gain time** um Zeit zu gewinnen; 2 profitieren; **to gain by something** von etwas profitieren.

◇ IRREGULAR VERB: *See the verb table in the centre of the dictionary*

gale noun Sturm der (PL die Stürme).

gallery noun Galerie die (PL die Galerien).

gamble verb spielen (for money).

game noun 1 Spiel das (PL die Spiele); **game of chance** das Glücksspiel; **board game** das Brettspiel; 2 **to have a game of cards** eine Partie Karten spielen; 3 **to have a game of football** Fußball spielen; 4 **games** (at school) Sport der.

gang noun Bande die (PL die Banden); **all the gang were there** die ganze Bande war da.

gap noun 1 (hole) Lücke die (PL die Lücken); 2 (in time) Pause die (PL die Pausen); **a two-hour gap** eine zweistündige Pause; 3 **age gap** der Altersunterschied.

garage noun 1 (for keeping your car) Garage die (PL die Garagen); 2 (for repairing cars) Autowerkstatt die (PL die Autowerkstätten); 3 (for petrol) Tankstelle die (PL die Tankstellen).

garden noun Garten der (PL die Gärten).

gardener noun Gärtner der (PL die Gärtner), Gärtnerin die (PL die Gärtnerinnen).

gardening noun Gartenarbeit die.

garlic noun Knoblauch der.

garment noun Kleidungsstück das (PL die Kleidungsstücke).

gas noun Gas das.

gas cooker noun Gasherd der (PL die Gasherde).

gas fire noun Gasofen der (PL die Gasöfen).

gas meter noun Gaszähler der (PL die Gaszähler).

gate noun 1 (in garden) Pforte die (PL die Pforten); 2 (in field) Gatter das (PL die Gatter); 3 (at an airport) Flugsteig der (PL die Flugsteige).

gather verb 1 (of people) sich versammeln; 2 sammeln (fruit, vegetables, flowers); 3 **as far as I can gather** soweit ich weiß.

gay adjective (homosexual) schwul (informal).

gaze verb **to gaze at something** etwas anstarren SEP.

gear noun 1 (in a car) Gang der (PL die Gänge); **to change gear** schalten; 2 (equipment) Ausrüstung die; **camping gear** die Campingausrüstung; 3 (things) Sachen (plural); **I've left all my gear at Gary's** ich habe alle meine Sachen bei Gary gelassen.

gear lever noun Schalthebel der (PL die Schalthebel).

gel noun Gel das (PL die Gele).

Gemini noun Zwillinge (plural); **Steph's Gemini** Steph ist Zwilling.

gender noun (of a word) Geschlecht das (PL die Geschlechter); **what is the gender of 'Haus'?** welches Geschlecht hat 'Haus'?

△ NEW SPELLING: See page xlii

general noun General der (PL die Generäle).
adjective allgemein; **in general** im Allgemeinen; **the general election** die allgemeinen Wahlen.

general knowledge noun Allgemeinwissen das.

generally adverb im Allgemeinen △.

generation noun Generation die (PL die Generationen).

generous adjective großzügig.

genetics noun Genetik die.

Geneva noun Genf das; **Lake Geneva** der Genfer See.

genius noun Genie das (PL die Genies; **Lisa, you're a genius!** Lisa, du bist ein Genie!

gentle adjective sanft.

gentleman noun Herr der (PL die Herren); **ladies and gentlemen!** meine Damen und Herren!

gently adverb sanft.

gents noun (lavatory) Herrentoilette die (PL die Herrentoiletten); (on a sign) 'Gents' 'Herren'; **where's the gents?** wo ist die Toilette?

genuine adjective 1 (real, authentic) echt; **a genuine diamond** ein echter Brillant; 2 aufrichtig (person); **she's very genuine** sie ist sehr aufrichtig.

geography noun Geographie die; (at school) Erdkunde die.

germ noun 1 Keim der (PL die Keime); 2 (causing a cold) **germs** Bazillen (plural).

German noun (person) 1 Deutsche der/die (PL die Deutschen); 2 (language) Deutsch das; **in German** auf Deutsch. adjective deutsch; **he is German** er ist Deutscher; **she is German** sie ist Deutsche; **our German teacher** unser Deutschlehrer, unsere Deutschlehrerin.

Germany Deutschland das; **to Germany** nach Deutschland; **from Germany** aus Deutschland.

get verb 1 (obtain, receive) bekommen ✧, kriegen (informal); **I got a bike for my birthday** ich habe ein Rad zum Geburtstag bekommen; **Fred got the job** Fred hat die Stelle bekommen; **she got a shock** sie hat einen Schreck gekriegt; **I got a good mark for my German homework** ich habe eine gute Note für meine Deutschhausaufgaben gekriegt; 2 **he's got lots of money** er hat viel Geld; **she's got long hair** sie hat lange Haare; **I've got a headache** ich habe Kopfschmerzen; 3 (fetch) holen; **I'll get some bread** ich hole Brot; **I'll get your bag for you** ich hole dir deine Tasche; 4 **to have got to do something** etwas tun müssen ✧; **I've got to phone before midday** ich muss vor Mittag anrufen; 5 **to get (to) somewhere** irgendwo ankommen ✧ SEP (PERF sein); **when I got to London** als ich in London ankam; **we got here this morning** wir sind heute Morgen angekommen; **what time did they get there?** wann sind sie angekommen? 6 (become) werden ✧ (PERF sein); **it's getting**

✧ IRREGULAR VERB: See the verb table in the centre of the dictionary

late es wird spät; **it's getting dark** es wird dunkel; **7 to get something done** etwas machen lassen ✧; **I'm getting my hair cut today** ich lasse mir heute die Haare schneiden.

● **to get back** zurückkommen ✧ SEP (PERF *sein*); **Mum gets back at six** Mutti kommt um sechs zurück.

● **to get something back** etwas zurückbekommen ✧ SEP, etwas zurückkriegen SEP (*informal*); **did you get your books back?** hast du deine Bücher zurückbekommen?

● **to get into something** (*a vehicle*) in etwas ←(ACC) einsteigen ✧ SEP (PERF *sein*); **he got into the car** er ist ins Auto eingestiegen.

● **to get off something** (*a vehicle*) aus etwas ←(DAT) aussteigen ✧ SEP (PERF *sein*); **I got off the train at Banbury** ich bin in Banbury aus dem Zug ausgestiegen.

● **to get on: how's Amanda getting on?** wie geht's Amanda?

● **to get on something** (*a vehicle*) in etwas ←(ACC) einsteigen ✧ SEP (PERF *sein*); **she got on the train at Reading** sie ist in Reading in den Zug eingestiegen.

● **to get on with somebody** sich mit jemandem verstehen ✧; **she doesn't get on with her brother** sie versteht sich nicht mit ihrem Bruder.

● **to get out of something** (*a vehicle*) aus etwas ←(DAT) aussteigen ✧ SEP (PERF *sein*); **Laura got out of the car** Laura ist aus dem Auto ausgestiegen.

● **to get together** sich wieder sehen ✧ SEP △; **we must get together soon** wir müssen uns bald mal wieder sehen.

● **to get up** aufstehen ✧ SEP (PERF *sein*); **I get up at seven** ich stehe um sieben auf.

ghost noun Geist der (PL die Geister).

gift noun **1** Geschenk das (PL die Geschenke); **a Christmas gift** ein Weihnachtsgeschenk; **2** Begabung die; **to have a gift for something** für etwas ←(ACC) begabt sein; **Jo has a real gift for languages** Jo ist richtig sprachbegabt.

gigantic adjective riesig.

gin noun Gin der (PL die Gins).

ginger noun Ingwer der (PL die Ingwer).

girl noun Mädchen das (PL die Mädchen); **three boys and four girls** drei Jungen und vier Mädchen; **when I was a little girl I had ...** als kleines Mädchen hatte ich ...

girlfriend noun Freundin die (PL die Freundinnen).

give verb **1** geben ✧; **to give something to somebody** jemandem etwas geben; **I'll give you my address** ich gebe dir meine Adresse; **give me the key** gib mir den Schlüssel; **Yasmin's dad gave her the money** Yasmins Vater hat ihr das Geld gegeben; **2** (*give as a gift*) schenken; **to give somebody a present** jemandem etwas schenken.

● **to give something away** etwas weggeben ✧ SEP; **she's given away all her books** sie hat alle ihre Bücher weggegeben.

△ **NEW SPELLING: See page xii**

● **to give something back to somebody** jemandem etwas zurückgeben ◆ SEP; **I gave her back the keys** ich habe ihr die Schlüssel zurückgegeben.

● **to give in** nachgeben ◆ SEP; **my mum said no but she gave in in the end** meine Mutti hat nein gesagt, aber schließlich hat sie nachgegeben.

● **to give up** aufgeben ◆ SEP; **I give up!** ich gebe auf!

● **to give up doing something** etwas aufgeben ◆ SEP; **she's given up smoking** sie hat das Rauchen aufgegeben.

glad adjective froh; **I'm glad to hear he's better** ich bin froh, dass es ihm besser geht; **I'm glad to be back** ich bin froh, dass ich wieder zurück bin.

glass noun Glas das (PL die Gläser); **a glass of water** ein Glas Wasser; **a glass table** ein Glastisch.

glasses plural noun Brille die (PL die Brillen); **to wear glasses** eine Brille tragen.

glove noun Handschuh der (PL die Handschuhe); **a pair of gloves** ein Paar Handschuhe.

glove compartment noun Handschuhfach das (PL die Handschuhfächer).

glue noun Klebstoff der (PL die Klebstoffe).

go noun 1 (in a game) **whose go is it?** wer ist dran?; **it's my go** ich bin dran; 2 **to have a go at doing something** versuchen, etwas zu tun; **I'll have a go at mending it** ich versuche, es zu reparieren.

verb 1 (on foot) gehen ◆ (PERF sein); **to go to school** in die Schule gehen; **Mark's gone to the dentist's** Mark ist zum Zahnarzt gegangen; **to go shopping** einkaufen gehen; 2 (in a vehicle) fahren ◆ (PERF sein); **we're going to London** wir fahren nach London; **we're planning to go early** wir wollen früh fahren; **to go on holiday** in die Ferien fahren; 3 (by plane) fliegen ◆ (PERF sein); 4 **to go for a walk** spazieren gehen ◆ SEP (PERF sein); 5 (with another verb) **I'm going to do it** ich werde es tun; **I'm going to make some tea** ich mache Tee; **he was going to phone you** er wollte dich anrufen; **how did your evening go?** wie ist dein Abend verlaufen?; **the party went well** die Party war gut.

● **to go away** weggehen ◆ SEP (PERF sein); **go away!** geh weg!; 2 (on holiday) verreisen (PERF sein).

● **to go back** 1 zurückgehen ◆ SEP (PERF sein); **I'm going back to Germany in March** ich gehe im März nach Deutschland zurück; **I'm not going back there again!** ich gehe da nicht wieder zurück!; 2 **I went back home** ich bin nach Hause gegangen.

● **to go down** 1 hinuntergehen ◆ SEP (PERF sein); **she's gone down to the kitchen** sie ist in die Küche

◆ **IRREGULAR VERB:** See the verb table in the centre of the dictionary

hinuntergegangen; **to go down the stairs** die Treppe hinuntergehen; **2** (*price, temperature*) fallen ◇ SEP (PERF *sein*); **3** (*tyre, balloon, airbed*) Luft verlieren ◇.

● **to go in** hineingehen ◇ SEP (PERF *sein*); **he went in and shut the door** er ist hineingegangen und hat die Tür zugemacht.

● **to go into 1** (*person*) gehen in (+ACC) (PERF *sein*); **Fran went into the kitchen** Fran ging in die Küche; **2** (*object*) passen in (+ACC); **this book won't go into my bag** dieses Buch passt nicht in meine Tasche.

● **to go off 1** (*bomb*) hochgehen ◇ SEP (PERF *sein*); **2** (*alarm clock*) klingeln; **my alarm clock went off at six** mein Wecker hat um sechs geklingelt; **3** (*fire or burglar alarm*) losgehen ◇ SEP (PERF *sein*); **the fire alarm went off** der Feuermelder ging los.

● **to go on 1** what's going on? was ist los?; **2** to go on doing something weiter etwas tun; **she went on talking** sie hat weiter geredet; **3** to go on about something stundenlang von etwas (DAT) reden; **he's always going on about his dog** er redet stundenlang von seinem Hund.

● **to go out 1** (*for an evening*) ausgehen ◇ SEP, weggehen ◇ SEP (PERF *sein*) (*informal*); **we're going out tonight** wir gehen heute Abend aus; **2** (*leave*) she went out of the kitchen sie ist aus der Küche gegangen; **3** to be going out with somebody mit jemandem gehen ◇ (PERF *sein*) (*informal*); **she's going out with my brother** sie geht mit

meinem Bruder; **4** (*light, fire*) ausgehen ◇ SEP (PERF *sein*); **the light went out** das Licht ist ausgegangen.

● **to go past something** an etwas ←(DAT) vorbeigehen ◇ SEP; **we went past your house** wir sind an eurem Haus vorbeigegangen.

● **to go round: to go round to somebody's house** jemanden besuchen; **we went round to Fred's last night** wir haben gestern Abend Fred besucht.

● **to go round something 1** um etwas ←(ACC) herumgehen ◇ SEP (PERF *sein*) (*building, park, garden*); **2** besichtigen (*museum, monument*).

● **to go through 1** the train goes through Cologne der Zug fährt durch Köln; **2** to go through a room durch ein Zimmer gehen; **3** (*search*) durchsuchen.

● **to go up 1** (*person*) hinaufgehen ◇ SEP (PERF *sein*); **she's gone up to her room** sie ist in ihr Zimmer hinaufgegangen; **to go up the stairs** die Treppe hinaufgehen; **2** (*prices*) steigen ◇ (PERF *sein*); **the price of petrol has gone up** die Benzinpreise sind gestiegen.

goal *noun* Tor *das* (PL die Tore); **to score a goal** ein Tor schießen.

goalkeeper *noun* Torwart *der* (PL die Torwarte).

goat *noun* Ziege *die* (PL die Ziegen).

god *noun* Gott *der* (PL die Götter).

God *noun* Gott *der*; **to believe in God** an Gott glauben.

△ NEW SPELLING: See page xii

godchild noun Patenkind das (PL die Patenkinder).

goddaughter noun Patentochter die (PL die Patentöchter).

goddess noun Göttin die (PL die Göttinnen).

godfather noun Pate der (PL die Paten).

godmother noun Patin die (PL die Patinnen).

godson noun Patensohn der (PL die Patensöhne).

gold noun Gold das; a gold bracelet ein Goldarmband.

goldfish noun Goldfisch der (PL die Goldfische).

golf noun Golf das; to play golf Golf spielen.

golf club noun 1 (place) Golfklub der (PL die Golfklubs); 2 (iron) Golfschläger der (PL die Golfschläger).

golf course noun Golfplatz der (PL die Golfplätze).

good adjective 1 gut; she's a good teacher sie ist eine gute Lehrerin; the cherries are very good die Kirschen sind sehr gut; 2 to be good for you gesund sein; tomatoes are good for you Tomaten sind gesund; 3 good at gut in (+DAT); she's good at maths sie ist gut in Mathe; he's good at drawing er ist gut im Zeichnen; 4 (well-behaved) brav; be good! sei brav!; 5 (kind) nett; she's been very good to me sie ist sehr nett zu mir gewesen; 6 for

good endgültig; I've stopped smoking for good ich habe das Rauchen endgültig aufgegeben.

good afternoon exclamation guten Tag!

goodbye exclamation auf Wiedersehen!

good evening exclamation guten Abend!

Good Friday noun Karfreitag der (PL die Karfreitage).

good-looking adjective gut aussehend △.

good morning exclamation guten Morgen!

goodness exclamation meine Güte!; for goodness sake! um Himmels willen!

good night exclamation gute Nacht!

goods plural noun Waren (plural).

goods train noun Güterzug der (PL die Güterzüge).

goose noun Gans die (PL die Gänse).

gorgeous adjective herrlich; it's a gorgeous day es ist ein herrlicher Tag.

gorilla noun Gorilla der (PL die Gorillas).

gosh exclamation Mensch!

gossip noun 1 (person) Klatschbase die (PL die Klatschbasen); 2 (scandal) Klatsch der. verb klatschen.

◇ **IRREGULAR VERB:** See the verb table in the centre of the dictionary

government noun Regierung die (PL die Regierungen).

grab verb 1 packen; **she grabbed my arm** sie packte mich am Arm; 2 **to grab something from somebody** jemandem etwas ←(ACC) entreißen ◇; **he grabbed the book from me** er hat mir das Buch entrissen.

grade noun (mark) Note die (PL die Noten); **to get good grades** gute Noten bekommen.

gradual adjective allmählich.

gradually adverb allmählich; **the weather got gradually better** das Wetter wurde allmählich besser.

graffiti plural noun Graffiti (plural).

gram noun Gramm das; **100 grams of salami** hundert Gramm Salami.

grammar noun Grammatik die.

grammar school noun Gymnasium das (PL die Gymnasien).

gran noun Oma die (PL die Omas).

grandchildren plural noun Enkelkinder (plural).

granddad noun Opa der (PL die Opas).

granddaughter noun Enkelin die (PL die Enkelinnen).

grandfather noun Großvater der (PL die Großväter).

grandma noun Oma die (PL die Omas).

grandmother noun Großmutter die (PL die Großmütter).

grandpa noun Opa der (PL die Opas).

grandparents plural noun Großeltern (plural).

grandson noun Enkel der (PL die Enkel).

granny noun Omi die (PL die Omis).

grape noun Weintraube die (PL die Weintrauben); **a grape** eine Weintraube; **to buy some grapes** Weintrauben kaufen; **do you like grapes?** magst du Weintrauben?; **a bunch of grapes** eine ganze Weintraube.

grapefruit noun Grapefruit die (PL die Grapefruits).

grasp verb festhalten ◇ SEP.

grass noun 1 Gras das; **to lie on the grass** im Gras liegen; 2 (lawn) Rasen der (PL die Rasen); **to cut the grass** den Rasen mähen.

grasshopper noun Heuschrecke die (PL die Heuschrecken).

grate verb reiben ◇; **grated cheese** geriebener Käse.

grateful adjective dankbar; **to be grateful to somebody** jemandem dankbar sein.

grater noun Reibe die (PL die Reiben).

grave noun Grab das (PL die Gräber).

△ NEW SPELLING: See page xii

graveyard *noun* Friedhof *der* (PL die Friedhöfe).

gravy *noun* Soße *die* (PL die Soßen).

grease *noun* Fett *das*.

greasy *adjective* 1 fettig; **to have greasy skin** fettige Haut haben; 2 (*food*) fett.

great *adjective* 1 groß; **a great poet** ein großer Dichter; 2 (*terrific*) großartig; **it was a great party** das war eine großartige Party; **great!** großartig!, prima! (*informal*); 3 **a great deal of** sehr viel; **a great many** sehr viele.

Great Britain *noun* Großbritannien *das*.

Greece *noun* Griechenland *das*.

greedy *adjective* gierig; (*with food*) gefräßig.

Greek *noun* 1 (*person*) Grieche *der* (PL die Griechen), Griechin *die* (PL die Griechinnen); 2 (*language*) Griechisch *das*. *adjective* griechisch; **she's Greek** sie ist Griechin.

green *noun* 1 (*colour*) Grün *das*; **a pale green** ein Hellgrün; 2 **the Greens** (*ecologists*) die Grünen. *adjective* 1 grün; **a green door** eine grüne Tür; 2 **the Green Party** die Grünen (*plural*).

greengrocer *noun* Obst- und Gemüsehändler *der* (PL die Obst- und Gemüsehändler).

greenhouse *noun* Gewächshaus *das* (PL die Gewächshäuser).

greenhouse effect *noun* Treibhauseffekt *der*.

greetings *plural noun* Grüße (*plural*); **Season's Greetings** fröhliche Weihnachten und ein glückliches neues Jahr.

greetings card *noun* Glückwunschkarte *die* (PL die Glückwunschkarten).

grey *adjective* grau.

grief *noun* Trauer *die*.

grill *noun* Grill *der* (PL die Grills). *verb* grillen; **I'm going to grill the sausages** ich grille die Würstchen.

grin *verb* grinsen.

grind *verb* mahlen.

grip *verb* (*hold on to*) festhalten ◇ SEP.

groan *noun* Stöhnen *das*. *verb* stöhnen.

grocer *noun* Lebensmittelhändler *der* (PL die Lebensmittelhändler).

groceries *plural noun* Lebensmittel (*plural*).

grocer's *noun* Lebensmittelgeschäft *das* (PL die Lebensmittelgeschäfte).

groom *noun* Bräutigam *der* (PL die Bräutigame); **the bride and groom** das Brautpaar.

gross *adjective* 1 **a gross injustice** ein schreiendes Unrecht; 2 grob; **a gross error** ein grober Fehler; 3 (*disgusting*) ekelhaft; **the food was gross!** das Essen war ekelhaft!

◇ **IRREGULAR VERB: See the verb table in the centre of the dictionary**

ground noun 1 Boden der; **to sit on the ground** auf dem Boden sitzen; 2 (for sport) Sportplatz der (PL die Sportplätze); **football ground** der Fußballplatz.
adjective gemahlen; **ground coffee** gemahlener Kaffee.

ground floor noun Erdgeschoss △ das; **they live on the ground floor** sie wohnen im Erdgeschoss.

group noun Gruppe die (PL die Gruppen).

grow verb (get bigger) 1 wachsen ◇ (PERF sein); **your hair grows very quickly** deine Haare wachsen sehr schnell; **my little sister's grown quite a bit this year** meine kleine Schwester ist dieses Jahr ein ganzes Stück gewachsen; **the number of students is still growing** die Zahl der Studenten wächst noch; 2 anbauen SEP (fruit, vegetables); 3 **to grow a beard** sich ←(DAT) einen Bart wachsen lassen; 4 (become) werden ◇ (PERF sein); **to grow old** alt werden.
• **to grow up** 1 erwachsen werden; **the children are growing up** die Kinder werden erwachsen; 2 aufwachsen SEP (PERF sein); **she grew up in Scotland** sie ist in Schottland aufgewachsen.

growl verb knurren.

grown-up noun Erwachsene der/die (PL die Erwachsenen).

growth noun Wachstum das.

grudge noun **to bear a grudge against somebody** etwas gegen

jemanden haben; **she bears me a grudge** sie hat etwas gegen mich.

grumble verb 1 murren; **he's always grumbling** er murrt immer; 2 **to grumble about something** sich über etwas ←(ACC) beklagen; **what's she grumbling about?** worüber beklagt sie sich?

guarantee noun Garantie die (PL die Garantien); **a year's guarantee** ein Jahr Garantie.
verb garantieren.

guard noun 1 prison **guard** der Gefängniswärter, die Gefängniswärterin; 2 (on a train) Zugführer der (PL die Zugführer), Zugführerin die (PL die Zugführerinnen); 3 security **guard** der Wächter, die Wächterin.
verb bewachen.

guard dog noun Wachhund der (PL die Wachhunde).

guess noun **have a guess!** rate mal!; **it's a good guess** gut geraten.
verb 1 raten ◇; **guess who I saw last night** rate mal, wen ich gestern Abend gesehen habe; 2 (guess something correctly) erraten ◇; **you'll never guess!** du errätst es nie!

guest noun Gast der (PL die Gäste); **we've got guests coming tonight** wir haben heute Abend Gäste; **a paying guest** ein zahlender Gast.

guide noun 1 (person) Führer der (PL die Führer), Führerin die (PL die Führerinnen); 2 (book) Reiseführer der (PL die Reiseführer);

3 (*girl guide*) Pfadfinderin *die* (PL *die* Pfadfinderinnen).

guidebook *noun* **1** Reiseführer *der* (PL *die* Reiseführer); **2** (*to a museum or monument*) Handbuch *das* (PL *die* Handbücher).

guide dog *noun* Blindenhund *der* (PL *die* Blindenhunde).

guilty *adjective* **1** schuldig; **2** to feel guilty ein schlechtes Gewissen haben; I felt guilty about the noise ich hatte ein schlechtes Gewissen wegen des Lärms.

guinea pig *noun*
1 (*pet*) Meerschweinchen *das* (PL *die* Meerschweinchen);
2 (*in an experiment*) Versuchskaninchen *das* (PL *die* Versuchskaninchen).

guitar *noun* Gitarre *die* (PL *die* Gitarren); to play the guitar Gitarre spielen.

gum *noun* **1** (*in your mouth*) Zahnfleisch *das*; **2** (*chewing gum*) Kaugummi *der* (PL *die* Kaugummi).

gun *noun* **1** Pistole *die* (PL *die* Pistolen); **2** (*rifle*) Gewehr *das* (PL *die* Gewehre).

guy *noun* Typ *der* (PL *die* Typen); (*informal*); he's a nice guy er ist ein netter Typ; that guy from Newcastle der Typ aus Newcastle.

gym *noun* **1** (*school lesson*) Turnen *das*; **2** (*building*) Turnhalle *die* (PL *die* Turnhallen); **3** (*health club*) Fitnesscenter △ *das* (PL *die* Fitnesscenter); to go to the gym ins Fitnesscenter gehen.

gymnasium *noun* Turnhalle *die* (PL *die* Turnhallen).

gymnast *noun* Turner *der* (PL *die* Turner), Turnerin *die* (PL *die* Turnerinnen).

gymnastics *noun* Turnen *das*.

gym shoe *noun* Turnschuh *der* (PL *die* Turnschuhe).

H h

habit *noun* Gewohnheit *die* (PL *die* Gewohnheiten); it's a bad habit es ist eine schlechte Gewohnheit.

haddock *noun* Schellfisch *der*; smoked haddock *der* Haddock.

hail *noun* Hagel *der*.

hailstone *noun* Hagelkorn *das* (PL *die* Hagelkörner).

hailstorm *noun* Hagelschauer *der* (PL *die* Hagelschauer).

hair *noun* **1** Haare (*plural*); to comb your hair sich ←(DAT) die Haare kämmen; to wash your hair sich ←(DAT) die Haare waschen; to have your hair cut sich ←(DAT) die Haare schneiden lassen; she's had her hair cut sie hat sich die Haare schneiden lassen; **2** a hair ein Haar.

hairbrush *noun* Haarbürste *die* (PL *die* Haarbürsten).

haircut *noun* **1** Haarschnitt *der* (PL *die* Haarschnitte); **2** to have a haircut sich ←(DAT) die Haare schneiden lassen.

◇ **IRREGULAR VERB: See the verb table in the centre of the dictionary**

hairdresser noun Friseur der (PL die Friseure), Friseuse die (PL die Friseusen); **at the hairdresser's** beim Friseur.

hair drier noun Föhn △ der (PL die Föhne).

hair gel noun Haargel das (PL die Haargele).

hairgrip noun Haarklemme die (PL die Haarklemmen).

hairslide noun Haarspange die (PL die Haarspangen).

hairspray noun Haarspray das (PL die Haarsprays).

hairstyle noun Frisur die (PL die Frisuren).

half noun 1 Hälfte die (PL die Hälften); **half of** die Hälfte von (+DAT); **I gave him half of the money** ich habe ihm die Hälfte von dem Geld gegeben; **half of it** die Hälfte davon; **2 half an apple** ein halber Apfel; **3 to cut something in half** etwas halbieren; **4** (as a fraction) halb; **three and a half** dreieinhalb; **5** (in time) halb; **half an hour** eine halbe Stunde; **an hour and a half** anderthalb Stunden; **it's half past three** es ist halb vier (literally: half on the way to four); **6** (in weights and measures) halb; **half a litre** ein halber Liter.

half hour noun halbe Stunde die; **every half hour** jede halbe Stunde.

half price adjective, adverb zum halben Preis; **half-price CDs** CDs zum halben Preis.

half-time noun Halbzeit die; **at half-time the score is 0–0** zur Halbzeit steht es null zu null.

halfway adverb 1 auf halbem Weg; **halfway to Frankfurt** auf halbem Weg nach Frankfurt; **2 to be halfway through doing something** halb fertig mit etwas sein; **I'm halfway through my homework** ich bin halb fertig mit meinen Hausaufgaben.

hall noun 1 (in a house) Diele die (PL die Dielen); **2** (public) Saal der (PL die Säle); **village hall** der Gemeindesaal; **concert hall** der Konzertsaal.

Hallowe'en noun der Tag vor Allerheiligen (in Germany there are no particular customs for this date).

ham noun Schinken der; **a ham sandwich** ein Schinkenbrot.

hamburger noun Hamburger der (PL die Hamburger).

hammer noun Hammer der (PL die Hammer).

hamster noun Hamster der (PL die Hamster).

hand noun 1 Hand die (PL die Hände); **to have something in your hand** etwas in der Hand haben; **to hold somebody's hand** jemandes Hand halten; **2 to give somebody a hand** jemandem helfen ◇; **can you give me a hand to move the table into the corner?** kannst du mir helfen, den Tisch in die Ecke zu rücken?; **do you need a hand?** kann ich dir helfen?; **3 on the other hand** ... andererseits ...; **4** (of a watch or clock) Zeiger der (PL die Zeiger); **the**

hour hand der Stundenzeiger.
verb **to hand something to somebody** jemandem etwas geben ◇; **I handed him the keys** ich gab ihm die Schlüssel.

● **to hand something in** etwas abgeben ◇ SEP; **hand in your homework** gebt eure Hausaufgaben ab.

● **to hand something out** etwas austeilen SEP.

handbag *noun* Handtasche *die* (PL die Handtaschen).

handcuffs *plural noun* Handschellen (*plural*).

handful *noun* **a handful of** eine Hand voll △.

handicapped *adjective* behindert.

handkerchief *noun* Taschentuch *das* (PL die Taschentücher).

handle *noun* 1 (*of a door, drawer, bag, or knife*) Griff *der* (PL die Griffe); 2 (*on a cup, jug, or basket*) Henkel *der* (PL die Henkel); 3 (*of a frying pan or broom*) Stiel *der* (PL die Stiele).
verb 1 erledigen; **Gina handles the correspondence** Gina erledigt die Korrespondenz; 2 umgehen ◇ SEP (PERF sein) mit; **she's good at handling people** sie kann gut mit Menschen umgehen; 3 fertig werden △ ◇ (PERF sein) mit; **he can't handle problems** er kann mit Problemen nicht fertig werden.

handlebars *plural noun* Lenkstange *die* (PL die Lenkstangen).

hand luggage *noun* Handgepäck *das*.

handmade *adjective* handgemacht.

handsome *adjective* gut aussehend △; **he's a handsome guy** er ist ein gut aussehender Typ.

handwriting *noun* Handschrift *die* (PL die Handschriften).

handy *adjective* 1 praktisch; **this little knife's very handy** dieses kleine Messer ist sehr praktisch; 2 griffbereit; **I always keep a notebook handy** ich habe immer ein kleines Notizbuch griffbereit.

hang *verb* 1 hängen ◇; **there was a mirror hanging on the wall** an der Wand hing ein Spiegel; 2 aufhängen SEP; **to hang a mirror on the wall** einen Spiegel an der Wand aufhängen.

● **to hang around** rumhängen ◇ SEP (PERF sein) (*informal*); **we were hanging around outside the cinema** wir haben vor dem Kino rumgehangen.

● **to hang on** warten; **hang on a second!** warten Sie einen Moment!

● **to hang up** (*on the phone*) auflegen SEP; **she hung up on me** sie hat einfach aufgelegt.

● **to hang something up** etwas aufhängen SEP.

hangover *noun* Kater *der* (PL die Kater).

happen *verb* 1 passieren (PERF sein); **what happened?** was ist passiert?; **it happened in June** es ist im Juni passiert; 2 **what's happening?** was ist los?; **what's happened to Jill?** was ist mit Jill los?; 3 **what's happened to the can-opener?** wo ist der Dosenöffner?; 4 **if you happen to see him** wenn du ihn zufällig triffst; **Leila happened to be there** Leila war zufällig da.

happily adverb 1 glücklich; 2 (willingly) gerne; **I'll happily do it for you** ich tu es gerne für dich.

happiness noun Glück das.

happy adjective glücklich; **a happy child** ein glückliches Kind; **Happy Birthday** herzlichen Glückwunsch zum Geburtstag.

harbour noun Hafen der (PL die Häfen).

hard adjective 1 hart; 2 (difficult) schwer; **a hard question** eine schwere Frage; **it's hard to know ...** es ist schwer zu wissen ... adverb 1 **to work hard** hart arbeiten; 2 **to try hard** sich sehr bemühen.

hard disk noun Festplatte die (PL die Festplatten).

hardly adverb 1 kaum; **I can hardly hear him** ich kann ihn kaum hören; **there was hardly anybody there** es war kaum jemand da; **we've got hardly any milk** wir haben kaum Milch; **hardly anything** kaum etwas; **he ate hardly anything** er hat kaum etwas gegessen; 2 **hardly ever** fast nie; **I hardly ever see him** ich sehe ihn fast nie.

hard up adjective **to be hard up** knapp bei Kasse sein.

harm noun **it won't do any harm** es kann nichts schaden. verb 1 **to harm somebody** jemandem etwas tun; **they didn't harm him** sie haben ihm nichts

getan; 2 schaden (+DAT) (health, environment, reputation); **a cup of coffee won't harm you** eine Tasse Kaffee schadet nicht.

harmful adjective schädlich.

harmless adjective unschädlich.

hat noun Hut der (PL die Hüte).

hate verb hassen; **I hate geography** ich hasse Erdkunde.

hatred noun Hass △ der.

have verb 1 haben ✧; **Anna has three brothers** Anna hat drei Brüder; **how many sisters do you have?** wie viele Schwestern hast du?; 2 **what have you got in your hand?** was hast du in der Hand?; **he has (got) flu** er hat die Grippe; 3 (to form past tenses, some verbs in German take 'haben' and others 'sein') **I've finished** ich bin fertig; **have you seen the film?** hast du den Film gesehen?; **Rosie hasn't arrived yet** Rosie ist noch nicht angekommen; 4 **to have to do something** etwas tun müssen ✧; **I have to phone my mum** ich muss meine Mutter anrufen; 5 ('have' is often translated by a more specific German verb) **we had a coffee** wir haben einen Kaffee getrunken; **what will you have?** was nehmen Sie?; **I'll have an omelette** ich nehme ein Omelett; **I'm going to have a shower** ich dusche jetzt; **to have lunch** zu Mittag essen; **to have dinner** (in the evening) zu Abend essen; 6 (get) bekommen ✧; **Emma had a letter from Sam yesterday**

gestern bekam Emma einen Brief von Sam; **she had a baby** sie hat ein Baby bekommen; **something done** etwas machen lassen ✧; **I'm going to have my hair cut** ich lasse mir die Haare schneiden; **8 to have on** (*be wearing*) anhaben ✧ SEP; **to have nothing on** nichts anhaben.

hay fever *noun* Heuschnupfen *der*.

hazelnut *noun* Haselnuss △ *die* (PL *die* Haselnüsse).

he *pronoun* er; **he lives in Manchester** er wohnt in Manchester.

head *noun* 1 Kopf *der* (PL *die* Köpfe); **he shook his head** er schüttelte den Kopf; **2** (*of a school*) Direktor *der* (PL *die* Direktoren), Direktorin *die* (PL *die* Direktorinnen); **3** (*of a firm*) Chef *der* (PL *die* Chefs), Chefin *die* (PL *die* Chefinnen); **4** (*when tossing a coin*) **'heads or tails?'** 'Kopf oder Zahl?'.

● **to head for something** auf etwas ←(ACC) zusteuern SEP (PERF *sein*); **Liz headed for the door** Liz steuerte auf die Tür zu.

headache *noun* Kopfschmerzen (*plural*); **I've got a headache** ich habe Kopfschmerzen.

headlight *noun* Scheinwerfer *der* (PL *die* Scheinwerfer).

headline *noun* Schlagzeile *die* (PL *die* Schlagzeilen).

headmaster *noun* Direktor *der* (PL *die* Direktoren).

headmistress *noun* Direktorin *die* (PL *die* Direktorinnen).

headphones *noun* Kopfhörer *der* (PL *die* Kopfhörer).

headteacher *noun* Direktor *der* (PL *die* Direktoren), Direktorin *die* (PL *die* Direktorinnen).

health *noun* Gesundheit *die*.

health centre *noun* Ärztezentrum *das* (PL *die* Ärztezentren).

healthy *adjective* gesund.

heap *noun* Haufen *der* (PL *die* Haufen); **I've got heaps of work** ich habe einen Haufen Arbeit (*informal*).

hear *verb* hören; **I can't hear anything** ich kann überhaupt nichts hören; **I hear you've bought a dog** ich habe gehört, dass ihr einen Hund gekauft habt.

● **to hear about something** von etwas ←(DAT) hören; **have you heard about the concert?** hast du von dem Konzert gehört?

● **to hear from somebody** von jemandem hören.

heart *noun* 1 Herz *das* (PL *die* Herzen); **2 to learn something by heart** etwas auswendig lernen; **3** (*in cards*) Herz *das*; **the jack of hearts** der Herzbube.

heat *noun* Hitze *die*.
verb **1 to heat something** etwas heiß machen; **I'll go and heat the soup** ich mache die Suppe heiß; **2 the soup's heating** die Suppe wird warm; **3** heizen (*a room*);

✧ IRREGULAR VERB: *See the verb table in the centre of the dictionary*

● **to heat something up** etwas
aufwärmen SEP; **I'm heating the
sauce up** ich wärme die Soße auf.

heater noun Heizgerät das (PL die
Heizgeräte).

heather noun Heidekraut das.

heating noun Heizung die.

heatwave noun Hitzewelle die (PL
die Hitzewellen).

heaven noun Himmel der.

heavy adjective **1** schwer; **my
rucksack's really heavy** mein
Rucksack ist sehr schwer; **2** (busy)
I've got a heavy day tomorrow ich
habe morgen viel zu tun; **3** (in
quantity) stark; **heavy rain** starker
Regen.

hectic adjective hektisch; **a hectic
day** ein hektischer Tag.

hedge noun Hecke die (PL die
Hecken).

hedgehog noun Igel der (PL die
Igel).

heel noun **1** (of foot or sock)
Ferse die (PL die Fersen); **2** (of a shoe)
Absatz der (PL die Absätze).

height noun **1** (of a person)
Größe die; **what height are you?**
wie groß bist du?; **2** (of a building,
mountain) Höhe die; **what height
is it?** wie hoch ist es?

helicopter noun
Hubschrauber der (PL die
Hubschrauber).

hell noun Hölle die; **hell!**
verdammt! (informal).

hello exclamation **1** (polite) guten
Tag!; **2** (informal, and on the phone)
hallo!

helmet noun Helm der (PL die
Helme).

help noun Hilfe die; **do you need
any help?** kann ich dir helfen?; (in
a shop) kann ich Ihnen behilflich
sein?
verb **1** helfen ✧ (+DAT); **to help
somebody (to) do something**
jemandem helfen, etwas zu tun; **can
you help me lay the table?** kannst
du mir helfen, den Tisch zu decken?;
2 to help yourself to something
sich ←(DAT) etwas nehmen ✧; **help
yourself to vegetables** nimm dir
Gemüse; **help yourself!** greif zu!;
3 help! Hilfe!; **4** he can't help it
er kann nichts dafür.

helpful adjective (person)
hilfsbereit.

hen noun Henne die (PL die
Hennen).

her pronoun (in German this
pronoun changes according to the
function it has in the sentence or the
preposition it follows) **1** (as a direct
object in the accusative) sie; **I know
her** ich kenne sie; **I saw her last
week** ich habe sie letzte Woche
gesehen; **2** (after prepositions +ACC)
sie; **without her** ohne sie; **we've
heard a lot about her** wir haben
viel über sie gehört; **3** (as an indirect
object or after verbs that take the
dative) ihr; **I gave her my address**
ich habe ihr meine Adresse gegeben;
we helped her wir haben ihr

geholfen; 4 (after prepositions +DAT) ihr; **with her** mit ihr; 5 (in comparisons) sie; **he's older than her** er ist älter als sie; 6 (in the nominative) sie; **it was her** sie war es.

adjective 1 (before a masculine noun) ihr; **her brother** ihr Bruder; 2 (before a feminine noun) ihre; **her sister** ihre Schwester; 3 (before a neuter noun) ihr; **her house** ihr Haus; 4 (before a plural noun) ihre; **her children** ihre Kinder; 5 (with parts of the body) der/die/das, die (plural); **she had a glass in her hand** sie hatte ein Glas in der Hand; **she's washing her hands** sie wäscht sich die Hände.

herb noun Kraut das (PL die Kräuter).

here adverb 1 (in or at this place) hier; **not far from here** nicht weit von hier; **here's my address** hier ist meine Adresse; **I want to stay here** ich möchte hier bleiben; 2 (to this place) hierher; **when Peter came here** als Peter hierher kam; 3 **here they are!** da sind sie!; **Tom isn't here at the moment** Tom ist im Moment nicht da.

hero noun Held der (PL die Helden).

heroin noun Heroin das.

heroine noun Heldin die (PL die Heldinnen).

herring noun Hering der (PL die Heringe).

hers pronoun 1 (for a masculine noun) ihrer; **my coat is blue and hers is red** mein Mantel ist blau und

ihrer ist rot; **I took my hat and she took hers** ich nahm meinen Hut und sie nahm ihren; 2 (for a feminine noun) ihre; **I gave Ann my address and she gave me hers** ich habe Ann meine Adresse gegeben und sie hat mir ihre gegeben; 3 (for a neuter noun) ihr(es); **my bike is new but hers is old** mein Rad ist neu, aber ihrs ist alt; 4 (for masculine/ feminine/neuter plural nouns) ihre; **I showed Emma my photos and she showed me hers** ich habe Emma meine Fotos gezeigt und sie hat mir ihre gezeigt; 5 **the CDs are hers** die CDs gehören ihr; **it's hers** das gehört ihr.

herself pronoun 1 (reflexive) sich; **she's hurt herself** sie hat sich wehgetan; 2 (stressing something) selbst; **she said it herself** sie hat es selbst gesagt; 3 **she did it by herself** sie hat es ganz allein gemacht.

hesitate verb zögern.

heterosexual adjective heterosexuell.
noun Heterosexuelle der/die (PL die Heterosexuellen).

hi exclamation hallo!

hiccups plural noun **to have the hiccups** einen Schluckauf haben.

hidden adjective verborgen.

hide verb 1 sich verstecken; **she hid behind the door** sie hat sich hinter der Tür versteckt; 2 **to hide something** etwas verstecken.

hi-fi noun Hi-Fi-Anlage die (PL die Hi-Fi-Anlagen).

◇ IRREGULAR VERB: See the verb table in the centre of the dictionary

high *adjective* **1** hoch; **how high is the wall?** wie hoch ist die Mauer?; **the wall is two metres high** die Mauer ist zwei Meter hoch; **the shelf is too high** das Regal ist zu hoch; (*the adjective 'hoch' loses its c when it has an ending, becoming hoher/hohe/hohes*) **a high tower** ein hoher Turm; **a high wall** eine hohe Mauer; **at high speed** mit hoher Geschwindigkeit; **a high voice** eine hohe Stimme; **2 high winds** starker Wind.
adverb hoch.

high-heeled *adjective* hochhackig.

high jump *noun* Hochsprung *der*.

hijack *verb* **to hijack a plane** ein Flugzeug entführen.

hijacker *noun* Entführer *der* (PL die Entführer).

hike *noun* Wanderung *die* (PL die Wanderungen).

hilarious *adjective* lustig.

hill *noun* **1** (*large hill*) Berg *der* (PL die Berge); **you can see the hills** man kann die Berge sehen; **2** (*smaller*) Hügel *der* (PL die Hügel); **to walk up the hill** den Hügel hinaufgehen; **3** (*hillside*) Hang *der* (PL die Hänge); **the house on the hill** das Haus am Hang.

him *pronoun* (*in German this pronoun changes according to the function it has in the sentence or the preposition it follows*) **1** (*as a direct object in the accusative*) ihn; **I know him** ich kenne ihn; **I saw him last week** ich habe ihn letzte Woche gesehen; **2** (*after prepositions* +ACC) ihn; **he fought against him** er hat gegen ihn gekämpft; **without him** ohne ihn; **3** (*as an indirect object or after verbs that take the dative*) ihm; **I gave him my address** ich habe ihm meine Adresse gegeben; **you must help him** du musst ihm helfen; **4** (*after prepositions* +DAT) ihm; **with him** mit ihm; **5** (*in comparisons*) er; **she's older than him** sie ist älter als er; **6** (*in the nominative*) er; **it was him** er war es.

himself *pronoun* **1** (*reflexive*) sich; **he's hurt himself** er hat sich wehgetan; **2** (*stressing something*) selbst; **he said it himself** er hat es selbst gesagt; **3 he did it by himself** er hat es ganz allein gemacht.

Hindu *adjective* hinduistisch.

hip *noun* Hüfte *die* (PL die Hüften).

hippie *noun* Hippie *der* (PL die Hippies).

hire *noun* **1** Vermietung *die*; **car hire** die Autovermietung; **2 for hire** zu vermieten.
verb mieten.

his *adjective* **1** (*before a masculine noun*) sein; **his brother** sein Bruder; **2** (*before a feminine noun*) seine; **his sister** seine Schwester; **3** (*before a neuter noun*) sein; **his house** sein Haus; **4** (*before a plural noun*) seine; **his children** seine Kinder; **5** (*with parts of the body*) der/die/das, die (*plural*); **he had a glass in his hand** er hatte ein Glas in der Hand; **he's washing his hands** er wäscht sich ←(DAT) die Hände.

△ NEW SPELLING: See page xii

pronoun 1 (for a masculine noun)
seiner; **my hat is red and his is blue**
mein Hut ist rot und seiner ist blau;
2 (for a feminine noun) seine; **I gave
him my address and he gave me
his** ich habe ihm meine Adresse
gegeben und er hat mir seine
gegeben; **3** (for a neuter noun)
sein(e)s; **my book is new but his is
old** mein Buch ist neu, aber seins ist
alt; **4** (for masculine/feminine/
neuter plural nouns) seine; **I've
invited my parents and Steve's
invited his** ich habe meine Eltern
eingeladen und Steve hat seine
eingeladen; **5 the green car's his**
das grüne Auto gehört ihm; **it's his**
das gehört ihm.

history noun Geschichte die.

hit noun **1** (song) Hit der (PL die
Hits); **their latest hit** ihr neuester
Hit; **2** (success) Erfolg der (PL die
Erfolge); **the film is a huge hit** der
Film ist ein großer Erfolg.
verb **1** treffen ◇; **to hit the ball** den
Ball treffen; **2 to hit your head
on something** sich ←(DAT) den Kopf
an etwas ←(DAT) stoßen; **I hit my head
on the door** ich habe mir den Kopf
an der Tür gestoßen; **3** prallen gegen
(+ACC) (PERF sein); **the car hit a wall**
das Auto ist gegen eine Wand
geprallt; **4 to be hit by a car** von
einem Auto angefahren werden.

hitch noun Problem das (PL die
Probleme); **there's been a slight
hitch** ein kleines Problem ist
aufgetaucht.
verb **to hitch a lift** per Anhalter
fahren ◇ (PERF sein).

hitchhike verb per Anhalter
fahren ◇ (PERF sein); **we hitchhiked
to Heidelberg** wir sind per Anhalter
nach Heidelberg gefahren.

hitchhiker noun Anhalter der (PL
die Anhalter), Anhalterin die (PL die
Anhalterinnen).

HIV-negative adjective HIV-
negativ.

HIV-positive adjective HIV-positiv.

hobby noun Hobby das (PL die
Hobbys).

hockey noun Hockey das.

hockey stick noun
Hockeyschläger der (PL die
Hockeyschläger).

hold verb **1** halten ◇; **to hold
something in your hand** etwas in
der Hand halten; **can you hold the
torch?** kannst du die Taschenlampe
halten?; **2** (be able to contain)
fassen; **the jug holds a litre** der Krug
fasst einen Liter; **3 to hold a
meeting** eine Versammlung
abhalten ◇ SEP; **4 can you hold the
line, please?** bleiben Sie bitte am
Apparat; **5 hold on!** (wait) warten
Sie!; (on the phone) bleiben Sie am
Apparat.
● **to hold on to something** (to stop
yourself from falling) sich an etwas
←(DAT) festhalten ◇ SEP.
● **to hold somebody up** (delay)
jemanden aufhalten ◇ SEP; **I was
held up at the dentist's** ich bin beim
Zahnarzt aufgehalten worden.
● **to hold something up** (raise) etwas
hochhalten ◇ SEP.

hold-up noun **1** Verzögerung die (PL

die Verzögerungen); **2** (*traffic jam*) Stau der (PL die Staus); **3** (*robbery*) Überfall der (PL die Überfälle).

hole noun Loch das (PL die Löcher).

holiday noun **1** Ferien (*plural*), Urlaub der (PL die Urlaube) (*students, schoolchildren, and families usually have 'Ferien'; people in paid employment usually have 'Urlaub'*); **where are you going for your holiday?** wo fahrt ihr in den Ferien hin?; **have a good holiday!** schöne Ferien!, schönen Urlaub!; **to be away on holiday** auf Urlaub sein, in Ferien sein; **to go on holiday** in Urlaub fahren, in die Ferien fahren; **the school holidays** die Schulferien; **2** (*day off work*) freie Tag der (PL die freien Tage); **I'm taking two days' holiday next week** ich nehme mir nächste Woche zwei Tage frei; **3 public holiday** der Feiertag; **Monday's a holiday** Montag ist ein Feiertag.

Holland noun Holland das.

holy adjective heilig.

home noun **1 I was at home** ich war zu Hause; **to stay at home** zu Hause bleiben; **2 make yourself at home** mach es dir bequem.
adverb **1** (*to home*) nach Hause; **Susie's gone home** Susie ist nach Hause gegangen; **on my way home** auf dem Weg nach Hause; **to get home** nach Hause kommen; **we got home at midnight** wir sind um Mitternacht nach Hause gekommen; **2** (*at home*) zu Hause; **I'll be home in the afternoon** ich bin am Nachmittag zu Hause.

homeless adjective obdachlos; **the homeless** die Obdachlosen.

homemade adjective selbst gemacht △; **homemade biscuits** selbst gebackene Kekse.

homeopathic adjective homöopathisch.

homesick adjective **to be homesick** Heimweh haben.

homework noun Hausaufgaben (*plural*); **I did my homework** ich habe meine Hausaufgaben gemacht; **my German homework** meine Deutschhausaufgaben.

homosexual adjective homosexuell.
noun Homosexuelle der/die (PL die Homosexuellen).

honest adjective ehrlich.

honestly adverb ehrlich.

honesty noun Ehrlichkeit die.

honey noun Honig der (PL die Honige).

hood noun **1** Kapuze die (PL die Kapuzen); **2** (*on a car*) Verdeck das (PL die Verdecke).

hook noun **1** Haken der (PL die Haken); **2 to take the phone off the hook** das Telefon aushängen SEP.

hooligan noun Hooligan der (PL die Hooligans).

hooray exclamation hurra!

hoover verb saugen; **I hoovered my bedroom** ich habe mein Schlafzimmer gesaugt.

△ NEW SPELLING: *See page xii*

Hoover™ noun Staubsauger der (PL die Staubsauger).

hope noun Hoffnung die (PL die Hoffnungen); **to give up hope** die Hoffnung aufgeben.
verb 1 hoffen; **we hope you'll be able to come** wir hoffen, ihr könnt kommen; **I'm hoping to see you on Friday** ich hoffe, dich am Freitag zu sehen; 2 **I hope so** hoffentlich; **I hope not** hoffentlich nicht.

hopefully adverb hoffentlich; **hopefully, the film won't have started** hoffentlich hat der Film noch nicht angefangen.

hopeless adjective miserabel (informal); **I'm hopeless at geography** ich bin miserabel in Erdkunde.

horn noun 1 (of an animal, instrument) Horn das (PL die Hörner); 2 (of a car) Hupe die (PL die Hupen).

horoscope noun Horoskop das (PL die Horoskope).

horrible adjective 1 furchtbar; **the weather was horrible** das Wetter war furchtbar; 2 (person) gemein; **she's really horrible** sie ist richtig gemein; **he was really horrible to me** er war richtig gemein zu mir.

horror noun Entsetzen das.

horror film noun Horrorfilm der (PL die Horrorfilme).

horse noun Pferd das (PL die Pferde).

hospital noun Krankenhaus das (PL die Krankenhäuser); **in hospital** im Krankenhaus; **to be taken into hospital** ins Krankenhaus kommen.

hospitality noun Gastfreundschaft die.

host noun 1 Gastgeber der (PL die Gastgeber); 2 (on a TV programme) Moderator der (PL die Moderatoren).

hostage noun Geisel die (PL die Geiseln).

hostel noun youth hostel die Jugendherberge.

hostess noun 1 Gastgeberin die (PL die Gastgeberinnen); 2 (on a TV programme) Moderatorin die (PL die Moderatorinnen); 3 air hostess die Stewardess.

hot adjective 1 heiß; **be careful, the plates are hot** sei vorsichtig, die Teller sind heiß; **it's hot today** heute ist es heiß; 2 (person) **I'm very hot** mir ist sehr heiß; 3 (spicy) scharf; **the curry's too hot for me** das Curry ist mir zu scharf; 4 **a hot meal** ein warmes Essen.

hotel noun Hotel das (PL die Hotels).

hour noun Stunde die (PL die Stunden); **two hours later** zwei Stunden später; **we waited for two hours** wir haben zwei Stunden lang gewartet; **I've been waiting for hours** ich warte schon seit Stunden; **two hours ago** vor zwei Stunden; **to be paid by the hour** pro Stunde bezahlt werden; **every hour** jede Stunde; **half an hour** eine halbe Stunde; **a quarter of an hour** eine Viertelstunde; **an hour and a half** anderthalb Stunden.

house noun 1 Haus das (PL die

◇ IRREGULAR VERB: See the verb table in the centre of the dictionary

Häuser); **2 at somebody's house**
bei jemandem; **I'm at Judy's house**
ich bin bei Judy; **I'm going to Sid's
house tonight** ich gehe heute Abend
zu Sid; **I phoned from Jill's house**
ich habe von Jill angerufen.

housewife noun Hausfrau die (PL
die Hausfrauen).

housework noun Hausarbeit die;
he does the housework er macht
den Haushalt (informal).

hovercraft noun
Luftkissenfahrzeug das (PL die
Luftkissenfahrzeuge).

how adverb **1** wie; **how did you do
it?** wie hast du das gemacht?; **how
are you?** wie geht es dir?; **how
many?** wie viele?; **how many
brothers do you have?** wie viele
Brüder hast du?; **how old are you?**
wie alt bist du?; **how far is it?** wie
weit ist es?; **how far is it to York?**
wie weit ist es bis York?; **how long
will it take?** wie lange dauert es?;
how long have you known her? wie
lange kennst du sie?; **2 how much?**
wie viel?; **how much money do you
have?** wie viel Geld hast du?; **how
much is it?** wie viel kostet das?

however adverb **1** jedoch; **2** (in
questions) however did she do it?
wie hat sie das nur gemacht?;
3 however famous he is wie
berühmt er auch sein mag.

hug noun **to give somebody a hug**
jemanden umarmen; **she gave me
a hug** sie hat mich umarmt.

huge adjective riesig.

hum verb summen.

human adjective menschlich.

human being noun Mensch der
(PL die Menschen).

humour noun Humor der; **to have
a sense of humour** Humor haben.

hundred number hundert; **two
hundred** zweihundert; **two
hundred and ten** zweihundertzehn;
a hundred people hundert
Menschen; **about a hundred** um die
hundert; **hundreds of people**
hunderte von Menschen.

Hungary noun Ungarn das.

hunger noun Hunger der.

hungry adjective **to be hungry**
Hunger haben; **I'm hungry** ich habe
Hunger.

hunting noun Jagd die; **fox-
hunting** die Fuchsjagd.

hurry noun **to be in a hurry** es eilig
haben; **I'm in a hurry** ich habe es
eilig; **there's no hurry** es eilt nicht.
verb **1** sich beeilen; **I must hurry** ich
muss mich beeilen; **hurry up!** beeil
dich!; **2 he hurried home** er ging
schnell nach Hause.

hurt verb **1 to hurt somebody**
jemandem wehtun ◇ SEP; **you're
hurting me!** du tust mir weh!; **that
hurts!** das tut weh!; **2 my arm
hurts** der Arm tut mir weh; **3 to hurt
yourself** sich ~(DAT) wehtun ◇ SEP;
did you hurt yourself? hast du dir
wehgetan?
adjective **1** (in an accident) verletzt;
three people were hurt drei
Menschen wurden verletzt; **2** (in

feelings) gekränkt; **she felt hurt** sie fühlte sich gekränkt.

husband *noun* Ehemann *der* (PL *die* Ehemänner).

hymn *noun* Kirchenlied *das* (PL *die* Kirchenlieder).

hypermarket *noun* Großmarkt *der* (PL *die* Großmärkte).

hyphen *noun* Bindestrich *der* (PL *die* Bindestriche).

I i

I *pronoun* ich; **I have two sisters** ich habe zwei Schwestern.

ice *noun* Eis *das*.

ice cream *noun* Eis *das*; **two chocolate ice creams** zwei Schokoladeneis.

ice hockey *noun* Eishockey *das*.

ice rink *noun* Eisbahn *die* (PL *die* Eisbahnen).

ice-skating *noun* **to go ice-skating** Schlittschuh laufen ✧ (PERF *sein*).

icy *adjective* 1 vereist (*road*); 2 (*very cold*) eiskalt.

idea *noun* 1 Idee *die* (PL *die* Ideen); **what a good idea!** was für eine gute Idee!; 2 **I've no idea** ich habe keine Ahnung.

ideal *adjective* ideal.

identical *adjective* identisch.

identification *noun* 1 Identifizierung *die*; 2 (*proof of identity*) Ausweispapiere (*plural*).

identity card *noun* Personalausweis *der* (PL *die* Personalausweise).

idiot *noun* Idiot *der* (PL *die* Idioten).

idiotic *adjective* idiotisch.

i.e. *abbreviation* d.h. (*das heißt*).

if *conjunction* 1 wenn; **if it rains** wenn es regnet; **if I won the lottery** wenn ich in der Lotterie gewinnen sollte; **if not** wenn nicht; **if only** wenn nur; **if only you'd told me** wenn du mir das nur gesagt hättest; 2 **even if** selbst wenn; **even if it snows** selbst wenn es schneit; 3 **if I were you** an deiner Stelle; **I wonder if he'll come** ich bin gespannt, ob er kommt; **as if** als ob.

ignore *verb* 1 ignorieren; 2 überhören (*what somebody says*).

ill *adjective* krank; **to fall ill, to be taken ill** krank werden; **I feel ill** ich fühle mich krank.

illegal *adjective* illegal.

illustration *noun* Illustration *die* (PL *die* Illustrationen).

image *noun* Bild *das* (PL *die* Bilder); ★ **he's the spitting image of his father** er ist das Ebenbild seines Vaters.

imagination *noun* Phantasie *die*.

imaginative *adjective* phantasievoll.

✧ **IRREGULAR VERB:** *See the verb table in the centre of the dictionary*

imagine *verb* sich ←(DAT) vorstellen; **imagine that you're very rich** stell dir vor, du bist sehr reich; **you can't imagine how hard it was** du kannst dir nicht vorstellen, wie schwer es war.

imitate *verb* nachahmen SEP.

immediate *adjective* 1 (*without delay*) unmittelbar; 2 **the immediate family** die engste Familie.

immediately *adverb* 1 sofort; **I rang them immediately** ich habe sie sofort angerufen; 2 **immediately before** unmittelbar davor; **immediately after** unmittelbar danach.

immigrant *noun* Einwanderer *der* (PL *die* Einwanderer), Einwanderin *die* (PL *die* Einwanderinnen).

immigration *noun* Einwanderung *die*.

impatience *noun* Ungeduld *die*.

impatient *adjective* 1 ungeduldig; 2 **to be impatient with somebody** ungeduldig mit jemandem sein.

impatiently *adverb* ungeduldig.

importance *noun* Wichtigkeit *die*.

important *adjective* wichtig.

impossible *adjective* unmöglich; **it's impossible to find a telephone** es ist unmöglich, ein Telefon zu finden.

impressed *adjective* beeindruckt; **to be impressed by something** von etwas ←(DAT) beeindruckt sein.

impressive *adjective* eindrucksvoll.

improve *verb* 1 **to improve something** etwas verbessern; 2 (*get better*) besser werden; **the weather is improving** das Wetter wird besser.

improvement *noun* Verbesserung *die* (PL *die* Verbesserungen).

in *preposition* 1 in (+DAT *or, with movement into*, +ACC); **it is in my pocket** es ist in meiner Tasche; (*with movement*) **he put it in his pocket** er hat es in die Tasche gesteckt; **she sat in the sun** sie saß in der Sonne; **I read it in the newspaper** ich habe es in der Zeitung gelesen; **in Oxford** in Oxford; **in Germany** in Deutschland; 2 **the biggest city in the world** die größte Stadt auf der Welt; **a house in the country** ein Haus auf dem Land; **in the street** auf der Straße; 3 (*wearing and with colours*) in (+DAT); **the girl in the pink shirt** das Mädchen im rosa Hemd; 4 **in German** auf Deutsch; 5 (*time expressions*) in (+DAT); **in May** im Mai; **in 1994** (im Jahre) 1994; **in winter** im Winter; **in summer** im Sommer; **in the night** in der Nacht; **I'll phone you in ten minutes** ich rufe dich in zehn Minuten an; **she was ready in five minutes** sie war in fünf Minuten fertig; 6 **in the morning** am Morgen; **at eight in the morning** um acht Uhr morgens; 7 (*among people or in literature*) bei (+DAT); **it's rare in children** das ist selten bei Kindern; **in Shakespeare** bei

△ NEW SPELLING: *See page xii*

Shakespeare; **in the army** beim
Militär; **8 in time** rechtzeitig.
adverb **1** (*inside*) hinein-, herein-,
rein- (*informal*); (Herein-, hinein-,
and rein- form prefixes to separable
verbs. 'Herein-' is used with verbs like
kommen, which have the sense of
moving towards the speaker. 'Hinein-'
is used with verbs like gehen, which
have the sense of going away from the
speaker. The informal 'rein-' can be
used with either movement.) **to
come in** hereinkommen ◇ SEP (PERF
sein); **to go in** hineingehen ◇ SEP
(PERF *sein*); **he was not allowed to
go into the room** er durfte nicht ins
Zimmer reingehen; **to run in**
reinlaufen ◇ SEP (PERF *sein*)
(*informal*); **2 to be in** da sein;
Mick's not in at the moment Mick
ist im Moment nicht da; **3** (*at home*)
zu Hause; **4** (*indoors*) drinnen; **in
here** hier drinnen; **in there** da
drinnen.

include *verb* einschließen ◇ SEP;
service is included in the price die
Bedienung ist im Preis inbegriffen.

including *preposition*
1 einschließlich (+GEN); **everyone,
including the children** alle,
einschließlich der Kinder; **£50
including postage** fünfzig Pfund
einschließlich Porto; **including
Sundays** einschließlich sonntags;
2 not including Sundays außer
sonntags.

income *noun* Einkommen *das* (PL
die Einkommen).

income tax *noun*
Einkommensteuer *die* (PL *die*
Einkommensteuern).

increase *noun* Erhöhung *die* (PL *die*
Erhöhungen) (*in price, for example*).
verb **1** steigen ◇ (PERF *sein*); **the
price has increased by £10** der
Preis ist um zehn Pfund gestiegen;
2 erhöhen (*salary*).

incredible *adjective* unglaublich.

incredibly *adverb* (*very*)
unwahrscheinlich; **the film's
incredibly boring** der Film ist
unwahrscheinlich langweilig.

indeed *adverb* **1** (*to emphasize*)
wirklich; **she's very pleased indeed**
sie hat sich wirklich sehr gefreut; **2**
(*certainly*) natürlich; **'can you
hear the radio?'** – **'indeed I can!'**
'kannst du das Radio hören?' – 'ja,
natürlich!'; **3 thank you very much
indeed** vielen herzlichen Dank.

indefinite article *noun*
unbestimmte Artikel *der*.

independence *noun*
Unabhängigkeit *die*.

independent *adjective*
unabhängig; **independent school**
die Privatschule.

India *noun* Indien *das*.

Indian *noun* **1** Inder *der* (PL *die*
Inder), Inderin *die* (PL *die*
Inderinnen); **2** (*a Native American*)
Indianer *der* (PL *die* Indianer),
Indianerin *die* (PL *die*
Indianerinnen).

◇ IRREGULAR VERB: *See the verb table in the centre of the dictionary*

adjective 1 indisch; **he's Indian** er ist Inder; 2 (*Native American*) indianisch; **she's Indian** sie ist Indianerin.

indicate *verb* 1 zeigen auf (+ACC) (*a person or a thing*); 2 (*of a car or driver*) blinken.

indigestion *noun* Magenverstimmung *die* (PL *die* Magenverstimmungen).

individual *noun* Einzelne △ *der/die* (PL *die* Einzelnen).
adjective 1 einzeln (*serving, contribution*); 2 **individual tuition** *der* Einzelunterricht.

indoor *adjective* **an indoor swimming pool** ein Hallenbad; **indoor games** Spiele im Haus; (*in sports*) Hallenspiele.

indoors *adverb* drinnen; **it's cooler indoors** drinnen ist es kühler; **to go indoors** ins Haus gehen.

industrial *adjective* industriell.

industrial estate *noun* Industriegebiet *das* (PL *die* Industriegebiete).

industry *noun* Industrie *die* (PL *die* Industrien); **the car industry** die Autoindustrie.

inevitable *adjective* unvermeidlich.

inevitably *adverb* zwangsläufig.

inexperienced *adjective* unerfahren.

infant school *noun* Vorschule *die* (PL *die* Vorschulen).

infection *noun* Infektion *die* (PL *die* Infektionen); **eye infection** *die* Augeninfektion; **throat infection** *die* Halsentzündung.

infectious *adjective* ansteckend.

infinitive *noun* Infinitiv *der* (PL *die* Infinitive).

inflammable *adjective* feuergefährlich.

inflatable *adjective* **inflatable mattress** *die* Luftmatratze; **inflatable boat** *das* Schlauchboot.

influence *noun* Einfluss △ *der* (PL *die* Einflüsse); **to be a good influence on somebody** einen guten Einfluss △ auf jemanden haben.
verb beeinflussen.

inform *verb* informieren; **to inform somebody of something** jemanden über etwas ←(ACC) informieren.

informal *adjective* 1 zwanglos (*meal or event*); 2 ungezwungen (*language, tone*).

information *noun* Auskunft *die*; **where can I get information about flights to Berlin?** wo kann ich Auskunft über Flüge nach Berlin bekommen?

information desk, information office *noun* Auskunftsbüro *das* (PL *die* Auskunftsbüros).

information technology *noun* Informatik *die*.

ingredient *noun* Zutat *die* (PL *die* Zutaten).

△ NEW SPELLING: *See page xii*

inhabitant *noun* Einwohner *der* (PL die Einwohner), Einwohnerin *die* (PL die Einwohnerinnen).

initials *plural noun* Initialen (*plural*).

injection *noun* Spritze *die* (PL die Spritzen).

injure *verb* verletzen.

injury *noun* Verletzung *die* (PL die Verletzungen).

ink *noun* Tinte *die* (PL die Tinten).

in-laws *noun* Schwiegereltern (*plural*).

innocent *adjective* unschuldig.

insane *adjective* **1** geisteskrank; **2** (*foolish*) wahnsinnig.

insect *noun* Insekt *das* (PL die Insekten); **insect bite** *der* Insektenstich.

insect repellent *noun* Insektenvertilgungsmittel *das*.

inside *noun* **on the inside** innen; **the inside of the oven is black** innen ist der Herd schwarz. *preposition* in (+DAT, *or, with movement towards a place*, +ACC); **inside the cinema** im Kino, **to go inside (the house)** ins Haus gehen. *adverb* drinnen; **she's inside, I think** ich glaube, sie ist drinnen.

inside out *adjective, adverb* (*clothing*) links.

insist *verb* darauf bestehen ◊; **if you insist** wenn du darauf bestehst; **to insist on doing something** darauf bestehen, etwas zu tun; **he insists**

on paying er besteht darauf zu zahlen; **to insist that ...** darauf bestehen, dass ...; **Ruth insisted I was wrong** Ruth hat darauf bestanden, dass ich Unrecht hatte.

inspector *noun* **1** (*on a bus or train*) Kontrolleur *der* (PL die Kontrolleure), Kontrolleurin *die* (PL die Kontrolleurinnen); **2** (*in the police*) Kommissar *der* (PL die Kommissare), Kommissarin *die* (PL die Kommissarinnen).

install *verb* installieren.

instalment *noun* (*of a story or serial*) Folge *die* (PL die Folgen).

instance *noun* **for instance** zum Beispiel.

instant *noun* Augenblick *der* (PL die Augenblicke); **come here this instant!** komm sofort her! *adjective* **1** Instant- (*coffee, tea*); **2** (*immediate*) sofortig.

instantly *adverb* sofort.

instead *adverb* **1** **Ted couldn't come, so I came instead (of him)** Ted konnte nicht kommen, also bin ich an seiner Stelle gekommen; **2 instead of** statt (+GEN *or* +DAT); **he bought a bike instead of a car** er hat ein Fahrrad statt eines Autos gekauft; **instead of cake I had cheese** statt Kuchen habe ich Käse genommen; **instead of playing tennis we went swimming** statt Tennis zu spielen, sind wir schwimmen gegangen.

instinct *noun* Instinkt *der* (PL die Instinkte).

◊ IRREGULAR VERB: *See the verb table in the centre of the dictionary*

institute *noun* Institut *das* (PL *die* Institute).

instructions *plural noun* Anweisung *die* (PL *die* Anweisungen); **follow the instructions on the packet** befolgen Sie die Anweisung auf der Packung; '**instructions for use**' 'Gebrauchsanweisung'.

instructor *noun* Lehrer *der* (PL *die* Lehrer), Lehrerin *die* (PL *die* Lehrerinnen); **my skiing instructor** mein Skilehrer.

instrument *noun* Instrument *das* (PL *die* Instrumente); **to play an instrument** ein Instrument spielen.

insulin *noun* Insulin *das*.

insult *noun* Beleidigung *die* (PL *die* Beleidigungen).
verb beleidigen.

insurance *noun* Versicherung *die* (PL *die* Versicherungen); **travel insurance** die Reiseversicherung.

intelligence *noun* Intelligenz *die*.

intelligent *adjective* intelligent.

intend *verb* beabsichtigen; **as I intended** wie beabsichtigt; **to intend to do something** beabsichtigen, etwas zu tun; **we intend to spend the night in Rome** wir beabsichtigen, in Rom zu übernachten.

intention *noun* Absicht *die* (PL *die* Absichten); **I have no intention of paying** ich habe nicht die Absicht zu zahlen.

interest *noun* 1 Interesse *das* (PL *die* Interessen); **to have lots of interests** viele Interessen haben; **he has an interest in jazz** er hat Interesse an Jazz; 2 (*financial*) Zinsen (*plural*).
verb interessieren; **that doesn't interest me** das interessiert mich nicht.

interested *adjective* **to be interested in something** sich für etwas ←(ACC) interessieren; **Sean's interested in cooking** Sean interessiert sich für Kochen.

interesting *adjective* interessant.

interfere *verb* 1 **to interfere with something** (*to fiddle with it*) sich ←(DAT) an etwas ←(DAT) zu schaffen machen; **don't interfere with my computer!** mach dir nicht an meinem Computer zu schaffen!; 2 **to interfere in something** sich in etwas ←(ACC) einmischen SEP (*somebody else's affairs*).

interior designer *noun* Innenarchitekt *der* (PL *die* Innenarchitekten), Innenarchitektin *die* (PL *die* Innenarchitektinnen).

international *adjective* international.

Internet *noun* Internet *das*; **on the Internet** im Internet.

interpret *verb* (*act as an interpreter*) dolmetschen.

interpreter *noun* Dometscher *der* (PL *die* Dolmetscher), Dolmetscherin *die* (PL *die* Dometscherinnen).

interrupt *verb* unterbrechen ✧.

△ NEW SPELLING: **See page xii**

interruption noun
Unterbrechung die (PL die
Unterbrechungen).

interval noun (in a play or concert)
Pause die (PL die Pausen).

interview noun 1 (for a job)
Vorstellungsgespräch das (PL die
Vorstellungsgespräche); **to go for an
interview** sich vorstellen SEP; 2 (in
a newspaper, on TV, or radio)
Interview das (PL die Interviews).
verb interviewen (on TV, radio).

interviewer noun Interviewer der
(PL die Interviewer), Interviewerin
die (PL die Interviewerinnen).

into preposition 1 in (+ACC); **he's
gone into the garden** er ist in den
Garten gegangen; **I put the ball into
the bag** ich habe den Ball in die
Tasche getan; **we all got into the car**
wir sind alle ins Auto eingestiegen; **to
go into town** in die Stadt gehen; **to
get into bed** ins Bett gehen; **to
translate into German** ins Deutsche
übersetzen; **to change pounds into
marks** Pfund in Mark wechseln;
2 (against) gegen (+ACC); **he drove
into the wall** er ist gegen die Wand
gefahren; 3 **to be into jazz** auf Jazz
abfahren ◇ SEP (PERF sein)
(informal).

introduce verb vorstellen SEP; **she
introduced me to her brother** sie
hat mich ihrem Bruder vorgestellt;
she introduced her brother to me
sie hat mir ihren Bruder vorgestellt;
can I introduce you to my mother?
darf ich Sie meiner Mutter
vorstellen?

introduction noun (in a book)
Einleitung die (PL die Einleitungen).

invade verb einfallen ◇ SEP in (PERF
sein) (+ACC).

invalid noun Kranke der/die (PL die
Kranken).

invent verb erfinden ◇.

invention noun Erfindung die (PL
die Erfindungen).

inverted commas plural noun
Anführungszeichen (plural);
in inverted commas in
Anführungszeichen.

investigation noun
Untersuchung die (PL die
Untersuchungen); **an investigation
into the incident** eine
Untersuchung des Vorfalls.

invisible adjective unsichtbar.

invitation noun Einladung die (PL
die Einladungen); **an invitation to
dinner** eine Einladung zum
Abendessen.

invite verb einladen ◇ SEP; **Kirsty
invited me to lunch** Kirsty hat mich
zum Mittagessen eingeladen; **he's
invited me out on Tuesday** er hat
mich eingeladen, Dienstag mit ihm
auszugehen; **they invited us round**
sie haben uns zu sich eingeladen.

inviting adjective verlockend.

involve verb 1 erfordern; **it involves
a lot of time** es erfordert viel Zeit;
2 (include) beteiligen; **the game will
involve everybody** alle können sich
an dem Spiel beteiligen; **to be
involved in something** an etwas
←(DAT) beteiligt sein; **I am involved in
the new project** ich bin an dem

◇ IRREGULAR VERB: See the verb table in the centre of the dictionary

neuen Projekt beteiligt;
3 (*implicate*) verwickeln; **to get involved in something** in etwas ←(ACC) verwickelt werden; **two cars were involved in the accident** zwei Autos waren in den Unfall verwickelt; **4 to get involved with somebody** sich mit jemandem einlassen ◇ SEP

Iran *noun* Iran *der*.

Iraq *noun* Irak *der*.

Ireland *noun* Irland *das*; **the Republic of Ireland** die Republik Irland.

Irish *noun* **1** (*the language*) Irisch *das*; **2** (*the people*) **the Irish** die Iren.
adjective irisch; **he's Irish** er ist Ire; **she's Irish** sie ist Irin.

Irishman *noun* Ire *der* (PL die Iren).

Irish Sea *noun* Irische See *die*.

Irishwoman *noun* Irin *die* (PL die Irinnen).

iron *noun* **1** (*for clothes*) Bügeleisen *das* (PL die Bügeleisen); **2** (*the metal*) Eisen *das*.
verb bügeln.

ironing *noun* Bügeln *das*; **to do the ironing** bügeln.

ironing board *noun* Bügelbrett *das* (PL die Bügelbretter).

ironmonger's *noun* Haushaltswarengeschäft *das* (PL die Haushaltswarengeschäfte).

irregular *adjective* unregelmäßig.

irritable *adjective* reizbar.

irritate *verb* ärgern.

irritating *adjective* ärgerlich.

Islam *noun* Islam *der*.

Islamic *adjective* islamisch.

island *noun* Insel *die* (PL die Inseln).

isolated *adjective* **1** (*remote*) abgelegen; **2** (*single*) einzeln; **isolated cases** Einzelfälle.

Israel *noun* Israel *das*.

Israeli *noun* Israeli *der*/die (PL die Israelis).
adjective israelisch.

issue *noun* **1** (*something you discuss*) Frage *die* (PL die Fragen); **a political issue** eine politische Frage; **2** (*of a magazine*) Ausgabe *die* (PL die Ausgaben).
verb (*hand out*) ausgeben ◇ SEP.

it *pronoun* **1** (*as the subject*) er (*standing for a masculine noun*), sie (*standing for a feminine noun*), es (*standing for a neuter noun*); **'where's my key?'** – **'it's in the kitchen'** 'wo ist mein Schlüssel?' – 'er ist in der Küche'; **'where's my bag?'** – **'it's in the living-room'** 'wo ist meine Tasche?' – 'sie ist im Wohnzimmer'; **'how old is your car?'** – **'it's five years old'** 'wie alt ist dein Auto?' – 'es ist fünf Jahre alt'; **2** (*as the direct object, in the accusative*) ihn (*standing for a masculine noun*), sie (*standing for a feminine noun*), es (*standing for a neuter noun*); **'where's your umbrella?'** – **'I've lost it'** 'wo ist dein Regenschirm?' – 'ich habe ihn verloren'; **'have you seen my bag?'** –

'I saw it in the kitchen' 'hast du meine Tasche gesehen?' – 'ich habe sie in der Küche gesehen'; **'have you read his new book? – 'I've just bought it'** 'hast du sein neues Buch gelesen?' – 'ich habe es gerade gekauft'; **3 to it** ihm (*masculine*), ihr (*feminine*), ihm (*neuter*); **4 yes, it's true** ja, das stimmt; **it doesn't matter** das macht nichts; **5 who is it?** wer ist da?; **it's me** ich bins; **what is it?** was ist los?; **6 it's raining** es regnet; **it's Monday** es ist Montag; **it's two o'clock** es ist zwei Uhr; **7 of it** davon; **8 out of it** daraus.

Italian noun **1** (*the language*) Italienisch *das*; **2** (*person*) Italiener *der* (PL die Italiener), Italienerin *die* (PL die Italienerinnen). adjective **1** italienisch; **Italian food** die italienische Küche; **2 my Italian class** mein Italienischunterricht.

italics noun Kursivschrift *die*; **in italics** kursiv.

Italy noun Italien *das*.

itch verb **1 my back's itching** mein Rücken juckt; **2 this jumper itches** dieser Pullover kratzt.

item noun **1** Gegenstand *der* (PL die Gegenstände); **2** (*for sale in a shop*) Artikel *der* (PL die Artikel).

its adjective **1** sein (*for a masculine noun*), ihr (*for a feminine noun*), sein (*for a neuter noun*); **the dog has lost its collar** der Hund hat sein Halsband verloren; **the cat's in its basket** die Katze ist in ihrem Korb; **the horse is brown and its mane is black** das Pferd ist braun und seine

Mähne ist schwarz; **2** (*for a plural noun*) seine (*standing for a masculine noun*), ihre (*standing for a feminine noun*), seine (*standing for a neuter noun*); **its toys** seine Spielsachen, ihre Spielsachen.

itself pronoun **1** (*reflexive*) sich; **the cat's washing itself** die Katze wäscht sich; **2 he left the dog by itself** er hat den Hund allein gelassen.

ivy noun Efeu *der*.

J j

jack noun **1** (*in cards*) Bube *der* (PL die Buben); **the jack of clubs** der Kreuzbube; **2** (*for a car*) Wagenheber *der* (PL die Wagenheber).

jacket noun Jacke *die* (PL die Jacken).

jackpot noun Jackpot *der* (PL die Jackpots); **to win the jackpot** das große Los ziehen.

jam noun **1** Marmelade *die* (PL die Marmeladen); **raspberry jam** die Himbeermarmelade; **2 traffic jam** der Stau.

January noun Januar *der*; **in January** im Januar.

Japan noun Japan *das*.

Japanese noun **1** (*the language*) Japanisch *das*; **2** (*person*) Japaner *der* (PL die Japaner),

◊ IRREGULAR VERB: *See the verb table in the centre of the dictionary*

Japanerin die (PL die Japanerinnen); **the Japanese** die Japaner. adjective japanisch.

jar noun 1 (small) Glas das (PL die Gläser); **a jar of jam** ein Glas Marmelade; 2 (large) Topf der (PL die Töpfe).

javelin noun Speer der (PL die Speere).

jaw noun Kiefer der (PL die Kiefer).

jazz noun Jazz der.

jealous adjective eifersüchtig; **to be jealous of somebody** eifersüchtig auf jemanden sein.

jeans plural noun Jeans (plural); **my jeans** meine Jeans; **a pair of jeans** ein Paar Jeans.

jelly noun 1 Gelee das (PL die Gelees); 2 (dessert) Götterspeise die (PL die Götterspeisen).

jellyfish noun Qualle die (PL die Quallen).

jersey noun 1 (jumper) Pullover der (PL die Pullover); 2 (for football) Trikot das (PL die Trikots).

Jesus noun Jesus der; **Jesus Christ** Jesus Christus.

jet noun (a plane) Jet der (PL die Jets).

Jew noun Jude der (PL die Juden), Jüdin die (PL die Jüdinnen).

jewel noun Edelstein der (PL die Edelsteine).

jeweller noun Juwelier der (PL die Juweliere).

jeweller's noun Juweliergeschäft das.

jewellery noun Schmuck der.

Jewish adjective jüdisch.

jigsaw noun Puzzlespiel das (PL die Puzzlespiele).

job noun 1 (paid work) Stelle die (PL die Stellen), Job der (PL die Jobs) (informal); **a job as a secretary** eine Stelle als Sekretärin; 2 (a task) Arbeit die (PL die Arbeiten); **it's not an easy job** das ist keine leichte Arbeit; 3 **she made a good job of it** sie hat es gut gemacht.

jobless adjective ◇ arbeitslos.

jog verb joggen ◇ (PERF sein).

join verb 1 (become a member of) beitreten ◇ SEP (+DAT) (PERF sein); **I've joined the tennis club** ich bin dem Tennisklub beigetreten; 2 (to meet up with) treffen ◇; **I'll join you later** ich treffe euch später.

● **to join in** 1 mitmachen SEP; **Kylie never joins in** Kylie macht nie mit; 2 **to join in something** bei etwas ←(DAT) mitmachen SEP; **won't you join in the game?** willst du bei dem Spiel nicht mitmachen?

joint noun 1 (of meat) Braten der (PL die Braten); **a joint of beef** ein Rinderbraten; 2 (in your body) Gelenk das (PL die Gelenke).

joke noun Witz der (PL die Witze); **to tell a joke** einen Witz erzählen. verb Witze machen; **you must be joking!** du machst wohl Witze!

joker noun (in cards) Joker der (PL die Joker).

journalism noun
Journalismus der.

journalist noun Journalist der (PL
die Journalisten), Journalistin die (PL
die Journalistinnen); **Sean's a
journalist** Sean ist Journalist.

journey noun 1 (a long one)
Reise die (PL die Reisen); **on our
journey to Italy** auf unserer Reise
nach Italien; 2 (shorter; to work or
school) Fahrt die (PL die Fahrten);
bus journey die Busfahrt.

joy noun Freude die (PL die Freuden).

judge noun 1 (in court) Richter der
(PL die Richter); 2 (in sporting
events) Schiedsrichter der (PL die
Schiedsrichter); 3 (in a
competition) Preisrichter der (PL die
Preisrichter).
verb schätzen (time or distance).

judo noun Judo das; **he does judo**
er macht Judo.

jug noun Krug der (PL die Krüge).

juice noun Saft der; **two orange
juices please** zwei Orangensaft
bitte.

juicy adjective saftig.

jukebox noun Jukebox die (PL die
Jukeboxes).

July noun Juli der; **in July** im Juli.

jumble sale noun Basar der (PL die
Basare).

jump noun Sprung der (PL die
Sprünge); **parachute jump** der
Fallschirmsprung.
verb springen ♦ (PERF sein).

jumper noun Pullover der (PL die
Pullover).

June noun Juni der; **in June** im
Juni.

jungle noun Dschungel der.

junior adjective jünger; **junior
school** die Grundschule; **the
juniors** (at primary school) die
Grundschüler, die
Grundschülerinnen.

junk noun Trödel der.

junk food noun ungesunde
Essen das.

just adverb 1 (very recently) gerade;
to have just done something gerade
etwas getan haben; **Tom has just
arrived** Tom ist gerade
angekommen; 2 **to be just doing
something** gerade dabei sein, etwas
zu tun; **I'm just doing the food** ich
bin gerade dabei, Essen zu machen;
3 **just before midday** kurz vor
Mittag; **just after 4 o'clock** kurz
nach vier Uhr; 4 (only) nur; **just for
fun** nur zum Vergnügen; **he's just a
child** es ist doch nur ein Kind; **just
me and Justine are coming** nur ich
und Justine kommen; 5 **just a
minute!** einen Moment!; 6 **just
coming!** ich komme schon!;
7 (exactly) **just as** genauso wie;
he's got just as many friends
er hat genauso viele Freunde.

justice noun Gerechtigkeit die.

♦ **IRREGULAR VERB: See the verb table in the centre of the dictionary**

K k

kangaroo noun Känguru △ das (PL die Kängurus).

karate noun Karate das.

kebab noun Kebab der (PL die Kebabs).

keen adjective 1 (enthusiastic or committed) begeistert; **he's a keen photographer** er ist ein begeisterter Fotograf; **you don't seem too keen** du scheinst nicht gerade begeistert zu sein; 2 **to be keen on** mögen ◇; **I'm not keen on fish** ich mag Fisch nicht; 3 **to be keen on doing (or to do) something** etwas gerne tun.

keep verb 1 behalten ◇; **you can keep the book** du kannst das Buch behalten; **to keep a secret** ein Geheimnis für sich behalten; 2 **will you keep my seat?** können Sie meinen Platz freihalten?; 3 **to keep somebody waiting** jemanden warten lassen; 4 (store) aufbewahren SEP; **can I keep my watch in your desk?** kann ich meine Uhr in deinem Schreibtisch aufbewahren?; **where do you keep saucepans?** wo hast du die Töpfe?; 5 (not throw away) aufheben ◇ SEP; **I kept all his letters** ich habe alle seine Briefe aufgehoben; 6 **to keep on doing something** etwas weiter tun; **she kept on talking** sie hat weitergeredet; **keep straight on** weiter geradeaus gehen; 7 **to keep**

on doing something (time after time) dauernd etwas tun; **he keeps on ringing me up** er ruft mich dauernd an; 8 (maintain) halten ◇; **to keep the food warm** das Essen warm halten; **to keep a promise** ein Versprechen halten; 9 (stay) bleiben ◇ (PERF sein); **to keep calm** ruhig bleiben; **to keep out of the sun** im Schatten bleiben.

kerb noun Randstein der.

kettle noun Kessel der (PL die Kessel); **to put the kettle on** Wasser aufsetzen.

key noun 1 (for a lock) Schlüssel der (PL die Schlüssel); **bunch of keys** das Schlüsselbund; 2 (on a piano or keyboard) Taste die.

keyboard noun (for a computer) Tastatur die (PL die Tastaturen).

keyring noun Schlüsselring der (PL die Schlüsselringe).

kick noun 1 (from a person or a horse) Tritt der (PL die Tritte); **to give somebody a kick** jemandem einen Tritt geben; 2 (in football) Schuss △ der (PL die Schüsse); ★ **to get a kick out of doing something** etwas nur zum Spaß tun.
verb 1 **to kick somebody** jemandem einen Tritt geben; 2 **to kick the ball** den Ball schießen.
• **to kick off** anstoßen ◇ SEP.

kick-off noun Anstoß der.

kid noun (child) Kind das (PL die Kinder); **Dad's looking after the kids** Vati passt auf die Kinder auf.

kidnap verb entführen

△ NEW SPELLING: See page xii

kidney noun Niere die (PL die Nieren).

kill verb 1 töten (an animal); 2 (murder) umbringen ✧ SEP; he killed the girl er brachte das Mädchen um; 3 she was killed in a car accident sie kam bei einem Autounfall ums Leben.

killer noun Mörder der (PL die Mörder), Mörderin die (PL die Mörderinnen).

kilo noun Kilo das (PL die Kilo); a kilo of sugar ein Kilo Zucker; ten marks a kilo zehn Mark das Kilo.

kilogram noun Kilogramm das.

kilometre noun Kilometer der (PL die Kilometer).

kilt noun Kilt der (PL die Kilts).

kind noun 1 Art die (PL die Arten); this kind of book diese Art Buch; all kinds of people alle möglichen Leute; 2 (brand) Sorte die (PL die Sorten).
adjective nett; she was very kind to me sie war sehr nett zu mir.

kindness noun Freundlichkeit die.

king noun König der (PL die Könige); the king of hearts der Herzkönig.

kingdom noun Königreich das (PL die Königreiche); the United Kingdom das Vereinigte Königreich.

kipper noun Räucherhering der (PL die Räucherheringe).

kiss noun Kuss △ der (PL die Küsse); to give somebody a kiss jemandem einen Kuss geben.
verb küssen; kiss me! küss mich!;

we kissed each other wir haben uns geküsst.

kit noun 1 (of tools) Werkzeug das; 2 (in a box) a tool kit ein Werkzeugkasten; 3 (clothes) Sachen (plural); where's my football kit? wo sind meine Fußballsachen?; 4 (for making a model, a piece of furniture, etc.) Bausatz der (PL die Bausätze).

kitchen noun Küche die (PL die Küchen); the kitchen table der Küchentisch.

kitchen foil noun Alufolie die.

kitchen roll noun Küchenrolle die (PL die Küchenrollen).

kite noun Drachen der; to fly a kite einen Drachen steigen lassen.

kitten noun Kätzchen das (PL die Kätzchen).

kiwi fruit noun Kiwi die (PL die Kiwis).

knee noun Knie das (PL die Knie); on (your) hands and knees auf allen vieren.

kneel verb knien; to kneel (down) sich hinknien SEP.

knickers plural noun Schlüpfer der (PL die Schlüpfer); two pairs of knickers zwei Schlüpfer.

knife noun Messer das (PL die Messer).
verb einstechen ✧ SEP auf (+ACC); (kill) erstechen ✧.

knight noun (in chess) Springer der (PL die Springer).

knit verb stricken.

✧ IRREGULAR VERB: See the verb table in the centre of the dictionary

knitting noun Strickerei die.

knob noun 1 (on a door or walking stick) Knauf der (PL die Knäufe); 2 (control on a radio or machine) Knopf der (PL die Knöpfe); 3 knob of butter das Butterklümpchen.

knock noun Schlag der (PL die Schläge); a knock on the head ein Schlag auf den Kopf; a knock at the door ein Klopfen an der Tür. verb 1 (to bang) stoßen ◇; I knocked my arm on the table ich habe mir den Arm am Tisch gestoßen; 2 to knock on something an etwas ←(ACC) klopfen.

● to knock down 1 (in a traffic accident) anfahren ◇ SEP (a person); 2 (to demolish) abreißen ◇ SEP (an old building).

● to knock out 1 (to make unconscious) bewusstlos △ schlagen ◇; 2 (in sport, to eliminate) k.o. schlagen ◇.

knot noun Knoten der (PL die Knoten); to tie a knot einen Knoten machen.

know verb 1 (know a fact) wissen ◇; do you know where Tim is? weißt du, wo Tim ist?; I know they've moved house ich weiß, dass sie umgezogen sind; yes, I know ja, weiß ich; you never know! man kann nie wissen!; I know how to get to town ich weiß, wie man in die Stadt kommt; 2 (be personally acquainted with) kennen ◇; do you know the Jacksons? kennst du die Jacksons?; all the people I know alle Leute, die ich kenne; I don't know his mother ich kenne seine Mutter

nicht; 3 to know how to do something etwas tun können; Steve knows how to make potato salad Steve kann Kartoffelsalat machen; Liz knows how to mend it Liz kann es reparieren; 4 to know about Bescheid wissen über (+ACC) (items in the news); 5 to know about sich auskennen ◇ SEP mit (machines, cars, etc.); Lindy knows about computers Lindy kennt sich mit Computern aus; 6 to get to know somebody jemanden kennen lernen △.

knowledge noun Wissen das.

Koran noun Koran der.

kosher adjective koscher.

L l

lab noun Labor das (PL die Labors).

label noun Etikett das (PL die Etikette).

laboratory noun Labor das (PL die Labors).

lace noun 1 (for a shoe) Schnürsenkel der (PL die Schnürsenkel); to tie your laces sich ←(DAT) die Schnürsenkel binden; 2 (fabric or trimming) Spitze die.

ladder noun 1 (for climbing) Leiter die (PL die Leitern); 2 (in your tights) Laufmasche die (PL die Laufmaschen).

ladies noun (lavatory)
Damentoilette die (PL die
Damentoiletten); (on a sign)
'Ladies' 'Damen'.

lady noun Dame die (PL die Damen);
ladies and gentlemen meine
Damen und Herren.

lager noun helle Bier das (PL die
hellen Biere), Helle das (PL die
Hellen) (informal); **a lager, please**
ein Helles bitte.

laid-back adjective gelassen.

lake noun See der (PL die Seen); **Lake
Geneva** der Genfer See.

lamb noun Lamm das (PL die
Lämmer); **leg of lamb** die
Lammkeule.

lamp noun Lampe die (PL die
Lampen).

lamp-post noun
Laternenpfahl der (PL die
Laternenpfähle).

lampshade noun
Lampenschirm der (PL die
Lampenschirme).

land noun 1 (when at sea) Land das;
2 (property) Grundstück das; **piece
of land** das Grundstück.
verb 1 (plane, passenger) landen
(PERF sein); 2 (leave a ship) an Land
gehen.

landing noun 1 (between flights of
stairs) Treppenabsatz der (PL die
Treppenabsätze); (passage)
Treppenflur der; 2 (of a plane or
ship) Landung die (PL die
Landungen).

landlady noun 1 (of a house or
room) Vermieterin die (PL die

Vermieterinnen); 2 (of a pub)
Gastwirtin die (PL die
Gastwirtinnen).

landlord noun 1 (of a house or room)
Vermieter der (PL die Vermieter);
2 (of a pub) Gastwirt der (PL die
Gastwirte).

lane noun 1 (small road) Weg der
(PL die Wege); 2 (of a motorway)
Spur die (PL die Spuren).

language noun 1 (German, Italian,
etc.) Sprache die (PL die Sprachen);
foreign language die
Fremdsprache; (way of speaking)
Ausdrucksweise die; **bad language**
Kraftausdrücke (plural).

lap noun 1 Schoß der (PL die
Schöße); 2 (in races) Runde die (PL
die Runden).

laptop noun Laptop der (PL die
Laptops).

larder noun Speisekammer die (PL
die Speisekammern).

large adjective groß.

last adjective letzte/letzte/letztes;
last week letzte Woche; **for the last
time** zum letzten Mal; **last night**
gestern Nacht.
adverb 1 (in final position) als
Letzter/als Letzte/als Letztes; **Rob
arrived last** Rob kam als Letzter an;
2 **at last!** endlich!; 3 (most
recently) zuletzt; **I last saw him in
May** ich habe ihn zuletzt im Mai
gesehen.
verb dauern; **the film lasted two
hours** der Film dauerte zwei
Stunden.

⬦ **IRREGULAR VERB: See the verb table in the centre of the dictionary**

late *adjective, adverb* 1 spät; **I'm late** ich bin spät dran; **we were five minutes late** wir haben uns fünf Minuten verspätet; **they arrived late** sie sind zu spät angekommen; **to be late for something** zu spät zu etwas ←(DAT) kommen; **we were late for the party** wir kamen zu spät zur Party; 2 **to be late** (*of a bus or train*) Verspätung haben; **the train was an hour late** der Zug hatte eine Stunde Verspätung; 3 (*late in the day*) spät; **we got up late** wir sind spät aufgestanden; **the chemist is open late** die Apotheke hat bis spät auf; **late last night** gestern spät in der Nacht; **too late!** zu spät!

lately *adverb* in letzter Zeit.

later *adverb* später; **I'll explain later** ich erkläre es später; **see you later!** bis später!

latest *adjective* 1 neuester/neueste/ neuestes; **the latest news** die neuesten Nachrichten; 2 **at the latest** spätestens.

Latin *noun* Latein *das*.

laugh *noun* Lachen *das*; **to do something for a laugh** etwas aus Spaß machen.
verb 1 lachen; **everybody laughed** alle haben gelacht; **to laugh about something** über etwas ←(ACC) lachen; 2 **to laugh at somebody** jemanden auslachen SEP; **they'll only laugh at me** sie lachen mich bestimmt aus.

launderette *noun* Waschsalon *der* (PL *die* Waschsalons).

lavatory *noun* Toilette *die* (PL *die* Toiletten); **to go to the lavatory** auf die Toilette gehen.

lavender *noun* Lavendel *der*.

law *noun* 1 Gesetz *das* (PL *die* Gesetze); **to break the law** gegen das Gesetz verstoßen; 2 **it's against the law** das ist verboten; 3 (*subject of study*) Jura (*plural*).

lawn *noun* Rasen *der* (PL *die* Rasen).

lawnmower *noun* Rasenmäher *der* (PL *die* Rasenmäher).

lawyer *noun* Rechtsanwalt *der* (PL *die* Rechtsanwälte), Rechtsanwältin *die* (PL *die* Rechtsanwältinnen).

lay *verb* 1 (*put*) legen; **she laid the cards on the table** sie legte die Karten auf den Tisch; 2 **to lay the table** den Tisch decken.

lay-by *noun* Parkplatz *der* (PL *die* Parkplätze).

layer *noun* Schicht *die* (PL *die* Schichten).

lazy *adjective* faul.

lead¹ *noun* 1 (*when you are ahead*) Führung *die*; **to be in the lead** in Führung liegen; **Baxter's in the lead** Baxter liegt in Führung; **to take the lead** in Führung gehen; 2 (*electric*) Schnur *die* (PL *die* Schnüre); 3 (*for a dog*) Leine *die* (PL *die* Leinen); **on a lead** an der Leine; 4 (*role*) Hauptrolle *die* (PL *die* Hauptrollen); 5 (*an actor*) Hauptdarsteller *der* (PL *die* Hauptdarsteller), Hauptdarstellerin *die* (PL *die* Hauptdarstellerinnen).

△ NEW SPELLING: *See page xii*

verb **1** führen; **the path leads to the sea** der Weg führt zum Meer; **to lead by three points** mit drei Punkten führen; **2** to lead the way vorangehen ◇ SEP (PERF *sein*); **3** to lead to something zu etwas ←(DAT) führen (*an accident or problems, for example*).

lead² *noun* (*metal*) Blei *das*.

leader *noun* **1** (*of a political party*) Vorsitzende *der* (PL die Vorsitzenden); **2** (*of an expedition or group*) Leiter *der* (PL die Leiter), Leiterin *die* (PL die Leiterinnen); **3** (*in a competition*) Erste *der/die* (PL die Ersten); **4** (*of a gang*) Anführer *der* (PL die Anführer), Anführerin *die* (PL die Anführerinnen).

lead singer *noun* Leadsänger *der* (PL die Leadsänger), Leadsängerin *die* (PL die Leadsängerinnen).

leaf *noun* Blatt *das* (PL die Blätter).

leaflet *noun* **1** (*with instructions*) Merkblatt *das* (PL die Merkblätter); **2** (*for advertising*) Reklameblatt *das* (PL die Reklameblätter).

leak *noun* **1** (*in a roof, tent*) undichte Stelle *die* (PL die undichten Stellen); **2** gas leak *der* Gasausfluss Δ; **3** (*in a boat*) Leck *das* (PL die Lecks). *verb* (*of a bottle or a roof*) undicht sein.

lean *adjective* (*meat*) mager. *verb* **1** to lean on something sich an etwas ←(ACC) lehnen; **he leaned against the door** er hat sich gegen die Tür gelehnt; **2** sich lehnen; **she was leaning out of the window** sie

lehnte sich aus dem Fenster; **3** to lean forward sich vorbeugen SEP.

leap year *noun* Schaltjahr *das* (PL die Schaltjahre).

learn *verb* lernen; **to learn German** Deutsch lernen; **to learn (how) to drive** Auto fahren lernen.

learner *noun* Lerner *der* (PL die Lerner); **to be a fast learner** schnell lernen; **2** (*beginner*) Anfänger *der* (PL die Anfänger), Anfängerin *die* (PL die Anfängerinnen).

least *adjective, pronoun* **1** wenigster/wenigste/wenigstes; **to have least time** am wenigsten Zeit haben; **Tony has the least money** Tony hat das wenigste Geld; **2** (*the slightest*) geringster/ geringste/geringstes; **I haven't the least idea** ich habe nicht die geringste Ahnung. *adverb* **1** am wenigsten; **I like the blue shirt least** ich mag das blaue Hemd am wenigsten; **2** the least expensive hotel das billigste Hotel; **3** at least (*at a minimum*) mindestens; **at least twenty people** mindestens zwanzig Leute; **4** at least (*at any rate*) wenigstens; **she's a teacher, at least I think she is** sie ist Lehrerin, glaube ich wenigstens.

leather *noun* Leder *das*; **leather jacket** die Lederjacke.

leave *noun* Urlaub *der*; **three days' leave** drei Tage Urlaub. *verb* **1** (*go away*) gehen ◇ (PERF *sein*); (*by car*) fahren ◇ SEP (PERF *sein*); (*a train or bus*) abfahren ◇ SEP

◇ **IRREGULAR VERB:** *See the verb table in the centre of the dictionary*

(PERF *sein*); **they're leaving tomorrow evening** sie fahren morgen Abend; **we left at six** wir sind um sechs Uhr gegangen; **the train leaves Munich at ten** der Zug fährt um zehn Uhr von München ab; **2** (*go away from or go out of*) verlassen ◇; **I left the office at five** ich habe das Büro um fünf verlassen; **he left his wife** er hat seine Frau verlassen; **3** (*deposit or allow to remain in the same state*) lassen ◇; **you can leave your coats in the hall** Sie können Ihre Mäntel in der Diele lassen; **to leave the door open** die Tür offen lassen; **leave it until tomorrow** lass es bis morgen; **4** to **leave somebody something** jemandem etwas hinterlassen ◇ (*a message or money*); **he hasn't left a message** er hat keine Nachricht hinterlassen; **5** (*not do*) stehen lassen ◇ △; **leave the washing up** lass den Abwasch stehen; **6** (*forget*) vergessen ◇; **he left his umbrella on the train** er hat seinen Regenschirm im Zug vergessen; **7 be left** übrig sein (PERF *sein*); **there are two pancakes left** zwei Pfannkuchen sind noch übrig; **I don't have any money left** ich habe kein Geld mehr übrig; **we have ten minutes left** wir haben noch zehn Minuten Zeit.

lecture *noun* **1** (*at university*) Vorlesung *die* (PL *die* Vorlesungen); **2** (*public*) Vortrag *der* (PL *die* Vorträge).

leek *noun* Lauch *der*.

left *noun* **on the left** links; **to drive on the left** links fahren; **on my left**

links von mir.
adverb links; **turn left at the church** an der Kirche links abbiegen.
adjective linker/linke/linkes; **his left foot** sein linker Fuß.

left-hand *adjective* **the left-hand side** die linke Seite.

left-handed *adjective* linkshändig.

leg *noun* **1** Bein *das* (PL *die* Beine); **my left leg** mein linkes Bein; **to break your leg** sich ←(DAT) das Bein brechen; **2** (*in cooking*) Keule *die* (PL *die* Keulen); **leg of lamb** die Lammkeule; ★ **to pull somebody's leg** jemanden auf den Arm nehmen.

leggings *plural noun* Leggings (*plural*).

leisure *noun* Freizeit *die*; **in my leisure time** in meiner Freizeit.

lemon *noun* Zitrone *die* (PL *die* Zitronen).

lemonade *noun* Limonade *die* (PL *die* Limonaden).

lemon juice *noun* Zitronensaft *der* (PL *die* Zitronensäfte).

lend *verb* leihen ◇; **to lend something to somebody** jemandem etwas leihen; **I lent Judy my bike** ich habe Judy mein Rad geliehen; **will you lend it to me?** kannst du es mir leihen?

length *noun* Länge *die* (PL *die* Längen).

lens *noun* **1** (*in a camera*) Objektiv *das* (PL *die* Objektive); **2** (*in spectacles*) Brillenglas *das* (PL *die* Brillengläser); **3 contact lenses** Kontaktlinsen (*plural*).

△ NEW SPELLING: *See page xii*

Lent noun Fastenzeit die.

lentil noun Linse die (PL die Linsen).

less pronoun, adjective, adverb weniger ('weniger' never changes); **Ben eats less** Ben isst weniger; **less time** weniger Zeit; **less than** weniger als; **less than three hours** weniger als drei Stunden; **you spent less than me** du hast weniger als ich ausgegeben; **less and less** immer weniger.

lesson noun (class) Stunde die (PL die Stunden); **German lesson** die Deutschstunde; **driving lesson** die Fahrstunde.

let¹ verb 1 (allow) lassen ◇; **to let somebody do something** jemanden etwas tun lassen; **she lets me drive her car** sie lässt mich mit ihrem Auto fahren; **the police let us through** die Polizei hat uns durchgelassen; **let me in** lass mich herein; 2 (as a suggestion or a command) **let's go!** gehen wir!; **let's not talk about it** reden wir nicht mehr darüber; **let's eat out** essen wir im Restaurant.

- **to let off** 1 hochgehen lassen ◇ (fireworks); 2 (to excuse from) befreien von (+DAT) (homework).

let² verb (to rent out) vermieten; **'flat to let'** 'Wohnung zu vermieten'.

letter noun 1 Brief der (PL die Briefe); **a letter for you from Delia** ein Brief für dich von Delia; 2 (of the alphabet) Buchstabe der (PL die Buchstaben).

letter box noun Briefkasten der (PL die Briefkästen).

lettuce noun Salat der; **two lettuces** zwei Kopf Salat.

level noun Höhe die; **at eye level** in Augenhöhe. adjective 1 eben (ground or floor); 2 (horizontal) waagerecht (shelf); 3 (at the same height) auf gleicher Höhe; **to be level with the ground** auf gleicher Höhe mit dem Boden sein.

level crossing noun Bahnübergang der (PL die Bahnübergänge).

lever noun Hebel der (PL die Hebel).

liar noun Lügner der (PL die Lügner), Lügnerin die (PL die Lügnerinnen).

liberal adjective 1 tolerant; 2 (in politics) liberal; **the Liberal Democrats** die Liberaldemokraten.

Libra noun Waage die; **Sean's Libra** Sean ist Waage.

librarian noun Bibliothekar der (PL die Bibliothekare), Bibliothekarin die (PL die Bibliothekarinnen).

library noun Bibliothek die (PL die Bibliotheken); **public library** die öffentliche Bücherei.

licence noun 1 (for a TV) Genehmigung die (PL die Genehmigungen); 2 (driving licence) Führerschein der (PL die Führerscheine).

lick verb lecken.

lid noun Deckel der (PL die Deckel).

lie noun Lüge die (PL die Lügen); **to tell a lie (or lies)** lügen ◇. verb 1 (to be stretched out) liegen ◇;

◇ **IRREGULAR VERB: See the verb table in the centre of the dictionary**

he's lying on the sofa er liegt auf dem Sofa; **my coat lay on the bed** mein Mantel lag auf dem Bett; **2 to lie down** (*for a rest*) sich hinlegen SEP; **I'm going to lie down for a little** ich lege mich ein bisschen hin; **3** (*tell lies*) lügen ✧.

lie-in *noun* **to have a lie-in** ausschlafen ✧ SEP

life *noun* Leben *das* (PL die Leben); **all her life** ihr ganzes Leben lang; **full of life** voller Leben; **that's life!** so ist das Leben!

life-style *noun* Lebensstil *der* (PL die Lebensstile).

lift *noun* **1** Aufzug *der* (PL die Aufzüge); **let's take the lift** fahren wir mit dem Aufzug; **2** (*a ride*) **to give somebody a lift to the station** jemanden zum Bahnhof mitnehmen ✧ SEP; **Khaled's giving me a lift** Khaled nimmt mich mit; **would you like a lift?** möchtest du mitfahren?
verb hochheben ✧ SEP; **he lifted the box** er hob die Kiste hoch.

light *noun* **1** Licht *das*; **will you turn the light on?** kannst du das Licht anmachen?; **to turn off the light** das Licht ausmachen; **are your lights on?** hast du Licht an?; **2** (*in the street*) Straßenlampe *die* (PL die Straßenlampen); **3** (*a lamp*) Lampe *die* (PL die Lampen); **4 traffic lights** die Ampel (*singular*); **the lights are green** die Ampel ist grün; **5** (*for a cigarette*) **have you got a light?** hast du Feuer?
adjective **1** (*not dark*) hell; **a light blue dress** ein hellblaues Kleid; **it**

gets light at six es wird um sechs hell; **2** (*not heavy*) leicht; **a light coat** ein leichter Mantel; **a light breeze** eine leichte Brise.
verb **1** anzünden SEP (*the fire, a match, the gas*); **we lit a fire** wir zündeten ein Feuer an; **2 to light a cigarette** sich ←(DAT) eine Zigarette anzünden.

light bulb *noun* Glühbirne *die* (PL die Glühbirnen).

lighter *noun* Feuerzeug *das* (PL die Feuerzeuge).

lightning *noun* Blitz *der*; **flash of lightning** der Blitz; **to be struck by lightning** vom Blitz getroffen werden.

like¹ *preposition, conjunction* **1** wie; **like me** wie ich; **like a duck** wie eine Ente; **like I said** wie gesagt; **what's it like?** wie ist es?; **what was the weather like?** wie war das Wetter?; **2 like this/that** so; **3** ähnlich (+DAT); **to look like somebody** jemandem ähnlich sehen; **Cindy looks like her father** Cindy sieht ihrem Vater ähnlich.

like² *verb* **1** mögen ✧; **I like vegetables** ich mag Gemüse; **I don't like meat** ich mag Fleisch nicht; **I like Dürer best** ich mag Dürer am liebsten; **2 to like doing something** etwas gerne tun; **Mum likes reading** Mutti liest gerne; **3 I would like ...** ich möchte gerne ...; **would you like a coffee?** möchten Sie einen Kaffee?; **what would you like to eat?** was möchten Sie essen?; **yes, if you like** ja, wenn du willst; **4 I like**

△ NEW SPELLING: *See page xii*

the dress das Kleid gefällt mir; **how do you like it?** wie gefällt es dir?

likely *adjective* wahrscheinlich; **she's likely to phone** wahrscheinlich ruft sie an.

lime *noun* Kalk *der*.

limit *noun* Grenze *die* (PL *die* Grenzen); **speed limit** die Geschwindigkeitsbeschränkung.

limp *noun* **to have a limp** hinken.

line *noun* **1** Linie *die* (PL *die* Linien); **a straight line** eine gerade Linie; **to draw a line** eine Linie ziehen; **2** (*in writing*) Zeile *die* (PL *die* Zeilen); **six lines of text** sechs Zeilen Text; **3** (*railway*) Bahnlinie *die* (PL *die* Bahnlinien) (*from one place to another*); **on the line** (*the track*) auf der Strecke; **4** (*a queue of people or cars*) Schlange *die* (PL *die* Schlangen); **to stand in line** Schlange stehen; **5** (*telephone*) Leitung *die* (PL *die* Leitungen); **the line's bad** die Verbindung ist schlecht; **hold the line, please** bitte bleiben Sie am Apparat.
verb füttern (*a coat*).

linen *noun* Leinen *das*; **a linen jacket** eine Leinenjacke.

lining *noun* Futter *das* (PL *die* Futter).

link *noun* Verbindung *die* (PL *die* Verbindungen); **what's the link between the two?** was für eine Verbindung besteht zwischen den beiden?
verb verbinden ◊ (*two places*); **the two towns are linked by a railway line** die beiden Städte sind durch

eine Bahnlinie miteinander verbunden.

lion *noun* Löwe *der* (PL *die* Löwen).

lip *noun* Lippe *die* (PL *die* Lippen).

lip-read *verb* von den Lippen lesen ◊.

lipstick *noun* Lippenstift *der* (PL *die* Lippenstifte).

liquid *noun* Flüssigkeit *die* (PL *die* Flüssigkeiten).
adjective flüssig.

list *noun* Liste *die* (PL *die* Listen).

listen *verb* **1** zuhören SEP; **I wasn't listening** ich habe nicht zugehört; **to listen to somebody** jemandem zuhören; **you're not listening to me** du hörst mir nicht zu; **2 to listen to something** etwas ←(ACC) hören; **to listen to the radio** Radio hören.

listener *noun* (*to the radio*) Hörer *der* (PL *die* Hörer), Hörerin *die* (PL *die* Hörerinnen).

litre *noun* Liter *der* (PL *die* Liter); **a litre of milk** ein Liter Milch.

litter *noun* (*rubbish*) Abfall *der*.

litter bin *noun* Abfalleimer *der* (PL *die* Abfalleimer).

little *adjective, pronoun* **1** (*small*) klein; **a little boy** ein kleiner Junge; **a little break** eine kleine Pause; **2** (*not much*) wenig; **we have very little time** wir haben sehr wenig Zeit; **3 a little** ein wenig; **we have a little left** wir haben ein wenig übrig; **4 just a little, please** nur ein bisschen, bitte; **it's a little late** es ist ein bisschen spät;

◊ IRREGULAR VERB: *See the verb table in the centre of the dictionary*

a little more ein bisschen mehr; **a little less** ein bisschen weniger; ★ **little by little** nach und nach.

live[1] *verb* **1** (*in a house or town*) wohnen; **she lives in York** sie wohnt in York; **we live in a flat** wir wohnen in einer Wohnung; **2** (*be or stay alive, spend one's life*) leben; **we're living in the country now** wir leben jetzt auf dem Land; **they live on fruit** sie leben von Obst; **they live apart** sie leben getrennt.

live[2] *adjective, adverb* **1** live (*broadcast*); **a live programme** eine Livesendung; **live music** die Livemusik; **a broadcast live from Wembley** eine Übertragung live aus Wembley; **to broadcast a concert live** ein Konzert live senden; **2** (*alive*) lebend.

lively *adjective* lebhaft.

liver *noun* Leber die (PL die Lebern).

living *noun* Lebensunterhalt der; **to earn a living** sich ←(DAT) seinen Lebensunterhalt verdienen.

living room *noun* Wohnzimmer das (PL die Wohnzimmer).

load *noun* **1** (*on a lorry*) Ladung die (PL die Ladungen); **a (lorry-)load of bricks** eine Ladung Ziegelsteine; **2 a bus-load of tourists** ein Bus voll Touristen; **3 loads of** massenhaft (*informal*); **loads of tourists** massenhaft Touristen; **they've got loads of money** die haben einen Haufen Geld (*informal*).
verb **1** beladen ◇ (*a vehicle*);

2 to load a camera einen Film einlegen SEP.

loaf *noun* Brot das (PL die Brote); **a loaf of white bread** ein Weißbrot.

loathe *verb* hassen; **I loathe getting up early** ich hasse es, früh aufzustehen.

local *noun* **1** (*a pub*) Stammkneipe die (PL die Stammkneipen); **2 the locals** (*people*) die Einheimischen.
adjective **1** hiesig; **the local library** die hiesige Bücherei; **2 local newspaper** die Lokalzeitung.

lock *noun* Schloss △ das (PL die Schlösser).
verb abschließen ◇ SEP (*a door, room, or bicycle*); **have you locked the door?** hast du abgeschlossen?

lodger *noun* Untermieter der (PL die Untermieter), Untermieterin die (PL die Untermieterinnen).

loft *noun* Dachboden der (PL die Dachböden).

log *noun* **1** Baumstamm der (PL die Baumstämme); **2** (*as firewood*) Holzscheit das (PL die Holzscheite); **a log fire** ein offenes Feuer.

lollipop *noun* Lutscher der (PL die Lutscher).

London *noun* London das.

Londoner *noun* Londoner der (PL die Londoner), Londonerin die (PL die Londonerinnen).

lonely *adjective* einsam; **to feel lonely** sich einsam fühlen.

△ **NEW SPELLING: See page xii**

long *adjective, adverb* **1** lang; **a long film** ein langer Film; **a long day** ein langer Tag; **it's five metres long** es ist fünf Meter lang; **the film is an hour long** der Film dauert eine Stunde; **2 a long time** lange; **he stayed for a long time** er ist lange geblieben; **I've been here for a long time** ich bin schon lange hier; **a long time ago** vor langer Zeit; **this won't take long** das dauert nicht lange; **3 how long?** wie lange?; **how long have you been here?** wie lange sind Sie schon hier?; **long ago** vor langer Zeit; **4 a long way** weit; **it's a long way to the cinema** bis zum Kino ist es weit; **5 all night long** die ganze Nacht; **6 no longer** nicht mehr; **he doesn't work here any longer** er arbeitet nicht mehr hier.
verb **to long to do something** sich danach sehnen, etwas zu tun; **I'm longing to see you** ich sehne mich danach, dich zu sehen.

long jump *noun* Weitsprung *der*.

longlife milk *noun* H-Milch *die*.

loo *noun* Klo *das* (PL die Klos) (*informal*).

look *noun* **1** (*a glance*) Blick *der* (PL die Blicke); **to take a look at somebody** einen Blick auf jemanden werfen; **2** (*a tour*) **to have a look at the school** sich ←(DAT) die Schule ansehen; **to have a look round the town** sich ←(DAT) die Stadt ansehen; **3 to have a look for** suchen.
verb **1** sehen ◇; **to look out of the window** aus dem Fenster sehen; **I**

wasn't looking ich habe nicht hingesehen; **2 to look at** ansehen ◇ SEP; **he looked at the girl** er hat das Mädchen angesehen; **to look at something** sich ←(DAT) etwas ansehen; **I'm looking at the photos** ich sehe mir die Fotos an; **3** (*to seem*) aussehen ◇ SEP; **she looks sad** sie sieht traurig aus; **the salad looks delicious** der Salat sieht köstlich aus; **to look like** aussehen wie; **what does the house look like?** wie sieht das Haus aus?; **4** (*resemble*) **to look like somebody** jemandem ähnlich sehen; **she looks like her aunt** sie sieht ihrer Tante ähnlich; **they look like each other** sie sehen sich ähnlich.

● **to look after 1** sich kümmern um (+ACC); **Dad's looking after the children** Vati kümmert sich um die Kinder; **2** aufpassen SEP auf (+ACC) (*luggage*).

● **to look for** suchen; **I'm looking for my keys** ich suche meine Schlüssel.

● **to look forward to** sich freuen auf (+ACC) (*a party or a trip, for example*).

● **to look out** (*to be careful*) aufpassen SEP; **look out, it's hot!** pass auf, das ist heiß!

● **to look up** nachschlagen ◇ SEP (*in a dictionary or directory*); **he's looking it up in the dictionary** er schlägt es im Wörterbuch nach.

loose *adjective* **1** (*screw or knot*) locker; **2** (*garment*) weit; **3 loose change** das Kleingeld; ★ **I'm at a loose end** ich habe nichts zu tun.

lorry *noun* Lastwagen *der* (PL die Lastwagen).

◇ **IRREGULAR VERB: See the verb table in the centre of the dictionary**

lorry driver noun
Lastwagenfahrer der (PL die
Lastwagenfahrer).

lose verb 1 verlieren ◇; we lost wir
haben verloren; we lost the match
wir haben das Spiel verloren; Sam's
lost his watch Sam hat seine Uhr
verloren; 2 to get lost sich
verlaufen ◇; we got lost in the
woods wir haben uns im Wald
verlaufen; 3 to lose weight
abnehmen ◇ SEP.

loss noun Verlust der (PL die
Verluste).

lost property noun Fundsachen
(plural).

lot noun 1 a lot viel; Wilbur eats a
lot Wilbur isst viel; I spent a lot ich
habe viel ausgegeben; he's a lot
better es geht ihm viel besser; a lot
of viel; a lot of coffee viel Kaffee;
2 (many) a lot of viele; a lot of
books viele Bücher; 3 lots of eine
Menge (informal); lots of people
eine Menge Leute.

lottery noun Lotterie die (PL die
Lotterien); to win the lottery in der
Lotterie gewinnen.

loud adjective 1 laut; in a loud voice
mit lauter Stimme; 2 to say
something out loud etwas laut
sagen.

loudly adverb laut.

loudspeaker noun
Lautsprecher der (PL die
Lautsprecher).

lounge noun 1 (in a house)
Wohnzimmer das (PL die
Wohnzimmer); 2 (in a hotel or an
airport) Halle die (PL die Hallen);
departure lounge die Abflughalle.

love noun 1 Liebe die; for love aus
Liebe; 2 to be in love with
somebody in jemanden verliebt
sein; she's in love with Jake sie ist
in Jake verliebt; 3 Gina sends her
love Gina lässt grüßen; with love
from Charlie herzliche Grüße von
Charlie; 4 (in tennis) null.
verb 1 lieben (a person); I love you
ich liebe dich; 2 sehr gerne
mögen ◇ (a place or food); she loves
London sie mag London sehr gerne;
Wayne loves chocolate Wayne mag
Schokolade sehr gerne; 3 to love
doing something etwas sehr gerne
tun; I love dancing ich tanze sehr
gerne; 4 I'd love to come ich würde
sehr gerne kommen.

lovely adjective schön; a lovely
dress ein schönes Kleid; we had a
lovely weather wir hatten schönes
Wetter; we had a lovely day es war
sehr schön.

low adjective 1 niedrig; a low table
ein niedriger Tisch; at a low price
zu einem niedrigen Preis; 2 (not
loud) leise; in a low voice mit leiser
Stimme.

lower adjective (not as high) tiefer.
verb senken.

luck noun 1 Glück das; good luck!
viel Glück!; with a bit of luck wenn
wir Glück haben; 2 bad luck! so ein
Pech!

luckily adverb zum Glück; luckily
for them zu ihrem Glück.

△ NEW SPELLING: See page xii

lucky adjective 1 to be lucky Glück haben; we were lucky wir haben Glück gehabt; 2 to be lucky (bringing luck) Glück bringen; it's supposed to be lucky es soll Glück bringen; my lucky number meine Glückszahl.

luggage noun Gepäck das; my luggage is in the boot mein Gepäck ist im Kofferraum.

lump noun 1 Klumpen der (PL die Klumpen); 2 (of sugar or butter) Stück das (PL die Stücke).

lunch noun Mittagessen das (PL die Mittagessen); to have lunch zu Mittag essen; we had lunch in Oxford wir haben in Oxford zu Mittag gegessen.

lunch break noun Mittagspause die (PL die Mittagspausen).

lunch hour, lunch time noun Mittagszeit die.

lung noun Lungenflügel der; lungs die Lunge (singular).

luxurious adjective luxuriös.

lyrics plural noun Text der.

M m

mac noun Regenmantel der (PL die Regenmäntel).

macaroni noun Makkaroni (plural).

machine noun 1 Maschine die (PL die Maschinen); 2 (a slot machine) Automat der (PL die Automaten).

mackerel noun Makrele die (PL die Makrelen).

mad adjective 1 verrückt; she's completely mad! sie ist total verrückt!; 2 (angry) wütend; to be mad at somebody wütend auf jemanden sein; 3 to be mad about something ganz verrückt auf etwas ←(ACC) sein; she's mad about horses sie ist ganz verrückt auf Pferde.

madman noun Verrückte der (PL die Verrückten).

madness noun Wahnsinn der.

magazine noun 1 Zeitschrift die (PL die Zeitschriften); (with mostly photos) Magazin das (PL die Magazine).

magic noun Zauber der; (conjuring tricks) Zauberei die.
adjective 1 Zauber-; magic wand der Zauberstab; 2 (great) super (informal).

magician noun 1 (wizard) Zauberer der (PL die Zauberer); 2 (conjurer) Zauberkünstler der (PL die Zauberkünstler).

magnifying glass noun Lupe die (PL die Lupen).

maiden name noun Mädchenname der (PL die Mädchennamen).

mail noun Post die.

mail order noun Bestellung per Post die; to buy something by mail

◆ IRREGULAR VERB: See the verb table in the centre of the dictionary

order etwas bei einem Versandhaus bestellen; **mail order catalogue** der Versandhauskatalog.

main *adjective* Haupt-; **main entrance** der Haupteingang.

mainly *adverb* hauptsächlich.

main road *noun* Hauptstraße die (PL die Hauptstraßen).

major *adjective* 1 (*important*) groß; 2 (*serious*) schwer; **a major accident** ein schwerer Unfall.

Majorca *noun* Mallorca das.

majority *noun* Mehrheit die.

make *noun* Marke die (PL die Marken); **the make of a car** die Automarke.
verb 1 machen; **to make a meal** Essen machen; **I made breakfast** ich habe Frühstück gemacht; **she made her bed** sie hat ihr Bett gemacht; **to make somebody happy** jemanden glücklich machen; **it makes you tired** das macht einen müde; 2 herstellen SEP; **they make computers** sie stellen Computer her; **'made in Germany'** 'in Deutschland hergestellt'; 3 **he made me wait** er ließ mich warten; **she makes me laugh** sie bringt mich zum Lachen; 4 verdienen; **he makes forty pounds a day** er verdient vierzig Pfund pro Tag; **to make a living** seinen Lebensunterhalt verdienen; 5 (*force*) zwingen ◇; **to make somebody do something** jemanden zwingen, etwas zu tun; **she made him give the money back** sie hat ihn gezwungen, das

Geld zurückzugeben; 6 (*the verb 'make' is often translated by a more specific verb*) **to make a cake** einen Kuchen backen; **to make a phone call** telefonieren; **to make a dress** ein Kleid nähen; 7 **to make friends with somebody** sich mit jemandem anfreunden SEP; 8 **I can't make it tonight** ich kann heute Abend nicht kommen; 9 **two and three make five** zwei und drei ist fünf.
● **to make something up** 1 etwas erfinden ◇; **she made up an excuse** sie hat eine Ausrede erfunden; 2 **to make it up** (*after a quarrel*) sich versöhnen; **they've made it up again** sie haben sich wieder versöhnt.

make-up *noun* 1 Make-up das; **I don't wear make-up** ich trage kein Make-up; 2 **to put on your make-up** sich schminken; **Jo's putting on her make-up** Jo schminkt sich.

male *adjective* 1 männlich; **male voice** die Männerstimme; 2 **male animal** das Männchen; **male rat** das Rattenmännchen; 3 **male student** der Student.

male chauvinist *noun* Chauvi der (PL die Chauvis) (*informal*).

man *noun* 1 Mann der (PL die Männer); **an old man** ein alter Mann; 2 (*the human race*) der Mensch.

manage *verb* 1 leiten (*a business, team*); **she manages a travel agency** sie leitet ein Reisebüro; 2 (*cope*) zurechtkommen ◇ SEP (PERF *sein*); **I can manage** ich

△ NEW SPELLING: *See page xii*

komme schon zurecht; **3 to manage
to do something** es schaffen, etwas
zu tun; **he managed to push the
door open** er hat es geschafft, die
Tür aufzustoßen; **I didn't manage to
get in touch with her** ich habe es
nicht geschafft, sie zu erreichen.

management noun
1 Management das (PL die
Managements); **management
course** der Managementkurs;
2 Leitung die.

manager noun **1** (of a company or
bank) Direktor der (PL die
Direktoren); **2** (of a shop or
restaurant) Geschäftsführer der (PL
die Geschäftsführer); **3** (in football)
Trainer der (PL die Trainer); **4** (in
entertainment) Manager der (PL die
Manager).

manageress noun (of a shop or
restaurant) Geschäftsführerin die
(PL die Geschäftsführerinnen).

mania noun Manie die (PL die
Manien).

maniac noun Wahnsinnige der/die
(PL die Wahnsinnigen); **she drives
like a maniac** sie fährt wie eine
Wahnsinnige.

man-made adjective **man-made
fibre** die Kunstfaser.

manner noun **1 in a manner of
speaking** mehr oder weniger;
2 manners Manieren (plural); **to
have good manners** gute Manieren
haben; **it's bad manners to talk like
that** es gehört sich nicht, so zu reden.

mantelpiece noun Kaminsims der
(PL die Kaminsimse).

manual noun Handbuch das (PL die
Handbücher).

manufacture verb herstellen SEP.

manufacturer noun
Hersteller der (PL die Hersteller).

many adjective, pronoun **1** viele;
does she have many friends? hat
sie viele Freunde?; **we didn't see
many people** wir haben nicht viele
Leute gesehen; **not many** nicht
viele; **many of them forgot** viele
haben es vergessen; **there were too
many people** es waren zu viele
(Leute) da; **how many?** wie viele?;
how many were there? wie viele
waren da?; **how many sisters have
you got?** wie viele Schwestern hast
du?; **how many are there left?** wie
viele sind übrig geblieben?; **I've
never had so many presents** ich
habe noch nie so viele Geschenke
bekommen; **2** (a lot) **so many** so
viel; **I have so many things to do**
ich habe so viel zu tun; **3** (as much
as) **as many as** so viel wie; **take as
many as you like** nimm so viel wie
du willst; **4** (too much) **that's far too
many** das ist viel zu viel.

map noun **1** Karte die (PL die
Karten); **2** (of a town) Stadtplan (PL
die Stadtpläne).

marathon noun Marathonlauf der
(PL die Marathonläufe).

marble noun **1** Marmor der;
2 (for playing) Murmel die (PL die
Murmeln); **to play marbles**
Murmeln spielen.

March noun März der; **in March** im
März.

◇ IRREGULAR VERB: See the verb table in the centre of the dictionary

march noun Marsch der (PL die Märsche).
verb marschieren (PERF sein).

mare noun Stute die (PL die Stuten).

margarine noun Margarine die.

margin noun Rand der (PL die Ränder).

marijuana noun Marihuana das.

mark noun 1 (at school) Note die (PL die Noten); I got a good mark in German ich habe eine gute Note in Deutsch bekommen; 2 (stain) Fleck der (PL die Flecke); 3 (German money) Mark die (PL die Mark).
verb 1 korrigieren; the teacher marks our homework die Lehrerin korrigiert unsere Hausaufgaben; 2 (in sports) decken.

market noun Markt der (PL die Märkte).

marketing noun Marketing das.

marmalade noun Orangenmarmelade die.

maroon adjective kastanienbraun.

marriage noun 1 Ehe die; 2 (wedding) Hochzeit die (PL die Hochzeiten).

married adjective 1 verheiratet; they've been married for twenty years sie sind seit zwanzig Jahren verheiratet; 2 married couple das Ehepaar.

marry verb 1 to marry somebody jemanden heiraten; she married a Frenchman sie hat einen Franzosen geheiratet; 2 to get married

heiraten; they got married in July sie haben im Juli geheiratet.

marvellous adjective wunderbar.

marzipan noun Marzipan das.

mascara noun Wimperntusche die.

masculine noun (in German and other grammars) männlich.

mash verb stampfen.

mashed potatoes plural noun Kartoffelbrei der (singular).

mask noun Maske die (PL die Masken).

mass noun 1 a mass of eine Menge; 2 masses of massenhaft (informal); they've got masses of money sie haben massenhaft Geld; there's masses left over es ist massenhaft übrig geblieben; 3 (religious) Messe die (PL die Messen); to go to mass zur Messe gehen.

massage noun Massage die (PL die Massagen).

massive adjective riesig.

master verb 1 meistern; 2 to master a language eine Sprache beherrschen.

mat noun 1 (doormat) Matte die (PL die Matten); 2 (to put under a hot dish) Untersetzer der (PL die Untersetzer); 3 table mat das Platzdeckchen.

match noun 1 (for lighting) Streichholz das (PL die Streichhölzer); box of matches die Streichholzschachtel; 2 (in sports)

Spiel das (PL die Spiele); **football match** das Fußballspiel; **to watch the match** das Spiel sehen; **to win the match** das Spiel gewinnen; **to lose the match** das Spiel verlieren; *verb* passen zu (+DAT); **the jacket matches the skirt** die Jacke passt zu dem Rock.

mate *noun* Freund der (PL die Freunde); **I'm going to the pub with my mates** ich gehe mit meinen Freunden in die Kneipe.

material *noun* **1** *(fabric, also information)* Stoff der (PL die Stoffe); **2** *(substance)* Material das (PL die Materialien).

mathematics *noun* Mathematik die.

maths *noun* Mathe *(informal)*; **I like maths** ich mag Mathe gerne; **Anna's good at maths** Anna ist gut in Mathe.

matter *noun* **what's the matter?** was ist los?
verb **1 that's what matters most** das ist am wichtigsten; **it matters a lot to me** es ist mir sehr wichtig; **does it really matter?** ist das wirklich so wichtig?; **2 it doesn't matter** es macht nichts; **it doesn't matter if it rains** es macht nichts, wenn es regnet; **3 you can write it in German or English, it doesn't matter** du kannst es auf Deutsch oder Englisch schreiben, das ist egal; **4 to matter to somebody** jemandem etwas ausmachen SEP; **does it matter to you if I leave earlier?** macht es dir etwas aus, wenn ich früher gehe?

mattress *noun* Matratze die (PL die Matratzen).

May *noun* Mai der; **in May** im Mai.

may *verb* **1 she may be ill** vielleicht ist sie krank; **we may go to Spain** wir fahren vielleicht nach Spanien; **2** *(expressing permission)* dürfen ◇; **may I close the door?** darf ich die Tür zumachen?

maybe *adverb* vielleicht; **maybe they've got lost** vielleicht haben sie sich verlaufen.

May Day *noun* der Erste Mai.

mayonnaise *noun* Majonäse △ die.

mayor *noun* Bürgermeister der (PL die Bürgermeister); Bürgermeisterin die (PL die Bürgermeisterinnen).

me *pronoun* *(in German this pronoun changes according to the function it has in the sentence or the preposition it follows)* **1** *(as a direct object in the accusative)* mich; **she knows me** sie kennt mich; **2** *(after a preposition that takes the accusative)* mich; **they left without me** sie sind ohne mich abgefahren; **wait for me!** warte auf mich !; **3** *(as an indirect object or following a verb that takes the dative)* mir; **can you give me your address?** kannst du mir deine Adresse geben?; **he helped me** er hat mir geholfen; **4** *(after a preposition that takes the dative)* mir; **she never talks to me** sie redet nie mit mir; **5** *(in comparisons)* than me als ich; **she's older than me** sie ist älter als ich; **6** *(in the nominative)* ich; **it's me** ich bin's; **not me** ich nicht.

◇ IRREGULAR VERB: *See the verb table in the centre of the dictionary*

meal noun 1 Essen das (PL die Essen); **to cook a meal** Essen kochen; 2 **to go for a meal** essen gehen.

mean verb 1 (signify) bedeuten; **what does that mean?** was bedeutet das?; 2 (intend to say) meinen; 3 **what do you mean?** was meinst du?; **that's not what I meant** das habe ich nicht gemeint; **I meant to phone my mother** ich wollte meine Mutter anrufen; 5 **to be meant to do something** etwas tun sollen; **she was meant to be here at six** sie sollte um sechs hier sein.
adjective 1 (with money) geizig; 2 (unkind) gemein; **she's really mean to her brother** sie ist richtig gemein zu ihrem Bruder; **what a mean thing to do!** das ist gemein!

meaning noun Bedeutung die (PL die Bedeutungen).

means noun 1 Mittel das (PL die Mittel); **means of transport** das Verkehrsmittel; 2 **a means of earning money** eine Möglichkeit, Geld zu verdienen; 3 **by means of** mit Hilfe (+GEN); 4 **by all means!** selbstverständlich!

meantime adverb **for the meantime** einstweilen; **in the meantime** in der Zwischenzeit.

measles noun Masern (plural).

measure verb messen ◇.

measurements plural noun Maße (plural); **the measurements of the**

room die Maße des Zimmers; **my measurements** meine Maße.

mechanic noun Mechaniker der (PL die Mechaniker), Mechanikerin die (PL die Mechanikerinnen).

mechanical adjective mechanisch.

medal noun Medaille die (PL die Medaillen); **the gold medal** die Goldmedaille.

media noun **the media** die Medien (plural).

medical noun 1 ärztliche Untersuchung die (PL die ärztlichen Untersuchungen); 2 **to have a medical** sich untersuchen lassen.
adjective 1 medizinisch; 2 ärztlich (examination, treatment).

medicine noun 1 (drug) Medikament das (PL die Medikamente); 2 (subject of study) Medizin die; **she's studying medicine** sie studiert Medizin; 3 **alternative medicine** die Alternativmedizin.

Mediterranean noun **the Mediterranean (Sea)** das Mittelmeer.

medium adjective mittlerer/mittlere/mittleres.

medium-sized adjective mittelgroß.

meet verb 1 (by chance) treffen ◇; **I met Rosie at the baker's** ich habe Rosie beim Bäcker getroffen; 2 (by appointment) sich treffen mit (+DAT); **I'll meet you outside the cinema** ich treffe mich mit dir vor dem Kino; 3 sich treffen; **we're**

meeting at six wir treffen uns um sechs; **4** (*get to know*) kennen lernen▵; **I met a German girl last week** ich habe letzte Woche eine Deutsche kennen gelernt; **5 I've never met Oskar** ich kenne Oskar nicht; **6** (*off a train or bus, for example*) abholen SEP; **my dad's meeting me at the station** mein Vater holt mich vom Bahnhof ab.

meeting *noun* **1** (*by arrangement*) Treffen *das* (PL die Treffen); **2** (*in business*) Besprechung *die* (PL die Besprechungen); **she's in a meeting** sie ist in einer Besprechung; **3** (*by chance, in sports*) Begegnung *die* (PL die Begegnungen).

melon *noun* Melone *die* (PL die Melonen).

melt *verb* **1** schmelzen ◇ (PERF *sein*); **the snow has melted** der Schnee ist geschmolzen; **2** (*in cookery*) zerlassen ◇ (*butter, fat*); **melt the butter in a saucepan** Butter im Topf zerlassen.

member *noun* Mitglied *das* (PL die Mitglieder).

Member of Parliament *noun* Abgeordnete *der/die* (PL die Abgeordneten).

membership *noun* Mitgliedschaft *die*.

membership card *noun* Mitgliedskarte *die* (PL die Mitgliedskarten).

membership fee *noun* Mitgliedsbeitrag *der* (PL die Mitgliedsbeiträge).

memorize *verb* **to memorize something** etwas auswendig lernen.

memory *noun* **1** (*of a person*) Gedächtnis *das*; **you have a good memory** du hast ein gutes Gedächtnis; **2** (*of the past*) Erinnerung *die* (PL die Erinnerungen); **I have good memories of our stay in Italy** ich habe schöne Erinnerungen an unseren Urlaub in Italien; **3** (*of a computer*) Speicher *der*.

mend *verb* **1** reparieren; **2** (*by sewing*) ausbessern SEP.

mental *adjective* **1** geistig; **2 mental illness** die Geisteskrankheit; **mental hospital** die psychiatrische Klinik.

mention *verb* erwähnen.

menu *noun* **1** (*in a restaurant*) Speisekarte *die* (PL die Speisekarten); **2** (*in computing*) Menü *das* (PL die Menüs).

meringue *noun* Baiser *das* (PL die Baisers).

merit *noun* **1** Verdienst *das* (PL die Verdienste); **2** (*good feature or advantage*) Vorzug *der* (PL die Vorzüge).

merry *adjective* **1** fröhlich; **Merry Christmas** fröhliche Weihnachten!; **2** (*from drinking*) angeheitert.

mess *noun* **1** Durcheinander *das*; **my papers are in a complete mess** meine Unterlagen sind ein einziges Durcheinander; **what a mess!** was für ein Durcheinander!; **2 to make**

◇ IRREGULAR VERB: *See the verb table in the centre of the dictionary*

a mess Unordnung machen; 3 to clear up the mess aufräumen SEP.

● to mess about herumalbern SEP; stop messing about! hör auf herumzualbern!

● to mess about with something mit etwas ←(DAT) herumspielen SEP; it's dangerous to mess about with matches es ist gefährlich, mit Streichhölzern herumzuspielen.

● to mess something up 1 etwas durcheinander bringen ⋄; you've messed up all my papers Sie haben meine Unterlagen völlig durcheinander gebracht; 2 (make dirty) etwas schmutzig machen; 3 (botch) etwas verpfuschen.

message noun 1 Nachricht die (PL die Nachrichten); a telephone message eine telefonische Nachricht; 2 to give somebody a message jemandem etwas ausrichten SEP.

messy adjective 1 (dirty) it's a messy job das ist ein dreckiger Job; 2 he's a messy eater er bekleckert sich beim Essen; 3 her writing's really messy sie hat eine furchtbare Schrift; 4 (untidy) she's very messy sie ist sehr unordentlich.

metal noun Metall das (PL die Metalle).

meter noun 1 (electricity, gas, taxi) Zähler der (PL die Zähler); to read the meter den Zähler ablesen ⋄ SEP; 2 parking meter die Parkuhr.

method noun Methode die (PL die Methoden).

Methodist noun Methodist der (PL die Methodisten), Methodistin die (PL die Methodistinnen).

metre noun Meter der (PL die Meter).

metric adjective metrisch.

microphone noun Mikrofon das (PL die Mikrofone).

microscope noun Mikroskop das (PL die Mikroskope).

microwave (oven) noun Mikrowellenherd der (PL die Mikrowellenherde).

midday noun Mittag der; at midday mittags.

middle noun 1 Mitte die; in the middle of the room in der Mitte des Zimmers; in the middle of June Mitte Juni; in the middle of the night mitten in der Nacht; 2 to be in the middle of doing something gerade dabei sein, etwas zu tun; when she phoned I was in the middle of washing my hair als sie anrief, war ich gerade dabei, mir die Haare zu waschen.

middle-aged adjective mittleren Alters; a middle-aged lady eine Dame mittleren Alters.

middle-class adjective der Mittelschicht; a middle-class family eine Familie der Mittelschicht.

Middle-East noun the Middle East der Nahe Osten.

midge noun Mücke die (PL die Mücken).

midnight noun Mitternacht die; at midnight um Mitternacht.

△ NEW SPELLING: See page xii

Midsummer's Day noun
Sommersonnenwende die.

might verb 1 'are you going to
phone him?' – 'I might' 'rufst du
ihn an?' – 'vielleicht'; I might invite
Jo vielleicht lade ich Jo ein; he
might have forgotten vielleicht hat
er es vergessen; 2 she might be
right sie könnte Recht haben.

mike noun (microphone) Mikro das
(PL die Mikros) (informal).

mild adjective mild.

mile noun 1 Meile die (PL die Meilen)
(Germans use kilometres for
distances; to convert miles to
kilometres, multiply by 8 and divide
by 5); it's ten miles to Oxford es
sind sechzehn Kilometer bis Oxford;
2 it's miles better das ist viel besser.

milk noun Milch die; full-cream
milk die Vollmilch; skimmed milk
die Magermilch; semi-skimmed
milk die fettarme Milch.
verb melken.

milk chocolate noun
Milchschokolade die.

milkman noun Milchmann der (PL
die Milchmänner).

milk shake noun
Milchmixgetränk das (PL die
Milchmixgetränke).

millimetre noun Millimeter der (PL
die Millimeter).

million noun Million die (PL die
Millionen); a million people eine
Million Menschen; two million
people zwei Millionen Menschen.

millionaire noun Millionär der (PL
die Millionäre), Millionärin die (PL
die Millionärinnen).

mince noun Hackfleisch das.

mind noun 1 Sinn der; it never
crossed my mind to ask them for
help es kam mir überhaupt nicht in
den Sinn, sie um Hilfe zu bitten;
2 Meinung die; to change your
mind seine Meinung ändern; I've
changed my mind ich habe meine
Meinung geändert; 3 to make up
your mind to do something sich
entschließen ◇, etwas zu tun; I can't
make up my mind which dress to
wear ich kann mich nicht
entschließen, welches Kleid ich
anziehe; 4 I've made up my mind
ich habe mich entschieden.
verb 1 aufpassen SEP auf (+ACC); can
you mind my bag for me? können
Sie auf meine Handtasche
aufpassen?; could you mind the
baby for ten minutes? könntest du
zehn Minuten auf das Baby
aufpassen?; 2 do you mind closing
the door? würden Sie bitte die Tür
zumachen?; 3 do you mind if ...?
würde es Ihnen etwas ausmachen SEP,
wenn ...?; do you mind if I open the
window? würde es Ihnen etwas
ausmachen, wenn ich das Fenster
aufmache?; I don't mind es macht
mir nichts aus; I don't mind the heat
die Hitze macht mir nichts aus;
4 never mind macht nichts.

mine[1] noun Bergwerk das (PL die
Bergwerke); coal mine das
Kohlenbergwerk.

mine[2] pronoun 1 (for a masculine

noun) mein; **she took her coat and I took mine** sie hat ihren Mantel genommen und ich habe meinen genommen; **2** (*for a feminine noun*) meine; **she gave me her address and I gave her mine** sie hat mir ihre Adresse gegeben und ich habe ihr meine gegeben; **3** (*for a neuter noun*) meins; **her dress is red and mine is blue** ihr Kleid ist rot und meins ist blau; **4** (*for masculine/ feminine/neuter plural nouns*) meine; **she showed me her photos and I showed her mine** sie hat mir ihre Fotos gezeigt und ich habe ihr meine gezeigt; **5 a friend of mine** ein Freund von mir; **it's mine** das gehört mir.

miner noun Bergarbeiter der (PL die Bergarbeiter).

mineral water noun Mineralwasser das.

minibus noun Kleinbus der (PL die Kleinbusse).

minimum noun Minimum das (PL die Minima); **a minimum of** ein Minimum von.
adjective Mindest-; **the minimum age** das Mindestalter; **minimum wage** der Mindestlohn.

miniskirt noun Minirock der (PL die Miniröcke).

minister noun **1** (*in government*) Minister der (PL die Minister), Ministerin die (PL die Ministerinnen); **2** (*of a church*) Geistliche der/die (PL die Geistlichen).

ministry noun Ministerium das (PL die Ministerien).

mint noun **1** (*herb*) Minze die (PL die Minzen); **2** (*sweet*) Pfefferminzbonbon der (PL die Pfefferminzbonbons).

minus preposition minus (+GEN); **seven minus three is four** sieben minus drei ist vier; **it was minus ten this morning** es war minus zehn heute Morgen.

minute¹ noun **1** Minute die (PL die Minuten); **I'll be ready in two minutes** ich bin in zwei Minuten fertig; **it's five minutes' walk from here** es ist fünf Minuten zu Fuß von hier; **2** Moment der; **just a minute!** einen Moment bitte!; **3 in a minute** gleich.

minute² adjective winzig; **the bedrooms are minute** die Schlafzimmer sind winzig.

miracle noun Wunder das (PL die Wunder).

mirror noun Spiegel der (PL die Spiegel); **he looked at himself in the mirror** er hat sich im Spiegel betrachtet.

misbehave verb sich schlecht benehmen ◇.

miserable adjective **1** unglücklich; **he was miserable without her** er war unglücklich ohne sie; **2 I feel really miserable today** ich fühle mich heute richtig elend; **3** mies; **it's miserable weather** das Wetter ist mies; **she gets paid a miserable salary** sie bekommt ein mieses Gehalt.

△ NEW SPELLING: See page xii

miss *verb* 1 verpassen; **she missed her train** sie hat ihren Zug verpasst; **I missed the film** ich habe den Film verpasst; **to miss an opportunity** eine Gelegenheit verpassen; 2 nicht treffen ◇; **the stone missed me** der Stein hat mich nicht getroffen; **the ball missed the goal** der Schuss ging am Tor vorbei; **missed!** nicht getroffen!; 3 versäumen; **he's missed his classes** er hat den Unterricht versäumt; 4 vermissen (*a person or thing*); **I miss you** ich vermisse dich; **she's missing her sister** sie vermisst ihre Schwester; **I miss England** ich vermisse England.

Miss *noun* Fräulein *das*; **Miss Jones** Fräulein Jones, Frau Jones (*adult women are usually addressed as 'Frau', whether or not they are married*).

missing *adjective* 1 fehlend; **she's found the missing pieces** sie hat die fehlenden Teile gefunden; **the missing link** das fehlende Glied; 2 **to be missing** fehlen; **there's a plate missing** ein Teller fehlt; **there are three forks missing** drei Gabeln fehlen; 3 **to go missing** verschwinden ◇ (PERF *sein*); **several things have gone missing lately** mehrere Sachen sind kürzlich verschwunden; 4 **three children are missing** drei Kinder werden vermisst.

missionary *noun* Missionar *der* (PL die Missionare), Missionarin *die* (PL die Missionarinnen).

mist *noun* Nebel *der*.

mistake *noun* 1 Fehler *der* (PL die Fehler); **spelling mistake** *der* Rechtschreibfehler; **you've made lots of mistakes** du hast viele Fehler gemacht; 2 **to make a mistake** (*be mistaken*) sich irren; **sorry, I made a mistake** Entschuldigung, ich habe mich geirrt; 3 **by mistake** aus Versehen.
verb **I mistook you for your brother** ich habe dich mit deinem Bruder verwechselt.

mistaken *adjective* **to be mistaken** sich täuschen; **you're mistaken** du täuschst dich.

mistletoe *noun* Mistel *die* (PL die Misteln).

misty *adjective* dunstig; **a misty morning** ein dunstiger Morgen.

misunderstand *verb* missverstehen ◇; **I misunderstood** ich habe es missverstanden.

misunderstanding *noun* Missverständnis △ *das* (PL die Missverständnisse); **there's been a misunderstanding** da liegt ein Missverständnis vor.

mix *noun* Mischung *die* (PL die Mischungen); **a good mix** eine gute Mischung; **cake mix** *die* Backmischung.
verb 1 vermischen; **mix the ingredients together** mix die Zutaten vermischen; **mix the cream into the sauce** die Sahne in die Soße rühren; 2 **to mix with** verkehren mit (+DAT); **she mixes with lots of interesting people** sie verkehrt mit vielen interessanten Leuten.

◇ IRREGULAR VERB: *See the verb table in the centre of the dictionary*

● **to mix up** 1 durcheinander bringen△✧; **you've mixed up all the papers** du hast alle Unterlagen durcheinander gebracht; **you've got it all mixed up** du hast alles durcheinander gebracht; 2 (*confuse*) verwechseln; **I get him mixed up with his brother** ich verwechsle ihn mit seinem Bruder.

mixed *adjective* 1 bunt; **a mixed programme** ein buntes Programm; 2 gemischt; **a mixed salad** ein gemischter Salat.

mixture *noun* Mischung *die* (PL *die* Mischungen); **it's a mixture of jazz and rock** es ist eine Mischung aus Jazz und Rock.

moan *verb* (*complain*) jammern; **stop moaning!** hör auf zu jammern!

mobile home *noun* Wohnwagen *der* (PL *die* Wohnwagen).

mobile phone *noun* Mobiltelefon *das* (PL *die* Mobiltelefone), Handy *das* (PL *die* Handys).

mock *noun* (*mock exam*) Übungsprüfung *die* (PL *die* Übungsprüfungen); *verb* sich lustig machen über (+ACC); **stop mocking me** hör auf, dich über mich lustig zu machen.

model *noun* 1 Modell *das* (PL *die* Modelle); **his car is the latest model** sein Auto ist das neueste Modell; **a model of Westminster Abbey** ein Modell von der Westminsterabtei; 2 (*fashion*

model) Mannequin *das* (PL *die* Mannequins); **she's a i..odel** sie ist Mannequin.

model aeroplane *noun* Modellflugzeug *das* (PL *die* Modellflugzeuge).

model railway *noun* Minieisenbahn *die* (PL *die* Minieisenbahnen).

modem *noun* Modem *der* (PL *die* Modems).

modern *adjective* modern.

modernize *verb* modernisieren.

modern languages *noun* neuere Sprachen (*plural*).

modest *adjective* bescheiden.

modify *verb* abändern SEP.

moisture *noun* Feuchtigkeit *die*.

moisturizer *noun* Feuchtigkeitscreme *die*.

mole *noun* 1 (*animal*) Maulwurf *der* (PL *die* Maulwürfe); 2 (*on the skin*) Leberfleck *der* (PL *die* Leberflecke).

moment *noun* 1 Moment *der* (PL *die* Momente); **at any moment** jeden Moment; **at the moment** im Moment, im Augenblick; **at the right moment** im richtigen Moment; 2 Augenblick *der* (PL *die* Augenblicke); **wait a moment!** einen Augenblick!; 3 **he'll be ready in a moment** er ist gleich fertig.

monarchy *noun* Monarchie *die*.

Monday *noun* 1 Montag *der*; **on Monday** am Montag; **I'm going to**

see him on Monday ich sehe ihn am Montag; see you on Monday! bis Montag!; every Monday jeden Montag; last Monday letzten Montag; next Monday nächsten Montag; 2 on Mondays montags; the museum is closed on Mondays das Museum ist montags geschlossen.

money noun Geld das; I don't have enough money ich habe nicht genug Geld; to make money Geld verdienen.

monitor noun (of a computer) Monitor der (PL die Monitoren).

monkey noun Affe der (PL die Affen).

monotonous adjective eintönig.

monster noun Ungeheuer das (PL die Ungeheuer).

month noun Monat der; in the month of May im Mai; this month diesen Monat; next month nächsten Monat; last month letzten Monat; for three months drei Monate lang; every month jeden Monat; every three months alle drei Monate; in two months' time in zwei Monaten; at the end of the month am Monatsende.

monthly adjective monatlich; monthly payment die monatliche Zahlung; monthly ticket die Monatskarte.

monument noun Denkmal das (PL die Denkmäler).

mood noun 1 Laune die (PL die Launen); to be in a good mood gute Laune haben; to be in a bad mood schlechte Laune haben; 2 I'm not in the mood ich habe keine Lust dazu; I'm not in the mood for working ich habe keine Lust zum Arbeiten.

moon noun Mond der (PL die Monde); by the light of the moon im Mondschein; ★ to be over the moon im siebten Himmel sein (literally: to be in seventh heaven).

moonlight noun Mondschein der; by moonlight im Mondschein.

moped noun Moped das (PL die Mopeds).

moral noun Moral die; the moral of the story die Moral der Geschichte. adjective moralisch.

morals noun Moral die.

more adverb 1 (followed by an adjective) (in German the ending '-er' is added to the adjective to show the comparative) more interesting interessanter; the book's more interesting than the film das Buch ist interessanter als der Film; more difficult schwieriger; more slowly langsamer; more easily einfacher; books are getting more and more expensive Bücher werden immer teurer; 2 not any more (no longer) nicht mehr; she doesn't live here any more sie wohnt nicht mehr hier. adjective 1 mehr ('mehr' never changes); more friends mehr Freunde; more … than mehr … als; they have more money than we do sie haben mehr Geld als wir; 2 no more kein; there's no more milk es ist keine Milch mehr da; **3** (*of something you have already*); **would you like some more cake?** möchtest du noch etwas Kuchen?; **a few more glasses** noch ein paar Gläser.

pronoun **1** mehr; **he eats more than me** er isst mehr als ich; **no more, thank you** nichts mehr, danke; **2** (*of something you have already*) noch; **we need three more** wir brauchen noch drei; **any more?** noch etwas?; **3 more and more** immer mehr; **it takes more and more time** es beansprucht immer mehr Zeit; **4 more or less** mehr oder weniger; **it's more or less finished** es ist mehr oder weniger fertig.

morning *noun* **1** Morgen *der* (PL *die* Morgen); **in the morning** am Morgen; **this morning** heute Morgen; **tomorrow morning** morgen früh; **yesterday morning** gestern Morgen; **on Friday morning** am Freitagmorgen; **2 in the morning** (*regularly*) morgens; **she doesn't work in the morning** sie arbeitet morgens nicht; **on Friday mornings** freitagmorgens; **at six o'clock in the morning** um sechs Uhr morgens; **3** (*as opposed to afternoon*) Vormittag *der* (PL *die* Vormittage); **I spent the whole morning waiting for him** ich habe den ganzen Vormittag auf ihn gewartet.

Moscow *noun* Moskau *das*.

Moslem *noun* Moslem *der* (PL *die* Moslems), Moslime *die* (PL *die* Moslimen).

mosque *noun* Moschee *die* (PL *die* Moscheen).

mosquito *noun* Mücke *die* (PL *die* Mücken); **mosquito bite** *der* Mückenstich.

most *adjective, pronoun* **1** (*followed by a plural noun*) die meisten; **most children like chocolate** die meisten Kinder mögen Schokolade; **most of my friends** die meisten von meinen Freunden; **2** (*followed by a singular noun*) der meiste/die meiste/das meiste; **they've eaten most of the ice-cream** sie haben das meiste Eis gegessen; **3 the most** (*followed by a noun or a verb*) am meisten; **I've got the most time** ich habe am meisten Zeit; **4 most of the time** die meiste Zeit; **most of them** die meisten.

adverb **1** (*followed by an adjective*) (*in German the ending '-(e)st' is added to the adjective to show the superlative*) **the most interesting film** der interessanteste Film; **the most exciting story** die spannendste Geschichte; **the most boring book** das langweiligste Buch; **2** am meisten; **the noise bothers me most** der Lärm stört mich am meisten; **3** (*very*) höchst; **it's most unlikely** es ist höchst unwahrscheinlich.

moth *noun* **1** Nachtfalter *der* (PL *die* Nachtfalter); **2** (*clothes moth*) Motte *die* (PL *die* Motten).

mother *noun* Mutter *die* (PL *die* Mütter); **Kate's mother** Kates Mutter.

△ NEW SPELLING: See page xii

mother-in-law *noun*
Schwiegermutter *die* (PL *die* Schwiegermütter).

Mother's Day *noun* Muttertag *der* (PL *die* Muttertage).

motor *noun* Motor *der* (PL *die* Motoren).

motorbike *noun* Motorrad *das* (PL *die* Motorräder).

motorcyclist *noun*
Motorradfahrer *der* (PL *die* Motorradfahrer), Motorradfahrerin *die* (PL *die* Motorradfahrerinnen).

motorist *noun* Autofahrer *der* (PL *die* Autofahrer), Autofahrerin *die* (PL *die* Autofahrerinnen).

motor racing *noun*
Autorennen *das*.

motorway *noun* Autobahn *die* (PL *die* Autobahnen).

mouldy *adjective* schimmelig.

mountain *noun* Berg *der* (PL *die* Berge); **in the mountains** in den Bergen.

mountain bike *noun*
Mountainbike *das* (PL *die* Mountainbikes).

mountaineer *noun*
Bergsteiger *der* (PL *die* Bergsteiger), Bergsteigerin *die* (PL *die* Bergsteigerinnen).

mountaineering *noun*
Bergsteigen *das*; **to go mountaineering** Bergsteigen gehen.

mountainous *adjective* gebirgig.

mouse *noun* Maus *die* (PL *die* Mäuse) (*also for a computer*).

moustache *noun* Schnurrbart *der* (PL *die* Schnurrbärte).

mouth *noun* 1 (*of a person*) Mund *der* (PL *die* Münder); 2 (*of an animal*) Maul *das* (PL *die* Mäuler); 3 (*of a river*) Mündung *die* (PL *die* Mündungen).

mouthful *noun* (*food*) Happen *der* (PL *die* Happen) (*informal*).

mouth organ *noun*
Mundharmonika *die* (PL *die* Mundharmonikas); **to play the mouth organ** Mundharmonika spielen.

move *noun* 1 (*to a different house*) Umzug *der* (PL *die* Umzüge); 2 (*in a game*) Zug *der* (PL *die* Züge); **your move!** du bist am Zug!
verb 1 sich bewegen; **she didn't move** sie hat sich nicht bewegt; 2 **to move up** vorrücken SEP (PERF *sein*); **move up a bit** rücken Sie etwas vor; 3 wegnehmen ◇ SEP; **can you move your bag, please?** können Sie Ihre Handtasche bitte wegnehmen?; 4 **to move something somewhere else** etwas woandershin stellen; **I've moved the chest into the cellar** ich habe die Truhe in den Keller gestellt; 5 (*car*) fahren ◇ (PERF *sein*); 6 (*traffic*) vorwärtskommen ◇ SEP (PERF *sein*); 7 (*driver*) wegfahren ◇ SEP; **could you move your car, please?** würden Sie bitte Ihr Auto wegfahren?; 8 **to move forward** (*person*) vorrücken SEP (PERF *sein*); (*vehicle*) vorwärts fahren ◇ (PERF *sein*); 9 (*move house*) umziehen ◇ SEP (PERF *sein*); **we're moving on Tuesday** wir ziehen am Dienstag

◇ IRREGULAR VERB: *See the verb table in the centre of the dictionary*

um; **they've moved to London** sie sind nach London umgezogen; **10 to move away** (live somewhere else) wegziehen ◇ SEP (PERF sein); **11 to move in** einziehen ◇ SEP (PERF sein); **she's moving in with friends** sie zieht bei Freunden ein.

movement noun Bewegung die (PL die Bewegungen).

movie noun Film der (PL die Filme); **to go to the movies** ins Kino gehen.

moving adjective **1** fahrend; **a moving car** ein fahrendes Auto; **2** (emotionally) ergreifend.

mow verb mähen.

mower noun Rasenmäher der (PL die Rasenmäher).

MP noun Abgeordnete der/die (PL die Abgeordneten).

Mr noun Herr der; (in an address) **Mr Angus Brown** Herrn Angus Brown; (in a letter) **Dear Mr Brown** Sehr geehrter Herr Brown.

Mrs noun Frau die; **Mrs Mary Hendry** Frau Mary Hendry; (in a letter) **Dear Mrs Hendry** Sehr geehrte Frau Hendry.

Ms noun Frau die (there is no direct equivalent to 'Ms' in German, but 'Frau' may be used whether the woman is married or not).

much adjective, adverb, pronoun **1** viel; **she doesn't eat much for breakfast** sie isst nicht viel zum Frühstück; **much more** viel mehr; **much quicker** viel schneller; **we**

don't have much time wir haben nicht viel Zeit; **2 not much** nicht viel; **'do you have a lot of work?'** – **'no, not much'** 'hast du viel Arbeit?' – ' nein, nicht viel'; **3 so much** so viel; **I have so much to do** ich habe so viel zu tun; **you shouldn't have given me so much** du hättest mir nicht so viel geben sollen; **4 as much as** so viel; **take as much as you like** nimm so viel du willst; **5 too much** zu viel △; **she gets too much money from her parents** sie bekommt zu viel Geld von ihren Eltern; **that's far too much** das ist viel zu viel; **6 how much?** wie viel? △; **how much is it?** wie viel kostet es?; **how much do you want?** wie viel möchten Sie?; **how much money do you need?** wie viel Geld brauchst du?; **7** (greatly) sehr; **he loved her very much** er hat sie sehr geliebt; **too much** zu sehr; **so much** (so) sehr; **we liked it so much** es hat uns sehr gefallen; **8** (often) oft; **I don't watch television much** ich sehe nicht oft fern; **we don't go out much** wir gehen nicht oft aus; **9 thank you very much** vielen Dank.

mud noun Schlamm der.

muddle noun **1** Durcheinander das; **2 to be in a muddle** durcheinander sein.

mug noun Becher der (PL die Becher); **a mug of milk** ein Becher Milch.
verb **to mug somebody** jemanden überfallen ◇; **to be mugged** überfallen werden.

△ NEW SPELLING: See page xii

multiplication noun
Multiplikation die.

multiply verb multiplizieren; **six multiplied by four** sechs multipliziert mit vier.

mum, mummy noun Mutti die (PL die Muttis); **Tom's mum** Toms Mutti; **I'll ask my mum** ich frage die Mutti.

mumps noun Mumps der.

Munich noun München das.

murder noun Mord der (PL die Morde).
verb ermorden.

murderer noun Mörder der (PL die Mörder), Mörderin die (PL die Mörderinnen).

muscle noun Muskel der (PL die Muskeln).

muscular adjective muskulös.

museum noun Museum das (PL die Museen); **to go to the museum** ins Museum gehen.

mushroom noun Pilz der (PL die Pilze), Champignon der (PL die Champignons); **mushroom salad** der Champignonsalat.

music noun Musik die; **pop music** die Popmusik; **classical music** die klassische Musik.

musical noun Musical das (PL die Musicals).
adjective **1 musical instrument** das Musikinstrument; **2 they're a very musical family** sie sind eine sehr musikalische Familie.

musician noun Musiker der (PL die Musiker), Musikerin die (PL die Musikerinnen).

Muslim noun Moslem der (PL die Moslems), Moslime die (PL die Moslimen).

mussel noun Muschel die (PL die Muscheln).

must verb **1** müssen ◇; **we must leave now** wir müssen jetzt gehen; **you must learn the vocabulary** du musst die Vokabeln lernen; **2** (with a negative) dürfen ◇; **you mustn't do that** das darfst du nicht tun; **3** (expressing probability) müssen ◇; **you must be tired** ihr müsst müde sein; **it must be five o'clock** es muss fünf Uhr sein; **he must have forgotten** er muss es vergessen haben.

mustard noun Senf der (PL die Senfe).

mutter verb murmeln.

my adjective **1** (before a masculine noun) mein; **my brother** mein Bruder; **they don't like my dog** sie mögen meinen Hund nicht; **2** (before a feminine noun) meine; **my sister** meine Schwester; **3** (before a neuter noun) mein; **that's my new car** das ist mein neues Auto; **we can go in my car** wir können mit meinem Auto fahren; **4** (before masculine/feminine/neuter plural nouns) meine; **my children** meine Kinder; **5** (with parts of the body) der/die/das (plural: die); **I had a glass in my hand** ich hatte ein Glas in der Hand; **I'm washing my hands** ich wasche mir die Hände.

◇ IRREGULAR VERB: See the verb table in the centre of the dictionary

myself *pronoun* **1** (*reflexive and after a preposition taking the accusative*) mich; **I've cut myself** ich habe mich geschnitten; **I've addressed the letter to myself** ich habe den Brief an mich adressiert; **2** (*reflexive and after a preposition taking the dative*) mir; **I've hurt myself** ich habe mir wehgetan; **I said to myself** ich habe mir gesagt; **3** (*stressing something*) selbst; **I said it myself** ich habe es selbst gesagt; **4 by myself** allein.

mysterious *adjective* rätselhaft.

mystery *noun* **1** Rätsel *das* (PL die Rätsel); **2** (*book*) Krimi *der* (PL die Krimis) (*informal*).

mythology *noun* Mythologie *die* (PL die Mythologien).

N n

nail *noun* (*on your finger or toe, also metal*) Nagel *der* (PL die Nägel). *verb* nageln.

nailbrush *noun* Nagelbürste *die* (PL die Nagelbürsten).

nailfile *noun* Nagelfeile *die* (PL die Nagelfeilen).

nail polish *noun* Nagellack *der*.

nail polish remover *noun* Nagellackentferner *der*.

name *noun* **1** Name *der* (PL die Namen); **I've forgotten her name** ich habe ihren Namen vergessen; **what's your name?** wie heißt du?; **my name's Joy** ich heiße Joy; **2** (*of a book or film*) Titel *der* (PL die Titel).

napkin *noun* Serviette *die* (PL die Servietten).

nappy *noun* Windel *die* (PL die Windeln).

narrow *adjective* schmal; **a narrow street** eine schmale Straße.

nasty *adjective* **1** (*mean*) gemein; **that was a nasty thing to do** das war gemein; **2** (*unpleasant, bad*) scheußlich; **that's a nasty job** das ist eine scheußliche Arbeit; **a nasty smell** ein scheußlicher Geruch.

nation *noun* Nation *die* (PL die Nationen).

national *adjective* national.

national anthem *noun* Nationalhymne *die* (PL die Nationalhymnen).

nationality *noun* Nationalität *die* (PL die Nationalitäten).

national park *noun* Nationalpark *der* (PL die Nationalparks).

natural *adjective* natürlich.

naturally *adverb* natürlich.

nature *noun* Natur *die*.

nature reserve *noun* Naturschutzgebiet *das* (PL die Naturschutzgebiete).

naughty *adjective* unartig.

△ NEW SPELLING: See page xii

navy noun Marine die; **my uncle's in the navy** mein Onkel ist bei der Marine.

navy-blue adjective marineblau.

near adjective 1 nah(e); 2 (the superlative of nah(e) is der/die/das nächste) **the nearest park** der nächste Park; **the nearest bank** die nächste Bank; **the nearest shop** das nächste Geschäft.
preposition nahe an (+DAT); **near (to) the station** nahe am Bahnhof.
adverb 1 nah(e) (in spoken German 'nah' is more common); **they live quite near** sie wohnen ganz nah; 2 **to come nearer** näher kommen.

nearly adverb fast; **nearly empty** fast leer.

neat adjective 1 (well organized, tidy) ordentlich; **a neat room** ein ordentliches Zimmer; 2 adrett (clothes or the way you look).

necessarily adverb not necessarily nicht unbedingt.

necessary adjective nötig; **if necessary** falls nötig.

neck noun 1 (of a person) Hals der (PL die Hälse); 2 (of a garment) Kragen der (PL die Kragen).

necklace noun Halskette die (PL die Halsketten).

need noun **there's no need, I've already done it** das ist nicht nötig, ich habe es schon gemacht; **there's no need to wait** du brauchst nicht zu warten.
verb 1 brauchen; **we need bread** wir brauchen Brot; **everything you need** alles, was man braucht; 2 (to

have to) müssen ◇; **I need to go to the bank** ich muss zur Bank gehen; 3 (with a negative) **you needn't wait** du brauchst nicht zu warten.

needle noun Nadel die (PL die Nadeln).

negative noun (of a photo) Negativ das (PL die Negative).

neighbour noun Nachbar der (PL die Nachbarn), Nachbarin die (PL die Nachbarinnen); **we're going round to the neighbours'** wir besuchen die Nachbarn.

neighbourhood noun Nachbarschaft die; **in our neighbourhood** in unserer Nachbarschaft.

neither conjunction 1 **neither ... nor** weder ... noch; **I have neither the time nor the money** ich habe weder die Zeit noch das Geld; 2 **neither do I** ich auch nicht; **'I don't like fish' – 'neither do I'** 'ich mag keinen Fisch' – 'ich auch nicht'; **'I didn't like the film' – 'neither did Kirsty'** 'mir hat der Film nicht gefallen' – 'Kirsty hat er auch nicht gefallen'.
pronoun keiner von beiden/keine von beiden/keins von beiden; **'which do you like?' – 'neither'** 'welches gefällt dir?' – 'keins von beiden'.

nephew noun Neffe der (PL die Neffen).

nerve noun Nerv der (PL die Nerven); 1 **to lose your nerve** die Nerven verlieren; **you've got a nerve!** du hast Nerven! (informal);

2 what a nerve! so eine Frechheit!;
★ **he gets on my nerves** er geht mir
auf die Nerven (*informal*).

nervous *adjective* **1** (*afraid*)
ängstlich; **to feel nervous about
something** Angst vor etwas ←(DAT)
haben; **2** (*highly strung*) nervös
(*person*).

net *noun* Netz *das* (PL die Netze).

Netherlands *noun* Niederlande
(*plural*); **in the Netherlands** in den
Niederlanden.

nettle *noun* Nessel *die* (PL die
Nesseln).

neutral *noun* (*neutral gear*)
Leerlauf *der*; **to be in neutral** im
Leerlauf sein.
adjective neutral.

never *adverb* **1** nie; **Ben never
smokes** Ben raucht nie; **I've never
told him** ich habe es ihm nie gesagt;
never again nie wieder; **2** noch nie;
'**have you ever been to Spain?**' –
'**no, never**' 'warst du schon mal in
Spanien?' – 'nein, noch nie'; **3** never
mind macht nichts.

new *adjective* neu; **have you seen
their new house?** hast du ihr neues
Haus gesehen?

news *noun* **1** (*new information*)
Nachricht *die* (PL die Nachrichten);
I've got good news ich habe gute
Nachrichten; **2 a piece of news**
eine Neuigkeit; **any news?** was gibt
es Neues?; **3** (*on TV or the radio*)
Nachrichten (*plural*); **we saw it on
the news** wir haben es in den
Nachrichten gesehen.

newsagent *noun*
Zeitungshändler *der* (PL die
Zeitungshändler).

newspaper *noun* Zeitung *die* (PL
die Zeitungen).

newsreader *noun*
Nachrichtensprecher *der* (PL die
Nachrichtensprecher),
Nachrichtensprecherin *die* (PL die
Nachrichtensprecherinnen).

New Year *noun* Neujahr *das*;
Happy New Year! ein gutes neues
Jahr!

New Year's Day *noun*
Neujahr *das*.

New Year's Eve *noun*
Silvester *der*.

New Zealand *noun*
Neuseeland *das*.

next *adjective* **1** nächster/nächste/
nächstes; **the next train leaves at
ten** der nächste Zug fährt um zehn
ab; **next week** nächste Woche; **next
Thursday** nächsten Donnerstag; **next
time I see you** nächstes Mal, wenn ich
dich sehe; **2** (*following*) **next
please!** der Nächste bitte/die
Nächste bitte; **the next thing** das
Nächste; **the next day** am nächsten
Tag; **the letter arrived the next day**
der Brief kam am nächsten Tag an;
3 (*week after next*) übernächste
Woche; **4** (*next-door*) nebenan; **I'm
in the next room** ich bin nebenan.
adverb **1** (*afterwards*) danach; **what
did he say next?** was hat er danach
gesagt?; **2** (*now*) als Nächstes; **what**

△ **NEW SPELLING:** *See page xii*

shall we do next? was machen wir als Nächstes?; **3 next to** neben (+DAT, *or* +ACC *with movement towards a place*); **the house next to the baker's** das Haus neben dem Bäcker; **I sat down next to her** ich habe mich neben sie gesetzt.

next door *adverb* nebenan; **they live next door** sie wohnen nebenan; **the girl next door** das Mädchen von nebenan.

nice *adjective* **1** (*pleasant*) schön; **we had a nice evening** wir haben einen schönen Abend verbracht; **Brighton's a nice town** Brighton ist eine schöne Stadt; **we had nice weather** wir hatten schönes Wetter; **2 to have a nice time** sich amüsieren; **have a nice day!** viel Spaß!; **3** (*attractive to look at*) hübsch; **that's a nice dress** das ist ein hübsches Kleid; **4** (*kind, friendly*) nett (*person*); **she's really nice** sie ist wirklich nett; **5 to be nice to somebody** nett zu jemandem sein; **she's been very nice to me** sie war sehr nett zu mir; **6** (*tasting good*) gut; **it tastes nice** es schmeckt gut.

niece *noun* Nichte *die* (PL *die* Nichten).

night *noun* **1** (*after bedtime*) Nacht *die* (PL *die* Nächte); **during the night** während der Nacht; **Sunday night** Sonntag Nacht; **it's cold at night** nachts ist es kalt; **to stay the night** über Nacht bleiben; **I stayed the night at Emma's** ich habe bei Emma übernachtet; **2** (*before you go to bed*) Abend *der*

(PL *die* Abende); **what are you doing tonight?** was macht ihr heute Abend?; **one night** eines Abends; **tomorrow night** morgen Abend; **I met Greg last night** ich habe Greg gestern Abend getroffen; **on Friday night** am Freitagabend; **see you tonight!** bis heute Abend!

night club *noun* Nachtklub *der* (PL *die* Nachtklubs).

nightie *noun* Nachthemd *das* (PL *die* Nachthemden).

nightmare *noun* Alptraum *der* (PL *die* Alpträume).

nil *noun* (*in sport*) null; **they won four-nil** sie haben vier zu null gewonnen.

nine *number* neun.

nineteen *number* neunzehn.

ninety *number* neunzig.

ninth *number* neunter/neunte/neuntes; **on the ninth floor** im neunten Stock; **on the ninth of June** am neunten Juni.

no *adverb* nein; **I said no** ich habe nein gesagt; **no thank you** nein danke.
adjective **1** kein; **we've got no bread** wir haben kein Brot; **no problem!** kein Problem!; **2** (*on a notice*) **'no smoking'** 'Rauchen verboten'; **'no parking'** 'Parken verboten'.

nobody *pronoun* niemand; **'who's there?' – 'nobody'** 'wer ist da?' – 'niemand'; **there's nobody in the kitchen** es ist niemand in der

---

✦ **IRREGULAR VERB:** *See the verb table in the centre of the dictionary*

Küche; **nobody was at home**
niemand war zu Hause.

nod *verb* nicken; **he nodded in agreement** er hat zustimmend
genickt.

noise *noun* Lärm *der*; **to make a noise** Lärm machen.

noisy *adjective* laut.

none *pronoun* 1 (*not one*)
keiner/keine/keins; **none of us**
keiner von uns/ keine von uns; '**how
many students failed the exam?' –
'none'** 'wie viele Schüler sind durch
die Prüfung gefallen?' – 'keine';
none of the boys knows him keiner
der Jungen kennt ihn; 2 **there's
none left** es ist nichts mehr übrig.

nonsense *noun* Unsinn *der*; **to talk
nonsense** Unsinn reden;
nonsense! Unsinn!

non-stop *adjective* durchgehend
(*train*); Nonstop- (*flight*).
adverb ununterbrochen;
she talks non-stop sie redet
ununterbrochen.

noon *noun* Mittag *der*; **at (twelve)
noon** um zwölf (Uhr mittags).

no-one *pronoun* niemand; '**who's
there?' – 'no-one'** 'wer ist da?' –
'niemand'; **there's no-one in the
kitchen** es ist niemand in der
Küche; **no-one was at home**
niemand war zu Hause.

nor *conjunction* 1 **neither ... nor**
weder ... noch; **I have neither the
time nor the money** ich habe weder
die Zeit noch das Geld; 2 **nor do I**
ich auch nicht; '**I don't like fish'** –

'**nor do I**' 'ich mag keinen Fisch' –
'ich auch nicht'; **nor do we** wir
auch nicht.

normal *adjective* normal.

normally *adverb* 1 (*usually*)
normalerweise; 2 (*in a normal way*)
normal.

north *noun* Norden *der*; **in the
north** im Norden.
adjective nördlich, Nord-; **the north
side** die Nordseite; **north wind** *der*
Nordwind.
adverb 1 (*towards the north*) nach
Norden; **to travel north** nach
Norden fahren; 2 **north of London**
nördlich von London.

North America *noun*
Nordamerika *das*.

northeast *noun* Nordosten *der*.
adjective **in northeast England** in
Nordostengland.

Northern Ireland *noun*
Nordirland *das*.

North Pole *noun* Nordpol *der*.

North Sea *noun* **the North Sea** die
Nordsee.

northwest *noun* Nordwesten *der*.
adjective **in northwest England** in
Nordwestengland.

Norway *noun* Norwegen *das*.

Norwegian *noun* 1 (*person*)
Norweger *der* (PL *die* Norweger),
Norwegerin *die* (PL *die*
Norwegerinnen); 2 (*language*)
Norwegisch *das*.
adjective norwegisch.

△ NEW SPELLING: *See page xii*

nose noun Nase die (PL die Nasen);
to blow your nose sich ←(DAT) die
Nase putzen.

not adverb 1 nicht; not on Sundays
sonntags nicht; not all alone! nicht
ganz allein!; not bad nicht schlecht;
not at all überhaupt nicht; not yet
noch nicht; Sam didn't phone Sam
hat nicht angerufen; I hope not
hoffentlich nicht; 2 not a
kein/keine; he's not a specialist er
ist kein Fachmann; not a bit kein
bisschen.

note noun 1 (a short letter)
Zettel der (PL die Zettel) (informal),
Brief der (PL die Briefe); 2 (in a class)
Notiz die (PL die Notizen); to take
notes sich ←(DAT) Notizen machen;
3 (a banknote) Schein der (PL die
Scheine); a ten-pound note ein
Zehnpfundschein; 4 (in music)
Note die (PL die Noten).

notebook noun Notizbuch das (PL
die Notizbücher).

notepad noun Notizblock der (PL
die Notizblöcke).

nothing pronoun nichts; 'what did
you say?' – 'nothing' 'was hast du
gesagt?' – 'nichts'; nothing special
nichts Besonderes; nothing new
nichts Neues; I saw nothing ich
habe nichts gesehen; there's nothing
left es ist nichts mehr übrig.

notice noun 1 (a sign) Anschlag der
(PL die Anschläge); 2 (an
advertisement) Anzeige die (PL die
Anzeigen); 3 (advance warning)
Ankündigung die; 4 don't take any
notice of her nimm keine Notiz von
ihr; 5 at short notice kurzfristig.
verb bemerken; I didn't notice
anything ich habe nichts bemerkt.

notice board noun
Anschlagbrett das (PL die
Anschlagbretter).

nought noun Null die (PL die
Nullen).

noun noun Substantiv das (PL die
Substantive).

novel noun Roman der (PL die
Romane).

novelist noun Romanautor der (PL
die Romanautoren), Romanautorin
die (PL die Romanautorinnen).

November noun November der; in
November im November.

now adverb 1 jetzt; where is he
now? wo ist er jetzt?; from now on
von jetzt an; 2 he left just now er
ist gerade eben gegangen; I saw her
just now in the corridor ich habe
sie gerade eben im Gang gesehen;
3 do it right now! mach es sofort!;
4 now and then hin und wieder.

nowhere adjective nirgends;
there's nowhere to park man kann
nirgends parken.

nuclear adjective Kern-; nuclear
power die Kernenergie; nuclear
power station das Kernkraftwerk.

nude noun in the nude nackt.
adjective nackt.

nuisance noun it's a nuisance das
ist ärgerlich; what a nuisance! wie
ärgerlich!

⬦ IRREGULAR VERB: See the verb table in the centre of the dictionary

numb adjective 1 (with cold) gefühllos; 2 (emotionally) benommen.

number noun 1 (of a house, telephone, or account) Nummer die (PL die Nummern); I live at number five ich wohne Nummer fünf; my new phone number meine neue Telefonnummer; 2 (a written figure) Zahl die (PL die Zahlen); 3 (amount) Anzahl die; the number of visitors die Anzahl der Besucher.

number plate noun Nummernschild das (PL die Nummernschilder).

nun noun Nonne die (PL die Nonnen).

nurse noun Krankenschwester die (PL die Krankenschwestern); Janet's a nurse Janet ist Krankenschwester.

nursery noun 1 (for children) Kindertagesstätte die (PL die Kindertagesstätten); 2 (for plants) Gärtnerei die (PL die Gärtnereien).

nursery school noun Kindergarten der (PL die Kindergärten).

nut noun 1 Nuss△ die (PL die Nüsse); 2 (for a bolt) Mutter die (PL die Muttern).

nylon noun Nylon das.

O o

oak noun Eiche die (PL die Eichen).

oar noun Ruder das (PL die Ruder).

oats noun Hafer der; porridge oats Haferflocken (plural).

obedient adjective gehorsam.

obey verb 1 gehorchen (+DAT); to obey somebody jemandem gehorchen; 2 to obey the rules sich an die Vorschriften halten ◊.

object noun 1 (thing) Gegenstand der (PL die Gegenstände); 2 (aim) Zweck der; 3 (in grammar) Objekt das (PL die Objekte).
verb etwas dagegen haben ◊; if you don't object wenn Sie nichts dagegen haben.

objection noun Einwand der (PL die Einwände).

observe verb beobachten.

obsessed adjective besessen; she's really obsessed with her diet sie ist von ihrer Schlankheitskur ganz besessen.

obstinate adjective starrsinnig.

obtain verb erhalten ◊.

obvious adjective eindeutig.

obviously adverb 1 (of course) natürlich; 2 (looking at something) offensichtlich; the house is

obviously empty das Haus steht offensichtlich leer.

occasion noun Gelegenheit die (PL die Gelegenheiten); **on special occasions** zu besonderen Gelegenheiten.

occasionally adverb gelegentlich.

occupation noun Beruf der (PL die Berufe).

occupied adjective 1 (taken) besetzt; **the seat is occupied** der Platz ist besetzt; 2 (lived in) bewohnt.

occur verb 1 **to occur to somebody** jemandem einfallen ◊SEP (PERF sein); **it occurs to me that ...** mir fällt ein, dass ...; 2 **it never occurred to me** darauf wäre ich nie gekommen; 3 (happen) sich ereignen.

ocean noun Ozean der (PL die Ozeane).

o'clock adverb **at ten o'clock** um zehn Uhr; **it's three o'clock** es ist drei Uhr.

October noun Oktober der; **in October** im Oktober.

odd adjective 1 (strange) komisch; **that's odd, I'm sure I heard the bell** das ist komisch, ich habe es bestimmt klingeln gehört; 2 (number) ungerade; **three is an odd number** drei ist eine ungerade Zahl; 3 **the odd one out** die Ausnahme.

odds and ends plural noun Kleinkram der.

of preposition 1 von (+DAT); (instead of translating 'of' with 'von', the

genitive case can be used) **the parents of the children** die Eltern von den Kindern, die Eltern der Kinder; **the name of the flower** der Name der Blume; **it's very kind of you** das ist sehr nett von Ihnen; 2 (with quantities 'of' is not translated) **a kilo of tomatoes** ein Kilo Tomaten; **a bottle of milk** eine Flasche Milch; **the three of us** wir drei; 3 **of it/them** davon (things); **of them** von ihnen (people); **how many of them didn't pay?** wie viele von ihnen haben nicht gezahlt?; **Ray has four cars but he's selling three of them** Ray hat vier Autos, aber er verkauft drei davon; **half of it** die Hälfte davon; **we ate a lot of it** wir haben viel davon gegessen; 4 **the sixth of June** der sechste Juni; 5 **made of** aus; **a bracelet made of silver** ein Armband aus Silber.

off adverb, adjective, preposition 1 (switched off) aus; **is the telly off?** ist der Fernseher aus?; **to turn off the lights** das Licht ausmachen SEP; 2 (electricity, water, gas) abgestellt; **the gas and electricity were off** Gas und Strom waren abgestellt; **to turn off the tap** den Wasserhahn zudrehen SEP; 3 **to be off** (to leave) gehen ◊ (PERF sein); (in a vehicle) fahren ◊ (PERF sein); **I must be off** ich muss gehen; 4 **on my day off** an meinem freien Tag; **to take three days off work** sich ←(DAT) drei Tage frei nehmen; **we were given two days off school** wir hatten zwei Tage schulfrei; **to be off sick** wegen Krankheit fehlen; **Maya's off school today** Maya fehlt heute in der

◊ IRREGULAR VERB: See the verb table in the centre of the dictionary

Schule; **5** (*cancelled*) abgesagt; **the match is off** das Spiel ist abgesagt worden; **6 '20% off shoes'** 'Schuhe 20% reduziert'.

offence *noun* **1** (*crime*) Straftat *die* (PL die Straftaten); **2 to take offence** beleidigt sein; **he takes offence easily** er ist schnell beleidigt.

offer *noun* **1** Angebot *das* (PL die Angebote); **job offer** das Stellenangebot; **2 on special offer** im Sonderangebot.
verb anbieten ◇ SEP (*a present, a reward, or a job*); **he offered her a chair** er bot ihr einen Stuhl an; **to offer to do something** anbieten, etwas zu tun; **he offered to drive me to the station** er hat angeboten, mich zum Bahnhof zu fahren.

office *noun* Büro *das* (PL die Büros); **he's still at the office** er ist noch im Büro.

office block *noun* Bürohaus *das* (PL die Bürohäuser).

official *adjective* offiziell.

off-licence *noun* Wein- und Spirituosenhandlung *die* (PL die Wein- und Spirituosenhandlungen).

often *adverb* **1** oft; **he's often late** er kommt oft zu spät; **how often?** wie oft?; **2 more often** öfter; **couldn't you come more often?** könntest du nicht öfter kommen?

oil *noun* **1** (*crude oil*) Öl *das*; **2 olive oil** das Olivenöl; **suntan oil** das Sonnenöl.

ointment *noun* Salbe *die* (PL die Salben).

okay *adjective* **1** okay (*informal*); **tomorrow at ten, okay?** morgen um zehn, okay?; **is it okay if I don't come till Friday?** ist es okay, wenn ich erst Freitag komme?; **2** (*person*) in Ordnung; **Daisy's okay** Daisy ist in Ordnung; **3** (*nothing special, not ill*) ganz gut; **the film was okay** der Film war ganz gut; **I've been ill but I'm now okay** ich war krank, aber jetzt geht es mir ganz gut; **how are you?** – **'okay'** 'wie geht's?' – 'ganz gut'; **4 it's okay by me** mir ist es recht.

old *adjective* **1** (*not young, not new, previous*) alt; **an old man** ein alter Mann; **an old lady** eine alte Dame; **an old tree** ein alter Baum; **old people** alte Leute; **old clothes** bring ein paar alte Sachen mit; **I've only got their old address** ich habe nur ihre alte Adresse; **2** (*talking about age*) **how old are you?** wie alt bist du?; **James is ten years old** James ist zehn Jahre alt; **3 a two-year-old child** ein zweijähriges Kind; **4 my older sister** meine ältere Schwester; **she's older than me** sie ist älter als ich; **he's a year older than me** er ist ein Jahr älter als ich.

old age *noun* Alter *das*.

old age pensioner *noun* Rentner *der* (PL die Rentner), Rentnerin *die* (PL die Rentnerinnen).

old-fashioned *noun* altmodisch.

olive *noun* Olive *die* (PL die Oliven).

△ NEW SPELLING: *See page xii*

olive oil noun Olivenöl das (PL die Olivenöle).

Olympic Games, Olympics plural noun Olympische Spiele (plural).

omelette noun Omelett das (PL die Omelette); **a cheese omelette** ein Käseomelett.

on preposition 1 auf (+DAT, or +ACC with movement towards a place); **it's on the desk** es ist auf dem Schreibtisch; 2 (attached to) an (+DAT, or +ACC with movement towards a place); **on the wall** an der Wand; 3 **on the beach** am Strand; **on the right/left** rechts/links; 4 (in expressions of time) **on March 21st** am 21. März; **he's arriving on Tuesday** er kommt am Dienstag an; **it's shut on Sundays** es ist sonntags geschlossen; **on rainy days** an Regentagen; 5 (for buses, trains, etc.) **to go on the bus** mit dem Bus fahren; **I met Jackie on the train** ich habe Jackie im Zug getroffen; **let's go on our bikes** fahren wir mit dem Rad; 6 **on TV** im Fernsehen; **on the radio** im Radio; **on video** auf Video; 7 **on holiday** in den Ferien. adjective 1 (switched on) **to be on** an sein; **the lights are on** das Licht ist an; **is the radio on?** ist das Radio an?; 2 (happening) **what's on TV?** was gibt's im Fernsehen?; **what's on this week at the cinema?** was läuft diese Woche im Kino?

once adverb 1 einmal; **I've tried once already** ich habe es schon einmal versucht; **try once more** versuch es noch einmal; **once a day**

einmal täglich; 2 **more than once** mehrmals; 3 **at once** (immediately) sofort; **the doctor came at once** der Arzt kam sofort; 4 **at once** (at the same time) gleichzeitig; **I can't do two things at once** ich kann nicht zwei Sachen gleichzeitig machen.

one number (when counting) eins; (with a noun) ein; **one son** ein Sohn; **one apple** ein Apfel; **if you want a biro I've got one** falls du einen Kugelschreiber brauchst, habe ich einen; **at one o'clock** um ein Uhr. pronoun 1 einer/eine/eins; **I saw the photos, can I have one of them?** ich habe die Fotos gesehen, kann ich eins davon haben?; 2 **this one** dieser/diese/dieses; **I'd prefer that bike, but this one's cheaper** ich würde lieber das Rad haben, aber dieses ist billiger; 3 **that one** der/die da/das da; **'which video?' – 'that one'** 'welches Video?' – 'das da'; 4 **which one?** welcher/welche/welches?; **'my foot's hurting' – 'which one?'** 'mir tut der Fuß weh' – 'welcher?'; **she borrowed a skirt from me' – 'which one?'** 'sie hat sich einen Rock von mir geliehen' – 'welchen?'; 5 (you) man; **one never knows** man kann nie wissen.

one's adjective sein/seine/sein; **one pays for one's car** man zahlt für sein Auto.

oneself pronoun 1 (reflexive) sich; **to wash oneself** sich waschen; 2 (stressing something) selbst; **one**

⬥ **IRREGULAR VERB:** See the verb table in the centre of the dictionary.

has to do everything oneself man muss alles selbst machen.

one-way street noun Einbahnstraße die (PL die Einbahnstraßen).

onion noun Zwiebel die (PL die Zwiebeln).

only adjective 1 einziger/einzige/einziges; **the only free seat** der einzige freie Platz; **the only thing you could do** das Einzige, was du machen könntest; 2 **an only child** ein Einzelkind.
adverb, conjunction 1 nur; **they've only got two bedrooms** sie haben nur zwei Schlafzimmer; **Anne's only free on Fridays** Anne ist nur freitags frei; **there are only three left** es sind nur noch drei übrig; **I'd walk, only it's raining** ich würde zu Fuß gehen, nur regnet es; 2 (very recently) gerade erst; **he's only just got the message** er hat die Nachricht gerade erst bekommen; 3 (barely) gerade noch; **we've only just made it on time** wir sind gerade noch rechtzeitig angekommen.

onto preposition auf (+ACC).

open noun in the open im Freien.
· adjective 1 offen; **the door's open** die Tür ist offen; **the baker's is not open** die Bäckerei ist nicht geöffnet; 2 **in the open air** im Freien.
verb 1 aufmachen SEP; **can you open the door for me?** kannst du mir die Tür aufmachen?; **the bank opens at nine** die Bank macht um neun auf; 2 (open up) sich öffnen; **the door opened slowly** die Tür öffnete sich langsam.

opera noun Oper die (PL die Opern).

operation noun 1 Operation die (PL die Operationen); 2 **to have an operation** operiert werden.

opinion noun Meinung die (PL die Meinungen); **in my opinion** meiner Meinung nach.

opinion poll noun Meinungsumfrage die (PL die Meinungsumfragen).

opportunity noun Gelegenheit die (PL die Gelegenheiten); **to have the opportunity of doing something** die Gelegenheit haben, etwas zu tun.

opposite noun Gegenteil das (PL die Gegenteile); **no, quite the opposite** nein, ganz im Gegenteil.
adjective 1 entgegengesetzt (direction); **she went off in the opposite direction** sie ging in die entgegengesetzte Richtung; 2 (facing) gegenüberliegend; **in the house opposite** im gegenüberliegenden Haus.
adverb gegenüber; **they live opposite** sie wohnen gegenüber.
preposition gegenüber (+DAT); **opposite the station** gegenüber dem Bahnhof.

optician noun Optiker der (PL die Optiker), Optikerin die (PL die Optikerinnen).

option noun Wahl die; **we have no option** wir haben keine andere Wahl.

optional adjective auf Wunsch erhältlich; **optional subject** das Wahlfach.

△ NEW SPELLING: See page xii

or *conjunction* **1** oder; **English or German?** Englisch oder Deutsch?; **today or Tuesday?** heute oder Dienstag?; **2** (*in negatives*) noch; **I don't have a cat or a dog** ich habe weder eine Katze noch einen Hund; **not in June or July** weder im Juni noch im Juli; **3** (*or else*) sonst; **phone Mum, or she'll worry** ruf Mutti an, sonst macht sie sich Sorgen.

oral *noun* (*an exam*) Mündliche *das* (*informal*); **my German oral** mein Deutschmündliches.

orange *noun* (*the fruit*) Orange *die* (PL *die* Orangen); **orange juice** *der* Orangensaft.
adjective orange ('*orange*' *never changes*); **my orange socks** meine orange Socken.

orchestra *noun* Orchester *das* (PL *die* Orchester).

order *noun* **1** (*sequence*) Reihenfolge *die* (PL *die* Reihenfolgen); **in the right order** in der richtigen Reihenfolge; **in the wrong order** nicht in der richtigen Reihenfolge; **in alphabetical order** in alphabetischer Reihenfolge; **2** (*in a restaurant, café, or shop*) Bestellung *die* (PL *die* Bestellungen); **3** '**out of order**' 'außer Betrieb'; **4** **in order to do something** um etwas zu tun.
verb **1** (*in a restaurant or a shop*) bestellen; **we ordered soup** wir haben Suppe bestellt; **have you ordered?** haben Sie schon bestellt?; **2** bestellen (*a taxi*).

ordinary *adjective* normal.

organ *noun* **1** (*the instrument*) Orgel *die* (PL *die* Orgeln); **2** (*of the body*) Organ *das* (PL *die* Organe).

organic *adjective* Bio- (*food*); **organic food** *die* Biokost.

organization *noun* Organisation *die* (PL *die* Organisationen).

organize *verb* **1** organisieren; **2** veranstalten (*a conference or festival*).

original *adjective* **1** ursprünglich; **the original plan was better** der ursprüngliche Plan war besser; **2** originell; **it's a really original novel** das ist ein wirklich origineller Roman.

originally *adverb* ursprünglich; **originally we wanted to go by car** ursprünglich wollten wir mit dem Auto fahren.

other *adjective* **1** anderer/andere/anderes; **we took the other road** wir haben die andere Straße genommen; **where are the others?** wo sind die anderen?; **the other two cars** die anderen beiden Autos; **2** **give me the other one** gib mir den anderen/die andere/das andere (*the translation of 'the other one' depends on the gender of the noun it refers to*); **3** **the other day** neulich; **4** **every other week** jede zweite Woche; **5** **somebody or other** irgendjemand; **something or other** irgendetwas; **somewhere or other** irgendwo; **6** **any other questions?** sonst noch Fragen?

◈ IRREGULAR VERB: *See the verb table in the centre of the dictionary*

otherwise *adverb, conjunction*
sonst.

ought *verb* ('*ought' is usually
translated by the subjunctive of
'sollen'*) **I ought to go** ich sollte
eigentlich gehen; **they ought to
have known the address** sie
hätten die Adresse kennen sollen;
**you oughtn't to have any
problems** du solltest keine
Probleme haben.

our *adjective* **1** (*before a masculine
noun*) unser; **our father** unser
Vater; **2** (*before a feminine noun*)
unsere; **our mother** unsere Mutter;
3 (*before a neuter noun*) unser; **our
house** unser Haus; **4** (*before
masculine/feminine/neuter plural
nouns*) unsere; **our parents** unsere
Eltern; **5** (*with parts of the body*)
der/die/das (*plural:* die); **we'll go
and wash our hands** wir waschen
uns die Hände.

ours *pronoun* **1** (*for a masculine
noun*) unserer; **their garden's
bigger than ours** ihr Garten ist
größer als unserer; **2** (*for a feminine
noun*) unsere; **their kitchen is
smaller than ours** ihre Küche ist
kleiner als unsere; **3** (*for a neuter
noun*) unsere; **their child is younger
than ours** ihr Kind ist jünger als
unsers; **4** (*for plural nouns*) unsere;
**they've invited their friends and
we've invited ours** sie haben ihre
Freunde eingeladen und wir haben
unsere eingeladen; **5 the green car
is ours** das grüne Auto gehört uns;
it's ours es gehört uns; **a friend of
ours** ein Freund von uns.

ourselves *pronoun* **1** (*reflexive*)
uns; **we introduced ourselves** wir
haben uns vorgestellt; **2** (*for
emphasis*) selbst; **in the end we did
it ourselves** schließlich haben wir
es selbst gemacht.

out *adverb* **1** (*outside*) draußen; **it's
cold out there** es ist kalt da
draußen; **they're out in the garden**
sie sind draußen im Garten; **2 to go
out** hinausgehen ◇ SEP (PERF *sein*),
rausgehen ◇ SEP (PERF *sein*)
(*informal*); **to go out shopping**
einkaufen gehen; **3 get out!** raus!
(*informal*); **4 the ball is out** der Ball
ist aus; **5** (*absent*) **to be out** nicht
da sein; **Mr Barnes is out** Herr
Barnes ist nicht da; **6 to go out** (*for
an evening or to the theatre or
cinema*) ausgehen ◇ SEP (PERF *sein*),
weggehen ◇ SEP (PERF *sein*)
(*informal*); **are you going out this
evening?** gehst du heute Abend
weg?; **to be going out with
somebody** mit jemandem gehen;
Alison's going out with Danny now
Alison geht jetzt mit Danny; **7 to ask
somebody out** jemanden
einladen ◇ SEP; **he's asked me out**
er hat mich eingeladen; **8** (*light,
fire*) aus; **are all the lights out?** ist
das Licht aus?
preposition **out of** aus (+DAT); **to go
out of the room** aus dem Zimmer
gehen; **he threw it out of the
window** er hat es aus dem Fenster
geworfen; **to drink out of a glass**
aus einem Glas trinken; **she took the
photo out of her bag** sie hat das
Foto aus der Tasche genommen.

△ NEW SPELLING: *See page xii*

outdoor adjective (activity or sport) im Freien; **outdoor games** Spiele im Freien.

outdoors adverb draußen; **to go outdoors** nach draußen gehen.

outing noun Ausflug der (PL die Ausflüge); **to go on an outing** einen Ausflug machen.

outline noun (of an object) Umriss der (PL die Umrisse).

out-of-date adjective 1 (no longer valid) ungültig; **my passport's out of date** mein Pass ist ungültig; 2 (old-fashioned) altmodisch (clothes, music).

outside noun Außenseite die; **it's blue on the outside** auf der Außenseite ist es blau.
adjective Außen-.
adverb draußen; **it's cold outside** es ist kalt draußen.
preposition vor (+DAT); **I'll meet you outside the cinema** ich treffe mich vor dem Kino mit dir.

oven noun Ofen der (PL die Öfen); **to put something in the oven** etwas in den Ofen tun.

over preposition 1 (above) über ←(DAT); **there's a mirror over the sink** über dem Waschbecken hängt ein Spiegel; 2 (involving movement) über (+ACC); **he threw the ball over the wall** er hat den Ball über die Mauer geworfen; 3 **over here** hier drüben; **the food is over here** das Essen ist hier drüben; 4 **over there** da drüben; **she's over there** sie ist da drüben; 5 (more than) über; **it will cost over**

a hundred pounds es wird über hundert Pfund kosten; **he's over sixty** er ist über sechzig; 6 (during) über (+ACC); **over Christmas** über Weihnachten; **over the weekend** übers Wochenende; 7 (finished) zu Ende; **when the meeting's over** wenn die Besprechung zu Ende ist; **it's all over** es ist vorbei; 8 **over the phone** am Telefon; **to ask someone over** jemanden einladen ◇ SEP; **to come over** herüberkommen ◇ SEP; **come over on Saturday** komm am Samstag zu uns herüber; 9 **all over the place** überall; **I've been looking for it all over** ich habe überall danach gesucht.

overtake verb überholen.

overtime noun **to work overtime** Überstunden machen.

overweight adjective **to be overweight** Übergewicht haben.

owe verb schulden; **I owe him ten pounds** ich schulde ihm zehn Pfund.

owing adjective 1 (outstanding) ausstehend; **there's five pounds owing** fünf Pfund stehen aus; 2 **owing to** wegen (+GEN); **owing to the snow** wegen des Schnees.

owl noun Eule die (PL die Eulen).

own adjective 1 eigen; **my own computer** mein eigener Computer; **I've got my own room** ich habe mein eigenes Zimmer; 2 **on your own** allein; **Annie did it on her own** Annie hat es allein gemacht.
verb besitzen ◇.

◇ IRREGULAR VERB: See the verb table in the centre of the dictionary

owner noun Besitzer der (PL die Besitzer), Besitzerin die (PL die Besitzerinnen).

oxygen noun Sauerstoff der.

ozone layer noun Ozonschicht die.

P p

pace noun 1 (a step) Schritt der (PL die Schritte); 2 (the speed you walk at) Tempo das (PL die Tempos).

Pacific noun the Pacific (Ocean) der Pazifik.

pack noun 1 Packung die (PL die Packungen); a pack of cards ein Kartenspiel.
verb 1 packen (your case); I haven't packed yet ich habe noch nicht gepackt; I'll pack my case tonight ich packe meinen Koffer heute Abend; 2 einpacken SEP (clothes, shoes, etc.); have you packed my red shirt? hast du mein rotes Hemd eingepackt?

package noun Paket das (PL die Pakete).

packed lunch noun Lunchpaket das (PL die Lunchpakete).

packet noun 1 Päckchen das (PL die Päckchen); a packet of tea ein Päckchen Tee; 2 (box) Schachtel die (PL die Schachteln); 3 (bag) Tüte die (PL die Tüten); a packet of crisps eine Tüte Chips.

pad noun (of paper) Block der (PL die Blöcke).

page noun Seite die (PL die Seiten); on page seven auf Seite sieben.

pain noun Schmerz der (PL die Schmerzen); to be in pain Schmerzen haben; I've got a pain in my leg ich habe Schmerzen im Bein; ★ Eric's a real pain (in the neck) Eric geht einem richtig auf den Wecker (informal).

painful adjective schmerzhaft.

paint noun Farbe die (PL die Farben); 'wet paint' 'frisch gestrichen'.
verb malen (a picture); streichen ✧ (a room); to paint a room pink ein Zimmer rosa streichen.

paintbrush noun Pinsel der (PL die Pinsel).

painter noun Maler der (PL die Maler), Malerin die (PL die Malerinnen).

painting noun (picture) Gemälde das (PL die Gemälde); a painting by Picasso ein Gemälde von Picasso.

pair noun 1 Paar das (PL die Paare); a pair of socks ein Paar Socken; 2 a pair of scissors eine Schere; 3 a pair of trousers eine Hose; a pair of knickers eine Unterhose; 4 to work in pairs paarweise arbeiten.

Pakistan noun Pakistan das.

palace noun Palast der (PL die Paläste).

pale adjective blass △; to turn pale blass werden; pale green zartgrün.

palm noun 1 (of your hand)
Handfläche die (PL die
Handflächen); 2 (a palm tree)
Palme die (PL die Palmen).

pan noun 1 (saucepan) Topf der (PL
die Töpfe); a pan of water ein Topf
Wasser; 2 (frying-pan) Pfanne die
(PL die Pfannen).

pancake noun Pfannkuchen der
(PL die Pfannkuchen).

panel noun 1 (for a discussion)
Diskussionsrunde die; (for a quiz)
Rateteam das; 2 (a piece of wood)
Tafel die (PL die Tafeln).

panic noun Panik die.
verb in Panik geraten ◇; don't
panic! keine Panik!

pantomime noun
Märchenvorstellung die (PL die
Märchenvorstellungen).

pants plural noun Unterhose die (PL
die Unterhosen).

paper noun 1 Papier das; a sheet of
paper ein Blatt Papier; 2 paper
hanky das Papiertaschentuch;
3 paper cup der Pappbecher;
4 (newspaper) Zeitung die (PL die
Zeitungen); it was in the paper es
stand in der Zeitung; 5 papers
(documents) Unterlagen (plural).

paperback noun Taschenbuch das
(PL die Taschenbücher).

paperclip noun Büroklammer die
(PL die Büroklammern).

paper towel noun
Papierhandtuch das (PL die
Papierhandtücher).

parachute noun Fallschirm der (PL
die Fallschirme).

parade noun Umzug der (PL die
Umzüge).

paragraph noun Absatz der (PL die
Absätze); 'new paragraph' 'Absatz'.

paralysed adjective gelähmt.

parcel noun Paket das (PL die
Pakete).

pardon noun I beg your pardon (as
an apology) Entschuldigung!;
pardon? wie bitte?

parent noun Elternteil der;
parents Eltern (plural); my parents
live in Germany meine Eltern
wohnen in Deutschland; parents'
evening der Elternabend.

park noun 1 Park der (PL die Parks);
theme park der (thematische)
Freizeitpark; 2 car park der
Parkplatz.
verb 1 parken; you can park outside
the house du kannst vor dem Haus
parken; 2 to find somewhere to
park einen Parkplatz finden.

parking noun Parken das; 'no
parking' 'Parken verboten'.

parking meter noun Parkuhr die
(PL die Parkuhren).

parking space noun
Parklücke die (PL die Parklücken).

parking ticket noun
Strafzettel der (PL die Strafzettel).

parliament noun Parlament das
(PL die Parlamente).

parrot noun Papagei der (PL die
Papageien).

◇ IRREGULAR VERB: See the verb table in the centre of the dictionary

parsley noun Petersilie die.

part noun 1 Teil der (PL die Teile); part of the garden Teil des Gartens; the last part of the book der letzte Teil des Buches; 2 that's part of your job das gehört dazu; 3 to take part in something an etwas ←(DAT) teilnehmen ✧ SEP; 4 (spare part) Teil das (PL die Teile) (for a machine or an engine); 5 (a role in a play) Rolle die (PL die Rollen).

particular adjective besonderer/besondere/besonderes; nothing in particular nichts Besonderes.

particularly adverb besonders; not particularly interesting nicht besonders interessant.

partly adverb teilweise.

partner noun Partner der (PL die Partner), Partnerin die (PL die Partnerinnen).

part-time adjective Teilzeit-; part-time work die Teilzeitarbeit. adverb to work part-time Teilzeit arbeiten.

party noun 1 (small, private) Party die (PL die Partys), Feier die (PL die Feiern); a Christmas party eine Weihnachtsfeier; to have a birthday party eine Geburtstagsparty machen; 2 (more formal, in the evening) Gesellschaft die (PL die Gesellschaften); we've been invited to a party at the Smiths' house wir sind zu einer Gesellschaft bei Smiths eingeladen worden; 3 (group) Gruppe die (PL die Gruppen); a party of schoolchildren eine Gruppe

Schulkinder; 4 (in politics) Partei die (PL die Parteien).

party game noun Gesellschaftsspiel das (PL die Gesellschaftsspiele).

pass noun 1 (to let you in) Ausweis der (PL die Ausweise); 2 bus pass die Buskarte; 3 (over the mountains) Pass ∆ der (PL die Pässe); 4 (in an exam) to get a pass in maths die Mathematikprüfung bestehen.
verb 1 (walk past) vorbeigehen ✧ SEP (PERF sein) an (+DAT) (a place or building); we passed your house wir sind an deinem Haus vorbeigegangen; 2 (drive past) vorbeifahren ✧ SEP (PERF sein) an (+DAT) (a place or building); 3 (overtake) überholen (a car); 4 (give) reichen; could you pass me the sugar please? könnten Sie mir bitte den Zucker reichen?; 5 (time) vergehen ✧ (PERF sein); the time passed slowly die Zeit verging langsam; 6 bestehen ✧ (an exam); to pass an exam eine Prüfung bestehen; did you pass in German? hast du die Deutschprüfung bestanden?

passenger noun 1 (in a plane or ship) Passagier der (PL die Passagiere); 2 (in a train or bus) Fahrgast der (PL die Fahrgäste); 3 (in a car) Mitfahrer der (PL die Mitfahrer).

Passover noun Passah das.

passport noun Reisepass ∆ der (PL die Reisepässe), Pass ∆ der (PL die Pässe).

∆ NEW SPELLING: See page xii

password noun Kennwort das (PL die Kennwörter).

past noun Vergangenheit die; **in the past** in der Vergangenheit.
adjective 1 (recent) letzter/letzte/letztes; **in the past few weeks** in den letzten paar Wochen; 2 (over) vorbei; **winter is past** der Winter ist vorbei.
preposition, adverb 1 **to walk past something** an etwas ~(DAT) vorbeigehen ◇ SEP (PERF sein); **we went past the school** wir sind an der Schule vorbeigegangen; **to go past** vorbeifahren ◇ (PERF sein); 2 (after) nach (+DAT); **it's just past the post office** es ist kurz nach der Post; 3 (talking about time) **ten past six** zehn nach sechs; **half past four** halb fünf; **a quarter past two** Viertel nach zwei.

pasta noun Nudeln (plural); **I don't like pasta** ich mag keine Nudeln.

pastry noun 1 (for baking) Teig der; 2 (cake) Gebäck das.

path noun Weg der (PL die Wege); (very narrow) Pfad der (PL die Pfade).

pathetic adjective (useless, hopeless) jämmerlich.

patience noun 1 Geduld die; 2 (card game) Patience die.

patient noun Patient der (PL die Patienten), Patientin die (PL die Patientinnen).
adjective geduldig.

patiently adverb geduldig.

patio noun Terrasse die (PL die Terrassen).

pattern noun 1 (on wallpaper or fabric) Muster das (PL die Muster); 2 (dressmaking, knitting) Schnitt der (PL die Schnitte).

pause noun Pause die (PL die Pausen).

pavement noun Bürgersteig der (PL die Bürgersteige); **on the pavement** auf dem Bürgersteig.

paw noun Pfote die (PL die Pfoten).

pawn noun (in chess) Bauer der (PL die Bauern).

pay noun (wage) Lohn der (PL die Löhne); (salary) Gehalt das (PL die Gehälter).
verb 1 zahlen; **I'm paying** ich zahle; **to pay cash** bar zahlen; **to pay by credit card** mit Kreditkarte zahlen; **they pay £8 an hour** sie zahlen acht Pfund pro Stunde; **to pay by cheque** mit Scheck zahlen; 2 bezahlen ('bezahlen' is used when you pay a person, a bill or for something); **to pay for something** etwas bezahlen; **Tony paid for the drinks** Tony hat die Getränke bezahlt; **it's all paid for** es ist alles bezahlt; 3 **to pay somebody back** (money) jemandem Geld zurückzahlen SEP; 4 **to pay attention** aufpassen SEP; 5 **to pay a visit to somebody** jemanden besuchen.

payment noun 1 Bezahlung die (of sum, bill, debt, or fine); 2 Zahlung die (PL die Zahlungen) (of interest, tax, or fee).

pay phone noun Münzfernsprecher der (PL die Münzfernsprecher).

◇ **IRREGULAR VERB: See the verb table in the centre of the dictionary**

PC noun (computer) PC der
(PL die PC).

pea noun Erbse die (PL die Erbsen).

peace noun Frieden der.

peaceful adjective friedlich.

peach noun Pfirsich der (PL die
Pfirsiche).

peak period (for holidays)
Hauptferienzeit die (PL die
Hauptferienzeiten).

peak rate noun (for phoning)
Höchsttarif der (PL die Höchsttarife).

peak time noun (for traffic)
Stoßzeit die (PL die Stoßzeiten).

peanut noun Erdnuss△ die (PL die
Erdnüsse).

peanut butter noun
Erdnussbutter△ die.

pear noun Birne die (PL die Birnen).

pearl noun Perle die (PL die Perlen).

pebble noun Kieselstein der (PL die
Kieselsteine).

peculiar adjective komisch.

pedal noun Pedal das (PL die
Pedale).
verb (on a bike) **to pedal off** (mit
dem Rad) wegfahren ◇ (PERF sein).

pedestrian noun Fußgänger der
(PL die Fußgänger), Fußgängerin die
(PL die Fußgängerinnen).

pedestrian crossing noun
Fußgängerüberweg der (PL die
Fußgängerüberwege).

pedestrian precinct noun
Fußgängerzone die (PL die
Fußgängerzonen).

pee noun **to have a pee** pinkeln
(informal).

peel noun Schale die (PL die
Schalen).
verb schälen (fruit, vegetables).

peg noun 1 (hook) Haken der (PL die
Haken); 2 **clothes peg** der
Kleiderhaken; 3 (for a tent)
Pflock der (PL die Pflöcke).

pen noun (ball-point)
Kugelschreiber der (PL die
Kugelschreiber); **felt pen** der
Filzstift.

penalty noun 1 (a fine)
Geldstrafe die (PL die Geldstrafen);
2 (in football) Elfmeter der (PL die
Elfmeter).

pence plural noun Pence (plural).

pencil noun Bleistift der (PL die
Bleistifte); **to write in pencil** mit
Bleistift schreiben.

pencil case noun
Federmäppchen das (PL die
Federmäppchen).

pencil sharpener noun
Bleistiftanspitzer der (PL die
Bleistiftanspitzer).

penfriend noun Brieffreund der (PL
die Brieffreunde), Brieffreundin die
(PL die Brieffreundinnen); **my
German pen-friend is called Heidi**
meine deutsche Brieffreundin heißt
Heidi.

penis noun Penis der (PL die
Penisse).

△ NEW SPELLING: See page xii

penny noun Penny der (PL die Pence).

pension noun Rente die (PL die Renten).

pensioner noun Rentner der (PL die Rentner), Rentnerin die (PL die Rentnerinnen).

people plural noun 1 Leute (plural), Menschen (plural); ('Menschen' is used in a more formal context); most people round here die meisten Leute hier; several people verschiedene Leute; nice people nette Leute; all the people in the world alle Menschen auf der Welt; a crowd of people eine Menschenmenge; 2 (when you're counting them) Personen (plural); for ten people für zehn Personen; how many people have you invited? wie viele Personen hast du eingeladen?; 3 people say that ... man sagt, dass ...

pepper noun 1 (spice) Pfeffer der; 2 (vegetable) Paprikaschote die (PL die Paprikaschoten).

peppermill noun Pfeffermühle die (PL die Pfeffermühlen).

peppermint noun (plant) Pfefferminze die; peppermint tea der Pfefferminztee.

per preposition pro (+ACC); ten pounds per person zehn Pfund pro Person.

per cent adverb Prozent das; sixty per cent of students sechzig Prozent der Studenten.

percentage noun Prozentsatz der (PL die Prozentsätze).

percussion noun Schlagzeug das; to play percussion Schlagzeug spielen.

perfect adjective 1 perfekt; she speaks perfect English sie spricht perfekt Englisch; 2 (ideal) herrlich (day or weather).

perfectly adverb 1 (absolutely) vollkommen; 2 (faultlessly) perfekt.

perform verb 1 spielen (a piece of music or a part); 2 singen ◇ (a song); 3 to perform a play ein Theaterstück aufführen SEP.

performance noun 1 (playing or acting) Darstellung die (PL die Darstellungen); his performance as Hamlet seine Darstellung des Hamlet; 2 (show or film) Vorstellung die (PL die Vorstellungen); the performance starts at eight die Vorstellung fängt um acht Uhr an; 3 (of a play or opera) Aufführung die (PL die Aufführungen).

performer noun Künstler der (PL die Künstler), Künstlerin die (PL die Künstlerinnen).

perfume noun Parfüm das (PL die Parfüme).

perhaps adverb vielleicht; perhaps he's missed the train vielleicht hat er den Zug verpasst.

period noun 1 (length of time) Zeit die (PL die Zeiten); trial period die Probezeit; 2 (a portion of time) Zeitraum der; a two-year period

◇ IRREGULAR VERB: See the verb table in the centre of the dictionary

ein Zeitraum von zwei Jahren;
3 (*in school*) Stunde *die* (PL *die*
Stunden); **4** (*menstruation*)
Periode *die* (PL *die* Perioden).

perm *noun* Dauerwelle *die* (PL *die*
Dauerwellen).

permanent *adjective* **1** ständig;
2 fest (*job or address, for example*).

permanently *adverb* **1** dauernd;
2 to be permanently employed fest
angestellt sein.

permission *noun* Erlaubnis *die*; to
get permission to do something
Erlaubnis zu etwas ←(DAT) erhalten.

permit *noun* Genehmigung *die* (PL
die Genehmigungen).
verb **1** erlauben; to permit
somebody to do something
jemandem erlauben, etwas zu tun;
smoking is not permitted Rauchen
ist nicht gestattet; **2** weather
permitting bei entsprechendem
Wetter.

person *noun* **1** Person *die* (PL *die*
Personen); there's still room for
one more person wir haben noch
Platz für eine Person; **2** in person
persönlich.

personal *adjective* persönlich.

personality *noun*
Persönlichkeit *die* (PL *die*
Persönlichkeiten).

personally *adverb* persönlich;
personally, I'm against it ich
persönlich bin dagegen.

perspiration *noun* Schweiß *der*.

persuade *verb* überreden; to
persuade somebody to come
jemanden überreden zu kommen.

pessimistic *adjective*
pessimistisch.

pest *noun* **1** (*greenfly, for example*)
Schädling *der* (PL *die* Schädlinge);
2 (*annoying person*) Nervensäge *die*
(PL *die* Nervensägen) (*informal*).

pet *noun* **1** Haustier *das* (PL *die*
Haustiere); do you have a pet?
habt ihr Haustiere?; a pet dog ein
Hund; **2** Julie is teacher's pet Julie
ist der Liebling des Lehrers.

petrol *noun* Benzin *das* (PL *die*
Benzine); to fill up with petrol
tanken; to run out of petrol kein
Benzin mehr haben.

petrol station *noun* Tankstelle *die*
(PL *die* Tankstellen).

pharmacy *noun* Apotheke *die* (PL
die Apotheken).

pheasant *noun* Fasan *der* (PL *die*
Fasane).

phone *noun* Telefon *das* (PL *die*
Telefone); she's on the phone sie
telefoniert; I was on the phone to
Sophie ich habe mit Sophie
telefoniert; you can book by phone
du kannst telefonisch buchen.
verb **1** telefonieren; while I was
phoning während ich telefonierte;
2 to phone somebody jemanden
anrufen ◆ SEP; I'll phone you
tonight ich rufe dich heute Abend
an.

phone book *noun* Telefonbuch
das (PL *die* Telefonbücher).

△ NEW SPELLING: See page xii

phone box noun Telefonzelle die (PL die Telefonzellen).

phone call noun 1 Anruf der (PL die Anrufe); **to get a phone call** einen Anruf erhalten; 2 **to make a phone call** ein Telefongespräch führen; **phone calls are free** Telefongespräche sind gebührenfrei.

phone card noun Telefonkarte die (PL die Telefonkarten).

phone number noun Telefonnummer die (PL die Telefonnummern).

photo noun Foto das (PL die Fotos); **to take a photo** ein Foto machen; **to take a photo of somebody** ein Foto von jemandem machen.

photocopier noun Fotokopiergerät das (PL die Fotokopiergeräte).

photocopy noun Fotokopie die (PL die Fotokopien).
verb fotokopieren.

photograph noun Fotografie die (PL die Fotografien); **to take a photograph** ein Foto machen.
verb fotografieren.

photographer noun Fotograf der (PL die Fotografen), Fotografin die (PL die Fotografinnen).

photography noun Fotografie die.

physics noun Physik die.

physiotherapist noun Physiotherapeut der (PL die Physiotherapeuten), Physiotherapeutin die (PL die Physiotherapeutinnen).

physiotherapy noun Physiotherapie die.

piano noun Klavier das (PL die Klaviere); **to play the piano** Klavier spielen; **piano lesson** die Klavierstunde.

pick noun **to take your pick** sich ←(DAT) etwas aussuchen SEP.
verb 1 (to select) wählen; **he picked his words carefully** er wählte seine Worte mit Bedacht; 2 (choose for oneself) sich ←(DAT) aussuchen SEP; **pick any book** such dir irgendein Buch aus; 3 **to pick a team** eine Mannschaft aufstellen; 4 pflücken (fruit); **to pick strawberries** Erdbeeren pflücken.
● **to pick up** 1 (lift) (in die Hand) nehmen ◇; **he picked up the papers** er hat die Unterlagen genommen; 2 (collect) abholen SEP; **I'll pick you up at six** ich hole dich um sechs Uhr ab; **I'll pick up the keys tomorrow** ich hole die Schlüssel morgen ab.

pickpocket noun Taschendieb der (PL die Taschendiebe).

picnic noun Picknick das (PL die Picknicke); **to have a picnic** ein Picknick machen.

picture noun 1 Bild das (PL die Bilder); 2 **to go to the pictures** (the cinema) ins Kino gehen.

pie noun 1 (sweet) Kuchen der (PL die Kuchen); **apple pie** der Apfelkuchen; 2 (savoury) Pastete die (PL die Pasteten).

piece noun 1 (a bit) Stück das (PL die Stücke); **a big piece of cheese**

ein großes Stück Käse; **2** (*that you fit together*) Teil das (PL *die* Teile); **the pieces of a jigsaw** die Teile von einem Puzzle; **to take something to pieces** etwas in Einzelteile zerlegen; **3** *piece of furniture* das Möbelstück; **a piece of information** eine Information; **a piece of luck** ein Glücksfall; **4** (*coin*) Stück das (PL *die* Stücke); **a five-pence piece** ein Fünf-Pence-Stück.

pierce *verb* **1** durchstechen ◆ SEP; **2 to have pierced ears** Löcher in den Ohrläppchen haben.

pig *noun* Schwein das (PL *die* Schweine).

pigeon *noun* Taube die (PL *die* Tauben).

pigtail *noun* Zopf der (PL *die* Zöpfe).

pile *noun* **1** (*a neat stack*) Stapel der (PL *die* Stapel); **a pile of plates** ein Stapel Teller; **2** (*a heap*) Haufen der (PL *die* Haufen).

● **to pile something up** (*neatly*) etwas aufstapeln SEP; (*in a heap*) etwas auftürmen SEP.

pill *noun* Pille die (PL *die* Pillen).

pillow *noun* Kopfkissen das (PL *die* Kopfkissen).

pilot *noun* Pilot der (PL *die* Piloten), Pilotin die (PL *die* Pilotinnen).

pimple *noun* Pickel der (PL *die* Pickel).

pin *noun* **1** (*for sewing*) Stecknadel die (PL *die* Stecknadeln); **2 a three-pin plug** ein dreipoliger Stecker.

● **to pin up 1** hochstecken SEP (*a hem*); **2** anschlagen ◆ SEP (*a notice*).

PIN *noun* (*personal identification number*) Geheimnummer die.

pinball *noun* Flippern das; **to play pinball** flippern; **pinball machine** der Flipper.

pinch *noun* (*of salt, for example*) Prise die (PL *die* Prisen).
verb **1** kneifen ◆; **she pinched my arm** sie hat mich in den Arm gekniffen; **2** klauen; **somebody's pinched my bike** jemand hat mein Rad geklaut.

pine *noun* Kiefer die (PL *die* Kiefern); **pine furniture** Kiefernmöbel (*plural*).

pineapple *noun* Ananas die (PL *die* Ananas).

ping-pong *noun* Tischtennis das; **to play ping-pong** Tischtennis spielen.

pink *adjective* rosa ('*rosa*' never changes); **pink hats** rosa Hüte.

pip *noun* (*in a fruit*) Kern der (PL *die* Kerne).

pipe *noun* **1** (*for gas or water*) Rohr das (PL *die* Rohre); **2** (*for smoking*) Pfeife die (PL *die* Pfeifen); **he smokes a pipe** er raucht Pfeife.

Pisces *noun* Fische (*plural*); **Amanda is Pisces** Amanda ist Fisch.

pitch *noun* Platz der (PL *die* Plätze); **football pitch** der Fußballplatz.
verb **to pitch a tent** ein Zelt aufstellen SEP.

△ NEW SPELLING: *See page xii*

pity noun 1 (*feeling sorry for somebody*) Mitleid *das*; 2 **what a pity!** wie schade!; **it would be a pity to miss the beginning** es wäre schade, den Anfang zu verpassen.
verb **to pity somebody** jemanden bemitleiden.

place noun 1 Ort *der* (PL die Orte); **Salzburg is a wonderful place** Salzburg ist ein schöner Ort; **in place** an Ort und Stelle; 2 **all over the place** überall; 3 (*a space*) Platz *der* (PL die Plätze); **a place for the car** ein Platz für das Auto; **is there a place for me?** gibt es Platz für mich?; **will you keep my place?** kannst du mir den Platz freihalten?; **to change places** die Plätze tauschen; 4 (*spot*) Stelle *die* (PL die Stellen); **this is a good place to stop** das ist eine gute Stelle zum Halten; 5 (*in a race*) Platz *der* (PL die Plätze); **to gain first place** den ersten Platz belegen; 6 **at your place** bei dir; **we'll go round to Zafir's place** wir gehen zu Zafir; 7 **to take place** stattfinden ◇ SEP; **the competition will take place at four** der Wettbewerb findet um vier Uhr statt.
verb (*upright*) stellen; (*lying flat*) legen.

plain noun Ebene *die* (PL die Ebenen).
adjective 1 einfach; **plain food** einfaches Essen; 2 (*unflavoured*) Natur-; **plain yoghurt** der Naturjoghurt; 3 (*not patterned*) einfarbig; **plain curtains** einfarbige Vorhänge.

plait noun Zopf *der* (PL die Zöpfe).

plan noun Plan *der* (PL die Pläne); **we've made plans for the summer** wir haben Pläne für den Sommer gemacht; **to go according to plan** nach Plan gehen; **everything went according to plan** alles ist nach Plan gegangen.
verb 1 **to plan to do something** etwas vorhaben ◇ SEP; **we're planning to leave at eight** wir haben vor, um acht abzufahren; 2 (*make plans for, organize, design*) planen; **she's planning a trip to Italy** sie plant eine Reise nach Italien.

plane noun Flugzeug *das* (PL die Flugzeuge); **we went by plane** wir sind geflogen.

planet noun Planet *der* (PL die Planeten).

plant noun Pflanze *die* (PL die Pflanzen); **a house plant** eine Topfpflanze.
verb pflanzen.

plaster noun 1 (*sticking plaster*) Pflaster *das* (PL die Pflaster); 2 (*for walls*) Verputz *der*; 3 Gips *der*; **to have your leg in plaster** das Bein in Gips haben.

plastic noun Plastik *das*; **plastic bag** die Plastiktüte.

plate noun Teller *der* (PL die Teller).

platform noun 1 (*in a station*) Bahnsteig *der* (PL die Bahnsteige); 2 **the train is arriving at platform six** der Zug fährt auf Gleis sechs ein; 3 (*for lecturing or performing*) Podium *das* (PL die Podien).

play noun (*in the theatre*) Stück *das* (PL die Stücke); **television play** das

◇ **IRREGULAR VERB:** See the verb table in the centre of the dictionary

Fernsehspiel; **we are putting on a play by Brecht at school** wir führen ein Stück von Brecht in der Schule auf.

verb **1** spielen; **the children are playing with a ball** die Kinder spielen Ball; **they play the piano and the guitar** sie spielen Klavier und Gitarre; **who's playing Hamlet?** wer spielt Hamlet?; **to play tennis** Tennis spielen; **they were playing cards** sie haben Karten gespielt; **2** (*in sport*) **to play somebody** gegen jemanden spielen; **Italy is playing Germany** Italien spielt gegen Deutschland; **3** (*music*) spielen (*a tape, CD, or record*); **play your new CD** spiele mal deine neue CD.

player *noun* **1** Spieler *der* (PL die Spieler), Spielerin *die* (PL die Spielerinnen); **football player** *der* Fußballspieler; **2** (*in the theatre*) Schauspieler *der* (PL die Schauspieler), Schauspielerin *die* (PL die Schauspielerinnen).

playground *noun* Spielplatz *der* (PL die Spielplätze); **school playground** *der* Schulhof.

playgroup *noun* Kindergarten *der* (PL die Kindergärten).

playing field *noun* Sportplatz *der* (PL die Sportplätze).

pleasant *adjective* angenehm.

please *adverb* bitte; **two coffees, please** zwei Kaffee bitte; **could you turn the TV off, please?** könntest du bitte den Fernseher ausmachen?

pleased *adjective* **1** erfreut; **I'm really pleased!** das freut mich wirklich!; **2** she was pleased with

her present sie hat sich über ihr Geschenk gefreut; **3 pleased to meet you!** freut mich!

pleasure *noun* **1** (*amusement*) Vergnügen *das*; **2** (*joy*) Freude *die*; **to get a lot of pleasure out of something** viel Freude an etwas ←(DAT) haben.

plenty *pronoun* **1** (*lots*) viel; **he's got plenty of money** er hat viel Geld; **2** (*enough*) genug; **that's plenty!** das ist genug!; **we've got plenty of time left** wir haben noch genug Zeit.

plot *noun* (*of a film or novel*) Handlung *die*.

plug *noun* **1** (*electrical*) Stecker *der* (PL die Stecker); **2** (*in a bath or sink*) Stöpsel *der* (PL die Stöpsel); **to pull out the plug** den Stöpsel herausziehen.

plum *noun* Pflaume *die* (PL die Pflaumen); **plum tart** *der* Pflaumenkuchen.

plumber *noun* Installateur *der* (PL die Installateure).

plural *noun* Mehrzahl *die*, Plural *der*; **in the plural** in der Mehrzahl, im Plural.

plus *preposition* plus (+DAT); **three children plus a baby** drei Kinder und ein Baby.

p.m. *abbreviation* nachmittags (*for times up to 6 p.m.*); abends (*for times after 6 p.m.*); **at two p.m.** um zwei Uhr nachmittags, um vierzehn Uhr; **at nine p.m.** um neun Uhr abends, um einundzwanzig Uhr (*in German you usually express times after*

△ NEW SPELLING: See page xii

midday in terms of the 24-hour clock).

pocket noun Tasche die (PL die Taschen).

pocket money noun Taschengeld das.

poem noun Gedicht das (PL die Gedichte).

poet noun Dichter der (PL die Dichter), Dichterin die (PL die Dichterinnen).

poetry noun Dichtung die.

point noun 1 (tip) Spitze die (PL die Spitzen); **the point of a nail** die Spitze eines Nagels; 2 (a tiny mark or dot) Punkt der (PL die Punkte); 3 (in time) Zeitpunkt der (PL die Zeitpunkte); **at that point** zu diesem Zeitpunkt; **to be on the point of doing something** gerade etwas tun wollen; 4 **that's not the point** darum geht es nicht; **there's no point phoning, he's out** es hat keinen Sinn anzurufen, er ist nicht da; **what's the point?** wozu?; 5 **that's a good point!** das stimmt!; **the point is …** es geht darum …; 6 **point of view** der Standpunkt; **from my point of view** von meinem Standpunkt aus; 7 **her strong point** ihre Stärke; 8 (in scoring) Punkt der (PL die Punkte); **to win by fifteen points** mit fünfzehn Punkten Vorsprung gewinnen; 9 (in decimals) 6 **point 4** sechs Komma vier (in German, a comma is used for the decimal point).
verb 1 hinweisen ◇ SEP auf (+ACC); **a notice pointing to the station** ein Schild, das auf den Bahnhof

hinweist; 2 (with your finger) zeigen auf (+ACC); **he pointed at Tom** er zeigte auf Tom.

pointless adjective sinnlos; **it's pointless to keep on ringing** es ist sinnlos, dauernd zu klingeln.

poison noun Gift das (PL die Gifte). verb vergiften.

poisonous adjective giftig.

Poland noun Polen das.

pole noun 1 (for a tent) Stange die (PL die Stangen); 2 (for skiing) Stock der (PL die Stöcke); 3 **the North Pole** der Nordpol.

Pole noun (a Polish person) Pole der (PL die Polen), Polin die (PL die Polinnen).

police noun **the police** die Polizei; **the police are coming** die Polizei kommt.

police car noun Streifenwagen der (PL die Streifenwagen).

policeman noun Polizist der (PL die Polizisten).

police station noun Polizeiwache die (PL die Polizeiwachen).

policewoman noun Polizistin die (PL die Polizistinnen).

polish noun 1 (for furniture) Politur die; 2 (for shoes) Schuhcreme die; 3 (for the floor) Bohnerwachs das. verb 1 polieren (furniture, silver); 2 **to polish your shoes** seine Schuhe putzen.

◇ IRREGULAR VERB: See the verb table in the centre of the dictionary

Polish noun (language)
Polnisch das.
adjective polnisch.

polite adjective höflich; **to be polite
to somebody** höflich zu jemandem
sein.

political adjective politisch.

politician noun Politiker der (PL die
Politiker), Politikerin die (PL die
Politikerinnen).

politics noun Politik die.

polluted adjective verschmutzt.

pollution noun
Verschmutzung die.

polo-necked adjective Rollkragen-;
a polo-necked jumper ein
Rollkragenpullover.

pond noun Teich der (PL die Teiche).

pony noun Pony das (PL die Ponys).

ponytail noun Pferdeschwanz der
(PL die Pferdeschwänze).

poodle noun Pudel der (PL die
Pudel).

pool noun 1 (swimming pool)
Schwimmbecken das (PL die
Schwimmbecken); 2 (pond)
Tümpel der (PL die Tümpel);
3 (puddle) Lache die (PL die
Lachen); 4 (game) Poolbillard das;
5 **the football pools** das Toto; **to do
the pools** Toto spielen.

poor adjective 1 arm; **a poor country**
ein armes Land; **a poor family** eine
arme Familie; 2 **poor Tanya's failed
her exam** die arme Tanya ist durch
die Prüfung gefallen; 3 (bad)

schlecht; **that's a poor result** das
ist ein schlechtes Ergebnis; **the
weather was pretty poor** das Wetter
war ziemlich schlecht.

pop noun Popmusik die; **pop
concert** das Popkonzert; **pop star**
der Popstar; **pop song** der Schlager.
● **to pop into: I'll just pop into the
bank** ich gehe kurz auf die Bank.

popcorn noun Puffmais der.

pope noun Papst der (PL die Päpste).

poppy noun Mohn der.

popular adjective beliebt.

population noun Bevölkerung die
(PL die Bevölkerungen).

porch noun Vorbau der (PL die
Vorbauten).

pork noun Schweinefleisch das;
pork chop das Schweinekotelett.

porridge noun Haferbrei der.

port noun 1 Hafen der (PL die
Häfen); 2 (wine) Portwein der (PL
die Portweine).

porter noun 1 (at a station or an
airport) Gepäckträger der (PL die
Gepäckträger); 2 (in a hotel)
Portier der (PL die Portiers).

portion noun (of food) Portion die
(PL die Portionen).

portrait noun Porträt das (PL die
Porträts).

Portugal noun Portugal das.

Portuguese noun 1 (language)
Portugiesisch das; 2 (a person)
Portugiese der (PL die Portugiesen),

Portugiesin die (PL die Portugiesinnen).
adjective portugiesisch.

posh *adjective* vornehm; **a posh area** eine vornehme Gegend.

position *noun* 1 Platz der (PL die Plätze); 2 (*situation*) Lage die (PL die Lagen); 3 (*status, job*) Stellung die (PL die Stellungen).

positive *adjective* 1 (*sure*) sicher; **I'm positive he's left** ich bin mir sicher, dass er gegangen ist; 2 (*enthusiastic*) positiv; **her reaction was very positive** ihre Reaktion war sehr positiv.

possessions *plural noun* Sachen (*plural*); **all my possessions are in the flat** alle meine Sachen sind in der Wohnung.

possibility *noun* Möglichkeit die (PL die Möglichkeiten).

possible *adjective* möglich; **it's possible** es ist gut möglich; **if possible** wenn möglich; **as quickly as possible** so schnell wie möglich.

possibly *adverb* 1 (*maybe*) möglicherweise; **'will you be at home at midday?'** – **'possibly'** 'bist du mittags zu Hause?' – 'möglicherweise'; 2 **how can you possibly believe that?** wie kannst du das nur glauben?; **I can't possibly arrive before Thursday** ich kann unmöglich vor Donnerstag ankommen.

post *noun* 1 Post die; **to send something by post** etwas per Post schicken; (*letters*) **is there any post for me?** ist Post für mich

gekommen?; 2 (*a pole*) Pfosten der (PL die Pfosten); 3 (*a job*) Stelle die (PL die Stellen).
verb **to post a letter** einen Brief abschicken SEP.

postbox *noun* Briefkasten der (PL die Briefkästen).

postcard *noun* Postkarte die (PL die Postkarten).

postcode *noun* Postleitzahl die (PL die Postleitzahlen).

poster *noun* 1 (*for decoration*) Poster das (PL die Poster); **I've bought an Oasis poster** ich habe ein Poster von Oasis gekauft; 2 (*advertising*) Plakat das (PL die Plakate); **I saw a poster for the concert** ich habe ein Plakat für das Konzert gesehen.

postman *noun* Briefträger der (PL die Briefträger).

post office *noun* Post die; **the post office is on the right** die Post ist auf der rechten Seite.

postpone *verb* verschieben ◇; **we've postponed the meeting until next week** wir haben die Besprechung auf nächste Woche verschoben.

postwoman *noun* Briefträgerin die (PL die Briefträgerinnen).

pot *noun* 1 (*jar*) Topf der (PL die Töpfe); **a pot of honey** ein Topf Honig; 2 (*teapot*) Kanne die (PL die Kannen); 3 **the pots and pans** die Töpfe und Pfannen.

◇ **IRREGULAR VERB: See the verb table in the centre of the dictionary**

potato noun Kartoffel die (PL die Kartoffeln); **fried potatoes** Bratkartoffeln (plural); **mashed potatoes** der Kartoffelbrei.

potato crisps plural noun Kartoffelchips (plural).

pottery noun 1 (craft) Töpferei die; 2 (objects) Töpferwaren (plural).

pound noun 1 (money) Pfund das (PL die Pfunde); **fourteen pounds** vierzehn Pfund; **three marks to the pound** drei Mark für ein Pfund; **a five pound note** ein Fünfpfundschein; 2 (in weight) Pfund das; **two pounds of apples** zwei Pfund Äpfel.

pour verb 1 gießen ◇ (liquid); **he poured milk into the pan** er hat Milch in den Topf gegossen; 2 eingießen ◇ SEP (a drink); **to pour the tea** den Tee eingießen; **I poured him a drink** ich habe ihm zu trinken eingegossen; 3 (with rain) **it's pouring** es gießt.

poverty noun Armut die.

powder noun 1 Pulver das (PL die Pulver); 2 (for face or body) Puder der (PL die Puder).

power noun 1 (electricity) Strom der; **a power cut** eine Stromsperre; 2 (energy) Energie die; **nuclear power** die Kernenergie; 3 (strength) Kraft die; 4 (over other people) Macht die; **to be in power** an der Macht sein.

powerful adjective (strong) stark; (influential) mächtig.

power station noun Kraftwerk das (PL die Kraftwerke).

practical adjective praktisch.

practice noun 1 (for sport) Training das; **hockey practice** das Hockeytraining; 2 Übung die; **to do your piano practice** Klavier üben; **to be out of practice** außer Übung sein.

practise verb 1 üben (an instrument, exercise, or skill); **to practise the piano** Klavier üben; 2 anwenden SEP (a language); **a week in Berlin to practise my German** eine Woche in Berlin, um mein Deutsch anzuwenden; 3 (in sport) trainieren; **the team practises on Wednesday** die Mannschaft trainiert Mittwoch.

praise verb loben; **to praise somebody for something** jemanden für etwas ←(ACC) loben.

pram noun Kinderwagen der (PL die Kinderwagen).

prawn noun Garnele die (PL die Garnelen).

pray verb beten.

prayer noun Gebet das (PL die Gebete).

precinct noun **shopping precinct** das Einkaufszentrum; **pedestrian precinct** die Fußgängerzone.

precisely adverb genau; **at eleven o'clock precisely** um genau elf Uhr.

prefer verb 1 vorziehen ◇ SEP; **I prefer Anna to her sister** ich ziehe Anna ihrer Schwester vor; 2 **to prefer to do something** etwas lieber tun; **I prefer to stay at home** ich bleibe lieber zu Hause.

△ NEW SPELLING: See page xii

pregnant *adjective* schwanger.

prejudice *noun* Vorurteil *das* (PL die Vorurteile); **to fight against racial prejudice** gegen Rassenvorurteile ankämpfen.

prejudiced *adjective* **to be prejudiced** voreingenommen sein.

prep *noun* Hausaufgaben (*plural*); **my English prep** meine Englischhausaufgaben.

preparation *noun* Vorbereitung *die* (PL die Vorbereitungen); **in preparation for something** in Vorbereitung auf etwas ←(ACC); **our preparations for Christmas** unsere Weihnachtsvorbereitungen.

prepare *verb* 1 vorbereiten SEP; **to prepare somebody for something** jemanden auf etwas ←(ACC) vorbereiten; 2 **to be prepared for the worst** sich auf das Schlimmste gefasst machen.

prepared *adjective* bereit; **I'm prepared to pay half** ich bin bereit, die Hälfte zu zahlen.

preposition *noun* Präposition *die* (PL die Präpositionen).

prep school *noun* private Grundschule *die*.

prescription *noun* Rezept *das* (PL die Rezepte); **on prescription** auf Rezept.

present *noun* 1 (*a gift*) Geschenk *das* (PL die Geschenke); **to give somebody a present** jemandem ein Geschenk machen; 2 (*the time now*) Gegenwart *die*;

in the present (tense) in der Gegenwart; 3 **that's all for the present** das ist vorläufig alles. *adjective* 1 (*attending*) anwesend; **Mr Blair is not present** Herr Blair ist nicht anwesend; **to be present at something** bei etwas ←(DAT) anwesend sein; **fifty people were present at the funeral** fünfzig Personen waren bei der Beerdigung anwesend; 2 (*existing now*) gegenwärtig; **the present situation** die gegenwärtige Lage; 3 **at the present time** zur Zeit. *verb* 1 (*a prize*) überreichen; 2 (*introduce*) vorstellen SEP; 3 (*on TV, radio*) moderieren (*a programme*).

presenter *noun* (*on TV*) Moderator *der* (PL die Moderatoren), Moderatorin *die* (PL die Moderatorinnen).

president *noun* Präsident *der* (PL die Präsidenten), Präsidentin *die* (PL die Präsidentinnen).

press *noun* **the press** die Presse. *verb* 1 (*to push*) drücken; **press here!** hier drücken!; 2 drücken auf (+ACC) (*a button or switch*); **she pressed the button** sie hat auf den Knopf gedrückt.

press conference *noun* Pressekonferenz *die* (PL die Pressekonferenzen).

pressure *noun* Druck *der*; **to put pressure on somebody** jemanden unter Druck setzen.

pressure group *noun* Interessengruppe *die* (PL die Interessengruppen).

✧ IRREGULAR VERB: *See the verb table in the centre of the dictionary*

pretend verb to pretend that ... so tun, als ob ...; he's pretending not to hear er tut so, als ob er nicht hört.

pretty adjective hübsch; a pretty dress ein hübsches Kleid.
adverb ziemlich; it was pretty silly das war ziemlich blöd.

prevent verb to prevent somebody from doing something jemanden daran hindern, etwas zu tun; there's nothing to prevent you from leaving niemand kann dich daran hindern wegzugehen.

previous adjective 1 (earlier) früher (years, opportunity, or job); 2 (immediately preceding) vorig; on the previous Tuesday am vorigen Dienstag.

price noun Preis der (PL die Preise); the price per kilo der Preis pro Kilo; CDs have gone up in price CDs sind im Preis gestiegen; what is the price of this? was kostet das?

price list noun Preisliste die (PL die Preislisten).

price ticket noun Preisschild das (PL die Preisschilder).

prick verb stechen ◇; to prick your finger sich in den Finger stechen.

pride noun Stolz der.

priest noun Priester der (PL die Priester).

primary school noun Grundschule die (PL die Grundschulen).

primary (school) teacher noun Grundschullehrer der (PL die Grundschullehrer),

Grundschullehrerin die (PL die Grundschullehrerinnen).

prime minister noun Premierminister der (PL die Premierminister), Premierministerin die (PL die Premierministerinnen).

prince noun Prinz der (PL die Prinzen).

princess noun Prinzessin die (PL die Prinzessinnen).

principal noun (of a college) Direktor der (PL die Direktoren), Direktorin die (PL die Direktorinnen).
adjective (main) Haupt-.

principle noun Prinzip das (PL die Prinzipien); on principle im Prinzip; that's true in principle im Prinzip stimmt das.

print noun 1 (letters) Druck der; in small print klein gedruckt; 2 (a photo) Abzug der (PL die Abzüge); colour print der Farbabzug.

printer noun (for a computer) Drucker der (PL die Drucker).

print-out noun Ausdruck der (PL die Ausdrucke).

prison noun Gefängnis das (PL die Gefängnisse); in prison im Gefängnis.

prisoner noun Gefangene der/die (PL die Gefangenen).

private adjective 1 Privat-, privat; private school die Privatschule; private property das Privateigentum; to have private

△ NEW SPELLING: See page xii

lessons Privatstunden nehmen;
2 in private privat.

prize noun Preis der (PL die Preise);
to win a prize einen Preis
gewinnen.

prize-giving noun
Preisverleihung die (PL die
Preisverleihungen).

prizewinner noun Gewinner der
(PL die Gewinner), Gewinnerin die
(PL die Gewinnerinnen).

probable adjective wahrscheinlich.

probably adverb wahrscheinlich.

problem noun Problem das (PL die
Probleme); **it's a serious problem**
das ist ein ernstes Problem; **no
problem!** kein Problem!

process noun 1 Prozess△ der (PL die
Prozesse); **2 to be in the process of
doing something** dabei sein, etwas
zu tun.

produce noun (food) Erzeugnisse
(plural).
verb 1 herstellen SEP (goods, food);
2 vorzeigen SEP (a ticket, document);
I produced my passport ich habe
meinen Pass vorgezeigt; **3** erzeugen
(interest, tension); **it produces heat**
es erzeugt Wärme; **4 to produce a
film** einen Film produzieren; **5 to
produce a play** ein Theaterstück
inszenieren.

producer noun (of a film or
programme) Produzent der (PL die
Produzenten).

product noun Produkt das (PL die
Produkte).

production noun 1 (of a film or an
opera) Produktion die (PL die
Produktionen); **2** (of a play)
Inszenierung die (PL die
Inszenierungen); **a new production
of Hamlet** eine neue Inszenierung
von Hamlet; **3** (by a factory)
Produktion die.

profession noun Beruf der (PL die
Berufe).

professional noun 1 (a trained
person) Fachmann der (PL die
Fachleute); **2** (in sport) Profi der (PL
die Profis).
adjective 1 professionell (work,
sportsman); **a professional
footballer** ein professioneller
Fußballer; **2** beruflich (career,
success); **she's a professional
singer** sie ist Sängerin von Beruf.

professor noun Professor der (PL
die Professoren), Professorin die (PL
die Professorinnen).

profile noun Profil das (PL die
Profile).

profit noun Gewinn der (PL die
Gewinne).

profitable adjective rentabel.

program noun computer program
das Programm.

programme noun 1 (for a play or an
event) Programm das (PL die
Programme); **2** (on TV or radio)
Sendung die (PL die Sendungen).

progress noun 1 Fortschritt der (PL
die Fortschritte); **to make progress**
Fortschritte machen; **2 to be in
progress** im Gange sein.

◇ IRREGULAR VERB: See the verb table in the centre of the dictionary

project noun 1 (at school) Arbeit die (PL die Arbeiten); 2 (a plan) Projekt das (PL die Projekte); **a project to build a bridge** ein Brückenbauprojekt.

promise noun Versprechen das (PL die Versprechen); **to make somebody a promise** jemandem ein Versprechen geben; **to keep a promise** ein Versprechen halten; **it's a promise!** ganz bestimmt!
verb **to promise something** etwas versprechen ◊; **I've promised to ring my mother** ich habe versprochen, meine Mutter anzurufen.

promote verb **to be promoted** (in football) aufsteigen ◊ SEP (PERF sein); (at work) befördert werden.

promotion noun 1 Beförderung die; 2 (in football) Aufstieg der; 3 (in advertising) Reklame die.

pronoun noun Pronomen das (PL die Pronomen).

pronounce verb aussprechen ◊ SEP; **you don't pronounce the 'c'** das 'c' spricht man nicht aus.

pronunciation noun Aussprache die.

proof noun Beweis der (PL die Beweise); **there's no proof that ...** es gibt keine Beweise dafür, dass ...

propaganda noun Propaganda die.

propeller noun Propeller der (PL die Propeller).

proper adjective 1 (correct, real, genuine) richtig; **the proper answer** die richtige Antwort; **he's not a proper doctor** er ist kein richtiger Arzt; 2 (decent) anständig; **I need a proper meal** ich brauche ein anständiges Essen; 3 **in its proper place** an Ort und Stelle.

properly adverb 1 richtig; 2 (decent) anständig.

property noun 1 (your belongings) Eigentum das; 2 (land, premises) Besitz der; **'private property'** 'Privatbesitz'; 3 (house) Haus das (PL die Häuser).

propose verb 1 (suggest) vorschlagen ◊ SEP; 2 (marriage) **he proposed to her** er hat ihr einen Heiratsantrag gemacht.

protect verb schützen; **to protect somebody from something** jemanden vor etwas ←(DAT) schützen.

protection noun Schutz der.

protein noun Protein das (PL die Proteine).

protest noun 1 Beschwerde die (PL die Beschwerden); **to make a protest** eine Beschwerde einlegen SEP; 2 (disapproval) Protest der (PL die Proteste); **in protest against something** aus Protest gegen etwas ←(ACC).
verb protestieren; **to protest about something** gegen etwas ←(ACC) protestieren.

Protestant noun Protestant der (PL die Protestanten), Protestantin die (PL die Protestantinnen).
adjective protestantisch.

△ NEW SPELLING: See page xii

protest march noun
Protestmarsch der (PL die
Protestmärsche).

proud adjective stolz; **to be proud
about something** stolz auf etwas
←(ACC) sein.

prove verb beweisen ✧.

provide verb zur Verfügung stellen.

provided, providing conjunction
vorausgesetzt; **provided it doesn't
rain** vorausgesetzt, es regnet nicht.

prune noun Backpflaume die (PL die
Backpflaumen).

psychiatrist noun Psychiater der
(PL die Psychiater), Psychiaterin die
(PL die Psychiaterinnen).

psychological adjective
psychologisch.

psychologist noun
Psychologe der (PL die
Psychologen), Psychologin die (PL
die Psychologinnen).

psychology noun Psychologie die.

PTO abbreviation b.w. (bitte
wenden).

pub noun Kneipe die (PL die
Kneipen; informal).

public noun **the public** die
Öffentlichkeit; **in public** in aller
Öffentlichkeit.
adjective öffentlich.

public holiday noun gesetzliche
Feiertag der (PL die gesetzlichen
Feiertage); **January 1st is a public
holiday** der erste Januar ist ein
gesetzlicher Feiertag.

publicity noun 1 Publicity die;
2 (advertising) Werbung die.

public school noun
Privatschule die (PL die
Privatschulen).

public transport noun öffentliche
Verkehrsmittel (plural).

publish verb veröffentlichen.

publisher noun 1 Verleger der (PL
die Verleger), Verlegerin die (PL die
Verlegerinnen); 2 (company)
Verlag der (PL die Verlage).

pudding noun (dessert)
Nachtisch der (PL die Nachtische);
**for pudding we've got
strawberries** zum Nachtisch gibt es
Erdbeeren.

puddle noun Pfütze die (PL die
Pfützen).

puff noun (of smoke) Wölkchen das
(PL die Wölkchen).

puff pastry noun Blätterteig der.

pull verb 1 ziehen ✧; **to pull a cart**
einen Wagen ziehen; 2 ziehen an
(+DAT); **to pull a rope** an einem Seil
ziehen; **he pulled a letter out of his
pocket** er hat einen Brief aus der
Tasche gezogen; ★ **he's pulling
your leg!** er nimmt dich auf den Arm
(literally: he's picking you up in his
arms).
● **to pull down** 1 herunterziehen ✧
SEP; 2 (demolish) abreißen ✧ SEP (a
building).
● **to pull in** (at the roadside) an den
Straßenrand fahren ✧ (PERF sein).

pullover noun Pullover der (PL die
Pullover).

pump noun Pumpe die (PL die
Pumpen); **bicycle pump** die

✧ IRREGULAR VERB: See the verb table in the centre of the dictionary

Fahrradpumpe.
verb pumpen.
● **to pump up** aufpumpen SEP.

punch *noun* **1** (*in boxing*)
Faustschlag *der* (PL *die*
Faustschläge); **2** (*drink*) Bowle *die*
(PL *die* Bowlen).
verb **1** **he punched me in the
stomach** er hat mich in den Magen
geboxt; **2** lochen (*a ticket*).

punctual *adjective* pünktlich.

punctuation *noun*
Interpunktion *die*.

punctuation mark *noun*
Satzzeichen *das* (PL *die*
Satzzeichen).

puncture *noun* (*flat tyre*)
Reifenpanne *die* (PL *die*
Reifenpannen).

punish *verb* bestrafen.

punishment *noun* Strafe *die* (PL *die*
Strafen).

pupil *noun* Schüler *der* (PL *die*
Schüler), Schülerin *die* (PL *die*
Schülerinnen).

puppet *noun* Puppe *die* (PL *die*
Puppen).

puppy *noun* junge Hund *der* (PL *die*
jungen Hunde); **a boxer puppy** ein
junger Boxer.

pure *adjective* rein.

purple *adjective* lila ('lila' *never
changes*).

purpose *noun* **1** Zweck *der* (PL *die*
Zwecke); **what's the purpose of it?**
was hat das für einen Zweck?; **2 on
purpose** absichtlich; **she did it on**

purpose das hat sie absichtlich
getan; **he closed the door on
purpose** er hat die Tür absichtlich
zugemacht.

purr *verb* schnurren.

purse *noun* Portemonnaie *das* (PL
die Portemonnaies).

push *noun* **to give something a
push** etwas schieben ✧.
verb **1** schubsen; **he pushed me** er
hat mich geschubst; **2** (*to press*)
drücken auf (+ACC) (*a bell or button*);
**3 to push somebody to do
something** jemanden zu etwas
drängen; **his teacher is pushing him
to sit the exam** sein Lehrer drängt
ihn, die Prüfung zu machen; **4 to
push your way through the crowd**
sich durch die Menge drängen.
● **to push something away** etwas
wegschieben ✧ SEP; **she pushed her
plate away** sie schob ihren Teller
weg.

pushchair *noun* Sportwagen *der*
(PL *die* Sportwagen).

put *verb* **1** (*place generally*) tun ✧;
put some milk in your tea tu etwas
Milch in den Tee; **you can put the
butter in the fridge** du kannst die
Butter in den Kühlschrank tun; **2** (*lay
flat*) legen; **she put the pencil on the
desk** sie hat den Bleistift auf den
Schreibtisch gelegt; **3** (*place
upright*) stellen; **where did you put
my bag?** wo hast du meine
Handtasche hingestellt?; **4** (*write*)
schreiben ✧; **put your address
here** schreiben Sie Ihre Adresse
hierhin.
● **to put away** wegräumen SEP; **put**

△ NEW SPELLING: *See page xii*

away your things räume deine Sachen weg.

● **to put back 1** zurücklegen SEP, zurückstellen SEP, zurücktun SEP (*the translation of 'put back' depends on the way it is done: if it's placed lying down, use 'zurücklegen', if placed upright use 'zurückstellen' and if it could be either, use 'zurücktun'*); **I put it back in the drawer** ich habe es in die Schublade zurückgetan; **2** (*postpone*) verschieben ◇; **the meeting has been put back until Thursday** die Besprechung ist auf Donnerstag verschoben worden.

● **to put down** (*lying down*) hinlegen SEP; (*upright*) hinstellen SEP; **where can I put the vase down?** wo kann ich die Vase hinstellen?

● **to put off 1** (*postpone*) verschieben ◇; **he's put off my lesson till Thursday** er hat meine Stunde auf Donnerstag verschoben; **2** (*turn off*) ausmachen SEP; **don't forget to put off the lights** vergiss nicht, das Licht auszumachen; **3** to put somebody off something jemandem die Lust an etwas ←(DAT) verderben ◇; **it really put me off my food** das hat mir wirklich die Lust am Essen verdorben; **4** to put somebody off doing something jemanden davon abbringen ◇ SEP, etwas zu tun; **don't be put off** lass dich nicht davon abbringen.

● **to put on 1** anziehen ◇ SEP (*clothes*); **I'll just put my shoes on** ich ziehe nur schnell meine Schuhe an; **2** auflegen SEP (*a CD or record*); **I'm putting on Oasis** ich lege Oasis auf; **3** (*switch on*) anmachen SEP (*a light*

or the heating); **could you put the lamp on?** kannst du die Lampe anmachen?

● **to put out 1** (*put outside*) hinaustun ◇ SEP, raustun ◇ SEP (*informal*); **have you put the rubbish out?** hast du den Müll rausgetan?; **2** ausmachen SEP (*a light or cigarette*); **I've put the lights out** ich habe das Licht ausgemacht; **3** to put out your hand die Hand ausstrecken SEP.

● **to put up 1** heben ◇ (*your hand*); **2** aufhängen SEP (*a picture or poster*); **I've put up some posters in my room** ich habe ein paar Poster in meinem Zimmer aufgehängt; **3** anschlagen ◇ SEP (*a notice*); **4** erhöhen (*the price*); **they've put up the fare** sie haben den Fahrpreis erhöht; **5** (*for the night*) friends put me up ich habe bei Freunden übernachtet; **can you put me up on Friday?** kann ich Freitag bei euch übernachten?

● **to put up with something** etwas aushalten ◇ SEP; **I don't know how she puts up with it** ich weiß nicht, wie sie das aushält.

puzzle noun (*jigsaw*) Puzzle das (PL die Puzzles).

puzzled adjective verdutzt.

pyjamas plural noun Schlafanzug der (PL die Schlafanzüge); **a pair of pyjamas** ein Schlafanzug; **where are my pyjamas?** wo ist mein Schlafanzug?

◇ IRREGULAR VERB: *See the verb table in the centre of the dictionary*

Q q

qualification noun 1 (ability, experience) Qualifikation die (PL die Qualifikationen); 2 (on paper) Zeugnis das (PL die Zeugnisse).

qualified adjective 1 ausgebildet; she's a qualified ski instructor sie ist eine ausgebildete Skilehrerin; 2 (having a degree or a diploma) Diplom-; a qualified engineer ein Diplomingenieur.

quality noun Qualität die; good quality products Waren von guter Qualität.

quantity noun Menge die (PL die Mengen).

quarrel noun Streit der (PL die Streite); to have a quarrel Streit haben.
verb sich streiten ◇; they're always quarrelling sie streiten sich dauernd.

quarter noun 1 Viertel das (PL die Viertel); a quarter of the price ein Viertel des Preises; three quarters of the class drei Viertel der Klasse; it's a quarter past ten es ist Viertel nach zehn; it's a quarter to ten es ist Viertel vor zehn; 2 we meet at quarter to eight wir treffen uns um Viertel vor acht; 3 a quarter of an hour eine Viertelstunde; 4 three quarters of an hour eine Dreiviertelstunde; 5 an hour and a quarter eineinviertel Stunden.

queen noun 1 Königin die (PL die Königinnen); 2 (in chess, cards) Dame die (PL die Damen).

question noun Frage die (PL die Fragen); to ask somebody a question jemandem eine Frage stellen; I asked her a question ich habe ihr eine Frage gestellt; it's out of the question das kommt nicht in Frage.
verb befragen (a person).

question mark noun Fragezeichen das (PL die Fragezeichen).

questionnaire noun Fragebogen der (PL die Fragebögen).

queue noun (of people, cars) Schlange die (PL die Schlangen); to stand in a queue Schlange stehen; a queue of cars eine Autoschlange.

quick adjective schnell; to have a quick lunch schnell etwas zu Mittag essen; it's quicker on the motorway auf der Autobahn geht es schneller; to have a quick look at something sich ←(DAT) schnell etwas ansehen; be quick! mach schnell!

quickly adverb schnell; I'll just quickly phone my mother ich rufe schnell meine Mutter an.

quiet adjective 1 (silent) still; to keep quiet still sein; please keep quiet sei bitte still; 2 (not loud) leise; the children are very quiet die Kinder sind ganz leise; in a quiet voice mit leiser Stimme; 3 (peaceful) ruhig; a quiet street eine ruhige Straße.

△ NEW SPELLING: See page xii

quietly adverb 1 (speak, move) leise; he got up quietly er ist leise aufgestanden; 2 (read or play) ruhig; to sit quietly ruhig sitzen.

quilt noun Steppdecke die (PL die Steppdecken).

quite adverb 1 (fairly) ziemlich; it's quite cold outside es ist ziemlich kalt draußen; quite often ziemlich oft; quite a few ziemlich viele; quite a few of our friends came ziemlich viele unserer Freunde sind gekommen; quite a few people ziemlich viele Leute; that's quite a good idea das ist eine ganz gute Idee; 2 (completely) völlig; it was quite amazing es war einfach fantastisch; not quite nicht ganz; she's not quite ready sie ist noch nicht ganz fertig; 3 genau; I don't quite know what he wants ich weiß nicht genau, was er will; quite! genau!

quiz noun Quiz das (PL die Quiz).

quotation noun (from a book) Zitat das (PL die Zitate).

quotation marks plural noun Anführungszeichen (plural); in quotation marks in Anführungszeichen.

quote noun 1 (from a book) Zitat das (PL die Zitate); 2 (estimate) Kostenvoranschlag der (PL die Kostenvoranschläge). verb zitieren.

R r

rabbi noun Rabbi der (PL die Rabbis).

rabbit noun Kaninchen das (PL die Kaninchen).

race noun 1 (a sports event) Rennen das (PL die Rennen); cycle race das Radrennen; 2 to have a race (running) um die Wette laufen ◇ (PERF sein); (swimming) um die Wette schwimmen ◇ (PERF sein); 3 (an ethnic group) Rasse die (PL die Rassen).

racetrack noun Rennbahn die (PL die Rennbahnen).

racial adjective rassisch, Rassen-; racial discrimination die Rassendiskriminierung.

racing car noun Rennwagen der (PL die Rennwagen).

racing driver noun Rennfahrer der (PL die Rennfahrer).

racism noun Rassismus der.

racist noun Rassist der (PL die Rassisten), Rassistin die (PL die Rassistinnen). adjective rassistisch.

racket noun 1 (for tennis) Schläger der (PL die Schläger); my tennis racket mein Tennisschläger; 2 (noise) Krach der.

radiator noun Heizkörper der (PL die Heizkörper).

◇ IRREGULAR VERB: See the verb table in the centre of the dictionary

radio noun Radio das (PL die Radios); **to listen to the radio** Radio hören; **to hear something on the radio** etwas im Radio hören.

radioactive adjective radioaktiv.

radio station noun Rundfunkstation die (PL die Rundfunkstationen).

radish noun Radieschen das (PL die Radieschen).

rag noun Lumpen der (PL die Lumpen).

rage noun Wut die; **to fly into a rage** in Wut geraten ◇ (PERF sein); **she's in a rage** sie ist wütend; ★ **it's all the rage** das ist der letzte Schrei (literally: it's the last scream).

rail noun 1 (for a train) Schiene die (PL die Schienen); 2 (the railway) **to go by rail** mit der Bahn fahren; 3 (on a balcony, bridge, or stairs) Geländer das (PL die Geländer).

rail card noun Bahnpass△ der (PL die Bahnpässe).

railing(s) noun Geländer das (PL die Geländer).

railway noun 1 (the system) Bahn die; **the railways** die Bahn; 2 **railway line** (from one place to another) die Bahnstrecke; 3 **on the railway line** (the track) auf dem Gleis.

railway carriage noun Eisenbahnwagen der (PL die Eisenbahnwagen).

railway station noun Bahnhof der (PL die Bahnhöfe).

rain noun Regen der; **in the rain** im Regen.
verb regnen; **it's raining** es regnet; **it's going to rain** es wird regnen.

rainbow noun Regenbogen der (PL die Regenbogen).

raincoat noun Regenmantel der (PL die Regenmäntel).

rainy adjective regnerisch.

raise verb 1 (lift up) hochheben ◇ SEP; 2 (increase) erhöhen (prices); 3 **to raise money for something** Geld für etwas aufbringen ◇ SEP.

raisin noun Rosine die (PL die Rosinen).

rally noun 1 (a meeting) Versammlung die (PL die Versammlungen); 2 (for cars) Rallye die (PL die Rallyes); 3 (in tennis) Ballwechsel der (PL die Ballwechsel).

rambler noun Wanderer der (PL die Wanderer), Wanderin die (PL die Wanderinnen).

rambling noun Wandern das.

range noun 1 (a choice) Auswahl die; **a wide range of travel brochures** eine große Auswahl an Reiseprospekten; 2 **a range of subjects** verschiedene Fächer; **in a range of colours** in verschiedenen Farben; 3 **a computer in this price range** ein Computer in dieser Preislage; **that's out of my price range** das kann ich mir nicht leisten.

rap noun Rap der (music).

△ NEW SPELLING: See page xii

rape noun Vergewaltigung die (PL die Vergewaltigungen).
verb vergewaltigen.

rare adjective 1 selten; a rare bird ein seltener Vogel; 2 englisch gebraten (steak).

rarely adverb selten.

rash noun Ausschlag der (PL die Ausschläge).
adjective voreilig.

raspberry noun Himbeere die (PL die Himbeeren); raspberry jam die Himbeermarmelade.

rat noun Ratte die (PL die Ratten).

rate noun 1 (a charge) Gebühren (plural); postage rates Postgebühren; 2 are there special rates for children? gibt es Sonderpreise für Kinder?; at reduced rates zu ermäßigten Preisen; 3 rate of exchange der Wechselkurs; 4 rate of pay der Lohnsatz; 5 (a level) Rate die (PL die Raten); a high cancellation rate eine hohe Absagerate; 6 at any rate auf jeden Fall.

rather adverb 1 lieber; I'd rather wait ich warte lieber; I'd rather you didn't go es wäre mir lieber, wenn du nicht gingst; 2 ziemlich; I'm rather busy ich habe ziemlich viel zu tun; I've got rather a lot of shopping to do ich muss noch ziemlich viel einkaufen; 3 rather than eher als; in summer rather than winter eher im Sommer als im Winter.

rave noun (party) Fete die (PL die Feten) (informal).

raw adjective roh.

razor noun Rasierapparat der (PL die Rasierapparate).

razor blade noun Rasierklinge die (PL die Rasierklingen).

RE noun Religionsunterricht der.

reach noun Reichweite die; out of reach außer Reichweite; within reach leicht erreichbar; to be within easy reach of Munich von München aus leicht erreichbar sein.
verb 1 ankommen ◇ SEP (PERF sein) an (+DAT) (a place or point), ankommen ◇ SEP (PERF sein) in (+DAT) (a town or country); when you reach the station wenn du am Bahnhof ankommst; 2 kommen ◇ (PERF sein) zu (+DAT) (an agreement, a conclusion); to reach a decision zu einer Entscheidung kommen; 3 to reach for something nach etwas ←(DAT) greifen ◇.

react verb reagieren.

reaction noun Reaktion die (PL die Reaktionen).

read verb 1 lesen ◇; what are you reading at the moment? was liest du zur Zeit?; I'm reading a detective novel ich lese einen Krimi; 2 to read out vorlesen ◇ SEP; he read out the list to the students er hat die Liste den Studenten vorgelesen.

reading noun 1 (action) Lesen das; 2 (reading matter) Lektüre die; some easy reading for the holidays eine leichte Lektüre für die Ferien.

ready adjective 1 fertig; supper's not ready yet das Essen ist noch nicht

◇ IRREGULAR VERB: See the verb table in the centre of the dictionary

fertig; **we are not quite ready** wir sind noch nicht ganz fertig; **are you ready to leave?** seid ihr fertig?; (*on a journey*) seid ihr reisefertig?; **to get ready** sich fertig machen; **I'm getting ready to play tennis** ich mache mich zum Tennisspielen fertig; **I was getting ready for bed** ich war gerade dabei, ins Bett zu gehen; **2 to get something ready** (*complete*) etwas fertig machen, etwas vorbereiten SEP (*a room or food*); **I'll get your room ready** ich bereite dein Zimmer vor.

real *adjective* **1** (*genuine*) echt; **it's a real diamond** das ist ein echter Brillant; **he's a real coward** er ist ein echter Feigling; **2** (*true*) richtig; **is that her real name?** ist das ihr richtiger Name?; **3** (*not imagined*) wirklich; **it's a real pity you can't come** es ist wirklich schade, dass du nicht kommen kannst.

realistic *adjective* realistisch.

realize *verb* wissen ✧; **I hadn't realized** das wusste ich nicht; **I didn't realize he was French** ich habe nicht gewusst, dass er Franzose ist; **do you realize what time it is?** weißt du, wie viel Uhr es ist?

really *adverb* **1** wirklich; **the film was really good** der Film war wirklich gut; **really?** wirklich?; **2 not really** eigentlich nicht.

reason *noun* Grund *der* (PL *die* Gründe); **for that reason** aus diesem Grund; **the reason why I phoned** der Grund meines Anrufs.

reasonable *adjective* vernünftig.

receipt *noun* Quittung *die* (PL *die* Quittungen).

receive *verb* erhalten ✧.

receiver *noun* Hörer *der* (PL *die* Hörer); **to pick up the receiver** den Hörer abnehmen ✧ SEP.

recent *adjective* **1** kürzlich erfolgter/kürzlich erfolgte/kürzlich erfolgtes; **the recent closure** die kürzlich erfolgte Schließung; **2 in recent years** in den letzten Jahren.

recently *adverb* **1** (*at a time not long ago*) kürzlich; **2** (*over the recent period*) in letzter Zeit.

reception *noun* **1** Rezeption *die* (PL *die* Rezeptionen); **he's waiting at reception** er wartet in der Rezeption; **2** Empfang *der* (PL *die* Empfänge); **a big wedding reception** ein großer Hochzeitsempfang; **3 to get a good reception** gut aufgenommen werden.

receptionist *noun* **1** Empfangsdame *die* (PL *die* Empfangsdamen); **2** (*in a doctor's surgery*) Sprechstundenhilfe *die* (PL *die* Sprechstundenhilfen).

recipe *noun* Rezept *das* (PL *die* Rezepte).

reckon *verb* glauben; **I reckon it's a good idea** ich glaube, das ist eine gute Idee.

recognize *verb* erkennen ✧.

recommend *verb* empfehlen ✧; **can you recommend a dentist?** kannst du mir einen Zahnarzt

△ **NEW SPELLING: See page xii**

empfehlen?; **I recommend the fish soup** ich empfehle die Fischsuppe.

record noun **1** Rekord der (PL die Rekorde); **it's a world record** das ist ein Weltrekord; **record sales** Verkaufsrekorde; **2** (of events) Aufzeichnung die (PL die Aufzeichnungen); **on record** aufgezeichnet; **to keep a record of something** sich ←(DAT) etwas notieren; **3** (music) Platte die (PL die Platten); **a Miles Davis record** eine Platte von Miles Davis; **4** records (office files) Unterlagen (plural); **I'll just check your records** ich prüfe nur Ihre Unterlagen.
verb (on tape) aufnehmen ✧ SEP; **I'm recording it on cassette** ich nehme es auf Kassette auf.

recorder noun **1** Blockflöte die (PL die Blockflöten); **to play the recorder** Blockflöte spielen; **2** cassette recorder der Kassettenrekorder; **video recorder** der Videorekorder.

recording noun (on tape or CD) Aufnahme die (PL die Aufnahmen); (on video) Aufzeichnung die (PL die Aufzeichnungen).

record player noun Plattenspieler der (PL die Plattenspieler).

recover verb sich erholen; **she's recovered now** sie hat sich wieder erholt.

recovery noun (from an illness) Erholung die; **to make a good recovery** sich gut erholen.

recycle verb recyceln.

red adjective rot; **a red car** ein rotes Auto; **to go red** rot werden; **to have red hair** rote Haare haben.

Red Cross noun **the Red Cross** das Rote Kreuz.

redcurrant noun Johannisbeere die (PL die Johannisbeeren); **redcurrant jelly** das Johannisbeergelee.

redecorate verb (with paint) neu streichen ✧; (with wallpaper) neu tapezieren ✧; **they've redecorated the kitchen** sie haben die Küche neu gestrichen.

redo verb noch einmal machen.

reduce verb **1** to reduce prices die Preise herabsetzen SEP; **2** to reduce speed die Geschwindigkeit verringern.

reduction noun **1** (in price) Ermäßigung die (PL die Ermäßigungen); **2** (in speed or number) Verringerung die.

redundant adjective **to be made redundant** entlassen werden.

referee noun (in sport) Schiedsrichter der (PL die Schiedsrichter), Schiedsrichterin die (PL die Schiedsrichterinnen).

reference noun Referenz die (PL die Referenzen); (for a job) **she gave me a good reference** sie hat mir gute Referenzen ausgestellt.

reference book noun Nachschlagewerk das (PL die Nachschlagewerke).

refill verb nachfüllen SEP.

✧ **IRREGULAR VERB: See the verb table in the centre of the dictionary**

reflect verb spiegeln; **to be reflected** sich spiegeln.

reflection noun **1** (in a mirror or on water) Spiegelung die (PL die Spiegelungen); **to see your reflection in the mirror** sich im Spiegel sehen; **2** (thought) Überlegung die; **on reflection** nach nochmaliger Überlegung.

reflexive adjective **a reflexive verb** ein reflexives Verb.

refreshing adjective erfrischend.

refrigerator noun Kühlschrank der (PL die Kühlschränke).

refugee noun Flüchtling der (PL die Flüchtlinge).

refund noun Rückzahlung die (PL die Rückzahlungen). verb zurückerstatten SEP.

refusal noun **1** Weigerung die (PL die Weigerungen); **2** (for a job) Absage die (PL die Absagen); **to get a refusal** eine Absage bekommen.

refuse noun (rubbish) Abfall der. verb sich weigern; **I refused** ich habe mich geweigert; **he refuses to help** er weigert sich zu helfen.

regards plural noun Grüße (plural); **regards to your parents** viele Grüße an deine Eltern; **Nat sends his regards** Nat lässt grüßen.

reggae noun Reggae der.

region noun Gebiet das (PL die Gebiete).

regional adjective regional.

register noun (in school) Anwesenheitsliste die (PL die Anwesenheitslisten), Klassenbuch das (PL die Klassenbücher) (kept by the teacher, it also contains notes about students' achievements). verb **1** eintragen ◆ SEP (a name); **2** (report) anmelden SEP.

registered letter noun Einschreiben das (PL die Einschreiben).

registration number noun Autonummer die (PL die Autonummern).

regret verb bedauern.

regular adjective regelmäßig; **regular visits** regelmäßige Besuche.

regularly adverb regelmäßig.

regulation noun Vorschrift die (PL die Vorschriften).

rehearsal noun Probe die (PL die Proben).

rehearse verb proben.

reheat verb aufwärmen SEP.

reject verb ablehnen SEP.

related adjective verwandt; **we're not related** wir sind nicht verwandt.

relation noun Verwandte der/die (PL die Verwandten).

relationship noun Beziehung die (PL die Beziehungen); **I have a good relationship with my parents** ich habe eine gute Beziehung zu meinen Eltern.

△ NEW SPELLING: See page xii

relative noun Verwandte der/die
(PL die Verwandten).

relatively adverb relativ.

relax verb entspannen; **I'm going to
relax and watch telly tonight** heute
Abend entspanne ich und sehe fern.

relaxed adjective entspannt.

relaxing adjective entspannend.

relay race noun Staffel die (PL die
Staffeln).

release noun (a film, CD, or book)
1 Neuerscheinung die (PL die
Neuerscheinungen); **this week's
new releases** die neuen Filme der
Woche; 2 (of a prisoner or hostage)
Freilassung die (PL die
Freilassungen).
verb 1 herausbringen ◇ SEP (a
record, film, or video);
2 freilassen ◇ SEP (a person).

reliable adjective zuverlässig.

relief noun Erleichterung die; **what
a relief!** da bin ich aber erleichtert!

relieve verb stillen (pain).

relieved adjective erleichtert; **I was
relieved to hear you'd arrived** es
hat mich erleichtert zu hören, dass
du angekommen bist.

religion noun Religion die (PL die
Religionen).

religious adjective religiös.

rely verb 1 (trust) **to rely on
somebody** sich auf jemanden
verlassen ◇; **I'm relying on your
help for Saturday** ich verlasse mich
darauf, dass du mir am Samstag

hilfst; 2 (be dependent on) **to rely
on** angewiesen sein auf (+ACC).

remain verb (be left over) übrig
bleiben ◇ Δ (PERF sein); (stay)
bleiben ◇ (PERF sein).

remark noun Bemerkung die (PL die
Bemerkungen); **to make remarks
about something** Bemerkungen
über etwas ← (ACC) machen.

remarkable adjective
bemerkenswert.

remarkably adverb
bemerkenswert.

remember verb 1 sich erinnern ◇
(+ACC) (a person or an occasion); **I
don't remember** daran kann ich
mich nicht erinnern; **do you
remember the holiday in Italy?**
erinnerst du dich noch an die Ferien
in Italien?; 2 **I can't remember his
number** seine Nummer fällt mir
nicht ein; 3 **to remember to do
something** daran denken ◇, etwas
zu tun; **remember to lock the door**
denk daran abzuschließen; **I
remembered to bring the CDs** ich
habe daran gedacht, die CDs
mitzubringen.

remind verb 1 erinnern; **to remind
somebody to do something**
jemanden daran erinnern, etwas zu
tun; **remind your mother to pick me
up** erinnere deine Mutter daran,
mich abzuholen; **he reminds me of
my brother** er erinnert mich an
meinen Bruder; 2 **oh, that reminds
me** ... dabei fällt mir ein, ...

remote adjective abgelegen.

◇ IRREGULAR VERB: See the verb table in the centre of the dictionary

emote control noun 1 (for a car or plane) Fernsteuerung die (PL die Fernsteuerungen); 2 (for TV or video) Fernbedienung die (PL die Fernbedienungen).

emove verb 1 entfernen (a stain, mark, or obstacle); 2 ausziehen ◇ SEP (clothes).

enew verb verlängern (a passport or licence).

ent noun Miete die (PL die Mieten). verb mieten; **Simon's rented a flat** Simon hat eine Wohnung gemietet.

eorganize verb umorganisieren.

epair noun Reparatur die (PL die Reparaturen). verb reparieren; **to get something repaired** etwas reparieren lassen; **we've had the television repaired** wir haben unseren Fernseher reparieren lassen.

epay verb zurückzahlen SEP.

epeat noun Wiederholung die (PL die Wiederholungen). verb wiederholen.

epeatedly adverb wiederholt.

epetitive adjective eintönig.

eplace verb ersetzen.

eply noun Antwort die (PL die Antworten); **I didn't get a reply to my letter** ich habe keine Antwort auf meinen Brief bekommen; **there's no reply** niemand antwortet. verb antworten; **I still haven't replied to the letter** ich habe immer noch nicht auf den Brief geantwortet.

report noun 1 (of an event) Bericht der (PL die Berichte); 2 (school report) Zeugnis das (PL die Zeugnisse). verb 1 melden (a problem or an accident); **we've reported the theft** wir haben den Diebstahl gemeldet; 2 sich melden; **I had to report to reception** ich musste mich an der Rezeption melden; 3 (in the news) berichten; **to report on the strike** über den Streik berichten.

reporter noun Reporter der (PL die Reporter), Reporterin die (PL die Reporterinnen).

represent verb 1 darstellen SEP (a word, a thing, an idea); 2 verteten ◇ (a group or company).

representative noun Vertreter der (PL die Vertreter), Vertreterin die (PL die Vertreterinnen).

republic noun Republik die (PL die Republiken).

reputation noun 1 Ruf der; **to have a good reputation** einen guten Ruf haben; 2 **she has a reputation for honesty** sie gilt als ehrlich.

request noun Bitte die (PL die Bitten); **at my mother's request** auf Bitte meiner Mutter. verb bitten ◇; **to request something** um etwas ←(ACC) bitten.

rescue noun Rettung die; **rescue operation** die Rettungsaktion; **to come to somebody's rescue** jemandem zu Hilfe kommen. verb retten; **they rescued the dog** sie haben den Hund gerettet.

△ NEW SPELLING: See page xii

rescue party noun
Rettungsmannschaft die (PL die
Rettungsmannschaften).

research noun 1 Forschung die;
for research into Aids für die
Aidsforschung; 2 to do research
forschen.
verb to research into something
etwas erforschen.

resemblance noun
Ähnlichkeit die (PL die
Ähnlichkeiten).

reservation noun (a booking)
Reservierung die (PL die
Reservierungen); to make a
reservation (for a room) (ein
Zimmer) reservieren lassen.

reserve noun 1 Reserve die (PL die
Reserven); we have a few in
reserve wir haben ein paar in
Reserve; 2 nature reserve das
Naturschutzgebiet; 3 (for a match)
Reservespieler der (PL die
Reservespieler), Reservespielerin
die (PL die Reservespielerinnen).
verb reservieren; this table is
reserved dieser Tisch ist reserviert.

resident noun Bewohner der (PL die
Bewohner), Bewohnerin die (PL die
Bewohnerinnen).

residential adjective Wohn-; a
residential area eine Wohngegend.

resign verb 1 (from your job)
kündigen; 2 (from an official post)
zurücktreten ◇ SEP.

resignation noun 1 Kündigung die
(PL die Kündigungen); 2 (from an
official post) Rücktritt der.

resist verb widerstehen ◇ (+DAT)
(an offer or temptation).

resit verb wiederholen (an exam).

resort noun 1 (for holidays) holiday
resort der Urlaubsort; ski resort
der Skiurlaubsort; seaside resort
das Seebad; 2 as a last resort als
letzter Ausweg.

respect noun Respekt der.
verb respektieren.

respectable adjective anständig.

responsibility noun
Verantwortung die (PL die
Verantwortungen).

responsible adjective
1 verantwortlich; he was
responsible for the accident er war
für den Unfall verantwortlich; I'm
responsible for booking the rooms
ich bin für die Zimmerreservierung
verantwortlich; 2 (reliable)
verantwortungsbewusst Δ; he's not
very responsible er ist nicht sehr
verantwortungsbewusst.

rest noun 1 the rest der Rest; the
rest of the day der Rest des Tages;
the rest of the bread das Brotrest,
der Rest von dem Brot; 2 (the others)
the rest die Übrigen; the rest have
gone home die Übrigen sind nach
Hause gegangen; 3 Erholung die;
he's going to the mountains for a
rest er fährt zur Erholung ins
Gebirge; ten days' rest zehn Tage
Erholung; to have a rest sich
ausruhen SEP; 4 (a short break)
Pause die (PL die Pausen); to stop for
a rest eine Pause machen.
verb (have a rest) sich ausruhen SEP

◇ IRREGULAR VERB: See the verb table in the centre of the dictionary

restaurant noun Restaurant das
(PL die Restaurants).

restful adjective erholsam.

restless adjective unruhig.

restrain verb zurückhalten ✧ SEP.

result noun 1 Ergebnis das (PL die
Ergebnisse); **the exam results** die
Prüfungsergebnisse; 2 **as a result**
infolgedessen; **as a result we
missed the train** infolgedessen
haben wir den Zug verpasst.

retire verb 1 (from work) aufhören
zu arbeiten; (civil servant, teacher,
soldier) sich pensionieren lassen;
she retires in June sie lässt sich im
Juni pensionieren; 2 **to be retired**
nicht mehr arbeiten.

retirement noun Ruhestand der;
since his retirement seitdem er in
den Ruhestand gegangen ist.

return noun 1 (coming back)
Rückkehr die; **the return journey**
die Rückreise; 2 **by return of post**
postwendend; 3 **in return for** für;
in return for his help für seine Hilfe;
4 **in return** dafür; ★ **many happy
returns !** herzlichen Glückwunsch
zum Geburtstag.
verb 1 (come back)
zurückkommen ✧ SEP (PERF sein); **he
returned ten minutes later** er kam
zehn Minuten später zurück; **to
return from holiday** aus den Ferien
zurückkommen; 2 (go back)
zurückgehen ✧ SEP (PERF sein);
(drive) zurückfahren ✧ SEP (PERF
sein); **we are planning to return in
the evening** wir wollen am Abend
zurückfahren; 3 (to give back)

zurückgeben ✧ SEP; **Gemma's never
returned the video** Gemma hat das
Video nie zurückgegeben.

return fare noun Preis für eine
Rückfahrkarte der; (for a flight)
Preis für einen Rückflugschein der.

return ticket noun
Rückfahrkarte die (PL die
Rückfahrkarten); (for a flight)
Rückflugschein der (PL die
Rückflugscheine).

reveal verb enthüllen.

reverse verb 1 (in a car) rückwärts
fahren ✧ (PERF sein); 2 **to reverse
the charges** ein R-Gespräch führen.

review noun (of a book, play, or film)
Kritik die (PL die Kritiken).
verb rezensieren (a book, play, or
film).

revise verb 1 lernen (for an exam);
**Tessa's busy revising for her
exams** Tessa lernt jetzt für ihre
Prüfung; 2 wiederholen; **to revise
maths** Mathe wiederholen.

revision noun Wiederholung die.

revolting adjective eklig.

revolution noun Revolution die (PL
die Revolutionen).

reward noun Belohnung die (PL die
Belohnungen).
verb belohnen.

rewind verb zurückspulen SEP (a
cassette or video).

rhubarb noun Rhabarber der.

rhyme noun Reim der (PL die
Reime).

△ NEW SPELLING: See page xii

rhythm noun Rhythmus der (PL die Rhythmen).

ribbon noun Band das (PL die Bänder).

rice noun Reis der; **rice pudding** der Milchreis.

rich adjective 1 reich; **they are very rich** sie sind sehr reich; 2 **the rich** die Reichen.

rid adjective **to get rid of something** etwas loswerden ◊ SEP (PERF sein) (informal); **we got rid of the car** wir sind das Auto losgeworden.

riddle noun Rätsel das (PL die Rätsel).

ride noun Fahrt die (PL die Fahrten); **to go for a ride (on a bike)** eine Fahrt machen; **to go for a ride (on a horse)** reiten gehen ◊ (PERF sein). verb 1 **to ride a bike** Rad fahren ◊ △ (PERF sein); **can you ride a bike?** kannst du Rad fahren?; **I've never ridden a bike** ich bin noch nie Rad gefahren; 2 **to ride (a horse)** reiten ◊ (PERF sein); **I've never ridden a horse** ich bin noch nie auf einem Pferd geritten.

ridiculous adjective lächerlich.

riding noun Reiten das; **to go riding** reiten gehen.

riding school noun Reitschule die (PL die Reitschulen).

right noun 1 (not left) rechte Seite die; **on the right** auf der rechten Seite; **on my right** rechts von mir; 2 (to do something) Recht das (PL die Rechte); **to have the right to something** ein Recht

auf etwas ←(ACC) haben; **the right to work** das Recht auf Arbeit; **you have no right to say that** du hast kein Recht, das zu sagen.
adjective 1 (not left) rechter/rechte/rechtes; **my right hand** meine rechte Hand; 2 (correct) richtig; **the right answer** die richtige Antwort; **is this the right address?** ist das die richtige Adresse?; 3 **to be right** (of a person) Recht haben; **you see, I was right** siehst du, ich hatte Recht; 4 **you were right not to say anything** du hattest Recht, nichts zu sagen; 5 **the clock is right** die Uhr geht richtig; 6 **yes, that's right** ja, das stimmt; **is that right?** stimmt das?
adverb 1 (direction) rechts; **turn right at the lights** biege an der Ampel rechts ab; 2 (correctly) richtig; **you're not doing it right** du machst das nicht richtig; 3 (completely) ganz; **right at the bottom** ganz unten; **right at the beginning** ganz am Anfang; 4 (exactly) genau; **right in the middle** genau in der Mitte; 5 **right now** sofort; 6 (okay) gut; **right, let's go** gut, gehen wir.

right-hand adjective **on the right-hand side** rechts.

right-handed adjective rechtshändig.

ring noun 1 (on the phone) **to give somebody a ring** jemanden anrufen ◊ SEP; 2 (for your finger) Ring der (PL die Ringe); 3 (circle) Kreis der (PL die Kreise); 4 **there was a ring at the door** es hat geklingelt.

◊ IRREGULAR VERB: *See the verb table in the centre of the dictionary*

verb 1 (*a bell or phone*) klingeln; **the phone rang** das Telefon hat geklingelt; **2** (*phone*) anrufen ◇ SEP; **I'll ring you tomorrow** ich rufe dich morgen an; **3 to ring for a taxi** ein Taxi rufen.

▸ **to ring back** zurückrufen ◇ SEP; **I'll ring you back later** ich rufe dich später zurück.

▸ **to ring off** auflegen SEP

ring road *noun* Ringstraße *die* (PL *die* Ringstraßen).

rinse *verb* spülen.

riot *noun* Aufstand *der* (PL *die* Aufstände).

rioting *noun* Unruhen (*plural*).

rip *verb* zerreißen ◇.

ripe *adjective* reif; **are the tomatoes ripe?** sind die Tomaten reif?

rip-off *noun* **it's a rip-off** das ist Nepp (*informal*).

rise *noun* **1** Anstieg *der*; **a rise in temperature** ein Temperaturanstieg; **2 pay rise** *die* Gehaltserhöhung.
verb 1 (*the sun*) aufgehen ◇ SEP (PERF *sein*); **2** (*prices*) steigen ◇ (PERF *sein*).

risk *noun* Risiko *das* (PL *die* Risiken); **to take a risk** ein Risiko eingehen.
verb riskieren; **he risks losing his job** er riskiert es, seine Stelle zu verlieren.

river *noun* Fluss △ *der* (PL *die* Flüsse).

road *noun* **1** Straße *die* (PL *die* Straßen); **the road to London** die Straße nach London; **2 the baker's is on the other side of the road** die Bäckerei ist auf der anderen Straßenseite; **3 across the road** gegenüber; **they live across the road from us** sie wohnen bei uns gegenüber.

road accident *noun* Verkehrsunfall *der* (PL *die* Verkehrsunfälle).

road map *noun* Straßenkarte *die* (PL *die* Straßenkarten).

roadside *noun* **by the roadside** am Straßenrand.

road sign *noun* Straßenschild *das* (PL *die* Straßenschilder).

roadworks *plural noun* Straßenarbeiten (*plural*).

roast *noun* Braten *der* (PL *die* Braten).
adjective gebraten; **roast potatoes** Bratkartoffeln; **roast beef** *der* Rinderbraten.

rob *verb* **1** berauben (*a person*); **2** ausrauben SEP (*a bank*).

robber *noun* Räuber *der* (PL *die* Räuber).

robbery *noun* Raub *der* (PL *die* Raube); **bank robbery** *der* Bankraub.

rock *noun* **1** (*a big stone*) Felsen *der* (PL *die* Felsen); **2** (*the material*) Fels *der*; **3** (*music*) Rock *der*; **rock band** *die* Rockband; **to dance rock and roll** Rock'n'Roll tanzen.

rock climbing *noun* Klettern *das*; **to go rock climbing** zum Klettern gehen.

△ NEW SPELLING: See page xii

rock star noun Rockstar der (PL die Rockstars).

rocky adjective felsig.

rod noun a fishing rod eine Angel.

role noun Rolle die (PL die Rollen); **to play the role of Hamlet** die Rolle des Hamlet spielen.

roll noun 1 Rolle die (PL die Rollen); **a roll of film** eine Rolle Film; **a toilet roll** eine Rolle Toilettenpapier; **2 bread roll** das Brötchen, die Semmel (South German). verb rollen (PERF sein).

roller noun 1 (for hair) Lockenwickler der (PL die Lockenwickler); **2** (for paint) Rolle die (PL die Rollen).

rollerblades plural noun Inlineskates (plural), Inliners (plural).

roller skates plural noun Rollschuhe (plural).

Roman Catholic adjective römisch-katholisch.

romantic adjective romantisch.

roof noun Dach das (PL die Dächer).

roof rack noun Gepäckträger der (PL die Gepäckträger).

room noun 1 Zimmer das (PL die Zimmer); **she's in the other room** sie ist im anderen Zimmer; **a three-room flat** eine Dreizimmerwohnung; **2** (space) Platz der; **enough room for two** genug Platz für zwei; **very little room** wenig Platz; **to make room** Platz machen.

root noun Wurzel die (PL die Wurzeln).

rope noun Seil das (PL die Seile).

rose noun Rose die (PL die Rosen).

rot verb verfaulen (PERF sein).

rotten adjective verfault.

rough adjective 1 (scratchy) rauh; **2** (vague) grob (plan or estimate); **3 a rough idea** eine vage Vorstellung; **4** (stormy) stürmisch; **a rough sea** eine stürmische See; **5** (difficult) **to have a rough time** e schwer haben; **6 to sleep rough** ir Freien schlafen.

roughly adverb (approximately) ungefähr; **roughly ten per cent** ungefähr zehn Prozent; **it takes roughly three hours** es dauert ungefähr drei Stunden.

round noun Runde die (PL die Runden); **a round of talks** eine Gesprächsrunde; **a round of drinks** eine Runde. adjective rund; **a round table** ein runder Tisch. preposition 1 um (+ACC); **round the city** um die Stadt; **round my arm** um meinen Arm; **they were sitting round the table** sie haben um den Tisch gesessen; **it's just round the corner** es ist gleich um die Ecke; **2 to go round a museum** ein Museum besuchen. adverb 1 **to go round to somebody's house** jemanden besuchen←(DAT); **2 to invite somebody round** jemanden zu sich←(DAT) einladen ◇ SEP; **we invited Sally round for lunch** wir

◇ IRREGULAR VERB: See the verb table in the centre of the dictionary

haben Sally zum Mittagessen eingeladen; **3 to look round the shops** sich in den Geschäften umsehen ◇ SEP; **4 all the year round** das ganze Jahr hindurch.

roundabout noun 1 (*for traffic*) Kreisverkehr der; 2 (*in a fairground*) Karussell das (PL die Karussells).

route noun 1 (*that you plan*) Route die (PL die Routen); **the best route is via Calais** die beste Route ist über Calais; **2 bus route** die Linie.

row[1] noun 1 Reihe die (PL die Reihen); **in the front row** in der ersten Reihe; **in the back row** in der letzten Reihe; **2 in a row** hintereinander; **four times in a row** viermal hintereinander.
verb (*in a boat*) rudern (PERF sein/haben); **we rowed across the lake** wir sind über den See gerudert; **he rowed us across the lake** er hat uns über den See gerudert.

row[2] noun 1 (*a quarrel*) Krach der (*informal*) (PL die Kräche); **to have a row** Krach haben; **they've had a row** sie haben Krach gehabt; **I had a row with my parents** ich habe Krach mit meinen Eltern gehabt; **2** (*noise*) Krach der; **they were making a terrible row** sie haben einen furchtbaren Krach gemacht.

rowing noun Rudern das; **to go rowing** rudern gehen.

rowing boat noun Ruderboot das (PL die Ruderboote).

royal adjective königlich; **the royal family** die königliche Familie.

rub verb reiben ◇; **to rub your eyes** sich ←(DAT) die Augen reiben.
● **to rub something out** etwas ausradieren SEP.

rubber noun 1 (*an eraser*) Radiergummi der (PL die Radiergummis); 2 (*material*) Gummi der; **rubber soles** Gummisohlen.

rubbish noun 1 (*for the bin*) Müll der; 2 (*nonsense*) Quatsch der (*informal*); **you're talking rubbish!** du redest Quatsch.
adjective blöd; **the film was rubbish** der Film war blöd; **they're a rubbish band** sie sind eine blöde Band.

rubbish bin noun Mülleimer der (PL die Mülleimer).

rucksack noun Rucksack der (PL die Rucksäcke).

rude adjective 1 unhöflich; **that's rude** das ist unhöflich; 2 unanständig; **a rude joke** ein unanständiger Witz.

rug noun 1 Teppich der (PL die Teppiche); 2 (*a blanket*) Decke die (PL die Decken).

rugby noun Rugby das.

ruin noun (*remains*) Ruine die (PL die Ruinen); **in ruins** in Trümmern.
verb 1 ruinieren; **you'll ruin your jacket** du ruinierst dir die Jacke; **2 verderben** ◇ (*day, holiday*); **it ruined my evening** das hat mir den Abend verdorben.

rule noun 1 Regel die (PL die Regeln); **the rules of the game** die

△ NEW SPELLING: *See page xii*

Spielregeln; **as a rule** in der Regel; **2** (*administrative*) Vorschrift *die* (PL *die* Vorschriften); **according to the school rules** nach den Schulvorschriften.

ruler *noun* Lineal *das* (PL *die* Lineale); **I've lost my ruler** ich habe mein Lineal verloren.

rumour *noun* Gerücht *das* (PL *die* Gerüchte).

run *noun* **1** (*in games, sport, and for fitness*) Lauf *der* (PL *die* Läufe); **to go for a run** einen Lauf machen, joggen (PERF *sein*); **2** (*of a play*) Laufzeit *die*; **3** (*in skiing*) Abfahrt *die* (PL *die* Abfahrten); **4 in the long run** auf lange Sicht.
verb **1** laufen ◇ (PERF *sein*); **I ran ten kilometres** ich bin zehn Kilometer gelaufen; **he ran across the pitch** er ist über das Spielfeld gelaufen; **2** (*run fast*) rennen ◇ (PERF *sein*); **Kitty ran for the bus** Kitty rannte, um den Bus zu kriegen; **3** (*drive*) fahren ◇; **I'll run you home later** ich fahre dich später nach Hause; **4** (*organize*) veranstalten (*a course or competition*); **who's running this competition?** wer veranstaltet diesen Wettbewerb?; **5** (*manage*) leiten (*a business*); **she's been running the firm for years** sie leitet die Firma schon seit Jahren; **to run a shop** ein Geschäft führen; **6** (*a train or a bus*) fahren ◇ (PERF *sein*); **the buses don't run on Sundays** sonntags fahren keine Busse; **7 to run a bath** ein Bad einlaufen lassen.

● **to run away** weglaufen ◇ SEP (PERF *sein*).

● **to run into something** gegen etwas ←(ACC) fahren ◇ (PERF *sein*); **the car ran into a tree** das Auto ist gegen einen Baum gefahren.

● **to run out of something: we've run out of bread** wir haben kein Brot mehr; **I'm running out of money** ich habe kaum noch Geld.

● **to run somebody over** jemanden überfahren ◇; **he nearly got run over** er ist beinahe überfahren worden.

runner *noun* Läufer *der* (PL *die* Läufer), Läuferin *die* (PL *die* Läuferinnen).

runner-up *noun* Zweite *der/die* (PL *die* Zweiten).

running *noun* (*for exercise*) Laufen *das*, Jogging *das*.
adjective **1 running water** fließendes Wasser; **2 three days running** drei Tage hintereinander; **to win three times running** dreimal hintereinander gewinnen.

runway *noun* **1** (*for take-off*) Startbahn *die* (PL *die* Startbahnen); **2** (*for landing*) Landebahn *die* (PL *die* Landebahnen).

rush *noun* (*a hurry*) **to be in a rush** in Eile sein; **sorry, I'm in a rush** Entschuldigung, ich bin in Eile.
verb **1** (*hurry*) sich beeilen; **I must rush!** ich muss mich beeilen; **2** (*run*) rasen (PERF *sein*); **she rushed out** sie raste raus (*informal*); **3 Louise was rushed to hospital** Louise ist schnellstens ins Krankenhaus gebracht worden.

◇ **IRREGULAR VERB:** *See the verb table in the centre of the dictionary*

rush hour *noun* Stoßzeit *die* (PL *die* Stoßzeiten); **in the rush hour** während der Stoßzeit.

Russia *noun* Russland Δ *das.*

Russian *noun* 1 (*a person*) Russe *der* (PL *die* Russen), Russin *die* (PL *die* Russinnen); 2 (*the language*) Russisch *das.* *adjective* russisch; **he's Russian** er ist Russe.

rust *noun* Rost *der.*

rusty *adjective* rostig.

rye *noun* Roggen *der.*

S s

Sabbath *noun* 1 (*Jewish*) Sabbat *der* (PL *die* Sabbate); 2 (*Christian*) Sonntag *der* (PL *die* Sonntage).

sack *noun* 1 Sack *der* (PL *die* Säcke); 2 **to get the sack** rausgeschmissen werden (*informal*). *verb* **to sack somebody** jemanden rausschmeißen ◆ SEP (*informal*).

sad *adjective* traurig.

saddle *noun* Sattel *der* (PL *die* Sättel).

sadly *adverb* 1 traurig; **she looked at me sadly** sie hat mich traurig angesehen; 2 (*unfortunately*) leider.

safe *adjective* 1 (*out of danger*) sicher; **to feel safe from something** sich vor etwas ←(DAT) sicher fühlen;

2 **she's safe** sie ist in Sicherheit; 3 (*not dangerous*) ungefährlich; **the path is safe** der Weg ist ungefährlich; **it's not safe** das ist gefährlich.

safety *noun* Sicherheit *die.*

safety belt *noun* Sicherheitsgurt *der* (PL *die* Sicherheitsgurte).

safety pin *noun* Sicherheitsnadel *die* (PL *die* Sicherheitsnadeln).

Sagittarius *noun* Schütze *der*; **Kylie's Sagittarius** Kylie ist Schütze.

sail *noun* Segel *das* (PL *die* Segel).

sailing *noun* Segeln *das*; **to go sailing** segeln.

sailing boat *noun* Segelboot *das* (PL *die* Segelboote).

sailor *noun* Seemann *der* (PL *die* Seeleute).

saint *noun* Heilige *der/die.*

sake *noun* 1 **for your mother's sake** deiner Mutter zuliebe; 2 **for heaven's sake** um Gottes willen.

salad *noun* Salat *der* (PL *die* Salate); **tomato salad** *der* Tomatensalat.

salad dressing *noun* Salatsoße *die* (PL *die* Salatsoßen).

salary *noun* Gehalt *das* (PL *die* Gehälter).

sale *noun* 1 (*selling*) Verkauf *der* (PL *die* Verkäufe); **the sale of the house** der Verkauf des Hauses; **'for sale'** 'zu verkaufen'; 2 **the sales**

Δ NEW SPELLING: *See page xii*

der Ausverkauf; **I bought it in the sales** ich habe es im Ausverkauf gekauft.

sales assistant noun
Verkäufer der (PL die Verkäufer), Verkäuferin die (PL die Verkäuferinnen).

salesman noun Verkäufer der (PL die Verkäufer).

saleswoman noun
Verkäuferin die (PL die Verkäuferinnen).

salmon noun Lachs der (PL die Lachse).

salt noun Salz das.

salty adjective salzig.

same adjective **the same** der gleiche/die gleiche/das gleiche; **she said the same thing** sie hat das gleiche gesagt; **her birthday's the same day as mine** sie hat am gleichen Tag Geburtstag wie ich; **at the same time** zur gleichen Zeit; **their car's the same as ours** sie haben das gleiche Auto wie wir. adverb **1 the same** gleich; **the two bikes look the same** die beiden Fahrräder sehen gleich aus; **2 all the same** trotzdem.

sample noun Muster das (PL die Muster); **a free sample** ein unverkäufliches Muster, eine Warenprobe.

sand noun Sand der.

sandal noun Sandale die (PL die Sandalen); **a pair of sandals** ein Paar Sandalen.

sandwich noun Sandwich das (PL die Sandwichs), belegte Brot das (PL die belegten Brote); **ham sandwich** das Schinkenbrot.

sanitary towel noun
Damenbinde die (PL die Damenbinden).

Santa Claus noun der Weihnachtsmann.

sarcastic adjective sarkastisch.

sardine noun Sardine die (PL die Sardinen).

satchel noun Ranzen der (PL die Ranzen).

satellite noun Satellit der (PL die Satelliten).

satellite dish noun
Satellitenschüssel die (PL die Satellitenschüsseln).

satellite television noun
Satellitenfernsehen das.

satisfactory adjective befriedigend.

satisfied adjective zufrieden.

satisfy verb befriedigen.

satisfying adjective **1** befriedigend; **2 a satisfying meal** ein sättigendes Essen.

Saturday noun **1** Samstag der (PL die Samstage), Sonnabend der (North German) (PL die Sonnabende); **on Saturday** am Sonnabend/am Samstag; **I'm going out on Saturday** ich gehe Sonnabend aus; **see you on Saturday!** bis Samstag!; **every Saturday** jeden Samstag; **last**

Saturday vorigen Sonnabend; **next Saturday** nächsten Sonnabend; **2 on Saturdays** samstags, sonnabends (*North German*); **the museum is closed on Saturdays** das Museum ist sonnabends/ samstags geschlossen; **to have a Saturday job** sonnabends/ samstags arbeiten.

sauce *noun* Soße die (PL die Soßen).

saucepan *noun* Kochtopf der (PL die Kochtöpfe).

saucer *noun* Untertasse die (PL die Untertassen).

sausage *noun* Wurst die (PL die Würste).

save *verb* 1 retten (*life*); **to save somebody's life** jemandem das Leben retten; **the doctors saved his life** die Ärzte haben ihm das Leben gerettet; 2 sparen (*money*); **I've saved £60** ich habe sechzig Pfund gespart; **I cycle to school to save money** ich fahre mit dem Rad zur Schule, um Geld zu sparen; **we'll take a taxi to save time** um Zeit zu sparen, nehmen wir ein Taxi; 3 (*on a computer*) speichern; 4 (*stop*) abwehren SEP (*a shot*); **to save a penalty** einen Elfmeter abwehren.

● **to save up** sparen; **I'm saving up for a car** ich spare auf ein Auto.

savings *plural noun* Ersparnisse (*plural*).

savoury *adjective* (*not sweet*) pikant.

sax *noun* Saxophon das (PL die Saxophone).

saxophone *noun* Saxophon das (PL die Saxophone); **to play the saxophone** Saxophon spielen.

say *verb* 1 sagen; **what did you say?** was hast du gesagt?; **she says she's tired** sie sagt, dass sie müde ist; **he said to wait here** er hat gesagt, wir sollen hier warten; **they say** man sagt; 2 **to say something again** etwas wiederholen; 3 **that's to say** das heißt.

saying *noun* Redensart die (PL die Redensarten); **it's just a saying** das ist so eine Redensart; **as the saying goes** wie man so sagt.

scale *noun* 1 (*of a map or model*) Maßstab der (PL die Maßstäbe); 2 (*extent*) Ausmaß das (PL die Ausmaße); **the scale of the disaster** das Ausmaß der Katastrophe; 3 (*in music*) Tonleiter die (PL die Tonleitern).

scales *noun* Waage die (PL die Waagen); **bathroom scales** die Personenwaage.

scandal *noun* 1 Skandal der (PL die Skandale); 2 (*gossip*) Klatsch der (*informal*).

Scandinavia *noun* Skandinavien das.

Scandinavian *adjective* skandinavisch.

scar *noun* Narbe die (PL die Narben).

scarce *adjective* knapp.

scare *noun* 1 Schrecken der (PL die Schrecken); **to give somebody a scare** jemandem einen Schrecken einjagen SEP; 2 (*general alarm*)

Panik die (PL die Paniken); **to cause a scare** eine Panik auslösen; **3 bomb scare** die Bombendrohung. *verb* **to scare somebody** jemanden erschrecken; **you scared me!** du hast mich erschreckt!

scared *adjective* **1 to be scared** Angst haben; **I'm scared** ich habe Angst; **to be scared of something** vor etwas ←(DAT) Angst haben; **he's scared of dogs** er hat vor Hunden Angst; **2 to be scared of doing something** sich nicht trauen, etwas zu tun; **I'm scared of telling him the truth** ich traue mich nicht, ihm die Wahrheit zu sagen.

scarf *noun* **1** (*silky*) Tuch das (PL die Tücher); **2** (*long, warm*) Schal der (PL die Schals).

scary *adjective* unheimlich.

scene *noun* **1** (*of an incident or event*) Schauplatz der (PL die Schauplätze); **to be on the scene** am Schauplatz sein; **the scene of the crime** der Tatort; **2** (*world*) **the music scene** die Musikszene; **on the fashion scene** in der Modewelt; **3** (*argument*) Szene die (PL die Szenen); **to make a scene** eine Szene machen.

scenery *noun* **1** (*landscape*) Landschaft die (PL die); **2** (*in the theatre*) Bühnenbild das.

schedule *noun* Programm das (PL die Programme).

scheme *noun* Projekt das (PL die Projekte).

scholarship *noun* Stipendium das (PL die Stipendien).

school *noun* Schule die (PL die Schulen); **at school** in der Schule; **to go to school** zur Schule gehen.

schoolbook *noun* Schulbuch das (PL die Schulbücher).

schoolboy *noun* Schüler der (PL die Schüler).

schoolchildren *plural noun* Schulkinder (*plural*).

schoolfriend *noun* Schulfreund der (PL die Schulfreunde), Schulfreundin die (PL die Schulfreundinnen).

schoolgirl *noun* Schülerin die (PL die Schülerinnen).

science *noun* Wissenschaft die (PL die Wissenschaften).

science fiction *noun* Sciencefiction△ die.

scientific *adjective* wissenschaftlich.

scientist *noun* Wissenschaftler der (PL die Wissenschaftler), Wissenschaftlerin die (PL die Wissenschaftlerinnen).

scissors *plural noun* Schere die (PL die Scheren); **a pair of scissors** eine Schere.

scooter *noun* **1** (*motor scooter*) Motorroller der (PL die Motorroller); **2** (*for a child*) Roller der (PL die Roller).

score *noun* Spielstand der (PL die Spielstände); **the score was three two** es stand drei zu zwei. *verb* **1 to score a goal** ein Tor schießen ◇; **2 to score three**

◇ IRREGULAR VERB: See the verb table in the centre of the dictionary

points drei Punkte erzielen; **3** (*keep score*) zählen.

Scorpio *noun* Skorpion *der*; **Neil is Scorpio** Neil ist Skorpion.

Scot *noun* Schotte *der* (PL *die* Schotten), Schottin *die* (PL *die* Schottinnen); **the Scots** die Schotten.

Scotland *noun* Schottland *das*; **from Scotland** aus Schottland; **Pauline's from Scotland** Pauline kommt aus Schottland; **to Scotland** nach Schottland.

Scots *adjective* schottisch.

Scotsman *noun* Schotte *der* (PL *die* Schotten).

Scotswoman *noun* Schottin *die* (PL *die* Schottinnen).

Scottish *adjective* schottisch; **he's Scottish** er ist Schotte.

scout *noun* Pfadfinder *der* (PL *die* Pfadfinder).

scrambled eggs *noun* Rührei *das*.

scrap *noun* Stück *das* (PL *die* Stücke); **a scrap of paper** ein Stück Papier.

scrapbook *noun* Album *das* (PL *die* Alben).

scrape *verb* **1** schaben (*potatoes or carrots*); **2** (*remove dirt or paint*) abkratzen SEP; **3** (*damage*) verschrammen.

scratch *noun* (*on your skin or a surface*) Kratzer *der* (PL *die* Kratzer); ★ **to start from scratch** von vorn anfangen ◇ SEP.

verb (*scratch yourself*) sich kratzen; **to scratch your head** sich am Kopf kratzen.

scream *noun* Schrei *der* (PL *die* Schreie).

verb schreien ◇.

screen *noun* **1** Bildschirm *der* (PL *die* Bildschirme) (*of a TV or computer*); **on the screen** auf dem Bildschirm; **2** (*in the cinema*) Leinwand *die* (PL *die* Leinwände).

screw *noun* Schraube *die* (PL *die* Schrauben).

verb schrauben.

screwdriver *noun* Schraubenzieher *der* (PL *die* Schraubenzieher).

scribble *verb* kritzeln.

scrub *verb* scheuern (*a saucepan or the floor*); **to scrub your nails** sich ←(DAT) die Nägel bürsten.

sculptor *noun* Bildhauer *der* (PL *die* Bildhauer), Bildhauerin *die* (PL *die* Bildhauerinnen); **Rebecca's a sculptor** Rebecca ist Bildhauerin.

sculpture *noun* Skulptur *die* (PL *die* Skulpturen).

sea *noun* Meer *das* (PL *die* Meere), See *die*; **by the sea** am Meer, an der See.

seafood *noun* Meeresfrüchte (*plural*); **I love seafood** ich esse Meeresfrüchte sehr gern.

search *verb* **1** absuchen SEP; **I've searched my desk but I can't find the letter** ich habe meinen Schreibtisch abgesucht, aber ich

△ NEW SPELLING: *See page xii*

kann den Brief nicht finden;
**2 durchsuchen; they searched the
building for him** sie haben das
Gebäude nach ihm durchsucht;
**3 suchen; to search for
something** nach etwas ←(DAT) suchen; **I've been
searching everywhere for my
scissors** ich habe überall nach
meiner Schere gesucht.

seasick *adjective* **to be seasick**
seekrank sein.

seaside *noun* **at the seaside** am
Meer.

season *noun* **1** Jahreszeit *die* (PL die
Jahreszeiten); **the four seasons** die
vier Jahreszeiten; **2** (*period of social
or sporting activity*) Saison *die* (PL
die Saisons); **the tennis season** die
Tennissaison; **off-season prices**
Preise außerhalb der Saison;
**3 strawberries are not in season at
the moment** jetzt ist nicht die
richtige Zeit für Erdbeeren.

season ticket *noun*
Dauerkarte *die* (PL die
Dauerkarten).

seat *noun* **1** Sitz *der* (PL die Sitze);
the front seat (*in a car*) der
Vordersitz; **the back seat** der
Rücksitz; **take a seat** nehmen Sie
Platz (*formal*); setz dich (*informal*);
2 (*on a bus, in the theatre, etc.*)
Platz *der* (PL die Plätze); **to book a
seat** einen Platz reservieren; **can
you keep my seat?** kannst du mir
meinen Platz freihalten?

seatbelt *noun* Sicherheitsgurt *der*
(PL die Sicherheitsgurte).

second *noun* Sekunde *die* (PL die
Sekunden); **can you wait a
second?** kannst du eine Sekunde
warten?
adjective **1** zweiter/zweite/zweites;
for the second time zum zweiten
Mal; **2 the second of July** der
zweite Juli.

secondary school *noun* **1** höhere
Schule *die* (PL die höheren Schulen)
(*Germans define the type of secondary
school*); **2** Gymnasium *das* (PL die
Gymnasien) (*grammar school, from
age 10 to 19 when Abitur is taken*);
3 Realschule *die* (PL die
Realschulen) (*from age 10 to 16, less
academic than a Gymnasium*).

secondhand *adjective, adverb*
gebraucht; **a secondhand bike** ein
gebrauchtes Fahrrad; **secondhand
car** der Gebrauchtwagen; **I bought
it secondhand** ich habe es
gebraucht gekauft.

secondly *adverb* zweitens.

secret *noun* Geheimnis *das* (PL die
Geheimnisse); **to tell somebody a
secret** jemandem ein Geheimnis
verraten; **in secret** heimlich.
adjective geheim; **a secret plan** ein
geheimer Plan; **to keep something
secret** etwas geheim halten.

secretary *noun* Sekretär *der* (PL die
Sekretäre), Sekretärin *die* (PL die
Sekretärinnen); **the secretary's
office** das Sekretariat.

secretly *adverb* heimlich.

sect *noun* Sekte *die* (PL die Sekten).

section *noun* Teil *der* (PL die Teile).

security *noun* Sicherheit *die*.

✧ **IRREGULAR VERB: See the verb table in the centre of the dictionary**

security guard noun Wächter der (PL die Wächter), Wächterin die (PL die Wächterinnen).

see verb 1 sehen ◇; I saw Lindy yesterday ich habe Lindy gestern gesehen; have you seen the film? hast du den Film gesehen?; I can't see anything ich kann überhaupt nichts sehen; 2 to go and see nachsehen ← SEP; I'll go and see ich sehe nach; 3 (visit) besuchen; why don't you come and see us in the summer? warum besucht ihr uns nicht im Sommer?; 4 to see somebody home jemanden nach Hause begleiten; see you! tschüs! (informal); see you on Saturday! bis Samstag!; see you soon! bis bald!

● **to see to something** sich um etwas ←(ACC) kümmern; Jo's seeing to the drinks Jo kümmert sich um die Getränke.

seed noun Samen der (PL die Samen).

seem verb 1 scheinen ◇; his story seems odd to me seine Geschichte kommt mir komisch vor; he seems shy er scheint schüchtern zu sein; the museum seems to be closed das Museum scheint geschlossen zu sein; 2 it seems (that) ... anscheinend ...; it seems he's left anscheinend ist er weggegangen; it seems that there are problems anscheinend gibt es Probleme.

select verb auswählen SEP.

self-confidence noun Selbstbewusstsein Δ das; she doesn't have much self-

confidence sie hat sehr wenig Selbstbewusstsein.

self-employed adjective to be self-employed selbstständig Δ sein; my parents are self-employed meine Eltern sind selbstständig.

selfish adjective egoistisch.

self-service adjective a self-service restaurant ein Selbstbedienungsrestaurant.

sell verb 1 verkaufen; to sell something to somebody jemandem etwas verkaufen; I sold him my bike ich habe ihm mein Rad verkauft; the house sold for a million das Haus wurde für eine Million verkauft; 2 the concert's sold out das Konzert ist ausverkauft; the tickets sold out very quickly die Karten waren schnell ausverkauft.

sell-by date noun Verfallsdatum das (PL die Verfallsdaten).

Sellotape™ noun Tesafilm™ der. verb to sellotape something etwas mit Tesafilm kleben.

semi noun Doppelhaushälfte die (PL die Doppelhaushälften).

semi-detached house noun Doppelhaushälfte die (PL die Doppelhaushälften).

semi-final noun Halbfinale das (PL die Halbfinale).

send verb schicken; to send something to somebody jemandem etwas schicken; I sent her a present for her birthday ich habe

Δ NEW SPELLING: See page xii

ihr zum Geburtstag ein Geschenk geschickt.
- to **send somebody back** jemanden zurückschicken SEP.
- to **send something back** etwas zurückschicken SEP.

sender noun Absender der (PL die Absender).

senior citizen noun Senior der (PL die Senioren), Seniorin die (PL die Seniorinnen).

sensational adjective sensationell.

sense noun 1 (common sense) Verstand der; 2 (faculty) Sinn der (PL die Sinne); **sense of smell** der Geruchssinn; **sense of touch** der Tastsinn; **to have a sense of humour** Humor haben; **she has no sense of humour** sie hat keinen Sinn für Humor; 3 (meaning) Sinn der; **this sentence makes no sense** dieser Satz ergibt keinen Sinn; **it doesn't make sense to do that** es ist Unsinn, das zu machen; **it makes sense to collect her first** es ist sinnvoll, sie erst abzuholen.

sensible adjective vernünftig; **be sensible** sei vernünftig; **that's a sensible suggestion** das ist ein vernünftiger Vorschlag.

sensitive adjective empfindlich; **for sensitive skin** für empfindliche Haut.

sentence noun 1 (words) Satz der (PL die Sätze); 2 (prison) Strafe die (PL die Strafen); **the death sentence** die Todesstrafe.
verb verurteilen; **to be sentenced to death** zum Tode verurteilt

werden; **to sentence somebody to a year in prison** jemanden zu einem Jahr Gefängnis verurteilen.

separate adjective 1 extra ('extra never has an ending'); **a separate pile** ein extra Stapel; **she wrote it on a separate sheet of paper** sie hat es auf ein anderes Blatt Papier geschrieben; **the drinks are separate** die Getränke gehen extra; 2 (different) verschieden; **two separate problems** zwei verschiedene Probleme; 3 **they have separate rooms** sie haben getrennte Zimmer.
verb 1 trennen; 2 (a couple) sich trennen.

separately adverb 1 extra; 2 getrennt; **they live separately** sie leben getrennt.

separation noun Trennung die (PL die Trennungen).

September noun September der; **in September** im September.

sequel noun Folge die (PL die Folgen).

sergeant noun 1 (in the police) Polizeimeister der (PL die Polizeimeisterin), Polizeimeisterin die (PL die Polizeimeisterinnen); 2 (in the army) Feldwebel der (PL die Feldwebel).

serial noun
1 Fortsetzungsgeschichte die (PL die Fortsetzungsgeschichten); 2 (on TV or radio) Serie die (PL die Serien).

series noun Serie die (PL die Serien); **television series** die Fernsehserie.

◇ **IRREGULAR VERB: See the verb table in the centre of the dictionary**

serious *adjective* 1 ernst; **a serious discussion** eine ernste Unterhaltung; **to be serious about something** etwas ernst nehmen; **are you serious?** ist das dein Ernst?; 2 schwer (*accident or mistake*).

seriously *adverb* 1 im Ernst; **seriously, I have to go now** im Ernst, ich muss jetzt gehen; **seriously?** im Ernst?; 2 **to take somebody seriously** jemanden ernst nehmen; 3 (*gravely*) schwer; **she is seriously ill** sie ist schwer krank.

serve *noun* (*in tennis*) Aufschlag *der* (PL die Aufschläge); **it's my serve** ich habe Aufschlag. *verb* 1 (*in tennis*) aufschlagen ◇ SEP; **Becker is serving** Becker schlägt auf; 2 servieren; **can you serve the vegetables, please?** können Sie bitte das Gemüse servieren?; ★ **it serves him right** das geschieht ihm recht.

service *noun* 1 (*in a restaurant, shop, etc.*) Bedienung *die*; **service is included** inklusive Bedienung; 2 (*from a company or firm to a customer*) Service *der*; 3 **the emergency services** der Notdienst; 4 (*church service*) Gottesdienst *der* (PL die Gottesdienste); 5 (*of a car or machine*) Wartung *die* (PL die Wartungen).

service charge *noun* Bedienung *die*; **there is no service charge** die Bedienung wird nicht extra berechnet.

service station *noun* Tankstelle *die* (PL die Tankstellen).

serviette *noun* Serviette *die* (PL die Servietten).

session *noun* Sitzung *die* (PL die Sitzungen).

set *noun* 1 (*for playing a game*) Spiel *das* (PL die Spiele); **chess set** das Schachspiel; 2 **train set** die Spielzeugeisenbahn; 3 (*in tennis*) Satz *der* (PL die Sätze). *adjective* 1 fest (*hours, habits*); **a set date** ein festes Datum; **at a set time** zu einer festgesetzten Zeit; 2 **set menu** das Menü. *verb* 1 festlegen SEP (*a date, time*); 2 aufstellen SEP (*a record*); 3 **to set the table** den Tisch decken; **to set an alarm clock** einen Wecker stellen; **I've set my alarm for seven** ich habe meinen Wecker auf sieben gestellt; 4 **to set your watch** seine Uhr richtig stellen; 5 (*sun*) untergehen ◇ SEP;

• **to set off** aufbrechen ◇ SEP (PERF sein); **we're setting off at ten** wir brechen um zehn auf; **they set off for Vienna yesterday** sie sind gestern nach Wien aufgebrochen.

• **to set off something** 1 etwas auslösen SEP (*an alarm, reaction*); 2 etwas abbrennen ◇ SEP (*a firework*); 3 etwas explodieren lassen (*a bomb*).

• **to set out** aufbrechen ◇ SEP (PERF sein); **they set out for Hamburg at ten** sie sind um zehn nach Hamburg aufgebrochen.

settee *noun* Sofa *das* (PL die Sofas).

settle verb 1 bezahlen (a bill); 2 lösen (a problem); 3 beilegen SEP (an argument).

seven number sieben; **Rosie's seven** Rosie ist sieben.

seventeen number siebzehn; **I'm seventeen** ich bin siebzehn.

seventh adjective siebter/siebte/siebtes; **on the seventh floor** im siebten Stock; **the seventh of July** der siebte Juli.

seventies plural noun **the seventies** die Siebzigerjahre △; **in the seventies** in den Siebzigerjahren.

seventieth adjective siebzigster/siebzigste/siebzigstes; **it's her seventieth birthday** es ist ihr siebzigster Geburtstag.

seventy number siebzig; **my granny's seventy** meine Oma ist siebzig.

several adjective, pronoun 1 mehrere; **I've read several of her novels** ich habe mehrere ihrer Romane gelesen; 2 **I've seen her several times** ich habe sie mehrmals gesehen.

sew verb nähen.

sewing noun Nähen das; **I like sewing** ich nähe gern.

sewing machine noun Nähmaschine die (PL die Nähmaschinen).

sex noun 1 (gender) Geschlecht das (PL die Geschlechter); 2 (sexuality) Sex der.

sex education noun Aufklärungsunterricht der.

sexism noun Sexismus der.

sexist adjective sexistisch; **sexist remarks** sexistische Bemerkungen.

sexual adjective sexuell.

sexual harassment noun sexuelle Belästigung die.

sexuality noun Sexualität die.

sexy adjective sexy.

shabby adjective schäbig.

shade noun 1 Ton der (PL die Töne); **a shade of green** ein Grünton; 2 Schatten der; **in the shade** im Schatten.

shadow noun Schatten der (PL die Schatten).

shake verb 1 (tremble) zittern; **I was shaking with fear** ich zitterte vor Angst; 2 **to shake something** etwas schütteln; **to shake your head** (meaning no) den Kopf schütteln; 3 **to shake hands with somebody** jemandem die Hand geben ◇; **she shook hands with me** sie hat mir die Hand gegeben; **we shook hands** wir gaben uns die Hand.

shaken adjective erschüttert; **I was shaken by the news** die Nachricht hat mich erschüttert.

shall verb **shall I come with you?** soll ich mitkommen? **shall we stop now?** sollen wir jetzt aufhören?

shallow adjective flach; **stay in the shallow end of the pool** bleib am flachen Ende des Beckens.

◇ IRREGULAR VERB: See the verb table in the centre of the dictionary

shambles noun Chaos das; it was a total shambles! es war ein völliges Chaos!

shame noun 1 Schande die; the shame of it! was für eine Schande!; 2 what a shame! wie schade!; it's a shame she can't come schade, dass sie nicht kommen kann.

shampoo noun Shampoo das (PL die Shampoos), Schampon das (PL die Schampons); I bought some shampoo ich habe Shampoo gekauft.

shamrock noun Klee der.

shandy noun Radler der (PL die Radler) (South German), Alsterwasser das (PL die Alsterwasser) (North German).

shape noun Form die (PL die Formen).

share noun 1 Anteil der (PL die Anteile); your share of the money dein Anteil am Geld; he paid his share er hat seinen Anteil gezahlt; 2 (in a company) Aktie die (PL die Aktien).
verb teilen; I'm sharing a room with Lucy ich teile ein Zimmer mit Lucy.

sharp adjective 1 (knife) scharf; this knife isn't very sharp dieses Messer ist nicht sehr scharf; 2 (pointed) spitz; a sharp pencil ein spitzer Bleistift; 3 a sharp bend eine scharfe Kurve; 4 (clever) clever.

shave verb 1 (have a shave) sich rasieren; 2 to shave your legs sich ←(DAT) die Beine rasieren; 3 to shave off your beard den Bart abrasieren SEP.

shaver noun Rasierapparat der (PL die Rasierapparate); **electric shaver** der Elektrorasierer.

shaving cream noun Rasiercreme die (PL die Rasiercremes).

shaving foam noun Rasierschaum der.

she pronoun sie; she's a student sie ist Studentin; she's a very good teacher sie ist eine sehr gute Lehrerin.

shed noun Schuppen der (PL die Schuppen).

sheep noun Schaf das (PL die Schafe).

sheepdog noun Schäferhund der (PL die Schäferhunde).

sheet noun 1 (for a bed) Laken das (PL die Laken); 2 a sheet of paper ein Blatt Papier; a blank sheet ein leeres Blatt; 3 (of glass or metal) Platte die (PL die Platten); ★ to be as white as a sheet leichenblass △ sein.

shelf noun 1 (in the home or a shop) Regal das (PL die Regale); a set of shelves ein Regal; 2 (in an oven) Schiene die (PL die Schienen).

shell noun 1 (of an egg or a nut) Schale die (PL die Schalen); 2 (seashell) Muschel die (PL die Muscheln).

shellfish noun 1 Schalentier das (PL die Schalentiere); 2 (in cookery) Meeresfrüchte (plural).

shelter noun Schutz der; in the shelter of im Schutz (+GEN); to take

shelter from the rain sich unterstellen SEP.

sherry noun Sherry der (PL die Sherrys).

Shetland Islands noun Shetlandinseln (plural).

shift noun Schicht die (PL die Schichten); **the night shift** die Nachtschicht; **to be on night shift** Nachtschicht haben.
verb **to shift something** etwas verrücken.

shifty adjective verschlagen; **he looks shifty** er sieht verschlagen aus; **a shifty-looking guy** ein verschlagener Typ.

shine verb scheinen ◇; **the sun is shining** die Sonne scheint.

shiny adjective glänzend.

ship noun Schiff das (PL die Schiffe).

shipyard noun Werft die (PL die Werften).

shirt noun 1 (man's) Hemd das (PL die Hemden); 2 (woman's) Bluse die (PL die Blusen).

shiver verb zittern.

shock noun 1 Schock der (PL die Schocks); **to get a shock** einen Schock bekommen; **it gave me a shock** das hat mir einen Schock versetzt; 2 **electric shock** der Schlag.
verb (upset) erschüttern; (cause scandal) schockieren.

shocked adjective schockiert.

shocking adjective schockierend.

shoe noun Schuh der (PL die Schuhe); **a pair of shoes** ein Paar Schuhe.

shoelace noun Schnürsenkel der (PL die Schnürsenkel).

shoe polish noun Schuhcreme die (PL die Schuhcremes).

shoe shop noun Schuhgeschäft das (PL die Schuhgeschäfte).

shoot verb 1 (fire) schießen ◇; **to shoot at somebody** auf jemanden schießen; **she shot him in the leg** sie hat ihm ins Bein geschossen; **he was shot in the arm** er wurde am Arm getroffen; 2 (kill, execute) erschießen ◇; **he was shot by terrorists** er wurde von Terroristen erschossen; 3 (in football, hockey) schießen ◇; 4 **to shoot a film** einen Film drehen.

shop noun Geschäft das (PL die Geschäfte), Laden der (PL die Läden); **shoe shop** das Schuhgeschäft; **to go round the shops** einen Ladenbummel machen.

shop assistant noun Verkäufer der (PL die Verkäufer), Verkäuferin die (PL die Verkäuferinnen).

shopkeeper noun Ladenbesitzer der (PL die Ladenbesitzer), Ladenbesitzerin die (PL die Ladenbesitzerinnen).

shoplifter noun Ladendieb der (PL die Ladendiebe), Ladendiebin die (PL die Ladendiebinnen).

◇ IRREGULAR VERB: See the verb table in the centre of the dictionary

shoplifting *noun*
Ladendiebstahl *der*.

shopping *noun* 1 Einkäufe (*plural*);
can you put the shopping away?
kannst du die Einkäufe wegräumen?;
2 (*activity*) Einkaufen *das*;
shopping is fun Einkaufen macht
Spaß; **to go shopping** einkaufen
gehen.

shopping trolley *noun*
Einkaufswagen *der* (PL die
Einkaufswagen).

shop window *noun*
Schaufenster *das* (PL die
Schaufenster).

short *adjective* 1 kurz; **a short dress**
ein kurzes Kleid; **she has short hair**
sie hat kurze Haare; 2 **a short break**
eine kurze Pause; **to go for a short
walk** einen kurzen Spaziergang
machen; **it's a short walk from the
bus stop** es ist nicht weit zu Fuß von
der Bushaltestelle; 3 **to be short of
something** knapp mit etwas ←(DAT)
sein; **we're a bit short of money at
the moment** wir sind im Moment
etwas knapp mit Geld; **we're getting
short of time** wir sind knapp mit der
Zeit.

shortage *noun* Mangel *der*.

shortbread *noun*
Buttergebäck *das*.

shortcrust pastry *noun*
Mürbeteig *der*.

short cut *noun* Abkürzung *die* (PL
die Abkürzungen).

shortly *adverb* gleich; **shortly
before I left** kurz bevor ich ging;
shortly after kurz danach.

shorts *plural noun* Shorts (*plural*);
a pair of shorts ein Paar Shorts; **my
red shorts** meine roten Shorts.

short-sighted *adjective*
kurzsichtig; **I'm short-sighted** ich
bin kurzsichtig.

shot *noun* 1 (*from a gun*)
Schuss △ *der* (PL die Schüsse);
2 (*a photo*) Aufnahme *die* (PL die
Aufnahmen).

should *verb* 1 sollen ✧ ('*should' is
usually translated by the imperfect
subjunctive of 'sollen'*); **you should
ask Simon** du solltest Simon fragen;
the potatoes should be ready now
die Kartoffeln sollten jetzt fertig
sein; 2 ('*should have' is translated by
'hätte sollen'*) **you should have told
me** du hättest es mir sagen sollen;
I shouldn't have stayed ich hätte
nicht bleiben sollen; **you shouldn't
have said that** das hättest du nicht
sagen sollen; 3 ('*should' meaning
'would' is translated by 'würde'*)
I should forget it if I were you an
deiner Stelle würde ich es vergessen;
4 **I should think** ich würde sagen;
I should think he's forgotten ich
würde sagen, er hat's vergessen;
5 **this should be enough** das
müsste eigentlich reichen.

shoulder *noun* Schulter *die* (PL die
Schultern).

shoulder bag *noun*
Umhängetasche *die* (PL die
Umhängetaschen).

shout *noun* Schrei *der* (PL die
Schreie).
verb 1 schreien ✧; **stop shouting!**

△ NEW SPELLING: See page xii

hör auf zu schreien!; 2 (*call*) rufen ◇; he shouted at us to come back er rief uns zu, wir sollten zurückkommen.

show *noun* 1 (*on stage*) Show *die* (PL *die* Shows); we went to see a show wir haben eine Show gesehen; 2 (*on TV, radio*) Sendung *die* (PL *die* Sendungen); 3 (*exhibition*) Ausstellung *die* (PL *die* Ausstellungen); **fashion show** *die* Modenschau.
verb 1 zeigen; to show something to somebody jemandem etwas zeigen; I'll show you my photos ich zeige dir meine Fotos; to show somebody how something works jemandem zeigen, wie etwas funktioniert; he showed me how to make pancakes er hat mir gezeigt, wie man Pfannkuchen macht; 2 it shows! das sieht man!
● to show off angeben ◇ SEP

shower *noun* 1 (*in a bathroom*) Dusche *die* (PL *die* Duschen); to have a shower duschen; 2 (*of rain*) Schauer *der* (PL *die* Schauer).

show-jumping *noun* Springreiten *das*.

show-off *noun* Angeber *der* (PL *die* Angeber), Angeberin *die* (PL *die* Angeberinnen).

shriek *verb* kreischen.

shrimp *noun* Krabbe *die* (PL *die* Krabben).

shrink *verb* 1 schrumpfen (PERF *sein*); 2 (*clothes*) einlaufen ◇ SEP (PERF *sein*); my sweater has shrunk mein Pullover ist eingelaufen.

Shrove Tuesday *noun* Fastnachtsdienstag *der*.

shrug *verb* to shrug your shoulders die Achseln zucken.

shuffle *verb* to shuffle the cards die Karten mischen.

shut *adjective* zu; the shops are shut die Geschäfte haben zu.
verb zumachen SEP; can you shut the door please? kannst du die Tür bitte zumachen?; the shops shut at six die Geschäfte machen um sechs zu.
● to shut up den Mund halten ◇ (*informal*); shut up! halt den Mund!

shuttlecock *noun* Federball *der* (PL *die* Federbälle).

shy *adjective* schüchtern.

shyness *noun* Schüchternheit *die*.

Sicily *noun* Sizilien *das*.

sick *adjective* 1 (*ill*) krank; 2 to be sick (*vomit*) sich übergeben ◇; I was sick several times ich habe mich mehrmals übergeben; 3 I feel sick mir ist schlecht; 4 übel; a sick joke ein übler Witz; 5 to be sick of something etwas satt haben; I'm sick of staying at home every day ich habe es satt, jeden Tag zu Hause zu sitzen.

sickness *noun* Krankheit *die* (PL *die* Krankheiten).

side *noun* 1 Seite *die* (PL *die* Seiten); on the other side of the street auf der anderen Straßenseite; on the wrong side auf der falschen Seite;

◇ IRREGULAR VERB: See the verb table in the centre of the dictionary

I'm on your side (*I agree with you*) ich bin auf deiner Seite; **2** (*edge*) Rand der (PL die Ränder) (*of a pool, river*); **at the side of the road** am Straßenrand; **3** (*team*) Mannschaft die (PL die Mannschaften); **the winning side** die siegreiche Mannschaft; **she plays on our side** sie spielt bei uns mit; **4 to take sides** Partei ergreifen ◇; **he always takes sides against her** er ergreift immer gegen sie Partei; **5 side by side** nebeneinander.

sideboard noun Anrichte die (PL die Anrichten).

sideburns noun Koteletten (*plural*).

side-effect noun Nebenwirkung die (PL die Nebenwirkungen).

side street noun Seitenstraße die (PL die Seitenstraßen).

sieve noun Sieb das (PL die Siebe).

sigh noun Seufzer der (PL die Seufzer). verb seufzen.

sight noun **1** (*Anblick*) der; **it was a marvellous sight** es war ein herrlicher Anblick; **2 at first sight** auf den ersten Blick; **3** (*eyesight*) **to have poor sight** schlechte Augen haben; **to know somebody by sight** jemanden vom Sehen kennen; **out of sight** außer Sicht; **to lose sight of somebody** jemanden aus den Augen verlieren; **4 the sights** die Sehenswürdigkeiten; **to see the**

sights die Sehenswürdigkeiten besichtigen.

sightseeing noun Sightseeing das; **to do some sightseeing** Sehenswürdigkeiten besichtigen.

sign noun **1** (*notice*) Schild das (PL die Schilder); **there's a sign on the door** da hängt ein Schild an der Tür; **2** (*trace, indication*) Zeichen das (PL die Zeichen); **3** (*of the zodiac*) Sternzeichen das (PL die Sternzeichen); **what sign are you?** was für ein Sternzeichen bist du? verb **1** unterschreiben ◇; **to sign a cheque** einen Scheck unterschreiben; **2** (*using sign language*) sich durch Zeichen verständigen.

• **to sign on** sich arbeitslos melden.

signal noun Signal das (PL die Signale).

signature noun Unterschrift die (PL die Unterschriften).

significant adjective bedeutend.

sign language noun Zeichensprache die (PL die Zeichensprachen).

signpost noun Wegweiser der (PL die Wegweiser).

silence noun Stille die.

silent adjective still.

silk noun Seide die (PL die Seiden). adjective Seiden-; **a silk blouse** eine Seidenbluse.

silky adjective seidig.

silly *adjective* dumm; **it was a really silly thing to do** das war wirklich dumm.

silver *noun* Silber *das*.
adjective Silber-; **a silver medal** eine Silbermedaille.

similar *adjective* ähnlich; **it looks similar to my old bike** es sieht so ähnlich wie mein altes Rad aus.

similarity *noun* Ähnlichkeit *die* (PL die Ähnlichkeiten).

simple *adjective* einfach.

simply *adverb* einfach.

sin *noun* Sünde *die* (PL die Sünden).

since *preposition* 1 seit (+DAT); *(notice that German uses the present tense for an action starting in the past and still going on in the present)* **I have been in Berlin since Saturday** ich bin seit Samstag in Berlin; **since when?** seit wann?; 2 *(with a negative the perfect tense is used)* **I haven't seen her since Monday** ich habe sie seit Montag nicht gesehen. *conjunction* 1 seit; **since I have known him** seit ich ihn kenne; **since I've been learning German** seitdem ich Deutsch lerne; 2 *(because)* da; **since it was raining, the match was cancelled** da es regnete, wurde das Spiel abgesagt. *adverb* seitdem; **I haven't seen him since** ich habe ihn seitdem nicht mehr gesehen.

sincere *adjective* aufrichtig.

sincerely *adverb* **Yours sincerely** Mit freundlichen Grüßen.

sing *verb* singen ✧.

singer *noun* Sänger *der* (PL die Sänger), Sängerin *die* (PL die Sängerinnen).

singing *noun* 1 Singen *das*; **a singing lesson** eine Singstunde; 2 **I like singing** ich singe gern.

single *noun* 1 *(ticket)* einfache Fahrkarte *die* (PL die einfachen Fahrkarten); **a single to Munich, please** eine einfache Fahrkarte nach München bitte; 2 *(record, CD)* Single *die* (PL die Singles). *adjective* 1 *(not married)* allein stehend Δ; **a single woman** eine allein stehende Frau; *(one)* ledig; 2 *(just one)* einzig; **I haven't had a single reply** ich habe keine einzige Antwort bekommen; 3 **not a single one** kein Einziger/keine Einzige/kein Einziges Δ; 4 **single room** das Einzelzimmer; **single bed** das Einzelbett.

single parent *noun* allein Erziehende Δ *der/die* (PL die allein Erziehenden); **she's a single parent** sie ist allein erziehende Mutter; **a single-parent family** eine Eineiternfamilie.

singles *plural noun* *(in tennis)* Einzel *das* (PL die Einzel); **the women's singles** das Dameneinzel; **the men's singles** das Herreneinzel.

singular *noun* Einzahl *die*; **in the singular** in der Einzahl.

sink *noun* Spülbecken *das* (PL die Spülbecken). *verb* sinken ✧ (PERF *sein*).

✧ IRREGULAR VERB: *See the verb table in the centre of the dictionary*

sir noun Herr der (PL die Herren); (in German,' Sir' is usually not translated) **would you like another one, sir?** möchten Sie noch eins?; **yes, sir** ja, mein Herr.

sister noun Schwester die (PL die Schwestern); **my sister's ten** meine Schwester ist zehn.

sister-in-law noun Schwägerin die (PL die Schwägerinnen).

sit verb 1 (to sit down) sich setzen; **you can sit on the sofa** ihr könnt euch aufs Sofa setzen; **sit on the floor** setz dich auf den Boden; 2 (to be sitting) sitzen ◇; **Leila was sitting on the sofa** Leila saß auf dem Sofa; **to sit on the floor** auf dem Boden sitzen; 3 **to sit an exam** eine Prüfung machen.

● **to sit down** sich setzen; **he sat down on the chair** er setzte sich auf den Stuhl; **do sit down** setzen Sie sich.

sitcom noun Situationskomödie die (PL die Situationskomödien).

site noun 1 **building site** die Baustelle; 2 **camping site** der Campingplatz; 3 **archaeological site** die archäologische Stätte.

sitting room noun Wohnzimmer das (PL die Wohnzimmer).

situated adjective **to be situated** liegen ◇; **the house is situated in a small village** das Haus liegt in einem kleinen Dorf.

situation noun 1 (location) Lage die (PL die Lagen);

2 (circumstances) Situation die (PL die Situationen).

six number sechs; **Harry's six** Harry ist sechs.

sixteen number sechzehn; **Alice is sixteen** Alice ist sechzehn.

sixth adjective sechster/sechste/sechstes; **on the sixth floor** im sechsten Stock; **on the sixth of July** am sechsten Juli.

sixty number sechzig; **she's sixty** sie ist sechzig.

size noun 1 Größe die (PL die Größen); **it depends on the size of the house** es kommt auf die Größe des Hauses an; 2 **what size is the window?** wie groß ist das Fenster?; 3 (in clothes) Größe die (PL die Größen); **what size do you take?** welche Größe haben Sie?; 4 (of shoes) Schuhgröße die (PL die Schuhgrößen); **I take a size thirty-eight** ich habe Schuhgröße achtunddreißig.

skate noun 1 (an ice skate) Schlittschuh der (PL die Schlittschuhe); 2 (a roller skate) Rollschuh der (PL die Rollschuhe). verb 1 (ice-skate) Schlittschuh laufen ◇ (PERF sein); 2 (roller-skate) Rollschuh laufen ◇ (PERF sein).

skateboard noun Skateboard das (PL die Skateboards).

skateboarding noun Skateboardfahren das; **to go skateboarding** Skateboard fahren ◇ (PERF sein).

skating noun 1 (on ice) Schlittschuhlaufen das; **to go**

skating Schlittschuh laufen ✧ (PERF *sein*); 2 (*roller-skating*) Rollschuhlaufen *das*; **to go roller-skating** Rollschuh laufen ✧ (PERF *sein*).

skating rink noun 1 (*ice rink*) Eisbahn *die* (PL die Eisbahnen); 2 (*for roller-skating*) Rollschuhbahn *die* (PL die Rollschuhbahnen).

sketch noun 1 Skizze *die* (PL die Skizzen); 2 (*comedy routine*) Sketch *der* (PL die Sketche).

ski noun Ski *der* (PL die Skier); *verb* Ski fahren ✧ (PERF *sein*); **he can ski** er kann Ski fahren.

ski boot noun Skistiefel *der* (PL die Skistiefel).

skid verb schleudern (PERF *sein*); **the car skidded** das Auto ist geschleudert.

skiing noun Skifahren *das*; **to go skiing** Ski fahren ✧ (PERF *sein*).

ski lift noun Skilift *der* (PL die Skilifte).

skin noun Haut *die* (PL die Häute).

skinhead noun Skinhead *der* (PL die Skinheads).

skinny adjective dünn.

skip noun (*for rubbish*) Container *der* (PL die Container); *verb* 1 auslassen ✧ SEP (*a meal, part of a book*); **I skipped a few chapters** ich ließ ein paar Kapitel aus; 2 **to skip a lesson** eine Stunde schwänzen (*informal*).

skirt noun Rock *der* (PL die Röcke); **a long skirt** ein langer Rock; **a tight skirt** ein enger Rock; **a mini-skirt** ein Minirock.

sky noun Himmel *der* (PL die Himmel).

skyscraper noun Wolkenkratzer *der* (PL die Wolkenkratzer).

slam verb zuknallen SEP; **she slammed the door** sie hat die Tür zugeknallt; **the door slammed** die Tür ist zugeknallt.

slang noun Slang *der* (PL die Slangs).

slap noun Klaps *der* (PL die Klapse); (*in the face*) Ohrfeige *die* (PL die Ohrfeigen); *verb* **to slap somebody** (*across the face*) jemanden ohrfeigen; (*on the bottom*) jemandem einen Klaps geben.

sledge noun Schlitten *der* (PL die Schlitten).

sledging noun **to go sledging** Schlitten fahren ✧ (PERF *sein*).

sleep noun Schlaf *der*; **you need more sleep** du brauchst mehr Schlaf; **I had a good sleep** ich habe gut geschlafen; **to go to sleep** einschlafen ✧ SEP (PERF *sein*); **he's gone back to sleep** er ist wieder eingeschlafen. *verb* schlafen ✧; **she's sleeping** sie schläft.

sleeping bag noun Schlafsack *der* (PL die Schlafsäcke).

sleeping pill noun Schlaftablette *die* (PL die Schlaftabletten).

✧ IRREGULAR VERB: *See the verb table in the centre of the dictionary*

sleepy *adjective* **to be sleepy** schläfrig sein; **he was getting sleepy** er wurde schläfrig.

sleet *noun* Schneeregen *der.*

sleeve *noun* Ärmel *der* (PL die Ärmel); **a long-sleeved jumper** ein Pullover mit langen Ärmeln; **a short-sleeved shirt** ein Hemd mit kurzen Ärmeln; **to roll up your sleeves** die Ärmel hochkrempeln.

slice *noun* Scheibe *die* (PL die Scheiben); **a slice of bread** eine Scheibe Brot.
verb **to slice something** etwas in Scheiben schneiden ◇.

slide *noun* **1** (*photo*) Dia *das* (PL die Dias); **2** (*hairslide*) Haarspange *die* (PL die Haarspangen); **3** (*for sliding down*) Rutschbahn *die* (PL die Rutschbahnen).

slight *adjective* klein; **there is a slight problem** es gibt ein kleines Problem.

slightly *adverb* etwas.

slim *adjective* schlank.
verb abnehmen ◇ SEP; **I'm slimming** ich mache eine Schlankheitskur.

sling *noun* Schlinge *die* (PL die Schlingen); **to have your arm in a sling** den Arm in der Schlinge haben.

slip *noun* **1** (*mistake*) Fehler *der* (PL die Fehler); **2** (*petticoat*) Unterrock *der* (PL die Unterröcke).
verb **1** (*slide*) ausrutschen SEP (PERF sein); **2 it slipped my mind** es ist mir entfallen.
● **to slip up** einen Fehler machen.

slipper *noun* Hausschuh *der* (PL die Hausschuhe).

slippery *adjective* glatt.

slope *noun* Hang *der* (PL die Hänge).

slot *noun* Schlitz *der* (PL die Schlitze).

slot machine *noun* **1** (*vending machine*) Automat *der* (PL die Automaten); **2** (*games machine*) Spielautomat *der* (PL die Spielautomaten).

slow *adjective* **1** langsam; **the service is a bit slow** die Bedienung ist etwas langsam; **2** (*of a clock or watch*) **to be slow** nachgehen ◇ SEP (PERF sein); **my watch is slow** meine Uhr geht nach.
● **to slow down** langsamer werden.

slowly *adverb* langsam; **he got up slowly** er ist langsam aufgestanden; **can you speak more slowly, please?** können Sie bitte etwas langsamer sprechen?

sly *adjective* gerissen (*a person*); ★ **on the sly** heimlich.

smack *noun* Klaps *der* (PL die Klapse).
verb **to smack somebody** jemandem einen Klaps geben ◇.

small *adjective* klein; **a small dog** ein kleiner Hund.

smart *adjective* **1** (*well-dressed, posh*) elegant; **a smart restaurant** ein elegantes Restaurant; **2** (*clever*) clever.

smash *noun* (*collision*) Zusammenstoß *der* (PL die Zusammenstöße).

△ NEW SPELLING: *See page xii*

verb 1 (break) zerschlagen ✧; **they smashed a window pane** sie haben eine Fensterscheibe zerschlagen; **2** (get broken) zerbrechen ✧ (PERF sein); **the plate smashed** der Teller ist zerbrochen.

smashing adjective klasse (informal).

smell noun Geruch der (PL die Gerüche); **a nasty smell** ein scheußlicher Geruch; **a smell of gas** ein Gasgeruch.
verb **1** riechen ✧; **I can't smell anything** ich kann nichts riechen; **to smell of perfume** nach Parfüm riechen; **2** (smell bad) stinken ✧; **the drains smell** der Abfluss stinkt.

smelly adjective **1** stinkend; **her smelly dog** ihr stinkender Hund; **2 to be smelly** stinken ✧.

smile noun Lächeln das.
verb lächeln; **to smile at somebody** jemanden anlächeln SEP.

smoke noun Rauch der.
verb rauchen; **she doesn't smoke** sie raucht nicht.

smoking noun 'no smoking' 'Rauchen verboten'; **to give up smoking** mit dem Rauchen aufhören.

smooth adjective **1** glatt; **a smooth surface** eine glatte Oberfläche; **2** (person) aalglatt.

smug adjective selbstgefällig.

smuggle verb **to smuggle something** etwas schmuggeln.

smuggler noun **1** Schmuggler der (PL die Schmuggler), Schmugglerin die (PL die Schmugglerinnen); **2 drugs smuggler** der Drogenschmuggler.

snack noun Snack der (PL die Snacks).

snail noun Schnecke die (PL die Schnecken).

snake noun Schlange die (PL die Schlangen).

snap noun (card game) Schnippschnapp das (PL die Schnippschnapp).
verb **1** (break) brechen ✧ (PERF sein); **2 to snap something** etwas zerbrechen ✧; **3 to snap your fingers** mit den Fingern schnalzen.

snapshot noun Schnappschuss △ der (PL die Schnappschüsse).

snarl verb knurren.

snatch verb **1** entreißen ✧; **to snatch something from somebody** jemandem etwas entreißen ✧; **she had her bag snatched** man hat ihr die Handtasche entrissen; **2** he **snatched it out of my hand** er hat es mir aus der Hand gerissen.

sneak verb **1 to sneak in** sich hineinschleichen ✧ SEP; **to sneak out** sich hinausschleichen ✧ SEP; **2 to sneak on somebody** jemanden verpetzen (informal).

sneeze verb niesen.

sniff verb schnüffeln.

snob noun Snob der (PL die Snobs).

snobbery noun Snobismus der.

snooker noun Snooker das.

snore verb schnarchen.

snow noun Schnee der.
verb schneien; **it's snowing** es
schneit.

snowball noun Schneeball der (PL
die Schneebälle).

snowman noun Schneemann der
(PL die Schneemänner).

so conjunction, adverb 1 so; **he's so
lazy** er ist so faul; **not so** nicht so;
**our house is a bit like yours, but not
so big** unser Haus ist so ähnlich wie
eures, aber nicht so groß; 2 **so much**
so sehr; **I hate it so much** ich hasse
es so sehr; 3 **so much** so viel; **I have
so much work** ich habe so viel
Arbeit; 4 **so many** so viele; **we've
got so many problems** wir haben
so viele Probleme; 5 (therefore) also;
**he got up late, so he missed his
train** er ist spät aufgestanden, also
hat er den Zug verpasst; **so what
shall we do?** also, was machen wir?;
6 **so what?** na und?; 7 (also) **so do
I, so did I** ich auch; **'I live in Leeds' –
'so do I'** 'ich wohne in Leeds' – 'ich
auch'; **I liked the film and so did he**
ich fand den Film gut und er auch; **so
am I** ich auch; **so do we** wir auch;
8 **I think so** ich glaube schon;
9 **I hope so** hoffentlich.

soak verb einweichen SEP.

soaked adjective patschnass △;
★ **to be soaked to the skin**
patschnass sein.

soap noun 1 Seife die (PL die Seifen);
2 (soap opera) Seifenoper die (PL die
Seifenopern).

soap powder noun
Seifenpulver das.

sober adjective nüchtern.
● **to sober up** nüchtern werden ◆
(PERF sein).

soccer noun Fußball der.

social adjective 1 sozial; **social
problems** soziale Probleme;
2 gesellschaftlich (engagement,
ambition); **social engagements**
gesellschaftliche Verpflichtungen;
social class die gesellschaftliche
Schicht; 3 (sociable) gesellig
(evening, person).

socialism noun Sozialismus der.

socialist noun, adjective
Sozialist der (PL die Sozialisten),
Sozialistin die (PL die
Sozialistinnen).

social security noun
1 Sozialhilfe die; **to be on social
security** Sozialhilfe bekommen;
2 (the system) Sozialversicherung
die.

social worker noun
Sozialarbeiter der (PL die
Sozialarbeiter), Sozialarbeiterin die
(PL die Sozialarbeiterinnen).

society noun Gesellschaft die (PL
die Gesellschaften).

sociology noun Soziologie die.

sock noun Socke die (PL die Socken);
a pair of socks ein Paar Socken.

socket noun (power point)
Steckdose die (PL die Steckdosen).

△ NEW SPELLING: See page xii

sofa noun Sofa das (PL die Sofas).

sofa bed noun Schlafcouch die (PL die Schlafcouchs).

soft adjective 1 weich; 2 a soft option eine bequeme Lösung; ★ to have a soft spot for somebody eine Vorliebe für jemanden haben.

soft drink noun alkoholfreie Getränk das (PL die alkoholfreien Getränke).

soft toy noun Stofftier das (PL die Stofftiere).

software noun Software die.

soil noun Erde die.

solar energy noun Sonnenenergie die.

soldier noun Soldat der (PL die Soldaten).

solicitor noun 1 (dealing with lawsuits) Rechtsanwalt der (PL die Rechtsanwälte), Rechtsanwältin die (PL die Rechtsanwältinnen); 2 (dealing with property or documents) Notar der (PL die Notare), Notarin die (PL die Notarinnen).

solid adjective 1 (not flimsy) stabil; a solid structure ein stabiler Bau; 2 massiv; a table made of solid oak ein Tisch aus massiver Eiche; solid silver massives Silber.

solo noun Solo das (PL die Solos); guitar solo das Gitarrensolo.
adjective Solo-; a solo act eine Solonummer.
adverb solo.

soloist noun Solist der (PL die Solisten), Solistin die (PL die Solistinnen).

solution noun Lösung die (PL die Lösungen).

solve verb lösen.

some adjective, adverb 1 (followed by a singular noun) etwas; would you like some salad? möchtest du etwas Salat?; can you lend me some money? kannst du mir etwas Geld leihen?; have you got some bread? (some is often not translated) hast du Brot?; 2 (followed by a plural noun) (a few) ein paar; I've bought some apples ich habe ein paar Äpfel gekauft; 3 (followed by a plural noun) (a certain number but not all) einige; some of his films are too violent einige von seinen Filmen sind zu brutal; 4 (referring to something that has been mentioned) 'would you like tea?' – 'thanks, I've got some' 'möchten Sie Tee?' – 'nein danke, ich habe schon welchen'; he's eaten some of it er hat etwas davon gegessen; I'd like some ich möchte etwas; (with a plural noun) ich möchte welche; 5 (certain people or things) manche; some people think he's right manche Leute glauben, dass er Recht hat; 6 some day eines Tages.

somebody, someone pronoun jemand; there's somebody in the garden da ist jemand im Garten.

somehow adverb irgendwie; I've got to finish this essay somehow ich muss diesen Aufsatz irgendwie fertig schreiben.

✧ IRREGULAR VERB: See the verb table in the centre of the dictionary

something *pronoun* 1 etwas; there's something I've got to tell you ich muss dir etwas erzählen; something new etwas Neues; something interesting etwas Interessantes; there's something wrong irgendetwas stimmt nicht; 2 their house is really something! ihr Haus ist einfach Klasse!

sometime *adverb* irgendwann; give me a ring sometime next week ruf mich irgendwann nächste Woche an.

sometimes *adverb* manchmal; I sometimes take the train manchmal fahre ich mit der Bahn.

somewhere *adverb* 1 (*in a place*) irgendwo; I've left my bag somewhere here ich habe meine Handtasche hier irgendwo liegen lassen; 2 (*to a place*) irgendwohin; I'd like to go somewhere warm ich möchte irgendwohin fahren, wo es warm ist.

son *noun* Sohn *der* (PL *die* Söhne).

song *noun* Lied *das* (PL *die* Lieder).

son-in-law *noun* Schwiegersohn *der* (PL *die* Schwiegersöhne).

soon *adverb* 1 bald; we'll soon be on holiday wir haben bald Ferien; see you soon! bis bald!; 2 as soon as she arrives sobald sie ankommt; as soon as possible so bald wie möglich; 3 it's too soon es ist zu früh.

sooner *adverb* 1 früher; we should have started sooner wir hätten früher anfangen sollen; sooner or later früher oder später; 2 I'd sooner wait ich würde lieber warten.

soprano *noun* Sopran *der* (PL *die* Soprane).

sore *noun* wunde Stelle *die* (PL *die* wunden Stellen).
adjective 1 (*inflamed*) wund; to have a sore throat Halsschmerzen haben; 2 he has a sore leg ihm tut das Bein weh; my arm's sore mir tut der Arm weh; ★ it's a sore point das ist ein wunder Punkt.

sorry *adjective* 1 I'm really sorry es tut mir wirklich Leid △; sorry to disturb you es tut mir Leid, dass ich dich störe; I'm sorry I forgot your birthday es tut mir Leid, dass ich deinen Geburtstag vergessen habe; I'm sorry, were closing es tut mir Leid, aber wir machen jetzt zu; 2 sorry! Entschuldigung!; 3 sorry? wie bitte?; 4 I feel sorry for him er tut mir Leid △.

sort *noun* Art *die* (PL *die* Arten); a sort of dance music eine Art Tanzmusik; what sort of car have you got? was für ein Auto hast du?; all sorts of people alle möglichen Leute; for all sorts of reasons aus allen möglichen Gründen.
● to sort something out 1 Ordnung schaffen ◇ in (+DAT) (*papers, desk, room, possessions*); I must sort out my room tonight ich muss heute Abend in meinem Zimmer Ordnung schaffen; 2 klären (*a problem, arrangement*); Liz is sorting it out Liz klärt es.

△ NEW SPELLING: See page xii

so-so *adjective* so lala (*informal*); **'how was the film?' - 'so-so'** 'wie war der Film?' - 'so lala'.

soul *noun* 1 Seele *die* (PL *die* Seelen); 2 (*music*) Soul *der*.

sound *noun* 1 (*noise*) Geräusch *das* (PL *die* Geräusche); 2 (*of voices, laughter, bell*) Klang *der*; **the sound of her voice** der Klang ihrer Stimme; **I can hear the sound of voices** ich kann Stimmen hören; 3 **without a sound** lautlos; 4 (*volume*) Lautstärke *die*; **to turn the sound down** leiser stellen. *verb* 1 **it sounds easy** es hört sich einfach an; 2 **it sounds as if she's happy** sie scheint glücklich zu sein.

sound asleep *adverb* **to be sound asleep** fest schlafen ✧.

sound effect *noun* Geräuscheffekt *der* (PL *die* Geräuscheffekte).

soundtrack *noun* Soundtrack *der* (PL *die* Soundtracks).

soup *noun* Suppe *die* (PL *die* Suppen); **mushroom soup** *die* Pilzsuppe.

soup plate *noun* Suppenteller *der* (PL *die* Suppenteller).

soup spoon *noun* Suppenlöffel *der* (PL *die* Suppenlöffel).

sour *adjective* sauer.

south *noun* Süden *der*; **in the south** im Süden. *adjective* Süd-, südlich; **the south side** die Südseite; **south wind** *der* Südwind.

adverb **south of Berlin** südlich von Berlin; **they went south** sie sind nach Süden gefahren.

South Africa *noun* Südafrika *das*.

South America *noun* Südamerika *das*.

southeast *noun* Südosten *der*. *adjective* **in southeast England** in Südostengland.

South Pole *noun* Südpol *der*.

southwest *noun* Südwesten *der*. *adjective* **in southwest England** in Südwestengland.

souvenir *noun* Souvenir *das* (PL *die* Souvenirs).

soya *noun* Soja *die*.

space *noun* 1 (*room*) Platz *der*; **there's enough space** es ist genug Platz da; **we've got enough space for two** wir haben genug Platz für zwei; 2 (*gap*) Zwischenraum *der* (PL *die* Zwischenräume); **to leave a large space between lines** einen großen Zwischenraum zwischen den Zeilen lassen; 3 (*parking*) space *die* Lücke; 4 (*outer space*) Weltraum *der*; **in space** im Weltraum.

spacecraft *noun* Raumschiff *das* (PL *die* Raumschiffe).

spade *noun* 1 Spaten *der* (PL *die* Spaten); 2 (*in cards*) Pik *das*; **the queen of spades** die Pikdame.

Spain *noun* Spanien *das*; **from Spain** aus Spanien; **to Spain** nach Spanien.

✧ IRREGULAR VERB: *See the verb table in the centre of the dictionary*

Spaniard noun Spanier der (PL die Spanier), Spanierin die (PL die Spanierinnen).

spaniel noun Spaniel der (PL die Spaniels).

Spanish noun 1 (language) Spanisch das; I'm learning Spanish ich lerne Spanisch; 2 the Spanish (people) die Spanier. adjective spanisch; Pedro is Spanish Pedro ist Spanier.

spare adjective Extra-; we have a spare ticket wir haben eine Extrakarte. verb to have time to spare Zeit haben; can you spare a moment? hast du einen Moment Zeit?

spare room noun Gästezimmer das (PL die Gästezimmer).

spare time noun Freizeit die; in my spare time in meiner Freizeit.

spare wheel noun Reserverad das (PL die Reserveräder).

sparkling adjective sparkling mineral water Mineralwasser mit Kohlensäure; sparkling wine der Schaumwein.

sparrow noun Spatz der (PL die Spätze).

speak verb 1 sprechen ◇; do you speak German? sprechen Sie Deutsch?; spoken German gesprochenes Deutsch; to speak to somebody about something mit jemandem über etwas ←(ACC) sprechen; she's speaking to Mike about it sie spricht mit Mike

darüber; 2 who's speaking? (on the phone) wer ist am Apparat?

speaker noun 1 (on a music system) Lautsprecher der (PL die Lautsprecher); 2 (at a public lecture) Redner der (PL die Redner), Rednerin die (PL die Rednerinnen).

special adjective 1 besonderer/ besondere/besonderes; on special occasions bei besonderen Anlässen; 2 special offer das Sonderangebot.

specialist noun Fachmann der (PL die Fachleute), Fachfrau die (PL die Fachfrauen).

specially adverb 1 besonders; not specially nicht besonders; it's specially good for babies es ist besonders gut für Babys; 2 (specifically) speziell; I made this cake specially for you ich habe diesen Kuchen speziell für dich gebacken.

spectacles noun Brille die (PL die Brillen).

spectacular adjective spektakulär.

spectator noun Zuschauer der (PL die Zuschauer), Zuschauerin die (PL die Zuschauerinnen).

speech noun Rede die (PL die Reden); to make a speech eine Rede halten.

speed noun 1 Geschwindigkeit die (PL die Geschwindigkeiten); at top speed mit Höchstgeschwindigkeit; what speed was he doing? wie schnell ist er gefahren?; 2 (gear) Gang der (PL die Gänge); a twelve-speed bike ein Rad mit zwölf Gängen.

△NEW SPELLING: See page xii

● **to speed up 1** beschleunigen (*a car*); **2** (*of a person, car*) schneller werden.

speeding *noun* zu schnelle Fahren *das*; **he was fined for speeding** er hat wegen zu schnellen Fahrens einen Strafzettel bekommen.

speed limit *noun* Geschwindigkeitsbeschränkung *die*.

spell *noun* **1** (*of time*) Weile *die*; **for a spell** eine Weile; **2 cold spell** die Kälteperiode; **sunny spells** sonnige Wetterabschnitte.
verb **1** (*in writing*) schreiben ◇; **how do you spell it?** wie schreibt man das?; **how do you spell your surname?** wie schreibt man Ihren Nachnamen?; **2** (*out loud*) buchstabieren.

spelling *noun* Rechtschreibung *die*; **spelling mistake** *der* Rechtschreibfehler.

spend *verb* **1** ausgeben ◇ SEP (*money*); **I've spent all my money** ich habe mein ganzes Geld ausgegeben; **2** verbringen ◇ (*time*); **we spent three days in Munich** wir haben drei Tage in München verbracht; **she spends her time reading** sie verbringt ihre Zeit mit Lesen.

spice *noun* Gewürz *das* (PL die Gewürze).

spicy *adjective* scharf; **he doesn't like spicy food** er mag kein scharfes Essen.

spider *noun* Spinne *die* (PL die Spinnen).

spill *verb* verschütten; **I've spilled my wine on the carpet** ich habe meinen Wein auf dem Teppich verschüttet.

spinach *noun* Spinat *der*.

spire *noun* Kirchturm *der* (PL die Kirchtürme).

spirit *noun* **1** (*energy*) Energie *die*; **2 in the right spirit** mit der richtigen Einstellung.

spirits *noun* **1** (*alcohol*) Spirituosen (*plural*); **2 to be in good spirits** guter Laune sein.

spit *verb* **1** spucken; **2 to spit something out** etwas ausspucken SEP; **spit it out!** spuck es aus!

spite *noun* **1 in spite of** trotz (+GEN); **we decided to go in spite of the rain** wir beschlossen trotz des Regens zu gehen; **2** (*nastiness*) Boshaftigkeit *die*; **to do something out of spite** etwas aus Boshaftigkeit tun.

spiteful *adjective* gehässig.

splash *noun* **1** (*noise*) Platsch *der*; **2 splash of colour** *der* Farbfleck.
verb bespritzen.

splendid *adjective* herrlich.

split *verb* **1** (*with an axe or a knife*) spalten; **to split wood** Holz spalten; **2** (*come apart*) zerreißen ◇ (PERF *sein*); **the lining has split** das Futter ist zerrissen; **3** (*divide up*) teilen; **they split the money between**

◇ IRREGULAR VERB: *See the verb table in the centre of the dictionary*

them sie haben das Geld untereinander geteilt.
- **to split up 1** (*a group or crowd*) sich auflösen SEP; **2** (*a couple*) sich trennen; **she's split up with her husband** sie hat sich von ihrem Mann getrennt; **she's split up with Sam** sie hat mit Sam Schluss gemacht. (*informal*).

spoil *verb* verderben ◇; **it completely spoiled our evening** das hat uns den Abend völlig verdorben; **to spoil somebody's fun** jemandem den Spaß verderben.

spoiled *adjective* verwöhnt; **a spoiled child** ein verwöhntes Kind.

spokesman *noun* Sprecher *der* (PL die Sprecher).

spokeswoman *noun* Sprecherin *die* (PL die Sprecherinnen).

sponge *noun* Schwamm *der* (PL die Schwämme).

sponge cake *noun* Rührkuchen *der* (PL die Rührkuchen).

sponsor *noun* Sponsor *der* (PL die Sponsoren).
verb sponsern.

spooky *adjective* gruselig; **a spooky story** eine gruselige Geschichte.

spoon *noun* Löffel *der* (PL die Löffel); **a spoon of sugar** ein Löffel Zucker; **soup spoon** der Suppenlöffel; **teaspoon** der Teelöffel.

spoonful *noun* Löffel *der* (PL die Löffel).

sport *noun* **1** Sport *der*; **to be good at sport** gut im Sport sein; **my favourite sport** mein Lieblingssport; **2** (*in games*) **to be a good sport** ein guter Verlierer sein.

sports bag *noun* Sporttasche *die* (PL die Sporttaschen).

sports car *noun* Sportwagen *der* (PL die Sportwagen).

sports centre *noun* Sportzentrum *das* (PL die Sportzentren).

sports club *noun* Sportverein *der* (PL die Sportvereine).

sportsman *noun* Sportler *der* (PL die Sportler).

sportswear *noun* Sportbekleidung *die*.

sportswoman *noun* Sportlerin *die* (PL die Sportlerinnen).

spot *noun* **1** (*pattern in fabric*) Punkt *der* (PL die Punkte); **a red shirt with black spots** ein rotes Hemd mit schwarzen Punkten; **2** (*on your skin*) Pickel *der* (PL die Pickel); **I've got spots** ich habe Pickel; **to be covered in spots** völlig verpickelt sein; **3** (*stain*) Fleck *der* (PL die Flecke); **you've got a spot on your shirt** du hast einen Fleck auf dem Hemd; **4** (*spotlight*) Scheinwerfer *der* (PL die Scheinwerfer); (*in the home*) Spot *der* (PL die Spots); **5 on the spot** (*immediately*) auf der Stelle; **we'll do it for you on the spot** wir machen es Ihnen auf der Stelle; **6** (*at hand*) **on the spot** zur Stelle; **7** (*at the same place*) **on the spot** an Ort

△ NEW SPELLING: See page xii

und Stelle.
verb entdecken; **he spotted his friend in the crowd** er entdeckte seinen Freund in der Menge.

spotlight *noun* 1 Scheinwerfer *der* (PL die Scheinwerfer); 2 (*in the home*) Spot *der* (PL die Spots).

spotty *adjective* (*pimply*) pickelig.

sprain *noun* Verstauchung *die* (PL die Verstauchungen).
verb **to sprain your ankle** sich ←(DAT) den Fuß verstauchen.

spray *noun* (*spray can*) Spray *das* (PL die Sprays).
verb sprühen.

spread *noun* Brotaufstrich *der*; **cheese spread** *der* Streichkäse.
verb 1 (*of news or a disease*) sich verbreiten; 2 streichen ✧ (*butter, jam, glue*).

spreadsheet *noun* (*on a computer*) Tabellenkalkulation *die*.

spring *noun* 1 (*the season*) Frühling *der* (PL die Frühlinge); **in the spring** im Frühling; **spring flowers** Frühlingsblumen; 2 (*made of metal*) Feder *die* (PL die Federn); 3 (*providing water*) Quelle *die* (PL die Quellen).

springtime *noun* Frühjahr *das*; **in springtime** im Frühjahr.

spring water *noun* Quellwasser *das*.

sprint *noun* Sprint *der* (PL die Sprints).
verb rennen ✧ (PERF sein).

sprinter *noun* Sprinter *der* (PL die Sprinter), Sprinterin *die* (PL die Sprinterinnen).

sprout *noun* (*Brussels sprout*) Rosenkohl *der*; **he likes sprouts** er mag Rosenkohl.

spy *noun* Spion *der* (PL die Spione), Spionin *die* (PL die Spioninnen).
verb **to spy on somebody** jemandem nachspionieren SEP; **he's spying on me** er spioniert mir nach.

squabble *verb* sich zanken.

square *noun* 1 (*shape*) Quadrat *das* (PL die Quadrate); 2 (*in a town or village*) Platz *der* (PL die Plätze); **the village square** *der* Dorfplatz.
adjective quadratisch; **a square box** eine viereckige Schachtel; **three square metres** drei Quadratmeter; **the room is four metres square** das Zimmer ist vier mal vier Meter; ★ **to go back to square one** noch einmal von vorn anfangen.

squash *noun* 1 (*drink*) Saft *der*; **orange squash** *der* Orangensaft; 2 (*sport*) Squash *das*.
verb zerquetschen.

squeak *verb* 1 (*door, hinge*) quietschen; 2 (*person, animal*) quieken.

squeeze *verb* 1 **to squeeze somebody's hand** jemandem die Hand drücken; 2 drücken (*toothpaste*).

stab *verb* stechen ✧; **to stab somebody** (*kill*) jemanden erstechen ✧.

✧ IRREGULAR VERB: *See the verb table in the centre of the dictionary*

stable noun Stall der (PL die Ställe). adjective stabil.

stack noun 1 Stapel der (PL die Stapel); 2 stacks of ein Haufen; she's got stacks of CDs sie hat einen Haufen CDs.

stadium noun Stadion das (PL die Stadien).

staff noun 1 (of a company) Personal das; 2 (in a school) Lehrkräfte (plural).

stage noun 1 (for a performance) Bühne die (PL die Bühnen); on stage auf der Bühne; 2 (phase) Phase die (PL die Phasen); at this stage of the project; at this stage it's hard to say im Augenblick ist es schwer zu sagen.

staggered adjective (amazed) verblüfft.

stain noun Fleck der (PL die Flecke). verb beflecken.

stainless steel noun Edelstahl der; a stainless steel sink ein Spülbecken aus Edelstahl.

stair noun 1 (step) Stufe die (PL die Stufen); 2 the stairs die Treppe (singular); I met her on the stairs ich habe sie auf der Treppe getroffen.

staircase noun Treppe die (PL die Treppen).

stale adjective alt.

stalemate noun (in chess) Patt das (PL die Patts).

stall noun 1 (at a market or fair) Stand der (PL die Stände); 2 (in a theatre) the stalls das Parkett.

stammer noun to have a stammer stottern.

stamp noun Briefmarke die (PL die Briefmarken). verb 1 frankieren (a letter); 2 to stamp your foot mit dem Fuß aufstampfen.

stamp album noun Briefmarkenalbum das (PL die Briefmarkenalben).

stamp collection noun Briefmarkensammlung die (PL die Briefmarkensammlungen).

stand verb 1 stehen ✧; several people were standing viele Leute standen; we stood outside the cinema wir haben vor dem Kino gestanden; 2 (bear) ausstehen ✧ SEP; I can't stand her ich kann sie nicht ausstehen; I can't stand waiting ich kann es nicht ausstehen, wenn man warten muss; 3 (keep going) aushalten ✧ SEP; I can't stand it any longer ich halte es nicht mehr aus. noun (in a stadium) Tribüne die (PL die Tribünen).

• **to stand for something** (be short for) bedeuten; UN stands for United Nations UN bedeutet United Nations.

• **stand up** aufstehen ✧ SEP (PERF sein); everybody stood up alle standen auf.

standard noun 1 (level) Niveau das; of high standard von hohem Niveau; 2 standard of living

der Lebensstandard; **3 she sets herself high standards** sie stellt hohe Ansprüche an sich selbst.
adjective normal; **the standard size** die Normalgröße.

staple *noun* Heftklammer *die* (PL *die* Heftklammern);
verb heften; **to staple the pages together** die Seiten zusammenheften.

stapler *noun* Hefter *der* (PL *die* Hefter).

star *noun* **1** (*in the sky*) Stern *der* (PL *die* Sterne); **2** (*person*) Star *der* (PL *die* Stars); **he's a film star** er ist ein Filmstar.
verb **to star in a film** in einem Film die Hauptrolle spielen; **starring ...** in der Hauptrolle ...

stare *verb* **1** starren; **what are you staring at?** was starrst du so?; **2 to stare at somebody** jemanden anstarren SEP; **he's staring at the wall** er starrt die Wand an.

start *noun* **1** Anfang *der*; **at the start** am Anfang; **at the start of the film** am Anfang des Films; **from the start** von Anfang an; **we knew from the start that it was dangerous** wir wussten von Anfang an, dass es gefährlich war; **2 to make a start on something** mit etwas ←(DAT) anfangen ✧ SEP; **I've made a start on my homework** ich habe mit meinen Hausaufgaben angefangen; **3** (*of a race*) Start *der* (PL *die* Starts).
verb **1** anfangen ✧ SEP; **the film starts at eight** der Film fängt um acht an; **I've started the book** ich habe das Buch angefangen; **to start**

doing something anfangen, etwas zu tun; **I've started learning Spanish** ich habe angefangen, Spanisch zu lernen; **to start crying** anfangen zu weinen; **2 to start a business** ein Geschäft gründen; **3 to start a car** ein Auto starten; **she started the car** sie hat das Auto gestartet; **4 the car won't start** das Auto springt nicht an.

starter *noun* (*first course*) Vorspeise *die* (PL *die* Vorspeisen).

starve *verb* verhungern; **I'm starving!** ich bin schon am Verhungern!

state *noun* **1** Zustand *der* (PL *die* Zustände); **the house is in a very bad state** das Haus ist in einem sehr schlechten Zustand; **2** (*country*) Staat *der* (PL *die* Staaten); **the state** der Staat; **3 the States** (*USA*) die Staaten; **they live in the States** sie leben in den Staaten.
verb **1** erklären (*intention, reason*); **2** angeben ✧ SEP (*an address, income, a reason*).

stately home *noun* Schloss △ *das* (PL *die* Schlösser).

statement *noun* Erklärung *die* (PL *die* Erklärungen).

station *noun* **1** Bahnhof *der* (PL *die* Bahnhöfe); **at the railway station** am Bahnhof; **bus station** der Busbahnhof; **2 police station** die Polizeiwache; **3 radio station** der Rundfunksender.

stationer's *noun* Schreibwarengeschäft *das* (PL *die* Schreibwarengeschäfte).

✧ **IRREGULAR VERB: See the verb table in the centre of the dictionary**

statistics noun (subject)
Statistik die; **the statistics** (figures)
die Statistik.

statue noun Statue die (PL die
Statuen).

stay noun Aufenthalt der (PL die
Aufenthalte); **our stay in Cologne**
unser Aufenthalt in Köln; **enjoy your
stay!** einen schönen Aufenthalt!
verb **1** bleiben ♦ (PERF sein); **I'll stay
here** ich bleibe hier; **how long are
you staying?** wie lange bleibst du?;
2 (spend the night) **you can stay
with us** du kannst bei uns
übernachten; **to stay the night with
friends** bei Freunden übernachten;
3 (be temporarily lodged) wohnen;
where are you staying? wo wohnst
du?; **I'm staying in a hotel** ich
wohne im Hotel; **to stay** ♦ (PERF sein)
sein ♦ (PERF sein); **I'm going to stay
with my sister this weekend** ich bin
am Wochenende bei meiner
Schwester; **I stayed in Munich for a
couple of days** ich war ein paar
Tage in München.

● **to stay in** zu Hause bleiben ♦ (PERF
sein); **I'm staying in tonight** heute
Abend bleibe ich zu Hause.

steady adjective **1** fest; **a steady job**
eine feste Stelle; **2** gleichmäßig; **at a
steady pace** mit gleichmäßiger
Geschwindigkeit; **3** (hand, voice)
ruhig; **to hold something steady**
etwas ruhig halten; **4** (dependable)
zuverlässig.

steak noun Steak das (PL die Steaks);
steak and chips Steak mit Pommes
frites.

steal verb stehlen ♦.

steam noun Dampf der.

steel noun Stahl der.

steep adjective steil; **a steep slope**
ein steiler Hang.

steeple noun (spire) Kirchturm der
(PL die Kirchtürme).

steering wheel noun
Lenkrad das (PL die Lenkräder).

step noun **1** Schritt der (PL die
Schritte); **to take a step forwards**
einen Schritt nach vorn machen; **to
take a step backwards** einen
Schritt zurück machen; **2** (stair)
Stufe die (PL die Stufen);

● **to step back** zurücktreten ♦ SEP
(PERF sein).

● **to step forward** vortreten ♦ SEP (PERF
sein).

stepbrother noun Stiefbruder der
(PL die Stiefbrüder).

stepdaughter noun
Stieftochter die (PL die Stieftöchter).

stepfather noun Stiefvater der (PL
die Stiefväter).

stepladder noun Trittleiter die (PL
die Trittleitern).

stepmother noun Stiefmutter die
(PL die Stiefmütter).

stepsister noun Stiefschwester die
(PL die Stiefschwestern).

stepson noun Stiefsohn der (PL die
Stiefsöhne).

stereo noun Stereoanlage die (PL die
Stereoanlagen).

sterling noun Sterling der; **in
sterling** in Pfund (Sterling).

△ NEW SPELLING: See page xii

stew noun Eintopf der (PL die Eintöpfe).

steward noun Steward der (PL die Stewards).

stewardess noun Stewardess △ die (PL die Stewardessen).

stick noun 1 Stock der (PL die Stöcke); 2 hockey stick der Hockeyschläger.
verb 1 (with glue) kleben; 2 (put) tun ♢; stick them on my desk tu sie auf meinen Schreibtisch.

sticker noun Aufkleber der (PL die Aufkleber).

sticky adjective 1 klebrig; I've got sticky hands ich habe klebrige Hände; 2 a sticky label ein Aufkleber.

sticky tape noun Klebestreifen der.

stiff adjective 1 steif; to feel stiff steif sein; (after exercise) Muskelkater haben; to have a stiff neck einen steifen Hals haben; 2 to be bored stiff sich zu Tode langweilen; 3 to be scared stiff furchtbare Angst haben.

still adjective 1 sit still! sitz still!; keep still! halt still!; 2 still mineral water Mineralwasser ohne Kohlensäure.
adverb 1 noch; do you still live in London? wohnst du noch in London? I've still not finished ich bin immer noch nicht fertig; he's still working er arbeitet noch; 2 (nevertheless) trotzdem; I told her not to, but she still did it ich habe

es ihr verboten, aber sie hat es trotzdem gemacht; 3 better still noch besser.

sting noun Stich der (PL die Stiche).
verb stechen ♢.

stink noun Gestank der.
verb stinken ♢; it stinks of fish in here es stinkt hier nach Fisch.

stir verb rühren.

stitch noun 1 (in sewing, surgical) Stich der (PL die Stiche); 2 (in knitting) Masche die (PL die Maschen); 3 (pain) Seitenstechen das.

stock noun 1 (in a shop) Warenbestand der; to have something in stock etwas auf Lager haben; to be out of stock ausverkauft sein; 2 (supply) Vorrat der (PL die Vorräte); I always have a stock of pencils ich habe immer einen Bleistiftvorrat; 3 (for cooking) Brühe die; chicken stock die Hühnerbrühe.
verb (in a shop) führen; they don't stock books sie führen keine Bücher.

stock cube noun Brühwürfel der (PL die Brühwürfel).

stocking noun Strumpf der (PL die Strümpfe).

stomach noun Magen der (PL die Mägen).

stomach-ache noun Magenschmerzen (plural); to have stomach-ache Magenschmerzen haben.

♢ IRREGULAR VERB: See the verb table in the centre of the dictionary

stone noun Stein der (PL die Steine); **stone wall** die Steinmauer.

stool noun Hocker der (PL die Hocker).

stop noun Haltestelle die (PL die Haltestellen); **bus stop** die Bushaltestelle.
verb 1 halten ◇; **does the train stop in Stuttgart?** hält der Zug in Stuttgart?; 2 **to stop somebody/something** jemanden/etwas anhalten ◇ SEP; **the police stopped the car** die Polizei hielt den Wagen an; 3 (cease) aufhören SEP; **the noise has stopped** der Lärm hat aufgehört; **to stop doing something** aufhören, etwas zu tun; **he's stopped smoking** er hat aufgehört zu rauchen; **she never stops asking questions** sie hört nie auf, Fragen zu stellen; **stop it!** hör auf!; 4 **to stop somebody doing something** jemanden daran hindern, etwas zu tun; **I can't stop her ringing him** ich kann sie nicht daran hindern, ihn anzurufen; 5 (prevent) verhindern (an accident, a crime).

stopwatch noun Stoppuhr die (PL die Stoppuhren).

store noun (shop) Geschäft das (PL die Geschäfte); **department store** das Kaufhaus.
verb 1 aufbewahren SEP; (in a warehouse) lagern; 2 (on a computer) speichern.

storey noun Stockwerk das (PL die Stockwerke); **a four-storey house** ein vierstöckiges Haus.

storm noun 1 Sturm der (PL die Stürme); 2 (thunderstorm) Gewitter das (PL die Gewitter).

stormy adjective stürmisch.

story noun Geschichte die (PL die Geschichten); **to tell a story** eine Geschichte erzählen.

stove noun (cooker) Herd der (PL die Herde).

straight adjective 1 gerade; **a straight line** eine gerade Linie; 2 **to have straight hair** glatte Haare haben.
adverb 1 (in direction) straight ahead geradeaus; **to go straight ahead** geradeaus gehen; 2 (immediately, directly) sofort; **straight away** sofort; **he went straight to the doctor's** er ging sofort zum Arzt.

straightforward adjective einfach.

strain noun Stress △ der; **the strain of the last few weeks** der Stress in den letzten Wochen; **to be a strain** anstrengend sein.
verb 1 zerren (a muscle); 2 verrenken (your arm, back); **he's strained his back** er hat sich ◇ (DAT) den Rücken verrenkt.

strange adjective seltsam; **his strange behaviour** sein seltsames Verhalten.

stranger noun Fremde der/die (PL die Fremden).

strap noun 1 (on a case, bag, camera) Riemen der (PL die Riemen); 2 (on a garment) Träger der (PL die Träger);

△ NEW SPELLING: See page xii

3 (*of a watch*) Armband *das* (PL *die* Armbänder).

strapless *adjective* trägerlos.

straw *noun* 1 (*for drinking*) Strohhalm *der* (PL *die* Strohhalme); 2 (*the material*) Stroh *das*; **straw hat** *der* Strohhut.

strawberry *noun* Erdbeere *die* (PL *die* Erdbeeren); **strawberry jam** *die* Erdbeermarmelade.

stray *adjective* **a stray dog** ein streunender Hund.

stream *noun* Bach *der* (PL *die* Bäche).

street *noun* Straße *die* (PL *die* Straßen); **I met Simon in the street** ich habe Simon auf der Straße getroffen.

streetlamp *noun* Straßenlampe *die* (PL *die* Straßenlampen).

street map *noun* Stadtplan *der* (PL *die* Stadtpläne).

streetwise *adjective* gewieft.

strength *noun* Kraft *die* (PL *die* Kräfte).

stress *noun* Stress △ *der*. *verb* betonen; **to stress the importance of something** die Wichtigkeit von etwas betonen.

stretch *verb* 1 (*garment, shoes*) sich dehnen; **this jumper has stretched** der Pullover hat sich gedehnt; 2 **to stretch your legs** sich ←(DAT) die Beine vertreten ◇.

stretcher *noun* Trage *die* (PL *die* Tragen).

stretchy *adjective* elastisch.

strict *adjective* streng.

strike *noun* Streik *der* (PL *die* Streiks); **to go on strike** in den Streik treten ◇ (PERF *sein*); **to be/go on strike** streiken. *verb* 1 (*hit*) schlagen ◇; **the clock struck six** die Uhr schlug sechs; 2 (*be/go on strike*) streiken.

striker *noun* 1 (*in football*) Stürmer *der* (PL *die* Stürmer, Stürmerin *die* (PL *die* Stürmerinnen); 2 (*person on strike*) Streikende *der/die* (PL *die* Streikenden).

string *noun* 1 (*for tying*) Schnur *die* (PL *die* Schnüre); 2 (*on a musical instrument*) Saite *die* (PL *die* Saiten).

strip *noun* Streifen *der* (PL *die* Streifen). *verb* 1 (*undress*) sich ausziehen ◇ SEP; 2 (*remove paint from*) abbeizen SEP.

strip cartoon *noun* Comicstrip △ *der* (PL *die* Comicstrips).

stripe *noun* Streifen *der* (PL *die* Streifen).

striped *adjective* gestreift.

stroke *noun* 1 (*style of swimming*) Stil *der* (PL *die* Stile); 2 (*medical*) Schlaganfall *der* (PL *die* Schlaganfälle); **to have a stroke** einen Schlaganfall bekommen; ★ **a stroke of luck** ein glücklicher Zufall; **to have a stroke of luck** Glück haben. *verb* streicheln.

strong *adjective* 1 (*person, drink, feeling*) stark; 2 (*sturdy*) stabil (*furniture*); **strong shoes** feste Schuhe.

strongly *adverb* 1 (*believe, oppose*) fest; 2 (*support*) nachdrücklich; 3 (*advise, recommend*) dringend; 4 **she smelt strongly** of garlic sie hat stark nach Knoblauch gerochen.

struggle *noun* Kampf *der* (PL die Kämpfe); **the struggle for freedom** der Kampf für die Freiheit; **it's been a struggle** es war ein Kampf.
verb 1 (*to obtain something*) kämpfen; **to struggle to do something** kämpfen, um etwas zu tun; **she struggled for a place** sie kämpfte um einen Platz; 2 (*physically, in order to escape or reach something*) sich wehren; 3 (*have difficulty in doing something*) sich abmühen SEP; **they are struggling to pay the rent** sie mühen sich ab, ihre Miete zu zahlen; **he's struggling with his homework** er müht sich mit seinen Hausaufgaben ab.

stub *noun* cigarette stub die Kippe.
● **to stub out** ausdrücken SEP.

stubborn *adjective* stur.

stuck *adjective* 1 (*jammed*) **it's stuck** es klemmt; **the drawer's stuck** die Schublade klemmt; 2 **to get stuck** (*person*) stecken bleiben △ ◇ (*in a lift, traffic jam, or place*).

stud *noun* 1 (*on clothes*) Niete *die* (PL die Nieten); 2 (*on a boot*) Stollen *der* (PL die Stollen);

3 (*earring*) Ohrstecker *der* (PL die Ohrstecker).

student *noun* 1 (*at college or university*) Student *der* (PL die Studenten), Studentin *die* (PL die Studentinnen); 2 (*at school*) Schüler *der* (PL die Schüler), Schülerin *die* (PL die Schülerinnen).

studio *noun* 1 (*film, TV*) Studio *das* (PL die Studios); 2 (*artist's*) Atelier *das* (PL die Ateliers).

study *verb* 1 lernen; **he's busy studying for his exams** er lernt fleißig für seine Prüfung; 2 studieren; **she's studying medicine** sie studiert Medizin.

stuff *noun* (*things, personal belongings*) Zeug *das* (*informal*); **we can put all that stuff in the attic** wir können das ganze Zeug auf den Boden bringen; **you can leave your stuff at my house** du kannst dein Zeug bei mir lassen.
verb 1 (*shove*) stopfen; **she stuffed some things into a suitcase** sie hat ein paar Sachen in einen Koffer gestopft; 2 füllen (*vegetables, turkey*); **stuffed peppers** gefüllte Paprikaschoten.

stuffing *noun* (*in cooking*) Füllung *die* (PL die Füllungen).

stuffy *adjective* (*airless*) stickig.

stunned *adjective* sprachlos.

stunning *adjective* toll (*informal*).

stunt *noun* (*in a film*) Stunt *der* (PL die Stunts).

stuntman *noun* Stuntman *der* (PL die Stuntmen).

△ NEW SPELLING: See page xii

stupid *adjective* blöd; **that was really stupid** das war so blöd; **I did something stupid** ich habe etwas Blödes gemacht.

stutter *noun* **to have a stutter** stottern.
verb stottern.

style *noun* **1** Stil *der* (PL die Stile); **style of living** *der* Lebensstil; **he has his own style** er hat seinen eigenen Stil; **2** (*fashion*) Mode *die*; **it's the latest style** das ist die neueste Mode.

subject *noun* **1** Thema *das* (PL die Themen); **the subject of my talk** das Thema meiner Rede; **2** (*at school*) Fach *das* (PL die Fächer); **my favourite subject is biology** mein Lieblingsfach ist Biologie.

subscription *noun* Abonnement *das* (PL die Abonnements); **to take out a subscription to a magazine** eine Zeitschrift abonnieren.

subsidize *verb* subventionieren.

subsidy *noun* Subvention *die* (PL die Subventionen).

substance *noun* Substanz *die* (PL die Substanzen).

substitute *noun* (*in sport*) Ersatzspieler *der* (PL die Ersatzspieler), Ersatzspielerin *die* (PL die Ersatzspielerinnen).
verb ersetzen.

subtitled *adjective* mit Untertiteln.

subtitles *plural noun* Untertitel (*plural*).

subtract *verb* abziehen ◊ SEP.

suburb *noun* Vorort *der* (PL die Vororte); **a suburb of Edinburgh** ein Vorort von Edinburgh; **in the suburbs of London** in den Londoner Vororten.

suburban *adjective* Vorort-; **a suburban train** ein Vorortzug.

subway *noun* (*underpass*) Unterführung *die* (PL die Unterführungen).

succeed *verb* gelingen ◊ (PERF sein); **we've succeeded in contacting her** es ist uns gelungen, sie zu erreichen.

success *noun* Erfolg *der* (PL die Erfolge); **a great success** ein großer Erfolg.

successful *adjective* **1** erfolgreich; **he's a successful writer** er ist ein erfolgreicher Schriftsteller; **2 to be successful in doing something** etwas mit Erfolg tun.

successfully *adverb* mit Erfolg.

such *adjective, adverb* **1** so; **they're such nice people** das sind so nette Leute; **I've had such a busy day** ich habe so einen hektischen Tag gehabt; **it's such a long way** es ist so weit; **it's such a pity** es ist so schade; **2 such a lot of** (*followed by a singular noun*) so viel; **they've got such a lot of money** sie haben so viel Geld; **3 such a lot of** (*followed by a plural noun*) so viele; **she's got such a lot of problems** sie hat so viele Probleme; **4 such as** wie; **in big cities such as Glasgow** in großen Städten wie Glasgow;

◊ **IRREGULAR VERB: See the verb table in the centre of the dictionary**

5 there's no such thing so etwas gibt es nicht.

suck verb lutschen; **to suck your thumb** am Daumen lutschen.

sudden adjective plötzlich; ★ **all of a sudden** plötzlich.

suddenly adverb plötzlich; **he suddenly started to laugh** plötzlich hat er angefangen zu lachen; **suddenly the light went out** plötzlich ging das Licht aus.

suede noun Wildleder das; **suede jacket** die Wildlederjacke.

suffer verb leiden ◇; **to suffer from asthma** an Asthma leiden.

sufficiently adverb genug.

sugar noun Zucker der; **do you take sugar?** nimmst du Zucker?

suggest verb vorschlagen ◇ SEP; **he suggested I should speak to you about it** er hat vorgeschlagen, dass ich mit dir darüber sprechen soll.

suggestion noun Vorschlag der (PL die Vorschläge); **to make a suggestion** einen Vorschlag machen.

suicide noun Selbstmord der (PL die Selbstmorde); **to commit suicide** Selbstmord begehen.

suit noun 1 (man's) Anzug der (PL die Anzüge); 2 (woman's) Kostüm das (PL die Kostüme).
verb 1 (be convenient) passen (+DAT); **does Monday suit you?** passt Ihnen Montag?; 2 (look good on) stehen ◇ (+DAT); **hats suit her** ihr stehen Hüte gut.

suitable adjective 1 geeignet; **to be suitable for something** für etwas geeignet sein; **it's suitable for children** es ist für Kinder geeignet; 2 (convenient) passend; **at a suitable time** zur passenden Zeit; **Saturday is the most suitable day for me** Samstag passt mir am besten; 3 (for a social occasion) angemessen (clothes).

suitcase noun Koffer der (PL die Koffer).

sulk verb schmollen.

sum noun 1 Summe die (PL die Summen); **a sum of money** eine Geldsumme; 2 (calculation) Rechenaufgabe die (PL die Rechenaufgaben).
● **to sum up** zusammenfassen SEP.

summarize verb zusammenfassen SEP.

summary noun Zusammenfassung die (PL die Zusammenfassungen).

summer noun Sommer der (PL die Sommer); **in summer** im Sommer; **summer clothes** die Sommerkleidung; **the summer holidays** die Sommerferien.

summertime noun Sommer der; **in summertime** im Sommer.

summit noun Gipfel der (PL die Gipfel).

sun noun Sonne die (PL die Sonnen); **in the sun** in der Sonne.

sunbathe verb sich sonnen.

△ NEW SPELLING: See page xii

sunblock noun Sun-Block-Creme
die (PL die Sun-Block-Cremes).

sunburned adjective **to get
sunburned** einen Sonnenbrand
bekommen.

Sunday noun 1 Sonntag der (PL die
Sonntage); **on Sunday** am Sonntag;
I'm going to the cinema on Sunday
ich gehe (am) Sonntag ins Kino; **see
you on Sunday!** bis Sonntag!; **every
Sunday** jeden Sonntag; **last
Sunday** vorigen Sonntag; **next
Sunday** nächsten Sonntag; 2 **on
Sundays** sonntags; **the museum is
closed on Sundays** das Museum ist
sonntags geschlossen.

sunflower noun Sonnenblume die
(PL die Sonnenblumen); **sunflower
oil** das Sonnenblumenöl.

sunglasses plural noun
Sonnenbrille die (PL die
Sonnenbrillen).

sunlight noun Sonnenlicht das.

sunny adjective sonnig; **a sunny day**
ein sonniger Tag; **sunny intervals**
Aufheiterungen.

sunrise noun Sonnenaufgang der
(PL die Sonnenaufgänge).

sunscreen noun
Sonnenschutzcreme die (PL die
Sonnenschutzcremes).

sunset noun Sonnenuntergang der
(PL die Sonnenuntergänge).

sunshine noun Sonnenschein der.

sunstroke noun Sonnenstich der
(PL die Sonnenstiche); **to get
sunstroke** einen Sonnenstich
bekommen.

suntan noun Bräune die; **to have a
suntan** braun sein; **to get a suntan**
braun werden.

suntan lotion noun
Sonnenmilch die.

suntan oil noun Sonnenöl das.

super adjective klasse (informal)
('klasse' never changes); **we had a
super time** es war wirklich klasse.

supermarket noun
Supermarkt der (PL die
Supermärkte).

supernatural adjective
übernatürlich.

superstitious adjective
abergläubisch.

supervise verb beaufsichtigen.

supper noun Abendessen das (PL
die Abendessen); **I had supper at
Sandy's** ich war bei Sandy zum
Abendessen.

supplement noun 1 (to newspaper)
Beilage die (PL die Beilagen); 2 (to
fare) Zuschlag der (PL die
Zuschläge).

supply noun 1 (stock) Vorrat der (PL
die Vorräte); 2 **to be in short supply**
knapp sein.
verb 1 stellen; **the school supplies
the books** die Schule stellt die
Bücher; 2 (deliver) liefern; **to
supply somebody with something**
jemandem etwas liefern.

supply teacher noun
Aushilfslehrer der (PL die
Aushilfslehrer), Aushilfslehrerin die
(PL die Aushilfslehrerinnen).

◇ IRREGULAR VERB: See the verb table in the centre of the dictionary

support noun Unterstützung die; **in support** zur Unterstützung.
verb 1 (back up) unterstützen; **her teachers have really supported her** die Lehrer haben sie sehr unterstützt; **to support somebody financially** jemanden finanziell unterstützen; **2 Will supports Chelsea** Will ist ein Chelsea-Fan; **what team do you support?** für welche Mannschaft bist du?; **3** (keep, provide for) ernähren; **to support a family** eine Familie ernähren.

supporter noun 1 Fan der (PL die Fans); **she's a Manchester United supporter** sie ist ein Manchester-United-Fan; **2** (of a party or cause) Anhänger der (PL die Anhänger), Anhängerin die (PL die Anhängerinnen).

suppose verb annehmen ◊ SEP; **I suppose she's forgotten** ich nehme an, sie hat es vergessen.

supposed adjective **to be supposed to do something** etwas tun sollen; **you were supposed to be here at six** du solltest um sechs hier sein.

sure adjective 1 sicher; **are you sure?** bist du sicher?; **are you sure you saw her?** bis du sicher, dass du sie gesehen hast?; **2 sure!** klar!

surely adverb doch sicherlich; **surely she hasn't forgotten** sie hat es doch sicherlich nicht vergessen.

surface noun Oberfläche die (PL die Oberflächen).

surfboard noun Surfbrett das (PL die Surfbretter).

surfing noun Surfen das.

surgeon noun Chirurg der (PL die Chirurgen), Chirurgin die (PL die Chirurginnen).

surgery noun 1 **to have surgery** operiert werden; **2** (doctor's) Praxis die (PL die Praxen); **the dentist's surgery** die Zahnarztpraxis; **3** (surgery hours) Sprechstunde die.

surname noun Nachname der (PL die Nachnamen).

surprise noun Überraschung die (PL die Überraschungen); **what a surprise!** was für eine Überraschung!

surprised adjective überrascht; **I was surprised to see her** ich war überrascht, sie zu sehen.

surprising adjective überraschend.

surround verb umgeben; **surrounded by** umgeben von (+DAT); **she was surrounded by friends** sie war von Freunden umgeben.

survey noun Umfrage die (PL die Umfragen).

survive verb überleben.

survivor noun Überlebende der/die (PL die Überlebenden).

suspect noun Verdächtige der/die (PL die Verdächtigen).
adjective verdächtig.
verb verdächtigen.

suspend verb 1 **to be suspended** (from school) vom Unterricht ausgeschlossen werden; **2** (from a

△ NEW SPELLING: See page xii

team) sperren; **to suspend a player for four weeks** einen Spieler für vier Wochen sperren.

suspense *noun* Spannung *die*.

suspicious *adjective*
1 misstrauisch △; **to be suspicious of somebody** jemandem misstrauen; 2 (*suspicious looking*) verdächtig.

swallow *noun* (*bird*) Schwalbe *die* (PL *die* Schwalben).
verb schlucken.

swan *noun* Schwan *der* (PL *die* Schwäne).

swap *verb* tauschen; **do you want to swap?** willst du tauschen?; **he swapped his bike for a computer** er hat sein Rad gegen einen Computer getauscht; **we swapped seats** wir tauschten die Plätze.

swear *verb* (*use bad language*) fluchen.

swearword *noun* Kraftausdruck *der* (PL *die* Kraftausdrücke).

sweat *noun* Schweiß *der*.
verb schwitzen.

sweater *noun* Pullover *der* (PL *die* Pullover).

Swede *noun* Schwede *der* (PL *die* Schweden), Schwedin *die* (PL *die* Schwedinnen).

Sweden *noun* Schweden *das*; **from Sweden** aus Schweden; **to Sweden** nach Schweden.

Swedish *noun* (*the language*) Schwedisch *das*.

adjective schwedisch; **he's Swedish** er ist Schwede; **she's Swedish** sie ist Schwedin.

sweep *verb* fegen.

sweet *noun* 1 Bonbon *der* (PL *die* Bonbons); 2 (*dessert*) Nachtisch *der* (PL *die* Nachtische).
adjective 1 süß; **I try not to eat sweet things** ich versuche keine Süßes zu essen; **she looks really sweet in that hat** sie sieht richtig süß mit dem Hut aus; 2 (*kind*) lieb; **she's a really sweet person** sie ist wirklich ein sehr lieber Mensch; **how sweet of him** wie lieb von ihm.

sweetcorn *noun* Mais *der*.

swell *verb* (*part of the body*) anschwellen ✧ SEP (PERF *sein*).

swim *noun* **to go for a swim** schwimmen gehen ✧ (PERF *sein*).
verb schwimmen ✧ (PERF *sein*); **can he swim?** kann er schwimmen?; **to swim across a lake** über einen See schwimmen.

swimmer *noun* Schwimmer *der* (PL *die* Schwimmer), Schwimmerin *die* (PL *die* Schwimmerinnen); **she's a strong swimmer** sie ist eine gute Schwimmerin.

swimming *noun* Schwimmen *das*; **to go swimming** schwimmen gehen.

swimming cap *noun* Badekappe *die* (PL *die* Badekappen).

swimming costume *noun* Badeanzug *der* (PL *die* Badeanzüge).

✧ IRREGULAR VERB: See the verb table in the centre of the dictionary

swimming pool noun Schwimmbecken das (PL die Schwimmbecken).

swimming trunks noun Badehose die (PL die Badehosen).

swimsuit noun Badeanzug der (PL die Badeanzüge).

swing noun Schaukel die (PL die Schaukeln).

Swiss noun (person) Schweizer der (PL die Schweizer), Schweizerin die (PL die Schweizerinnen); **the Swiss** die Schweizer. adjective schweizerisch; **she is Swiss** sie ist Schweizerin.

switch noun (for a light, radio, etc.) Schalter der (PL die Schalter). verb (change) wechseln; **to switch places** die Plätze wechseln.

to switch something off etwas ausschalten SEP.

to switch something on etwas anschalten SEP.

Switzerland noun die Schweiz; **from Switzerland** aus der Schweiz; **in Switzerland** in der Schweiz; **to Switzerland** in die Schweiz.

swollen adjective geschwollen.

swop verb SEE swap.

syllabus noun Lehrplan der (PL die Lehrpläne); **to be on the syllabus** auf dem Lehrplan stehen.

symbol noun Symbol das (PL die Symbole).

sympathetic adjective verständnisvoll.

sympathize verb to sympathize with somebody mit jemandem mitfühlen SEP; **I sympathize with you** ich kann mit Ihnen mitfühlen.

sympathy noun Mitleid das.

symptom noun Symptom das (PL die Symptome).

synthesizer noun Synthesizer der (PL die Synthesizers).

synthetic adjective synthetisch.

syringe noun Spritze die (PL die Spritzen).

system noun System das (PL die Systeme).

T t

table noun Tisch der (PL die Tische); **to lay the table** den Tisch decken; **to clear the table** den Tisch abräumen SEP.

tablecloth noun Tischdecke die (PL die Tischdecken).

tablespoon noun Esslöffel △ der (PL die Esslöffel); **a tablespoon of flour** ein Esslöffel Mehl.

tablet noun Tablette die (PL die Tabletten).

table tennis noun Tischtennis das.

tackle verb 1 (in football or hockey) angreifen ◇ SEP; 2 angehen ◇ SEP (PERF sein) (a job or a problem).

tact noun Takt der.

△ NEW SPELLING: See page xii

tactful *adjective* taktvoll; **that wasn't very tactful** das war nicht sehr taktvoll.

tail *noun* **1** Schwanz *der* (PL *die* Schwänze); **2** **'heads or tails?'** – **'tails'** 'Kopf oder Zahl?' – 'Zahl'.

take *verb* **1** nehmen ◇; **he took a sweet** er nahm einen Bonbon; **take my hand** nimm meine Hand; **I took the bus** ich habe den Bus genommen; **do you take sugar?** nimmst du Zucker?; **2** (*with time*) dauern; **it takes two hours** es dauert zwei Stunden; **3** (*react to*) aufnehmen ◇ SEP; **he took the news calmly** er hat die Nachricht gelassen aufgenommen; **4** (*take to a place*) bringen ◇; **I'm taking Jake to my parents** ich bringe Jake zu meinen Eltern; **I took the car to the garage** ich muss das Auto in die Werkstatt bringen; **to take somebody home** jemanden nach Hause bringen; **5** **to take something up(stairs)** etwas heraufbringen ◇ SEP; **could you take the towels up?** könntest du die Handtücher heraufbringen?; **6** **to take something down(stairs)** etwas herunterbringen ◇ SEP; **Cheryl's taken the cups down** Cheryl hat die Tassen heruntergebracht; **7** (*carry with you*) mitnehmen ◇ SEP; **she's taken some of the files home** sie hat einige der Akten mit nach Hause genommen; **I'm taking my Walkman** ich nehme meinen Walkman mit; **I'll take him next time** nächstes Mal nehme ich ihn mit; **8** annehmen ◇ SEP (*a credit card or a*

cheque); **do you take cheques?** nehmen Sie Schecks an?; **9** machen (*an exam, a holiday, or a photo*); **she's taking her driving test tomorrow** sie macht morgen ihre Fahrprüfung; **to take a holiday** Ferien machen; **10** (*need*) brauchen; **it takes a lot of courage** dazu braucht man viel Mut; **it takes me at least two hours to read it** ich brauche mindestens zwei Stunden, um es zu lesen; **11** haben ◇ (*clothes size*); **what size do you take?** welche Größe haben Sie?

● **to take something apart** etwas auseinander nehmen △ ◇ SEP.
● **to take something back** etwas zurückbringen ◇ SEP.
● **to take off 1** (*plane*) abfliegen ◇ SEP (PERF *sein*); **2** ausziehen ◇ SEP (*clothes, shoes*); **take your jacket off** zieh die Jacke aus; **to take your clothes off** sich ausziehen; **3** abziehen ◇ SEP (*money*); **he took five pounds off the price** er hat fünf Pfund vom Preis abgezogen.
● **to take out something** (*from a bag or pocket*) etwas herausnehmen ◇ SEP; **Eric took out his wallet** Eric nahm seine Brieftasche heraus.
● **to take somebody out** jemanden einladen ◇ SEP; **to take somebody out for a meal** jemanden zum Essen einladen ◇ SEP.

takeaway *noun* **1** (*meal*) Essen zum Mitnehmen *das* (PL *die* Essen zum Mitnehmen); **an Indian takeaway** ein indisches Essen zum Mitnehmen; **2** (*where you buy it*) Restaurant mit Straßenverkauf *das* (PL *die* Restaurants mit Straßenverkauf).

◇ IRREGULAR VERB: *See the verb table in the centre of the dictionary*

ake-off noun (of a plane)
Abflug der (PL die Abflüge).

Talent noun Talent das (PL die
Talente); **to have a talent for
painting** ein Talent zum Malen
haben.

Talented adjective talentiert; **he's
really talented** er ist wirklich
talentiert.

Talk noun 1 (a chat) Gespräch das
(PL die Gespräche); **we had a serious
talk about it** wir hatten ein ernstes
Gespräch darüber; 2 Vortrag der (PL
die Vorträge); **she's giving a talk on
Hungary** sie hält einen Vortrag über
Ungarn.
verb 1 reden; **to talk to somebody**
mit jemandem reden; **we talked
about football** wir haben über
Fußball geredet; **what's he talking
about?** wovon redet er?; **we'll talk
about it later** darüber reden wir
später; **they're always talking** sie
reden immer; 2 **to talk to
somebody on the phone** mit
jemandem telefonieren.

all adjective 1 groß; **she's very tall**
sie ist sehr groß; **I'm 1.7 metres tall**
ich bin ein Meter siebzig groß;
2 hoch (building or tree).

ampon noun Tampon der (PL die
Tampons).

an noun Bräune die; **to have a tan**
braun sein; **to get a tan** braun
werden.

ank noun 1 (for petrol or water)
Tank der (PL die Tanks); 2 **fish tank**
das Aquarium; 3 (army) Panzer der
(PL die Panzer).

tanned adjective braun.

tap noun Wasserhahn der (PL die
Wasserhähne); **to turn on the tap**
den Wasserhahn aufdrehen SEP; **to
turn off the tap** den Wasserhahn
zudrehen SEP; **the hot tap** der
Warmwasserhahn.
verb klopfen; **to tap on the door** an
die Tür klopfen.

tap-dancing noun
Stepptanzen das.

tape noun 1 Kassette die (PL die
Kassetten); **my tape of the Stones**
meine Kassette von den Stones; **I've
got it on tape** ich habe es auf Band;
2 **sticky tape** der Klebestreifen.
verb aufnehmen ✧ SEP; **I want to
tape the film** ich will den Film
aufnehmen.

tape measure noun
Metermaß das (PL die Metermaße).

tape recorder noun
Tonbandgerät das (PL die
Tonbandgeräte).

target noun Ziel das (PL die Ziele).

tart noun Kuchen der (PL die
Kuchen); **apple tart** der
Apfelkuchen.

tartan adjective Schotten-; **a tartan
skirt** ein Schottenrock.

task noun Aufgabe die (PL die
Aufgaben).

taste noun 1 Geschmack der (PL die
Geschmäcke); **a taste of onions** ein
Zwiebelgeschmack; **she's got no
taste** sie hat keinen Geschmack;
2 **in bad taste** geschmacklos.
verb 1 schmecken; **the soup tastes**

△ NEW SPELLING: See page xii

horrible die Suppe schmeckt furchtbar; **2 to taste of something** nach etwas ←(DAT) schmecken; **it tastes of garlic** es schmeckt nach Knoblauch; **3** (*try a little*) probieren; **do you want to taste?** möchtest du mal probieren?

tasty *adjective* schmackhaft.

tattoo *noun* Tätowierung die (PL die Tätowierungen); **he's got a tattoo on his arm** er hat eine Tätowierung am Arm.

Taurus *noun* Stier der; **Josephine's Taurus** Josephine ist (ein) Stier.

tax *noun* Steuer die (PL die Steuern) (*on goods, income*).

taxi *noun* Taxi das (PL die Taxis); **to go by taxi** mit dem Taxi fahren; **to take a taxi** ein Taxi nehmen.

taxi driver *noun* Taxifahrer der (PL die Taxifahrer), Taxifahrerin die (PL die Taxifahrerinnen).

taxi rank *noun* Taxistand der (PL die Taxistände).

tea *noun* **1** Tee der (PL die Tees); **a cup of tea** eine Tasse Tee; **to have tea** Tee trinken; **2** (*evening meal*) Abendessen das (PL die Abendessen).

teabag *noun* Teebeutel der (PL die Teebeutel).

teach *verb* **1** beibringen ◇ SEP; **she's teaching me to drive** sie bringt mir das Autofahren bei; **2 to teach yourself something** sich ←(DAT) etwas beibringen ◇ SEP; **I taught myself Italian** ich habe mir Italienisch beigebracht; **3 that'll**

teach you! das wird dir eine Lehre sein!; **4** unterrichten; **her mum teaches maths** ihre Mutter unterrichtet Mathematik.

teacher *noun* Lehrer der (PL die Lehrer), Lehrerin die (PL die Lehrerinnen).

teaching *noun* Unterrichten das.

team *noun* Mannschaft die (PL die Mannschaften); **football team** die Fußballmannschaft.

teapot *noun* Teekanne die (PL die Teekannen).

tear¹ *noun* (*a rip*) Riss △ der (PL die Risse).
verb **1** zerreißen ◇; **she tore up my letter** sie hat meinen Brief zerrissen; **2** reißen ◇ (PERF sein); **the net has torn** das Netz ist gerissen; **be careful, it tears easily** sei vorsichtig, es reißt leicht.

tear² *noun* (*when you cry*) Träne die (PL die Tränen); **to be in tears** in Tränen aufgelöst sein; **to burst into tears** in Tränen ausbrechen.

tease *verb* **1** necken (*a person*); **2** quälen (*an animal*).

teaspoon *noun* Teelöffel der (PL die Teelöffel); **a teaspoon of vinegar** ein Teelöffel Essig.

teatime *noun* (*evening meal*) Abendessenszeit die (PL die Abendessenszeiten); **it's teatime!** es gibt Abendessen!

tea towel *noun* Geschirrtuch das (PL die Geschirrtücher).

technical *adjective* technisch.

◇ IRREGULAR VERB: See the verb table in the centre of the dictionary.

technical college noun
Fachhochschule die (PL die
Fachhochschulen).

technician noun Techniker der (PL
die Techniker), Technikerin der (PL
die Technikerinnen).

technique noun Technik die (PL die
Techniken).

techno noun (music) Techno der.

technology noun
1 Technologie die; 2 information
technology die Informatik.

teddy bear noun Teddybär der (PL
die Teddybären).

teenage adjective 1 Teenage-;
2 they have a teenage son sie
haben einen Sohn im Teenageralter;
3 (films, magazines, etc.) für
Teenager; a teenage magazine eine
Zeitschrift für Teenager.

teenager noun Teenager der (PL die
Teenager); a group of teenagers
eine Gruppe von Teenagern.

teens plural noun the teens die
Teenagerjahre; he's in his teens er
ist ein Teenager.

tee-shirt noun T-Shirt das
(PL die T-Shirts).

telephone noun Telefon das (PL die
Telefone); on the telephone am
Telefon.
verb anrufen ◇ SEP; I'll telephone
the bank ich rufe die Bank an.

telephone box noun
Telefonzelle die (PL die
Telefonzellen).

telephone call noun
Telefongespräch das (PL die
Telefongespräche).

telephone directory noun
Telefonbuch das (PL die
Telefonbücher).

telephone number noun
Telefonnummer die (PL die
Telefonnummern).

televise verb im Fernsehen
übertragen ◇; they're televising
the match sie übertragen das Spiel
im Fernsehen.

television noun 1 Fernsehen das;
I saw it on television ich habe es
im Fernsehen gesehen; 2 to watch
television fernsehen ◇ SEP; I'm
watching television ich sehe fern.

television programme noun
Fernsehsendung die (PL die
Fernsehsendungen).

tell verb 1 sagen; to tell somebody
something jemandem etwas sagen;
if she asks, tell her sag's ihr, wenn
sie fragt; 2 to tell somebody to do
something jemandem sagen, er/sie
soll etwas tun; he told me to do it
myself er hat mir gesagt, ich soll es
selbst machen; she told me not to
wait sie hat mir gesagt, ich soll nicht
warten; 3 (explain) can you tell me
how to do it? kannst du mir sagen,
wie man das macht?; 4 erzählen (a
story); tell me about your holiday
erzähl mir von deinen Ferien; 5 (to
see) sehen ◇; you can tell it's old
man sieht, dass es alt ist; I can't tell
them apart ich kann sie nicht
unterscheiden.

△ NEW SPELLING: See page xii

telly noun 1 (set) Fernseher der (PL die Fernseher); 2 to watch telly fernsehen ⟡ SEP; I saw her on telly ich habe sie im Fernsehen gesehen.

temp noun Aushilfskraft die (PL die Aushilfskräfte).

temper noun to lose your temper wütend werden.

temperature noun
1 Temperatur die (PL die Temperaturen); what is the temperature? wie viel Grad sind es?; 2 to have a temperature Fieber haben.

temporary adjective vorübergehend.

temptation noun Versuchung die (PL die Versuchungen).

tempted adjective versucht; I'm really tempted to come ich bin wirklich versucht zu kommen.

tempting adjective verlockend.

ten number zehn; Harry's ten Harry ist zehn.

tend verb to tend to do something dazu neigen, etwas zu tun.

tender adjective 1 (loving) zärtlich; 2 (painful) empfindlich.

tennis noun Tennis das; to play tennis Tennis spielen.

tennis ball noun Tennisball der (PL die Tennisbälle).

tennis court noun Tennisplatz der (PL die Tennisplätze).

tennis player noun Tennisspieler der (PL die Tennisspieler), Tennisspielerin die (PL die Tennisspielerinnen).

tennis racket noun Tennisschläger der (PL die Tennisschläger).

tenor noun Tenor der (PL die Tenöre).

tenpin bowling noun Bowling das.

tense noun Zeit die; the present tense das Präsens; in the future tense im Futur.
adjective gespannt.

tent noun Zelt das (PL die Zelte).

tenth number zehnter/zehnte/zehntes; on the tenth floor im zehnten Stock; the tenth of April der zehnte April.

term noun (in school) Halbjahr das (PL die Halbjahre); (at university) Semester das (PL die Semester).

terminal noun 1 (at an airport) Terminal der (PL die Terminals); 2 bus terminal die Endstation; 3 (computer terminal) Terminal das (PL die Terminals).

terrace noun 1 (outside a house) Terrasse die (PL die Terrassen); 2 (row of houses) Häuserreihe die (PL die Häuserreihen); 3 the terraces (at a stadium) die Ränge (plural).

terrible adjective furchtbar.

terribly adverb 1 (very) sehr; not terribly clean nicht sehr sauber; 2 (badly) furchtbar; I played terribly ich habe furchtbar gespielt.

terrific adjective 1 irre (informal); a terrific amount eine irre Menge; 2 terrific! super! (informal).

⟡ IRREGULAR VERB: See the verb table in the centre of the dictionary

rrified *adjective* verängstigt; **to be terrified** furchtbare Angst haben.

rrorism *noun* Terrorismus der.

rrorist *noun* Terrorist der (PL die Terroristen), Terroristin die (PL die Terroristinnen).

st *noun* 1 (*in school*) Klassenarbeit die (PL die Klassenarbeiten); **we've got a maths test tomorrow** wir schreiben morgen eine Mathearbeit; 2 (*medical check, trial*) Test der (PL die Tests); **eye test** der Sehtest; **blood test** die Blutprobe; 3 **driving test** die Fahrprüfung; **she's taking her driving test on Friday** sie macht am Freitag ihre Fahrprüfung; **he passed his driving test** er hat seine Fahrprüfung bestanden.
verb (*in school*) prüfen; **can you test me?** kannst du mich abfragen?

st tube *noun* Reagenzglas das (PL die Reagenzgläser).

ext *noun* Text der (PL die Texte).

extbook *noun* Lehrbuch das (PL die Lehrbücher).

hames *noun* **the Thames** die Themse.

han *conjunction* als; **they have more money than we do** sie haben mehr Geld als wir; **more than forty** mehr als vierzig; **more than thirty years** mehr als dreißig Jahre.

hank *verb* 1 **to thank somebody for something** sich bei jemandem für etwas ←(ACC) bedanken; 2 **thank you** danke; **thank you for looking after the children** danke, dass du auf die Kinder aufgepasst hast.

thanks *plural noun* 1 Dank der; **thanks a lot!** vielen Dank!; **many thanks** vielen Dank; 2 **no thanks** nein danke; **thanks for your letter** danke für deinen Brief; 3 **thanks to** dank (+DAT); **it was thanks to him that we made it** dank ihm haben wir es geschafft.

thank you *adverb* danke; **thank you very much for the cheque** herzlichen Dank für den Scheck; **no thank you** nein danke; **a thank-you letter** ein Dankbrief.

that *adjective* 1 dieser/diese/dieses; **that boy** dieser Junge; **that woman** diese Frau; **that house** dieses Haus; 2 **that one** der da/die da/das da; **'which cake would you like?' – 'that one, please'** 'welchen Kuchen möchten Sie?' – 'den da, bitte'; **I like all the dresses but I'm going to buy that one** mir gefallen alle Kleider, aber ich kaufe das da.
adverb so; **it's not that easy** es ist nicht so einfach.
pronoun 1 das; **what's that?** was ist das?; **who's that?** wer ist das?; **where's that?** wo ist das?; **is that Mandy?** ist das Mandy?; 2 das; **did you see that?** hast du das gesehen?; **that's my bedroom** das ist mein Schlafzimmer; 3 (*in relative clauses*) der/die/das (*depending on the gender of the noun 'that' refers to*); **the train that's leaving now** der Zug, der jetzt abfährt; **the flower that I picked** die Blume, die ich gepflückt habe; **the car that's red** das Auto, das rot ist.
conjunction dass △; **I knew that he was lying** ich wußte, dass er log.

△ NEW SPELLING: *See page xii*

the *definite article* **1** der/die/das (*the article changes according to the gender of the noun*); (*before a masculine noun*) **the dog** der Hund; (*before a feminine noun*) **the cat** die Katze; (*before a neuter noun*) **the car** das Auto; **2** (*before all plural nouns*) die; **the windows** die Fenster.

theatre *noun* Theater *das* (PL *die* Theater); **to go to the theatre** ins Theater gehen.

their *adjective* ihr; (*plural*) ihre; **their son** ihr Sohn; **their daughter** ihre Tochter; **their car** ihr Auto; **their presents** ihre Geschenke.

theirs *pronoun* **1** ihrer (*when standing for a masculine noun*); **our garden's smaller than theirs** unser Garten ist kleiner als ihrer; **2** ihre (*when standing for a feminine noun*); **your flat is bigger than theirs** deine Wohnung ist größer als ihre; **3** ihrs (*when standing for a neuter noun*); **our car was cheaper than theirs** unser Auto war billiger als ihrs; **4** ihre (*when standing for a plural noun*); **our children are older than theirs** unsere Kinder sind älter als ihre; **the yellow car's theirs** das gelbe Auto gehört ihnen; **it's theirs** das gehört ihnen.

them *pronoun* **1** (*as a direct object in the accusative*) sie; **I know them** ich kenne sie; **I don't know them** ich kenne sie nicht; **2** (*after prepositions* +ACC) sie; **it's for them** das ist für sie; **3** (*as an indirect object or following a verb that takes the dative*) ihnen; **I told them a story** ich habe

ihnen eine Geschichte erzählt; **4** (*to them*) ihnen; **I gave them my address** ich habe ihnen meine Adresse gegeben; **5** (*after prepositions* +DAT) ihnen; **I'll go wit them** ich gehe mit ihnen mit; **6** (*in comparisons*) **he's older than them** er ist älter als sie.

themselves *pronoun* **1** sich; **they enjoyed themselves** sie haben sich amüsiert; **2** (*for emphasis*) selbst; **the boys can do it themselves** die Jungen können es selbst machen.

then *adverb* **1** (*next*) dann; **I get up and then I make the bed** ich stehe auf und dann mache ich das Bett; **I went to the post office and then th bank** ich bin zur Post und dann au die Bank gegangen; **2** (*at that time*) damals; **we were living in York then** wir haben damals in York gewohnt; **3** (*in that case*) dann; **then why worry?** warum machst du dir dann Sorgen? **4** **since then** seitdem; **5 from then on** von da an.

theory *noun* **1** Theorie *die* (PL *die* Theorien); **2 in theory** theoretisch

there *adverb* **1** (*in a fixed location*) da; **up there** da oben; **down there** da unten; **in there** da drin; **stay there** bleib da; **2 over there** da drüben; **she's over there with Mark** sie ist da drüben mit Mark; **3** (*with movement to a place*) dahin; **put it there** leg es dahin; **we're going there on Tuesday** wir fahren am Dienstag dahin; **4** (*further away*) dort; **I've seen photos of Oxford bu I've never been there** ich habe Fotos von Oxford gesehen, aber ich

✧ **IRREGULAR VERB:** *See the verb table in the centre of the dictionary*

war noch nie dort; **5 there is** (*there exists*) da ist, es ist; **there's a cat in the garden** da ist eine Katze im Garten; **there's enough bread** es ist genug Brot da; **no, there's not enough** nein, es ist nicht genug da; **6 there is** es gibt; **there's only one hospital in this town** in dieser Stadt gibt es nur ein Krankenhaus; **7 there are** da sind, es sind; **there were lots of people in town** es waren viele Leute in der Stadt; **8 there are** (*there exist*) es gibt; **there are lots of museums here** es gibt hier viele Museen; **9** (*when drawing attention*) da; **there they are!** da sind sie!; **there's the bus coming!** da kommt der Bus!

therefore *adverb* deshalb.

thermometer *noun* Thermometer *das* (PL *die* Thermometer).

these *adjective* diese; **these glasses** diese Gläser. *pronoun* die; **these are cheaper** die sind billiger.

they *pronoun* **1** sie; **'where are the knives?' – 'they're in the drawer'** 'wo sind die Messer?' – 'sie sind in der Schublade'; **2** man; **they say** man sagt.

thick *adjective* dick; **a thick layer of butter** eine dicke Schicht Butter.

thief *noun* Dieb *der* (PL *die* Diebe), Diebin *die* (PL *die* Diebinnen).

thin *adjective* dünn.

thing *noun* **1** (*an object*) Ding *das* (PL *die* Dinge); **they have lots of nice things** sie haben viele schöne Dinge;

she told me some strange things sie hat mir ein paar seltsame Dinge erzählt; **that thing next to the hammer** das Ding da neben dem Hammer; **2 things** (*belongings*) Sachen (*plural*); **you can leave your things in my room** du kannst deine Sachen in meinem Zimmer lassen; **3 the best thing to do is …** am besten wäre es …; **4** (*subject, affair*) Sache *die* (PL *die* Sachen); **the thing is, I've lost her address** die Sache ist die, ich habe ihre Adresse verloren; **5 how are things?** wie geht's?

think *verb* **1** (*believe*) glauben; **do you think they'll come?** glaubst du, sie kommen?; **no, I don't think so** nein, ich glaube nicht; **I think so** ich glaube schon; **I think he's already paid** ich glaube, er hat schon gezahlt; **2** denken ◇; **I'm thinking about you** ich denke an dich; **what are you thinking about?** woran denkst du?; **3 what do you think of that?** was halten Sie davon?; **I don't think much of her proposal** ich halte nicht viel von ihrem Vorschlag; **4 what do you think of my new jacket?** wie findest du meine neue Jacke?; **5** (*remember*) **to think to do something** daran denken, etwas zu tun; **he didn't think of locking the door** er hat nicht daran gedacht, die Tür abzuschließen; **6** (*to think carefully*) nachdenken ◇ SEP; **he thought for a moment** er hat einen Moment lang nachgedacht; **think about it!** denk darüber nach!; **7 I've thought it over carefully** ich habe es mir genau überlegt;

△ NEW SPELLING: See page xii

8 (*imagine*) sich ←(DAT) vorstellen SEP; **just think, we'll soon be in Spain!** stell dir nur vor, bald sind wir in Spanien!; **I never thought it would be like this** ich habe mir nie vorgestellt, dass es so sein würde.

third *noun* Drittel *das* (PL *die* Drittel); **a third of the population** ein Drittel der Bevölkerung. *adjective* dritter/dritte/drittes; **on the third floor** im dritten Stock; **on the third of March** am dritten März.

thirdly *adverb* drittens.

Third World *noun* Dritte Welt △ *die*.

thirst *noun* Durst *der*.

thirsty *adjective* durstig; **to be thirsty** Durst haben; **I'm thirsty** ich habe Durst; **we were all thirsty** wir hatten alle Durst.

thirteen *number* dreizehn; **Ahmed's thirteen** Ahmed ist dreizehn.

thirty *number* dreißig.

this *adjective* **1** dieser/diese/dieses; **this boy** dieser Junge; **this flower** diese Blume; **this car** dieses Auto; **at the end of this week** Ende dieser Woche; **2 this morning** heute Morgen; **this evening** heute Abend; **this afternoon** heute Nachmittag; **3 this one** der/die/das; (*with more emphasis*) dieser/diese/dieses; **if you need a pen you can have this one** wenn du einen Kugelschreiber brauchst, kannst du den haben; **I'll take this one** ich nehme diesen. *pronoun* **1** das; **can you hold this?** kannst du das festhalten?; **what's**

this? was ist das?; **2 this is my sister Carla** (*in introductions*) das ist meine Schwester Carla; **3 this is Tracy speaking** (*on the phone*) hie spricht Tracy.

thistle *noun* Distel *die* (PL *die* Disteln).

those *adjective* diese; **those books** diese Bücher. *pronoun* die da; **if you need more knives you can take those** wenn du mehr Messer brauchst, kannst d die da nehmen.

though *conjunction* obwohl; **though it's cold** obwohl es kalt ist. *adverb* aber; **it was a good idea, though** es war aber eine gute Idee.

thought *noun* Gedanke *der* (PL *die* Gedanken).

thousand *number* **1** tausend; **a thousand** eintausend; **three thousand** dreitausend; **2 thousands of** Tausende von; **there were thousands of tourists i Venice** Tausende von Touristen waren in Venedig.

thread *noun* Faden *der* (PL *die* Fäden). *verb* einfädeln (*a needle*).

threat *noun* Drohung *die* (PL *die* Drohungen); **is that a threat?** soll das eine Drohung sein?

threaten *verb* drohen (+DAT); **he threatened her** er hat ihr gedroht; **to threaten to do something** dam drohen, etwas zu tun.

three *number* drei; **Oskar's three** Oskar ist drei.

◇ **IRREGULAR VERB: See the verb table in the centre of the dictionary**

three-quarters noun Dreiviertel das.
adverb **three-quarters full** drei viertel △ voll.

thrilled adjective **to be thrilled** sich wahnsinnig freuen.

thriller noun Thriller der (PL die Thriller).

thrilling adjective spannend.

throat noun Hals der (PL die Hälse); **to have a sore throat** Halsschmerzen haben.

through preposition 1 (across, via) durch (+ACC); **through the forest** durch den Wald; **the train goes through Leeds** der Zug fährt durch Leeds; **through the window** durch das Fenster; 2 **to let somebody through** jemanden durchlassen ◇ SEP; **the police let us through** die Polizei ließ uns durch; 3 **I know them through my cousin** ich kenne sie über meinen Vetter.

throw verb 1 werfen ◇; **I threw the letter in the bin** ich habe den Brief in den Mülleimer geworfen; 2 **to throw something to somebody** jemandem etwas zuwerfen ◇ SEP; **throw me the ball** wirf mir den Ball zu; **to throw something at somebody** etwas nach jemanden werfen.
to throw something away etwas wegwerfen ◇ SEP; **I'm throwing away the old newspapers** ich werfe die alten Zeitungen weg.
● **to throw somebody out** jemanden rauswerfen ◇ SEP.

● **to throw something out** etwas wegwerfen ◇ SEP (rubbish).

thumb noun Daumen der (PL die Daumen).

thunder noun Donner der; **peal of thunder** der Donnerschlag.

thunderstorm noun Gewitter das (PL die Gewitter).

Thursday noun 1 Donnerstag der (PL die Donnerstage); **on Thursday** (am) Donnerstag; **I'm leaving on Thursday** ich fahre am Donnerstag ab; **see you on Thursday** bis Donnerstag; **every Thursday** jeden Donnerstag; **last Thursday** vorigen Donnerstag; **next Thursday** nächsten Donnerstag; 2 **on Thursdays** donnerstags; **the museum is closed on Thursdays** das Museum ist donnerstags geschlossen.

thyme noun Thymian der.

tick verb 1 (clock, watch) ticken; 2 (on paper) abhaken SEP.

ticket noun 1 (for an exhibition, theatre, or cinema) Karte die (PL die Karten); **two tickets for the concert** zwei Karten für das Konzert; 2 (for the underground, a bus, or a train) Fahrkarte die (PL die Fahrkarten); **a plane ticket** ein Flugschein, ein Ticket; 3 (for left luggage, parking) Schein der (PL die Scheine); 4 (for a lottery or raffle) Los das (PL die Lose); 5 **parking ticket** der Strafzettel.

ticket office noun (at a station) Fahrkartenschalter der (PL die Fahrkartenschalter).

△ NEW SPELLING: See page xii

tickle verb kitzeln.

tidy adjective ordentlich.
verb aufräumen SEP; **I'll tidy (up) the kitchen** ich räume die Küche auf.

tie noun 1 (necktie) Krawatte die (PL die Krawatten); **2** (in a match) Unentschieden das.
verb 1 binden◇; **to tie your shoelaces** sich ←(DAT) die Schnürsenkel binden; **2 to tie a knot in something** einen Knoten in etwas ←(ACC) machen; **3** (in a match) **we tied two all** wir haben zwei zu zwei gespielt.

tiger noun Tiger der (PL die Tiger).

tight adjective (close-fitting) eng; **the skirt's a bit tight** der Rock ist etwas eng; **these shoes are too tight** diese Schuhe sind zu eng; **she was wearing tight jeans** sie hatte enge Jeans an.

tightly adverb fest.

tights plural noun Strumpfhose die (PL die Strumpfhosen); **a pair of purple tights** eine lila Strumpfhose.

tile noun 1 (on a floor) Fliese die (PL die Fliesen); **2** (on a wall) Kachel die (PL die Kacheln); **3** (on a roof) Ziegel der (PL die Ziegel).

till[1] preposition, conjunction **1** bis; **they're staying till Sunday** sie bleiben bis Sonntag; **till then** bis dann; **till now** bis jetzt; **2** (when 'till' is followed by a noun it is usually translated as 'bis zu' +DAT) **till the evening** bis zum Abend; **3 not till** erst; **she won't be back till ten** sie kommt erst um zehn zurück; **we**

won't know till Monday wir werden erst am Montag Bescheid wissen.

till[2] noun Kasse die (PL die Kassen); **please pay at the till** bitte zahlen Sie an der Kasse.

time noun 1 (on the clock) Zeit die; **it's time for breakfast** es ist Zeit zum Frühstücken; **2 what time is it?** wie viel △ Uhr ist es?; **at what time does it start?** um wie viel Uhr fängt es an?; **ten o'clock German time** zehn Uhr, deutsche Zeit; **3 on time** pünktlich; **4** (an amount of time) Zeit die; **we've got lots of time** wir haben viel Zeit; **I haven't got time now** ich habe jetzt keine Zeit; **there's no time left to do it** dafür bleibt keine Zeit mehr; **from time to time** von Zeit zu Zeit; **for a long time** lange; **5** (moment) Moment der (PL die Momente); **this isn't a good time to discuss it** das ist kein guter Moment, um sich darüber zu unterhalten; **at the right time** im richtigen Moment; **for the time being** im Moment; **any time now** jeden Moment; **6 at times** manchmal; **7** (in a series) Mal das (PL die Male); **eight times** achtmal; **for the first time** zum ersten Mal; **the first time I saw you** das erste Mal, als ich dich sah; **three times a year** dreimal jährlich; **8 three times two is six** drei mal zwei ist sechs; **9 to have a good time** sich amüsieren; **we had a really good time** wir haben uns richtig gut amüsiert; **have a good time!** viel Vergnügen!

timetable noun 1 (in school) Stundenplan der (PL die

Stundenpläne); **2** (*for trains or buses*) Fahrplan der (PL die Fahrpläne); **bus timetable** der Busfahrplan.

tin *noun* Dose die (PL die Dosen); **a tin of tomatoes** eine Dose Tomaten.

tinned *adjective* in Dosen; **tinned peas** Erbsen in Dosen.

tin opener *noun* Dosenöffner der (PL die Dosenöffner).

tiny *adjective* winzig.

tip *noun* **1** (*end*) Spitze die (PL die Spitzen); **2** (*money*) Trinkgeld das; **3** (*useful hint*) Tipp △ der (PL die Tipps) (*informal*).
verb (*give money*) ein Trinkgeld geben ◇ (+DAT); **we tipped the waiter** wir haben dem Kellner ein Trinkgeld gegeben.

tired *adjective* **1** müde; **I'm tired** ich bin müde; **you look tired** du siehst müde aus; **2** to be tired of something** etwas satt haben; **I'm tired of London** ich habe London satt; **I'm tired of watching TV every evening** ich habe es satt, jeden Abend fernzusehen.

tiring *adjective* ermüdend.

tissue *noun* (*a paper hanky*) Papiertaschentuch das (PL die Papiertaschentücher).

tissue paper *noun* Seidenpapier das.

title *noun* Titel der (PL die Titel).

to *preposition* **1** (*to a country or town*) nach; **to go to London** nach London fahren; **the motorway to Italy** die Autobahn nach Italien; **they're going to Switzerland** sie fahren in die Schweiz; **2** (*to the cinema, theatre, school, office*) in (+ACC); **I'm going to school** ich gehe in die Schule; **she's gone to the office** sie ist ins Büro gegangen; **we want to go to town** wir wollen in die Stadt gehen; **3** (*to a wedding, party, university, the toilet*) auf (+ACC); **she's gone to the toilet** sie ist auf die Toilette gegangen; **4** (*addressed or attached to*) an (+ACC); **a letter to my parents** ein Brief an meine Eltern; **5** **give the book to her** gib ihr das Buch; **he said to me that ...** er hat mir gesagt, dass ...; **6** (*to somebody's house, a particular place, or person*) zu (+DAT); **I went round to Paul's house** ich bin zu Paul nach Hause gegangen; **we're going to the Browns' for supper** wir gehen zu Browns zum Abendessen; **I'm going to the dentist tomorrow** morgen gehe ich zum Zahnarzt; **7** (*talking about the time*) **it's ten to nine** es ist zehn vor neun; **from eight to ten** von acht bis zehn; **from Monday to Friday** von Montag bis Freitag; **8** (*in order to*) um ... zu (+ infinitive); **he gave me some money to buy a sandwich** er hat mir Geld gegeben, um ein Sandwich zu kaufen; **9** (*in verbal phrases with the infinitive*) zu; **I have nothing to do** ich habe nichts zu tun; **have you got something to eat?** hast du etwas zu essen?

toast *noun* **1** Toast der (PL die Toasts); **two slices of toast** zwei Scheiben Toast; **2** (*to your health*)

△ NEW SPELLING: See page xii

Toast der (PL die Toasts); **to drink a toast to somebody** auf jemanden trinken.

toaster noun Toaster der (PL die Toaster).

tobacco noun Tabak der.

tobacconist's noun Tabakladen der (PL die Tabakläden).

today adverb heute; **today's her birthday** sie hat heute Geburtstag.

toe noun Zeh der (PL die Zehen).

toffee noun Karamell △ der.

together adverb 1 zusammen; **we did it together** wir haben es zusammen gemacht; **2** (at the same time) gleichzeitig; **they all left together** sie sind alle gleichzeitig weggegangen.

toilet noun Toilette die (PL die Toiletten); **she's gone to the toilet** sie ist auf die Toilette gegangen.

toilet paper noun Toilettenpapier das.

toilet roll noun Rolle Toilettenpapier die (PL die Rollen Toilettenpapier).

token noun 1 (for a machine or game) Marke die (PL die Marken); **2** (voucher) Gutschein der (PL die Gutscheine); **gift token** der Geschenkgutschein.

toll noun Gebühr die (PL die Gebühren).

tomato noun Tomate die (PL die Tomaten); **tomato salad** der Tomatensalat; **tomato sauce** die Tomatensoße.

tomorrow adverb 1 morgen; **I'll do it tomorrow** ich mache es morgen; **tomorrow afternoon** morgen Nachmittag; **tomorrow morning** morgen früh; **tomorrow night** morgen Abend; **2 the day after tomorrow** übermorgen.

tone noun (on an answerphone, of a voice, or letter) Ton der (PL die Töne).

tongue noun Zunge die (PL die Zungen); **to stick your tongue out at somebody** jemandem die Zunge herausstrecken; ★ **it's on the tip of my tongue** es liegt mir auf der Zunge.

tonic noun Tonic das (PL die Tonics); **a gin and tonic** ein Gin Tonic.

tonight adverb 1 (this evening) heute Abend △; **I'm going out with my friends tonight** ich gehe heute Abend mit meinen Freunden weg; **2** (after bedtime) heute Nacht △.

tonsillitis noun Mandelentzündung die; **Ahlem's got tonsillitis** Ahlem hat eine Mandelentzündung.

too adverb 1 zu; **it's too expensive** es ist zu teuer; **too often** zu oft; **2 too much** zu viel; **I've spent too much** ich habe zu viel ausgegeben; **too many** zu viele; **3** (as well) auch; **Karen's coming too** Karen kommt auch; **me too!** ich auch!

tool noun Werkzeug das (PL die Werkzeuge).

tool kit noun Werkzeug das.

tooth noun Zahn der (PL die Zähne).

◇ **IRREGULAR VERB: See the verb table in the centre of the dictionary**

to brush your teeth sich ←(DAT) die Zähne putzen.

toothache noun Zahnschmerzen (plural).

toothbrush noun Zahnbürste die (PL die Zahnbürsten).

toothpaste noun Zahnpasta die (PL die Zahnpasten).

top noun 1 (highest part) Spitze die (PL die Spitzen; (of a tree); 2 **at the top of** oben auf (+DAT); **at the top of the ladder** oben auf der Leiter; **it's on top of the chest of drawers** es liegt oben auf der Kommode; 3 **at the top** oben; **there are four rooms at the top** oben sind vier Zimmer; **from top to bottom** von oben bis unten; 4 (of a container, jar, or box) Deckel der (PL die Deckel); 5 (of a mountain) Gipfel der (PL die Gipfel); 6 (a lid) Kappe die (PL die Kappen; (of a pen); Verschluss △ der (PL die Verschlüsse) (of a bottle); 7 (of a garment) Oberteil das (PL die Oberteile); 8 (in sport) **the top of the table** die Tabellenspitze; ★ **and on top of all that** obendrein; ★ **it was a bit over the top** es war leicht übertrieben.
adjective oberster/oberste/oberstes (step or floor); **on the top floor** im obersten Stockwerk.

topic noun Thema das (PL die Themen).

torch noun Taschenlampe die (PL die Taschenlampen).

torn adjective zerrissen.

tortoise noun Schildkröte die (PL die Schildkröten).

torture noun 1 Folter die (PL die Foltern); 2 **the exam was torture** die Prüfung war die Hölle (informal).
verb quälen.

Tory noun Konservative der/die (PL die Konservativen).

total noun 1 (number) Gesamtzahl die (PL die Gesamtzahlen); 2 (result of addition) Summe die (PL die Summen).
adjective gesamt.

totally adverb völlig.

touch noun 1 (contact) **to get in touch with somebody** sich mit jemandem in Verbindung setzen; **to stay in touch with somebody** mit jemandem in Verbindung bleiben; 2 **we've lost touch** wir haben keinen Kontakt mehr miteinander; **I've lost touch with Peter** ich habe keinen Kontakt mehr mit Peter; 3 (a little bit) **a touch of salt** eine Spur Salz; **it was a touch embarrassing** es war ein bisschen peinlich.
verb 1 berühren; 2 (get hold of) anfassen SEP; **don't touch that** fass das nicht an.

touched adjective gerührt.

touching adjective rührend.

tough adjective 1 hart; **she's had a tough time** sie hat eine harte Zeit hinter sich; **a tough guy** ein harter Kerl; 2 zäh; **the meat's tough** das Fleisch ist zäh; 3 fest (material, shoes, etc).; 4 tough luck! Pech!; **tough, you're too late** so'n Pech, du bist zu spät dran.

△ NEW SPELLING: See page xii

tour noun 1 Besichtigung die (PL die Besichtigungen); **a tour of the city** eine Stadtbesichtigung; **we did a tour of the castle** wir haben das Schloss besichtigt; 2 **guided tour** die Führung; 3 **package tour** die Pauschalreise; 4 (by a band or theatre group) Tournee die (PL die Tournees); **to go on tour** auf Tournee gehen.
verb (performer) auf Tournee sein ✧ (PERF sein); **they're touring America** sie sind auf Tournee in Amerika.

tour guide noun Reiseleiter der (PL die Reiseleiter), Reiseleiterin die (PL die Reiseleiterinnen).

tourism noun Tourismus der.

tourist noun Tourist der (PL die Touristen), Touristin die (PL die Touristinnen).

tourist information office noun Fremdenverkehrsbüro das (PL die Fremdenverkehrsbüros).

tournament noun Turnier das (PL die Turniere); **tennis tournament** das Tennisturnier.

tow verb **to be towed away** abgeschleppt werden ✧ (PERF sein).

towards preposition zu (+DAT); **she went off towards the lake** sie ist zum See gegangen; **to come towards somebody** auf jemanden zukommen ✧ SEP (PERF sein).

towel noun Handtuch das (PL die Handtücher).

tower noun Turm der (PL die Türme).

tower block noun Hochhaus das (PL die Hochhäuser).

town noun Stadt die (PL die Städte); **to go into town** in die Stadt gehen.

town centre noun Stadtmitte die (PL die Stadtmitten).

town hall noun Rathaus das (PL die Rathäuser).

toy noun Spielzeug das.

toyshop noun Spielzeuggeschäft das (PL die Spielzeuggeschäfte).

trace noun Spur die (PL die Spuren); **there was no trace of the thieves** es fehlte jede Spur von den Dieben. verb 1 (find) finden ✧; 2 (follow) verfolgen; 3 (copy) durchpausen SEP.

tracing paper noun Pauspapier das.

track noun 1 (for sport) Bahn die (PL die Bahnen); **cycling track** die Radrennbahn; **racing track** (for cars) die Rennstrecke; 2 (a path) Weg der (PL die Wege); 3 (song) Stück das (PL die Stücke); **this is my favourite track** das ist mein Lieblingsstück.

track suit noun Trainingsanzug der (PL die Trainingsanzüge).

tractor noun Traktor der (PL die Traktoren).

trade noun 1 (a profession) Gewerbe das; 2 (skill, craft) Handwerk das; **to learn a trade** ein Handwerk erlernen.

trade union noun
Gewerkschaft die (PL die
Gewerkschaften).

tradition noun Tradition die (PL die
Traditionen).

traditional adjective traditionell.

traffic noun Verkehr der.

traffic jam noun Stau der (PL die
Staus).

traffic lights plural noun
Ampel die (PL die Ampeln).

traffic warden noun
Hilfspolizist der (PL die
Hilfspolizisten), Politesse die (PL die
Politessen).

tragedy noun Tragödie die (PL die
Tragödien).

tragic adjective tragisch.

trailer noun Anhänger der (PL die
Anhänger).

train noun Zug der (PL die Züge);
he's coming by train er kommt mit
dem Zug; I met her on the train ich
habe sie im Zug getroffen; the train
for York der Zug nach York.
verb 1 (for a career) ausbilden SEP;
2 she's training to be a nurse sie
lässt sich als Krankenschwester
ausbilden; 3 (in sport) trainieren;
the team trains on Wednesdays die
Mannschaft trainiert mittwochs.

trainer noun 1 (of an athlete or
horse) Trainer der (PL die Trainer),
Trainerin die (PL die Trainerinnen);
2 trainers Trainingsschuhe
(plural).

training noun 1 (for a career)
Ausbildung die (PL die
Ausbildungen); 2 (for sport)
Training das.

train ticket noun Fahrkarte die (PL
die Fahrkarten).

train timetable noun
Bahnfahrplan der (PL die
Bahnfahrpläne).

tram noun Straßenbahn die (PL die
Straßenbahnen).

tramp noun Landstreicher der (PL
die Landstreicher), Landstreicherin
die (PL die Landstreicherinnen).

transfer noun Abziehbild das (PL
die Abziehbilder).

transform verb verwandeln.

transistor noun Transistor der (PL
die Transistoren).

translate verb übersetzen; to
translate something into German
etwas ins Deutsche übersetzen.

translation noun Übersetzung die
(PL die Übersetzungen).

translator noun Übersetzer der (PL
die Übersetzer), Übersetzerin die (PL
die Übersetzerinnen).

transparent adjective
durchsichtig.

transport noun Transport der (PL
die Transporte); the transport of
goods der Warentransport; public
transport öffentliche
Verkehrsmittel (plural).

trap noun Falle die (PL die Fallen).

travel noun Reisen das; foreign
travel Auslandsreisen (plural).
verb reisen (PERF sein).

△ NEW SPELLING: See page xii

travel agency noun
Reisebüro das (PL die Reisebüros).

travel agent's noun
Reisebüro das (PL die Reisebüros).

traveller noun 1 Reisende der/die
(PL die Reisenden); 2 (gypsy)
Zigeuner der (PL die Zigeuner),
Zigeunerin die (PL die
Zigeunerinnen).

traveller's cheque noun
Reisescheck der (PL die
Reiseschecks).

tray noun Tablett das (PL die
Tabletts).

tread verb to tread on something
auf etwas ←(ACC) treten ✧ (PERF sein);
she trod on my foot sie ist mir auf
den Fuß getreten.

treasure noun Schatz der (PL die
Schätze).

treat noun 1 I took them to the
circus as a treat ich habe ihnen
eine besondere Freude gemacht und
sie in den Zirkus eingeladen;
2 (food) Leckerbissen der (PL die
Leckerbissen).
verb 1 behandeln; he treats his dog
well er behandelt seinen Hund gut;
the doctor who treated you der
Arzt, der dich behandelt hat; 2 to
treat somebody to something
jemandem etwas spendieren; I'll
treat you to an ice cream ich
spendiere euch ein Eis.

treatment noun Behandlung die
(PL die Behandlungen).

tree noun Baum der (PL die Bäume).

tremble verb zittern.

trend noun 1 (a fashion) Trend der
(PL die Trends); 2 (a tendency)
Tendenz die (PL die Tendenzen).

trendy adjective modern.

trial noun (in court) Prozess △ der
(PL die Prozesse).

triangle noun Dreieck das (PL die
Dreiecke).

trick noun 1 (a joke) Streich der (PL
die Streiche); to play a trick on
somebody jemandem einen Streich
spielen; 2 (a knack or by a conjuror)
Trick der (PL die Tricks); there must
be a trick to it da muss ein Trick
dabei sein.
verb hereinlegen SEP; he tricked
me! er hat mich hereingelegt!

tricky adjective verzwickt; it's a
tricky situation das ist eine
verzwickte Situation.

trim verb schneiden ✧ (hair).

trip noun 1 Reise die (PL die Reisen);
a trip to Florida eine Reise nach
Florida; he's going on a business
trip er macht eine Geschäftsreise;
2 (a day out) Ausflug der (PL die
Ausflüge); a day trip to France ein
Tagesausflug nach Frankreich.
verb (to stumble) stolpern (PERF
sein); Nicky tripped over a stone
Nicky ist über einen Stein gestolpert.

trolley noun 1 (for shopping)
Einkaufswagen der (PL die
Einkaufswagen); 2 (for luggage)
Kofferkuli der (PL die Kofferkulis).

trombone noun Posaune die (PL die
Posaunen).

✧ **IRREGULAR VERB: See the verb table in the centre of the dictionary**

troops plural noun Truppen (plural).

trophy noun Trophäe die (PL die Trophäen); (in competitions) Pokal der (PL die Pokale).

trot verb traben (PERF sein).

trouble noun 1 (general difficulties) Ärger der; **to make trouble** Ärger machen; **to get into trouble** Ärger bekommen; **we had trouble with the travel agency** wir hatten Ärger mit dem Reisebüro; 2 (problem) Problem das (PL die Probleme); **the trouble is, I've lost his phone number** das Problem ist, dass ich seine Telefonnummer verloren habe; **Steph's in trouble** Steph hat Probleme; **what's the trouble?** was ist los?; **it's no trouble!** das ist kein Problem; 3 (difficulty, effort) Mühe die; **to have trouble doing something** Mühe haben, etwas zu tun; **I had trouble finding a seat** ich hatte Mühe, einen Platz zu finden; **it's not worth the trouble** das ist nicht der Mühe wert.

trousers plural noun Hose die (PL die Hosen); **my old trousers** meine alte Hose; **a new pair of trousers** eine neue Hose.

trout noun Forelle die (PL die Forellen).

truck noun Lastwagen der (PL die Lastwagen).

true adjective 1 wahr; **a true story** eine wahre Geschichte; 2 **is that true?** stimmt das?; **it's true she's absent-minded** das stimmt, sie ist sehr vergesslich.

trump noun Trumpf der (PL die Trümpfe); **hearts are trumps** Herz ist Trumpf.

trumpet noun Trompete die (PL die Trompeten).

trunk noun 1 (of a tree) Stamm der (PL die Stämme); 2 (of an elephant) Rüssel der (PL die Rüssel).

trust noun Vertrauen das.
verb 1 (believe) **to trust somebody** jemandem vertrauen; 2 (rely on) **you can trust him** man kann sich auf ihn verlassen.

truth noun Wahrheit die.

try noun Versuch der (PL die Versuche); **it's my first try** es ist mein erster Versuch; **to have a try** es versuchen; **give it a try!** versuch's doch mal!
verb 1 versuchen; **to try to do something** versuchen, etwas zu tun; **I'm trying to open the door** ich versuche, die Tür aufzumachen; 2 (taste) probieren.
• **to try something on** etwas anprobieren SEP (a garment).

T-shirt noun T-Shirt das (PL die T-Shirts).

tube noun 1 Tube die (PL die Tuben); 2 (the Underground) **the Tube** die U-Bahn.

Tuesday noun 1 Dienstag der (PL die Dienstage); **on Tuesday** (am) Dienstag; **I'm going to the cinema on Tuesday** ich gehe Dienstag ins Kino; **see you on Tuesday!** bis Dienstag!; **every Tuesday** jeden Dienstag; **last Tuesday** vorigen Dienstag; **next Tuesday** nächsten

△ NEW SPELLING: See page xii

Dienstag; **2 on Tuesdays** dienstags; **the museum is closed on Tuesdays** das Museum ist dienstags geschlossen.

tuition noun **1** Unterricht der; **piano tuition** der Klavierunterricht; **2 extra tuition** Nachhilfestunden (plural).

tulip noun Tulpe die (PL die Tulpen).

tumble-drier noun Wäschetrockner der (PL die Wäschetrockner).

tuna noun Thunfisch der.

tune noun Melodie die (PL die Melodien).

tunnel noun Tunnel der (PL die Tunnel); **the Channel Tunnel** der Eurotunnel.

turkey noun Pute die (PL die Puten).

Turkey noun die Türkei; **from Turkey** aus der Türkei; **in Turkey** in der Türkei; **to Turkey** in die Türkei.

Turkish noun (language) Türkisch das.
adjective türkisch; **he is Turkish** er ist Türke; **she is Turkish** sie ist Türkin.

turn noun **1** (in a game) **it's your turn** du bist an der Reihe; **whose turn is it?** wer ist an der Reihe?; **it's Jane's turn** Jane ist an der Reihe; **2 to take turns** sich abwechseln; **to take it in turns to do something** abwechselnd etwas tun; **3** (in a road) Kurve die (PL die Kurven); **to take a right/left turn** nach rechts/links abbiegen.
verb **1** drehen; **turn the key to the**

right dreh den Schlüssel nach rechts; **turn your chair round** dreh deinen Stuhl herum; **2** (person, car) abbiegen ◇ SEP (PERF sein); **turn left at the next set of lights** biegen Sie an der nächsten Ampel links ab; **3** (become) werden ◇ (PERF sein); **she turned red** sie ist rot geworden.
● **to turn back** umkehren SEP (PERF sein).
● **to turn off 1** (from a road) abbiegen ◇ SEP (PERF sein); **2** (switch off) ausmachen SEP (a light, an oven, a TV, or radio); zudrehen SEP (a tap) abstellen SEP (gas, electricity, or water); ausschalten SEP (an engine).
● **to turn on** anmachen SEP (a TV, radio or light); aufdrehen SEP (a tap); anschalten SEP (an oven); anlassen ◇ SEP (an engine).
● **to turn out 1 to turn out well** gut ausgehen ◇ SEP (PERF sein); **the discussions turned out badly** die Gespräche sind schlecht ausgegangen; **it all turned out all right in the end** am Ende ging alles gut aus; **2 it turned out that I was right** es stellte sich heraus, dass ich Recht hatte.
● **to turn up 1** (to arrive) aufkreuzen SEP (PERF sein); **they turned up an hour later** sie sind eine Stunde später aufgekreuzt; **2** (to make louder) lauter machen.

turquoise adjective türkis.

turtle noun Schildkröte die (PL die Schildkröten).

TV noun Fernsehen das; **I saw her on TV** ich habe sie im Fernsehen gesehen.

◇ IRREGULAR VERB: See the verb table in the centre of the dictionary

tweezers noun Pinzette die (PL die Pinzetten).

twelfth number zwölfter/zwölfte/ zwölftes; **on the twelfth floor** im zwölften Stock; **the twelfth of May** der zwölfte Mai.

twelve number 1 zwölf; **Tara's twelve** Tara ist zwölf; 2 **at twelve o'clock** um zwölf Uhr.

twenty number zwanzig; **Marie's twenty** Marie ist zwanzig; **twenty- one** einundzwanzig.

twice adverb 1 zweimal; **I've asked him twice** ich habe ihn zweimal gefragt; **twice a day** zweimal täglich; 2 **twice as much** doppelt so viel.

twin noun Zwilling der (PL die Zwillinge); **Helen and Tim are twins** Helen und Tim sind Zwillinge; **her twin sister** ihre Zwillingsschwester. verb **Richmond is twinned with Konstanz** Richmond und Konstanz sind Partnerstädte.

twist verb 1 (bend out of shape) verbiegen ◇; 2 verdrehen (words, meaning); 3 **to twist your ankle** sich ←(DAT) den Knöchel verrenken.

two number zwei; **Ben's two** Ben ist zwei; **two by two** zu zweit.

type noun Art die; **what type of computer is it?** welche Art Computer ist es? verb (on a typewriter) Schreibmaschine schreiben ◇, tippen (informal); **I'm learning to type** ich lerne Schreibmaschine schreiben; **I'm just typing some letters** ich tippe gerade ein paar Briefe.

typewriter noun Schreibmaschine die (PL die Schreibmaschinen).

typical adjective typisch.

tyre noun Reifen der (PL die Reifen).

U u

ugly adjective hässlich △.

UK noun (United Kingdom) Vereinigte Königreich das.

Ulster noun Ulster; **from Ulster** aus Ulster.

umbrella noun Regenschirm der (PL die Regenschirme).

umpire noun Schiedsrichter der (PL die Schiedsrichter), Schiedsrichterin die (PL die Schiedsrichterinnen).

UN noun (United Nations) UN (plural).

unable adjective **to be unable to do something** etwas nicht tun können; **he's unable to come** er kann nicht kommen.

unavoidable adjective unvermeidlich.

unbearable adjective unerträglich.

unbelievable adjective unglaublich.

uncertain adjective 1 (not sure) to be uncertain whether ... sich ←(DAT) nicht sicher sein, ob ...; 2 (unpredictable) ungewiss △ (future or result).

uncle noun Onkel der (PL die Onkel).

uncomfortable adjective 1 unbequem (shoes, chair, or journey); 2 unangenehm (situation, heat).

unconscious adjective (out cold) bewusstlos △.

under preposition 1 (underneath) unter (+DAT, or +ACC when there is movement towards a place); the dog's under the bed der Hund ist unter dem Bett; the ball rolled under the bed der Ball ist unter das Bett gerollt; 2 under there da drunter; perhaps it's under there vielleicht ist es da drunter; 3 (less than) unter (+DAT); under £20 unter zwanzig Pfund; children under five Kinder unter fünf.

under-age adjective to be under-age minderjährig sein.

undercooked adjective nicht gar.

underestimate verb unterschätzen.

underground noun (railway) U-Bahn die (PL die U-Bahnen); I saw her on the underground ich habe sie in der U-Bahn gesehen; shall we go by underground? fahren wir mit der U-Bahn?
adjective unterirdisch (cave);

underground car park die Tiefgarage.

underline verb unterstreichen ✧.

underneath preposition unter (+DAT, or +ACC when there is movement towards a place); it's underneath the newspaper es ist unter der Zeitung I put it underneath the newspaper ich habe es unter die Zeitung gelegt.
adverb darunter; check underneath sieh darunter nach.

underpants plural noun Unterhose die (PL die Unterhosen); my underpants meine Unterhose.

underpass noun Unterführung die (PL die Unterführungen).

understand verb verstehen ✧; do you understand? verstehst du?; I couldn't understand what he was saying ich konnte ihn nicht verstehen; I can't understand why she doesn't want to see him ich kann nicht verstehen, warum sie ihn nicht sehen will.

understandable adjective that's understandable das ist verständlich.

understanding noun Verständnis das. adjective verständnisvoll.

underwear noun Unterwäsche die.

undo verb aufmachen SEP.

undone adjective to come undone aufgehen ✧ SEP (PERF sein).

undress verb to get undressed sich ausziehen ✧ SEP.

✧ IRREGULAR VERB: See the verb table in the centre of the dictionary

unemployed *noun* the
unemployed die Arbeitslosen
(*plural*).
adjective arbeitslos.

unemployment *noun*
Arbeitslosigkeit *die*.

unexpected *adjective* unerwartet.

unexpectedly *adverb* (*to happen,
arrive*) überraschend.

unfair *adjective* unfair; **it's unfair on
young people** es ist jungen Leuten
gegenüber unfair.

unfashionable *adjective*
unmodern.

unfasten *verb* aufmachen SEP.

unfit *adjective* nicht fit; **I'm terribly
unfit** ich bin nicht sehr fit.

unfortunate *adjective* unglücklich.

unfortunately *adverb* leider.

unfriendly *adjective* unfreundlich.

ungrateful *adjective* undankbar.

unhappy *adjective* 1 unglücklich;
2 (*not satisfied*) unzufrieden; **to be
unhappy about something** mit
etwas unzufrieden sein.

unhealthy *adjective* ungesund.

uniform *noun* Uniform *die* (PL *die*
Uniformen).

union *noun* (*trade union*)
Gewerkschaft *die* (PL *die*
Gewerkschaften).

Union Jack *noun* the Union Jack
die britische Nationalflagge.

unique *adjective* einzigartig.

unit *noun* 1 (*for measuring, for
example*) Einheit *die* (PL *die*
Einheiten); 2 (*in a kitchen*)
Einbauschrank der (PL *die*
Einbauschränke); 3 (*a department*)
Abteilung *die* (PL *die* Abteilungen);
the research unit die
Forschungsabteilung.

United Kingdom *noun* Vereinigte
Königreich *das*.

United Nations *noun* Vereinte
Nationen (*plural*).

United States (of America)
plural noun Vereinigte Staaten (von
Amerika) (*plural*).

universe *noun* Universum *das*,
Weltall *das*.

university *noun* Universität *die* (PL
die Universitäten); **to go to
university** auf die Universität gehen.

unkind *adjective* unfreundlich.

unknown *adjective* unbekannt.

unleaded petrol *noun* bleifreie
Benzin *das*.

unless *conjunction* es sei denn;
unless he does it es sei denn, er
macht es; **unless you write** es sei
denn, du schreibst.

unlike *adjective* 1 im Gegensatz zu
(+DAT); **unlike me, she hates dogs**
im Gegensatz zu mir hasst sie
Hunde; 2 **it's unlike her to be late**
es sieht ihr gar nicht ähnlich, zu spät
zu kommen.

unlikely *adjective*
unwahrscheinlich.

unload *verb* 1 ausladen ✧ SEP
(*luggage, car*); 2 entladen ✧ (*lorry*).

△ NEW SPELLING: *See page xii*

unlock *verb* aufschließen ◇ SEP.

unlucky *adjective* 1 **to be unlucky** (*person*) Pech haben; **I was unlucky, the shop was shut** ich hatte Pech, das Geschäft war zu; 2 (*bringing bad luck*) Unglücks-; **thirteen is an unlucky number** dreizehn ist eine Unglückszahl; **it's unlucky** es bringt Unglück.

unnecessary *adjective* unnötig.

unpack *verb* auspacken SEP; **I'm just unpacking my rucksack** ich packe gerade meinen Rucksack aus; **I'll just unpack and then come down** ich packe nur noch aus und dann komme ich runter.

unpaid *adjective* unbezahlt.

unpleasant *adjective* unangenehm.

unplug *verb* **to unplug the lamp** den Stecker von der Lampe herausziehen ◇ SEP.

unpopular *adjective* unbeliebt.

unreasonable *adjective* uneinsichtig; **he's being really unreasonable** er ist so uneinsichtig.

unreliable *adjective* unzuverlässig; **he's unreliable** er ist unzuverlässig.

unsafe *adjective* gefährlich (*wiring, for example*).

unsatisfactory *adjective* unbefriedigend.

unscrew *verb* aufschrauben SEP.

unshaven *adjective* unrasiert.

unsuccessful *adjective* 1 erfolglos; **an unsuccessful attempt** ein erfolgloser Versuch; 2 **to be unsuccessful** keinen Erfolg haben; **I tried, but I was unsuccessful** ich habe es versucht, aber ich hatte keinen Erfolg.

unsuitable *adjective* unpassend.

untidy *adjective* unordentlich; **the house is always untidy** das Haus ist immer unordentlich.

until *preposition, conjunction* 1 bis; **until Monday** bis Montag; **until now** bis jetzt; **until then** bis dahin; 2 (*when 'until' is followed by a noun it is usually translated as 'bis zu'* +DAT) **until the tenth** bis zum Zehnten; **until the morning** bis zum Morgen; 3 **not until** erst; **not until September** erst im September; **it won't be finished until Friday** es wird erst Freitag fertig sein.

unusual *adjective* ungewöhnlich; **an unusual face** ein ungewöhnliches Gesicht.

unwilling *adjective* **to be unwilling to do something** etwas nicht tun wollen.

unwrap *verb* auspacken SEP.

up *preposition, adverb* 1 (*out of bed*) **to be up** auf sein △ ◇ (PERF *sein*); **Liz isn't up yet** Liz ist noch nicht auf; **I was up late last night** ich war gestern bis spät auf; 2 **to get up** aufstehen ◇ SEP (PERF *sein*); **we got up at six** wir sind um sechs aufgestanden; 3 (*higher up*) auf (+DAT, *or* +ACC *when there is movement towards a place*); **up on the roof** auf

◇ **IRREGULAR VERB: See the verb table in the centre of the dictionary**

dem Dach; **4** up here hier oben; **up there** da oben; **to go up** (*upstairs*) nach oben gehen; **I went up** ich bin nach oben gegangen; **5 to go up the road** die Straße entlanggehen ◇ SEP (PERF **sein**); **it's further up the road** es ist weiter die Straße entlang; **6 to go up the hill** (*on foot*) hinaufgehen ◇ SEP (PERF **sein**); (*in a vehicle*) hinauffahren ◇ SEP (PERF **sein**); (*in spoken German the prefix 'rauf-' is most common*) **does the bus go up the hill?** fährt der Bus den Berg rauf?; **7 to come up** heraufkommen ◇ SEP (PERF **sein**), raufkommen ◇ SEP (PERF **sein**) (*informal*); **8** (*wrong*) **what's up?** was ist los? (*informal*); **what's up with him?** was ist mit ihm los?; **9 up to** bis; **up to here** bis hier; **up to last week** bis zur letzten Woche; **10 she came up to me** sie kam auf mich zu; **11 what's she up to?** was hat sie vor?; **12 it's up to you** (*it's for you to decide*) das hängt von dir ab; (*it concerns only you*) das ist deine Sache; ★ **time's up!** die Zeit ist um.

upheaval *noun* Unruhe *die* (PL *die* Unruhen).

upper-class *adjective* der Oberschicht; **an upper-class family** eine Familie der Oberschicht.

upright *adjective* aufrecht; **put it upright** stell es aufrecht; **to stand upright** aufrecht stehen.

upset *noun* **stomach upset** die Magenverstimmung.
adjective **1** (*annoyed*) ärgerlich; **he's upset** er ist ärgerlich; **2** (*distressed*) bestürzt; (*sad*)

betrübt.
verb **to upset somebody** (*hurt*) jemanden kränken; (*annoy*) jemanden ärgern.

upside down *adjective* verkehrt herum.

upstairs *adverb* **1** oben; **Mum's upstairs** Mutti ist oben; **2** (*with movement*) nach oben; **to go upstairs** nach oben gehen.

up-to-date *adjective* **1** (*in fashion*) modern; **2** (*information*) aktuell.

upwards *adjective* nach oben.

urgent *adjective* dringend.

US *noun* USA (*plural*).

us *pronoun* uns; **she knows us** sie kennt uns; **they saw us** sie haben uns gesehen; **with us** mit uns.

USA *noun* USA (*plural*).

use *noun* **1** Gebrauch *der*; **instructions for use** die Gebrauchsanweisung (*singular*); **2 it's no use** es hat keinen Zweck; **it's no use phoning** es hat keinen Zweck anzurufen.
verb benutzen; **we used the dictionary** wir haben das Wörterbuch benutzt; **to use something to do something** etwas zu etwas ←(DAT) benutzen; **I used a towel to dry myself** ich habe ein Handtuch zum Abtrocknen benutzt.
● **to use up 1** aufbrauchen SEP (*food*); **2** verbrauchen (*money*).

used *adjective* **1 to be used to something** an etwas ←(ACC) gewöhnt sein; **I'm used to cats** ich bin an Katzen gewöhnt; **I'm not used to it!**

ich bin nicht daran gewöhnt!; **I'm not used to eating in restaurants** ich bin nicht daran gewöhnt, in Restaurants zu essen; **2 to get used to something** sich an etwas ←(ACC) gewöhnen; **you'll soon get used to the new car** du wirst dich schnell an das neue Auto gewöhnen; **I've got used to living here** ich habe mich daran gewöhnt, hier zu wohnen; **you'll get used to it** du wirst dich schon daran gewöhnen. *verb* **they used to live in the country** sie haben früher auf dem Land gewohnt; **she used to smoke** sie hat früher geraucht.

useful *adjective* nützlich.

useless *adjective* **1** unbrauchbar; **this knife's useless** dieses Messer ist unbrauchbar; **you're completely useless!** du bist wirklich zu nichts zu gebrauchen!; **2** nutzlos (*advice, information, or facts, for example*); **useless knowledge** nutzloses Wissen; **3** (*pointless*) zwecklos.

user-friendly *adjective* benutzerfreundlich.

usual *adjective* **1** üblich; **it's the usual problem** es ist das übliche Problem; **as usual** wie üblich; **2** **it's colder than usual** es ist kälter als gewöhnlich.

usually *adjective* normalerweise; **I usually leave at eight** normalerweise gehe ich um acht weg.

V v

vacancy *noun* **1** (*in a hotel*) 'vacancies' 'Zimmer frei!'; 'no vacancies' 'belegt'; **2** **job vacancy** die freie Stelle.

vacant *adjective* frei.

vaccination *noun* Impfung *die* (PL die Impfungen).

vacuum *verb* saugen; **I'm going to vacuum my room** ich sauge mein Zimmer.

vacuum cleaner *noun* Staubsauger *der* (PL die Staubsauger).

vagina *noun* Vagina *die* (PL die Vaginen).

vague *adjective* vage.

vain *adjective* eitel; **in vain** vergeblich.

Valentine's Day *noun* Valentinstag *der* (PL die Valentinstage).

valid *adjective* gültig.

valley *noun* Tal *das* (PL die Täler).

valuable *adjective* wertvoll.

value *noun* Wert *der* (PL die Werte). *verb* schätzen.

van *noun* Lieferwagen *der* (PL die Lieferwagen).

vandal *noun* Rowdy *der* (PL die Rowdies).

✧ IRREGULAR VERB: *See the verb table in the centre of the dictionary*

vandalism noun
Wandalismus △ der.

vandalize verb mutwillig zerstören.

vanilla noun Vanille die; **vanilla ice cream** das Vanilleeis.

vanish verb verschwinden ✧ (PERF sein).

variety noun 1 Abwechslung die (in a routine, diet, or style); **for the sake of variety** zur Abwechslung; 2 (kind) Sorte die (PL die Sorten); **a new variety of apple** eine neue Apfelsorte; 3 (assortment) Auswahl die.

various adjective verschieden; **there are various ways of doing it** man kann es auf verschiedene Art und Weise machen.

vary verb 1 (become different) sich ändern; 2 **it varies a lot** es ist sehr unterschiedlich; 3 (make different) ändern (a programme or method).

vase noun Vase die (PL die Vasen).

VAT noun Mehrwertsteuer die (PL die Mehrwertsteuern).

VCR noun Videorecorder der (PL die Videorecorder).

VDU noun Bildschirm der (PL die Bildschirme).

veal noun Kalbfleisch das.

vegan noun Veganer der (PL die Veganer), Veganerin die (PL die Veganerinnen).

vegetable noun Gemüse das; **fresh vegetables** frisches Gemüse.

vegetarian noun Vegetarier der (PL die Vegetarier), Vegetarierin die (PL die Vegetarierinnen).
adjective vegetarisch.

vehicle noun Fahrzeug das (PL die Fahrzeuge).

vein noun Vene die (PL die Venen).

velvet noun Samt der.

vending machine noun
Automat der (PL die Automaten).

verb noun Verb das (PL die Verben).

verdict noun Urteil das (PL die Urteile).

verge noun 1 (roadside) Bankette die (PL die Banketten); 2 **to be on the verge of doing something** im Begriff sein, etwas zu tun; **I was on the verge of leaving** ich war im Begriff zu gehen.

version noun Version die (PL die Versionen).

versus preposition gegen (+ACC); **Arsenal versus Chelsea** Arsenal gegen Chelsea.

very adverb sehr; **it's very difficult** es ist sehr schwer; **very much** sehr viel.
adjective 1 **the very person I need!** genau der Mann, den ich brauche; genau die Frau, die ich brauche; **the very thing he's looking for** genau das, was er sucht; **in the very middle** genau in der Mitte; 2 **at the very end** ganz am Ende; **at the very front** ganz vorne.

vest noun Unterhemd das (PL die Unterhemden).

△ NEW SPELLING: See page xii

vet noun Tierarzt der (PL die Tierärzte), Tierärztin die (PL die Tierärztinnen); **she's a vet** sie ist Tierärztin.

via preposition über (+ACC); **we're going to Frankfurt via Brussels** wir fahren über Brüssel nach Frankfurt.

vicar noun Pfarrer der (PL die Pfarrer).

vicious adjective **1** bösartig (dog); **2** brutal (attack).

victim noun Opfer das (PL die Opfer).

victory noun Sieg der (PL die Siege).

video noun **1** (film, cassette) Video das (PL die Videos); **to watch a video** ein Video ansehen; **I've got it on video** ich habe es auf Video; **it's out on video** das gibt's als Video; **2** (video recorder) Videorecorder der (PL die Videorecorder). verb aufzeichnen SEP; **I'll video it for you** ich zeichne es für dich auf.

video camera noun Videokamera die (PL die Videokameras).

video cassette noun Videokassette die (PL die Videokassetten).

video game noun Videospiel das (PL die Videospiele).

video recorder noun Videorecorder der (PL die Videorecorder).

video shop noun Videothek die (PL die Videotheken).

Vienna noun Wien das; **to Vienna** nach Wien.

view noun **1** Aussicht die; **a room with a view of the lake** ein Zimmer mit Aussicht auf den See; **2** (opinion) Meinung die (PL die Meinungen); **in my view** meiner Meinung nach; **point of view** der Standpunkt.

viewer noun Zuschauer der (PL die Zuschauer), Zuschauerin die (PL die Zuschauerinnen).

vile adjective ekelhaft.

villa noun Villa die (PL die Villen).

village noun Dorf das (PL die Dörfer).

vine noun Weinrebe die (PL die Weinreben).

vinegar noun Essig der.

vineyard noun Weinberg der (PL die Weinberge).

violence noun Gewalt die.

violent adjective **1** gewalttätig (person, film, behaviour); **2** heftig (jolt, punch).

violin noun Geige die (PL die Geigen); **to play the violin** Geige spielen.

violinist noun Geiger der (PL die Geiger), Geigerin die (PL die Geigerinnen).

virgin noun Jungfrau die (PL die Jungfrauen).

Virgo noun Jungfrau die; **Robert's Virgo** Robert ist Jungfrau.

virtual reality noun virtuelle Realität die.

virus noun Virus das (PL die Viren).

✧ IRREGULAR VERB: See the verb table in the centre of the dictionary

isa noun Visum das (PL die Visa).

isit noun Besuch der (PL die Besuche); **I was in Berlin on a visit to friends** ich war in Berlin bei Freunden zu Besuch; **my last visit to Germany** mein letzter Deutschlandbesuch.
verb **1** besuchen (a person); **2** besichtigen (a building, town).

isitor noun **1** Besucher der (PL die Besucher), Besucherin die (PL die Besucherinnen); **we've got visitors tonight** wir haben heute Abend Besuch; **3** (in a hotel) Gast der (PL die Gäste).

isual adjective visuell.

ital adjective unbedingt erforderlich; **it's vital to book** man muss unbedingt buchen.

itamin noun Vitamin das (PL die Vitamine).

ivid adjective lebhaft (colours, memory); **to have a vivid imagination** eine lebhafte Phantasie haben.

vocabulary noun Wortschatz der.

vocational adjective beruflich.

vodka noun Wodka der (PL die Wodkas).

voice noun Stimme die (PL die Stimmen).

volcano noun Vulkan der (PL die Vulkane).

volleyball noun Volleyball der; **to play volleyball** Volleyball spielen.

volume noun **1** Lautstärke die; **could you turn down the volume?**

könntest du etwas leiser stellen?; **2** (book) Band der (PL die Bände).

voluntary adjective **1** freiwillig; **a voluntary worker** ein freiwilliger Helfer, eine freiwillige Helferin; **2 to do voluntary work** für einen wohltätigen Zweck arbeiten.

volunteer noun Freiwillige der/die (PL die Freiwilligen).
verb **to volunteer to do something** sich anbieten, etwas zu tun.

vote verb wählen; **to vote for somebody** jemanden wählen.

voucher noun Gutschein der (PL die Gutscheine).

vowel noun Vokal der (PL die Vokale).

vulgar adjective vulgär.

W w

wage(s) noun Lohn der (PL die Löhne).

waist noun Taille die (PL die Taillen).

waistcoat noun Weste die (PL die Westen).

waist measurement noun Taillenweite die.

wait noun Wartezeit die; **an hour's wait** eine Stunde Wartezeit.
verb **1** warten; **they're waiting in the car** sie warten im Auto; **she kept me waiting** sie hat mich warten lassen; **2 to wait for somebody** auf jemanden warten; **wait for me**

warte auf mich; **to wait for something** auf etwas ←(ACC) warten; **we waited for a taxi** wir haben auf ein Taxi gewartet; **3 to wait for somebody to do something** darauf warten, dass jemand etwas tut; **I'm waiting for him to ring up** ich warte darauf, dass er anruft; **4 I can't wait to open it** ich kann's kaum erwarten, es aufzumachen.

waiter noun Kellner der (PL die Kellner); **waiter!** Herr Ober!

waiting room noun Wartezimmer das (PL die Wartezimmer); (at a station) Warteraum der (PL die Warteräume).

waitress noun Kellnerin die (PL die Kellnerinnen); **waitress!** Fräulein!

wake verb **1** wecken (somebody); **Jess woke me at six** Jess hat mich um sechs geweckt; **2** aufwachen SEP (PERF sein); **I woke (up) at six** ich bin um sechs aufgewacht; **wake up!** wach auf!

Wales noun Wales das; **from Wales** aus Wales; **to Wales** nach Wales.

walk noun **1** Spaziergang der (PL die Spaziergänge); **to go for walk** einen Spaziergang machen; **we'll go for a little walk round the village** wir machen einen kleinen Spaziergang durchs Dorf; **2 to take the dog for a walk** mit dem Hund spazieren gehen ◇ (PERF sein); **3 it's about five minutes' walk from here** es ist ungefähr fünf Minuten zu Fuß von hier.
verb **1** (go, not run) gehen ◇ (PERF sein); **he walks very slowly** er geht

sehr langsam; **I'll walk to the bus stop with you** ich gehe mit dir zur Bushaltestelle; **2** (on foot rather than by car or bus) zu Fuß gehen ◇ (PERF sein); **it's not far, we can walk** es ist nicht weit, wir können zu Fuß gehen; **3** (walk around) spazieren gehen ◇ △ (PERF sein); **we walked around the old town** wir sind in der Altstadt spazieren gegangen; **4** (move on foot) laufen ◇ (PERF sein); **to learn to walk** laufen lernen; **the child can't walk yet** das Kind kann noch nicht laufen.

walking noun (hiking) Wandern das; **to go walking** wandern (PERF sein).

walking distance noun **to be within walking distance** zu Fuß zu erreichen sein; **it's within walking distance of the sea** man kann das Meer zu Fuß erreichen.

walkman™ noun Walkman™ der (PL die Walkmen).

wall noun **1** (inside a building) Wand die (PL die Wände); **there's a picture on every wall** an jeder Wand hängt ein Bild; **2** (outside) Mauer die (PL die Mauern).

wallet noun Brieftasche die (PL die Brieftaschen).

wallpaper noun Tapete die (PL die Tapeten).

walnut noun Walnuss △ die (PL die Walnüsse).

wander verb **to wander around town** durch die Stadt bummeln

◇ **IRREGULAR VERB:** See the verb table in the centre of the dictionary

(PERF *sein*); **to wander off** weggehen ◇ SEP (PERF *sein*).

want *verb* 1 wollen ◇; **do you want to come?** willst du mitkommen?; **what do you want to do?** was willst du machen?; **I don't want to bother him** ich will ihn nicht stören; 2 (*more polite*) mögen ◇ (*'ich möchte' is much politer than 'ich will'*); **do you want some more coffee?** möchtest du noch Kaffee?; **I want two pounds of apples please** ich möchte gern zwei Pfund Äpfel (*'möchte gern' is particularly used when shopping*).

war *noun* Krieg der (PL die Kriege).

wardrobe *noun* Kleiderschrank der (PL die Kleiderschränke).

warm *adjective* 1 warm; **a warm coat** ein warmer Mantel; **it's warm today** heute ist es warm; **I'll keep your dinner warm** ich halte dir das Essen warm; **it's warm inside** drinnen ist es warm; **I am warm** mir ist warm; 2 (*friendly*) herzlich; **a warm welcome** ein herzlicher Empfang.
verb wärmen; **to warm the plates** die Teller wärmen.
to warm up 1 (*weather*) warm werden; 2 (*an athlete*) sich aufwärmen SEP; 3 (*to heat up*) aufwärmen SEP; **I'll warm the soup up for you** ich wärme dir die Suppe auf.

warmth *noun* Wärme die.

warn *verb* 1 warnen; **I warn you, it's expensive** ich warne dich, es ist teuer; **to warn somebody not to do something** jemanden davor

warnen, etwas zu tun; **she warned me not to let him drive** sie hat mich davor gewarnt, ihn fahren zu lassen; 2 **he warned me to lock the car** er hat mich ermahnt, das Auto abzuschließen.

warning *noun* Warnung die (PL die Warnungen).

wash *noun* **to give something a wash** etwas waschen ◇; **to have a wash** sich waschen.
verb 1 waschen ◇; **I've washed your jeans** ich habe deine Jeans gewaschen; 2 (*have a wash*) sich waschen ◇; **to get washed** sich waschen; 3 **to wash your hands** sich ←(DAT) die Hände waschen; **I washed my hands** ich habe mir die Hände gewaschen; **to wash your hair** sich ←(DAT) die Haare waschen; 4 **to wash the dishes** abwaschen ◇ SEP.
● **to wash up** abwaschen ◇ SEP.

washbasin *noun* Waschbecken das (PL die Waschbecken).

washing *noun* Wäsche die; **to do the washing** Wäsche waschen.

washing machine *noun* Waschmaschine die (PL die Waschmaschinen).

washing powder *noun* Waschpulver das.

washing-up *noun* Abwasch der; **to do the washing-up** den Abwasch machen.

washing-up liquid *noun* Spülmittel das (PL die Spülmittel).

△ NEW SPELLING: *See page xii*

wasp noun Wespe die (PL die Wespen).

waste noun Verschwendung die; it's a waste of time das ist eine Zeitverschwendung.
verb verschwenden.

waste-bin noun Mülltonne die (PL die Mülltonnen).

waste-paper basket noun Papierkorb der (PL die Papierkörbe).

watch noun Uhr die (PL die Uhren); my watch is fast meine Uhr geht vor; my watch is slow meine Uhr geht nach.
verb 1 (to look at) sich ←(DAT) ansehen ◇ SEP; I was watching a film ich habe mir einen Film angesehen; 2 to watch TV fernsehen ◇ SEP; 3 (keep a check on, look after) achten auf (+ACC); watch the children achte auf die Kinder; 4 (to be careful) aufpassen SEP; watch you don't spill it pass auf, dass du es nicht verschüttest; watch out! pass auf!; 5 (observe) beobachten; they were being watched sie wurden beobachtet.

water noun Wasser das.
verb gießen ◇ (plants).

waterfall noun Wasserfall der (PL die Wasserfälle).

watering can noun Gießkanne die (PL die Gießkannen).

waterproof adjective wasserdicht.

water-skiing noun Wasserskifahren das; to go water-skiing Wasserski fahren.

wave noun 1 (in the sea) Welle die (PL die Wellen); 2 (with your hand) to give somebody a wave jemandem zuwinken SEP; she gave him a wave from the bus sie winkte ihm vom Bus zu.
verb 1 (with your hand) winken; 2 (flap) schwenken (a flag, for example).

wax noun Wachs das.

way noun 1 (a route or road) Weg der (PL die Wege); the way to town der Weg in die Stadt; we asked the way to the station wir haben gefragt, wie man zum Bahnhof kommt; on the way back auf dem Rückweg; on the way unterwegs; to be in the way im Weg sein; to be in somebody's way jemandem im Weg sein; to get out of the way aus dem Weg gehen; 2 to lose your way sich verlaufen ◇; (in a car) sich verfahren ◇; 3 'way in' 'Eingang'; 'way out' 'Ausgang'; 4 (direction) Richtung die (PL die Richtungen); which way did he go? in welche Richtung ist er gegangen?; this way in diese Richtung; 5 (side) the right way up richtig herum; the wrong way round falsch herum; the other way round andersherum; 6 (distance) it's a long way es ist weit weg; we still had a little way to go wir mussten noch ein kleines Stück gehen; 7 (manner) Art und Weise die; my way of learning German meine Art und Weise, Deutsch zu lernen; he does it his way er macht es auf seine Art und Weise; I've done it the wrong way ich habe es falsch gemacht; in a way in gewisser Weise; **8 no way!** auf keinen Fall!; **9 by the way** übrigens.

e *pronoun* wir; **we're going to the cinema tonight** wir gehen heute Abend ins Kino.

eak *adjective* **1** (*feeble*) schwach; **in a weak voice** mit schwacher Stimme; **2** dünn (*coffee or tea*).

ealthy *adjective* reich.

eapon *noun* Waffe *die* (PL *die* Waffen).

ear *noun* **children's wear** *die* Kinderkleidung; **sports wear** *die* Sportkleidung.
verb tragen ◇, anhaben ◇ SEP (*informal*); **she often wears red** sie trägt oft Rot; **Tamsin's wearing her jeans** Tamsin hat ihre Jeans an.

eather *noun* **1** Wetter *das*; **what's the weather like?** wie ist das Wetter?; **in fine weather** bei schönem Wetter; **the weather is terrible** das Wetter ist furchtbar; **2 in wet weather** wenn es regnet; **the weather was cold** es war kalt.

eather forecast *noun* Wettervorhersage *die*; **the weather forecast says it will rain** der Wettervorhersage zufolge soll es regnen.

edding *noun* Hochzeit *die* (PL *die* Hochzeiten).

Vednesday *noun* **1** Mittwoch *der* (PL *die* Mittwoche); **on Wednesday** (am) Mittwoch; **I'm going to the cinema on Wednesday** ich gehe Mittwoch ins Kino; **see you on Wednesday!** bis Mittwoch!; **every**

Wednesday jeden Mittwoch; **last Wednesday** vorigen Mittwoch; **next Wednesday** nächsten Mittwoch; **2 on Wednesdays** mittwochs; **the museum is closed on Wednesdays** das Museum ist mittwochs geschlossen.

weed *noun* Unkraut *das*.

week *noun* Woche *die* (PL *die* Wochen); **last week** vorige Woche; **next week** nächste Woche; **this week** diese Woche; **for weeks** wochenlang; **a week today** heute in einer Woche; **in three weeks' time** in drei Wochen.

weekday *noun* **on weekdays** wochentags.

weekend *noun* Wochenende *das* (PL *die* Wochenenden); **last weekend** voriges Wochenende; **next weekend** nächstes Wochenende; **they're coming for the weekend** sie kommen übers Wochenende; **I'll do it at the weekend** ich mache es am Wochenende; **have a nice weekend!** ein schönes Wochenende!

weigh *verb* **1** wiegen ◇; **to weigh something** etwas wiegen; **to weigh yourself** sich wiegen; **2 how much do you weigh?** wie viel wiegst du?; **I weigh 50 kilos** ich wiege fünfzig Kilo.

weight *noun* **1** Gewicht *das* (PL *die* Gewichte); **2 to put on weight** zunehmen ◇ SEP; **3 to lose weight** abnehmen ◇ SEP.

weird *adjective* seltsam.

△ NEW SPELLING: *See page xii*

welcome

ENGLISH–GERMAN

welcome noun **1** they gave us a warm welcome sie haben uns herzlich empfangen; **2** welcome to Oxford! herzlich willkommen in Oxford!
adjective willkommen; you're welcome any time du bist immer willkommen; 'thank you!' – 'you're welcome!' 'danke!' – 'bitte!'.
verb begrüßen; to welcome somebody jemanden begrüßen.

well adverb **1** to be well gesund sein; I'm very well, thank you danke, es geht mir gut; get well soon! gute Besserung!; **2** gut; Terry played well Terry hat gut gespielt; it's well paid es wird gut bezahlt; well done! gut gemacht!; **3** as well auch; Kevin's coming as well Kevin kommt auch; **4** na ja; well, never mind na ja, macht nichts; **5** gut; it may well be that … es ist gut möglich, dass …; very well then, you can go also gut, du kannst gehen.

well-behaved adjective artig.

well-done adjective durchgebraten (steak).

wellington (boot) noun Gummistiefel der (PL die Gummistiefel).

well-known adjective bekannt.

well-off adjective wohlhabend.

Welsh noun **1** the Welsh (people) die Waliser (plural); **2** (language) Walisisch das.
adjective walisisch; he's Welsh er ist Waliser; she's Welsh sie ist Waliserin.

Welshman noun Waliser der (PL die Waliser).

Welshwoman noun Waliserin die (PL die Waliserinnen).

west noun Westen der; in the west im Westen.
adjective West-; the west side die Westseite; west wind der Westwind; west of westlich von; it's west of Munich es liegt westlich von München.
adverb nach Westen.

western noun (film) Western der (PL die Western).

West Indian noun Westinder der (PL die Westinder), Westinderin die (PL die Westinderinnen).
adjective westindisch.

West Indies plural noun die Westindischen Inseln (plural); in the West Indies auf den Westindischen Inseln.

wet adjective **1** nass △; we got wet wir sind nass geworden; **2** a wet day ein regnerischer Tag.

whale noun Wal der (PL die Wale).

what pronoun, adjective **1** (in questions) was; what did you say? was hast du gesagt?; what's she doing? was macht sie?; what did you buy? was hast du gekauft?; what is it? was ist das?; what's the matter? was ist los?; what's happened? was ist passiert?; what? was?; **2** what's your address? wie ist Ihre Adresse?; what's her name? wie heißt sie?; what was it like? wie war's?; **3** (asking for an amount) wie viel △;

◊ **IRREGULAR VERB: See the verb table in the centre of the dictionary**

what time? um wie viel Uhr?; (*that which*) was (*relative pronoun*); she told me what had happened sie hat mir gesagt, was passiert ist; **do what I tell you** tu, was ich dir sage; 5 (*which*) welcher/welche/welches; **what country is it in?** in welchem Land ist es?; **what colour is it?** welche Farbe hat es?; **what make is it?** welche Marke ist es?; 6 **what for?** wozu?

wheat noun Weizen der.

wheel noun Rad das (PL die Räder); **the spare wheel** das Reserverad; **the steering wheel** das Lenkrad.

wheelbarrow noun Schubkarre die (PL die Schubkarren).

wheelchair noun Rollstuhl der (PL der Rollstühle).

when adverb wann; **when is she arriving?** wann kommt sie an?; **when's your birthday?** wann hast du Geburtstag?
conjunction 1 (*with the past*) als; **I was out shopping when you rang** ich war beim Einkaufen, als du anriefst; 2 (*with the present or future*) wenn; **when she comes I'll ring** wenn sie kommt, rufe ich an.

where adverb, conjunction wo; **where do you live?** wo wohnst du?; **where are you going?** wo gehst du hin?; **I don't know where they live** ich weiß nicht, wo sie wohnen.

whether conjunction ob; **I don't know whether he's back** ich weiß nicht, ob er schon zurück ist.

which adjective, pronoun
1 welcher/welche/welches; **which CD did you buy?** welche CD hast du gekauft?; 2 **which (one)** welcher/welche/welches (*depending on the gender of the noun the question refers back to*); **'I met your brother' – 'which one?'** 'ich habe deinen Bruder getroffen' – 'welchen?'; **'I met your sister' – 'which one?'** 'ich habe deine Schwester getroffen' – 'welche?'; **'have you seen my book?' – 'which one?'** 'hast du mein Buch gesehen?' – 'welches?'; 3 (*relative pronoun*) der/die/das (*depending on the gender of the noun 'which' refers to*); (*plural*) die; **the film which is showing now** der Film, der gerade läuft; **the lamp which is on the table** die Lampe, die auf dem Tisch steht; **the book which I lent you** das Buch, das ich dir geliehen habe; **the books which I've read** die Bücher, die ich gelesen habe.

while noun **for a while** eine Weile; **she worked here for a while** sie hat eine Weile hier gearbeitet; **after a while** nach einer Weile.
conjunction während; **you can make some coffee while I'm finishing my homework** du kannst Kaffee kochen, während ich meine Hausaufgaben fertig mache.

whip noun Peitsche die (PL die Peitschen).
verb schlagen ◇ (*cream*); **whipped cream** die Schlagsahne.

whisky noun Whisky der (PL die Whiskys).

△ NEW SPELLING: See page xii

whisper noun Flüstern das; **in a whisper** im Flüsterton.
verb flüstern.

whistle noun Pfeife die (PL die Pfeifen).
verb pfeifen ✧.

white noun Weiß das; **egg white** das Eiweiß.
adjective weiß; **a white shirt** ein weißes Hemd.

white coffee noun Kaffee mit Milch der (PL die Kaffees mit Milch).

Whitsun noun Pfingsten das (PL die Pfingsten).

who pronoun 1 (in questions) wer; **who wants some chocolate?** wer möchte Schokolade?; 2 (in the accusative) wen; **who did you ring?** wen hast du angerufen?; 3 (in the dative) wem; **who did you give it to?** wem hast du es gegeben?; 4 (relative pronoun) der/die/das (depending on the gender of the noun 'who' refers to); (plural) die; **my friend who lives in Liverpool** mein Freund, der in Liverpool wohnt; **my girl friend who lives in Berlin** meine Freundin, die in Berlin wohnt; **the child who's staying with us** das Kind, das bei uns wohnt; **the friends who are coming to see us tonight** die Freunde, die heute Abend kommen.

whole noun **the whole of the class** die ganze Klasse; **the whole of Germany** ganz Deutschland; **on the whole** im Großen und Ganzen.
adjective ganz; **the whole family** die ganze Familie; **the whole**

morning den ganzen Morgen; **the whole time** die ganze Zeit; **the whole world** die ganze Welt.

wholemeal adjective Vollkorn-; **wholemeal bread** das Vollkornbro[t]

whom pronoun 1 den/die/das; (plural) die; **the man whom I saw** der Mann, den ich sah; **the woman whom I saw** die Frau, die ich sah; **the child whom I saw** das Kind, d[as] ich sah; 2 (in the dative) dem/der/ dem; (plural) denen; **the girl to whom I wrote** das Mädchen, dem ich geschrieben habe; 3 (in questions) wen; **whom did you see?** wen haben Sie gesehen?; 4 **whom did you give it?** wem habe[n] Sie es gegeben?

whose pronoun, adjective 1 (in questions) wessen; **whose is this jacket?** wessen Jacke ist das?; **whose shoes are these?** wessen Schuhe sind das?; 2 **whose is it?** wem gehört das?; **I know whose it** is ich weiß, wem es gehört; 3 (as relative pronoun) dessen/deren/ dessen (depending on the gender o[f] the noun 'whose' refers to); (plural[)] deren; **the man whose car I'm buying** der Mann, dessen Auto ich kaufe; **the woman whose bag I** found die Frau, deren Tasche ich gefunden habe; **the girl whose sis[ter]** I know das Mädchen, dessen Schwester ich kenne; **the people whose children he teaches** die Leute, deren Kinder er unterricht[et]

why adverb 1 warum; **why did she phone?** warum hat sie angerufe[n?]; **why not?** warum nicht?; 2 that's

---

✧ IRREGULAR VERB: See the verb table in the centre of the dictionary

y I don't want to come darum
ll ich nicht kommen.

ked adjective **1** (*bad*) böse;
(*brilliant*) geil (*informal*).

le adjective **1** breit; **it's a very**
le road es ist eine sehr breite
aße; the shelf is 30 cm wide das
gal ist dreißig Zentimeter breit;
de screen das Breitbild; **2** groß;
de range eine große Auswahl.
verb the door was wide open
e Tür stand weit offen.

le awake adjective hellwach.

low noun Witwe die (PL die
twen).

lower noun Witwer der (PL die
atwer).

th noun Breite die.

e noun Ehefrau die (PL die
efrauen).

noun Perücke die (PL die
rücken).

d adjective **1** wild; **wild animals**
lde Tiere; 2 (*crazy*) verrückt (*idea*,
rty, person*); **3 to be wild about
mething scharf auf etwas ←(ACC)
in.

dlife noun Tierwelt die; **a**
ogramme on wildlife in Africa
e Sendung über die afrikanische
erwelt.

dlife park noun Wildpark der
**die Wildparks).

l verb **1** (*in German the present*
**nse is often used to express future*
ctions and intentions*) **I'll wait for
ou at the bus stop ich warte an

der Bushaltestelle auf dich; **he'll be**
pleased to help you er hilft dir gern;
that won't be a problem das ist kein
Problem; **I'll phone them at once**
ich rufe sie sofort an; **2** (*the German*
future tense is used when firm
intention is stressed, when referring
to the more distant future and when
some doubt about the future is
expressed) werden ◇; **he will**
definitely come er wird ganz
bestimmt kommen; **she'll probably**
ring before leaving sie wird
wahrscheinlich anrufen, bevor sie
geht; **3** (*in questions and requests*)
will you have some more tea?
möchten Sie noch Tee?; **will you help**
me? hilfst du mir?; **'will you write**
to me?' – 'of course I will!'
'schreibst du mir?' – 'ja, natürlich';
'he won't like it' – 'yes he will' 'es
wird ihm nicht gefallen' – 'doch';
4 wollen ◇; **he won't help us** er will
uns nicht helfen; **the car won't start**
das Auto will nicht anspringen.

willing adjective **to be willing to do**
something bereit sein, etwas zu
tun; **I'm willing to pay half** ich bin
bereit, die Hälfte zu zahlen.

willingly adverb gern.

win noun Sieg der (PL die Siege); **our**
win over Everton unser Sieg über
Everton.
verb **1** gewinnen ◇; **we won!** wir
haben gewonnen!; **2 to win a prize**
einen Preis bekommen.

wind¹ noun Wind der (PL die Winde).

wind² verb **1** wickeln (*a wire or rope,*
for example); **2** aufziehen ◇ SEP (*a*
clock).

△ NEW SPELLING: See page xii

wind instrument noun
Blasinstrument das (PL die
Blasinstrumente).

window noun 1 Fenster das (PL die
Fenster); **to look out of the window**
aus dem Fenster sehen; 2 (in a shop)
Schaufenster das (PL die
Schaufenster).

windscreen noun
Windschutzscheibe die (PL die
Windschutzscheiben).

windscreen wiper noun
Scheibenwischer der (PL die
Scheibenwischer).

windy adjective windig; **it's windy
today** heute ist es windig.

wine noun Wein der (PL die Weine);
a glass of white wine ein Glas
Weißwein.

wing noun Flügel der (PL die Flügel).

wink verb **to wink at somebody**
jemandem zuzwinkern SEP.

winner noun Sieger der (PL die
Sieger), Siegerin die (PL die
Siegerinnen).

winning adjective siegreich.

winnings plural noun Gewinn der.

winter noun Winter der (PL die
Winter); **in winter** im Winter.

wipe verb 1 abwischen SEP; **I'll just
wipe the table** ich wische schnell
den Tisch ab; **to wipe your nose** sich
←(DAT) die Nase abwischen; 2 **to wipe
the floor** den Boden wischen; 3 **to
wipe your feet** sich ←(DAT) die
Schuhe abtreten SEP.

• **to wipe up** abtrocknen SEP (dishes).

wire noun Draht der (PL die Dräh...
electric wire die Leitung.

wise adjective weise.

wish noun 1 Wunsch der (PL die
Wünsche); **to make a wish** sich
←(DAT) etwas wünschen; **make a
wish!** wünsch dir was!; 2 **best
wishes on your birthday** alles G...
zum Geburtstag; 3 (in a letter) **w...
best wishes** mit freundlichen
Grüßen.

verb 1 **I wish she were here** ich
wünschte, sie wäre hier; 2 **to wis...
for something** sich ←(DAT) etwas
wünschen; 3 **to wish somebody
happy Christmas** jemandem fro...
Weihnachten wünschen; **I wished
him happy birthday** ich habe ihr...
alles Gute zum Geburtstag
gewünscht.

with preposition 1 mit (+DAT); **wit...
me** mit mir; **with pleasure** mit
Vergnügen; **he went on holiday w...
his friends** er ist mit seinen
Freunden in die Ferien gefahren; **a
girl with red hair** ein Mädchen m...
roten Haaren; 2 (at the house of)
(+ACC); **we're staying the night w...
friends** wir übernachten bei
Freunden; 3 vor (+DAT); **to shiver
with cold** vor Kälte zittern; **to
tremble with fear** vor Angst zitte...
4 **I haven't got any money with r...**
ich habe kein Geld dabei.

without preposition ohne (+ACC);
without you ohne dich; **without ...
sweater** ohne einen Pullover;
without knowing ohne zu wisse...

◇ **IRREGULAR VERB: See the verb table in the centre of the dictionary**

…tness noun Zeuge der (PL die …eugen), Zeugin die (PL die …euginnen).

…ty adjective geistreich.

…man noun Frau die (PL die …rauen); **a woman friend** eine …reundin; **a woman doctor** eine …

…nder noun Wunder das (PL die …under); **it's no wonder you're** …red es ist kein Wunder, dass du …üde bist.
verb 1 sich fragen; **I wonder why she** …id that ich frage mich, warum sie …as getan hat; **2 I wonder who?** wer …ohl?; **I wonder where Jake is** wo …ake wohl ist?; **3** (in polite requests) …wonder if you could tell me …? …önnten Sie mir vielleicht sagen …?

…nderful adjective wunderbar.

…ood noun Holz das; **the lamp is** …nade of wood die Lampe ist aus …olz.

…ooden adjective Holz-, hölzern; …ooden toys das Holzspielzeug.

…oodwork noun (craft) …ischlerei die.

…ool noun Wolle die.

…rd noun 1 Wort das (PL die …Wörter) (the plural 'Wörter' is used …when the words are unrelated); **a** …ong word ein langes Wort; **what's** …he German word for 'window'? …vie heißt 'window' auf Deutsch?; …'ve learned ten German words …oday ich habe heute zehn deutsche …Wörter gelernt; **words in the** …dictionary Wörter im Wörterbuch; …2 Wort das (PL die Worte) (the plural

'Worte' is used when the words are connected in a text or conversation); **he wanted to say a few words** er wollte nur ein paar Worte sagen; **in other words** mit anderen Worten; **to have a word with somebody** mit jemandem sprechen; **3** (promise) Wort das; **to keep your word** sein Wort halten; **he broke his word** er hat sein Wort gebrochen; **4 the words of a song** der Text von einem Lied.

word processing noun Textverarbeitung die.

word processor noun Textverarbeitungssystem das.

work noun Arbeit die; **I enjoy my work** meine Arbeit macht mir Spaß; **she's looking for work** sie sucht Arbeit; **I've got some work to do** ich habe noch etwas Arbeit; **he's out of work** er hat keine Arbeit; **to be off work** (sick) Ben ist krank; **Ben's off work** (sick) Ben ist krank; **to go to work on the tube** mit der U-Bahn zur Arbeit fahren.
verb 1 arbeiten; **she works in an office** sie arbeitet in einem Büro; **Mum works as a dentist** Mutti ist Zahnärztin; **he works part-time** er arbeitet halbtags; **2** (to operate) sich auskennen ◇ SEP mit; **can you work the video?** kennst du dich mit dem Videorecorder aus?; **3** (function) funktionieren; **the washing machine's not working** die Waschmaschine funktioniert nicht; **4** (a plan or idea) klappen; **that worked really well** das hat prima geklappt.

△ NEW SPELLING: See page xii

● **to work out 1** (*understand*)
verstehen ◇; **I can't work out why**
ich kann nicht verstehen, warum;
2 (*exercise*) trainieren; **3** (*to go well*)
klappen; **4** (*calculate*) ausrechnen
SEP (*a sum*); **I'll work out how much
it would cost** ich rechne aus, wie
viel es kosten würde; **5** (*solve*) lösen
(*a problem*).

worker *noun* Arbeiter *der* (PL *die*
Arbeiter), Arbeiterin *die* (PL *die*
Arbeiterinnen).

work experience *noun*
Praktikum *das* (PL *die* Praktika); **to
do work experience** ein Praktikum
machen.

working-class *adjective* der
Arbeiterschicht; **a working-class
family** eine Familie der
Arbeiterschicht.

workshop *noun* Werkstatt *die* (PL
die Werkstätten).

world *noun* Welt *die*; **the biggest
tree in the world** der größte Baum
der Welt; **all over the world** auf der
ganzen Welt; **the Western world** die
westliche Welt.

World Cup *noun* **the World Cup**
die Weltmeisterschaft.

world war *noun* Weltkrieg *der* (PL
die Weltkriege); **the Second World
War** der Zweite Weltkrieg.

worm *noun* Wurm *der* (PL *die*
Würmer).

worn out *adjective* **1** (*person*)
erschöpft; **2** (*clothes or shoes*)
abgetragen.

worried *adjective* **1** besorgt; **his**

worried parents seine besorgten
Eltern; **2 to be worried about
somebody** sich ←(DAT) um
jemanden Sorgen machen; **we're
worried about Susan** wir machen
uns um Susan Sorgen.

worry *noun* Sorge *die* (PL *die*
Sorgen).
verb sich ←(DAT) Sorgen machen;
don't worry! keine Sorge !; **don't
worry about it** mach dir darum
keine Sorgen.

worrying *adjective* beunruhigen[d]

worse *adjective* **1** (*more unpleasa[nt]*)
schlimmer (*problem, pain, illness*);
things couldn't be worse es kan[n]
nicht schlimmer kommen; **2** (*less
good*) schlechter; **it was even wor[se]**
than the last time** es war noch
schlechter als letztes Mal; **to get
worse** schlechter werden; **the
weather's getting worse** das We[tter]
wird schlechter; **she's getting
worse** (*in health*) es geht ihr
schlechter.

worst *adjective* **1** (*most unpleasa[nt]*)
schlimmste/schlimmste/
schlimmste; **the worst** der/die/d[as]
Schlimmste; **it was the worst day
of my life** es war der schlimmste
Tag meines Lebens; **if the worst
comes to the worst** wenn es zum
Schlimmsten kommt; **2** (*least good*)
schlechteste/schlechteste/
schlechteste; **it's his worst film** d[as]
ist sein schlechtester Film; **French['s]
my worst subject** in Französisch
bin ich am schlechtesten.

worth *adjective* **to be worth** wert
sein; **how much is it worth?** wie
viel ist es wert?; **it's worth buying**

◇ **IRREGULAR VERB: See the verb table in the centre of the dictionary**

as lohnt sich zu kaufen; **it's worth** das lohnt sich nicht; **it's not worth it** es lohnt sich nicht.

uld verb **1 would you like omething to eat?** möchtest du was essen?; **what would you like?** as möchten Sie?; **2 I wouldn't do** ich würde das nicht machen; **I ould buy it, but I haven't got any oney at the moment** ich würde es aufen, aber ich habe zur Zeit kein eld; **I'd like to go to the cinema** ich würde gern ins Kino gehen; **she aid she'd help us** sie hat gesagt, e würde uns helfen; **3 that would e a good idea** das wäre ein gute dee; **if we had asked her she would ave helped us** wenn wir sie gefragt ätten, hätte sie uns geholfen; **4 he ouldn't answer** er wollte nicht ntworten; **the car wouldn't start** as Auto wollte nicht anspringen.

und noun Wunde die (PL die Vunden).
erb verwunden.

rap verb einwickeln SEP; **I'm going o wrap (up) my presents** ich wickele meine Geschenke ein; **could ou wrap it for me please?** können ie es bitte in Geschenkpapier inwickeln?

rapping paper noun Geschenkpapier das.

reck noun **1** Wrack das (PL die Vracks); **2 I feel a wreck** ich bin öllig kaputt.
erb **1** zerstören (a building or nachinery); **2** kaputtfahren ◇ SEP a car); **3** verderben ◇ (a party, olidays); **it completely wrecked**

my evening das hat mir den Abend völlig verdorben; **4** zunichte machen (plans).

wrestler noun Ringer der (PL die Ringer), Ringerin die (PL die Ringerinnen).

wrestling noun Ringen das.

wrist noun Handgelenk das (PL die Handgelenke).

write verb schreiben ◇; **to write to somebody** jemandem schreiben; **I'll write her a letter** ich schreibe ihr einen Brief; **to write to a firm** an eine Firma schreiben.
● **to write down** aufschreiben ◇ SEP; **I wrote down her name** ich schreibe ihren Namen auf; **she wrote it down for me** sie hat es mir aufgeschrieben.

writer noun Schriftsteller der (PL die Schriftsteller), Schriftstellerin die (PL die Schriftstellerinnen).

writing noun Schrift die.

wrong adjective **1** (not correct) falsch; **the wrong answer** die falsche Antwort; **it's the wrong address** das ist die falsche Adresse; **2 you've got the wrong number** Sie haben sich verwählt; **3 to be wrong** (be mistaken) sich irren; **I must have been wrong** ich muss mich geirrt haben; **4** (out of order) nicht stimmen; **there's something wrong** etwas stimmt nicht; **5** (dishonest) unrecht; **it's wrong to make him pay for it** es ist unrecht, dass er dafür zahlen muss; **he's wrong** er hat Unrecht; **you're quite wrong there**, cars pollute the

△ NEW SPELLING: See page xii

environment da haben Sie aber Unrecht, Autos verschmutzen die Umwelt; **6 what's wrong?** was ist los?

adverb **1** (*false*) falsch; **he's got it wrong** er hat es falsch gemacht; **2 to go wrong** (*break*) kaputtgehen ◇ SEP (PERF *sein*) (*informal*); **3 to go wrong** schief gehen △ ◇ (*plan*).

X x

xerox™ *noun* Fotokopie die (PL die Fotokopien).
verb fotokopieren.

X-ray *noun* Röntgenaufnahme die (PL die Röntgenaufnahmen); **to have an X-ray** geröntgt werden ◇ (PERF *sein*).
verb röntgen; **they X-rayed her ankle** sie haben ihren Knöchel geröntgt.

Y y

yacht *noun* **1** (*sailing boat*) Segelboot das (PL die Segelboote); **2** (*large luxury boat*) Jacht die (PL die Jachten).

yawn *verb* gähnen.

year *noun* **1** Jahr das (PL die Jahre; **six years ago** vor sechs Jahren; t**he whole year** das ganze Jahr; **2** he **lived in Moscow for years** sie haben jahrelang in Moskau gewohnt; **3 to be seventeen years old** siebzehn Jahre alt sein; **a two year-old child** ein zweijähriges Kind; **4** (*in school*) Klasse die (PL die Klassen) (*in German secondary schools the years go from the 'fünfte Klasse' to the 'dreizehnte Klasse'*); **I'm in Year 10** (*in Britain*) ich geh in die zehnte Klasse; **he'll be in Year 11** (*in Britain*) er kommt in e elfte Klasse.

yellow *adjective* gelb.

yes *adverb* **1** ja; **yes please** ja bit 'is Tom in his room?' – 'yes, he i 'ist Tom im Zimmer?' – 'ja'; **2** (*answering a negative*) doch; **'ye don't want to come with us, do you?'** – ' **yes, I do!**' 'du willst ni mitkommen?' – 'doch!'; **'you haven't finished, have you?'** – 'ye **I have**' 'Sie sind noch nicht fertig oder?' – 'doch!'.

yesterday *adverb* **1** gestern; **I saw her yesterday** ich habe sie gester gesehen; **yesterday afternoon** gestern Nachmittag; **yesterday morning** gestern früh; **2 the day before yesterday** vorgestern.

yet *adverb* **1 not yet** noch nicht; i **not ready yet** es ist noch nicht fertig; **2** (*in questions*) schon; **has she mentioned it yet?** hat sie es schon erwähnt?

yoghurt *noun* Joghurt der (PL die Joghurt).

◇ **IRREGULAR VERB: See the verb table in the centre of the dictionary**

olk noun Eigelb das (PL die Eigelbe).

ou pronoun 1 (as the subject of the sentence and in comparisons) du (familiar form, singular); Sie (polite form, singular and plural); ('du' is the familiar way of talking to family members, close friends, and people of your own age; 'Sie' is more polite) **do you want to go to the cinema tonight?** möchtest du heute Abend ins Kino gehen?; **can you tell me where the station is, please?** können Sie mir bitte sagen, wo der Bahnhof ist?; **he's older than you** er ist älter als du, er ist älter als Sie; 2 (the object form of 'du' and 'Sie', in the dative) dir (familiar form, singular); Ihnen (polite form, singular and plural); **I'll lend you my bike** ich leihe dir mein Rad; **I'll write to you** ich schreibe Ihnen; **I'll come with you** ich komme mit Ihnen mit; 3 (the object form of 'du' and 'Sie', in the accusative) dich (familiar form, singular); Sie (polite form, singular and plural); **I saw you** ich habe dich gesehen, ich habe Sie gesehen; 4 (as the subject of the sentence) ihr (familiar form, plural); **do you all want to come?** wollt ihr alle kommen?; 5 (the object form, in the accusative and the dative) euch; **I'll invite you all!** ich lade euch alle ein!; **I'll give it to you later** ich gebe es euch später.

young adjective jung; **young people** junge Leute; **he's younger than me** er ist jünger als ich; **Tessa's two years younger than me** Tessa ist zwei Jahre jünger als ich.

your adjective 1 (familiar form, singular) dein; (this is the familiar way of talking to family members, close friends, and people of your own age; 'Ihr' is more polite) **I met your brother** ich habe deinen Bruder getroffen; **I met your sister** ich habe deine Schwester getroffen; **I drove your car** ich bin mit deinem Auto gefahren; **I know your brothers** ich kenne deine Brüder; 2 (familiar form, plural) euer; **your brother** euer Bruder; **your sister** eure Schwester; **your car** euer Auto; **your friends are waiting downstairs** eure Freunde warten unten; 3 (polite form, singular and plural) Ihr; **your brother** Ihr Bruder; **your sister** Ihre Schwester; **your car is in the garage** Ihr Auto ist in der Garage; **you can all bring your friends** Sie können alle Ihre Freunde mitbringen.

yours pronoun 1 (familiar form, singular) deiner/deine/deins; (this is the familiar way of talking to family members, close friends, and people of your own age, 'Ihrer/Ihre/Ihrs' is more polite) **my brother's younger than yours** mein Bruder ist jünger als deiner; **my sister is older than yours** meine Schwester ist älter als deine; **I enjoyed that book – is it yours?** das Buch hat mir gefallen – ist es deins?; **my shoes are more expensive than yours** meine Schuhe sind teurer als deine; 2 (familiar form, plural) euer/eure/eures; **my children are younger than yours** meine Kinder sind jünger als eure; 3 (polite form, singular and

△ NEW SPELLING: See page xii

plural) Ihrer/Ihre/Ihrs; **his father must be older than yours** sein Vater muss älter als Ihrer sein; **4 she's a friend of yours** sie ist eine Freundin von Ihnen; **these books are yours** diese Bücher gehören Ihnen; **5** (*in letters*) **Yours sincerely** Mit freundlichen Grüßen.

yourself *pronoun* **1** (*when translated by a reflexive verb in German*) dich; (*formal*) sich; **ask yourself** frage dich, fragen Sie sich; **2** (*as a reflexive dative pronoun*) dir; (*formal*) sich; **did you hurt yourself?** hast du dir wehgetan?, haben Sie sich wehgetan?; **3** (*for emphasis*) selbst; **did you do it yourself?** hast du es selbst gemacht?; **4 all by yourself** ganz allein.

yourselves *pronoun* **1** euch; (*formal*) sich; **make yourselves comfortable** macht es euch gemütlich, machen Sie es sich gemütlich; **2** (*for emphasis*) selbst; **did you do it yourselves?** habt ihr es selbst gemacht?; **3 by yourselves** allein.

youth hostel *noun* Jugendherberge *die* (PL *die* Jugendherbergen).

Yugoslavia *noun* Jugoslawien *das*; **in the former Yugoslavia** im ehemaligen Jugoslawien.

Z z

zany *adjective* verrückt.

zebra *noun* Zebra *das* (PL *die* Zebras).

zebra crossing *noun* Zebrastreifen *der* (PL *die* Zebrastreifen).

zero *noun* Null *die* (PL *die* Nullen).

zigzag *verb* **1** im Zickzack laufen ◇ (PERF *sein*); **2** (*in a car*) im Zickzack fahren ◇ (PERF *sein*).

zip *noun* Reißverschluss Δ *der* (PL *die* Reißverschlüsse).

zodiac *noun* Tierkreis *der*; **the signs of the zodiac** die Sternzeichen (*plural*).

zone *noun* Zone *die* (PL *die* Zonen).

zoo *noun* Zoo *der* (PL *die* Zoos).

zoom lens *noun* Zoomobjektiv *das* (PL *die* Zoomobjektive).

◇ **IRREGULAR VERB: See the verb table in the centre of the dictionary**

Notes

Notes

Notes

Notes